Cases and Readings Manual

for use with

Cost Management
A Strategic Emphasis

Fourth Edition

Edward J. Blocher
University of North Carolina at Chapel Hill

David E. Stout
Youngstown State University

Gary Cokins
SAS Institute Inc.

Kung H. Chen
University of Nebraska at Lincoln

McGraw-Hill
Irwin

Boston   Burr Ridge, IL   Dubuque, IA   Madison, WI   New York   San Francisco   St. Louis
Bangkok   Bogotá   Caracas   Kuala Lumpur   Lisbon   London   Madrid   Mexico City
Milan   Montreal   New Delhi   Santiago   Seoul   Singapore   Sydney   Taipei   Toronto

Cases and Readings Manual for use with
COST MANAGEMENT: A STRATEGIC EMPHASIS
Edward J. Blocher, David E. Stout, Gary Cokins, and Kung H. Chen

Published by McGraw-Hill/Irwin, an imprint of The McGraw-Hill Companies, Inc., 1221 Avenue of the Americas, New York, NY 10020. Copyright © 2008 by The McGraw-Hill Companies, Inc. All rights reserved.

1 2 3 4 5 6 7 8 9 0 QPD/QPD 0 9 8 7 6

ISBN   978-0-07-312819-1
MHID   0-07-312819-8

www.mhhe.com

Preface

To extend the teaching materials of *Cost Management: A Strategic Emphasis*, this casebook provides additional cases and articles for each chapter. The cases and articles are an important part of the text and have the same teaching objectives. The problem material in the text includes short cases and exercises, while this casebook provides longer cases and articles to facilitate more extensive discussion and analysis. The casebook for the fourth edition has several new cases and readings plus some of our favorites from the prior edition.

As in the prior edition, this edition of the casebook also includes a case that utilizes the ABC costing system (©Oros) from SAS Institute software company. There is a comprehensive teaching note in the teaching notes supplement which explains in detail how to solve the case using the commercial ABC software system, ©Oros. The teaching note includes a link to a tutorial (requires approximately 2 hours) and a link to the ©Oros software (the assignment, done in student teams or individually, should require 3-4 hours). Additional ©Oros cases are available on the text web site.

We feel that cases serve a very important role in the cost management course. We know of many faculty who use cases from a variety of sources to supplement the text they are using. We have provided these materials in this book for easier access, greater convenience, and lower overall cost to the instructor and student.

Using cases has two important benefits. First, the use of a case requires the student to develop analytical skills by organizing the unstructured information in the case, devising appropriate analyses, and drawing appropriate conclusions. Second, the cases permit a more thorough strategic analysis of a given firm than would be possible with a problem or exercise. With a richer amount of information about the case firm and its environment, the student can more effectively apply the concepts of strategy and competitive advantage explained in chapters one and two in the text.

Each of the cases can be used as an exercise in competitive analysis to set the stage for the decision problem in the case, whatever that might be. A firm facing a lease-or-buy decision will want to assess the strategic, competitive situation of the firm before making the decision. Similarly, a firm considering the outsourcing of a department or activity will want to begin the analysis with an assessment of the strategic issues facing the firm, and then to make the outsourcing decision with these issues in mind. In this way, the cases can be used to effectively put each decision problem in a strategic context. Rather than to make a cost calculation and then "consider the qualitative factors," which can be done with problems and exercises, the case more readily allows an approach in which the strategic issues are considered an integral part of the solution of the case.

Articles are included for each chapter to provide an opportunity for more in-depth coverage. Key chapters have a larger number of cases and articles. We have included discussion questions for each article. Some of the articles are examples of how actual firms have implemented the cost management methods explained in the chapter. These stories show some of the implementation issues that arise in practical situations. Other articles report the results of surveys, which provide a perspective for how the cost management methods are used in practice. Others have a technical focus, and provide an opportunity to look more closely at the methods explained in the chapter and on the effects of using the methods.

We hope you will find these cases and readings helpful. We welcome feedback from students and instructors.

Edward Blocher
David Stout
Gary Cokins
Kung Chen

Acknowledgments

The following materials have been reprinted with permission from the **Institute of Management Accountants** (© Copyright by Institute of Management Accountants, Montvale, NJ):

Management Accounting

Robin Cooper and Regine Slagmulder, "Integrating Activity-Based Costing and the Theory of "Constraints," February 1999

Jack Bailes, James Nielsen, Stephen Lawton, "How Forest Product Companies Analyze Capital Budgets," October 1998.

Chee W. Chow, Kamal M. Haddad, James E. Williamson, "Applying the Balanced Scorecard to Small Companies," August 1997.

Steve Coburn, Hugh Grove, Tom Cook, "How ABC was
    Used in Capital Budgeting," May 1997.

Nick Fera, "Using Shareholder Value to Evaluate Strategic
    Choice," November 1997.

Robert S. Kaplan, Dan Weiss, Eyal Desheh, "Transfer Pricing with ABC," May 1997.

Gerald H. Lander, Mohamed E. Bayou, "Does ROI Apply to Robotic Factories?".

Peter J. Leitner, "Beyond the Numbers," May 1998.

Kenneth A. Merchant, "How Challenging Should Profit Budget Targets Be?" November 1990

Adel M. Novin, "How to Find the Right Bases and Rates," March 1992.

George Schmelze, Rolf Geier, Thomas El Buttross, "Target
    Costing at ITT Automotive," December 1996.

Bonnie P. Stivers, Teresa Joyce Covin, Nancy Green Hall, Steve W. Smalt, "How Nonfinancial Priscilla Performance Measures are Used," February 1998.

Dan W. Swenson, "Managing Costs Through Complexity
    Reduction at Carrier Corporation," April 1998.

Robert N. West, Amy N. Snyder, "How to Set Up a Budgeting and Planning System," January 1997.

Management Accounting Quarterly

Thomas L Burton and John B MacArthur, "Activity Based Costing and Predatory Pricing: The Case of the Petroleum Retail Industry," Spring 2003

Russell F. Briner, Mark Alford, and JoAnne Noble, "Activity Based Costing for State and Local Governments," Spring 2003

Bea Chiang, "Activity Based Benchmarking and Process Management – Managing the Case of Cardiac Surgery," Fall 2002

Lawrence A. Gordon and Martin P. Loeb, "Distinguishing Between Direct and Indirect Costs is Crucial for Internet Companies," Summer 2001.

Anthony J. Hayzen, James M. Reeve, "Examining the Relationships in Productivity Accounting," Summer 2000.

David Johnsen, Parvez Sopariwala, "Standard Costing is
    Alive and Well at Parker Brass," Winter 2000.

Ronald Kettering, "Accounting for Quality with Nonfinancial Measures: A Simple No-Cost Program for the Small Company," Spring 2001

Ted Mitchell and Mike Thomas, "Can Variance Analysis Make Media Marketing Managers More Accountable?" Fall 2005

Priscilla O'Clock and Kevin Devine, "The Role of Strategy and Culture in the Performance Evaluation of International Strategic Business Units," Winter 2003

Harper A. Roehm, Larry Weinstein, Joseph F. Castellano, "Management Control Systems: How SPC Enhances Budgeting and Standard Costing," Fall 2000.

Parvez R. Sopariwala, "Using Direct labor Cost in a Costs vs. Resources Framework," Spring 2004

William W. Stammerjohan, "Better Information Through the Marriage of ABC and Traditional Standard Costing Techniques," Fall 2001

Audrey G. Taylor and Savya Rafai, "Strategic Budgeting: A Case Study and Proposed Framework," Fall 2003

DeWayne L. Searcy, "Using Activity Based Costing to Assess Channel/Customer Profitability," Winter 2004

Lakshmi U. Tatikonda, and Rao J. Tatikonda, "Activity Based Costing for Higher Education Institutions," Fall 2001

"How to Report A Company's Sustainability Activities," Gwendolen H. White, Fall 2005.

Kennard T. Wing, "Using Enhanced Cost Models in Variance Analysis for Better Control and Decision Making," Winter 2000.

Strategic Finance

Terrell L. Carter, Ali Ml Sedghat, Thomas D. Williams, "How ABC Changed the Post Office," February 1998

Gunther Friedl, Hans-Ulrich Kupper and Buckhard Pedell, "Relevance Added: Combining ABC with German Cost Accounting," June 2005.

David Gebler, "Creating an Ethical Culture," May 2006.

Linda Holmes and Ann Hendricks, "Is TOC for You?" April 2005

Robert Kaplan and David Norton, "Strategy Maps," March 2004.

Frances Kennedy and Peter Brewer," Lean Accounting: What's it All About?" November 2005

Gregory T. Lucier, Sridhar Seshadri, "GE Takes Six Sigma Beyond the Bottom Line," May 2001. .

Gary Siegel, James E. Sorensen, and Sandra b. Richtermeyer, "Are You a Business Partner?" Parts 1 and 2, September and October 2003

Richard H. Snyder, "How I Reengineered a Small Business," May 1999.

Nancy Thurley Hill, Kevin T. Stevens, "Structuring Compensation to Achieve Better Financial Results," March 2001.

Ann Triplett, Jon Scheumann, "Managing Shared Services with ABM," February 2000.

Paul B. Weiss, "Buy or Lease" November 2003

Cases from Management Accounting Practice
Volume 1 (1985): The Pump Division
Volume 2 (1986): The Atlantic City Casino , Analysis
  of the Accounting Function; Polymer Products
  Company
Volume 4 (1987): Industrial Chemical Company
Volume 5 (1989): The Rossford Plant, The United
L/N Plant
Volume 6 (1992): Superior Valve Company

Volume 7 (1992): Toll Revenue Sharing
Volume 8 (1992): California Illini Manufacturing
Volumes 10/11 (1997): East River Manufacturing
Volume 12 (1998): Brookwood Medical Center, Precision
  System Inc.
Volume 14 (1998): OutSource, Inc.
Volume 14: (1998) Wellesley Paint, Letsgo Travel Trailers
Volume 15 (2000): Mercedes-Benz All Activity Vehicle
  (AAV), Columbo Soft-Serve Frozen Yogurt

The following materials have been reprinted with permission from the **American Accounting Association**:

Horizons
Wilton L. Accola, "Assessing Risk and Uncertainty in
New
  Technology Investments," September 1994.
Carole B. Cheatham, Leo R. Cheatham, "Redesigning
  Cost Systems: Is Standard Costing Obsolete?"
  December 1996.
Robert S. Kaplan, David P. Norton, "Transforming the
  Balanced Scorecard from Performance
Measurement to
  Strategic Management: Part 1," March 2001.
Robert E. Malcolm, "Overhead Control Implications
  of Activity Costing," December 1991.

Issues in Accounting Education
Ramji Balakrishnan, Utpal Bhattacharya, "Ace
  Company (B): The Option Value of Waiting and
  Capital Budgeting," Fall 1997.
Linda Smith Bamber and K. E. Hughes II, "Activity
  Based Costing in the Service Sector: The Buckeye
  National Bank," August 2001
Robert Bowen and James Wallace, "Interior Systems:
  The Decision to Adopt EVA® August 1999
Peter C. Brewer, Robert J. Campbell, and Richard H.
  McClure, "Wilson Electronics (A) and (B): An
  ABC Capstone Experience," August 2000
Robert Capettini, C.W. Chow, J.E. Williamson,
  "Instructional Case: The Proper Use of Feedback
  Information," Spring 1992.

Chee W. Chow, "Instructional Case: Vincent's Cappuccino
  Express – A Teaching Case to Help Students Master
  Basic Cost Terms and Concepts Through Interactive
  Learning," Spring 1995.
Chee W. Chow, Yuhchang, Dennis F. Togo, "Ace
  Company: A Case for Incorporating Competitive
  Consideration into Teaching of Capital Budgeting," Fall
  1995.
Dean Crawford, Eleanor G. Henry, "Budgeting and
  Performance Evaluation at the Berkshire Toy Company,"
  May 2000.
Vijay Govindarajan, John K. Shank, "Profit Variance
  Analysis: A Strategic Focus," Fall 1989.
Julie H. Hertenstein, "Component Technologies, Inc.:
  Adding Flexconnex Capacity," May 2000.
Alison Hubbard Ashton, Robert H. Ashton, Laureen
  Maines, "Instructional Case: General Medical Center --
  Evaluation of Diagnostic Imaging Equipment,"
  November 1998.
Jack M. Ruhl, Jerry G. Kreuze, "Startup, Inc.: Linking
  Financial Accounting, Managerial Accounting, and
  Strategic Management," Fall 1997.
George J. Staubus, "The Case of the Almost Identical
  Twins," Spring 1993.

Elsevier
Reprinted from the *Journal of Accounting Education*, Vol. 20, No. 3 (2002), Rouse et al., "Instructional Case:
  Capital Budgeting, pp. 235-247, with permission from Elsevier.

Journal of Accounting Education
"Instructional Case: Floating Investments," Paul Rouse and Leigh Houghton, Vol 2, 2002

Additional Acknowledgements:
Robert J. Bowlby, "How Boeing Tracks Costs A to
  Z," *The Financial Executive*. Reprinted with
  permission.
J. C. Cooper and J. D. Suver, "Variance Analysis
  Refines Overhead Cost Control, Healthcare
  Financial Management (February 1992) Used with
  permission

David A. Kunz, Keith A. Russell, "Midwest Petro-
  Chemical Company," Institute of Management
  Accountants, 1996. Used with permission.
Joseph San Miguel, "Target Costing," "Emerson Electric
  Company," "Dallas Consulting Group". Reprinted with
  permission.

Table of Contents

Chapter 1
Cost Management and Strategy: An Overview

Cases

Readings

1-1 "Are You a Business Partner?" Parts 1 and 2 by Gary Siegel, James E. Sorensen, and Sandra Richtermeyer, *Strategic Finance* (September and October 2003).

This article is based on interviews of 100 accountants who have made the transition to business partner. For firms such as McDonalds, Trane, and Boeing, they explain the transition from traditional accountant to accountant as business partner. The study is a follow-up to the 1995-1999 research by the same authors, shown below in "Counting More, Counting Less."

Discussion Questions:
1. What are the key findings of the recent research of 100 accountants, now business partners?
2. What are the implications of these findings for the education and training of management accountants?

1-2 "Creating an Ethical Culture" by David Gebler, *Strategic Finance* (May 2006) pp. 29-34.

This article takes a look at the financial fraud at WorldCom and other companies in recent years, and examines the role of controls and the ethical culture in the frauds that occurred in these companies. In considers the following questions. How does the ethical culture effect the risk of fraud? How does a company develop an ethical culture?

Discussion Questions:
1. According to the article, did WorldCom lack internal controls to detect fraud? Why was the fraud not detected earlier, or prevented all together?
2. According to the Culture Risk Assessment model, what are the levels of values of an organization and what are the objectives of each?
3. What are some of the ways a company can help to develop an ethical culture?

1-3 "How Intel Finance Uses Business Partnerships To Supercharge Results" by Russel R. Boedeker, CMA, CFM , and Susan B. Hughes, CPA, *Strategic Finance* (October 2005) pp. 27-34.

This article is a report on the program within Intel Corporation to develop a business partnering approach between the finance function in the company and the operating managers. The goal is to improve the relevance and effectiveness of the finance function to the managers, and thereby to improve the competitiveness and profitability of the business units.

Discussion Questions:
1. What is the vision of Intel's finance function, and what are the key objectives of this vision?
2. How does the finance function build its credibility at Intel?
3. What are the levels of the scale that finance personnel at Intel strive to achieve, from lowest to highest? Explain what is accomplished at each level.
4. How does Intel measure the success of the finance partnering effort?

Cases

Cost Management and Strategy: An Overview

1-1. Critical Success Factors

Kirsten Malon has found a way to profitably exploit her computer know-how. She has started a firm that offers consulting services for computer and software repair and analysis. Most of her customers have purchased computers or software systems with little vendor support and need help in installing and using the systems effectively. Kirsten has expanded her business recently to include 25 technicians besides herself, and her client base has grown to over 1,900. Many of these clients are on a retainer arrangement (a fixed fee per month which guarantees access to a certain number of hours of technician time) to stabilize her cash flow. With the success of the business, Kirsten is now thinking about beginning a related business which would publish books and newsletters on computer and software issues.

REQUIRED:

What are the critical success factors likely to be for Kirsten's business, now and into the future? What cost management information is she likely to need: management planning and decision making, management and operational control, or product and service costing, and why?

1-2. Contemporary Management Techniques

DeLight Inc., is a large manufacturer of lighting fixtures for both wholesalers and electrical contractors. An important aspect of the business with electrical contractors is Delight's ability to develop product leadership through innovation, quality, and service. In contrast, in the wholesale business, Delight competes primarily on the basis of lowest price. DeLight has prospered in the recent five years because of its careful attention to developing and maintaining a sustainable competitive advantage in each of its markets.

REQUIRED:

Which of the ten types of contemporary management techniques does DeLight probably use? Explain your answer.

Blocher, Stout, Cokins, Chen: *Cost Management, 4e*

1-3. Ethics, Pricing

AeroSpace Inc. is a manufacturer of airplane parts and engines for a variety of military as well as civilian aircraft. Though there are many commercial customers for most of the company's products, the U.S. government is the only buyer of the firm's rocket engines. Because AeroSpace is the sole provider of the engines, the government buys the engines at a price equal to cost plus a percent markup.

The cost system in place at AeroSpace is under review by top management, with the objective of developing a system which will provide more accurate and timelier cost management information.

At the current phase of the study of the cost system, it is now apparent that the new system, while more accurate and timely, will result in lower costs being assigned to the rocket engines and higher costs being assigned to the firm's other products. Apparently, the current (less accurate) cost system has over-costed the engines and under-costed the other products. On hearing of this, top management has decided to scrap the plans for the new cost system, because the rocket engine business with the government is a significant part of AeroSpace's business, and the reduced cost will reduce the price and thus the profits for this part of Aero-Space's business.

REQUIRED:

As a staff cost analyst on the cost review project, how do you see your responsibility when you hear of the decision of top management to cancel the plans for the new cost system?

1-4. Selected Ethics Cases

After his first two years at Bronson Beverages (BB), a publicly held wholesaler of beers and wines, Jim Best has advanced to a senior cost analyst position with a very good salary.

REQUIRED:

For each of the following situations Jim will face in the coming year, indicate how you see his responsibility, and how he should respond.

1. Jim learns that a significant portion of the firm's beer inventory has passed its shelf life and by local ordinance and company policy, should be destroyed. Because of concern about the effect on profits and his bonus, the chief operating officer decides that the beer should be sold anyway.

2. As part of his regular duties, Jim reviews BB's financial statements for inconsistencies and errors. While reviewing the recent report, Jim notices that non-trade accounts receivable (note: non-trade receivables arise from non-operating events, such as a loan to an employee, customer, etc; trade receivables arise from sales on credit) have increased sharply over the prior year. Upon inquiry, Jim finds out that the firm is lending money to one of its customers so that it can make purchases from BB. Jim knows that in his state, beer and wine purchases must be paid for in cash, by state law. Jim wonders if the treatment of the loan as a non-trade receivable is OK, or if it should be classified as a trade receivable?

3. Jim learns that BB has just been granted the franchise to sell a popular new line of custom-brewed beers. The franchise will improve BB's sales and profits substantially, and should mean a significant boost to BB's share price. Jim knows that, until the news of the franchise is made public, he is restricted by the SEC from using this insider information to trade in BB's shares and make unfair profits as a result. That evening, Jim and his wife have dinner with some friends, and one of them says she has heard there are some good things going on at BB, and asks Jim to comment. What should Jim say?

4. Jim is analyzing the sales and cost of sales in specialty wines when he discovers that one of the firm's customers has greatly increased purchases in this, the last month of the firm's fiscal year. Jim goes to talk to the salesperson for this customer to offer his congratulations. The salesperson says that he has simply shipped in advance the customer's order for the following month, so that it would appear on the current year's financial report. This tactic would help the salesperson meet his sales target and would also improve BB's sales and profits for the current year. The salesperson says there is a small chance that the customer will reject the shipment and send it back, but then says, "We will worry about that if it happens."

5. Working late one night, Jim notices that one of the top marketing executives has come into the office and is removing a box full of office supplies. He says in a joking manner to Jim as he leaves, "BB won't miss this stuff, and I really need it for my other business."

Blocher, Stout, Cokins, Chen: *Cost Management, 4e*

1-5 Strategy; Branding Beef

The steaks and roasts and hamburger you buy at the supermarket are what many would call a commodity. For a certain degree of lean, or a certain USDA grade, you have the same product from supermarket to supermarket.   As a commodity, beef is doing pretty well with annual supermarket sales of $60 billion relative to cereal sales of $7.5 billion or soda sales of $13.1 billion.   However, the taste for beef is down, and supermarket demand for beef has fallen by 41% over the last 25 years.   Some meatpackers attribute this to broad social and economic trends, including the fact that two-wage-earner families have less time to prepare meals, and cooking a roast can take hours.   So some meatpackers are working on new products that will improve the convenience of the meat product: pre-cooked roasts and specially-prepared cuts of meat which can be cooked at higher heat levels.

REQUIRED:
1. How would you describe the strategy of the meatpacking industry (cost leadership or differentiation), and why?
2. Do you think the meatpacker's new products will improve sales of beef? Why or why not?

1-6 Sales, Profits, and Competitive Strategy

The top ten U. S. Companies in sales and profits in 2004 are shown below.

	Sales	Profits
1	Wal-Mart	ExxonMobil
2	ExxonMobil	Citigroup
3	General Motors	General Electric
4	Ford Motor	Bank of America
5	Chevron Texaco	Chevron Texaco
6	General Electric	Pfizer
7	ConocoPhillips	AIG
8	CitiGroup	Microsoft
9	AIG	Wal-Mart
10	IBM	Altria Group

REQUIRED:

Which of the above companies do you think are cost leaders or differentiators, and why?

Blocher, Stout, Cokins, Chen: *Cost Management, 4e*

©The McGraw-Hill Companies, Inc 2008

Readings

1.1: ARE YOU A BUSINESS PARTNER?

by Gary Siegel, James E. Sorensen, and Sandra B. Richtermeyer

PART I

Business partners help run businesses. They are consulted on all major decisions. They are proactive with information, are focused on improving business processes, and are team leaders.

Their work is exciting, and they are enthusiastic about what they do. The financial professionals who have become business partners say they are thriving since they added this dimension to their work.

What is a business partner? It's difficult to define a business partner in two or three sentences because the work they do requires a variety of skills, encompasses several disciplines, and impacts the organization in various ways. Are they accountants? In one sense, you could say that business partners are accountants. They still hold fiduciary responsibility and carry out all of the traditional accounting functions. They just do it a lot faster and with a lot fewer people than they used to. But they definitely do more than accounting. They are involved in strategic planning, process improvement, team building, and a host of other activities.

Textbooks tell us that management accountants do scorekeeping, attention directing (for example, alerting management to problems with the management control system and established policies and procedures), and problem solving. Business partners do very little scorekeeping and a lot more problem solving. But they also do more than solve problems.

Business partners have transformed themselves from accountants to superaccountants—from accounting specialists to business generalists. Their perspective has changed. They still do the accounting work but don't see it as their mission. Their mission is business success and performance excellence. They focus on running the business, and accounting is a vehicle to improve performance and help people make better decisions.

So are these superaccountants still accountants? They'll tell you, no. They call themselves business partners. Their titles don't include the "A" word. Sure, if we point out to them that they are a CMA, CFM, or CPA, they will say, "Yes, we earned those credentials, but we don't do accounting." And, yes, they still have to know their debits and credits. But as a business partner at UPS told us, "Our business is delivering packages, not debits and credits."

Making the transition. They have transformed into business partners. They perceive themselves differently, and the people they work with see them differently. But do their colleagues refer to them as business partners? A controller at McDonald's explains:

We probably get called everything in the book—I hope all of it good. I don't know if they call us business partners or not. I hope they would. If you asked them a question about me or some of the other folks in accounting, I would hope they would say, "He is much more than just an accountant." If you asked them, "What types of things does this person do?," they will talk about strategic plans, they will talk about evaluations, they will talk about impact on the business, having an influence on—in my case—individual brands, striving for better business results. All these things are driven around the business, not debits and credits, not anything that is in a traditional accounting realm. Whether they call us a business partner or not, we are doing a lot more than traditional accounting.

Again, are they accountants? Technically, yes. But substantively, no. These financial professionals do much more than traditional accounting. They do decision support, but they are beyond decision support. They are business analysts, but they do more than simply analyze. They are valued for their business savvy and financial insight. They are focused on improving business processes. Their work is light years away from the work traditional accountants did as recently as 15-20 years ago.

Scope of change. Accountants' work had been pretty constant from the development of double entry bookkeeping in 1492, but it took a dramatic turn with the development of high-speed computers in the 1960s and again with the wide-spread diffusion of electronic spreadsheets in the early 1980s. The old accountant is dead or dying. Long live the new accountant! We aren't the same as we were in 1985 or even 1995, which should be a wakeup call to leaders in the profession, business school educators, and corporate executives.

Traditional accountants. To appreciate what a business partner does, let's contrast their role with the role of traditional accountants. Historically, accountants collected and manipulated data, manually worked spreadsheets, checked expense reports, produced inventory reports and standardized financial statements, complied with federal and local tax laws, prepared and maintained the budget, handled the treasury function, worked with outside auditors, held fiduciary responsibility for the company's assets,

"Yes, I'm a Business Partner. You have to know the business. You have to have some credibility, and you have to push your way into things. I have always done that. You have to get some understanding. This is a strongly engineering- and operations oriented company. You have to get to know the business and understand it and not be afraid to push outside of your sphere and then show the link. You just have to push that."—A controller at Trane

made sure that bills were paid and receivables collected, and were available to answer accounting- or tax-related questions. They were the keepers of financial records, preparers of financial reports, treasury officers, internal auditors, and compliance and fiduciary agents. They provided a vital service to their organizations, but they weren't central to running the business. In organization charts, accounting was off to the side—it was a staff function that supported line managers.

Accountants worked mainly with other accountants on accounting projects, such as cost reports, payables, yearend closings, and inventory. They worked in their own world, physically and psychologically isolated from the people who were running the business. In the actual work environment, there were "departments." Accountants worked in the accounting department, but the people running the business worked in other departments. This doesn't imply that accountants had no interaction with other people in the organization. They did. But the accountant's focus was on "doing the accounting": getting the report out on time, doing the payroll, working on the budget. The focus of the line people was on "running the business." Accountants weren't expected to be participants in this.

Accountants were psychologically distant as well. They were seen as numbers crunchers, bookkeepers, and bean counters. Because they prepared and enforced the budgets, they were the corporate cops, the people who could make a line manager's life miserable. They were the naysayers. They were seen as obstacles, not enablers. In the course of interviewing dozens of accountants over the past several years, we have heard many stories about their purposely being kept out of the decision making process. They simply weren't consulted about upcoming decisions involving expenditures. They learned about decisions only after they were made. Why? A frequent explanation is that they were seen as protectors of the budget—the guys (there were few women accountants in the old days) who always said no. So why bother asking?

Accountants were valued for the information system they maintained and the reports they provided. But they weren't valued for their interpretation of the information or the advice they could give on a business question. This implies that accountants weren't considered "big picture" people. They were seen as too focused on the numbers. The implication is that they really didn't sufficiently understand the complexities and nuances of the business, so few people sought their opinions.

Business partners. Then the business world changed. Manual spreadsheets disappeared, and management accountants no longer had to spend hours calculating and checking calculations. Bureaucracies were flattened. Company precedents were questioned. Shared services emerged. Technology made a quantum leap. Continuous improvement became a reality.

As accountants were liberated from the time-consuming, mechanical aspects of accounting, they had to move from the operational level in organizations to the strategic level for the profession to survive and remain relevant. Their knowledge of basic financial tools wasn't sufficient to keep them relevant; they had to enhance their knowledge and acquire advanced financial tools. In many companies, financial professionals used their freed-up time to create a new role for themselves as business partners, which required them to become generalists. Those who have successfully made the switch tell us that there are some lingering jokes about "bean counters" in their organizations, but that isn't how they are perceived anymore. Now they are considered proactive and available and are sought-after participants in the decision making process. They are seen as valued team members and enablers. As another business partner at McDonald's said, "We are not asked when the pro-

Blocher, Stout, Cokins, Chen: *Cost Management, 4e*

ject is almost done to come out here and run some numbers; we are invited early on."

The physical and psychological isolation has broken down. Physically, those who have become business partners have moved out of the accounting department. Many work with the groups they support. This means their desk could be in the marketing department, on the factory floor, or in an office adjacent to the president's. Most of their day is spent sharing information with others. Shared objectives and shared perspectives have erased the psychological isolation. The term "business partner" is itself very telling of a new identity. Partners have an equal voice and an equal vote on decisions. They have the right to challenge faulty logic or faulty assumptions, regardless of who makes a statement. Indeed, it is expected that a partner do this. A partner is actively involved in business decisions. Before accountants became business partners they "serviced their internal customers." Their mission was to satisfy their customers' needs. A principle of quality service is that the customer is always right. In practice, this meant that if a marketing vice president asked for a particular report, the accountant was expected to deliver it as ordered. It didn't matter if the requested information wasn't the most relevant to the decision or if interpreted in a particular way could result in a dysfunctional decision. "The customer was king," and it wasn't accounting's prerogative to second-guess the decision maker.

Not so with business partners. They have to understand what the business problem is and work with the team to determine which information is most relevant. Then they interpret the information and work with the team to make the decision. They have to understand how accounting information and practices impact behavior and, ultimately, performance. They have to foresee how company decisions and practices will impact accounting reports. And they educate their teams about the tax and financial implications of company actions.

A corporate controller from a large, publicly traded company describes the business partner philosophy: *"I just made a presentation to a group of 20-30 of our assistant regional controllers from around the country, and I told them that the most important thing they can do is move the business, which really doesn't have much to do with numbers. It has to do with understanding that you have fiduciary duty, but you can never fulfill your fiduciary duty and get the business moving in the right direction unless you have the right kind of relationships with your management. You start with your regional manager. You should be the first person the regional manager goes to when they want to*

ask a question. I don't think accountants can do their job unless they know almost as much about the business as everybody around them because we are supposed to assess the answers we get. If you are able to understand the various parts of the business, you are the best person for senior management to go to for advice and guidance. This doesn't just happen because you are an accountant or are good analytically. It happens because you go out of your way to create relationships that allow you to do that when the time comes. I think that's the biggest thing we are talking about nowadays—customer satisfaction at a very high level. It's very much about having the confidence of the people that you need to do this interpretation for to help run the business.

"Yes, I'm a Business Partner. ...it was an open dialogue and they [accountants] were treated as an equal at the table, and they were at the front end making the decision, not given the answer and go figure it out."—A controller at Boeing

In many organizations, business partners have taken leadership roles on teams. Unlike team members in marketing or engineering, accountants aren't seen as having their own agenda. As corporate insiders explained to us, the marketing person is focused on market share, and the engineer is focused on design issues. But the business partner is perceived as having an overview of the organization as a whole and an understanding of the financial implications of actions. They can point out to the marketing person or the engineer whether a proposed action will enhance the company's well being. In this way, business partners are perceived as committed to the organization's goals.

Skill set. What skills do business partners need to do all of this? They need excellent communication and interpersonal skills, team-building skills, and analytical skills.

"Yes, I'm a Business Partner. I see an overall trend that has been going on for some time of more empowerment at lower levels of the organization. More and more individual work teams and work groups are trying to make decisions that have a large financial component to them in managing their daily work, whereas they might not have been thinking about it in that way before. I think it is going to increase. There is more demand for financial support at a lower level—more demand for accountants to help. In wing manufacturing, [the staff focuses] on particular parts of

the process in building the airplane. The demand for financial support is insatiable. They want to know, and they need to know: What is the consequence of doing this? If we stream-line this, how does it impact us financially? What does that do to us? Does it impact the value stream? They need accountants to help them with that kind of information. I see a continued growth in that kind of activity and the need for accountants as the trusted busi-ness advisor. That is one aspect that I really think will continue to expand and grow."

—A financial director from Boeing

They need a thorough understanding of the business they work in. This is critical because, without that understanding, they can't add value. They should be familiar with the quality literature (cost of quality, Six Sigma, ISO 9000-2000, Criteria for Performance Excellence, and the like) and know how to use quality tools (affinity diagrams, interrelationship digraphs, cause-and-effect diagrams). And an understanding of psychology and social psychology will help them learn how to resolve conflicts and motivate people. What about accounting skills? This is a given. Any business partner is expected to have a comprehensive knowledge of accounting and tax laws.

Their work encompasses the disciplines of accounting, some finance, some systems, and some decision support. To be effective in their roles, they have to be familiar with all of the business functions (marketing, purchasing, engineering), the processes that run their organization, and how the processes, functions, and people work together. As another McDonald's controller observed regarding decision support: *When voice recognition becomes even more prevalent, the chief executive is just going to scream at a computer, and it is going to tell him the answers to the question. So the funda-mental basics of scorekeeping will be done by ma-chines, all of it, and also much of the analytical work. Accountants are basically interpreters. That doesn't mean that they just interpret numbers. They tell people what to do with them.*

The future. For accountants who have made the transition to business partner, or would like to make the transition, the way to remain rele-vant is perseverance, stamina, and a commitment to lifelong learning. For educators, the challenge is to prepare their students to become business partners, not "accountants." Accounting programs still have to teach students the intricacies of the accounting information system, cash flows, data flows, the relationships between the financial statements, and the like. But there has to be more emphasis on de-cision support and understanding a business—more emphasis on using the information. Students must learn how to handle qualitative data because they will be attending meetings and will have to make sense out of hours of back-and forth discussion. They should be introduced to the Baldrige Criteria for Performance Excellence. They should learn how to use some quality tools. But step one is that they need to be informed that there's a new occu-pation called business partner to which they can aspire.

For leaders in the profession, many issues have to be addressed. Do we continue to call our-selves accountants, or do we select a new name? How can the most appropriate continuing profes-sional education (CPE) be developed and deliv-ered? How should professional associations re-spond to the ongoing changes in work roles and responsibilities? The answers to these questions will determine the future of our profession. ∎

"Yes, I'm a Business Partner. ... once we went to business units, people started acting like [they were] their independent businesses. So suddenly it was more important for them to have broader business knowledge. At that point, I think in almost every profit center the senior accounting person became the right hand person to business unit managers be-cause they were the person they turned to with, 'Help me understand the financial data I'm getting. Help me understand what levers I can move to make the financial data to be what I want it to be.'"—A corporate accounting manager from Caterpillar.

PART II

There are many paths you can take to become a business partner. And it's up to you to select the path. Don't expect someone in your company to suddenly declare that you are a business partner; you're the only one who can make it happen. You have to want the role, and you have to work for it. As a controller at McDonald's put it *The account-ing department proved itself. It wasn't that all of a sudden we said we wanted to be business partners and everybody applauded. It was a process. We made sure we hired the best and the brightest. They are well rounded in technical skills and analytical skills, and one of the key competencies they had was the ability to communicate financial informa-tion. We set the tone by our higher-level financial organization...and, over time, the financial organi-*

Blocher, Stout, Cokins, Chen: *Cost Management, 4e*

zation proved its value in projects, in identifying certain business opportunities, and the like.

There are other necessary factors also. To become a business partner, it's a given that you know your accounting cold. You're expected to know the tax implications of proposed courses of action. You need to understand cost flows and information flows. You have to be very comfortable with technology and be an expert in the company's business and accounting software. You have to be a generalist. You need a working knowledge of what people do in marketing, engineering, human resources, and other departments. You need to understand how the processes, departments, and functions work together to run the business. You'll be expected to contribute ideas at planning meetings, so you have to see the big picture, keep a focus on the bottom line, and think strategically. Most important, you must understand the business. You have to know how the company makes money and how the industry is structured. Another controller from McDonald's explained:

McDonald's is very heavily operations oriented, which means that the operations guys are first, second, third, fourth, and fifth. We managed to create a situation in the U.K. where accounting was first and operations was second. The way we did that was understanding the business, building relationships, and showing we were willing to participate in the day-to-day operation of the business. For instance, in 1996, before I came to the U.S., I spent seven months going through full-time operations training in a restaurant, starting as a crew member and ending up as an assistant manager, so that I understood what the operations folks had to do on a day-to-day basis. Once I got to that level, the rest of it was just normal management practice. So it was a willingness to go well beyond just thinking about accounting to thinking about the business as a whole that generated that kind of reputation.

MAKING THE TRANSITION

The transformation to business partner requires vision, hard work, and perseverance. It occurred differently in each of the six companies we interviewed, so we thought it would be beneficial to concentrate on one company at a time. In this article we focus on Caterpillar, where changes were driven by a corporate reorganization. We'll tell Caterpillar's story in the words of the accountants who experienced the changes—a controller, a vice president, a financial reporting manager, and several business managers of product lines (business

managers are at the same level as product managers). Accounting at Caterpillar has always been held at a pretty high plane, partially because in the 1950s and 1960s, two of the Caterpillar chairmen were former controllers at Caterpillar. They and the whole organization realized the importance of accounting. Also, they were instrumental in creating Caterpillar's cost system, which we are very proud of and which is seen as a world-class cost system. Accounting wasn't just a function at Caterpillar—it was a vital function.

Changes started about 1986 when Caterpillar initiated a $2 billion worldwide modernization program, a large sum for any company. And Caterpillar is conservative. We run things by the numbers a lot, and this modernization program was such a big commitment that people really looked to the accounting organization for the objective and financial perspective on how things were going. They wanted to make sure that we got the returns we expected in terms of working capital improvements, labor efficiencies, and so on. They looked to the numbers to help support the direction in which we were going. This really created the partnership or cemented the partnership relationship. By 1989, I felt we were partners with the manufacturing people, the planning people, and the executive officers. Then in 1990, Caterpillar reorganized itself into profit centers. Before the reorganization, we were an extremely centralized, bureaucratic company, with decisions being made at the top. Then we changed from a functional organization to one that was organized on a profit-center basis with about 26 profit centers or business units. The person in charge of running a business unit was evaluated on return on investment and the unit's profitability. Each vice president had to run his business with a P&L. Each unit had a business manager reporting to the profit center in that organization. These business managers were accountants. With the creation of business units, obviously, you become a business manager rather than an accountant. As a business manager, you get involved in all aspects of the business, in finding ways and solutions to help the business achieve strategic objectives.

In the old days, you had a plant accountant who worked at the plant and didn't have much responsibility other than to cost the product. But after the reorganization we had an entrepreneurial relationship within that plant. Caterpillar created, for the first time, high-level managers at the plant level who had total responsibility for the product, for the design, manufacturing, pricing, and all those functions that used to be in a central location in the functional organization. Then the business manager was created at the business-unit level who was at as high a level as the product managers who ran the company.

What helped make the accountants partners and a big part of the management community is that each vice president relied on us to help run his business. We analyzed the results, answered questions about why things were better, and, maybe even more important, why things were worse. This is critical.

ORGANIZATIONAL EDUCATORS

The organizational change was advanced by a companywide educational program initiated by the accounting leadership. Caterpillar business partners describe that effort.

To get people to really understand what we were doing, we spent a large amount of time training this new organization that we split into business units. The accountants took on the burden of educating the various divisions about what the numbers meant and how they could impact them. We had a program called "Understanding the Business 101" that we presented to all 1,100 salaried people and all 2,000 hourly people. Everybody was interested because they knew it was going to impact their incentive plan. We taught them what financial results are, how we get the information, and how we measure it. We showed them how a welder impacts our business, how a purchasing person impacts our business. This put us in something like a counseling position because we were the teachers. One of the great things that the reorganization did in unbundling the corporation and developing 26 different business units was to create 1,000 businesspeople. Now, the best engineer is a general manager, and the best planning person is running a new business.

We accountants took the leadership role, became counselors, and helped cultivate a real business sense within Caterpillar. We would have floundered had we not done that. These businesspeople we created came back to us and involved us in running their business, which was a major transformation for the company.

LINES OF RESPONSIBILITY ARE IMPORTANT

The following vignette reveals the thought that went into building a new organization and the importance of clear lines of responsibility. Some of us were concerned about the control aspects of the new organization—we weren't very familiar with it. There was some thought given to the idea that maybe the business managers ought to report to the

corporate controller rather than up through the profit-center chain. While that might have made us feel better from a control standpoint, it wouldn't have cemented the partnership relationship. So our business managers report to the profit center. That was a big decision. As it turns out, control issues haven't been a problem over the years.

Coupled with the reorganization of the profit centers was a change in the function of the corporate offices, which were once accounting general offices that told people what to do. In our new organization, we had to charge for our services, which also makes for a partnership point of view. We had to become very customer friendly, and, rather than tell people what to do, we had to jointly agree on things, and we had to get them to agree to take charges for our services.

CHANGING ACCOUNTANTS' SELF-IMAGE

What effect did the change to business partner have on accountants' self-image? What were some of the challenges encountered in the process of change? Caterpillar business partners describe the events: First and foremost is the mental attitude—accepting the fact that you have a different role to play other than just reporting the results. That was the first thing the accountants had to learn.

Our purpose now was to help guide the different business units and profit centers—help them achieve their strategic goals and objectives. Accountants had to say: "We have a different role to play. We are no longer going to be people who just present data or monitor activities to ensure that people perform according to certain guidelines. We are here to identify opportunities that we could capture and lock in."

Everything started from defining our role. Was it simply to collect and present the data, or was it to analyze the data and look at opportunities outside the accounting functions and say, "How do we leverage that to make this more of a successful approach to doing the business?" We became involved in different aspects of the business. We got involved in marketing strategies, in acquisitions, in designing strategic directions. It became important that we were viewed as a partner with the different business units rather than their just viewing us as presenting information or monitoring.

ORGANIZATIONAL CULTURE

The change in self-image coincided with a change in the organizational culture at Caterpillar.

It used to be, "I'm an engineer; I design. I'm an accountant; I will keep track of the cost."

Blocher, Stout, Cokins, Chen: *Cost Management, 4e*

The culture evolved to where everybody's role was broadened in that they became part of a business and became better businesspeople. Engineers had to think: "How much does it cost to produce a part if I design it this way or that way?" They didn't think this way before. They used to design a part, give it to a manufacturing guy who had to provide it, and then down the road the accountant had to cost it. But now, as a result of the reorganization and the fact that every business unit has their own P&L responsibilities, everybody is more aware of the commercial aspects of what they are doing. Everybody's level was raised, and the accountant became a higher species in the food chain. They were looked to for guidance as things were thought about in a P&L commercial aspect, which wasn't the case before.

OBSTACLES

Common obstacles in making the transition to business partner are lack of time, expertise, top-management support, and operational support. In addition, difficulty changing the corporate culture, obtaining trust, and gaining access to information may also create roadblocks. Here's what the Caterpillar financial professionals say: The biggest obstacle on the path to becoming a business partner was the cultural change in getting people to think more broadly. Another challenge was having to come up with a balanced set of measures to measure the new organization—a set of measures that could be used for incentive pay to motivate the behavior the company wanted.

That was probably our biggest challenge. Some people found the change to be difficult. But the majority saw it as an opportunity to grow and contribute. In any kind of activity, there are those who are locked into the way they think and behave, but those who were open minded and had a broader perspective succeeded. As accountants and younger people saw the successes of some of the original participants, they tried to emulate that. They wanted to get outside the accounting pigeon-hole they had been identified with. The more they did differently and the more they participated, the more the enterprise valued them and the more in demand they became. The more they were in demand, the more activities they became involved in. The more activities they were involved in, the more attractive it became for the other managers to ask for their help.

EFFECT ON NONACCOUNTANTS

We also asked the Caterpillar accountants how the change to business partner affected non-accountants.

They told us: Many leaders in the business units were not accountants, not finance people. They were marketing people, manufacturing people, and others, so they tended to depend more and more heavily on the accountants for their success. As the rest of the organization began to recognize that the accountants not only talked about numbers but talked about strategies and approaches to business, they began to listen to them. It started at the top. It definitely didn't bubble from the bottom up. It started at the top by the business-unit managers and profit-center vice presidents depending more and more on the accountants and using the accountant as a right-hand man or woman in helping them guide their businesses. The organization, having seen that, was willing to listen to the accountants.

WILL YOU MAKE THE LEAP?

Once more, becoming a business partner takes a great deal of hard work, perseverance, vision, and spirit. Most of the financial professionals we interviewed who have made the transition say the effort was worth it and that they are thriving in their new roles. They say they feel more valued, more a part of the business, and more challenged to do excellent work. Will you make the leap and join them?

This article is based on interviews with more than 100 accountants who have made the transition to business partner. The interviews were part of the research project, "How to Become a Business Partner," the fourth in a series of applied IMA research studies that focus on the changes in accountants' work and work roles. The authors are the research team. Previous IMA projects are "What Corporate America Wants in Entry-Level Accountants" (1994), "The Practice Analysis of Management Accountants" (1996), and "Counting More, Counting Less: Transformations in the Management Accounting Profession" (1999). Executive summaries of the previous research are available on IMA's website at www.imanet.org. Click on Resources, then IMA Studies. Results of "How to Become a Business Partner" will be available this fall in hard copy form and also on the IMA-website.

1.2: CREATING AN ETHICAL CULTURE

by David Gebler

While the fate of former Enron leaders Kenneth Lay and Jeffrey Skilling is being determined in what has been labeled the "Trial of the Century," former WorldCom managers are in jail for pulling off one of the largest frauds in history. Yes, criminal activity definitely took place in these companies and in dozens more that have been in the news in recent years, but what's really important is to take stock of the nature of many of the perpetrators. Some quotes from former WorldCom executives paint a different picture of corporate criminals than we came to know in other eras:

"I'm sorry for the hurt that has been caused by my cowardly behavior."
—*Scott Sullivan, CFO*

"Faced with a decision that required strong moral courage, I took the easy way out....There are no words to describe my shame."
—*Buford Yates, director of general accounting*

"At the time I consider the single most critical character defining moment of my life, I failed. It's something I'll take with me the rest of my life."
—*David Myers, controller*

These are the statements of good people gone bad. But probably most disturbing was the conviction of Betty Vinson, the senior manager in the accounting department who booked billions of dollars in false expenses. At her sentencing, U.S. District Judge Barbara Jones noted that Vinson was among the lowest-ranking members of the conspiracy that led to the $11 billion fraud that sank the telecommunications company in 2002. Still, she said, "Had Ms. Vinson refused to do what she was asked, it's possible this conspiracy might have been nipped in the bud." Judge Jones added that although Ms. Vinson "was among the least culpable members of the conspiracy" and acted under extreme pressure, "that does not excuse what she did." Vinson said she improperly covered up expenses by drawing down reserve accounts—some completely unrelated to the expenses—and by moving expenses off income statements and listing them as assets on the balance sheet. Also the company's former director of corporate reporting, Vin-

son testified at Bernie Ebbers's trial that, in choosing which accounts to alter, "I just really pulled some out of the air. I used some spreadsheets." She said she repeatedly brought her concerns to colleagues and supervisors, once describing the entries to a coworker as "just crazy." In spring 2002, she noted, she told one boss she would no longer make the entries. "I said that I thought the entries were just being made to make the income statement look like Scott wanted it to look." Standing before the judge at her sentencing, Vinson said: "I never expected to be here, and I certainly won't do anything like this again." She was sentenced to five months in prison and five months of house arrest.

PRESSURE REIGNS

While the judge correctly said that her lack of culpability didn't excuse her actions, we must carefully note that Betty Vinson, as well as many of her codefendants, didn't start out as criminals seeking to defraud the organization. Under typical antifraud screening tools, she and others like her wouldn't have raised any red flags as being potential committers of corporate fraud. Scott Sullivan was a powerful leader with a well-known reputation for integrity. If any of us were in Betty Vinson's shoes, could we say with 100% confidence that we would say "no" to the CFO if he asked us to do something and promised that he would take full responsibility for any fallout from the actions we were going to take? Today's white-collar criminals are more likely to be those among us who are unable to withstand the blistering pressures placed on managers to meet higher and tougher goals. In this environment, companies looking to protect themselves from corporate fraud must take a hard look at their own culture. Does it promote ethical behavior, or does it emphasize something else? In most companies, "ethics" programs are really no more than compliance programs with a veneer of "do the right thing" messaging to create an apparent link to the company's values. To be effective, they have to go deeper than outlining steps to take to report misconduct. Organizations must understand what causes misconduct in the first place. We can't forget that Enron had a Code of Ethics. And it wasn't as if WorldCom lacked extensive internal controls. But both had cultures where engaging in unethical conduct was tacitly condoned, if not encouraged.

Blocher, Stout, Cokins, Chen: *Cost Management, 4e*

BUILDING THE RIGHT CULTURE

Now the focus has shifted toward looking at what is going on inside organizations that's either keeping people from doing the right thing or, just as importantly, keeping people from doing something about misconduct they observe. If an organization wants to reduce the risk of unethical conduct, it must focus more effort on building the right culture than on building a compliance infrastructure. The Ethics Resource Center's 2005 National Business Ethics Survey (NBES) clearly confirms this trend toward recognizing the role of corporate culture. Based on interviews with more than 3,000 employees and managers in the U.S., the survey disclosed that, despite the increase in the number of ethics and compliance program elements being implemented, desired outcomes, such as reduced levels of observed misconduct, haven't changed since 1994. Even more striking is the revelation that, although formal ethics and compliance programs have some impact, organizational culture has the greatest influence in determining program outcomes. The Securities & Exchange Commission (SEC) and the Department of Justice have also been watching these trends. Stephen Cutler, the recently retired SEC director of the Division of Enforcement, was matter of fact about the importance of looking at culture when it came to decisions of whether or not to bring an action. "We're trying to induce companies to address matters of tone and culture….What we're asking of that CEO, CFO, or General Counsel goes beyond what a pep walk or an enforcement action against another company executive might impel her to do. We're hoping that if she sees that a failure of corporate culture can result in a fine that significantly exceeds the proverbial 'cost of doing business,' and reflects a failure on her watch—and a failure on terms that everyone can understand: the company's bottom line—she may have a little more incentive to pay attention to the environment in which her company's employees do their jobs."

MEASURING SUCCESS

Only lagging companies still measure the success of their ethics and compliance programs just by tallying the percentage of employees who have certified that they read the Code of Conduct and attended ethics and compliance training. The true indicator of success is whether the company has made significant progress in achieving key program outcomes. The National Business Ethics Survey listed four key outcomes that help determine the success of a program:

- Reduced misconduct observed by employees,
- Reduced pressure to engage in unethical conduct,
- Increased willingness of employees to report misconduct, and
- Greater satisfaction with organizational response to reports of misconduct.

What's going to move these outcomes in the right direction? Establishing the right culture. Most compliance programs are generated from "corporate" and disseminated down through the organization. As such, measurement of the success of the program is often based on criteria important to the corporate office: how many employees certified the Code of Conduct, how many employees went through the training, or how many calls the hotline received. Culture is different—and is measured differently. An organization's culture isn't something that's created by senior leadership and then rolled out. A culture is an objective picture of the organization, for better or worse. It's the sum total of all the collective values and behaviors of all employees, managers, and leaders. By definition, it can only be measured by criteria that reflect the individual values of all employees, so understanding cultural vulnerabilities that can lead to ethics issues requires knowledge of what motivates employees in the organization. Leadership must know how the myriad human behaviors and interactions fit together like puzzle pieces to create a whole picture. An organization moves toward an ethical culture only if it understands the full range of values and behaviors needed to meet its ethical goals. The "full-spectrum" organization is one that creates a positive sense of engagement and purpose that drives ethical behavior. Why is understanding the culture so important in determining the success of a compliance program? Here's an example: Most organizations have a policy that prohibits retaliation against those who bring forward concerns or claims. But creating a culture where employees feel safe enough to admit mistakes and to raise uncomfortable issues requires more than a policy and "Code training." To truly develop an ethical culture, the organization must be aware of how its managers deal with these issues up and down the line and how the values they demonstrate impact desired behaviors. The organization must understand the pressures its people are under and how they react to those pressures. And it must know how its managers communicate and whether employees have a sense of accountability and purpose.

CATEGORIZING VALUES

Determining whether an organization has the capabilities to put such a culture in place requires careful examination. Do employees and managers demonstrate values such as respect? Do employees feel accountable for their actions and feel that they have a stake in the success of the organization? How does an organization make such a determination? One approach is to categorize different types of values in a way that lends itself to determining specific strengths and weaknesses that can be assessed and then corrected or enhanced. The Culture Risk Assessment model presented in Figure 1 has been adapted from the Cultural Transformation Tools® developed by Richard Barrett & Associates. Such tools provide a comprehensive framework for measuring cultures by mapping values. More than 1,000 organizations in 24 countries have used this technique in the past six years. In fact, the international management consulting firm McKinsey & Co. has adopted it as its method of choice for mapping corporate cultures and measuring progress toward achieving culture change. The model is based on the principle, substantiated through practice, that all values can be assigned to one of seven categories:

Levels 1, 2, and 3—The Organization's Basic Needs

Does the organization support values that enable it to run smoothly and effectively? From an ethics perspective, is the environment one in which employees feel physically and emotionally safe to report unethical behavior and to do the right thing?

Level 1—Financial Stability. Every organization needs to make financial stability a primary concern. Companies that are consumed with just surviving struggle to focus enough attention on how they conduct themselves. This may, in fact, create a negative cycle that makes survival much more difficult. Managers may exercise excessive control, so employees may be working in an environment of fear.

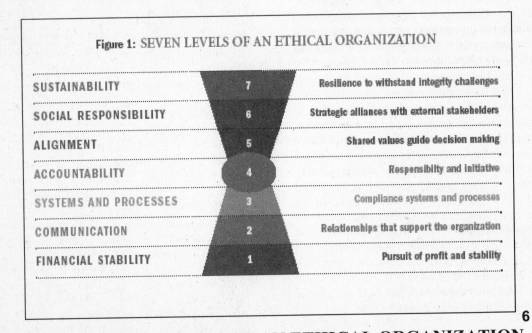

Figure 1: SEVEN LEVELS OF AN ETHICAL ORGANIZATION

SUSTAINABILITY	7	Resilience to withstand integrity challenges
SOCIAL RESPONSIBILITY	6	Strategic alliances with external stakeholders
ALIGNMENT	5	Shared values guide decision making
ACCOUNTABILITY	4	Responsibility and initiative
SYSTEMS AND PROCESSES	3	Compliance systems and processes
COMMUNICATION	2	Relationships that support the organization
FINANCIAL STABILITY	1	Pursuit of profit and stability

6

Figure 1: SEVEN LEVELS OF AN ETHICAL ORGANIZATION
© Working Values, Ltd. Based on Cultural Transformation Tools © Richard Barrett & Associates

In these circumstances, unethical or even illegal conduct can be rationalized. When asked to conform to regulations, organizations do the minimum with an attitude of begrudging compliance. Organizations with challenges at this level need to be confident that managers know and stand within clear ethical boundaries.

Level 2—Communication. Without good relationships with employees, customers, and suppliers, integrity is compromised. The critical issue at this level is to create a sense of loyalty and belonging among employees and a sense of caring and connection between the organization and its customers. The most critical link in the chain is between employees and their direct supervisors. If direct supervisors can't effectively reinforce mes-

Blocher, Stout, Cokins, Chen: *Cost Management, 4e*

sages coming from senior leadership, those messages might be diluted and confused by the time they reach line employees. When faced with conflicting messages, employees will usually choose to follow the lead of their direct supervisor over the words of the CEO that have been conveyed through an impersonal communication channel. Disconnects in how local managers "manage" these messages often mean that employees can face tremendous pressure in following the lead established by leadership. Fears about belonging and lack of respect lead to fragmentation, dissension, and disloyalty. When leaders meet behind closed doors or fail to communicate openly, employees suspect the worst. Cliques form, and gossip becomes rife. When leaders are more focused on their own success, rather than the success of the organization, they begin to compete with each other.

Level 3—Systems and Processes.

At this level, the organization is focused on becoming the best it can be through the adoption of best practices and a focus on quality, productivity, and efficiency. Level 3 organizations have succeeded in implementing strong internal controls and have enacted clear standards of conduct. Those that succeed at this level are the ones that see internal controls as an opportunity to create better, more efficient processes. But even those that have successfully deployed business processes and practices need to be alert to potentially limiting aspects of being too focused on processes. All organizations need to be alert to resorting to a "check-the-box" attitude that assumes compliance comes naturally from just implementing standards and procedures. Being efficient all too often leads to bureaucracy and inconsistent application of the rules.

When this goes badly, employees lose respect for the system and resort to self-help to get things done. This can lead to shortcuts and, in the worst case, engaging in unethical conduct under the guise of doing what it takes to succeed.

Level 4—Accountability

The focus of the fourth level is on creating an environment in which employees and managers begin to take responsibility for their own actions. They want to be held accountable, not micromanaged and supervised every moment of every day. For an ethics and compliance program to be successful, all employees must feel that they have a personal responsibility for the integrity of the organization. Everyone must feel that his or her voice is being heard. This requires managers and leaders to admit that they don't have all the answers and invite employee participation.

Levels 5, 6, and 7—Common Good,

Does the organization support values that create a collective sense of belonging where employees feel that they have a stake in the success of the ethics program?

Level 5—Alignment.

The critical issue at this level is developing a shared vision of the future and a shared set of values. The shared vision clarifies the intentions of the organization and gives employees a unifying purpose and direction. The shared values provide guidance for making decisions. The organization develops the ability to align decision making around a set of shared values. The values and behaviors must be reflected in all of the organization's processes and systems, with appropriate consequences for those who aren't willing to walk the talk. A precondition for success at this level is building a climate of trust.

Level 6—Social Responsibility.

At this level, the organization is able to use its relationships with stakeholders to sustain itself through crises and change. Employees and customers see that the organization is making a difference in the world through its products and services, its involvement in the local community, or its willingness to fight for causes that improve humanity. They must feel that the company cares about them and their future. Companies operating at this level go the extra mile to make sure they are being responsible citizens. They support and encourage employees' activities in the community by providing time off for volunteer work and/or making a financial contribution to the charities that employees are involved in.

Level 7—Sustainability.

To be successful at Level 7, organizations must embrace the highest ethical standards in all their interactions with employees, suppliers, customers, shareholders, and the community. They must always consider the long-term impact of their decisions and actions. Employee values are distributed across all seven levels. Through surveys, organizations learn which values employees bring to the workplace and which values are missing. Organizations don't operate from any one level of values: They tend to be clustered around three or four levels. Most are focused on the first three: profit and growth (Level 1), customer satisfaction (Level 2), and productivity, efficiency, and quality (Level 3). The most successful organizations operate across the full spectrum with particular focus in the upper levels of consciousness—the common good—accountability, leading to learning and innovation (Level 4), alignment (Level 5), sustainability (Level 6), and social responsibility (Level 7).

Some organizations have fully developed values around Levels 1, 2, and 3 but are lacking in Levels 5, 6, and 7. They may have a complete infrastructure of controls and procedures but may lack the accountability and commitment of employees and leaders to go further than what is required. Similarly, some organizations have fully developed values around Levels 5, 6, and 7 but are deficient in Levels 1, 2, and 3. These organizations may have visionary leaders and externally focused social responsibility programs, but they may be lacking in core systems that will ensure that the higher-level commitments are embedded into day-today processes. Once an organization understands its values' strengths and weaknesses, it can take specific steps to correct deficient behavior.

STARTING THE PROCESS

Could a deeper understanding of values have saved WorldCom? We will never know, but if the culture had encouraged open communication and fostered trust, people like Betty Vinson might have been more willing to confront orders that they knew were wrong. Moreover, if the culture had embodied values that encouraged transparency, mid-level managers wouldn't have been asked to engage in such activity in the first place. The significance of culture issues such as these is also being reflected in major employee surveys that highlight what causes unethical behavior. According to the NBES, "Where top management displays certain ethics-related actions, employees are 50 percentage points less likely to observe misconduct." No other factor in any ethics survey can demonstrate such a drastic influence. So how do compliance leaders move their organizations to these new directions?

1. The criteria for success of an ethics program must be outcomes based. Merely checking off program elements isn't enough to change behavior.

2. Each organization must identify the key indicators of its culture. Only by assessing its own ethical culture can a company know what behaviors are the most influential in effecting change.

3. The organization must gauge how all levels of employees perceive adherence to values by others within the company. One of the surprising findings of the NBES was that managers, especially senior managers, were out of touch with how nonmanagement employees perceived their adherence to ethical behaviors. Nonmanagers are 27 percentage points less likely than senior managers to indicate that executives engage in all of the ethics-related actions outlined in the survey.

4. Formal programs are guides to shape the culture, not vice versa. People who are inclined to follow the rules appreciate the rules as a guide to behavior. Formal program elements need to reflect the culture in which they are deployed if they are going to be most effective in driving the company to the desired outcomes. Culture may be new on the radar screen, but it isn't outside the scope or skills of forward-thinking finance managers and compliance professionals. Culture can be measured, and finance managers can play a leadership role in developing systematic approaches to move companies in the right direction.

Blocher, Stout, Cokins, Chen: *Cost Management, 4e*

1-3: HOW INTEL FINANCE USES BUSINESS PARTNERSHIPS TO SUPERCHARGE RESULTS

b y Russel R. Boedeker, CMA, CFM ,
and Susan B. Hughes, CPA

BEST PRACTICES IN FINANCE

The roles of the finance and accounting functions have changed over the past few years. In place of the traditional scorekeepers and tabulators, both accounting and finance personnel now find themselves operating in cross-functional teams working to identify new business opportunities, streamline operations, and improve profitability. Intel describes the active involvement of finance and accounting personnel in making decisions that affect the various operating units as a business partnership between finance and operations.

The business partnership concept began at Intel during the 1980s and accelerated to its current state during the leadership of CFO Andy Bryant. In a successful partnership, finance personnel use their business influence to help operating areas deliver above-average financial and business results, thereby increasing shareholder value. Since the finance function isn't involved in the daily activities of the operations area, it stays focused on the financial impact of various decisions. Operations gains a finance partner who is well versed in the business, is skilled at data analysis, and has the ability to clearly communicate the financial returns of various decisions. To better understand how Intel developed its finance partnerships into a best-practice approach to achieve operating and financial excellence, we interviewed senior controllers and operations managers within Intel. Their overwhelming conclusion is that when a highly competent general manager and a strong finance professional form an effective partnership, they can accomplish great things within the business unit.

THE FINANCE BUSINESS PARTNER

The Finance Vision and Charter (Table 1) emphasizes the importance of finance as a partner and identifies the potential for finance personnel to enhance profitability. Rather than working for a specific operating unit, finance personnel are employed within the finance function (see Figure 1) and partner with at least one operating area. This structure differs from that of organizations in which finance personnel work within specific operating areas and locations. An Intel finance professional may support operating areas as small as a single department or as large as an entire factory, depending on the experience level of the finance employee. The finance charter says finance employees are to "provide effective analysis, influence, leadership, and control as business partners" to their operating areas. Using its network across the company, Intel finance is able to tap expertise from finance employees who support other operational areas. For example, other finance employees may have developed expertise at solving particular pricing or valuation issues that are currently being analyzed within other parts of the organization. By staying in a separate reporting structure, Intel finance maintains an objective view across the company and works in the overall best interests of the stockholders. Maintaining finance as a separate function—one that's responsive to and anticipates the needs of the operations area—results in an environment in which finance guides operations to make better decisions for the company than the group would have made without finance's involvement. The final decisions, however, remain with the operations manager, either the general manager or vice president. This lack of decision-making authority for finance can lead to conflicts and requires finance personnel to use effective partnership techniques to achieve optimal decisions without needing to involve others. In order to form and maintain effective business partnerships, the finance partner must:

- **Understand the key business drivers.** This knowledge allows finance personnel to identify potential solutions and provide recommendations that operations can support effectively.
- **Develop and possess influencing skills.** The finance partner must clearly communicate the value-added components of the solution and provide compelling reasons to adopt them.

- **Be proactive.** The effective business partner actively scans the business horizon and works with the operations partner to identify potential opportunities and address items before they become problems.

DEVELOPING THE PARTNERSHIP

Partnerships don't happen overnight. The first step to developing effective partnerships is to target key operations partners, whether it's one person or several people who make the major decisions for the operating area. One way to identify the correct partners is by meeting with your finance manager to agree on a list of individuals to partner with and then review the list quarterly. Too little time spent on developing relationships with key personnel reduces the effectiveness of finance suggestions, but too much time developing relationships may slow down financial results. Second, it's important to understand how the business works. The finance partner should walk the factory floor with the production partners and ask them to explain the manufacturing process. When working with engineering operations, the finance partner must learn from the engineers how they design products. Meetings with the sales and marketing staff are critical if finance is to understand what drives the customer relationship. On all assignments it's important to meet with technical experts from operations and learn how

they do their jobs and what limits their effectiveness. No matter the area, the finance partner must move beyond the mind-set of simply running reports and looking at numbers. A clear, broad-based understanding is required to determine the areas in which value-added analysis and recommendations can be developed. Third, early in the relationship there's a need to build trust by delivering the basics of traditional financial analysis effectively. Again, meeting with the operations partners should provide insight into what data they need. Finance builds credibility by delivering the information on time and in a format that provides information, not simply data. This approach gives the operations partner the opportunity to suggest areas in which data collection, analysis, and reporting can be improved.

Once the finance partner has earned the reputation as a provider of valuable information, he or she should find more opportunities to influence decisions. When a business deal is being considered, the finance partner adds value by not only showing an analysis of the business deal in question but by also showing what might happen to the other portions of the business. For instance, the finance partner might prepare estimates of the impact of specific pricing changes on other customers and provide alternatives that meet customer requirements and Intel's financial objectives. Eric Anderson, engineering manager, explains what basic

Blocher, Stout, Cokins, Chen: *Cost Management, 4e*

©The McGraw-Hill Companies, Inc 2008

Figure 1: FINANCE AS A SEPARATE ORGANIZATION

- The finance chair at Intel is separate from that of operations.
- Finance reports on a dotted-line basis to the operational group that it supports.

financial data he considers valuable from his finance partner. "Provide me with financial metrics that help me run my business. How much time can we take on certain operations or spend on certain tasks and still make a positive ROI? Provide me rules of thumb on our operations that I can provide to a tech on the line so they know how they can do their job and help the company achieve our financial goals." Fourth, the finance partner should ask the operations partner about problems they are experiencing or information they need to make better decisions. This allows the finance partner to identify one or two value-added solutions for problems the operations partner currently faces. It may work best to start with simple problems and then work toward tackling more complex ones. The partnership will prosper when the finance partner maintains a high level of personal integrity and remembers there's an appropriate balance between the need for financial results for not only the operating unit but also the entire company. After all, the finance charter requires that finance work in the best interests of the shareholders, not the unit they assist.

When finance partners work with their operations partners to build effective partnerships, they can establish high levels of mutual credibility, and the finance personnel will find operations asking them for help in making key decisions. When operations asks finance's opinion on key issues before making decisions and invites finance into strategic meetings, finance knows it's part of a well functioning partnership. "The best indicators of partnership are the ones you can't easily measure," says Mark Henninger, an Intel controller, "things like a partner saying publicly how great finance is or receiving an award from your partner group."

Much of this is intangible, such as no longer having to push open a door to participate but instead being invited into the discussions by your operations [partner]." Intel finance views partnership as a continuum that runs from the irrelevant to full partner, and, in any given partnership, the finance professional may be at any point on the Degree of Involvement scale (see Figure 2). Finance personnel move up the scale as they find ways to work effectively with their partners. The five levels of the continuum can be described as:

Irrelevant: Operations perceives no value from their interactions with finance and works with finance only when required.

Listened to: Operations comes to finance for data and analysis, but finance is not invited into the decision making process.

Included: Operations proactively invites finance into the decision-making process and asks for and values finance's input.

Empowered: Finance uses its knowledge of the business and ability to leverage the finance network to actively drive changes that result in enhanced business value.

Full Partner: Finance and operations work as an almost indistinguishable unit to shape the direction of the business. To maintain the partnership at a high level requires constant maintenance. One-on-one meetings with partners outside the normal business calendar provide an opportunity to discuss the business and focus on developing issues. While the frequency of these meetings varies, experienced finance partners suggest meeting weekly early on and bi-weekly or even monthly once the relationship is firmly established.

Figure 2: THE PROGRESSIVE STAGES OF PARTNERSHIP

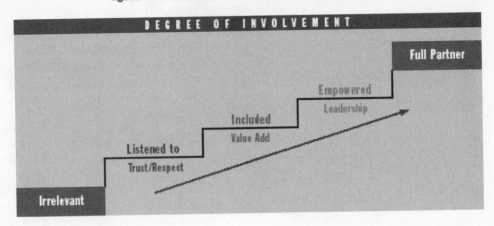

HOW TO MEASURE RESULTS

Effective partnerships should lead to measurable results and improvements. Intel evaluates finance partnering effectiveness via the following measures:

Strategic Influence Events: Significant changes to the business strategy or business direction in which finance played a central role;

Cash Savings: Instances in which finance successfully changed a decision operations made that resulted in a 12- month cash savings of at least $1 million after tax; and

Cash Maximization: Partnership results in which finance contributed at least 25% of the effort in a business decision or process change that resulted in at least $5 million of after-tax cash savings in the first 12 months.

Intel sets annual number and dollar goals for each measure. Achieving these goals is a tangible measure of the bottom-line benefit business partnership provides to the company.

REGULATORY AND ENVIRONMENTAL CHANGES

Since accounting and finance professionals are familiar with the ever-changing requirements of the Sarbanes- Oxley Act (SOX) and the Public Company Accounting Oversight Board (PCAOB), they can help operations partners minimize regulatory risk and exposure. Finance partners, especially those with an accounting background, should translate the accounting and reporting regulations into terms that operations personnel can understand and implement. Finance personnel can also communicate how these regulations and the application of generally accepted accounting principles affect the business. In addition, finance partners should an-

ticipate upcoming regulatory changes, assess their impact on the operating area, and communicate the implications of these potential changes to their operations partners. The Intel finance charter specifically includes the importance of monitoring financial compliance and controls. In today's heightened regulatory climate, finance and accounting partners may struggle to maintain the appropriate balance between the demands of their fiduciary duties and their need to work with partners on business issues. We asked finance partners if they believe that financial control and compliance have become so critical as to become the primary focus of finance activities, in turn reducing or eliminating the traditional activities of finance business partners. The answer was a resounding "no." Business partnership is too important to the company's success to reduce this level of activity. To adequately support both the demands of the regulatory environment and the supportive role of business partner, finance may need to move some routine data collection and analysis tasks to the operations side. This reallocation of duties requires a thorough examination of and agreement on roles and responsibilities between finance and operations. Accountants engaged in business partnerships are also in a unique position to investigate and correct erroneous accounting entries the business unit makes and to work with their partners to improve financial reporting. Accountants who have achieved full partnership can explain how accounting helps drive the strategic portion of the business and fix the accounting issues at the source rather than after the fact.

Blocher, Stout, Cokins, Chen: *Cost Management, 4e*

RESOLVING DISAGREEMENTS

What happens if the division manager wants to invest in a new plant that finance has determined will generate a substandard return on investment (ROI)? Under the Intel model, finance personnel don't have the final decision making authority, so to avoid taking such a decision to the next organizational level, finance professionals need to use effective data presentation and analysis to sway operations partners away from suboptimal decisions. As Keith Lewis, Intel manufacturing manager, explains, "Don't get lost in the details and financial numbers. Show me a summary with a simple answer. Understand what we do as a business and our common goals, and show me how to get there." When finance needs to elevate a decision because the operations area's decision isn't in the best interests of the unit or corporation, it's important that finance clearly explains why this is the appropriate decision and includes the operations partner in all upper-level meetings. How this is approached is critical. Prior to the meeting, finance should brief the operations partner on what it will present. Experienced finance partners recommend that the finance and operations partners go into the meeting together, and only under the most extreme circumstances, such as suspected fraud, should finance go without first informing its partner. Invoking a higher authority without first informing the partner destroys credibility, which is hard to regain. One way to avoid taking a decision to a higher level is by predefining the types of disagreements that will be appealed, such as those that exceed a certain dollar amount or that relate to specific types of expenditures. But too many or too few disagreements taken to upper levels may be signs of poor partnerships. Finance partners should anticipate that conflict may stem from pressure on the operating unit for near-term performance or reliance solely on P&L measurements that result in poor cash decisions. At Intel, part of finance's role is to establish some healthy tension between the short and long term and to focus the business on the right long-term cash decisions for the company. Many finance and accounting professionals have a natural tendency to avoid conflicts with operations. But by practicing effective conflict-resolution techniques they can work through tough decisions with their partners. Also, the partnership benefits if the finance partner gives in on the small stuff and saves any battles for the issues and decisions that will have a material impact on the business.

THE OPERATIONS PARTNER'S VIEWPOINT

When we asked Intel operations managers and general managers for their viewpoints on what makes a successful partnership, they said finance must have a keen understanding of the big picture of the business and must understand the issues and objectives from the operations viewpoint, develop a common understanding of costs and risks, and work toward the best financial solution. Finance should also help operations prioritize projects and investments that maximize the return to the business. One way to do this is to help operations understand the maximum amount of money they can spend to achieve their goals while still providing the expected ROI. What abilities does operations value in finance professionals? First, operations wants partners who can provide basic financial support. Second, they expect finance people to be skilled in their field and to be able to obtain and analyze all the relevant data, but operations partners don't want to receive reams of data or mountains of numbers. The best finance partner distills data into a clear and simple presentation. Third, operations personnel stress that they want finance to push back on nonvalue-added analysis and financial reports requested by operations personnel. Reducing these activities gives finance the time to help operations make better decisions. Partners value anything finance can do to streamline day-to-day duties to free up time to work on the problems of and opportunities for the business partner. "Finance employees should negotiate with their managers to free up time to work on partnership issues. Have enough buffer time available to allow for partnership relations, trust building, problem solving, and strategizing," says Ann Flatz, Intel accounting controller. Characteristics of a poor finance partner include not understanding the business, failing to stand up for the business in the face of a dominating operations partner, and not supporting his/her "no" response with clear reasoning and data. Operations doesn't want finance to just say "no" without presenting alternatives that show there's a better solution than the one being rejected. "Don't just tell me no," says Tom Swinford, co-GM of Intel's Lan Access Division. "Tell me no and why—and provide me with alternatives."

THE PITFALLS

As valuable and beneficial as it is to be a business partner, there are some potential downsides. Perhaps one of the most difficult aspects is an operations manager not wanting to partner.

Performance evaluations don't always capture operations partnering activities, so finance, whose performance evaluation includes the outcomes of partnering, is left struggling to partner with an unwilling operations manager. There's another pitfall. Some partnership activities result in very visible results. For example, finance may benefit from the cash savings generated by projects that were implemented only because finance took them to the next level of management. But it's harder to measure and to reward times when a good partnership results in good decisions without higher-level involvement. Guiding operations through the appropriate financial decisions is certainly less visible (but potentially more productive) than escalating decisions (see "Business Partnership in Action"). Fortunately, there are ways to mitigate these issues. To reward finance individuals for activities that are less visible, 360-degree feedback within performance reviews may be used. In the case of having to work with uncooperative operations managers, finance should employ effective partnership techniques, patience, and, under extreme circumstances, change finance personnel. At Intel, we find it may take a few finance rotations, each with a different finance partner, to fully engage some operations personnel in effective partnerships. Each person in the role helps develop the partnership from the irrelevant to the full-partner level.

BUSINESS PARTNERSHIP IN ACTION

Over the years some operational groups had gotten into a habit of ordering certain nonmanufacturing items directly from the vendors of their choice and then submitting receipts for reimbursement after the fact. While this may have sped up the purchasing process, it prevented Intel from obtaining discounts from our contracted suppliers. Finance identified and analyzed the problem and estimated the lost savings to Intel. Finance then formed cross-functional teams with the various stakeholders throughout the company. Using its business knowledge of how the operations worked, finance devised alternative solutions for procurement and payment that met the business unit's requirements and obtained purchasing discounts that resulted in annual savings for the company. In another area, operations developed a sales proposal to win business in a competitive emerging market area. Finance analyzed the proposal and, using its business knowledge of the markets and customers, determined that the pricing and structure of the deal would impact existing customers to the point of negative returns for the project. Finance escalated the decision to the unit general manager and not only showed the impact but offered alternative solutions and pricing structures that would prevent existing market erosion. The result? A winning proposal at acceptable financial returns.

IT'S A JOURNEY

Partnership is more of a journey than a destination. Each time a finance professional moves into a new job or an operations manager moves into a new role, the partnership progression starts again. Fortunately, Intel experience has shown that, once the operations managers are comfortable working in a finance business partnership relationship, the building of a new partnership relationship goes much faster.

Blocher, Stout, Cokins, Chen: *Cost Management, 4e*

Chapter 2
Implementing Strategy: The Balanced Scorecard and the Value Chain

Cases

Readings

2-1: "How to Report A Company's Sustainability Activities" by Gwendolen B. White, PH.D., CPA, *Management Accounting Quarterly* (Fall 2005), Vol. 7, No. 1 pp. 36-43.

This article explains the concept of sustainability and its role in the corporation. It describes how a firm can measure and report its outcomes and efforts regarding sustainability within a balances scorecard.

Discussion Questions:
1. What is meant by sustainability? What measures are included in a sustainability report?
2. How many companies issued sustainability reports in 2005? Cite your source for this information.
3. Are sustainability goals important to shareholders of public companies? Why or why not?
4. How can sustainability be included within the balances scorecard? Base your answer on the Global Reporting Initiative (GRI) reporting guidelines and its three categories of indicators:
   - economic indicators
   - environmental indicators
   - social indicators

2-2:"Applying the Balanced Scorecard to Small Companies" by Chee W. Chow, Kamal M. Haddad, and James E. Williamson, CPA, *Management Accounting* (August 1997).

This article reports the findings of a case study of four small firms to identify the potential use of the balanced scorecard in these firms and to determine the differences in the use of the scorecard across industries. The industries include a food ingredients company, a commercial bank, a biotechnology firm, and an electronics firm.

Discussion Questions:
1. Did these four firms adopt the balanced scorecard? Why or why not?
2. For each of the firms, examine the scorecard presented in the article and use it to determine what you think is likely to be or should be the competitive strategy of the firm. Does it seem that the balanced scorecard is consistent with the nature of the firm's business and strategy?
3. How do the scorecards differ across firms? Can you explain why?

2-1. Atlantic City Casino

Several years ago the management of a large hotel chain, Hotel Corporation of American (HCA) purchased a casino in Las Vegas. Pleased with the results HCA constructed another casino in Atlantic City shortly after casino gaming was legalized in that city. At the time the proposal in this case arose (see below) there were 9 other casinos operating and 2 additional casinos under construction.

The casino is an independent operating unit within the hotel chain. For example, all financial and accounting services are provided in-house. The casino has been profitable since the day it opened. However, the level of profits has not been satisfactory. Corporate management is well aware that HCA would have been better off if the huge sums involved in the construction of the casino had been invested in certificates of deposit.

THE PROPOSAL

Management of the Atlantic City Casino has employed several consulting services to study the market and the casino's position in the market. Consumer surveys have shown that the casino is viewed as an average casino, with no distinguishing characteristics. Coupled with its location (several blocks from where most of the casinos are located) this perception of blandness seems to explain the casino's relatively small walk-in trade (most visitors to Atlantic City visit more than one casino; people staying at one casino who visit a second are considered walk-ins at the second casino).

A proposal has been made to expand the casino and hotel (state law prescribes a fixed number of hotel rooms per square feet of casino space). As part of this expansion, the proposal includes the construction of a theme entertainment center. The center would be separate from, but attached to, the casino. The showpiece of the center would be a large Ferris wheel designed to look like a giant wheel of fortune. It would be visible from a large portion of the boardwalk. Additionally, the area would include a unique water slide, bumper cars, a space capsule ride and a fun house. Throughout the area would be a number of small souvenir and snack shops, push carts, tent shows and midway-type games to provide an old-fashioned style carnival atmosphere. An admission fee would be charged to enter the theme center and most of the rides and entertainment would be included in the admission fee. Management expects to be able to use free admission tickets to the center as a promotional item. There would be easy access from the center to the casino floor. It is anticipated that a large number of the visitors to the center would also visit the casino.

Although management is impressed by the plan and has already had detailed architectural plans prepared for the expansion, they are cautious. When the casino was first built, everyone was enthusiastic about the casino's potential, but the results have been disappointing. Management wants a thorough study made of the financial prospects for this expansion before committing funds to it.

Detailed financial data for every casino in Atlantic City are public information and are routinely exchanged. Thus, data such as that given in Tables A and B for the current year are readily available.

REQUIRED:

1. Complete a value chain analysis. Describe your understanding of the competitive position of the Atlantic City Casino. Identify areas for potential cost reduction and/or value added for customers.
2. Should HCA make the investment in the theme entertainment center? Why?
3. HCA is considering a balanced scorecard for the Atlantic City Casino. For each of the four areas within the balanced scorecard, list two or three examples of measurable critical success factors which should be included.

(IMA adapted)

Blocher, Stout, Cokins, Chen: *Cost Management, 4e*

TABLE A
Selected Annual Financial Data
(000s omitted)

| Property | Revenues | | | Net Income |
	Casino	Rooms	Food and Beverage	
Atlantic City Casino	$220,183	$14,862	$36,833	$23,921
Competitors				
1	254,753	17,604	36,457	40,979
2	224,077	14,836	34,493	18,834
3	237,700	15,787	35,168	47,146
4	158,602	9,897	18,788	1,574
5	210,848	13,870	35,265	64,765
6	251,675	17,665	33,867	17,904
7	147,037	10,191	35,020	(9,075)
8	121,581	13,469	21,863	2,246
9*	123,947	12,157	22,643	(1,176)

* In operation in for only 6.5 months

TABLE B
Selected Statistics

Property	Casino Space (square feet)	Number of Rooms	Number of Restaurants
Atlantic City Casino	50,850	521	7
Competitors			
1	59,857	727	9
2	59,296	645	9
3	59,439	512	9
4	49,639	501	14
5	52,083	750	7
6	40,814	504	8
7	50,516	500	5
8	34,408	504	6
9	60,000	612	8

2-2. Sovera Enterprises (Strategic Analysis)

Sovera Enterprises, an expanding conglomerate, was founded 35 years ago by Emil Sovera. The company's policy has been to acquire businesses that show significant profit potential; if a business fails to attain projected profits, it is usually sold. Currently, the company consists of eight businesses acquired throughout the years; three of those businesses are described here.

LaBue Videodiscs produces a line of videodisc players. The sale of videodisc players has not met expectations, but LaBue's management believes that the company will succeed in being the first to develop a moderately priced videodisc recorder/player. Market research predicts that the first company to develop this product will be a star.

Ulysses Travel Agencies also showed potential, and the travel industry is growing. However, Ulysses' market share has declined for the last two years even though Sovera has contributed a lot of money to Ulysses' operations. The travel agencies located in the Midwestern and eastern sections of the country have been the biggest drain on resources.

Reddy Self-Storage was one of the first self-storage companies to open. For the last three years, Reddy has maintained a large market share while growth in the self-storage market has slowed considerably.

Ron Ebert, chairman of Sovera, prepared the agenda for the company's annual planning meeting where the present businesses were evaluated and strategies for future acquisitions were formulated. The following statements of strategy for each of the subsidiary companies discussed were formulated on the basis of the master plan:

LaBue Videodiscs. Sovera's discretionary resources are to be employed to support the growth of this business. The future officers of Sovera are to be developed here.

Ulysses Travel Agencies. An orderly disposal of the least profitable locations is the initial objective. Once the disposals are complete, an acceptable profit and growth strategy for the remaining locations will be formulated.

Reddy Self-Storage. The strategy for this company is to maintain efficient operations and maximize the generation of cash for use in the further development of Sovera's other businesses.

These strategy statements were part of the strategic plan presented to Sovera's board of directors. The directors' only debate was whether Sovera should sell the entire Ulysses organization rather than parts of it. However, the board approved all three statements as presented and circulated them to managers throughout the three units as the corporation's "new marching orders."

REQUIRED:

1. Identify at least four general characteristics that differentiate the three businesses described above, and explain how these characteristics influenced the formulation of a different strategy for each business.
2. Discuss the likely effects of the three strategy statements on the behavior of top management and middle management of each of the three businesses.
   (CMA adapted)

Blocher, Stout, Cokins, Chen: *Cost Management, 4e*

2-3. Accounting and Tax Practices
(Strategic Analysis)[1]

Terry Merton, CPA, hardly noticed the bright sunshine as she drove down the freeway in late October, 2007 on her way to her job as controller for a small manufacturing company in her hometown of Brightside, California. She was contemplating the prospect of starting an accounting and tax practice. Although quite satisfied with her present employment, she was very excited about the possibility of owning her own business. Prior to her present position, Terry had worked for four years in the small business division of a Big 5 public accounting firm's Brightside office and had dreamed of opening her own practice. Terry had decided that 2008 is the year her dream will become a reality.

Arriving at her office early, Terry began to think about the possible market segments she might serve and the types of tax and accounting problems these potential clients might have. For instance, Terry might simply establish a tax practice which would focus on serving individuals who typically require only simple return preparation. Serving this target market segment would mean preparing simple tax returns, such as form 1040 and other schedules commonly completed for individuals along with the 1040.

On the other hand, Terry could establish both a tax and accounting practice. This would mean she would serve both individuals and small businesses, although her primary target market would be small businesses. Pursuing this alternative would mean that she would render tax services for individuals, small businesses, estates, trusts and pension plans. Further, she would provide compilation, review and audit services for small businesses, as well as advice on designing accounting information systems. Terry knew that her first step would be to identify the market segment she wished to serve. To be successful, she would have to serve the selected target market very well.

Once she identified her target market segment, Terry could then make a decision about her competitive strategy -- whether to implement a cost leadership of differentiation strategy.

Pursuing a cost leadership strategy meant that she would attract clients by keeping her prices (and her costs) low. At the same time, Terry would still be attentive to providing quality service on a timely basis. She would compete on the basis of price and monitor costs to be sure they were kept low.

Pursuing the differentiation strategy meant providing services which are considered to be unique. Differentiating her product probably meant that Terry would provide above-average service and develop a more personal relationship with clients. With the differentiation strategy, Terry would be able to charge above-average prices for the services provided to clients and would not have to be as attentive to cost control as she would under the cost leadership strategy.

In considering which strategy to pursue, Terry thought about a nationally known provider of tax preparation services for individuals, which had offices located throughout the U.S. This national firm used television, radio and billboard advertising to present 17 reasons why taxpayers should do business with their firm. Terry was certain that the national firm had a costly centralized administrative structure. The firm's tax preparers were typically not CPA's, but were graduates of a training program conducted by the firm. Terry felt that this nationally-known firm was pursuing a differentiation strategy, since it emphasized the 17 reasons but did not emphasize low price.

If Terry selected the individual tax market, she could employ the cost leadership strategy. The limited tax expertise required would allow Terry to remain at her present employment. She would hire Jim Wallace, an experienced semi-retired preparer of uncomplicated tax returns. Terry would locate her tax practice in a storefront in a nearby shopping mall. Rent was very low there, and there was a high volume of pedestrian traffic past the location. Given this heavy pedestrian traffic, Terry reasoned that she would incur little advertising cost. Terry expected that her costs could be kept low compared with the nationally-known firm for two reasons: (1) she would provide minimal training for Jim and (2) she would have minimal administrative and advertising costs.

Now, Terry thought about the small business market. Here, Terry thought about using the differentiation strategy. With the differentiation strategy, the services she would provide would be significantly different from the services provided by competitors. Terry would differentiate herself along a number of dimensions, many of which related to her extensive experience with the Brightside business community. First from her experience working in a Big 5 firm's small business division, Terry is

---

[1] Prepared by Jack M. Ruhl and Jerry G. Kreuze, © American Accounting Association, 1997. Used with permission.

acquainted with all the bankers in town. She knows how to prepare financial presentations for clients seeking loans in such a way that the loan applications are almost always approved. She also is familiar with virtually all the small business rental property in town, and can direct clients to the most reasonably priced locations. Finally, she is thoroughly familiar with the operation of a small business and can provide extremely useful insights to small business owners. Terry would provide small businesses with many reasons to patronize her new firm. If the small business strategy is pursued, Terry will leave her $40,000/year controller position to become the principal employee of Startup, Inc.

Terry would like to finance her new business start-up costs entirely from her personal savings. This is not possible, however, since she just recently purchased a new automobile for cash, which left her with a savings account balance of only $2,400. She will need a business loan to cover start-up costs including the purchase of a computer and software. Prior to contacting Bill Andersen, the loan officer at a nearby bank, Terry prepares some preliminary profit estimates. Terry's estimates of the revenues and costs associated with each strategy for the first year of operation, 2008, are presented in exhibit 1.

Terry projects revenues of $67,500 (450 Clients at $150/client) and $91,350 (203 clients at $450/client) under the cost leadership and differentiation strategies, respectively (see exhibit 1). Supplies average $10 per client and constitute the only variable costs for Startup, Inc. The fixed expenses vary between the strategies in several respects:

1. If she pursues the small business strategy, Terry will incur significantly higher liability insurance costs each year than she would under the cost leadership strategy. This is due to the fact that she has much more liability exposure since she will be doing attest work (reviews and audits).
2. Annual computer software costs will be greater under the small business strategy. This is because each year Terry will purchase specialized CD-ROM tax preparation disks needed to properly prepare the estate and trust returns. Additional software is also needed if she wishes to advise clients with regard to pensions.
3. If she pursues the small business strategy, Terry will incur additional expense for club membership dues and entertainment expenses compared with the cost leadership strategy. This is due to the fact that Terry knows that she can develop the estate and trust work through social contacts with bankers and attorneys.
4. Under the individual tax strategy, Terry will continue in her present employment position. She will hire Jim Wallace for $500/week. Although not a CPA, Jim is approaching retirement at the public accounting firm where Terry had been employed. Jim would be happy to work part-time at Startup, Inc. Terry is impressed with Jim's qualifications and is confident he could prepare uncomplicated tax returns. The differentiation strategy, however, will entail more complicated tax return preparations, which are beyond Jim's capabilities. Under the small business strategy, Terry would resign from her controller position and work full-time for Startup, Inc., drawing a salary of $600 per week.
5. Terry's home has a very large attached apartment which she presently leases to two college students at a rent of $500 per month. The students' lease expires on December 31, 20X0. Under the small business strategy, she will not renew the lease. Instead, she will set up the offices of Startup, Inc. in the apartment. Under the cost leadership provider strategy, the students would continue to occupy the apartment, since space in a nearby strip mall will be leased for Startup's offices. The strip mall space would provide needed pedestrian traffic and high visibility for Startup, Inc., and avoid traffic congestion in Terry's residential neighborhood.
6. Anticipating the complexity of clients under the small business strategy and considering the fact that she has been out of public accounting for three years, Terry estimates $8,000 in annual training costs. Minimal training costs are projected with the individual tax strategy since Jim Wallace already possesses the necessary experience, and the level of tax expertise required is minimal.

OBTAINING A BUSINESS LOAN

Terry faxed the financial projections in Exhibit 1 to Bill Andersen in early November 2007. As a loan officer, Bill must follow a set of specific guidelines in making his loan approval decisions. If Bill approves too many loans which ultimately are "bad," he will be dismissed from his job. For all loan applications, he must be able to justify after-the-fact his decision to the bank's board of directors, based largely on the loan applicant's financial statements. In assessing the credit worthiness of Terry's loan application, Bill plans to use operating income before depreciation and working capital as surrogates for cash-paying ability. Terry will offer her nearly new automobile as collateral. The bank's policy is to

Blocher, Stout, Cokins, Chen: *Cost Management, 4e*

approve loans only if the annual payments are less than the beginning working capital balance and the projected before depreciation operating income for the next 12 months. The bank has also instituted a policy to have all loans due and payable on demand at the end of any calendar year if the payee is not in compliance with the original loan requirements.

Bill's bank has a maximum loan period for startup companies of five years. At an interest rate of ten percent per annum, Startup, Inc. qualifies for an $8,000 maximum loan requiring a $2,110 annual payment. Consequently Startup's December 31 working capital balance and annual operating income (before depreciation expense) must not fall below $2,110, or the bank loan becomes due and payable.

REQUIRED:
1. From Bill Andersen's perspective, which practice strategy is better? Why?
2. From a managerial and strategic planning perspective, which practice strategy should Terry pursue? Why?

EXHIBIT 1
Startup, Inc.
Projected Income Statements Under Two Competitive Strategies
For the Twelve Months Ended December 31, 2008

		Strategies for Practice	
		Cost Leadership	**Differentiation**
Revenues	(450 clients at $150)	$67,500	
	(203 clients at $450)		$91,350
Variable Expenses			
	Supplies ($10 per client)	4,500	2,030
Contribution Margin		63,000	89,320
Fixed Expenses:			
	Depreciation—Computer	1,600	1,600
	Software	500	4,000
	Liability Insurance	2,400	11,680
	Rental—Furniture	5,660	5,660
	Club Membership & Entertainment	—	1,200
	Preparer Salary	26,000	31,200
	Secretarial Salary	16,000	16,000
	Advertising	200	1,180
	Rent—office	8,400	—
	Training	—	8,000
	Total Fixed Expenses	60,760	80,520
Operating Income		$ 2,240	$ 8,800

2-4. Strategy, International

Barry McDonald, CFO for Recreational Products, Inc (RPI), is convinced it would be profitable for his firm to invest in a manufacturing operation in Singapore. RPI makes a variety of recreational products, including sporting goods, sportware, and camping equipment. RPI is known as a very high quality producer, with features and prices greater than most in the industry. One of the largest divisions in RPI is the boating division, which makes a variety of sailboats and fishing boats from 16 feet up to large sailboats of 40+ feet in length. These boats are now manufactured in two US plants. Barry's idea is to utilize the available low cost labor, materials resources and the favorable business climate in Singapore to build a manufacturing plant there for producing the larger sailboats. The finished boats would be sold to existing customers (boat dealers) in the United States and Canada, and a new effort would be made to sell some of the product in Asia and Australia. Barry forecasts sales of US$50 million, cost of sales (manufacturing in the Singapore plant) of $34 million, and other expenses of approximately $10 million. The government of Singapore would provide a tax holiday for the project, but the return of profits to the United States would be taxed in the US at the US rate of 34%.

Barry's research showed that the cost of the plant in Singapore would be $20 million. Funds for the investment could come from the firm's own resources at a cost of approximately 12%, or through a subsidized loan from the government of Singapore at a 5% rate. With these figures and other estimates, Barry figured the after-tax cash flow of the plant would be a positive $4 million per year for the next 15 years, the expected life of the plant.

REQUIRED:

1. What does RPI's competitive position appear to be for the entire firm, and for the boating division? What are some of the likely critical success factors for the boating division?
2. Does Barry's plan for the Singapore plant fit the strategic competitive position you developed in (1) above?
3. What do you think are some of the key international issues that are relevant for Barry's proposal?

Blocher, Stout, Cokins, Chen: *Cost Management, 4e*

Readings

2.1: HOW TO REPORT A COMPANY'S SUSTAINABILITY ACTIVITIES

By combining two metrics, management accountants can create a comprehensive methodology for reporting a company's use of economic, environmental, and social resources.

by Gwendolen B. White, PH.D., CPA

"What is sustainability? It's more than environmentalism. It's about living and working in ways that don't jeopardize the future of our social, economic and natural resources. In business, sustainability means managing human and natural capital with the same vigor we apply to the management of financial capital. It means widening the scope of our awareness so we can understand fully the 'true cost' of every choice we make."—Ray Anderson, founder of Interface, Inc.

More and more, corporations and other organizations are reporting their "sustainability" activities—their responsibilities to keep the environment clean, treat people humanely, and achieve economic goals. In fact, sustainability reporting has become a vital part of the information that external and internal decision makers use. "For many corporations, sustainability is becoming not just 'a nice thing to do' but a core requirement, enabling them to increase their value and sustain profitability in the long term," Willem Bröcker of PricewaterhouseCoopers (PwC) says.[1]

Sustainability reporting includes economic, environmental, and social indicators that help monitor progress toward sustainable practices. Eighty-one percent of senior executives at large U.S.-based businesses report that sustainability practices will be essential or very important to their company's strategic mission.[2] That may be because the way a company manages its social and environmental responsibilities influences its financial success.[3] In this article I will discuss the emergence of sustainability reporting as a major source of information for external decision makers.

I will pay special attention to the Global Reporting Initiative's (GRI) *Sustainability Reporting Guidelines* and how they fit into the balanced scorecard (BSC).

EMERGENCE OF SUSTAINABILITY REPORTING

Sustainability reporting is becoming a mainstream practice.[4] Sustainability reports had primarily addressed environmental issues until 1999, when they began to include economic and social indicators as well. Fewer than 100 U.S. companies issued sustainability reports in 1993, but that number had grown to 1,500 by 2005.[5] That figure includes 68% of the top 250 companies in the *Fortune* 500. The increase in sustainability reporting has not gone unnoticed by the investment community. Since 1999, the Dow Jones Sustainability Indexes (DJSI) have been tracking the financial performance of companies that are "sustainability driven." In addition, the Dow Jones STOXX Indexes and Sustainable Asset Management provide asset managers with benchmarks to manage portfolios of issuers who practice sustainability. More than 50 asset managers in 14 countries are using the DJSI to manage €3.6 billion.[6]

The number of investment management companies that are evaluating companies' sustainability practices illustrates that, for investment purposes, some external users are no longer satisfied with historical financial reports as the predominant source of a company's reported information. Increased scrutiny of corporate behavior is being demanded by consumers, governments, employees, and local communities as well as investors. Large companies have a substantial impact on the people in their communities and on their employees. Corporate misbehavior is costly in many ways. It can harm workers, cultures, and the environment. Ultimately, corporate misbehavior damages reputations and profits. For example, in 1996, Nike suffered a consumer backlash, a boycott, and long-term damage to its reputation because it employed children to manufacture its products in Pakistan. Reports of poor working conditions and pollution in Nike's factories in Vietnam also plagued the company. Many other large companies also have come under scrutiny for their treatment of workers. For example, Wal-Mart's stakeholders have demanded more transparency because of the company's employee compensation practices. Sustainability reports can provide some of this transparency. Stakeholders are increasingly interested in evaluating profits and the processes that create them because processes that involve innovation, production, and worker and consumer safety are influenced by a company's values about the environment and financial and human capital. Jeffrey Immelt, GE's chairman and CEO, views execution, growth, great people, and being a good corporate citizen by helping to solve world problems as drivers of GE's success. Its practices of global citizenship affect how GE operates and treats its employees, the kinds of companies and countries it chooses to do business with, and the technologies it invests in, Immelt said in a news report. For example, GE is making better energy-efficient locomotives to protect the environment along with requiring supply chain audits to protect against the use of sweatshops. These values are important to stakeholders and can be communicated in terms of sustainable practices in sustainability reports. By embracing sustainable development, companies can improve their competitiveness, performance, and image.[8]

Another indication of the emerging relevance of sustainability reporting is the direct involvement of major public accounting firms. For example, KPMG in the U.K. offers a variety of services related to sustainable development: public opinions on environmental and social reports, assurance on environmental and social management systems, and advisory services (risk management, performance measurement, and reporting) in relation to "hot issues" in the marketplace, such as climate change, emerging standards and regulations, supply-chain risks, human rights, and stakeholder activism. PwC offers similar services. It sees sustainable reporting as a fast-growing market and an opportunity to expand its business.[9] The major accounting firms are already performing 65% of the verifications of companies' sustainability reports, a report from KPMG's Global Sustainability Services said.[10] Verifications of these reports are not the same as an audit of financial statements because sustainability reports are published in a variety of formats.

Unlike generally accepted accounting principles (GAAP), there are no generally accepted standards of sustainability reporting. In most instances, sustainability reports cover a company's economic, environmental, and social activities, but not all companies use the same indicators to gauge their activities, and this makes comparison difficult. To address this consistency problem, the Global Reporting Initiative, an independent institution, offers sustainability reporting guidelines that help make the reports more standardized.[11] The GRI began in 1997 and became independent in 2002. It is an official collaborating center of the United Nations Environment Programme. To develop reporting guidelines, the GRI works with representatives from business, accounting, investment, environmental, human rights, research, and labor organizations from around the world. There are 665 organizations that report their sustainable activities in accordance with the GRI's *Sustainability Reporting Guidelines*.

SUSTAINABILITY REPORTING AND THE BALANCED SCORECARD

Sustainability reports also help internal users better manage risks associated with environmental and social incidents. Rather than reacting to problems as they arise, managers can engage in proactive strategies to reduce problems. Many corporations report that adopting sustainable practices and reporting them reduces operating costs, improves efficiency, improves their reputation, helps them develop innovative products and services, and integrates risk management.[12] For example, Canon Corporation has been redesigning its production processes and products to reduce the use of hazardous materials to meet the company's environmental performance targets. Meeting its environmental targets results in progress toward economic and social objectives by reducing costs and increasing worker safety, respectively. One specific change in Canon's production process involves the production of lead-free cables for all of its printers.[13] By not using lead, Canon is able to reduce its costs, lessen the negative impact on the environment, and provide a safer workplace. Although the *Sustainability Reporting Guidelines*

Blocher, Stout, Cokins, Chen: *Cost Management, 4e*

are not a management system, they can provide companies with an approach to achieving sustainable practices that involves the entire company. Involving the entire company increases the likelihood of achieving successful outcomes. Many initiatives in managerial accounting, such as total quality management (TQM), activity-based costing (ABC), just-in-time (JIT) production and distribution systems, and reengineering, appeared promising but did not produce the desired economic benefits.[14] In many companies, the programs were fragmented and not tied to the overall corporate strategy. This could be the fate of sustainability reporting if it is not viewed from a strategic management viewpoint.

The balanced scorecard is considered a strategic management system that ties financial and nonfinancial performance measures to the overall mission of the organization. The measures on a BSC should be used to "articulate the strategy of the business, to communicate the strategy of the business, and to help align individual, organizational, and cross-departmental initiatives to achieve a common goal," according to Robert Kaplan and David Norton.[15] The BSC was not intended to be a system to achieve compliance with a predetermined plan but a system that fosters communication, informing, and learning. It is a set of measures derived from a top-down process and driven by the mission and strategy of the company. By incorporating the GRI sustainability indicators into the BSC, organizations can easily tie their sustainability measures to their overall mission. Sustainability practices can be instituted throughout a company with the intent of achieving an integrated strategy of sustainable development. Measurements involving the four perspectives of the BSC (financial, customer, internal business processes, and learning and growth) can be combined with the three components of sustainability reporting (economic, environmental, and social). This combination could result in obtaining the most from the external measures intended for shareholders and customers and the internal measures of business processes, innovation, and learning and growth. Let's examine the GRI's *Sustainability Reporting Guidelines* in connection with the BSC's four perspectives. First, the balanced scorecard measures of financial performance are revenue growth and mix, cost reduction/productivity improvement, asset utilization/investment strategy, and risk management, and they are aimed primarily at how a "company's strategy, implementation, and execution are contributing to bottom-line improvement."[16]

The BSC customer perspective includes core customer outcome measures such as satisfaction, loyalty, retention, acquisition, and profitability. In the BSC internal business processes perspective, objectives and measures are derived from explicit strategies to meet shareholder and targeted customer expectations. Kaplan and Norton recommend a value-chain model that includes innovation, operations, and post-sale service. In the learning and growth perspective, the BSC develops objectives and measures to help achieve the objectives in the financial, customer, and internal business processes perspectives. The three principal categories for learning and growth are employee capabilities, information systems capabilities, and alignment and empowerment. The BSC complements the sustainability goals of continuously improving financial performance (growth and value creation), environmental performance (integrating environmental and bioethical considerations), and social performance (integrating social, human rights, and health and safety). Many of the GRI indicators correspond to the financial, customer, internal business, and learning and growth perspectives of the BSC.

ECONOMIC INDICATORS

Rather than measuring changes in the organization, GRI economic performance measurements track economic changes that result because of an organization's sustainability activities that affect stakeholders. Although the GRI economic indicators are similar to the BSC financial perspective, they are broader. They focus more on the way an organization affects the stakeholders with whom it has direct and indirect economic interactions. For example, the GRI categorizes economic indicators in terms of stakeholders: customers, suppliers, employees, providers of capital, and the public sector, as shown in Table 1. This reporting blends the needs of the external and internal users because it enables external users to monitor progress toward sustainability, and internal users can identify areas that need corrective action. The GRI economic indicators involving customers include net sales and geographic breakdown of markets. Companies report their net sales by geographic region and type of product. From an internal perspective, managers are able to monitor whether they are on target for their financial goals in each of these markets. From a BSC financial perspective, GRI economic indicators correspond to revenue growth and sources of revenue. They can also be tied to the BSC customer perspective, which measures profitability of the core customer.

Stakeholders can also determine where the customer base is and what financial impact the company is having in different regions worldwide.

This information is also relevant to risk assessment from both external and internal viewpoints.

Table 1: Snapshot of Where Balanced Scorecard Perspectives Intersect with Economic Sustainability Indicators

Economic Sustainability Indicators[†]	Balanced Scorecard Perspectives[*]				
	FINANCIAL				CUSTOMER
	Revenue and Growth	Cost Reduction	Asset Utilization	Risk Management	Retention, Acquisition, and Profitability
Customer	✓				
Suppliers		✓		✓	
Employees		✓	✓		
Providers of Capital		✓			
Public Sector					✓

[*] Robert S. Kaplan and David P. Norton, *The Balanced Scorecard*, Harvard Business School Press, Boston, Mass., 1996.

[†] Global Reporting Initiative, *Sustainability Reporting Guidelines*, Boston, Mass., 2002.

Unpredictable events in different parts of the world can have a dramatic impact on a company's profits. For instance, if war or natural disaster affects a particular region of the world, a company's risk exposure to loss can be assessed by analyzing its customer base in that location. Economic indicators for suppliers are cost of all goods, materials, and services that suppliers provide and the percent of contracts that are paid in accordance with agreed terms, excluding agreed penalty arrangements. These indicators could help with cost reduction and with risk management in the BSC financial perspective. The cost of goods, materials, or services is often a major component of a company's expenses and can be evaluated in terms of its impact on profits. Whether a company is complying with contract terms helps internal and external users evaluate contract risk.

Indicators for employees are total payroll and benefits, such as wages, pension, and other benefits, broken down by country or region. From the BSC financial perspective, these indicators can be categorized under cost reduction and risk management. Internal users can monitor and control these costs for specific countries and regions. Stakeholders can assess the impact that the company has as a provider of employment and wealth to workers in different regions of the world. Stakeholders may be able to determine whether fair wages are being paid according to the standards of specific countries. Failure to pay fair wages puts a company at risk for charges of exploitation and may damage its reputation. Indicators about capital providers show distributions to creditors and shareholders. These indicators are interest on debt

and borrowings; dividends on all classes of shares, with any arrears of preferred dividends to be disclosed; and the change in retained earnings at the end of the period. The last item includes return on average capital employed, one of the BSC's financial measurements. Payments for interest can affect profitability, and their reduction would be considered part of cost reduction goals in the BSC. The public sector indicators include total sum of taxes of all types paid, broken down by country; subsidies received, broken down by country or region; and donations to community, civil society, and other groups, broken down in terms of cash and in-kind donations per type of group. These payments are a measure of the financial impact that a company has on the local economy through taxes and contributions. For example, in its sustainability report for 2003, British Petroleum reported its total charitable contributions as $74.4 million, broken down by projects in different countries. Many companies make these donations to local communities to generate goodwill, which can be viewed as an objective of the financial perspective of the BSC, measured by new local customer acquisition or revenue growth in the local communities.

ENVIRONMENTAL INDICATORS

GRI environmental indicators are divided into materials, energy, water, biodiversity, emissions, effluents, waste, products and services, and compliance, as shown in Table 2. These environmental sustainability indicators are then subdivided. For example, materials—other than

Blocher, Stout, Cokins, Chen: *Cost Management, 4e*

water—are grouped by type, use, and quantity. Materials that are waste are classified as those from internal sources and those from external sources. Energy indicators are divided into direct energy use, segmented by primary source, and indirect energy use. These measures would be useful as part of cost reduction in the BSC financial perspective. The environmental indicators are also relevant from the BSC internal business processes perspective. In particular, innovation is applicable. Companies can reduce their emissions by developing new products and/or processes that emit fewer greenhouse gases and other ozone-depleting substances. The environmental indicators are good measures to ensure that the company is moving to reduce environmental impacts. GRI environmental indicators are also important from a BSC risk management perspective because a company that does not manage its pollution problems faces the risk of fines and lawsuits for environmental damage. Biodiversity indicators include location and size of land owned, leased, or managed in biodiversity-rich habitats. These indicators also report the effect industrial activity has on the biodiversity in terrestrial, freshwater, and marine environments. Biodiversity indicators are important for the customer perspective of the BSC. Companies that are thoughtful about their growth in environmentally sensitive areas are likely to attract customers who are interested in sustainable practices.

This approach to sustainable development provides goodwill for the company. Total amount of waste by type and destination also is reported. Destination is the method by which waste is treated, such as composting or reuse. Companies are finding cost-effective ways to reuse their waste. By monitoring where their waste goes, companies can also focus on cost reduction and risk management. Canon, for example, uses large quantities of fresh water to clean its lenses during production. To reduce its costs and impact on the environment, the company redesigned its lens washing process to reduce water use and discharges into the environment. The water is now cleaned and reused. Other GRI environmental indicators are significant discharges into water and significant spills of chemicals, oils, and fuels. This information is relevant to cost reduction and risk assessment in the financial perspective of the BSC.

In addition, these measures could be useful for internal business processes. Companies can establish processes that are aimed at reducing the chances that spills will occur. Indicators for products and services include significant environmental impacts of principal products and services, percentage of the weight of products sold that is reclaimable at the end of the products' useful life, and percentage that is actually reclaimed. When companies report these impacts, they are more likely to look for ways to reduce the waste associated with the product at the end of its life. This can reduce costs and, in many instances, meet customers' specific needs. Interface, Inc., for example, is a carpet producer that has used these ideas about environmental impacts of products and services to meet its customers' needs. The company's customers lease its carpets, and, when the carpets need to be replaced, Interface replaces only the worn pieces. Then Interface reworks or composts the worn pieces.

GRI compliance reports include fines and incidents of noncompliance with all applicable international declarations/conventions/treaties and national, subnational, regional, and local regulations associated with environmental issues. These reports assist companies with their compliance so they can avoid costly fines and negative media attention. In addition, these GRI indicators address cost reduction and risk management in the financial perspective of the BSC.

SOCIAL INDICATORS

The social component of sustainability details an organization's impacts on the social systems within which it operates. Social performance analyzes an organization's impacts on stakeholders at the local, national, and global levels. Social performance indicators are grouped into labor practices and "decent" work, human rights, and product responsibility, as shown in Table 3. GRI labor practices and decent work indicators are measures related to employment, labor-management relations, health and safety, nondiscrimination, child labor, forced and compulsory labor, training and education, and diversity and opportunity. Employment indicators show, where possible, the breakdown of the workforce by region/country, status (employee/ non-employee), by employment type (full-time/part-time), and by employment contract (indefinite, permanent/fixed-term, or temporary). Net employment creation and average turnover segmented by region/ country are reported. High employee turnover can be an indication that the objectives of internal business processes are not being met. Health and safety indicators include the number of accidents and fatalities, and focusing on worker health and safety can reduce costs. Labor practice indicators that cover nondiscrimination policies, child labor policies, and compulsory labor policies are particularly relevant for the financial, internal business processes, and learning and growth perspectives of the BSC. GRI indicators for nondiscrimination, child labor, forced and compulsory labor, diversity, and opportunity are statements of a company's policies to prevent these activities. These indicators can be useful in risk management of the BSC financial perspective. Meanwhile, training and education indicators provide detail about employee training programs at all levels of the company. Training and education are part of the objectives of the BSC learning and growth because they deal with employee morale and productivity. Ultimately, employees who are treated fairly with regard to wages, a decent work environment, and a healthy and safe place to work are likely to be more productive. Human rights indicators cover community, bribery and corruption, and political contributions.

Table 2: Snapshot of Where Balanced Scorecard Perspectives Intersect with Environmental Sustainability Indicators

Environmental Sustainability Indicators[†]	Balanced Scorecard Perspectives[*]					
	FINANCIAL		CUSTOMER		INTERNAL BUSINESS PROCESSES	
	Cost Reduction/ Productivity Improvement	Risk Management	Satisfaction, Loyalty	Retention, Acquisition, and Profitability	Innovation	Operations
Materials	✓	✓		✓	✓	
Energy	✓	✓		✓	✓	
Water	✓	✓		✓	✓	
Biodiversity				✓		
Emissions		✓				
Effluents		✓				
Waste	✓	✓			✓	✓
Products and Services	✓		✓			
Compliance	✓	✓				

[*] Robert S. Kaplan and David P. Norton, *The Balanced Scorecard*, Harvard Business School Press, Boston, Mass., 1996.

[†] Global Reporting Initiative, *Sustainability Reporting Guidelines*, Boston, Mass., 2002.

Table 3: Snapshot of Where Balanced Scorecard Components Intersect with Social Sustainability Indicators

Social Sustainability Indicators[†]	Balanced Scorecard Perspectives[*]								
	FINANCIAL		CUSTOMER		INTERNAL BUSINESS PROCESSES		LEARNING AND GROWTH		
	Cost Reduction/ Productivity Improvement	Risk Management	Satisfaction, Loyalty	Retention, Acquisition, and Profitability	Operations	Post-Sale Service	Employee Capabilities	Information System Capabilities	Alignment and Empowerment
Labor Practices and Decent Work	✓	✓			✓		✓	✓	✓
Human Rights		✓			✓			✓	
Product Responsibility			✓	✓		✓		✓	

[*] Robert S. Kaplan and David P. Norton, *The Balanced Scorecard*, Harvard Business School Press, Boston, Mass., 1996.

[†] Global Reporting Initiative, *Sustainability Reporting Guidelines*, Boston, Mass., 2002.

Blocher, Stout, Cokins, Chen: *Cost Management, 4e*

Community indicators are descriptions of policies to manage impacts on communities in areas affected by a company's activities, as well as descriptions of procedures to address this issue, including monitoring systems and results of monitoring. Community indicators can be tied to the internal business processes objective of the BSC because companies can manage their operations better when they know how their activities affect communities in which they are located. Bribery and corruption indicators involve a description of the organization's policy, procedures/management systems, and compliance mechanisms for addressing bribery and corruption. Political contribution indicators are descriptions of policy, procedures/management systems, and compliance mechanisms for managing political lobbying and contributions. They also include the amount of money paid to political parties and institutions whose prime function is to fund political parties or their candidates. In terms of the BSC financial perspective, the bribery and corruption and political contributions indicators are useful for managing risk associated with the prevention of illegal activities on the part of the company. Customer health and safety indicators, part of product responsibility, include a description of policy for preserving customers' health and safety when they use the company's products and services. This includes the extent to which this policy is visibly stated and applied as well as a description of procedures to address this issue, including monitoring systems and results of monitoring. In addition, descriptions of policy, procedures/ management systems, and compliance mechanisms related to product information and labeling are part of this set of indicators. These indicators can be viewed as important from the customer perspective of the BSC, and they intersect specifically with customer satisfaction, loyalty, retention, and profitability.

A FUTURE OF SUSTAINABILITY REPORTING

Sustainability reporting is a growing trend that promises to become a competitive edge for many companies. It is proving to be a valuable tool internally and externally, giving management a means of analysis and stakeholders more transparency. By combining economic, environmental, and social indicators across Kaplan and Norton's balanced scorecard, management accountants can produce meaningful financial and non-financial sustainability measures that give decision makers a better view of a company's short-term and long-term profitability as well as long-term viability.

ENDNOTES

1 PricewaterhouseCoopers, "Discussion with PwC Managing Partner: Willem Bröcker," Amsterdam, The Netherlands, 2004.
2 PricewaterhouseCoopers, "Corporate Governance and Sustainability Survey," New York, N.Y., 2002.
3 KPMG International, "KPMG International Survey of Environmental Reporting," KPMG Environmental Consulting, Amsterdam, The Netherlands, 1999.
4 Ibid.
5 Association of Chartered Certified Accountants, "Towards Transparency: Progress on Global Sustainability Reporting 2004," London, England, 2004.
6 SAM Indexes GmbH, www.sustainability-indexes.com, Zurich, Switzerland.
7 Marc Gunther, "Money and Morals at GE," Fortune, November 10, 2004, p. 176.
8 PricewaterhouseCoopers, 2004.
9 PricewaterhouseCoopers, 2002.
10 KPMG International.
11 Global Reporting Initiative, Sustainability Reporting Guidelines, Boston, Mass., 2002.
12 PricewaterhouseCoopers, 2002.
13 Canon Inc., "Canon Sustainability Report 2004," Tokyo, Japan, 2004.
14 Robert S. Kaplan and David P. Norton, The Balanced Scorecard, Harvard Business School Press, Boston, Mass., 1996.
15 Ibid., p. 25.
16 Ibid.

2.2: APPLYING THE BALANCED SCORECARD TO SMALL COMPANIES

Companies are designing their performance goals—and keeping score—based on their unique needs and perceived critical success factors.

by Chee W. Chow, Kamal M. Haddad, and James E. Williamson, CPA

On October 30, 1996, Pacific Inland Bank of Anaheim, Calif., announced that it had changed its vision and strategy to such an extent that it was also changing its name to Security First Bank in a complete restructuring to transform it into "a true community bank, one that serves small businesses, professionals, and consumers."[1]

The restructuring at Security First is only one example of how American companies are making major changes in responding to an increasingly competitive global economy. Indeed, the need for fundamental change is so strong that some leading authorities from academia and industry have called for a complete rethinking and reengineering of Corporate America. For example, in their book, *Reengineering the Corporation,*[2] authors Hammer and Champy emphasize that it no longer is enough to do traditional tasks better. Rather, the realities of the current competitive environment require that the old "individual-based task-oriented" management concept be discarded completely and replaced with a "team-based process-oriented" management concept.

The current emphasis on restructuring has created a new problem for management because traditional measures of financial performance no longer are adequate to fully assess how the newly restructured organization is doing. Not only will successful restructuring require innovation in the way organizations view and measure performance, but developing, implementing, and evaluating such measures may be the greatest challenge that companies will have to face. In fact, a recent survey has found that "80% of large American companies want to change their performance measurement systems."[3] The "Balanced Scorecard" may be just what organizations need to help them restructure successfully to meet the demands of the 21st Century.

WHAT IS THE BALANCED SCORECARD?

Essentially, the Balanced Scorecard is a set of financial and nonfinancial measures relating to a company's critical success factors. What is innovative about the concept is that the components of the scorecard are designed in an integrative fashion such that they reinforce each other in indicating both the current and future prospects of the company. More than others, Kaplan and Norton probably deserve much of the credit for elucidating and increasing the awareness of this concept.[4]

When Kaplan and Norton introduced the concept of the Balanced Scorecard they were looking for ways to concentrate corporate focus on performance measurement innovation. This focus was considered necessary because traditional management reporting systems have been found to be not much help in measuring performance in the new manufacturing environment. While these backward-looking "task" or "cost object" oriented measurement systems generated financial results for numerous organizational units—including results by entity, lines of business, cost centers, and profit centers—they failed to supply the information necessary to pull strong future performance out of the organization.

Today's managers know that yesterday's accounting results tell little about what actually can help grow market share and profits—things like employee development and turnover, innovative services that enhance customer values, the quality of vendor services, and benefits from advancements in research and development. A key advantage of the Balanced Scorecard is that it puts strategy, structure, and vision at the center of management's focus.

Another advantage is that because the Balanced Scorecard emphasizes an integrated combination of traditional and nontraditional performance measures, it keeps management focused on the entire business process and helps ensure that actual current operating performance is in line with long-term strategy and customer values. In so doing, the Balanced Scorecard helps maintain a balance.

Blocher, Stout, Cokins, Chen: *Cost Management, 4e*

Figure 1. TRANSLATING STRATEGY INTO OPERATIONAL TERMS*

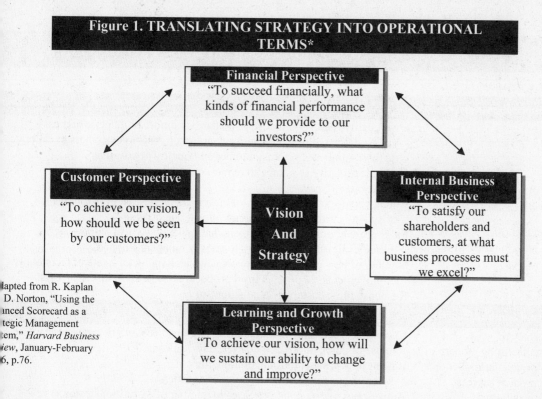

Financial Perspective
"To succeed financially, what kinds of financial performance should we provide to our investors?"

Customer Perspective
"To achieve our vision, how should we be seen by our customers?"

Vision And Strategy

Internal Business Perspective
"To satisfy our shareholders and customers, at what business processes must we excel?"

Learning and Growth Perspective
"To achieve our vision, how will we sustain our ability to change and improve?"

Adapted from R. Kaplan D. Norton, "Using the anced Scorecard as a tegic Management tem," *Harvard Business iew*, January-February 6, p.76.

Between building long-range competitive ilities and recognizing investors' attention to ancial reports. To this extent the Balanced corecard does retain traditional financial easures. But these financial measures are viewed the larger context of the company's competitive ategies for creating "future value through vestment in customers, suppliers, employees, cesses, technology, and innovation."[5]

Because of the way the Balanced Scorecard aids successful restructuring by linking together all bunits and members in a concerted effort to hance the overall goals and objectives of the ganization, many leading-edge companies have gun to adopt this new approach. For example, in e 1989, Bank of Montreal's "corporate rformance was heading downhill fast." Chairman d Chief Executive Officer Mathew Barrett and his m, deciding that "a successful turn-around strategy d to include a new approach to performance asurement," used the Balanced Scorecard to help ve the company's problems. A partial list of other pters includes KPMG Peat Marwick, Tenneco, state, AT&T, and Elf Atochem.[6]

AJOR COMPONENTS OF A BALANCED ORECARD

A well designed Balanced Scorecard nbines financial measures of past performance h measures of the firm's' drivers of future formance. The specific objectives and measures an organization's Balanced Scorecard are derived from the firm's vision and strategy. As such, the relevance perspectives and their relative importance can be expected to vary among firms. There is some agreement, however, that the framework for a Balanced Scorecard will include at least four major perspectives: financial, customer, internal business process, and learning and growth (Figure 1).

The financial perspective serves as the focus for the objects and measures in the other scorecard perspectives. This perspective reflects the concern in for-profit enterprises that every action should be part of a network of cause-and-effect relationships that culminate in improving short- and long-run financial performance. In the process of identifying goals and measures, different financial metrics may be appropriate for different units within the organization, linking that unit's financial objectives to the overall business unit strategy.

But how is a company to achieve its financial goals? Current wisdom is that every company needs to pay attention to the needs and desires of its customers because customers pay for the company's costs and provide for its profit. Companies need to identify the customer and market segments in which they choose to compete. This customer perspective allows companies to align their measures of customer values (i.e., satisfaction, loyalty, retention, acquisition, and profitability) with targeted customers and market segments.

RESPONSE FROM AN ELECTRONICS FIRM

Goals	Measures
Customer Perspective	
Quality	Own quality relative to industry standards; number of defects; first pass yields; delivered product quality; number of visits to customers to calibrate quality; number of returns; number and quality of customers.
Price	Own price relative to competitive market price; sales volume; customer willingness to pay.
Delivery	Actual versus planned; number of ontime deliveries; number of days early/late; current backlog; aging of past due orders.
Shipments	Sales growth; number of customers that make up 90% of shipments; % military sales; number of new-to-us part numbers shipped.
New products	Number of new products to support new semiconductors; rate of technology improvements; % of sales from products introduced in last two years.
Support	Response time; customer satisfaction surveys.
Internal Capabilities	
Efficiency of manufacturing process	Cycle time; lead time; manufacturing overhead cost/quarter; rate of increase in use of automation each quarter; days' sales in WIP; yield.
New product introduction	Rate of new product introduction/quarter
New product success	New products quarterly sales; number of orders.
Sales penetration	Actual sales versus plan; increases in number of $1 million customers each quarter.
New businesses	Number of new businesses each year.
Innovation	
Technology leadership	Product performance compared to competition; number of new products with patented technology in them; annual rate of increase in number of new products per engineer.
Cost leadership	Manufacturing overhead per quarter as a percent of sales; rate of decrease in cost of quality per quarter.
Market leadership	Market share in all major markets; number of systems developed to meet customer requests and requirements.
Research and development	Number of new products; number of patents.
Financial Perspective	
Sales	Annual growth in sales and profits.
Cost of sales	Extent it remains flat or decreases each year.
Profitability	Return on total capital employed.
Prosperity	Cash flows.
Employees and Community Perspective	
Competitive salaries and benefits	Salaries compared to norm in local area.
Opportunity	Individual contribution, personal satisfaction in job; opportunity to share in company financial success.
Citizenship	Company contributions to community and the institutions that generate the environment; extent to which employees are encouraged to contribute to the community.

Blocher, Stout, Cokins, Chen: *Cost Management,*

Another component of the scorecard focuses on those internal business processes that will deliver the objectives that the financial and customer perspectives have established for customers and shareholders. This component expands the focus beyond improving existing operating processes to defining a complete internal process value chain that includes identifying current and future customer needs and developing solutions for those needs. This perspective will be unique to each company as it identifies the complete chain of processes that add to the value customers receive from its products and services.

Based on the objectives established in the financial, customer, and internal business process perspectives, a company needs to identify objectives and measures to drive continuous organizational learning and growth. The objectives in the learning and growth perspective should be the drivers of successful outcomes in the first three perspectives.

Because the Balanced Scorecard expands the company's set of objectives beyond traditional financial measures, managers will be able to measure how their business units create value for current and future customers. The Balanced Scorecard also helps to measure the need to enhance internal capabilities and the firm's investment in people, systems, and those procedures necessary to improve future performance. In other words, the Balanced Scorecard is an attempt to capture the essence of the organization's critical value-creating activities. The Balanced Scorecard also aids in communicating the company's goals and rewarding those employees whose efforts enhance those goals. Because of the financial perspective, the Balanced Scorecard retains an interest in short-term performance but, at the same time, clearly reveals those drivers leading to long-term financial and competitive performance.

FITTING THE BALANCED SCORECARD TO THE ORGANIZATION

Developing a Balanced Scorecard involves a process of custom designing a strategic management measurement system for a specific organization. The process is begun by making a preliminary assessment of the overall business strategy of the organization. The focus is on integration of the entire business process but not overly emphasizing the individual tasks. Once the overall business process is identified, along with its goals and objectives, it should be possible to identify and rank the measures believed to capture the essence of the organization's progress toward those goals and objectives.

To date, reported applications of the Balanced Scorecard mostly have been confined to large, international companies. These companies tend to face more turbulent and competitive environments, have more dispersed and varied products and processes that they to coordinate and monitor, and also have more resources for undertaking change initiatives. In comparison, small or local companies may have different needs such that what works for large companies may be ineffective or unnecessary for them. To gain some insights into the potential applicability of the Balanced Scorecard in small or local companies, we undertook a dialogue with four such companies operating in Southern California whose size ranged from 100 to 1,200 employees. This dialogue with a top-level manager, either the CEO or a senior vice president from each company, was loosely structured in the form of a question and response survey asking to what extent the company had considered developing a Balanced Scorecard to fir its particular needs. Each company was asked to identify up to five major components, along with the goals and associated performance measures, that might form the basis for an effective Balanced Scorecard for it.

Another objective of our study was to explore how the Balanced Scorecard might vary across industries, so we looked at four companies from different industries: electronics manufacturing, food ingredients, banking, and biotechnology. The Balanced Scorecards suggested by these companies are shown in Tables 1-4. Because of space limitations, however, we will discuss only the responses from the electronics firm, as shown in Table 1, in any detail.

We also asked each of the top managers to what extent their company had implemented a performance monitoring system similar to the Balanced Scorecard and if they thought such a system could be beneficial to their company. Only one of the responding companies said it had totally implemented such a system, with the other companies reporting that their current implementation status ranged from 3 to 7 on a scale of 1 to 10. All responding companies, however, said they thought such a system would be extremely beneficial, with the lowest score being 8 on a scale of 1 to 10, and half of the companies gave the value of the concept a perfect 10 rating.

The electronics firm selected the customer perspective, emphasizing the goals of quality, price, delivery, and development of new products as of primary importance.

Table 2. RESPONSE FROM A FOOD INGREDIENTS COMPANY

Goals	Measures
Financial Perspective	
Capture an increasing share of industry growth.	Company growth versus industry growth.
Secure the base business while remaining the preferred supplier to our customers.	Volume trend by line of business; revenue trend by line of business; gross margin.
Expand aggressively in global markets.	Ratio of North American sales to international sales.
Commercialize a continuous stream of profitable new ingredients and services.	Percent of sales from products launched within the past five years; gross profit from new products.
Customer Perspective	
Become the lowest-cost supplier.	Total cost of using our products and services relative to total cost of using competitive products and services.
Tailor products and services to meet local needs.	Cross-sell ratio.
Expand those products and services that meet customers' needs better than competitors.	Percent of products in R&D pipeline that are being test-marketed by out customers (percent of pipeline value).
Customer satisfaction.	Customer surveys.
Internal Perspective	
Maintain lowest cost base in the industry.	Our total costs relative to number one competitor; inventory turns; plant utilization.
Maintain consistent predictable production processes.	First pass success rate.
Continue to improve distribution efficiency.	Percent of perfect orders.
Build capability to screen and identify profitable products and services.	Change in pipeline economic value (risk-adjusted decision tree approach similar to option pricing methodology).
Integrate acquisitions and alliances efficiently.	Revenues per salary dollar.
Learning and Growth Perspective	
Link the overall strategy to the reward and recognition system.	Net income per dollar of variable pay.
Foster a culture that supports innovation and growth.	Annual preparedness assessment; quarterly reports (done by VP-MGR).
Develop those competencies critical to the overall critical gaps to be filled.	Percent competency deployment matrix filled.

This selection probably is typical of the contemporary world view that customers and their values must come first if the company is going to maintain long-term financial stability and growth.

The second component selected is internal capabilities. But analysis of the goals and measures attached to this component indicates that customer values and market penetration are still on the minds of the company's management. There definitely is a linkage here that the management clearly recognizes.

Third, the company values innovation which, again, clearly reflects the linkage with customer values and market penetration. In this area, we also see that they are very concerned with quality, the

cost of quality, and its cause and effect competitive market prices.

Fourth, the company indicates, but with litt discussion, that there is a need to provi shareholders some relatively short-run tradition financial results. That the company places th component fourth is an indication that it se customer values, product development a innovation, and market penetration as drivers financial performance.

Finally, the company management's expli identification of an employee perspective refle its belief that a well-paid and satisfied workforce key to attaining the company's overall goals a objectives.

Blocher, Stout, Cokins, Chen: *Cost Management,*

DIFFERENT GOALS AND SCORECARDS

As we mentioned earlier, an important consideration in applying the Balanced Scorecard approach is to recognize that each organization is unique and, therefore, requires a different set of goals, objectives, and strategies to attain its mission. This fact is evident when we look at the items selected by some of the other companies for their scorecard.

A company in the food ingredients industry (Table 2) says it is first interested in the financial perspective but then proceeds to identify many goals and measures in the other perspectives that will enhance the financial goals along with the goals of perspective.

The responses from a commercial bank are illustrated in Table 3. An interesting observation about this scorecard is that it sets out a separate community perspective. This viewpoint probably reflects the traditional community role that bank managers think may be expected of them.

Finally, a biotechnology firm in its Balanced Scorecard (Table 4) selected the customer perspective as of primary importance. The financial perspective comes after customers and technological leadership. Thus, across the four types of companies considered there is a clear indication that management is designing the goals and measures to fit the company's unique needs and perceived role. Further, these responses suggest that the Balanced Scorecard can be an effective management tool for small companies as well.

FOUR NEW MANAGEMENT PROCESSES

Kaplan and Norton show how the Balanced Scorecard will let managers introduce "four new management processes that, separately and in combination, contribute to linking long-term strategic objectives with short-term actions."[7] Figure 2 shows how the integration of the four processes lead to the Balanced Scorecard.

The first process—translating the vision—helps managers build a consensus of opinion about the organization's vision and strategy. Because it is very important to translate vision and strategy into operational terms that employees can understand and use to guide actions at their local level, the vision and strategy statements must be expressed as an agreed-upon integrated set of objectives and measures that describe the long-term drivers of success.

The second process—communicating and linking—helps management tie overall objectives and strategies to department and individual objectives. This process replaces the traditional way departments are evaluated by financial performance and individual incentives. The advantages of this new approach is the way it ensures that all levels of the organization are made aware of and understand the company's long-term strategy. The scorecard also ensures that individual and departmental objectives are in agreement with the long-term strategy.

The third process—business planning—helps organizations integrate their business and financial plans. Kaplan and Norton explain that most organizations today are trying to implement a variety of change programs that are competing with each other for time, energy, and resources.[8] This competition can be so intense and inner focused that it is difficult to integrate these diverse initiatives to achieve the firm's overall strategic goals. The Balanced Scorecard can be used to set goals that provide a basis for allocating resources and setting priorities. The scorecard also can aid in eliminating some initiatives and selecting others that are more effective for moving the organization toward its long-term strategic objectives.

The fourth process—feedback and learning—helps management direct the organization toward strategic learning. This process is different from traditional feedback and review models that focus on whether the company, departments, or individuals have met their budgeted financial objectives. An advantage of the Balanced Scorecard approach over traditional models is that it focuses management's attention on managing results from the perspective of customers, internal business processes, and learning and growth. This real-time learning perspective can increase organizations' nimbleness in modifying strategies in response to changing circumstances.

THE PERSONAL SCORECARD

Because achieving a company's goals requires a concerted effort on the part of everyone, there is a need to translate the goals and objectives down to the individual level. Translating the company scorecard into specific goals and measures at the individual level is important for motivating and focusing the individuals and teams performing the work. There is no reason why all the individual scorecards should be identical because each member may have a unique role in the organization. The goals and needs of any organization are many and varied, and skills, talents, and interests also vary across individuals.

Table 3. RESPONSE FROM A COMMERCIAL BANK

Goals	Measures
Shareholders — Financial Perspective	
Return on assets of 1% or more and return on equity of 15% or more.	Net interest margin; noninterest income; noninterest expense.
Efficiency ratio of 68% or less.	Overhead expenses.
Growth in assets of 15% or more.	Asset growth.
Loan losses of .5% or less.	Number of problem loans; early detection rate.
Loan delinquencies over 30 days of 2% or less.	Number of bad loan underwriting; number of loan delinquencies.
Customer Perspective	
Personalized quality service	Number of complaints; amount spent on training; number of rewards and recognitions; customer satisfaction.
Competitive products	Sales volume; number of customers; number of products offered a year; extent products are "user friendly" compared to competition; degree of use of technology (where appropriate).
Pricing	Cost of doing business; own price relative to competition; extent service is better than competition.
Customer satisfaction	Customer surveys.
Employee Perspective	
Competitive wages and benefits.	Annual market review.
Participation in success of the organization.	Bonuses based on corporate and personal performance; sales incentives; recognition.
Enhanced job skills.	Training/schooling; coaching.
Objective evaluation of performance.	Performance standards; job descriptions.
Enhance upward career movement.	Number of promotions from within; posting of most open positions.
Community Perspective	
Support worthwhile community activities.	Extent of employee participation; extent of financial support.
Act as good corporate citizens.	Extent employees are encouraged to vote; extent of support and activities that foster this attitude.

To attain the greatest success as a whole requires organizations to exploit these individual differences and to seek and create synergies among its members. Thus, unlike a golf team, where the team score is simply the sum of individual team members' scores, most organizations are more like a football team, where the team outcome depends on coordination and cooperation in addition to specialization among team members. Accordingly, while the individual personal scorecards need to be consistent with the organization's overall strategies, goals, and measures, there also needs to be flexibility in accommodating individual strengths and weaknesses.

A question that remains is whether an organization's compensation system should be linked to its Balance Scorecard measures. Som companies believe that tying financial reward performance is a powerfully motivating incenti and have done so.[9] If an organization is consideri using such a linkage in its compensation schem however, it is important to realize that there a are risks involved with this approach. Does organization have the right measures on scorecard? Does the organization have valid a reliable data for the selected measures performance? Are there undesirable consequen that could arise from actions aimed at achieving established targets? Those types of questions n to be explored before an organization adopts incentive strategy based on achieving cert targeted goals.

Blocher, Stout, Cokins, Chen: *Cost Management*

Table 4. RESPONSE FROM A BIOTECHNOLOGY FIRM

Goals	Measures
Customer Perspective (How can we improve customer perceptions and relationships?)	
New products	Percent of sales from new products.
Early purchase of seasonal products	Percent of sales recorded by early purchase date.
Accurate invoices	Percent error-free invoices.
Early payment	Percent of customers who pay early.
Product quality	Product performance vs. industry quality standards.
Customer satisfaction	Customer satisfaction surveys.
Internal Business Perspective (Efficiency; how can we be more cost-effective?)	
Low-cost producer	Unit cost vs. competitors.
Reduce inventory	Inventory as percent of sales.
New products	Number of actual introductions vs. target.
Innovation Perspective (How can we establish and maintain technological leadership?)	
New active ingredients	Number of new ingredients identified by internal discovery program.
Proprietary positions	Number of patents that create exclusive marketing rights.
Financial Perspective (How do we build shareowner value?)	
Growth	Percent increase in top line revenue.
Profitability	Return on equity; earnings per share.
Industry leadership	Market share.

We do know that if the current trend of shifting emphasis from individual achievement to cooperation and teamwork continues, companies will need to reexamine their short-term formula-based incentive compensation systems. Moreover, when companies adopt the Balanced Scorecard approach, they move to a longer-term viewpoint and may need to set incentive rewards more objectively. According to Kaplan and Norton, the longer-term subjective evaluation process appears to have the advantage of being less susceptible to game playing and distortions associated with explicit, formula-based rules.[10] There is little doubt that the Balanced Scorecard has a role to play in incentive compensation systems. Exactly what that role will be will become clear as companies experiment with various ways to link rewards to scorecard measures.

IMPLEMENTING THE BALANCED SCORECARD

If the experience of other companies is any guide,[11] the design and implementation process for installing a Balanced Scorecard may take two years or more. A typical schedule may contain all or some of the following component stages.

Stage 1. A strategic planning retreat involving all levels of management is held to identify strategic issues and discuss possible solutions. A major purpose of this meeting is to achieve a consensus among the individual members concerning the company's overall vision and strategic goals and objectives. This step should lead to identifying the critical perspectives in the company's Balanced Scorecard.

Stage 2. A strategic planning committee is formed to formulate objectives for each previously identified perspective in the firm's Balanced Scorecard.

Stage 3. Using the Balanced Scorecard as a communication tool, the strategic planning committee seeks comments on and acceptance of the company's Balanced Scorecard from all members of the organization.

Stage 4. Based on feedback from the dialogue with the individual members, the strategic planning committee revises the company's Balanced Scorecard.

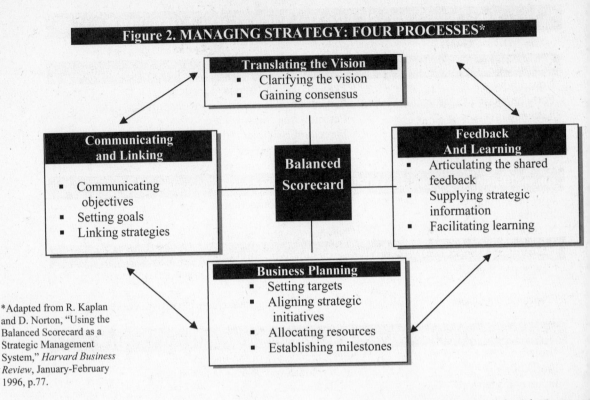

Figure 2. MANAGING STRATEGY: FOUR PROCESSES*

Translating the Vision
- Clarifying the vision
- Gaining consensus

Communicating and Linking
- Communicating objectives
- Setting goals
- Linking strategies

Balanced Scorecard

Feedback And Learning
- Articulating the shared feedback
- Supplying strategic information
- Facilitating learning

Business Planning
- Setting targets
- Aligning strategic initiatives
- Allocating resources
- Establishing milestones

*Adapted from R. Kaplan and D. Norton, "Using the Balanced Scorecard as a Strategic Management System," *Harvard Business Review*, January-February 1996, p.77.

Stage 5. The revised balanced Scorecard is communicated to the individual members. Thereupon, each individual member is required to develop a personal Balanced Scorecard that supports the company's overall goals and objectives described in its Balanced Scorecard.

Stage 6. The strategic planning committee reviews the individual Balanced Scorecards and may revise not only the personal scorecards but also the company's Balanced Scorecard.

Stage 7. Based on final Balanced Scorecards, management formulates a five-year strategic plan for the overall organization. The first-year plan is expanded into the annual operating plan for the following year.

Stage 8. Individual and company progress is reviewed quarterly to identify areas that need immediate attention and additional work.

Stage 9. Based on the individual personal Balanced Scorecards, the company's personnel committee in conjunction with each individual's supervisor evaluates each member's performance for the past year and makes recommendations relating to retention promotion, salary increases, or other rewards.

Stage 10. The strategic planning committee revises the company's Balanced Scorecard and the five-year strategic plan based on external and internal scanning of the company's current condition and changes in the economic environment.

Because the process is so lengthy, manage should lose no time in evaluating the Balanc Scorecard concept to see if they want to impleme it or other methods that will promote and supp change to better measurement and reward system

A SCORECARD FOR THE 21ST CENTURY

Maybe it is time to try something new. T Balanced Scorecard appears to be an exciting n idea that may help firms restructure to survive difficult times. The scorecard also appears to be concept that helps management direct its attent to those goals and objectives and the measures t drive the company toward achieving those go and objectives that will allow the company reengineer or restructure to meet the needs of 21st Century.

The Balanced Scorecard is not so structu that it can serve all organizations uniformly. F instead, its strength really lies in providing management the ability to design a uni scorecard that specifically firs the needs of t company, subunit, or individual employee.

Perhaps most important, while the Balan Scorecard is relatively new on the performa measurement scene, its perceived advantages at time indicate that it may be with us for quite awhil

Chee W. Chow, Ph.D., is Vern Odmark Professor of Accountancy, San Diego State University, San Diego, Calif. Kamal M. Haddad, Ph.D., is professor of finance, San Diego State University, and James E. Williamson, Ph.D., CPA, is director of the School of Accounting, San Diego State University. He is a member of the San Diego Chapter, through which he submitted this article. He may be contacted at (619) 594-6021 or e-mail jameswilliamson@sdsu.edu.

ENDNOTES

James Granelli, "Troubled Bank Tries Fresh Start," *Los Angeles Times*, October 31, 1996, pp. D1, D4

Michael Hammer and James Champy, *Reengineering the Corporation*, Harper Business, New York, N.Y., 1993.

Bill Birchard, "Making it Go," *CFO*, October 1995, pp. 42-51.

Robert Kaplan and David Norton, "The Balanced Scorecard—Measures That Drive Performance," *Harvard Business Review*, January-February 1992, pp. 71-79.

Robert S. Kaplan and David P. Norton, *Translating Strategy Into Action: The Balanced Scorecard,* Harvard Business School Press, Boston, Mass., 1996, p.7.

Birchard, pp. 49-51.

Robert Kaplan and David Norton, "Using the Balanced Scorecard as a Strategic Management System," *Harvard Business Review*, January-February 1996, p. 75.

Kaplan and Norton, p. 75.

Kaplan and Norton, p. 81.

Kaplan and Norton, p. 82.

Kaplan and Norton, p. 78-79.

Chapter 3
Basic Cost Management Concepts[1]

Cases

3-1   Strategy, CSFs, Cost Objects, and Performance Measures

3-2   Cost Drivers and Strategy

Readings

3-1 "Managing Costs Through Complexity Reduction at Carrier Corporation," by Dan W. Swenson, *Management Accounting*, April 1998.

This article, based on the experience of Carrier Corporation, a United Technologies company, and one of the world's largest manufacturers of heating and air conditioning products, explains how product complexity is a key driver of total costs. The article also explains how product complexity can be measured and some techniques for reducing complexity.

Discussion Questions:
1. Why does product complexity lead to increased costs?
2. Explain 3-4 useful measures of product complexity.
3. Identify and explain 2-3 techniques for reducing product complexity and cost.

3-2: "Using Direct Labor Cost in a Cost vs. Resources Framework" by Parvez Sopariwala

This article explains the traditional approach to usage of cost terms and proposed a new approach based on the concept of distinguishing the use of resources, cost of resources, and capacity of resources available.

Discussion Questions:
1. What are the key cost categories in the traditional view?
2. Why is it important to distinguish flexible and committed resources?
3. Explain the relationship between the costs of flexible and committed resources, usage of resources, cost behavior, and cost determination.

---

[1] Prepared by Chee W. Chow, © American Accounting Association, 1997. Used with permission.

Cases

3-1. Strategy, CSFs, Cost Objects, and Performance Measures

Three years ago, Vincent Chow completed his degree in accounting. The economy was in a depressed state at the time, and Vincent managed to get an offer of only $20,000 per year as a bookkeeper. In addition to its relatively low pay, this job had limited advancement potential.

Since Vincent was an enterprising and ambitious young man, he declined this offer and started a business of his own. He was convinced that because of changing lifestyles, a drive-through coffee establishment would be profitable. He was able to obtain backing from his parents to open such an establishment close to the industrial park area in town. Vincent named his business The Cappuccino Express and decided to sell only two type types of coffee; cappuccino and decaffeinated.

As Vincent had expected, the Cappuccino Express was very well received. Within three years, Vincent had added another outlet north of town. He left the day-to-day management of each site to a manager and focused his own attention on overseeing the entire enterprise. He also hired an assistant to do the record keeping and to perform selected other shores.

REQUIRED:

1. What is the competitive strategy of Vincent's business – cost leadership, differentiation, or focus?
2. What are the critical success factors of The Cappuccino Express? Which of these are controllable by Vincent?
3. What major tasks does Vincent have to undertake in managing The Cappuccino Express?
4. What are the costs of operating The Cappuccino Express? Choose a cost object and classify each of these costs as direct or indirect, fixed or variable, controllable or uncontrollable, product cost or period cost, or opportunity cost.
5. Vincent would like to monitor the performance of each site manager. What measure, or measures, should he use?
6. If you had suggested more than one measure, which of these should Vincent select if he could use only one?

Blocher, Stout, Cokins, Chen: *Cost Management, 4e*

3-2. Cost Drivers, Strategy

Joe Costanzo is owner of a growing chain of grocery stores in the Richmond, Virginia and the Washington, D.C. area. Joe's stores specialize in organic and other specialty foods and other specialty products, which have attracted a strong following. As his business matures, Joe is now more interested in understanding how he can better manage the profitability of his stores. In particular, he is interested in understanding what drives the costs in his business.

REQUIRED:

As a potential consultant to Joe, develop a proposal for a consulting engagement which would focus on the profitability and cost driver issues Joe is concerned about. The proposal should address which types of cost drivers should be studied and why. Also, the proposal should identify what are likely to be the important cost drivers in this business.

Readings

3.1: Managing Costs through Complexity Reduction at Carrier Corporation

By Dan W. Swenson, CMA

Carrier, a United Technologies' Company, is the world's largest manufacturer of air conditioning and heating products. Competition is intense, however, and among its six largest competitors, Carrier is the only one that is not Japanese owned. The director of cost improvement for Carrier's worldwide operations notes that Carrier's customers demand "a wide range of products that have unquestionable quality and include state-of-the-art features. Further, they expect these products to be delivered when needed, at a competitive price."

As the industry leader, Carrier strives to maintain its dominant position through innovative product design (product differentiation), high-quality low-cost manufacturing (zero defects and cost leadership), and time-based competition. (See Figure 1.) To achieve these objectives, Carrier implemented a series of improvement initiatives, including just-in-time, product and process standardization, strategic out-sourcing, supply chain management, target costing, and performance measurement. Complexity reduction is a common goal among each of these initiatives.

While Carrier's manufacturing environment was changing dramatically at the plant level, its parent company, United Technologies, continued to emphasize financial reporting and control at the corporate level and placed relatively little emphasis on developing modern cost management systems for its manufacturing plants. Therefore, the manufacturing plants lacked the cost management information that was needed to support the above improvement initiatives adequately, and profitability suffered. "The intense competition, coupled with ever increasing customer demands, have made it difficult to maintain adequate profit margins on many products. Accordingly, NAO's (Carrier's North American Operations) profitability had dropped significantly below historical levels."

Carrier needed what it describes as a set of "enablers" to support the development of cost effective product designs and manufacturing processes. Activity-based cost management was selected as the enabler, or tool, that provides the necessary financial and activity information. Following its implementation, ABCM has been used by Carrier to quantify the benefits of redesigning plant layouts, using common parts, outsourcing, strengthening supplier and customer relationships, and developing alternative product designs. In some cases, even though management knows intuitively how to improve its operations, until the improvements are quantified they are not acted upon.

COMPLEXITY REDUCTION PROGRAM

Carrier embarked upon its complexity reduction program to reduce the amount of complexity in both the design and manufacture of its products. In many ways the term complexity is analogous to variety. A company's complexity increases as the breadth of its product line expands, as each product uses more unique components, and as more process options are available to manufacture the product. The costs associated with this complexity fall as manufacturing processes are simplified and standardized and as companies offer fewer product options. At Carrier, a strategy to reduce complexity is the common thread that runs through each of its improvement initiatives (see Figure 1). Excessive product and process complexity drives costs up, increases lead time, and makes quality more difficult to control. According to Gonsalves and Eiler,[1] "Complexity factors are the biggest single driver of cost. They are also the single biggest inhibitors of throughput."

To measure its progress at reducing complexity costs, Carrier classifies manufacturing costs as being either unit-related, batch-related, product-sustaining, or structural. Unit-related costs fluctuate with the number of units produced. Direct material and direct labor are examples of unit-related costs. Batch-related costs vary according to the number of batches produced, and examples include material handling and first-part inspection costs. Product-sustaining costs change based on the number of different types of products produced. Designing new products and maintaining part numbers in the information system are examples of product-sustaining costs. Finally, structural costs tend to be fixed and are not related to the number of units, batches, or products produced.[2]

For most companies, batch and product-sustaining costs are closely associated with manufacturing complexity. These costs increase as product lines expand, as more component parts are developed, and as batch production is utilized. For measurement and control purposes, Carrier classifies all batch and product-sustaining costs as "costs of complexity." Furthermore, Carrier has developed financial and nonfinancial performance measures to benchmark its progress at removing complexity from its value chain. Financial performance measures include complexity costs as a percentage of overhead, complexity costs as a percentage of total product costs, and complexity costs as a percent of revenue. Nonfinancial performance measures include the number of common components and manufacturing process options available (which it tries to minimize) and the extent to which certified suppliers and strategic outsourcing are used (which it tries to encourage). Complexity reduction targets are in place for Carrier's current product line, and they also are used during the development of new products. Some of its complexity measures are illustrated in Table 1.[3]

Carrier's complexity reduction process has evolved into a formal, systematic program with corporate-wide visibility. The cost of complexity (COC) programs are administered at the plant level by COC teams. COC teams are formed by recruiting mid-level managers from each functional area including manufacturing, engineering, accounting, and materials management. Once a team is formed, it documents its goals, objectives, and deliverables. It then agrees to a methodology for financially evaluating complexity costs and potential cost reduction opportunities. The team also develops a process to target products and processes for standardization (a primary means of complexity reduction). The COC teams receive top management support from a steering committee that oversees and monitors the success of the COC program. Carrier considers this program to be one of its critical success factors.

STEPS TO COMPLEXITY REDUCTION

The complexity reduction process begins when someone (the originator) proposes an idea for complexity reduction, completes a Complexity

Reduction Form, and marks up the product's prints, specification sheets, and other applicable documents. The originator also can use the Complexity Reduction Form to suggest changes in parts, processes, or procedures. For example, the originator might see an opportunity to eliminate the use of single-application unique parts and replace them with common parts that have multiple applications. Originators also might propose process cost reductions, such as replacing a batch process with a point-of-use process.

The Complexity Reduction Form is forwarded to the plant coordinator who records the proposal in the Complexity Reduction Log. The coordinator also records a description of the proposal, the date it was received, its status, and potential outcomes.

The proposal then moves on to one of the area coordinators who evaluates its feasibility and uses an activity-based costing methodology to perform a financial analysis. (See Table 2.)

If the area coordinator rejects the complexity reduction proposal, he or she will provide the originator with a written explanation of reasons for the rejection within two weeks of receiving the proposal. (The originator can appeal a negative decision by resubmitting his or her proposal to the steering committee that oversees the COC program.)

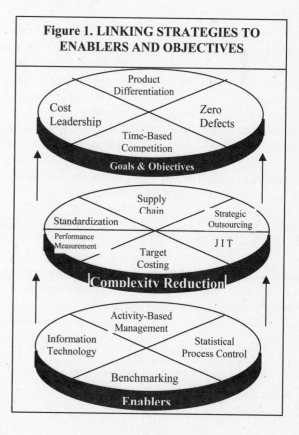

Figure 1. LINKING STRATEGIES TO ENABLERS AND OBJECTIVES

Table 1. Suggested Complexity Measures

Measures	Purpose	Objective	Benchmark
% of components that are standard—parts that are readily available and can be purchased in very short lead times (off the shelf).	To determine if we are taking advantage of opportunities to purchase components at low prices due to market pressures on suppliers.	To generate cost reductions by using standard components for noncore competency parts.	To be determined.
% of components that are unique—used in less than 50% of the models.	To determine the degree we use common components in our products.	To promote the use of common components.	To be determined.
% of purchased parts that are certified.	To determine the confidence level we have in our suppliers.	To encourage actions to eliminate incoming inspection of material.	100%.
# of suppliers by commodity code.	To determine progress made in establishing long-term strategic relationships with suppliers.	To promote actions to reduce the number of suppliers and development of long-term supplier relationships.	To be determined.
% of suppliers up on EDI.	To determine percent of supplier base that we use EDI technology to obtain material for production requirements.	To use EDI technology to reduce lead times and manufacturing material coordination cost.	To be determined.
Number of processes in plant (assembly 1,2 press, coil, paint, weld, etc.).	To determine degree of vertical integration.	To encourage focus on just a few key capabilities in each plant.	To be determined.
Number of process types (number of machines, i.e., brake presses, turrets).	To determine degree of process proliferation.	To reduce process-sustaining cost.	To be determined.
Capacity utilization by process type.	To identify the degree of excess capacity by process type.	To obtain the benefits of process rationalization.	80-85% utilization on a two-shift basis
Complexity cost batch cost + product sustaining cost.	To highlight the overhead cost associated with manufacturing complexity.	To establish targets and plans for reducing these costs. To track progress against plans.	To be determined.
Complexity cost % batch + product cost/total overhead.	To highlight the percent of overhead cost associated with manufacturing complexity.	To establish targets and plans for reducing these costs. To track progress against plans.	To be determined.
Complexity cost as a % of cost of completed production.	To highlight the percent complexity cost is of total product cost. To demonstrate impact of capacity utilization.	To encourage actions to increase capacity utilization of resources.	To be determined.
Complexity cost as a % of revenue.	To highlight the percent complexity cost is of revenue.	To ensure an adequate return is obtained in complexity cost.	To be determined.
Commonality index # of models/total # part.	To determine the degree modularity is used.	To encourage use of modularity in product designs.	To be determined.
Proliferation index/total # of different components used divided by the average # of components in a model.	To highlight the attention given to design for manufacturability and assembly.	To encourage the use of common components.	To be determined.
Total # of components.	To highlight the total number of components managed in the operation.	To encourage design for manufacturability and assembly actions to reduce the number of components.	To be determined.
% of components that are purchased.	To determine degree of vertical integration.	To encourage more strategic outsourcing.	To be determined.

Blocher, Stout, Cokins, Chen: *Cost Management, 4e*

Table 2. Standardization saving worksheet — ABC burden analysis

Nonstandardized*

Part Number	Unit Volume	WIP	Prime Costs		ABC Burden			
			Material	Labor	Unit	Batch	Product-Sustaining Cost	Structural
40RM500061	10,000		80.11	16.50	17.7665	2.1080	2.8693	2.4638
40RM500071	500		80.11	20.90	22.4731	4.5135	3.9245	3.0897
40RM500081	250		80.11	20.90	22.4731	6.4042	4.3440	3.1927
TOTAL EXTENSION BY VOLUME	10,750		$861,182.50	$180,675.00	$184,519.83	$24,937.80	$31,741.25	$26,981.03

Standardized

Part Number	Unit Volume	WIP	Prime Costs		ABC Burden			
			Material	Labor	Unit	Batch	Product-Sustaining Cost	Structural
40RM500061	10,750							
TOTAL EXTENSION BY VOLUME	10,750		$861,182.50	$177,375.00	$190,989.88	$22,633.05	$30,829.93	$26,981.03
Savings			$0.00	$3,300.00	$3,529.95	$2,304.75	$911.32	$0.00
Total Savings			$10,046.03					

* Note that in this example the nonstandardized costs represent the current costs (using ABC) for making the three component parts. The proposal is to eliminate the three components and replace them with one common component. This analysis illustrates how the proposed change would produce savings of $10,046 due to reductions in labor, unit, batch, and product-sustaining costs.

If the area coordinator approves the complexity reduction proposal, it is prioritized and scheduled for implementation by the production engineering coordinator.

Once the project is under way, its progress is monitored through a Complexity Reduction Project Status Report. This report identifies the responsible individuals, the planned implementation dates, and projected cost savings.

The Complexity Reduction Log and Project Status Reports are maintained in an online computer network. All projects are updated at least once a month. Hard copies of the log and status reports also are posted monthly on the plant bulletin boards.

LINKAGE TO OTHER INITIATIVES

Carrier implemented ABCM to support its complexity reduction programs.[4] The financial analysis in the previous example illustrates how ABCM information is used to compare the costs and benefits of changing to a standardized part. In addition to the cost/benefit analysis for complexity reduction proposals, ABCM also is used to support other improvment initiatives as illustrated at Carrier's McMinville manufacturing plant.

Just-in-time. The McMinville plant began its complexity reduction journey by simplifying and streamlining manufacturing processes. Just-in-time (JIT) production methods were adopted, and modular work cells were set up for equipment in the factory. These changes were supported by an activity analysis that pointed to material handling as a major cost driver. Furthermore, ABCM was used to calculate the financial benefits of reducing cycle times, raw material, work-in-process inventories, and storage space requirements. After implementing JIT, savings occurred through reduced material handling costs, lower inventory investments, and by avoiding a physical expansion of the plant (even though new products were transferred to McMinville from other Carrier factories).

In the early stages of the complexity reduction program, management realized that production

Cases and Readings

©The McGraw-Hill Companies, Inc 2008

workers were an untapped resource for productivity improvement ideas. Therefore, these workers were placed on work cell teams, and each team became responsible for workflow, quality, and throughput. Prior to these changes, the production supervisors spent most of their time troubleshooting problems and expediting work orders. These problems currently are being handled by the line worker teams, and the supervisors now have enough time to plan their workloads and monitor the financial results of their work cells.

CARRIER CORPORATION: A BEST PRACTICE COMPANY

The American Productivity and Quality Center (APQC) and the Consortium for Advanced Manufacturing-International (CAM-I) recently sponsored a study to benchmark best practices in the installation and use of activity-based cost management (ABCM) systems. Seven hundred and fifty manufacturing and service organizations were invited to participate in the study, and 166 responded by completing a 20-page survey instrument. Approximately 50% of the 750 companies that were invited to participate in the study had either not yet adopted ABCM or were in the early stages of implementation and thus could not complete the survey.

The survey results and telephone- interviews then were used to select 15 "best practice" companies. The best practice companies were selected based on their ABCM system's maturity, the breadth of their ABCM applications, the extent of their systems integration, and their level of success with ABCM.

Carrier Corporation participated in the survey and was selected as one of the best practice companies. Carrier currently has more than a dozen manufacturing sites located throughout the world, and it was Carrier's McMinville, Tenn., manufacturing plant (located near Nashville) that was identified as the best practice site. Carrier uses ABCM to support its complexity reduction program.

Standardization. Standardizing parts and manufacturing processes is another way in which the McMinville plant has achieved complexity reduction. The standardization process is divided into two different programs—one targets new product designs, and the other one targets existing products. The objective for both programs is to encourage the use of common components and manufacturing processes. For example, the plant has a preferred parts list for new products to minimize the proliferation of new component parts and thus control product-sustaining costs.

McMinville also has financial incentives (lower product costs) to reduce the number of components used in existing products. The plant currently maintains 280 different circuit breakers and 580 different fasteners to support its product lines. Its goal is to eliminate well over 50% of the circuit breakers and fasteners by promoting the use of common components. Maintaining an extensive parts list causes complexity whether the parts are components or finished goods. The high costs of unique components now are reflected in McMinville's product costs.

As a specific example of complexity reduction, product and process complexity was reduced at the McMinville plant when it developed common sizes for some of the sheet metal components that go into subassemblies. Each subassembly has a minimum size requirement for its sheet metal components. Therefore, if a sheet metal component will be used for multiple subassembly sizes, it must be cut large enough to fit the largest subassembly. The decision maker is now confronted with a cost-benefit tradeoff—he or she must balance the savings associated with using common components against the scrap produced by trimming the oversized sheet metal components to fit small subassemblies. The power of ABCM is its ability to compare the savings from lower batch-related and product sustaining costs with the additional cost of producing sheet metal scrap.

If common components are not practical, the next best alternative to reduce complexity is to use common manufacturing processes. In fact, some manufacturing processes become more cost effective when flexible, but expensive, computerized equipment is replaced with inexpensive dedicated equipment. The McMinville plant used dedicated equipment to achieve fewer and less expensive changeovers, to lower work-in-process, and to reduce cycle times. For this manufacturing process, JIT sparked the interest in dedicated equipment, but ABCM supported the

Blocher, Stout, Cokins, Chen: *Cost Management, 4e*

financial analysis that justified the changes. Change occurs much more quickly at McMinville when the financial impact is highly visible.

Strategic outsourcing. As McMinville's complexity reduction program evolved, management considered many change proposals to reduce complexity and improve productivity. One such proposal was to outsource the sheet metal painting operation. Intuitively, managers at the plant were confident that outsourcing the painting operation would be cost effective and improve productivity. At a higher level, however, management would not approve the change. These managers relied upon a traditional

Figure 2. NEED TO REDUCE COMPLEXITY

Drivers	Carrier Today	Objective
rnal benchmarks elate excess plexity with financial rperformance. petition intensifying :o: new competitors, ing competitors, ucturing and using systems, and ations. icial targets raised ing a current fall in profits.	Many activities under way to understand and reduce complexity • Eliminated product lines, • Moved subassemblies to point of use, • Consolidated like platforms, • Created press cells, • Outsourced paint/converted to pre-painted materials, • Outsourced product lines, • Greater understanding of how complexity affects cost, and • Organization-wide desire to tackle complexity issues. Costs remain too high • Complexity still overwhelming, • Excess capacity in noncore processes, • Mismatch between product and manufacturing process design.	Reshape Carrier and build its future by cost effectively focusing on core products, components, and processes to deliver necessary variety.

financial analysis that only considered the cost of direct materials, direct labor, and an overhead allocation. Using this analysis, outsourcing the painting operation appeared to have a negative payback.

Once ABCM data were available, however, an analysis produced results that were quite different from the traditional financial analysis. ABCM quantified the cost of many support activities that had not been considered previously, such as material handling, inspection, inventory holding, and environmental costs. After including the cost of these activities, managers at the plant found the cost of in-house painting to be considerably higher than the cost of outsourcing the painting operation. Furthermore, by purchasing pre-painted sheet metal, quality improved and in-plant cycle time fell by five days. In the final analysis, outsourcing the painting operation proved to be very cost effective, and it also supported the goals of JIT and complexity reduction.

Supply chain management. To further improve its competitiveness, Carrier has been strengthening its supplier relationships. Actions taken by its suppliers greatly influence the price, quality, and delivery speed of Carrier's products. For example, the McMinville plant has developed a partnership with a supplier of nonproduction service parts. This supplier now staffs McMinville's service parts warehouse and is fully responsible for purchasing, stocking, and scheduling service parts. McMinville's ABCM model illustrates how the supplier can source service parts and actually run the warehouse more cost effectively than McMinville can with its own employees.

The McMinville plant currently is considering a partnership with a supplier of copper tubing. This supplier would be responsible for managing the copper tubing portion of McMinville's raw materials warehouse. Through this partnership, the copper tubing supplier would exploit certain of its core competencies. It has detailed knowledge of material flow from its own plants, where the tubing is formed, to its customers. Many of the copper tubing suppliers also have the latest technology for copper tubing fabrication. Therefore, the partnership might be expanded to include some fabrication of copper tubing parts. (The vendor may choose to perform some operations at its own facility and others at McMinville.) As the vendor becomes directly involved in McMinville's production process, it can (or might be required to) propose improvement programs. These improvements might be in product functionality, the production process, or quality. And, finally, vendor management of this activity also will reduce cycle time. Once again, ABCM helps Carrier make better decisions by considering the entire cost of an activity and not just the "out-of-pocket" costs such as the cost of the raw materials.

Target costing. In the current competitive marketplace, customers often dictate the price they will pay for a given set of product features. Therefore, Carrier has eliminated "cost plus" pricing for its products and now uses a target costing approach. The target costing process begins when Carrier estimates the price customers will pay for a new product offering (the target selling price). After subtracting a desired profit margin from the target selling price, a target cost is established. The new product's target cost then is compared with its estimated cost. (Cost estimates are based on the new product's initial design and current manufacturing processes.) If the product's estimated cost is higher than its target cost, engineers will attempt to either design costs out of the product or improve the manufacturing process. In the end, if the target cost cannot be met, the product will not go into production.

Both the complexity reduction program and ABCM are linked to target costing at Carrier. These initiatives encourage engineers to control costs by designing products that use common components and standard manufacturing processes. Gone are the days when engineers prided themselves in developing unique, elegant parts.[5] When the new products do require new component designs, the engineers try to use existing manufacturing processes to build the components. To facilitate this new directive, product designers are now part of an engineering team that includes manufacturing engineers. The team uses a "design for manufacturability" philosophy in which the design team works with manufacturing to introduce product designs that use cost effective manufacturing processes.

Performance measures. An activity dictionary with common process definitions supports performance measurement among the Carrier plants. Managers at the plants use the dictionary to develop internal benchmarks for activity-based process costs. The managers also share information to learn from the low-cost producers. At the McMinville plant, the first line production supervisors also receive monthly reports with financial (labor, material usage, and scrap) and nonfinancial (production schedule targets) information. The supervisors are accountable for budgeted process costs in their areas, and the results influence their performance evaluation.

At the product level, Carrier uses ABCM to support product mix decisions. Its product mix at each site is based on a product profitability analysis. For example, unprofitable products are either dropped or moved to another Carrier location, and profitable products are emphasized. Essentially, this system encourages competition among the plants—the most efficient plants win bids for new products and take over production contracts from less efficient plants.

Even though the McMinville plant appropriately has dropped some product lines and added others, it has taken some missteps along the way. Some products that appeared to be unprofitable mistakenly were dropped (existing products) or avoided (new business). This scenario occurred because management did not conduct the following analysis:

- Before rejecting an unprofitable product, management should make every effort to remove costs from the product's design or production process.
- When the plant has excess capacity in the short run and sales revenue more than covers variable cost, new products should be considered for production (and existing products should not necessarily be dropped).

STAYING COMPETITIVE WITH HARD DATA

Carrier's complexity reduction program along with its other improvement initiatives have combined to produce quantifiable results (Figure 2). But more work needs to be done for Carrier to maintain its competitive edge. In the current competitive environment, Carrier is striving to better understand cost behavior and the steps it can take to maintain its position as the world's largest manufacturer of air conditioning and heating products. Even though Carrier's management believes that product and process complexity hurts profitability, it needs hard financial data. ABCM provides the information managers need to make difficult decisions.

Blocher, Stout, Cokins, Chen: *Cost Management, 4e*

ENDNOTES:

[1] F.A. Gonsalves and R. G. Eiler, "Managing Complexity Through Performance Measurement, *Management Accounting*, August 1996, p. 35.

[2] For an in-depth discussion of this classification scheme, see Robin Cooper, "Cost Classification in Unit-Based and Activity-Based Manufacturing Cost Systems," *Journal of Cost Management,* Fall 1990, pp. 1-14.

[3] In their article, "Managing complexity Through Performance Measurement," Gonsalves and Eiler provide additional examples of complexity performance measures.

[4] As part of the ABCM best practices study, sponsored by the APQC and CAM-I, the research team searched for characteristics that were common among the best practice companies. One finding was that each of the 15 best practice companies had linked ABCM to another improvement initiative. Total quality management (TQM). Just-in-time (JIT) manufacturing, and business process reengineering (IBPR) were some of the other initiatives that were linked to ABCM. This linkage provides direction for the ABCM implementation and a ready application for the ABCM information once it becomes available.

[5] A new product at the McMinville plant recently required three design attempts before its target cost was achieved. It was obtained only after the design team brought the part count down from 160 to 60 parts.

3.2: USING DIRECT LABOR COST IN A COST VS. RESOURCES FRAMEWORK

UPDATING THE TRADITIONAL TREATMENT OF COST TERMS CAN IMPROVE BUSINESS DECISIONS.

By Parvez R. Sopariwala

Activity-based costing measures resources used for an activity by the cost driver . . . The resources supplied to an activity are the expenditures or the amounts spent on the activity . . . The difference between resources supplied and resources used is unused capacity.[1] (Emphases authors) *Labor costs have caused both confusion and controversy in costing circles. Labor costs were originally flexible costs, because workers were paid in proportion to the hours they worked . . . scheduling and union considerations have changed most labor costs into capacity-related costs, because even though many workers are paid on an hourly basis, their wages are guaranteed to be paid, at least in the short run, regardless if work is available. For this reason, most organizations now treat labor costs as capacity related rather than flexible.[2]*

Two developments have influenced recent evolution in cost/managerial accounting literature. The first issue, suggested by Robin Cooper and Robert Kaplan, emphasizes the distinction between the cost of available, or supplied, resources and the cost of used resources.[3] It is argued that the difference between the cost of available resources and those used should not be allocated to the units produced but written off separately as a loss. Most traditional cost/managerial accounting textbooks, however, do not generate the cost of unused resources. The other issue brings accounting terminology in line with today's business environment. Most traditional cost/managerial accounting textbooks assume that direct or assembly labor is acquired when these services are required, thereby suggesting that direct labor costs are avoidable or are relevant for deciding the cost of a job that uses this labor. Assembly labor in today's business environment, however, is often acquired before it is used, in which case these direct labor costs are really not avoidable or relevant in determining the cost of a certain job that uses this labor because the direct labor has already been acquired. Following this line of thought, one might reasonably argue that direct labor cost

should be a fixed cost because it is paid for in advance and its payment does not vary with the number of units produced. I argue that direct labor cost (for example, assembly cost) will always be a variable cost, whether it is acquired in advance of use or acquired when needed. Many textbooks have incorporated this and other issues.[4] But such incorporation has generally been piecemeal, and no textbook, to my knowledge, has provided a comprehensive framework of cost terminology after incorporating these two developments.

TRADITIONAL TREATMENT OF COST TERMS

Traditional cost/managerial accounting usually defines three categories of costs. A cost can be:

- Fixed or variable with respect to a level of activity for cost estimation and cost prediction purposes.[5]
- Direct or indirect to a cost object, and, in particular, be direct (or traceable) to a unit of product (e.g., direct material and direct labor) or indirect (or allocated) to a unit of product (e.g., overhead and nonmanufacturing expenses) for cost determination purposes.[6]
- Relevant (or avoidable) or irrelevant (or unavoidable) when choosing between decision-making alternatives such as make-or-buy.[7] I use direct labor cost to highlight the differences between the traditional and contemporary treatments discussed later.[8] Assume two assembly line workers are hired at the rate of $10 per hour. Both work six hours assembling 120 units in batch #439, and together they are paid $120 (12 hours * $10 an hour) for their effort. Figure 1 shows how this transaction would be reflected using the traditional treatment of direct labor cost. For example:
- The actual cash outflow of $120 is an avoidable or relevant cost; that is, it would only be incurred if the 120 units in batch #439 need to be assembled. Hence, for direct labor to be an avoidable or relevant cost

Figure 1: A Traditional Treatment of Cost Terms

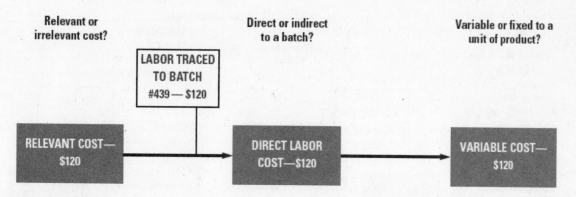

Relevant or irrelevant cost?	**Direct or indirect to a batch?**	**Variable or fixed to a unit of product?**

for short-term decision making, it needs to be paid on a piece-rate basis, that is, the resources of $120 are expended only after each assembly worker works six hours on batch #439.

- The direct labor cost is $120 because the use of 12 hours of assembly labor can be traced to the production of 120 units in batch #439—the work was performed solely for that batch of 120 units.
- The $120 cost is also a variable cost because the total direct labor cost is likely to vary with the number of units to be assembled in the batch. A smaller number of units in the batch, say 110 units, would have necessitated a smaller number of direct labor hours (11 or [(12 hours/120 units) * 110 units]) and, consequently, a smaller direct labor cost ($110 or [11 hours * $10 per hour]). The implication of the traditional treatment is that direct labor costs are variable costs because they are incurred in proportion to the units produced, and these variable costs are also relevant costs because direct labor was acquired on a piece-rate basis; that is, acquired only when it was needed for the job.[9] But what if direct labor were not piece-rate? Say it was paid a fixed amount per week or month irrespective of how many hours it worked? Would it still remain a variable cost, or would it now be classified as a fixed cost since it was acquired and paid for before it was actually used? I will look at these and other questions next.

CONTEMPORARY TREATMENT OF COST TERMS

Some cost/managerial accounting textbooks have attempted to update the traditional treatment of cost

terms to bring it more in line with the existing business environment where direct labor, for example, is often salaried; that is, it is not acquired on a piece-rate basis. This contemporary treatment can be seen in the following updated version of the previous example:

- Two assembly line workers are hired at $10 an hour.
- Worker A is hired on a piece-rate basis and works for six hours assembling 60 of the 120 units in batch #439 and is paid $60 (6 * $10).
- Worker B is hired on a nonpiece-rate basis, and she is paid at $10 for eight hours' work even though she may not work for eight hours on any job.[10]
- Worker B works six hours assembling the remaining 60 of the 120 units in batch #439, spends one hour familiarizing a new intern with the intricacies of her machine, and has no work for the remaining hour. She is paid $80 [(6 + 1 + 1) * $10] for her efforts. The example highlights the following facts:
- Labor may be acquired on a piece-rate basis where a worker would be paid only for the work she performed. Worker A is one such worker, and she bears all the risk—the employer can always send her home if there is no work for her.
- Labor may be acquired on a nonpiece-rate basis where a worker would get paid for being available to do eight hours of work. Worker B is such a worker and bears a fraction of the risk borne by Worker A. The employer bears all the risk, hypothesizing there will be enough work for Worker B to justify hiring her for the eight-hour day.

Figure 2: A Contemporary Treatment of Cost Terms

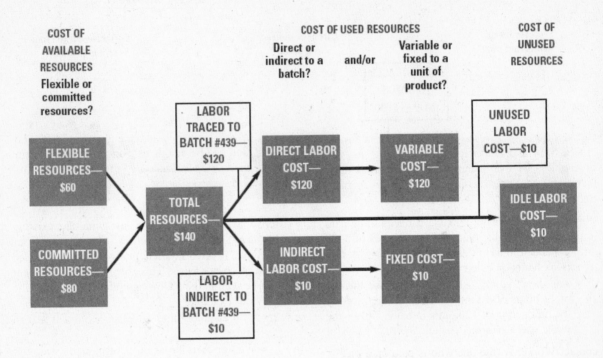

- If all labor acquired on a nonpiece-rate basis is not used for the purpose it was acquired, it might be justifiable for the employer to use the worker wherever she can contribute. So even though a worker may be contracted primarily as direct or assembly labor, she may end up spending some, or all, of her time with tasks that may not directly contribute to the product or batch, or, worst of all, she may have no work. Figure 2 shows this transaction, using a more contemporary treatment of direct labor cost.

COST OF AVAILABLE RESOURCES VS. COST OF USED RESOURCES VS. COST OF UNUSED RESOURCES

First, the contemporary treatment highlights the relatively recent development in the cost-management literature spearheaded by Cooper and Kaplan, who have emphasized the distinction between the cost of resources available (or supplied) and the cost of used resources. They suggest that products created and services provided during the year should be charged for the resources they actually use, and the balance should be considered as the cost of unused resources and written off as an expense on the income statement

and not be spread over the products created and services provided during the year. The traditional treatment, on the other hand, did not highlight this distinction because it assumed that direct labor was piece-rate, and, hence, the cost of resources available was automatically equal to the cost of resources used.

COST OF AVAILABLE RESOURCES: FLEXIBLE VS. COMMITTED RESOURCES

Second, Figure 2 partitions the cost of available resources into the cost of committed resources, or capacity-related resources, and the cost of flexible resources.[11] In the context of the earlier example, the $60 paid to Worker A represents a flexible resource because Worker A is paid on a piece-rate basis and worked six hours on batch #439. Other examples would include raw material, electricity, and hiring temporary workers. Similarly, the $80 paid to Worker B represents a committed resource as Worker B is not paid on a piece-rate basis and essentially is available for work during the eight-hour day. The fact that Worker B worked only six hours on batch #439 has no impact on the company's obligation to pay her $80 because they hired her for the eight-hour day. Other examples would include purchase of fixed assets, property

Blocher, Stout, Cokins, Chen: *Cost Management, 4e*

©The McGraw-Hill Companies, Inc 2008

taxes, and insurance. As a result, the total resources expended were $140, of which $60 were flexible resources and $80 were committed resources.

HOW IS DISTINGUISHING BETWEEN FLEXIBLE AND COMMITTED RESOURCES USEFUL?

The significant issue in differentiating between these resources is the "timing" of the acquisition of resources. That is, were the resources acquired in advance of use (were they committed resources) or were they acquired only when they were needed (were they flexible resources)? This distinction is critical for short-term decision making as the profitability of a short-term decision depends only on the resources that have to be acquired for that purpose; that is, the decision depends on the flexible resources. Let's assume that a customer wants a price quote on the assembly of 120 units of her product during the following week. You estimate that it would take 12 hours of work to assemble these 120 units. Based on your operating schedule, however, you find that Worker B (the worker who is not paid on piece-rate) is expected to be free for five hours during the next week. Because you would need seven more hours, you contact Worker A (the one who is paid on a piece-rate) and find that she is available to work for seven hours next week. Before contacting the manufacturer, you need to determine your cost. Because Worker B will be paid for the next week whether she works on this new job or not, you choose to ignore that cost and concentrate primarily on the cost of $70 (7 hours * $10) that you will have to pay Worker A. Assuming that there are no other costs, you might consider $70 as your only cost and price the job at the price you believe the manufacturer is willing to pay, but above $70. But would you always expect to spend $70 in the short run to assemble the 120 units? Not necessarily! That would depend on the number of hours that Worker B had available during that week. If Worker B had all eight hours available, the short-run cost of assembling the same 120 units would be $40. Or if Worker B had no hours available during that week, the short-run cost of assembling 120 units would be $120 because Worker A would have to be hired and paid $120 for 12 hours of work. Hence, the cost of assembling these 120 units on any future date would depend on the availability of Worker B. On the other hand, what did it really cost you to assemble the 120 units? In other words, what cost would you be willing to use as a long-term price quote for this manufacturer? Might it be $70? No! The cost of assembling the $120 units is $120, and

that cost has nothing to do with whether some of it is derived from using a flexible resource and whether some of it is derived from using a committed resource. Distinguishing between flexible and committed resources allows one to determine the short-term profitability of a business decision, which is very similar to what traditional cost/managerial accounting textbooks discuss in their "Relevant Costs for Decision Making" or "Differential Costs for Decision Making" chapters. This view is also consistent with direct or variable costing and its later extension, throughput costing, popularized by Eli Goldratt and Jeff Cox's *The Goal*, and can be distinguished from the long-term cost view popularized by the proponents of activity-based costing.

COST OF USED RESOURCES: DIRECT VS. INDIRECT TO A BATCH

Because 12 hours (six hours each by Workers A and B) were used to assemble 120 units in batch #439, a total of $120 still represents direct labor cost; that is, the cost of $120 can be traced to the 120 units in batch #439. Of the remaining two hours that were available from Worker B, one hour was spent educating a new intern on the intricacies of a machine. As this training had nothing to do with batch #439 or any other batch, $10, representing one hour, is indirect to all batches. Finally, Worker A had no work for one hour. This cost of $10 is neither direct nor indirect to any batch because the hour was not spent adding value directly or indirectly to any product or batch. Hence, even though the cost of available resources is $140, the total costs that are direct or indirect to a batch are $130 ($120 + $10). The balance of $10 is the cost of unused resources. On the other hand, if the total number of units in batch #439 was 110, and Worker A had still been hired for six hours, the direct labor cost would have been $110 (five hours from Worker B and six hours from Worker A), the indirect cost (B's one hour for training the intern) would have remained at $10, but the cost of unused resources (B's idle time of two hours) would have increased to $20. The cost of available resources would have remained $140.

COST OF USED RESOURCES: VARIABLE VS. FIXED TO A UNIT OF PRODUCT

As 12 hours (six hours each by Workers A and B) were used to assemble 120 units in batch #439, a total of $120 still represents a variable cost; that is, the assembly cost varies with the number of units assembled. Hence, the cost of $120 would double to $240 if the number of units in batch #439 doubled from 120 units to 240 units. Of the remaining two hours that were available from Worker B, one hour was spent educating a new intern. This training was independent of the 120 units manufactured in batch #439 or any other units manufactured in any other batch, so its cost of $10 is unlikely to be influenced by the size of this batch or any other batch. Hence, $10, representing one hour, is a fixed cost. Finally, Worker A had no work for one hour. This cost of $10 is neither variable nor fixed with respect to a unit of product and represents the cost of unused resources. Out of the cost of available resources of $140, the costs that are either variable to fixed with respect to units of product are $130 ($120 + $10), the balance of $10 being the cost of unused resources. On the other hand, if the total number of units in batch #439 was 110, and Worker A had still been hired for six hours, the variable cost would have been $110 (five hours from Worker B and six hours from Worker A). Worker B's one hour for training the intern would have remained a fixed cost at $10, but the cost of unused resources (B's idle time of two hours) would have increased to $20. The cost of available resources would have remained $140.

WHAT INFORMATION DOES THE COST OF USED RESOURCES PROVIDE?

While the cost of available resources represents the cost of committed and flexible resources, the cost of used resources represents how these resources were actually used. For example, were any of the resources used primarily for a certain product or batch of products? If so, the cost of those resources would be direct to the product or batch of products. Similarly, were any of the resources used in direct proportion to the number of units manufactured? If so, the cost of those resources would be variable with respect to the number of units manufactured. Now let's assume that a customer wants to offer you a long-term contract to assemble 120 units of her product a week. This time, however, she would like to sign a five-year contract. You estimate that it would take 12 hours of work to assemble these 120 units of product. But you are unlikely to check your operating schedule for the next week to see if Worker B is free then since you are attempting to provide a quote for the next five years and worker B may have different schedules during the next 260 weeks. For all you know, Worker B may not be with you for the next five years. You need to determine the cost of using 12 hours of your resources every week for the next five years, regardless of who will be doing the assembling or how you will be paying her (piece-rate or nonpiece-rate). If you assume that the wage rate

per hour will remain at $10 over the next five years, then the long-term cost for assembly would be $120 a week, which will be both direct to the job as well as variable to the number of units manufactured. Now it is possible that, during one week, you may find that Worker B (the worker not paid on piece-rate) works five hours on the job and Worker A (paid on a piece-rate) works the remaining seven hours. Even though you will only acquire resources for $70, your cost would still be $120 for that week—$120 being direct to the job as well as variable to the number of units. During another week, you may find that Worker B (the worker not paid on piece-rate) can work on the job all 12 hours, over two days, and Worker A (paid on a piece-rate) is not needed. Even though you have acquired no resources for this job, your cost would still be $120—again, $120 being direct to the job as well as variable to the number of units. Hence, the long-term cost of assembling the 120 units is $120, all of it being direct to the batch as well as variable with the number of units produced, and such longterm cost has nothing to do with whether a flexible resource (Worker A) or a committed resource (Worker B) is acquired. This long-term view is consistent with full or absorption costing and its later extension, activity-based costing, popularized by Robin Cooper, Robert Kaplan, and others.

WHAT INFORMATION DOES THE COST OF UNUSED RESOURCES PROVIDE?

Figure 2 reveals that $10, representing one hour of idle time by Worker B, is the cost of unused resources. Such cost of unused resources could represent waste or a myriad of causes needing management action.[12] One such action could be to create additional demand for the resource through additional production/sales, thereby transferring part or all of the cost of unused resources to the cost of used resources. For example, if the total number of units in batch #439 were 130, and Worker A had still been hired for six hours, the variable cost would have been $130 (seven hours from Worker B and six hours from Worker A). Worker B's one hour for training the intern would have remained a fixed cost at $10, but there would have been no cost of unused resources as the extra unused hour was used up by the assembly of 100 additional units. The cost of available resources would have remained $140.

Another action could be to sell or dispose of one or more "chunks" of resource if the demand placed on this resource is reduced. For example, assume the total number of units in batch #439 was

Blocher, Stout, Cokins, Chen: *Cost Management, 4e*

Figure 3: A Comprehensive Framework of Cost Terminology

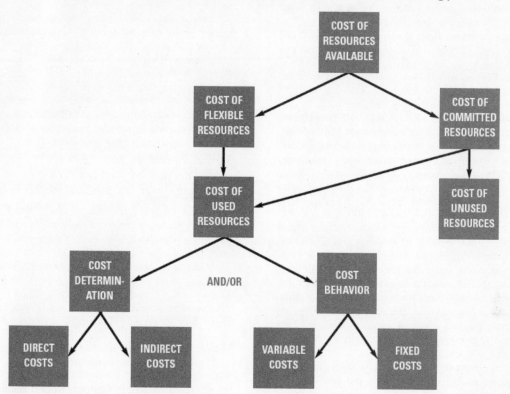

40 and Worker B has enough available time to work on this batch. In that case, Worker A would not be needed. Yet if Worker B had no other assignments, four hours of her time, or $40, would be the cost of unused resources. If such a scenario repeats itself quite often, you might have to consider letting

Worker B go and using Worker A whenever you have extra work. Such release of Worker B would be equivalent to disposing of a "chunk" of resource.

CAN THIS ALL BE SYNTHESIZED INTO A COMPREHENSIVE FRAMEWORK?

Figure 3 illustrates a comprehensive framework of cost terms that reveals the following steps:

1. The starting point for all discussions regarding cost terms should be the cost of resources acquired. In financial accounting terms, this is equivalent to acquiring an asset.

2. When you have determined the resources that were acquired, the next step is to decide if those resources are committed resources or flexible resources. This distinguishes the timing of the acquired resources and is useful for short-term decision making using direct or variable costing or its more recent version, throughput costing.

3. All flexible resources are used, so the cost of flexible resources is always converted into the cost of used resources. No cost of unused resources arises from the acquisition of flexible resources. On the other hand, all committed resources need not be used. The costs of committed resources are broken up into the cost of used resources and the cost of unused resources.

4. The cost of used resources is made up of the cost of flexible resources acquired (and used) and the cost of committed resources used. This cost of used resources is now the universe from which costs for cost determination purposes (direct vs. indirect cost) and costs for behavioral purposes (variable vs. fixed) are extracted. Many traditional cost/management accounting textbooks ignore these developments. First, they fail to make a distinction between the cost of available resources and the cost of used resources. Second, they assume that direct or assembly labor is acquired when these services are required, thereby suggesting that direct labor costs are avoidable or are relevant costs for decision making. Using the piecemeal advancements from many cost/managerial accounting textbooks, one can compile a comprehensive framework for cost terminology— one that attempts to incorporate these two cost/managerial accounting developments.

ENDNOTES:

1 Michael Maher, Clyde Stickney, and Roman Weil, *Managerial Accounting,* seventh edition, Harcourt College Publishers, Fort Worth, Texas, 2001.

2 Anthony Atkinson, Rajiv Banker, Robert Kaplan, and Mark Young, *Management Accounting,* third edition, Prentice-Hall, Upper Saddle River, N.J., 2001.

3 Robin Cooper and Robert Kaplan, "Activity-Based Systems: Measuring the Costs of Resource Usage," *Accounting Horizons*, September 1992, pp. 1-13.

4 Examples include Atkinson, et al., 2001; Don Hansen and Maryanne Mowen, *Cost Management,* third edition, South- Western College Publishing, Cincinnati, Ohio, 2000; Don Hansen and Maryanne Mowen, *Management Accounting,* fifth edition, South-Western College Publishing, Cincinnati, Ohio, 2000; Ronald Hilton, Michael Maher, and Frank Selto, *Cost Management*, Irwin McGraw-Hill, Boston, Mass., 2000; Maher, et al., 2001; and Cheryl McWatters, Dale Morse, and Jerold Zimmerman, *Management Accounting,* second edition, Irwin McGraw-Hill, Boston, Mass., 2001.

5 "A fixed cost is a cost that remains constant, in total, regardless of changes in the level of activity, "from Ray Garrison and Eric Noreen, *Managerial Accounting,* ninth edition, Irwin McGraw-Hill, Boston, Mass., 2000, p. 58; "A variable cost is a cost that varies, in total, in direct proportion to changes in the level of activity," Garrison and Noreen, 2000, p. 57.

6 "The term direct labor is reserved for those labor costs that can be easily (i.e., physically and conveniently) traced to individual units of product.... The labor costs of assembly-line workers, for example, would be direct labor costs, as would be the labor costs of carpenters, bricklayers, and machine operators," Garrison and Noreen, 2000, p. 45. For this discussion, I ignore nonmanufacturing costs like sales commissions and simplistically assume that all nonmanufacturing costs are indirect to a unit of product. I also ignore the important distinctions of indirect costs provided by activity-based costing.

7 "An avoidable cost is a cost that can be eliminated in whole or in part by choosing one alternative over another.... Avoidable costs are relevant costs. Unavoidable costs are irrelevant costs," Garrison and Noreen, 2000, p. 616.

8 I recognize that direct labor cost is no longer an important part of many companies' cost structures, but I use direct labor cost because it offers an opportunity to best differentiate the diverse treatments available in the cost/managerial accounting textbooks.

9 The only exception was the case of obsolete inventory where direct costs, such as direct materials and direct labor, were not relevant because they had already been acquired and used.

10 For simplicity, I ignore the possibility that Worker B, not being paid on a piece-rate basis, might cost less than the $10 an hour that Worker A, a piece-rate worker, is paid.

11 "Committed resources are purchased before they are used,"
Hansen and Mowen, 2000, p. 690; "capacity-related resources are acquired and paid for in advance of when the work is done," (Emphases authors), Atkinson, Banker, Kaplan, and Young, 2001, p. 74; "flexible resources can be easily purchased in the amount needed and at the time of use," Hansen and Mowen, 2000, p. 690.

12 CAM-I (Consortium for Advanced Manufacturing-International), in its attempt to explain the cost of unused resources or capacity, introduced the concepts of idle capacity and nonproductive capacity. For more details, see Thomas Klammer, *Capacity Measurement & Improvement*, Irwin Professional Publishing, Chicago, Ill., 1996.

Chapter 4
Job Costing

Cases

4-1   **Constructo Inc.** (Under or Over-Applied Overhead)
4-2   **East River Manufacturing (A)** (Problems of Traditional Job Costing)

Readings

4-1: "How I Reengineered a Small Business" by Richard H. Snyder, *Strategic Finance* (May 1999).

This article describes both the old and new job costing systems at James Street Fashions (also called Latt-Greene), a small textile knitting and converting operation in Vernon, California. The author is the controller of Latt-Greene. He instituted a spreadsheet-based job costing system that helped to reverse a $5 million loss on $65 million in sales revenue to a $3 million profit on just $32 million in sales revenue. He also eliminated unnecessary overtime and increased the overall quality of the company's product line.

Discussion Questions:
1. Briefly describe the company, its products and customers.
2. What problems did the author discover when he conducted his initial interviews?
3. Describe the company's old financial costing system, and identify its weaknesses as well as business operating and profit consequences cause by its poor costing system.
4. What are major impacts of the company's new computerized costing system on its business operations, product prices and quality, and company's profit?
5. What are general principles learned by the author for changing or reengineering a company's costing system?

4-2: "Distinguishing Between Direct and Indirect Costs Is Crucial For Internet Companies" by Lawrence A. Gordon, Ph.D., and Martin P. Loeb, Ph.D., *Management Accounting Quarterly* (Summer 2001) pp. 12-17.

This article points out the importance of distinguishing direct and indirect costs for internet companies. The cost objects are different for internet companies, a focus on customers instead of products.   However, the key issues of pricing, cost allocation, and cost management are still applicable.

Discussion Questions:
1. What characteristic must a company have to be referred to as an internet company?
2. What is the key element of competition for an internet company?
3. What is the key cost allocation issue for internet companies?
4. What is the key cost object for an internet company?

Cases

4-1 Under or Overapplied Overhead

Constructo Inc. is a manufacturer of furnishings for infants and children. The company uses a job cost system and employs a full absorption accounting method for cost accumulation. Constructo's work-in-process inventory at April 30, 2001 consisted of the following jobs.

Job No.	Items	Units	Accumulated Cost
CBS102	Cribs	20,000	$ 900,000
PLP086	Playpens	25,000	420,000
DRS114	Dressers	25,000	250,000
			$1,570,000

The company's finished goods inventory, which Constructo evaluates using the FIFO (First-in, first-out) method, consisted of five items.

Item	Quantity and Unit Cost	Accumulated Cost
Cribs	7,500 units @ $ 64 each	$ 480,000
Strollers	13,000 units @ $ 23 each	299,000
Carriages	11,200 units @ $102 each	1,142,400
Dressers	21,000 units @ $ 55 each	1,155,000
Playpens	19,400 units @ $ 35 each	679,999
		$3,755,400

Constructo applies factory overhead on the basis of direct labor hours. The company's factory overhead budget for the fiscal year ending May 31, 2001, totals $4,500,000, and the company plans to expend 600,000 direct labor hours during this period. Through the first eleven months of the year, a total of 555,000 direct labor hours were worked, and total factory overhead amounted to $4,273,500.

At the end of April, the balance in Constructo's Materials Inventory account, which includes both raw materials and purchased parts, was $668,000. Additions to and requisitions from the materials inventory during the month of May included the following.

	Raw Materials	Purchased Parts
Additions	$242,000	$396,000
Requisitions:		
Job CBS102	51,000	104,000
Job PLP086	3,000	10,800
Job DRS114	124,000	87,000
Job STR077		
(10,000 strollers)	62,000	81,000
Job CRG098		
(5,000 carriages)	65,000	187,000

Blocher, Stout, Cokins, Chen: *Cost Management, 4e*

©The McGraw-Hill Companies, Inc 2008

During the month of May, Constructo's factory payroll consisted of the following.

Account	Hours	Cost
CBS102	12,000	$122,400
PLP086	4,400	43,200
DRS114	19,500	200,500
STR077	3,500	30,000
CRG098	14,000	138,000
Indirect	3,000	29,400
Supervision		57,600
		$621,100

Listed below are the jobs that were completed and the unit sales for the month of May.

Job No.	Items	Quantity Complete
CBS102	Cribs	20,000
PLP086	Playpens	15,000
STR077	Strollers	10,000
CRG098	Carriages	5,000

Items	Quantity Shipped
Cribs	17,500
Playpens	21,000
Strollers	14,000
Dressers	18,000
Carriages	6,000

REQUIRED:

1. Describe when it is appropriate for a company to use a job cost system.
2. Calculate the dollar balance in Constructo's work-in-process inventory account as of May 31, 2001.
3. Calculate the dollar amount related to the playpens in Constructo's finished goods inventory as of May 31, 2001.
4. Explain the proper accounting treatment for overapplied or underapplied overhead balances when using a job cost system.

(CMA Adapted)

4-2 East River Manufacturing (A)

Power Services Industries has been in business since 1907. PSI's principal business is the design, manufacture, and erection of steam generation equipment for utility and industrial customers. PSI also serves the after-parts market, which includes individual boiler components and loose tubes for repair and replacement. Their primary product, coal-fired boilers, burns fossil fuels to heat water, which turns to steam, and is used either for electrical generation or industrial process. Boilers are highly engineered products which can take anywhere from six months to five years to complete from the design stage through manufacturing and erection phases.

The East River, Illinois plant is one of three manufacturing facilities of the Services Division of the Energy Group. The East River plant has over 503,000 square feet of fabrication area, nine fabrication bays, and a practical capacity load of 1,345,000 manhours. There are over 500 hourly and salaried employees at the East River plant.

MARKET AND COMPETITIVE ENVIRONMENT

Throughout the post-World War II period and up until the mid-1970s, the demand for power-generating capacity increased steadily. PSI was a prime beneficiary of this growth in demand for electricity. They were awash in orders for original equipment. Backlogs of orders for forty or more radiant boilers were common, and when measured in manhours, were equivalent to over five years of work. The typical order for original equipment boilers averaged $30 million. Prior to the eighties, the original-equipment market (OEM) made up more than 60 percent of East River's revenues. Throughout this period, PSI earned a very respectable return on its investment.

As a sideline to the OEM, East River also serviced the replacement-parts (known as loose tubes) market. Tubes wear out in the hostile environment (e.g., coal-fired boilers generate fly ash which is very corrosive when it continually beats against a tube wall) and need to be replaced. However, demand for service work (replacement parts and components or subassemblies) is extremely difficult to project. Replacement-parts business requires short lead times, on-time shipments, and competitive prices. Service work is made more demanding because customers want made-to-order replacement tubes in small quantities. The typical replacement-parts order was $50,000 and usually had to be delivered in less than ten days, although the need to expedite an order overnight was not unusual. Replacement orders made up about 40 percent of revenues. And while the reported gross profit margins on individual loose tubes were high, the absolute size of and total returns on OEM projects made that market more attractive.

In the early eighties, a combination of fuel price increases, high interest rates, and a global recession hit and the bottom fell out of the OEM. In the past, this was normally a temporary setback and orders always picked up once the economy recovered. But this time it was different. The steady growth in electricity consumption, which had been predictable for so long, leveled off and OEM orders plunged. A number of factors led to a permanent drop in demand by the OEM, including the sharp increase in the cost of energy, unsympathetic utility regulatory agencies, uncertainty related to deregulation, environmental concerns about acid-rain, and improved capabilities to transmit excess energy across markets.

This new environment was marked by wide swings in business and fluctuating manning requirements. OEM business picked up again in the mid-eighties, but total OEM business and profits never returned to their former high levels and the total workload at the East River facility continued to drop. The inevitable profit squeeze caused by excess capacity and by ever-rising costs led PSI to look to the replacement-parts business to offset the declining OEM business.

Demand for replacement parts expanded as orders for original equipment declined. The principal reason was that utility and industrial customers wanted to maintain and prolong the useful life of power-generating equipment by replacing worn out parts rather than build new capacity. In addition, PSI engineers worked closely with customers to achieve greater efficiencies and enhance the power output of existing power sources by redesigning components or adding additional parts.

Blocher, Stout, Cokins, Chen: *Cost Management, 4e*

The determinants of successful management of large and complex OEM projects are very different from the key success factors in the replacement-parts market. Critical market drivers in the loose-tube replacement market are:

- Increased flexibility

- Reduced lead time

- Low price

- On-time delivery

- High Quality

Except for high quality, these factors did not carry the same weight in the OEM. As a result, PSI had to quickly adapt. For example, fast turnaround of worn or damaged parts is crucial once a boiler is in operation. Replacement parts availability is critical to a pulp and paper customer like Weyerhaeuser. Customers can suffer losses in the tens of thousands of dollars daily if their boilers are shut down as a result of part failure. East River always tried to accommodate customers' needs for replacement parts. But East River was structured to capitalize on the returns to be made on large-scale OEM projects. Primary considerations on OEM projects were to complete the boiler on time, within budget, and according to contract specifications.

The urgency of meeting contract lead times and completion dates on new equipment was not as critical as it was for replacement parts. But now, replacement parts were the primary source of revenues. And while new boilers were still being sold, replacement parts for existing boilers now made up 70 percent of East River's workload. Since PSI's major competitors (e.g., Asea, Brown, Bovari/Combustion Engineering; Babcock & Wilcox; Riley, Foster, & Wheeler; and Zurn) were suffering from the same drop in OEM orders, they too started to compete aggressively for the growing replacement-parts business. The field was crowded with competitors. But the expanding replacement-parts business was not large enough to offset the lost OEM orders. By the early nineties, total OEM and replacement-parts business was significantly less than it was in the early eighties (Refer to Exhibit 1). There was now a glut of industry-wide capacity. By 1989, the industry was overcapitalized and demand from the OEM and replacement-parts markets was running at a level which utilized only 45-50 percent of East River's capacity. The inevitable outcome was constant pressure on prices, margins, and market share.

MAJOR PRODUCTS

The East River plant manufactures a wide variety of components for boilers including wall panels— a collection of steel tubes (carbon steel, stainless, or composites) which are welded together with membrane bars in between them; loose tubes that have a number of bends in them or studs applied to them for heat transfer capability; burners which can burn coal, oil, or gas; structural members which contain the tubes that make up the walls of the boiler; expansion joints; dampers; economizers; risers and supplies tubes.

The Bay 7 facility was configured and equipped to process straight lengths of loose tubes into various shapes and lengths, suitable for the repair and replacement-parts market or needed as component parts of other assemblies completed at East River. Replacement parts and components are custom-made from unique materials compositions and configurations so that the parts can function reliably in a power-generation environment where steam may be generated by burning any one of hundreds of different kinds of coal or other fossil fuels.

Exhibit 1
East River Plant (A)

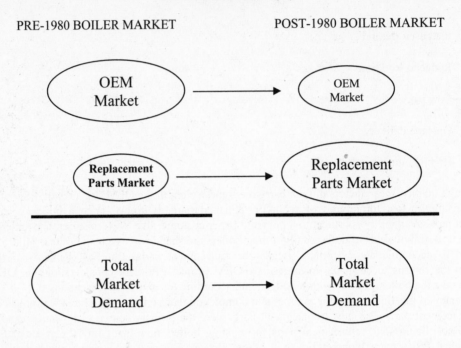

PRE-1980 BOILER MARKET   POST-1980 BOILER MARKET

Many of the tubes manufactured have difficult welds and intricate bends in several different planes. All of these bends are engineered to a certain size, dimension, and location on the tube. Quality has to be right the first time. Once parts are in the field, they have to fit exactly. There is no reworking on the line.

ENGINEERING AND PRODUCTION PROCESS

Customer orders for individual boiler components and loose tubes to be fabricated in Bay 7 are initially processed at PSI's Dallas, Texas headquarters. Since there are no off-the-shelf parts, preliminary tube designs are prepared by product design engineers from historical data. Cost estimators use these preliminary tube designs to prepare estimates of the tube's manufacturing and material cost. The base estimating data used by cost estimators was developed from industrial engineering time studies completed in the early seventies. There are enough similarities to previously-fabricated tube variations that customer requested quotes can be developed on a timely basis by querying the parts database. If the proposal is accepted and becomes a contract, the proposal becomes the base-line or "as-sold" estimate (i.e., the budgeted cost) for cost monitoring and measuring actual performance.

Once a proposal is accepted, product design engineers "start from scratch" and prepare detailed part and component designs on computer-aided design (CAD) systems. They also determine the materials composition for all tubes. This product structure and tube geometry, which describes the physical characteristics of the tube, is then transferred to draftsmen who transform the product structure into detailed graphics (blueprints). Draftsmen manually load information on the tube's geometry into three different computer systems: (1) the Bill of Material system; (2) the CAD drawing system; and (3) the Tube Detail file which converts tube geometry along with design, process, machine, and tooling constraints data into process plans. This information is downloaded to East River's mainframe computers.

Purchasing places orders for all stock and non-stock items, many of which have long leadtimes. The process engineering group uses the Tube Detail file to generate the route sheet generation program or RSGP. RSGP creates a routing for each part with specific work centers, operations descriptions, and estimated process times. Customer order information is entered into MAPICS II (Manufacturing Accounting Production Inventory Control System), an IBM MRP II system. MAPICS generates bill of materials, routing sheets, order quantities, and required delivery dates. Manufacturing orders released by MAPICS were hand delivered to their respective

Blocher, Stout, Cokins, Chen: *Cost Management, 4e*

©The McGraw-Hill Companies, Inc 2008

work centers. Exhibit 2 shows the sequential flow of a contract from the preliminary proposal through shipment to the customer.

The East River plant has nine manufacturing bays. By 1990, the average age of equipment in Bay 7 was greater than 29 years. Bay 7 has practical capacity of 160,000 manhours. Tubes were received by truck and unloaded by a radio controlled overhead crane with the assistance of two workers. Tubes moved through the shops by a series of overhead cranes, jib cranes hung from building supports, forklifts, and transfer cars.

Tubes were shotblasted, cut to length, and machined as required. Tubes may be welded together prior to moving to the stencil/layout table, where the tubes were paint marked for a variety of studding and bending patterns. Tubes were then moved to a staging area near the stud welders and benders. Tubes were processed through a series of stud welding and bending stations, which were machine-assisted but still highly labor-intensive. Exhibit 3 displays certain tube features. Bending dies were stored outside Bay 7 and, when needed, transported by forklift to the proper bending station. Tube bundles were moved from station to station through Bay 7 by a series of pendant operated overhead cranes. Tubes were then checked, inspected, finished, and cleaned prior to shipment to the customer or transferred to another bay where they were assembled into boiler components. Average throughput time in the bay was approximately 3-4 weeks with high work-in-process. About 40 percent of the manhours in Bay 7 were attributable to material handling at the work stations or movement between work stations. Exhibit 4 shows the process flow for Bay 7, including machine count and headcount.

Exhibit 2
East River Plant (A)
Proposal-to-Shipment Process

SEQUENTIAL FLOW TUBE PROCESS

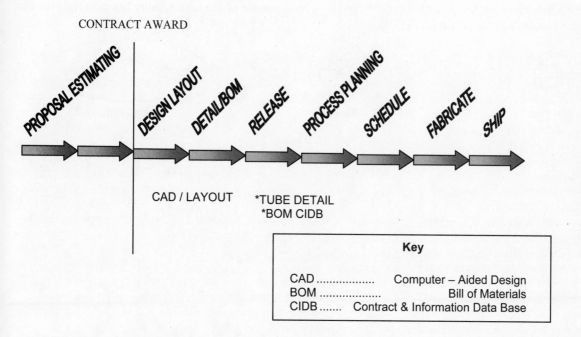

It was not unusual for bottlenecks and scheduling difficulties to arise during processing. Work-in-process was stored adjacent to work stations to alleviate any disruptions which might occur in upstream operations. There was approximately $7 million worth of inventory at East River at any given time.

Over the years, maintenance expenditures were kept at levels sufficient to sustain current operations. Competing on cost meant that operations management focused on high levels of equipment utilization.

However, machine downtime and costs to repair equipment were now rising rapidly. In addition, depreciation expenditures were not reinvested in new equipment.

Furthermore, the collective bargaining agreement with the union did not allow workers to be cross-trained to run multiple machines and perform a variety of functions. Part of the difficulty was that over the years the collective bargaining unit negotiated fifteen different job levels along with several classes within each level. But now competition was placing a premium on flexible work rules and East River was saddled with a labor agreement which made it difficult to respond quickly. With so much to disrupt shop floor control, it was hard to consistently maintain contract work schedules and meet customers' requested shipping dates.

Exhibit 3
East River Plant (A)

TUBE FEATURES

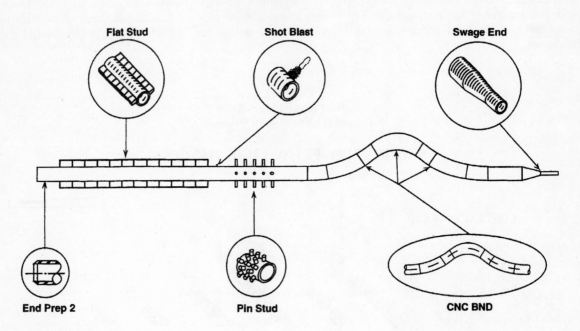

Exhibit 4
East River Plant (A)
Tube Shop Manual Line

EXISTING PROCESS FLOW/MACHINE COUNT/HEADCOUNT

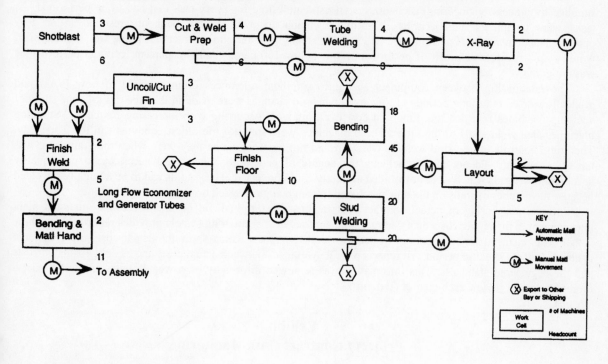

EXISTING COST SYSTEM

Traditionally, throughput in East River's labor-intensive shops was measured by manhours. The East River facility is on a job cost system. The same job cost system was installed in all plants built during the 1950s. In the case of East River, the job cost system was installed in 1951 and remained virtually unchanged until 1992, with two exceptions: (1) practical capacity replaced a three-year average of expected actual capacity for determining burden rates in 1982; and (2) a material burden rate was developed in the late 1980s. A job or contract cost system is necessary since PSI doesn't make a standard product. End products are manufactured to customer's specifications. The entire project is designed and engineered at PSI's Dallas, Texas headquarters. Materials composition and product structure are based upon the type of fossil fuel that will be used by the power generator and other environmental variables.

The contract is the primary cost object. Orders are grouped by contract, and costs are accumulated for purchase orders as well as manufacturing orders. The cost system charges materials and labor costs directly to the contract and to the part. Product design engineering, drafting or graphics, machine setup, and material handling costs are also directly charged to contracts. Burden rates are based upon practical capacity. A material burden rate of 5 percent of material cost covers the cost of purchasing and material control costs. Pressure Shop 415's overhead for three bays includes indirect labor and fringes, equipment-related costs, maintenance and repairs, and supplies. Shop 415 overhead was charged to contracts and other cost objects at 150 percent of direct labor cost. Plant support services, known as works-general costs, consist of production control, plant engineering, quality assurance, payroll, accounting, and other support services and are charged to contracts at the rate of 40 percent of direct labor cost. In addition, operating-all-works (OAW) costs associated with Dallas support services are charged to contracts at the rate of 15 percent of direct labor cost. OAW consists of manufacturing engineering support and the resource allocation group which plans and monitors plant loads, product mix, and production volume. These costing procedures were more than adequate given market conditions and the focus on large OEM projects throughout most of the post-war period.

In addition to costing the contract at practical capacity, the cost system was also capable of providing operating personnel with contract-related performance information. One of the most critical performance indicators was the monthly ratio of Estimated Man Hours to Actual Man Hours (E/A). Given that contracts could easily extend over a period of years, operating management could not wait until the project was completed to determine whether the contract was coming in over budget. It was essential to have some basis for monitoring progress on each project on an on-going Percentage-of-Completion basis. Using information supplied by process engineering, accounting staff estimated time for every task that had to be performed. As tasks were completed, comparisons of estimated manhours with actual manhours resulted in an E/A performance percentage. If performance was at 100 percent or better, the contract was going well and the plant would earn a respectable profit. If performance was below 100 percent, say 75 percent, contract performance was not going very well.

The relationship between equipment age and equipment tolerances is an example of how E/A could gradually worsen over long periods of time even when no changes were made in the tube design. One study of studding machines revealed that time and cost overruns were occurring with increasing frequency. Studding machines spot weld studs to the tubes. These machines were some of the oldest equipment in the Tube Bay. Therefore, controls on the stud welders were old and not as effective as they were when the equipment was newer. The welds did not always achieve the degree of penetration on a weld necessary to pass quality specifications. Studs which were not welded correctly could break off. These studs had to be manually rewelded because the number of studs on the tube precluded it from being rewelded on the studding machine.

Periodic monitoring of actual contract costs against the original bid or as-sold estimate assisted plant management in managing costs on a contract. The contract cost accounting system provides reports which show actual costs incurred for the contract to date, as well as reports which show the actual costs incurred for a contract during a specific period. All reports provide variances between actual costs and as-sold estimated costs and the engineered standards. This information was reviewed informally on a weekly basis and underwent a thorough, formal review each quarter (Exhibit 5).

Exhibit 5
Project / Contract Cost Monitoring

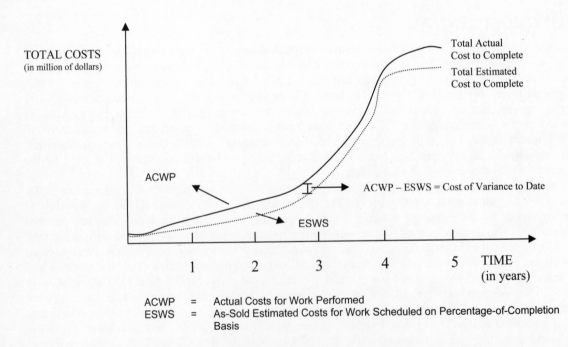

ACWP	=	Actual Costs for Work Performed
ESWS	=	As-Sold Estimated Costs for Work Scheduled on Percentage-of-Completion Basis

From a customer's perspective, there are two other critical performance indicators: (1) on-time delivery—meeting the customer-requested delivery schedule; and (2) quality. Often, customers have planned outages and want replacement parts delivered during a certain outage window—a specific date and time. If this window is

Blocher, Stout, Cokins, Chen: *Cost Management, 4e*

missed, at the very least, customers lose confidence in suppliers. In some cases, there are substantial liquidating damages associated with a missed delivery date.

Quality Assurance reports defects. If a defect will cost more than $1,000 to repair, a separate sub-account is established for the contract, called a C-order, and all costs of reworking the part(s) is charged to this account. Accounting supplies the cost information to QA, which then identifies what the problem was, where it occurred, what the root cause was, and who had primary responsibility for correcting it. Some defects are due to a design errors, referred to as a D-orders. Design flaws can be identified when parts don't assemble properly. It is important to determine the cause of design errors so that they do not repeat these mistakes on future contracts of a similar nature or, if the error is the result of a flaw in the manufacturing process, the process gets corrected. Guarantee-orders or G-orders accumulate the cost of corrective work on a unit in the field that doesn't meet its warranted performance. Reserves are set up for C-, D-, and G-orders to cover the estimated cost or liability. These costs are built into the base estimating data used for proposals and establish allowances for contract cost.

REQUIRED:

1. Briefly summarize and contrast the competitive environment in the pre-1980 era with that of the early nineties.
2. What are the problems that plant management has to resolve?
3. What potential problems may occur between the as-sold cost estimates and the actual contract cost?
4. Diagram the structure of the existing cost system and explain how cost information is used for decision-making, cost control, and performance evaluation purposes.
5. Is the labor-based cost system appropriate for this facility? Should activity-based costing be implemented to analyze product costs?
6. Prepare a set of recommendations for changes in the cost system. Describe a general framework for costing products in an automated facility.

Readings

4.1: HOW I REENGINEERED A SMALL BUSINESS

By *Richard H. Snyder, CPA*

Reengineering is not just for large businesses. It's true that only giant corporations can afford to pay the fees for high-powered consultants to come in and turn the organization upside down. But for those brave souls in small businesses willing to think the unthinkable, reengineering can be managed without huge money outlays.

The major stumbling block in reengineering a small business is the staff who has worked at the business for years and tends to develop an ownership in the current process and, as a result, may be unable or unwilling to consider a revolutionary change in the process. What is required is knowledge of the system that exists and a willingness to consider radical new processes that would dramatically improve the system. In such circumstances an outsider may he necessary in order to produce dramatic change.

Take as an example the case of James Street Fashions dba Latt-Greene, a knitting and converting operation in Vernon, Calif. I became controller of the company on January 2, 1990, at the request of the owner in order to introduce control into the activities of the company. I had a prior knowledge of the textile industry, having been in public accounting for many years and having had some textile companies as clients (not Latt-Greene). I also had controllership, internal auditing, and cost accounting experience and had guided businesses though bankruptcy.

Latt-Greene knits textiles for the women's and children's apparel market, dyes and prints designs on the textiles according to customer instructions, and delivers the product to the customer ready for cutting and sewing into clothing. The customers of the company consist of clothing manufacturers who sell to clothing retailers.

In the initial interviews at this family-owned and operated company, I discovered some of the concerns: severe negative cash flow, a belief that not all sales to customers were being billed or

collected, a paper-heavy system that was being crushed by its own weight. In my initial walk-

Table 1

YEAR ENDED 05/31	NET SALES	ROI
1985	16.5	11.3%
1986	19.8	(46%)
1987	24.8	(18%)
1988	33.6	33%
1989	39.2	11%
1990	54.8	(6%)
SEVEN MONTHS ENDED 12/31		
1990	31.3	63%
YEAR ENDED 12/31		
1991	54	61%
1992	30	7%
1993	32	41%
1994	38	53%
1995	31	28%
1996	30	30%
1997	36	43%
1998	30	24%

through, I was astonished to see that the accountant was still keeping records on a "one-write" system. There wasn't a single computer to be found on the premises. I told the owners that if I were hired I would be making some dramatic changes including introducing data processing.

UNRAVELING THE OLD

The first thing I did upon being hired was to purchase a personal computer. I purchased one

Blocher, Stout, Cokins, Chen: *Cost Management, 4e*

without any networking software because at that moment I had no one to network with. But I did look forward to that day in the future and purchased a computer with the capability of being turned into a central server at a future date. The only software that I installed at that time was a powerful spreadsheet, Quattro Pro. In order to gain insight and perspective into the problems of the system, I loaded into a spreadsheet all the invoices billed to customers during the month of November 1989, the most current period available at that time. I then began filling in columns with dyeing and printing costs from the subcontracting companies who did this work for Latt-Greene. I also calculated and added yarn costs and added a knitting cost, a tricky and inaccurate process because such costs had never been accumulated or calculated. The only financial records being prepared at this time were the general ledger, cash receipts journal and customer ledgers, and a cash disbursement journal. As yarn was knitted into unfinished textiles (called greige goods), sheets were manually prepared showing what pieces were assigned to what lot and what the lot weighed. But no attempt was made to cost the greige goods. When the finished goods were delivered to customers, they were billed as per the purchase order, but again no attempt was made to cost the product. The owners believed they knew what their knitting costs should be, and so I used that number as a starting point.

As I developed the cost sheet, several problems began to surface. One, I couldn't locate dyeing and printing invoices that could be matched up against the sales invoices. There was no controlling order number that followed the job through all its steps before the finished product was delivered to the customer. The dye house assigned its own number to the orders, and the print plant did the same. In some cases it was virtually impossible to determine to which order the costs applied. Two, I found purchase orders for which no shipment to the customer could be located. Three, I found many orders being delivered late. The person who placed orders into work kept the orders in an alphabetical file on her desk and each day rummaged through the file, pulled some orders from it, and told her assistant to put them into work. Many orders were delivered very late simply because they didn't get pulled from the file, and there was no control over the orders that were in process.

As I completed input for the month of November, I began seeing that a large number of the orders either had a too low gross margin to generate a profit on the sale, or even incurred a gross loss. I began analyzing these orders, and

several problems came to the surface. First, like a conscientious baker who regularly gives his customers a "baker's dozen' Latt-Greene was producing textiles that were heavier than required. If an order called for goods that weighed eight ounces to the running yard, we were filling it with goods that weighed nine ounces. This extra weight made for a nice finished product, but it also often meant the difference between a profit and a loss. Second, in many cases, while the weight was okay, and all other factors in the production were correct, the order didn't produce a profit. We came to the conclusion that in many cases the product was simply being sold for too low a price. No wonder the company's sales increased from $16 million to over $54 million in five short years.

During the time that I was developing this spreadsheet, the solutions to the problems being uncovered were becoming clearer. I developed a manual costing system whereby every new order coming in was costed as it progressed through the stages of production. When it was delivered to the customer we knew immediately whether we made or lost money and the reasons for an unsatisfactory result. But this manual costing system required a tremendous amount of time to maintain and keep current.

KNITTING THE NEW TOGETHER

While searching for computer software that would take the place of the manual system, I looked at several programs, but each had some faults or shortcomings that disqualified them. Finally, I was introduced to a company that had produced a textile conversion system for a business which was smaller than Latt-Greene, and which did no knitting. But I liked what I saw because it had many fine features and controls. Talking with the developer convinced me that the knitting operation could be added to produce a system that met our needs.

In October 1990, we installed a computer system using my old personal computer as the central server and added 10 stations using the Novell system. After installation, I had to train the employees to use the new system. For some who resisted abandoning "the way we had always done it' I had to warn them to either do it my way or I would get someone who would. Over several months they learned to become computer operators, and the old system was forgotten.

As better and better cost data was developed using the new system, we refined our sales prices. In some cases major customers were lost because we raised our prices. But most customers were retained because we improved our service to them in several ways. Delivery schedules were met on a more consistent basis, and product consistency and quality improved as the employees were able to spend more time on those aspects of the product and less time on paperwork and trying to track down product location.

The system developer and I were able to develop a system that works very well for us because we took the time to thoroughly understand the business of Latt-Greene and the problems that occur in the textile industry. I took the time to talk to everyone involved in the process of converting yarn into a dyed and printed textile. I looked at every piece of paper being produced and traced an entire month's orders through to the final invoicing of the finished product. This thorough analysis uncovered the problems. All that was left was the development of the systems necessary to fix the problems. I involved as many of the employees of Latt-Greene as possible in identifying the problems and in suggesting solutions. Then, when the final system was installed, many of the people who would be working with it already felt ownership of the system. The few who felt threatened by it and resisted it subsequently left the company.

How successful were we in turning the company around? The table on page 28 displays sales and return on owners investment (ROI) for the years 1985 to 1998.

The big ROI fluctuations up to the year ended May 31, 1990, represent the agonies the company was experiencing because of its rapid growth without corresponding improvements in the systems. The marked decline in ROI in 1992 was due to the upheavals introduced when the recession hit the clothing industry with a vengeance that year. But the important thing here is that even in the deep recession into which the clothing industry sank that year, Latt-Greene continued to be profitable. The 1998 numbers reflect the fact that tremendous quantities of Asian textiles were "dumped" in the United States at prices that we cannot compete against. Several of our clothing customers closed up because of this situation. Even during this "textile depression" however, Latt-Greene continued to be profitable.

The lesson here is that reengineering can have a dramatic impact upon a business. Huge costs to implement change aren't necessary. The entire cost of our new system was approximately $150,000. Turnaround was swift and dramatic. Downsizing did *not* take place. We have about the same size office staff as we did in 1990 (eight people). The difference is that now we know what our costs are, we bill all our sales, and collect all our receivables.

We are able to plan and to develop strategy. While marketing mistakes still occur (for example, when we miss a season because of incorrect designs), the cost of these mistakes is minimized because we can measure them and identify exactly what the nature of the mistake was and make corrections before the mistake becomes a catastrophe.

AN UPDATE

Nine years after inception, the system has changed considerably from the initial setup, but we have never had to do another reengineering. The staff today is still about the same size as it was in 1990. All the personnel that I hired in 1990 to assist in administering the system are still with us. The only office staff to leave were those who refused to work with the new system and had left by the end of 1990.

Some general principles that I learned from this reengineering and which may be helpful to others who would like to upgrade their operation:

- Be open with all employees regarding the process.
- Solicit input from all employees.
- Involve everyone in the implementation of the new system.
- Understand the system yourself because this understanding is more important than bringing in consultants and helps to ensure that costs are kept under control.

Blocher, Stout, Cokins, Chen: *Cost Management, 4e*

4.2: Distinguishing Between Direct and Indirect Costs Is Crucial For Internet Companies

By Lawrence A. Gordon, Ph.D., and Martin P. Loeb, Ph.D.

EXECUTIVE SUMMARY

People who argue that distinguishing between direct and indirect costs is of no relevance in today's Information Economy are dead wrong! Indeed, the importance of the direct vs. indirect costs dichotomy (as well as with many other management accounting techniques) may be even more crucial to an Internet-based firm's survival than to other companies. The key paradigm shift here is that, when separating direct from indirect costs, we need to think of customers as a primary cost objective in such an environment.

Cost management is an important aspect of running a corporation successfully. A crucial part of cost management is the proper allocation of costs to various products and services. Indeed, the way costs are allocated plays a key role in determining the reported profitability of individual products and/or services. In addition, product-line decisions and pricing decisions (of both an internal and external nature) often are affected by cost allocation decisions. At the heart of cost allocation decisions is the dichotomy between direct and indirect costs. Because a given cost can be direct with respect to one cost objective and indirect with respect to another cost objective, determining the appropriate cost objective is fundamental. This fact notwithstanding, there seems to be a growing concern, if not confusion, on the importance of the distinction between direct and indirect costs for Internet-based businesses. We argue that the distinction between direct and indirect costs is as important for Internetbased companies as it is for other companies. The e-commerce revolution, however, requires many companies to make a fundamental change in the way they consider the notion of a cost objective and, in turn, cost management. In particular, Internetbased companies need to view the *customer* as a primary cost objective for purposes of allocating costs.

DIRECT VS. INDIRECT COSTS: A TRADITIONAL VIEW

Direct costs can easily be traced to the cost objective and can be assigned to the cost objective in a straightforward manner. In contrast, *indirect costs* cannot be easily traced to the cost objective.[1] They need some sort of allocation scheme. Thus, the choice of cost objective is critical to the determination of whether a cost is considered direct or indirect. A *cost objective* is the purpose for which a cost is being measured. Further, it is quite common for a given cost to be measured for multiple purposes. Thus, a given cost may be direct with respect to one cost objective and indirect with respect to another cost objective.[2]

Traditionally, products, services, and departments have served as key cost objectives in managing the operations of a firm. In manufacturing firms, the primary cost objective is traditionally assumed to be the physical products being produced. A computer manufacturer, for example, would usually consider the need to determine the cost of producing a computer as the primary purpose for which costs (at least manufacturing costs) are being measured. As such, the costs of materials and labor that can easily be traced to the production of individual computers would be considered direct costs. Costs of materials and labor that cannot be directly related to the production of individual computers would be considered indirect costs.

In a similar vein, the costs associated with depreciating machinery, utilities, and accident insurance would be additional indirect costs in most manufacturing firms. Knowing the costs of manufacturing a product is important in determining the product's profitability, even where prices are market driven,[3] because in these markets the costs will determine the desirability of being in the market. In markets where prices are driven more by costs, knowing the cost of producing a product is all that more important. Further, many new cost management techniques, such as target costing, are focused on controlling product costs. Assessing the contribution of one subunit versus another subunit within a given company also requires a financial manager to determine product costs for transfer pricing purposes. Accordingly, choosing products as the primary cost objective seems quite logical for most manufacturing firms. Whereas tangible products are logical choices for primary cost objectives in most manufacturing firms, services are logical choices for primary cost objectives in other firms. For example, in the banking industry, the distinction between a direct and an indirect cost is usually considered in terms of whether the cost can or cannot be directly related to a particular service (e.g., processing a loan). Choosing departments as the primary cost objective seems to make sense in other firms. For example, in a retail department store, the distinction between direct and indirect costs is often thought of in terms of whether the cost can or cannot be related to a specific department (e.g., men's clothing). As with measuring the cost of products, measuring the cost of services and departments will facilitate profitability analysis as well as pricing decisions.[4] Yet a fundamental change in the way many companies do business has taken place over the past five years. This change falls under the rubric of e-commerce (i.e., electronic commerce) and is largely the result of the Internet. E-commerce has changed the way companies interact with their suppliers and, even more important, the way they interact with their customers.

In fact, Internet commerce has changed the very essence of the way many companies do business. Now, many companies generate a large portion of their revenues via the Internet, and a growing number generate the *majority* of their revenues that way. We refer to these companies as Internet-based because they epitomize the essence of the new Information Economy.[5] To date, most companies still consider costs as being direct or indirect in terms of products, services, or departments. This is true even for many Internet-based firms. Though the basic nature of doing business has changed for a large segment of our economy, the essence of cost management has not changed. In particular, many Internet-based firms have not abandoned the old way of thinking about cost objectives. Yet the important distinction between direct and indirect costs is becoming fuzzy. Some people even argue that distinguishing between direct and indirect costs is no longer a valid way to look at costs for a company operating in an e-commerce environment where intangible assets (e.g., intellectual capital) are so prevalent. For example, in the popular book *The Blur*, Davis and Myer argue that "direct costs are dead, and diminishing marginal returns died with them, a victim of intangibles."

We disagree! In our opinion, the need to differentiate between direct and indirect costs is as valid today in an e-commerce environment as it is in a traditional (brick-and-mortar) environment. Profitability analysis, product-line decisions, and pricing decisions are still significantly affected by the way costs are classified in terms of direct and indirect. The thing that is often no longer valid, however, is the focus on the old notion of cost objectives for firms that operate in an e-commerce environment. We believe companies actively involved in e-commerce need to view customers, as well as products, services, and departments, as key cost objectives. Nowhere is this need more important than in Internet-based firms.

DIRECT VS. INDIRECT COSTS IN INTERNET-BASED FIRMS

The number of firms that derive the majority of their sales over the Internet has grown at a rapid rate. The U.S. Bureau of Census conservatively estimated that $5.3 billion (0.64%) of retail sales in the fourth quarter of 1999 was conducted using the Internet.[6] Furthermore, this estimate excludes the huge number of Internet sales from business to business. Clearly, the growth of the Internet is changing all facets of commerce. Understanding the impact of these changes on corporate cost management systems is vital. The distinguishing feature of an e-commerce environment is that business transactions are handled electronically. The hallmark of such an environment has become the way firms interact with customers via the Internet.

A logical way to decide whether to classify a firm as being dominated by an e-commerce environment is to use the percentage of the firm's sales generated from the Internet. For a firm to be eligible for the Dow Jones Internet Composite Index (which is further subdivided into the Dow Jones Internet Commerce Index and the Dow Jones Internet Service Index), the company must generate at least half of its sales via the Internet.[7] Internet customers, be they households, businesses, or government agencies, can and do conduct quick and inexpensive shopping comparisons. These comparisons take place in a nanosecond, with the click of a mouse. Hence companies are required to continually adjust prices to respond to price changes initiated by competitors. At the same time, their competitors are making similar price adjustments. As a result, companies are required to expend continuous real-time efforts at attracting and tracking customers. In the e-commerce environment, where information search costs approach zero and competitors match price cuts almost instantaneously, competing only in price is not likely to be the means to attracting and maintaining a loyal customer base.

Pricing over the Internet has pushed firms to operate in highly competitive, if not purely competitive, economic markets. Businesses are

Blocher, Stout, Cokins, Chen: *Cost Management, 4e*

quickly learning that a comparative advantage in the cyber marketplace (or, as some have called it, the marketspace) can be secured only by competing effectively in quality customer service to the point of becoming customercentric. Understanding and managing such services requires the allocation of these costs among customers. The proper allocation, in this regard, requires that customers become a key, if not the primary, cost objective for the purposes of distinguishing between direct and indirect costs. Most Internet-based firms use business models that are classified as business-to-business (B2B) or business-to-consumer (B2C). As the names of these models indicate, B2B means that the firm is using the Internet to generate sales of goods and services to other businesses, while B2C means that the firm uses the Internet to generate sales directly to consumers (i.e., retail sales). In addition, the business models used by some Internet-based firms would be classified as business-to-government (B2G) or consumer-to-consumer (C2C). B2G means that the firm sells its products and services primarily to government agencies. C2C means that the firm (for example, eBay) facilitates direct trades among consumers by providing a central marketplace in cyberspace. A firm using a C2C business model typically generates revenues from fees and commissions paid by consumers for participating in the electronic marketplace. Of course, many major corporations use more than one of the above business models. Security analysts and the general investing public commonly use the B2B designation to refer to companies (e.g., Ariba and i2 Technologies) that produce products and services (e.g., software and consulting) to facilitate B2B transactions among businesses via the Internet. The products and services produced by such B2B firms use the Internet to help match sellers of inputs of production with the buyers of these inputs in an efficient manner so firms secure the right inputs at the right time at minimum cost. Such supply chain management benefits sellers by expanding their geographical market to the entire globe and benefits buyers by facilitating the search for low-cost suppliers, reducing the processing costs associated with materials acquisition, and reducing their inventory holding costs. While the companies designated in the media as B2B firms have often been associated with generating high growth in revenues and profits, the larger effects of the B2B revolution are seen outside the firms given the B2B designation. The larger impact on the economy comes from the rapidly expanding number of firms that have embraced B2B for their supply chain management and for sales of their products to other businesses. Irrespective of whether a firm uses the Internet to sell its products and/or services to other businesses, to consumers, or to government agencies, the environment of electronic commerce requires successful firms to focus data collection on customers or customer classes.

Because selling via the Internet empowers customers by reducing their information search costs and their costs of switching from one vendor to another, firms selling via the Internet have stronger motivation to treat customers as key cost objectives than do firms that sell through non-Internet sources. Whether using e-commerce for retail sales or business-to-business sales, companies must devote substantial resources to providing their customers with a user friendly, secure, and hassle-free shopping experience. The development, maintenance, and enhancement of software that keeps track of customer preferences is essential for ensuring such an experience. In essence, Internet-based firms rely much less on traditional infrastructure assets, such as buildings, and more on computers, specialized software, and intellectual capital that cater to customers in cyberspace. When comparing one seller with another, customers cannot compare the service level that would be provided as easily as they can compare quoted prices. Nevertheless, with the wealth of information on the Web, including the seller's website, websites of consumer groups, bulletin boards, and message boards, customers can gather information about the quality of service at a fraction of the cost of a decade earlier. These comparisons result in diminishing customer loyalty.

Moreover, with venture capitalists funding start-up companies on a regular basis and with more brick-and-mortar companies adding e-commerce divisions, new competition is constantly coming to the marketplace. Thus, companies face a dynamic, increasingly competitive environment. In this new environment, companies that are going to be competitive need to devote substantial resources to attracting customers through advertising on the Internet as well as in traditional media (e.g., newspapers, magazines, and television) that direct customers to the firm's Internet sales site. During the actual sales, it is easier for competitive Internet-based firms than traditional firms to customize the physical product (e.g., specifications of a machine being purchased by one firm from another) or service (e.g., loan agreement) being sold. Internet-based sales provide an easy mechanism for direct and instantaneous contact with customers so companies can quickly modify products to new specifications (e.g., the addition or deletion of a clause in a loan agreement). It is also incumbent upon e-commerce firms to provide a high level of post-sale services to customers because such services are often carried out in an easy, quick, and inexpensive manner.

Tracking delivery from the time of sale is a good example of the type of postsale service easily provided in an e-commerce environment. For all the reasons we have noted, tracing costs to individual customers and/or customer classes is an essential competitive strategy for Internet-based companies. In other words, the customer must be a primary cost objective for them. Furthermore, tracing costs to customers cannot be considered a onetime or even periodic investment. Instead, tracing costs to customers must be done on a continuous basis and requires a real-time cost system. For many Internet-based companies, this requires a major change from the way they accumulate costs.[8] In fact, Internet based firms that fail to treat customers as a primary cost objective face the danger of being outsmarted by the competition and left with the least profitable customers in the marketplace.[9] For an Internet-based retailer, the costs of products a customer buys would be classified as direct costs for the customer. For an Internet-based manufacturing firm, the manufacturing cost of products would represent an intermediate cost objective, and the total cost (including costs which are indirect with respect to products) would be traced directly to the customers. Because software can identify the specific Internet advertising that routes a particular customer to the firm's e-store, the cost of this advertising can also be allocated to customers in logical manner. It may even be possible to trace specific software-related costs to particular customers in an e-commerce environment, thereby treating these costs as direct costs in terms of customers.[10]

In essence, many of the costs of pre- and post-sale services, as well as the costs for services incurred during the actual sale, could be traced to individual customers and/or customer classes and treated as direct costs for e-commerce firms.[11] Costs that cannot be traced directly to individual customers and/or customer classes, such as the costs associated with computer hardware, would be treated as indirect costs. By treating the customer as a primary cost objective, effective resource allocation decisions will be enhanced. In addition, effective customer profitability analysis, pricing decisions, and marketing decisions will be greatly facilitated. Finally, and of no small consequence, the use of customers as a primary cost objective will facilitate the very essence of being an Internet-based firm (i.e., an Internet-based cost management system will facilitate e-commerce business). It is well known, and accepted, that focusing on the needs and desires of customers is fundamental to running a successful business. This is true whether the business is Internet-based or brick-and-mortar. Yet a fundamental cost objective for Internet-based firms needs to be the customer. In other words, in accumulating and allocating costs, Internet-based firms need to adopt a customer focus. Once they recognize this fact, it becomes clear that the distinction between direct and indirect costs is as important for them as it is for other firms. Of course, the fact that Internet-based firms need to adopt a customer focus in allocating costs in no way mitigates the potential importance of knowing the costs of individual products (or services) as well as departments. Thus, Internet-based firms may well consider other cost objectives in differentiating between direct and indirect costs. To the extent that this is the case, the argument that distinguishing between direct and indirect costs is a relevant and important activity for Internet-based firms is only strengthened.

USE MANAGEMENT ACCOUNTING TECHNIQUES PROPERLY

Cost allocations are fundamental to effective cost management, and, as we have emphasized, a key aspect of cost allocations is the distinction between direct and indirect costs. Nevertheless, the claim that this distinction is not relevant to Internet-based companies has been promulgated lately. We disagree with this claim, for the reasons given above. A fundamental aspect of our argument is the need for Internet-based firms to trace costs to customers. Hence, Internet-based firms need to treat the customer as a primary cost objective in differentiating between direct and indirect costs. The new Information Economy has important implications for the field of management accounting. Direct vs. indirect costs is only one such implication. Other implications include the way companies need to consider performance measures, profit planning, and the use of cost information for pricing decisions. While the sum of these implications represents a fundamental shift in the management accounting paradigm, it does not represent the demise of management accounting. Indeed, the proper use of management accounting techniques is more relevant to the survival of firms in today's dynamic information economy than ever before in the history of commerce.

Blocher, Stout, Cokins, Chen: *Cost Management, 4e*

ENDNOTES:

[1] Indirect costs are often referred to as overhead costs. Because the term overhead is misleading, we will use indirect to refer to such costs.

[2] For examples illustrating this point, see Chapter 3 of Gordon, *Managerial Accounting: Concepts and Empirical Evidence*, in Further Reading section.

[3] In the extreme case of prices being set by the marketplace, we have what economists refer to as a purely competitive market. In a purely competitive market, firms essentially take the market price as given and need to focus on cost management techniques to earn a desirable level of profit.

[4] Of course, firms are interested in many cost objectives. Hence, the designation of one cost objective as primary does not preclude the use of other cost objectives.

[5] Our definition of what constitutes an Internet-based firm is consistent with the way Dow Jones derives its list of such firms (i.e., for more information, see http://indexes.dowjones.com./djii/djiiabout.html).

[6] The U.S. Department of Commerce reports (*Digital Economy 2000*, June 2000, p.9), "private estimates for consumer e-commerce in the fourth quarter of 1999 ranged from approximately $4 billion to $14 billion."

[7] Clearly, the trend is for all firms to increase their Internetbased sales. Accordingly, the distinction between Internetbased firms and non-Internet-based firms is one of degree rather that absoluteness. Over time, it seems logical to expect more and more firms to become Internet-based.

[8] Although not the focus of this article, it is equally important for Internet-based firms to identify the revenues of individual customers and/or customer classes.

[9] The growing emphasis on linking customers to the production process in the emerging literature on supply chain management is consistent with this argument. For an interesting discussion on the use of "customer-product maps," in the context of supply chain management, see Cloud in the

Further Reading section.

[10] In a non-e-commerce environment, computer-related costs are traditionally considered to be indirect with respect to a firm's products and services. Given that these assets are an important aspect of an e-commerce firm's assets, this reclassification has nontrivial implications.

[11] Recent works in database design has centered on customer focused data models. This work has particular relevance to the arguments presented in this section.

Chapter 5
Activity-Based Costing and Management

Cases

Readings

5-1: "Activity-Based Costing and Predatory Pricing: The Case of the Petroleum Retail Industry" by Thomas L Burton and John B MacArthur, *Management Accounting Quarterly*, (Spring 2003).

The assignment of indirect costs in a volume-based costing system can lead to product-cost subsidization—overcost high-volume products and undercost low-volume products. Undercosted products can lead to the appearance of predatory pricing where it actually does not exist. This article focuses on a lawsuit brought against a major chain of retail motor fuel (gasoline) service centers for allegedly selling regular-grade gasoline below cost, as defined by state statutes. The defendant employed ABC analysis to support its position that it was not selling its regular gasoline below cost. After the ABC analysis was presented, the case was settled, and the judge lifted the initial injunction.

Discussion Questions:
1. What are product-cost subsidizations?
2. What are possible consequences of product-cost subsidizations?
3. List alternative approaches to assign costs in a gasoline service center.
4. Identify cost hierarchy level groups in classifying activities at the retail level of a gasoline service center and give at least one example each.
5. What are overheads activity-cost pools pertaining to selling gasoline in a retail gasoline service center and what is the activity level for each of the cost pools?
6. Identify the activity drivers for overheads activity-cost pools identified in this study and explain the reasons for the selection?
7. List examples of gasoline-dispensing facilities for a gasoline service center and identify whether each of the facilities is a common or a gasoline grade-specific asset.

5-2: "Activity-Based Benchmarking and Process Management—Managing the Case of Cardiac Surgery" by Bea Chiang, *Management Accounting Quarterly* (Fall 2002).

Through a study of resource consumption, hospitals can get a more accurate picture of how practices are linked to cost.

Discussion Questions:
1. Describe briefly hospital's costing system.
2. Describe steps in activity-based benchmarking for medical-care processes.

5-3 "Using Activity Based Costing To Assess Channel/Customer Profitability" by DeWayne L. Searcy, PhD., CMA, CPA, *Management Accounting Quarterly* (Winter 2004).

This article explains how ABC was used by a firm (TEC) in the temporary employment industry to better identify the profitability of its service distribution channels and individual customers.

Discussion Questions:
1. What are the four steps used in implementing ABC costing at TEC?
2. What are the activity consumption drivers that TEC has chosen for each of the three activities: filling work orders, hiring temporaries, and processing payroll?
3. Which customer channel is most profitable, clerical or industrial, and why?
4. Within the industrial channel, which class of customers is most profitable and why?
5. In the study of the four largest customers, which is the most profitable and why?

Blocher, Stout, Cokins, Chen: *Cost Management, 4e*

Cases

5-1 Blue Ridge Manufacturing

BACKGROUND:

Blue Ridge Manufacturing is one of a dozen companies that produces and sells towels for the U.S. "sports towel" market. A "sports towel" is a towel that has the promotion of an event or a logo printed on it. They're called sports towels because their most popular use is for distribution in connection with major sporting events such as the Super Bowl, NCAA Final Four, Augusta National Golf Tournament and the U.S. Open Tennis Tournament. Towels with college, NBA and NFL team logos, and promotions for commercial products such as soft drinks, beer, fast food chains, etc., are also big sellers.

The firm designs, knits, prints and embroiders towels. The firm knits all the towels it sells and tracks costs for towel production separately from the cost to customize the towels. Seventy-five percent of its orders include logo design, while the balance are print only and require the payment of a license fee for the logo used. However, about 15% of its orders include embroidery. Towels are made in three sizes: regular (18" x 30"), hand (12" x 20") and mid-range (15"x 24"). The normal production cycle for an order of white towels is three days. If a customer wants a colored towel, the basic white towel made by Blue Ridge is sent to a dyeing firm, which extends the production cycle of an order by three days. Also, occasionally, customers order towels in sizes other than the three standard sizes. These towels are called "special".

The firm now produces a "medium" quality towel. They have had some difficulty with the "staying power" of the material printed on these towels, which is attributed to the towel quality, the ink and the printing process. Customers have complained that the ink "lays on the surface" and it cracks and peels off.

Blue Ridge recently made a break-through in developing an ink that soaks into the towel, won't wash out and is non-toxic. A big advantage of this ink is that it avoids EPA disposal requirements because is can be "washed down the drain". Due to these characteristics of its new ink, Blue Ridge is considering upgrading the quality of the basic towel it produces because it will "take" the ink better, both the towel and the ink will last longer and the product will sell at a higher price. If it takes this step, the company will evaluate expanding its marketing and sales area with the objective of "going national".

CUSTOMERS:

Except for a few non-regional chains, Blue Ridge's sales are predominantly in the southeastern states. The company sells its products to 986 different customers. These customers differ primarily in the volume of their purchases, so management classifies each customer in one of three groups: large (8 customers), medium (154 customers) and small (824 customers). Large customers are primarily national chains, small customers are single store operations (including pro shops at golf courses) and medium-sized customers are small chains, large single stores or licensing agents for professional sports teams and manufacturers of consumer products. Table 1 gives the product and customer size statistics for 2001.

Blue Ridge has a different approach to customers in each of its three categories. A small group of in-house sales people sell directly to buyers in the large customer category. Independent manufacturer representatives, on commission, call on the license holder or the manager of a store in the medium customer category. Ads placed in regional and national magazines and newspapers target customers primarily in the small-customer segment, who call or mail in their orders.

Blue Ridge does not give discounts and it ships all order free on board (FOB) point of origin, i.e., customers pay their freight costs.

MANUFACTURING:

Blue Ridge has a modern knitting and printing plant in the foothills of North Carolina's Blue Ridge Mountains. Upgrading the facilities over recent years was accompanied by the introduction of an activity-based costing (ABC) system to determine product costs. The cost accounting system is fairly sophisticated and management has confidence in the accuracy of the manufacturing cost figures for each product line. Table 2 shows the firm's unit costs for various items.

Company management is committed to adopting advanced manufacturing techniques such as benchmarking and just-in-time (JIT). The corporate culture necessary for the success of such techniques is evolving and worker empowerment is already a major program. In addition, workers are allowed several hours away from regular work assignments each week for training programs conferring on budgets and work improvements and applying the ABC system.

PERFORMANCE:

The company is profitable. However, management has become concerned about the profitability of the customers in its three customer-size categories—large, medium and small. Different customers demand different levels of support. Management has no basis for identifying customers that generate high profits or to drop those that do not generate enough revenues to cover the expenses to support them. Under the previous accounting system, it wasn't possible to determine the costs of supporting individual customers.

With the introduction of ABC, it now may be possible to determine customer profitability. Table 3 shows how the administrative and selling costs are assigned and re-assigned between various functions within the selling and marketing areas and to sub-activities in the selling and marketing areas. Table 4 provides a list of selling and marketing activities and the activity base to use in assigning costs to each.

REQUIRED:

The managers of Blue Ridge Manufacturing have hired your consulting firm to advise them on the potential of using strategic cost analysis in assessing the profitability of their customer accounts.
Your analysis should include:

1. What is Blue Ridge's competitive strategy?
2. What type of cost system does Blue Ridge use, and is it consistent with their strategy?
3. Develop a spreadsheet analysis which can be used to assess the profitability of the three customer groups of Blue Ridge—large, medium and small customer account sizes. Use the information in Tables 1-4 to trace and allocate the costs necessary for the analysis.

Blocher, Stout, Cokins, Chen: *Cost Management, 4e*

TABLE 1
BLUE RIDGE MANUFACTURING
Sales Information

Product and Customer Size Statistics		Sales in Units by Customer Account Size			
		Large	Medium	Small	Total
Towel:	Regular	27,250	16,600	10,550	54,400
	Mid-Size	36,640	18,552	10,308	65,500
	Hand	35,880	19,966	95,954	151,800
	Special	480	3,426	594	4,500
Number of Units Sold		100,250	58,544	117,406	276,200
Number of Units Embroidered		5,959	6,490	29,394	41,842
Number of Units Dyed		20,536	9,935	12,328	42,798
Sales Volume Revenue		$308,762	$183,744	$318,024	$810,530
Number of Orders Received		133	845	5,130	6,108
Number of Shipments Made		147	923	5,431	6,501
Number of Invoices Sent		112	754	4,737	5,603
Accounts with Balance >60 Days		1	11	122	134

TABLE 2
BLUE RIDGE MANUFACTURING
Unit Cost Information

Line 1 Direct Manufacturing Costs Per Unit

		Quantity	Sales Price	Material	Labor	Overhead	Unit Cost
Towels:	Regular	54,400	$3.60	$0.60	$0.37	$0.22	$1.19
	Mid-Size	65,500	3.20	0.50	0.33	0.20	1.03
	Hand	151,800	2.55	0.39	0.31	0.19	0.89
	Special	4,500	4.00	0.67	0.48	0.29	1.44

Line 2 Direct Costs of Customizing Per Unit

	Quantity	Cost	Material	Labor	Overhead	Total
Inking (based on passes)	552,400	—	$0.0030	$0.0045	$0.0742	$0.0817
Dyeing	42,798	$0.11	—	—	0.0000	0.1100
Embroidery	41,842	—	0.0026	0.1750	1.0994	1.2770

Direct Labor Wage Rate: $9.00 (Including Fringes)

Inking requires one pass for each color used; average two colors per towel (i.e., 2 per unit), and is used on all towels.

TABLE 3
BLUE RIDGE MANUFACTURING
Selling and Administrative Costs and Activities

Costs Incurred in Each Function (Shipping, Sales, Marketing)

Directly Assigned To:

	Total	Shipping	Sales	Marketing	Other	Total Assigned	Unassigned
Administration	$170,000	$ 17,000	$ 37,400	$20,400	$56,100	$130,900	$39,100*
Selling	155,000	15,500	117,800	9,300	12,400	155,000	
	$325,000	$ 32,500	$155,200	$29,700	$68,500	$285,900	$39,100

Each function is used for the Following Activities

Percentage of:

Selling and Administrative Activities:	Shipping	Sales	Marketing	Other
Entering Purchase Orders		55		10
Commissions		10		
Shipping Activities	65			15
Invoicing				20
Cost to Make Sales Calls		30		10
Checking Credit				10
Samples, Catalog Info.	5		10	
Special Handling Charges	5			5
Distribution Management	10		10	
Marketing, by Customer Type		5		
Advertising/Promotion			30	
Marketing	15		50	5
Administrative Office Support				20
Licenses, Fees				5
	100	100	100	100

* Note that $39,100 of the SG&A cost was not directly assigned. This amount represents the facility-sustaining activity cost.

Blocher, Stout, Cokins, Chen: *Cost Management, 4e*

©The McGraw-Hill Companies, Inc 2008

TABLE 4
BLUE RIDGE MANUFACTURING
Activities and Cost drivers

Cost Drivers for Allocating Costs of Activities to Customer Groups (Large, Medium, Small)

Activity	Cost Driver
Entering Purchase Orders	Number of Orders
Commissions	Sales Dollars with Medium Customers
Shipping Activities	Number of Shipments
Invoicing	Number of Invoices
Cost to Make Sales Calls	Sales Dollars with Large Customers
Checking Credit	Percent Accounts >60 Days
Samples, Catalog Info.	Sales Dollars
Special Handling Charges	Management Estimate[1]
Distribution Management	Sales Dollars
Marketing, by Customer Type	Sales Dollars
Advertising/Promotion	Management Estimate[2]
Marketing	Number of Units Sold[3]
Administrative Office Support	Number of Units Sold[4]
Licenses, Fees	Sales Dollars with Medium Customers

[1]20% to medium-sized customers; 80% to small-sized customers.

[2]25% to medium-sized customers; 75% to small-sized customers.

[3]Excluding Specials

[4]Excluding Specials

5-2 Implementation of Activity Based Costing for Blue Ridge Manufacturing Company Using SAS Activity-Based Costing Software

REQUIRED:

Use the data for Blue Ridge Manufacturing Company in 5-1 to complete the following requirements:

1. Download and install the Oros Quick® ABC/M program from the textbook website: www.mhhe.com/blocher3e under Premium Content. (It's a WinZip file).
2. Download the Oros Quick® Tutorial from the text website: www.mhhe.com/blocher3e under Premium Content (It's an Adobe Acrobat file)
3. Work through the Oros tutorial (you can skip the sections on attributes and on the balanced scorecard)
4. Create a folder labeled "Blue Ridge." You will save the ABC model you create within that folder.
5. Use the information in the Blue Ridge Manufacturing Company Case (Case Number 5-1) and in the Tutorial to complete an ABC costing application using Oros; determine the ABC-based unit costs for Blue Ridge's three customer groups
6. Create and print a unit cost report for Blue Ridge, using the Oros system.

Blocher, Stout, Cokins, Chen: *Cost Management, 4e*
©The McGraw-Hill Companies, Inc 2008

5-3 Colombo Soft-Serve Frozen Yogurt

In 1994, General Mills Incorporated, a $6 billion consumer goods company, acquired Colombo Frozen Yogurt. General Mills Inc. (GMI) believed they could add Colombo frozen yogurt to their existing product lineup to increase net sales with little addition in marketing cost.

Frozen yogurt is sold through two distinct segments – independent shops and impulse locations such as cafeterias, colleges, and buffets. Frozen yogurt is the main business for the shops whereas yogurt is incremental to the impulse locations' main business. GMI's large sales force already served the impulse market.

The financial results in the first couple of years were mixed. Earnings increased slightly and then dropped each year even though sales volume was relatively flat. In total, merchandising costs dropped, while pricing promotion rates escalated. The GMI sales force focused on the impulse segments and pricing promotions were believed to be driving volume increases. However, volume in the shop segment declined at alarming rates and there was widespread dissatisfaction in the sales organization. While GMI knew sales by segment, they didn't track costs by segment. Instead costs were allocated based on sales dollars. The situation was ripe for a clearer look using ABC methods.

TODAY'S FROZEN YOGURT MARKET STRUCTURE:

When Colombo Yogurt Company began marketing soft-serve frozen yogurt in the early 1980's, their main distribution was through independent yogurt shops. In the early 90's, they faced competition from franchise operations such as TCBY and Freshens that replaced many of the independent yogurt shops. And the market changed as Foodservice operators such as cafeterias, colleges, and buffets started to add soft-serve yogurt to their business. By the late 90's, these Impulse locations accounted for 2/3 of the soft-serve market.

In the late 90's, Shop sales began to increase with the addition of distinctive new products such as smoothies, boosters, and granitas. The Shops make their living from the soft-serve business and must innovate or go out of business (as thousands have done in the last decade). On the other hand, the Impulse locations make their living from other items and the soft-serve trade is only performance topspin. These firms are unwilling to take any risk (new equipment or extra labor) to serve highly differentiated products like smoothies or granitas.

THE GMI-COLOMBO MARKETING PLAN:

The GMI Foodservice Division markets brands such as Cheerios, Yoplait, Betty Crocker, Gold Medal Flour, Hamburger Helper, Pop-Secret, and Chex Snack to Food Management Firms, Hospitals, and schools. Colombo yogurt was added to this product lineup and the Foodservice sales force covered both Shop and Impulse locations.

Salesforce: Colombo's salesforce was merged into the Foodservice salesforce. Customers were reassigned to salespeople who already serviced that geographical area. The salespeople varied in their reaction to the product. Some found shops easy to sell to while others avoided the shops despite the possible lost commission. Many spent a lot of time helping their impulse customers understand how to use the machinery.

Merchandising Promotions: Colombo traditionally charged the Shops for merchandising that was large scale and eye popping (neon signs). The Shops used these signs to draw customers inside. GMI chose not to charge for merchandising and to provide the same large scale merchandising to both Shops and Impulse locations. Shops were very interested in the kits while many Impulse locations didn't even hang them up.

Pricing Promotions: Pricing promotions are a mainstay of GMI's impulse location approach. GMI's salesforce generally used these promotion events as an opportunity to visit their accounts and take advantage of the occasion to meet service needs and sell other products that may not be featured.

GMI made price promotions available to both segments of the market. While the deals were typically around $5 per case, they averaged $3 per case against all the volume shipped during the year. GMI marketing knew price was not a major decision factor for Shops and they did not target pricing promotions to them. However, Shops were aware of the promotions and took advantage of them.

THE BUSINESS STATUS – PRE-ABC:

PROFIT AND LOSS BY SEGMENT – PRE-ABC

Category	Impulse Segment	Yogurt Shops	Total
Sales in cases	1,200,000	300,000	1,500,000
Sales revenue	$23,880,000	$5,970,000	$29,850,000
Less: Price Promotions	- $ 3,600,000	- $ 900,000	- $ 4,500,000
Net Sales	$20,280,000	$5,070,000	$25,350,000
Less: Cost of Goods Sold	- $13,800,000	- $3,450,000	- $17,250,000
Gross Margin	$ 6,480,000	$1,620,000	$ 8,100,000
Less: Merchandising	- $ 1,380,000	- $ 345,000	- $ 1,725,000
Less: SG&A	- $ 948,000	- $ 237,000	- $ 1,185,000
Net income	$ 4,152,000	$1,038,000	$ 5,190,000

ABC ANALYSIS OF COST OF GOODS SOLD:

Cost of Goods Sold is made up of $14,250,000 for ingredients, packaging, and storage and $3,000,000 for pick/pack and shipping. Since the product is the same across segments, the cost to produce should be the same. However, pick/pack and shipping costs were found to vary with whether or not the order was for a full pallet. Full pallets cost $75 to pick and ship whereas individual orders cost $2.25 per case. There are 75 cases in a pallet and the segments differ in their utilization of full pallets as shown below.

	Impulse Segment	Yogurt Shops	Total
Cases in full Pallets	60,000	240,000	300,000
Individual cases	1,140,000	60,000	1,200,000
Total cases	1,200,000	300,000	1,500,000

ABC ANALYSIS OF MERCHANDISING:

Merchandising costs consist mainly of kits costing $500 each. A review of where the kits were sent indicated that 3,450 kits were sent out and 90 of them were sent to shops.

ABC ANALYSIS OF SELLING, GENERAL AND ADMINISTRATIVE:

Since sales representatives service several products, their costs are allocated to the various products based on gross sales dollars. GMI gave diaries to 10% of the sales force in randomly selected markets of the country and asked them to track their time in activity classifications for 60 days. The diaries indicated that sales reps spent almost 3 times as much time on the yogurt than GMI had estimated. The total allocation to Yogurt jumped from $1,185,000 to $3,900,000. Of their time spent on Yogurt, only 1% of the time was spent on the shops.

REQUIRED:

1. Briefly summarize Colombo's competitive environment and General Mills' strategy in response to that environment.
2. Using the ABC analysis, determine new segment profitability statements.
3. Based on your analysis in Questions 1 and 2, what changes would you suggest to General Mills? Give specific examples and explain.

Blocher, Stout, Cokins, Chen: *Cost Management, 4e*
©The McGraw-Hill Companies, Inc 2008

5-4 Wilson Electronics (A)[*]

CASE OVERVIEW

During the afternoon of August 30th, a meeting was convened of the senior finance managers and the industrial engineering manager of Wilson Electronics Company. The meeting had been called by Alice Johnson, controller, following her disturbing conversation with the president, Bill Simms. Johnson had approached Simms to discuss the idea of committing the resources necessary to update Wilson's activity-based costing (ABC) model. This idea seemed reasonable, given that the previously designed ABC model relied upon information that was more than one year old. Much to Alice's surprise, Simms responded to her inquiry by questioning the value of ABC altogether. Simms commented that he was well aware of the time and money spent designing the ABC model; however, he was not comfortable that a game plan existed for starting to actually use the ABC system to help make business decisions. In fact, Simms was concerned that even though the ABC model-building process had been completed, the idea of educating the management team on the potential applications of ABC had completely stagnated since the recent departure of the former controller and ABC champion, Mike Foster.

Simms explained to Johnson that simply re-arranging the company's general ledger expenses into an activity-based format was not beneficial enough to justify the continued support and maintenance of the ABC system. Instead, the ABC system needed to help Wilson's management team make better decisions that would improve overall company profitability. He informed Johnson that the ABC system was on the agenda for the next management team meeting to be held in three weeks. Her task for this meeting would be to substantiate the potential value of ABC to Wilson's management team. Simms knew that if Johnson could not demonstrate the potential applications of ABC to his company, he would halt the finance department's intentions of committing additional resources to updating an offline ABC system that had yet to be used within his organization to support decision making.

Johnson concluded that for ABC to survive the upcoming management team meeting, she would have to demonstrate its value in terms of cost reduction rather than just cost reporting. In particular, she thought it would make sense to narrow the scope of her presentation to focus on a recent cost cutting proposal that called for a reduction in the number of different types of parts contained in the A12 junction box. This product line had recently been threatened by a major competitor's announcement to reduce its price by $0.40 per unit. Wilson's management team felt that it must find a way to meet the price cut without causing a decline in the company's profits. Johnson believed that the ABC system would survive Simms's scrutiny if she could use ABC data to help Wilson effectively respond to the A12 price reduction.

COMPANY BACKGROUND

Wilson, located in Middletown, Ohio, builds components, such as ducts, connectors, and junction boxes, which are used in the installation of power cable and data communication cable management systems. These systems are typically installed within concrete floors in office buildings and shopping malls. Wilson employs 300 people who are responsible for engineering, fabricating, and assembling these products for resale through its two primary regional customer channels-large contractors and wholesale electrical supply houses. The firm's strategy is to "offer superior quality products and customer service at competitive prices.

Wilson's 1999 revenues were $60 million. The company's sales growth has been steady over the past several years; however, profit margins have shrunk as the company has experienced an increase in expenses that cannot be passed on to its customers in the form of higher prices. In 1999, Wilson's average cost structure across all product lines was as follows: 59¢ of each sales dollar was material cost, 14.7¢ was conversion cost, 13¢ was fixed selling and administrative expenses, and 6¢ was sales commissions. This provided financial results in 1999 of a 7.3 percent before-tax profit margin and (given a 40 percent tax rate) an after tax return on sales of 4.4 percent, which compared unfavorably with industry norms of 10 percent and 6 percent, respectively. (See Exhibit 1 for summary financial information, by major product line.)

Wilson sells more than 100 different product types and models across four major product lines. It is currently operating at or near its practical capacity. Most of Wilson's products are commodity-type products that have standard designs and applications. The technology of these products does not change rapidly; therefore, each competitor

---

[*] Peter C. Brewer, Robert J. Campbell, and Richard H. McClure, *Issues in Accounting Education*, 15 (3), pp. 415-429.

offers similar functionality and design. However, a growing source of revenue for Wilson during the past five years has been customized production of orders with unique size and feature requirements for customers outside of Wilson's normal distribution channels. In 1999, Wilson secured record highs in its growing custom business in terms of number of orders received (740) and total number of units produced (68,500). Even though the volume is lower, Wilson's management team considers the custom business to be attractive because it utilizes previously idle plant capacity, earns reportedly high profit margins, and offers some pricing flexibility. Furthermore, Wilson has been able to adapt its existing manufacturing equipment to handle most of the custom business with minimal additional capital investment.

THE COST ACCOUNTING SYSTEM

In 1998, Wilson, with the support of Mike Foster, the controller at that time, decided to develop an ABC model that would encompass the materials acquisition and manufacturing departments. After this model gained acceptance within the company, Foster's long-term goal was to expand the ABC model's scope to include all of Wilson's departments. The model-building process included: (1) gathering activity definition, resource driver, and activity driver data; (2) creating an ABC cost model that had the ability to model the effect of changes in product design on activity frequencies; and (3) inputting data into the model. The ambitious goal of creating "what-if" activity-cost modeling capability was understood by Foster to be more time-consuming because of the need to create activity time standards, but he also viewed this capability as essential to managing the business from an activity-oriented perspective.

At the outset of the ABC project, Foster expressed the desire that the ABC model rely on activity charge rates that represented the cost of creating activity capacity. For example, a rate such as $100 per material move should reflect the investment in resources necessary to provide the capacity to make material moves. Therefore, unlike many ABC systems that use annual estimates of activity driver counts needed to satisfy demand, Wilson developed measures of activity driver capacities that were used as the denominators in its ABC rate calculations.

Foster decided that Wilson would state its activity driver capacities in terms of employee capacity. Accordingly, he worked with Wilson's Industrial Engineering group to develop activity time standards that could be used to determine activity capacity estimates. (See both Exhibit 2 for a summary of the estimates of employee capacity in each department and Exhibit 3 for a summary of the activity time standards and activity driver capacities established for each activity in the ABC model.) For example, the first activity, "analyze purchase decision reports," has a time standard of 50 minutes per batch. Purchase orders are prepared for specific customer orders produced in batches. The average time to review the order requirements and make the purchase decision represents a general range of time from 35 minutes to 70 minutes. Over many orders, the average time of 50 minutes was fairly representative and deemed adequate for the ABC project.

Foster's ABC philosophy was that periodic drops in activity frequency should be viewed as evidence that temporary levels of idle activity capacity existed, rather than as evidence that ABC rates should be raised. The ABC model was designed to isolate idle capacity as a cost to the company, rather than treating it as an expense to be borne by customers. This approach was intended to put pressure on management either to fully utilize existing activity capacity or to adjust that capacity downward when lower levels of activity frequency became permanent.

THE TRANSITION

After completing the ABC model (see Exhibit 4 for a summary of the model), Foster spent a month experimenting with activity-based report formatting. The primary type of report format that he designed for analyzing annual product-line profitability was called a "bill of activities," which Foster referred to as the activity-based alternative to a conventional "bill of materials." Foster was beginning the process of organizing a presentation for Wilson's management team that explained the full range of the ABC model's potential applications when he received an outstanding job opportunity to be the chief financial officer of a manufacturing firm near his hometown of Athens, Georgia. While Foster opted to take the job in Georgia, he agreed to remain at Wilson for six weeks to oversee the hiring and transition of his successor. Unfortunately, during his last six weeks, Foster was unable to complete his ABC presentation.

Once the new controller, Alice Johnson, was hired and briefly oriented to Wilson's operations, Foster departed for Georgia. His departure struck a blow to the momentum of Wilson's ABC system. Although a bright young prospect with ample financial accounting experience, Johnson did not have any prior ABC experience. Furthermore, none of Wilson's functional managers had familiarity with how to use output from the ABC model, given that they

Blocher, Stout, Cokins, Chen: *Cost Management, 4e*

were merely asked to provide some data inputs during the model-building process. In short, the core of Wilson's ABC knowledge base walked out the door with Foster's departure. Not surprisingly, after Foster's exit, the ABC model ended up sitting on the shelf for the next year as efforts to apply the data to real decisions took a back seat to the day-to-day tasks that demanded everyone's attention. During this time, the direct-labor-hour-based standard cost system continued to support all financial reporting and decision making at Wilson, while the ABC system and its offline computer terminal sat untouched in the finance department.

Aware that the ABC project had stagnated, and intrigued by thoughts of the system's potential, Alice Johnson contemplated the idea of dedicating resources within her department to update the ABC model. Since the original ABC project was started almost two years ago and finalized over one year ago, Johnson felt that refreshing the data in the ABC model made sense. In all likelihood, some changes within the organization and its manufacturing methods had likely occurred, thus calling into question certain assumptions built into the initial ABC model. Updating the model would require performing interviews again within each department and reassigning organizational expenses to activities. Of course, Johnson's unexpected conversation with Simms shifted her focus from refreshing the ABC model to defending its continued existence.

THE A12 JUNCTION BOX AND ITS COST-REDUCTION PROPOSAL

The A12 junction box product line accounted for approximately 18.5 percent of Wilson's sales in 1999. It has generated approximately 300 customer orders per year and an annual volume of 100,000 units that is expected to continue for the next several years. Wilson maintains a 20 percent market share in this product line, while its five major competitors each possess market shares ranging from 8 percent to 25 percent. Wilson offers little product differentiation on the junction box line; therefore, it must be price-competitive in this commodity business or risk loss of substantial market share.

Junction boxes are installed at intersections of tubes or ducts containing cables, allowing for turns and connections to other ducts. When installed in concrete floors, they provide limited access to the cable management system for additions or changes in the type and quantity of cable used. The outer shell of the junction box is assembled from a steel housing comprising a separately fabricated top and bottom. Assembly workers assemble and mount electronic components inside the junction box. The current model A12 junction box contains ten different types of parts and 26 total parts.

The A12 cost-reduction proposal was predicated on the belief that the number of different types of parts used in each model is an important cost driver, along with the total volume of parts used annually in production. Therefore, the product engineering group wanted to redesign the A12 model of the junction box so that it would require only 21 total parts (instead of 26) and eight different types of parts (instead of ten different types) with virtually no loss in quality or functionality. The group's expectation was that the primary savings would come through improving operational efficiencies.

Exhibit 5 provides an overview of the material cost impact of the redesign. Three old parts, labeled part numbers #3, #5, and #7, would be replaced by a single new part. The cost for the new part is $12.85. Since two of these new parts would be required per unit, the added product cost would be $25.70 per junction box. The three deleted parts have a cumulative cost per junction box of $24.70; therefore, the total increase in material costs based on 100,000 units of production would be $100,000 or $1.00 per unit.

As part of the cost-reduction proposal, the product-engineering group solicited numerous bids from potential suppliers of the new part. Applied Technologies was identified as the preferred supplier of the new part because of its competitive price ($12.85), reputation for high quality, and commitment to customer service. Wilson's engineers believe that, since Applied Technologies is ISO 9000 certified, incoming inspection of the parts would not be necessary. If this turns out not to be the case, three other potential suppliers (all ISO 9000 certified) could be called upon to source the new part at price and quality levels comparable to Applied Technologies, with slightly inferior customer service.

The estimates of the project's upfront costs include $10,000 for product engineering work and $9,500 for process engineering work. In the event the proposal resulted in any layoffs, Wilson would have to cover severance pay of approximately $5,000 per employee. Any future cash flows associated with the proposal would be evaluated using a 14 percent discount rate.

The product engineering group believes that the extra up-front costs and material costs associated with the A12 redesign would be more than offset by future savings created by activity reductions in procurement, material handling, and manufacturing. The product engineering group's problem has been trying to use existing information databases, such as the standard cost system, to estimate the potential savings associated with the A12 redesign. Data provided by the standard cost system, with its labor-based factory burden rate, makes it difficult for the group to predict credible changes in operating costs for the A12 product line.

THE AUGUST 30TH MEETING

Alice Johnson (Controller), Ed Branson (Head of the Industrial Engineering group), Phil Markley (Assistant Controller), and Sally Jones (Cost Accounting Manager) were all in attendance at the August 30th meeting. Alice began the meeting by saying:

As you know, Mr. Simms has put the ABC system on the agenda for the management team meeting in two weeks. My task at the meeting is to substantiate the potential value of our ABC system to this company. If my presentation bombs out, Simms may permanently revoke any additional support for maintaining the offline ABC system. I believe that to save the ABC system we need to shift our focus from cost reporting to cost reduction. More specifically, I believe that we have to prove ABC's worth by demonstrating how it can help management quantify the costs and benefits associated with the cost-reduction and profit-improvement proposals that have become more prevalent in recent months. Right now, the standard cost data that our managers look at to help make business decisions is misleading. I have reviewed the design of the ABC system and believe that the cost pools created and activity drivers chosen are reasonably accurate; therefore, I feel confident that the ABC system can do a much better job of supporting decision making than the standard cost system.

The A12 junction box proposal is our opportunity to show how ABC can make a difference. It can provide the "proof of concept" that we need to sustain the system. With the impending price reduction on the A12 product line, our target cost reduction is $0.40 per unit. The initial report on the re-design is not very encouraging. The re-engineering plan, while achieving a reduction in the number of different types of parts per unit from 10 to 8, projects that material costs will increase by $1.00 per unit. (See Exhibit 5.)

Ed Branson interrupted, saying:

So, the key to our analysis is determining if the potential cost savings associated with the reduction in number of different types of parts exceeds the $1.00 per unit increase in material costs by more than the $0.40 per unit market-driven price reduction. Given the annual product volume of 100,000 units, this means a total parts reduction of 500,000 parts per year, which should generate significant savings in employee time from the standpoint of buying, storing, moving, and assembling these parts into products. We know the savings are there; it is just a matter of properly quantifying them. Clearly, the standard cost system cannot do it, so this presents a good opportunity to show the value of the ABC system.

Alice interjected:

To that end, I asked Sally [cost accounting manager] and Ed [industrial engineering head] to use the "what-if" capability of the ABC model to estimate the impact of the parts reduction on the workload of the departments directly affected-Purchasing, Stores, Material Handling, and Assembly. I have further asked Sally to quantify the cost savings using our existing activity driver charge rates.

Sally Jones offered:

Ed and I began by reviewing the available ABC data on the A12 junction box as shown in the bill of activities (Exhibit 6). The current unit cost is $82.72, composed of $64.00 in direct materials, $13.51 in ABC costs, and $5.21 in overhead charges from departments that were not included in the ABC project. Of course, these costs are based upon the ten-parts version of A12.

We then used the ABC model to adjust the activity driver counts affected by the change in parts. The model assumes the same size and contents of parts containers. It also assumes that the distance traveled and carrying capacity of the forklift trucks would be unchanged. The projection of activity driver count changes is shown in the report that I prepared on "Estimated Cost Savings Using ABC" (Exhibit 7). For example, activity #5b (unload materials and put in stores-assembly) uses the activity driver "# parts containers." Notice the proposal calls for reducing the total number of parts used by 19 percent, from 26 to 21. However, adjusting for parts volume changes as well as parts size changes, the ABC model estimates that the number of parts containers will be reduced by 16 percent. This works out to be a reduction of 3,200 containers, from 20,000 to 16,800.

My report (Exhibit 7) shows how the ABC model estimated the related cost savings by taking the activity driver count reductions and multiplying them by their corresponding ABC rates. For example, activity #5b (unload materials and put in stores-assembly) has a potential cost savings of $6,016, determined by multiplying

Blocher, Stout, Cokins, Chen: *Cost Management, 4e*

the ABC rate of $1.88 per parts container times the projected reduction of 3,200 parts containers. As you can see, whenever we reduce activity counts, we achieve cost savings. Looking at the eight activities that are affected by the A12 redesign (#3, #4, #5b, #6b, #8, #13, #15, and #16), we can see that the total annual cost savings due to activity reductions will be $147,231, as shown in the Exhibit. This translates to a $0.47 per unit savings net of the increase in material costs.

The redesign proposal prepared by the product-engineering group relies upon the standard cost system to estimate the savings associated with the A12 redesign. The standard cost system is based on the assumption that direct labor is the only relevant cost driver and, therefore, reductions in direct labor will result in proportional reductions in overhead. Obviously, that assumption is flawed! We could never have identified all of these cost savings using the traditional labor-based overhead allocation method, because the plant-wide overhead rate effectively hides any specific changes in resource costs that might result from mix and volume changes. Thanks to the ABC model and its "what-if" capability, we can estimate with much greater certainty what our cost savings will be in each one of these support departments.

Ed Branson interrupted at this point:

Sally, that brings up an interesting point. You just used the term "cost savings." What does cost savings really mean to us? What does it mean to the line managers and to our company's top management? What does it mean to our stockholders?

I think that the estimates generated by the ABC model are flawed because they do not account for the fact that this type of proposal essentially boils down to quantifying cash savings-"cash" being the key word. Tangible reductions in cash outflows most often will be found by making specific reductions in employee headcount and payroll. Estimating these potential reductions in spending, particularly with respect to payroll, depends upon two factors: the aggregate change in activity demand within each department and the amount of idle capacity that may now be available within each department. For example, if eliminating 800 forklift moves freed up 333 hours of labor time, this would not necessarily save us any money. In other words, since each forklift operator provides 1,571 hours of productive capacity (see Exhibit 2), a reduction in demand of 333 hours does not allow us to let one forklift driver go without becoming shorthanded. On the other hand, if we knew that we had idle capacity in this activity area, say 1,250 hours of unused forklift driver time, we could now be confident that letting one driver go would still leave us with sufficient capacity among the remaining drivers to handle all workload needs. So, it is not a matter of how much we reduce activity levels and release employee time, but whether we can reduce our capacity by one or more workers. So, it seems to me the value of ABC for evaluating this type of proposal rests upon whether it can help us assess short-run changes in spending.

I propose that we consider the impact of the activity reductions identified by the ABC model on departmental workloads and savings in employee hours. As we know, no employee performs just one activity. Rather, within a departmental structure, employees are trained to perform a set of activities. Whether enough time can be saved to release an employee is dependent on what is happening to all the activities within a department. For example, within Purchasing we want to determine how much time is saved by the impact of the A12 proposal on two activities-#3, issuing purchase orders for parts, and #4, expediting open parts orders-and whether that time savings is sufficient to allow us to reduce the number of people we employ in that department. The cost savings materialize only if we can reduce our payroll expense.

Based on discussions with department heads, I have developed an estimate of idle employee time within each department. Believe me, they were not very happy about providing these estimates because our department heads are very protective of their staffing levels. Nonetheless, almost every manager did admit to having some idle capacity within his or her respective departments, as shown below:

Department	Estimate of Total Idle Capacity
Purchasing	0.75 full time equivalents
Stores	0.25 full time equivalents
Crane Operators	0.25 full time equivalents
Forklift Operators	0.50 full time equivalents
Fabrication	0.50 full time equivalents
Assembly	0.00 full time equivalents

For example, the Purchasing manager admitted to having three fourths of a person idle or 0.75 fulltime equivalents (FTEs). By using the practical capacity estimate of one purchasing agent (1,537 hours), we can determine that the parts reduction proposal needs only to produce a time savings of approximately 385 hours (0.25 x 1,537 hours) to generate the opportunity for real cost savings. Assembly was the only department that would not concede any idle time. Of course, that probably makes sense, given how backed up they have been lately, coupled with Mr. Simms' reservations about increasing payroll expense by hiring more people.

Alice Johnson interrupted with several questions:

Why are you bringing up the issue of existing idle time in the departments? Don't these crude estimates change from week-to-week? It seems that the inclusion, or exclusion, of existing idle time can have a significant impact on cost savings according to your point of view. Yet, the parts-reduction proposal on the table is not in any way responsible for the current level of idle capacity within each department. How can you justify linking these idle-capacity estimates to the analysis of this proposal? If I were seeking approval of a cost-reduction proposal, using your mode of thinking, I would wait for a down period in our business when capacity utilization drops and then make my pitch to the management team.

Phil Markley spoke up at this point:

I think an important point that we have yet to mention is the notion of time frame. What time horizon should we consider when trying to estimate the economic benefits of these types of cost-reduction proposals? Sally's approach to estimating cost savings seems to be more long-term oriented, while Ed's point of view is more short-term in nature. There is no doubt that Mr. Simms is pretty focused on getting short-run results to appease our creditors and investors. Yet, the rhetoric suggests that we are supposed to be managing for long-run success. Should our perspective of cost savings be focused on a 6-12 month time horizon, or something more long-term?

As the meeting progressed, little consensus emerged regarding how to measure the cost savings associated with the A12 proposal. Alice was becoming somewhat concerned. The management meeting was less than two weeks away and she was not confident about what to say regarding the A12 proposal.

SUGGESTED CASE DISCUSSION QUESTIONS

1. Describe the position taken by Sally Jones. Prepare a new bill of activities for the revised version of the A12 junction box, based on the old bill of activities provided in Exhibit 3. How much cost savings per unit will be realized? How does the capacity-based approach to designing an ABC system enable the measurement of changes in resource usage?
2. Describe the position taken by Ed Branson on what is meant by cost savings. Prepare a schedule of employee time savings and a schedule of cost savings according to this viewpoint. How much cost savings will be realized in the next year-in total and per unit for the A12 junction box-according to this viewpoint? Decide if you should recognize available idle time estimates in your analysis.
3. With which point of view (Question 1 or 2) do you agree? Why? What net dollar amount of savings, per unit and in total, would you use to analyze this proposal?
4. Does this proposal meet the strategic needs of the company, with respect to competition on the A12 junction box product line? What other advice would you give Alice Johnson to help her prepare for the management team meeting? What do you think the response of President Simms will be to Alice Johnson's presentation? Assuming Simms takes Alice Johnson's recommendation and commits the resources necessary to update Wilson's ABC model, do you think this overall ABC initiative will be successful?

Blocher, Stout, Cokins, Chen: *Cost Management, 4e*

©The McGraw-Hill Companies, Inc 2008

EXHIBIT 1
Wilson's Financial Performance vs. the Industry Average
(in thousands of dollars)

1997	Ducts	Connectors	Junction Boxes	Custom[a]	Total	(%)	Industry Average
Sales $17,515	$13,560	$20,905	$4,520	$56,500	100.0	100.0%	
Direct materials	10,118	8,040	12,125	2,600	32,883	58.2	58.0
Direct labor	650	450	750	150	2,000	3.5	4.0
Overhead	2,145	1,485	2,475	495	6,600	11.7	10.5
Gross margin	$ 4,602	$ 3,585	$ 5,555	$1,275	$15,017	26.6	27.5
S, G & A	2,978	2,305	3,554	768	9,605	17.0	17.0
Profit before tax	$ 1,624	$ 1,280	$ 2,001	$ 507	$ 5,412	9.6	10.5
Tax expense	650	512	800	203	2,165	3.8	4.2
Profit after tax	$ 975	$ 768	$ 1,201	$ 304	$ 3,247		
Profit margin	5.6%	5.7%	5.7%	6.7%	5.7%	5.7%	6.3%
1998							
Sales $16,820	$13,920	$20,880	$6,380	$58,000	100.0	100.0%	
Direct materials	10,183	8,213	12,110	3,365	33,871	58.4	58.0
Direct labor	442	394	734	230	1,800	3.1	4.0
Overhead	1,729	1,541	2,871	900	7,040	12.1	10.0
Gross Margin	$ 4,466	$ 3,772	$ 5,165	$1,885	$15,289	26.4	27.5
S, G & A	2,994	2,478	3,717	1,136	10,324	17.8	17.5
Profit before tax	$ 1,472	$ 1,294	$ 1,449	$ 750	$ 4,965	8.6	10.0
Tax expense	589	518	579	300	1,986	3.4	4.0
Profit after tax	$ 883	$ 777	$ 869	$ 450	$ 2,979		
Profit margin	5.3%	5.6%	4.2%	7.1%	5.1%	5.1%	6.0%
1999							
Sales $16,800	$14,200	$21,000	$8,000	$60,000	100.0	100.0%	
Direct materials	10,550	8,430	12,320	4,100	35,400	59.0	58.0
Direct labor	392	368	680	260	1,700	2.8	4.0
Overhead	1,646	1,546	2,856	1,092	7,140	11.9	10.0
Gross margin	$ 4,212	$ 3,856	$ 5,144	$2,548	$15,760	26.3	28.0
S, G & A	3,192	2,698	3,990	1,520	11,400	19.0	18.0
Profit before tax	$ 1,020	$ 1,158	$ 1,154	$1,028	$ 4,360	7.3	10.0
Tax expense	408	463	462	411	1,744	2.9	4.0
Profit after tax	$ 612	$ 695	$ 692	$ 617	$ 2,616		
Profit margin	3.6%	4.9%	3.3%	7.7%	4.4%	4.4%	6.0%

[a] The "Custom" segment represents the Ducts, Connectors, and Junction Boxes that were uniquely designed to meet specific customer requirements. The other three segments represent the standard versions of those products made for the customers in Wilson's normal distribution channels.

EXHIBIT 2
Employee Annual Capacity in Labor Hours
(excludes supervisory labor)

Employee Classification	Employee Headcount	Theoretical Capacity[a]	Practical Capacity[b]	Average Employee Practical Capacity	Average Wage + Fringe[c] per Employee	Average Hourly Wage per Employee
Purchasing Agents	15	30,000	23,050	1,537	$30,373.33	$12.66
Stores Employees	12	24,000	17,880	1,490	29,066.67	12.11
Crane Operators	2	4,000	3,230	1,615	31,100.00	12.96
Forklift Operators	13	26,000	20,420	1,571	29,509.54	12.30
Fabrication Workers	32	64,000	50,880	1,590	30,510.94	12.71
Assemblers	103	206,000	157,220	1,526	29,800.00	12.42

[a] Theoretical capacity is defined as 50 weeks/year multiplied by 40 hours/week, or 2,000 hours/employee/year.

[b] Practical capacity equals theoretical capacity less nonproductive times, such as vacation and sick time, planned idle time, scheduling, and other downtime. Idle capacity estimates were obtained from departmental managers in the form of FTEs.

[c] Fringe benefits are 20 percent of employee wages.

Activity Capacity Estimates in Hours

Activities	Allocation of Hours of Employee Capacity		Activity Driver	Activity Time Standards		Activity Capacity by Activity Driver Count	
Purchasing Department							
1. Analyze purchase decision reports	2,080	9%	# production batches	50	min./batch	2,496	batches
2. Issue purchase orders for sheets	1,850	8%	# production batches	45	min./batch	2,467	batches
3. Issue purchase orders for parts	,600	33%	# unique parts/batch	20	min./count	22,800	count
4. Expedite open parts orders	11,520	50%	# unique parts/batch	30	min./count	23,040	count
	23,050	100%					
Stores							
5. Unload materials and put in stores							
a. Fabrication-steel sheets	2,330	13%	# sheet bundles	16	min./bundle	8,738	bundles
b. Assembly-parts	10,190	57%	# parts containers	5	min./container	122,280	containers
6. Process material requisitions							
a. Fabrication-steel sheets	890	5%	# sheet bundles	5	min./bundle	10,680	bundles
b. Assembly-parts	4,470	25%	# parts containers	2	min./container	134,100	containers
	17,880	100%					
Material Handling							
7. Move sheets to Fabrication by crane	3,230	100%	# crane moves	60	min./crane move	3,230	crane moves
8. Move parts to Assembly	11,640	57%	# forklift moves	25	min./forklift move	27,936	forklift moves
9. Move steel housing to Assembly	5,100	25%	# forklift moves	45	min./forklift move	6,800	forklift moves
10. Move finished goods to warehouse	3,680	18%	# forklift moves	30	min./forklift move	7,360	forklift moves
	20,420	100%					
Fabrication							
11. Setup equipment	5,090	10%	# setups	150	min./setup	2,036	setups
12. Fabricate steel housing units	40,702	80%	# housing units	6	min./unit	407,020	units
13. Rework defective units	5,088	10%	# of rework hours	10	min./unit	30,528	hours
	50,880	100%					
Assembly							
14. Unload steel housing units	12,580	8%	# housing units	1.5	min./housing	503,200	units
15. Unload parts and hold	18,870	12%	# parts used	0.10	min./part	11,322,000	parts
16. Assemble finished products	94,330	60%	# parts used		see note below	11,322,000	parts
17. Inspect finished goods	17,290	11%	# finished units	2	min./unit	518,700	units
18. Package finished goods	14,150	9%	# finished units	1.5	min./unit	566,000	units
	157,220	100%					

Total assembly times (in minutes and hours) for the original A12 and the revised A12 are provided in Exhibit 5.

EXHIBIT 4 Activity Cost Pools

Process 1: Materials Procurement	Wage and Fringes	Supervision	Supplies and Utilities	Equipment	ABC Cost Pools	Activity Driver	Activity Cost Rate	Activity Driver Capacity
1. Analyze purchase decision reports	$ 41,004	$ 5,000	$ 3,000	$ 2,181	$ 51,185	# production batches	$20.51	2,496
2. Issue purchase orders for sheets	36,448	6,000	4,000	1,938	48,386	# production batches	19.61	2,467
3. Issue purchase orders for parts	150,348	10,000	8,000	6,481	174,829	# unique parts/batch	7.67	22,800
4. Expedite open parts orders	227,800	31,000	6,380	5,380	270,560	# unique parts/batch	11.74	23,040
Subtotal	$455,600	$52,000	$21,380	$10,600	$544,960			
Stores Personnel								
5. Unload material and put in stores								
a. Fabrication-steel sheets	$ 45,344	$ 8,160	$ 5,200	$ 4,440	$ 63,144	# sheet bundles	7.23	8,738
b. Assembly-parts	198,816	18,000	6,800	6,290	229,906	# parts containers	1.88	122,280
6. Process material requisitions								
a. Fabrication-steel sheets	17,440	5,780	8,500	3,145	34,865	# sheet bundles	3.26	10,680
b. Assembly-parts	87,200	16,860	7,000	4,625	115,685	# parts containers	0.86	134,100
Subtotal	$348,800	$48,800	$27,500	$18,500	$443,600			
Process 2: Manufacturing								
Material Handlers								
7. Move sheets to Fabrication by crane	$ 62,200	$11,200	$ 9,600	$42,800	$125,800	# crane moves	38.95	3,230
8. Move parts to Assembly	218,666	24,350	17,200	38,600	298,816	# forklift moves	10.70	27,936
9. Move steel housing to Assembly	95,906	7,525	10,600	32,250	146,281	# forklift moves	21.51	6,800
10. Move finished goods to warehouse	69,052	6,063	8,500	26,930	110,545	# forklift moves	15.02	7,360
Subtotal	$383,624	$37,938	$36,300	$97,780	$555,642			
Fabrication Workers								
11. Setup equipment	$ 97,635	$ 22,000	$14,400	$ 38,450	$ 172,485	# setups	84.72	2,036
12. Fabricate steel housing units	781,080	78,800	15,000	126,500	1,001,380	# housing units	2.46	407,020
13. Rework defective units	97,635	11,200	10,000	100,000	218,835	# of rework hours	7.17	30,528
Subtotal	$976,350	$112,000	$39,400	$264,950	$1,392,700			
Assembly Workers								
14. Unload steel housing units	$ 245,552	$ 52,600	$ 3,000	$ 17,200	$ 318,352	# housing units	0.63	503,200
15. Unload parts and hold	368,328	72,000	3,900	33,700	477,928	# parts used	0.04	11,322,000
16. Assemble finished products	1,841,640	86,000	18,100	66,500	2,012,240	# parts used	0.18	11,322,000
17. Inspect finished goods	337,634	94,200	11,300	23,000	466,134	# finished units	0.90	518,700
18. Package finished goods	276,246	66,000	6,500	33,000	381,746	# finished units	0.67	566,000
Subtotal	$3,069,400	$370,800	$42,800	$173,400	$3,656,400			
Total Activity Costs					$6,719,102			

EXHIBIT 5
Junction Box-Model A12
Summary of Direct Material Cost and Assembly Time per Unit

Direct Material Cost per Unit

Unique Part Number	Vendor Cost per Part	Original Number of Parts per Unit Model A12	Original Materials Cost Model A12	Model A12 Revised Parts List	Revised Materials Cost Model A12
1	$ 0.50	4	$ 2.00	4	$ 2.00
2	2.80	3	8.40	3	8.40
3	4.00	2	8.00 0 -		
4	2.50	1	2.50	1	2.50
5	3.50	3	10.50	0	
6	2.75	2	5.50	2	5.50
7	3.10	2	6.20	0	-
8	2.40	4	9.60	4	9.60
9	2.00	3	6.00	3	6.00
10	2.65	2	5.30	2	5.30
New part	12.85	0	-	2	25.70
		26	$64.00	21	$65.00

1997 Production Volume (units)			100,000	100,000	
1997 Direct Materials Estimate			$6,400,000	$6,500,000	

Assembly Time per Unit

Unique Part Number	Assembly Time in Minutes	Original Number of Parts per Unit Model A12	Assembly Time/Unit (Original A12)	Model A12 Revised Parts List	Assembly Time/Unit (Revised A12)
1	0.25	4	1.00	4	1.00
2	0.50	3	1.50	3	1.50
3	0.75	2	1.50	0	0.00
4	1.00	1	1.00	1	1.00
5	0.50	3	1.50	0	0.00
6	0.75	2	1.50	2	1.50
7	1.00	2	2.00	0	0.00
8	0.25	4	1.00	4	1.00
9	0.50	3	1.50	3	1.50
10	0.75	2	1.50	2	1.50
New part	1.71	0	0.00	2	3.42
Total		26	14.00	21	12.42

Production volume (units)		100,000		100,000
Total Assembly minutes		1,400,000		1,242,000
Minutes per hour		60		60
Total Assembly hours		**23,333**		**20,700**

EXHIBIT 6
Bill of Activities for Current Version of A12 Junction Box

Activity#	Quantity of Activity Driver		Activity Rate	Total Activity Charge	Volume of Production		Activity Charge/unit
1	300	batches	$20.51	$ 6,153	100,000	units	$ 0.06
2	300	batches	19.61	5,883	100,000	units	0.06
3	3,000	unique parts	7.67	23,010	100,000	units	0.23
4	3,000	unique parts	11.74	35,220	100,000	units	0.35
5a	1,500	bundles	7.23	10,845	100,000	units	0.11
5b	20,000	containers	1.88	37,600	100,000	units	0.38
6a	1,500	bundles	3.26	4,890	100,000	units	0.05
6b	20,000	containers	0.86	17,200	100,000	units	0.17
7	600	crane moves	38.95	23,370	100,000	units	0.23
8	3,333	forklift moves	10.70	35,663	100,000	units	0.36
9	1,500	forklift moves	21.51	32,265	100,000	units	0.32
10	1,500	forklift moves	15.02	22,530	100,000	units	0.23
11	300	setups	84.72	25,416	100,000	units	0.25
12	100,000	housing units	2.46	246,000	100,000	units	2.46
13	4,550	hours	7.17	32,624	100,000	units	0.33
14	100,000	housing units	0.63	63,000	100,000	units	0.63
15	2,600,000	parts	0.04	104,000	100,000	units	1.04
16	2,600,000	parts	0.18	468,000	100,000	units	4.68
17	100,000	finished units	0.90	90,000	100,000	units	0.90
18	100,000	finished units	0.67	67,000	100,000	units	0.67
Total Activity Charges				$1,350,669			$13.51
Overhead from departments not included in ABC study[a]				520,661			5.21
Total Material Costs				6,400,000			64.00
Total Product Cost				$8,271,330			$82.72

---

[a] The overhead charged from the departments not included in the ABC study continues to be the same amount as would be charged from these departments using the direct-labor-based standard cost system.

Estimated Cost Savings Using ABC (assumed annual volume = 100,000 units)

Activity	Activity Driver	Original Activity Frequency	Revised Activity Frequency	Change in Activity Frequency	ABC Rates	ABC Cost Savings
Purchasing Department						
1. Analyze purchase decision reports	# production batches	300	300	0	$20.51	
2. Issue purchase orders for sheets	# production batches	300	300	0	19.61	
3. Issue purchase orders for parts	# unique parts/batch	3,000	2,400	-600	7.67	($4,602)
4. Expedite open parts orders	# unique parts/batch	3,000	2,400	-600	11.74	(7,044)
Stores						
5. Unload materials and put in stores						
a. Fabrication-steel sheets	# sheet bundles	1,500	1,500	0	7.23	
b. Assembly-parts	# parts containers	20,000	16,800	-3,200	1.88	(6,016)[a]
6. Process material requisitions						
a. Fabrication-steel sheets	# sheet bundles	1,500	1,500	0	3.26	
b. Assembly-parts	# parts containers	20,000	16,800	-3,200	0.86	(2,752)[a]
Material Handling						
7. Move sheets to Fabrication by crane	# crane moves	600	600	0	38.95	
8. Move parts to Assembly	# forklift moves	3,333	2,800	-533	10.70	(5,703)[b]
9. Move steel housing to Assembly	# forklift moves	1,500	1,500	0	21.51	
10. Move finished goods to warehouse	# forklift moves	1,500	1,500	0	15.02	
Fabrication						
11. Setup equipment	# setups	300	300	0	84.72	
12. Fabricate steel housing units	# housing units	100,000	100,000	0	2.46	
13. Rework defective units	# of rework hours	4,550	3,000	-1,550	7.17	(11,114)[c]
Assembly						
14. Unload steel housing units	# housing units	100,000	100,000	0	0.63	
15. Unload parts and hold	# parts used	2,600,000	2,100,000	-500,000	0.04	(20,000)
16. Assemble finished products	# parts used	2,600,000	2,100,000	-500,000	0.18	(90,000)
17. Inspect finished goods	# finished units	100,000	100,000	0	0.90	
18. Package finished goods	# finished units	100,000	100,000	0	0.67	
Total savings						**($147,231)**

[a] The original activity frequency for activities #5b and #6b assumed an average of 130 units per container. The revised frequency is based on fewer although larger parts, which average 125 parts per container.

[b] For activity #8, each forklift move is assumed to carry 6 parts containers. Thus, 3,333 moves would be required to move 20,000 containers.

[c] For activity #13, the revised number is an estimate based on the presumption that the change in unique parts will reduce rework by approximately 1/3.

5-5 Wilson Electronics (B)[†]

As the date of the management team meeting approached, Alice Johnson was gaining confidence that her presentation concerning the A12 junction box would have a positive effect on her colleagues. The $0.47 per unit resource-usage-based savings associated with the A12 redesign provided her with the means to illustrate ABC's value to the company. However, a few days before the management team meeting, another one of Wilson's major competitors announced a $2.50 per unit price reduction on its version of the A12 junction box. Johnson is now convinced that her demonstration of a meager $0.47 per unit savings for the A12 junction box will have little influence on the management team; therefore, the credibility of her presentation is doomed. At a loss as to how to respond to this recent development, Alice decided to contact Mike Foster, the former corporate controller of Wilson Electronics. When Foster departed to pursue another job opportunity, he encouraged Alice to use him as a "sounding board" if any questions or concerns arose. Alice decided to take him up on his offer with a phone call.

Alice Johnson (AJ): Hello, Mike. This is Alice Johnson. How are you doing?

Mike Foster (MF): Good to hear from you. I'm doing fine, thanks. Things are a little hectic down here, but I'm hanging in. How are you doing at Wilson? Are you becoming comfortable with their systems and procedures?

AJ: Well, I'm fine, but I'm not so sure about our ABC system.

MF: What do you mean?

AJ: After you left, ABC ground to a screeching halt. In an effort to jump-start things again, I suggested to Mr. Simms that we update the model. He not only put that thought on hold, but he questioned the value of the ABC system altogether. To make a long story short, I have to make a presentation to the management team in a couple of days that explains how ABC can add value to the decision-making process within our company. If I fail to deliver a convincing argument, it's possible that Mr. Simms will essentially "pull the plug" on the ABC system entirely.

MF: Dumping ABC would be a mistake. It doesn't surprise me that, subsequent to my departure, the ABC system is on the chopping block. It was tough enough getting support for the initiative while I was there. Well anyway, what do you have up your sleeve for this presentation?

AJ: I decided that it probably makes sense to focus on a cost-reduction proposal as a way to demonstrate that ABC is capable of aiding the decision-making process. Therefore, I selected a cost-cutting proposal that relates to the redesign of the A12 junction box.

MF: Tell me a little bit about that particular proposal.

AJ: The proposal is designed to reduce the total number of parts in the A12 junction box from 26 to 21. Also, the number of different types of parts used in each junction box is being reduced from ten to eight. What is interesting about the proposal is that the revised bill of materials projects that raw material costs will increase $100,000 as a result of the product redesign. Since the standard cost system is unable to link the reduction in the number of parts to activity reductions and cost savings, this proposal provides a good opportunity to demonstrate the value of ABC.

MF: Sounds like an interesting proposal. So, how is your presentation to the management team shaping up?

AJ: Well, this is where the problem starts. A few months ago one of our major competitors announced a $0.40 per unit price reduction on its version of the A12 junction box. I concluded that if we could use ABC to document a net savings in excess of $0.40 per unit, then my presentation to the management team would be a

---

[†] Peter C. Brewer, Robert J. Campbell, and Richard H. McClure, *Issues in Accounting Education*, 15 (3), pp. 415-429.

Blocher, Stout, Cokins, Chen: *Cost Management, 4e*

success. I met with Sally and Phil from Accounting and Ed from Industrial Engineering to see if we could use the data from the ABC system to estimate the cost savings potential of the A12 redesign proposal.

MF: So, what did your cost savings estimates turn out to be?

AJ: We didn't exactly reach a consensus on this point. Sally applied what I now understand to be the resource-usage viewpoint to calculate an estimated cost savings of $0.47 per unit, net of the material cost increase. However, Ed took a more short-run-oriented perspective that focused on spending reduction. According to Ed's viewpoint, the A12 redesign doesn't generate enough savings to offset the increase in material cost.

MF: What was your reaction to these two sets of cost savings estimates?

AJ: I tend to agree with the long-run-oriented resource-usage-based perspective that Sally used to calculate her numbers. Therefore, I was going to build my presentation around the $0.47 per unit savings figure that she derived. I was intending to make the argument that ABC could enable us to make a data-driven decision to match the $0.40 per unit price reduction while maintaining profitability.

MF: You just said that you "were intending" to make this point, but it sounds like you've changed your mind.

AJ: Actually, I was forced to change my mind because yesterday another one of our primary competitors announced a $2.50 per unit price reduction on this product. So, if I go into the management team meeting bragging about a $0.47 savings on a product in need of a $2.50 per unit price cut, I'm going to look foolish! It's the proverbial "eleventh hour" and I'm feeling a little stressed out! So, I decided to call you to see if you could offer any advice as to where I should go from here.

MF: First of all, the work that you have done regarding the A12 redesign was not wasted time. The information that you've conveyed to me regarding your analysis is interesting and it should comprise a portion of your presentation. However, you're correct in assuming that the A12 proposal can't be the basis for your entire presentation.

AJ: But, should I use Sally's numbers or Ed's? I'm inclined to use Sally's, but what do you think?

MF: Personally, I prefer the usage model because I believe that it puts the focus on redeploying freed-up capacity as opposed to the spending model that tends to focus on headcount reduction. Nonetheless, I would present both modes of analysis as potentially useful sources of information 432 Issues in Accounting Education depending upon the decision context. Furthermore, I think that both modes of analysis are an improvement over the existing standard cost system.

AJ: Okay, what else can I build into the presentation beyond the usage-vs.-spending analysis of the A12 proposal?

MF: My suggestion is that you use the ABC cross model as a way to broaden the scope of your presentation to include some "big picture" issues that you're currently overlooking if your focus is exclusively on the cost-reduction potential of the A12 proposal. I'll have my assistant send you a copy of an article describing the ABC cross model, but for now, here is a thumbnail sketch. The ABC cross model will not only give you a platform for talking about applications of ABC from a "what-if" cost-modeling perspective, which you're already touching upon with the A12 proposal, but it will also enable you to discuss ABC applications from both a product-mix-strategy perspective and a process-cost-management perspective. Right now, your presentation game plan is overlooking these two potential applications of ABC that I've always felt are critical to Wilson. I think it's important for you to consider why the product-engineering group picked the A12 product line over other product lines as the focal point of its product redesign cost reduction efforts.

AJ: Probably it was a "knee-jerk" reaction to our competitor's announced price reduction of $0.40 per unit coupled with the already low 2.2 percent profit margin on this product reported by the standard cost system. Of course, you and I know that the 2.2 percent margin is probably distorted, but....

MF: So, in other words, management's perception was that the A12 junction box was marginally profitable before any price reduction, and a further reduction in price without taking any type of management action would drop this product into the "red." So, a response was necessary and cost reduction seemed to be the most likely option.

A "big picture" question that you should ask is: Should Wilson be focusing its attention on products such as A12? Is A12 really a loser even before the price cut? Products such as A12 are the perceived reason that overall company profits have been shrinking, but what about all those low-volume, custom products that look so great according to the standard cost system? Right now, nobody outside your finance department has a clue about the true relationship between the revenue being generated by the growing custom business and the costs being driven by that segment of Wilson's business.

AJ: Wow, I guess in the back of my mind I was aware of this issue, but I allowed myself to get caught up in the detail of A12 proposal, while turning a blind eye to the product-mix-strategy issue.

MF: Keep in mind that there's nothing wrong with the details of the A12 proposal that you've been wrestling with. After all, if Wilson reduces its price on the A12 junction box by $2.50 without any true accompanying cost reduction, your company will see its profits decline regardless of what the ABC system indicates about A12's profit margin. So the usage-vs.-spending issue is worth thinking over and incorporating into your presentation, but it's not the whole ABC story. While we're talking, here's another issue to think about.

Let's assume for a minute that your focus is the A12 junction box. You just told me moments ago that Sally's projected cost savings were well short of the market-driven $2.50 price cut. Look at the activity costs that are being charged to the A12 line and are being passed on to Wilson's customers. How many of those activities in the ABC model are value-added from the customer's perspective?

AJ: You're right-moving, storing, setting-up equipment, expediting-none of those activities adds any value. We could be spending time analyzing these non-value-added costs to find ways to reduce support costs without sacrificing product quality or customer service.

MF: Given the volume of sales associated with A12, it may make more sense to talk about cost reduction from a process-redesign perspective instead of a product redesign perspective. There is probably a big savings opportunity associated with creating a manufacturing cell for A12. I think the big dollars are there instead of the proposed product redesign. Obviously, Wilson cannot snap its fingers and have a manufacturing cell up and running, but the purpose of your presentation should be simply to create an awareness of this application of ABC data. In other words, how on earth would you quantify the resources being consumed in non-value-added work using the standard cost system? Furthermore, how would you use the standard cost system to estimate the cost savings associated with a process redesign initiative?

AJ: Good point. These process cost management issues definitely need to be included in my presentation.

MF: Listen, I have an appointment coming up, but I want to mention one last thing for you to think about for your presentation. Spend some time contemplating the tone of your message. If your sole focus is on cutting-cutting product lines and cutting nonvalue-added workers-your fellow managers may begin to get resentful and see you only in the role of the proverbial "bean counter." I know the people out on the manufacturing floor are going to want to talk about revenue growth, not just cost reduction. You probably should be prepared to offer some comments regarding ABC from a resource redeployment and revenue growth perspective. Make the point that once ABC has helped identify freed-up resources in support as well as production departments, those valuable resources do not necessarily need to be eliminated; rather, they can be channeled to growing revenue and contributions from other product lines. In that way, total profitability can be increased without sacrificing people. That will appease the manufacturing managers.

AJ: Good advice. I'll need to consider that point. Perhaps the theory of constraints [TOC] could come into play here since we are talking about revenue growth, and we have recently been operating at practical capacity. I know the Assembly Department has been particularly backed up in recent months.

Blocher, Stout, Cokins, Chen: *Cost Management, 4e*

©The McGraw-Hill Companies, Inc 2008

MF: You're right. I never really thought about that, but perhaps TOC could somehow work in a complementary fashion with ABC.

AJ: All right, I've taken up enough of your time. I know that you're busy and must go. You've given me a ton of great ideas to think about. Thanks a million!

MF: It was my pleasure to help. Give me a call after the meeting to let me know how it worked out.

AJ: Will do. Talk to you later and thanks again.

As Alice hung up the phone, she continued to fill her note pad with a summary of the insights provided by Mike Foster. Alice had become well aware that her original game plan for the management team presentation would probably have failed. Thanks to Mike's advice, Alice was beginning to crystallize in her mind a presentation that she felt was sure to impress Simms, thereby saving the ABC system from discontinuation.

DISCUSSION QUESTIONS:

Assuming that you hold the position of corporate controller (that of Alice Johnson), organize a written presentation to the Wilson management team attempting to sell the virtues of ABC. To help organize your thoughts and presentation, consider the following questions:

1. What is the ABC cross model? Define what is meant by the product costing, process costing, and the "what-if" cost-modeling perspectives of ABC.

2. Estimate an income statement for the current version of the A12 junction box using the direct-labor-based standard cost system. Compare the profitability of the current version of the A12 junction box as reported by the direct-labor-based system to the ABC system and relate these cost numbers to the competitor's announced price reduction of $2.50 per unit. What conclusions may be inferred from this information?

3. Estimate the average overhead charge per unit for the custom product lines using the direct-labor-based standard cost system. How do these charges compare to the per unit charges assessed against the A12 junction box using the standard cost system? What conclusions may be inferred from this information?

4. Estimate an income statement for the A12 junction box, assuming that Wilson implemented a manufacturing cell for the A12 line and was able to eliminate all non-value-added resource costs associated with producing A12. What other information could you present that would highlight the dollar value of resources that Wilson is channeling to non-value-added activities?

5. What role would the data from the resource usage vs. resource spending analysis play in your presentation? How could net present value analysis be incorporated into the usage-vs.-spending analysis?

6. How would you use data from Wilson's activity model to estimate the throughput growth potential associated with the A12 redesign?

5-6 The Buckeye National Bank

INTRODUCTION

The Buckeye National Bank began operations in the mid-1980s. The bank quickly grew by providing checking account services to many small businesses that preferred to do business with a "local" bank. Although Buckeye initially offered checking account services for individual accounts (retail customers), the bank primarily focused on serving its business customers. During the economic slowdown of the early 1990s that weakened the local economy, growth in business customer accounts began to decline. In response, Buckeye's senior management adopted a new strategy, focusing on increasing the number of retail customer accounts. By aggressively marketing individual retail accounts, Buckeye continued to grow. Today, the Buckeye National Bank strives to maintain a stable base of business customers, while actively competing for an increased market share of retail customers.

Recent income statements (Exhibit A) reveal a decline in the bank's profits. The bank's primary (noninterest) expense consists of salaries and employee benefits. Most full-time employees' first priority is providing services to customers; these employees conduct their administrative responsibilities during slack times. The Bank schedules additional part-time employees to work during peak demand times, from 11 AM–2 PM and Friday afternoons. Flexibility in scheduling part-time employees means that the bank's staff is lean and fully utilized. Buckeye's CEO, Rob Garrison, believes that this staffing arrangement allows the bank to provide speedy customer service, while operating at practical capacity. (That is, the bank's staff is fully utilized in efficient operations, after allowing for bank holidays and other scheduled staff activities such as training.)

To counter falling profits, Buckeye's directors took two actions last year, both aimed at increasing the bank's retail customer base. First, Buckeye established a service call center to respond to customer inquiries about account balances, checks cleared, fees charged, and other banking concerns. Second, Buckeye's directors authorized year-end bonuses to branch managers who met their branch's target increase in the number of customers. However, even though 80 percent of the branch managers met the targeted increase in customer accounts, the Bank's profits continued to decline. CEO Rob Garrison does not understand why profits are declining, given that the Bank is serving more customers. Buckeye's southeast regional manager, Erik Larsen, has also noticed that while small retail customers flock to the bank, the number of business customers is barely stable.

Erik Larsen suspects that Buckeye's costing system may be part of the problem. Buckeye developed its simple costing system when the bank began operations in 1985. The bank does not trace any costs directly to individual customers. It simply treats all (noninterest expense) operating costs identified in the Income Statement in Exhibit A as indirect with respect to the customer line. The bank allocates these indirect costs to either the retail customer line or the business customer line, based on the total dollar value of checks processed (which is readily available because each branch must provide the dollar values of daily transactions for internal control). For the current period, Buckeye processed a total of $95 million in checks, of which $9.5 million was written by retail customers, and $85.5 million was written by business customers. This costing approach was fairly typical of banks and other financial institutions at the time Buckeye developed its cost system.

In college, Erik learned about an alternative costing approach called activity-based costing (ABC). However, the examples he remembered involved manufacturing firms. He wondered whether Buckeye could develop an ABC system, with the business account customer line and the retail account customer line as the two primary cost objects. Erik approached Rob Garrison with this suggestion. Rob was skeptical, exclaiming, "Our profits are going down the tubes and you want me to spend money developing a new *accounting* system?" However, Erik persisted, and Rob eventually authorized a pilot ABC study using three local branches of the bank.

The ABC implementation team included Erik, the managers of each of the three bank branches, a bank teller, and a representative from the customer service call center. The team began by identifying the activities Buckeye National Bank performed. To start a simple pilot study, the team identified the three most important activities:

Source: Linda Smith Bamber and K. E. Hughes II, Activity-Based Costing in the Service Sector: The Buckeye National Bank. *Issues in Accounting Education, 16 (3) 381-87.*

Blocher, Stout, Cokins, Chen: *Cost Management, 4e*

EXHIBIT A
Buckeye National Bank
Consolidated Income Statement
For the three years ending December 31, 20x5

	20x5 ($000)	20x4 ($000)	20x3 ($000)
Net interest income[a]	$3,486	$3,417	$3,349
Provision for credit losses	484	475	465
Net interest income after provision for credit losses	3,002	2,942	2,884
Noninterest income	1,207	1,199	1,190
Income prior to noninterest expenses and income tax	4,209	4,141	4,074
Noninterest expenses	3,805	3,539	3,362
Income before income taxes	404	602	712
Income tax expense	130	194	230
Net income	$ 274	$408	$ 482

[a] Net interest income equals interest income less interest expense. The bank's primary income is from interest-bearing checking accounts. Noninterest income includes fees charged for various services, such as checking account fees charged if the account balance falls below the required minimum level. Noninterest expenses are all of the bank's operating costs, including those associated with paying checks, providing teller services, and responding to customer account inquires.

1. Paying checks
2. Providing teller services
3. Responding to customer account inquiries at the customer service call center

If this pilot study turned out to be successful, then the team planned to refine the system by conducting a more detailed activity analysis the following year. The ABC team began by determining the costs that are associated with each of the three activities. The team quickly discovered that, as is typical in service industries like banking, labor (personnel) costs dominate. The ABC team asked each employee to fill out a short questionnaire to find out how the employee spends his or her time. The team then followed up with an in-depth personal interview with each employee. The ABC team used this combined information to estimate the percentage of time each employee spent on each of the three activities: (1) paying checks, (2) providing teller services, and (3) responding to customer account inquiries.

The team then estimated the other (nonlabor) resources that each of the three activities consumed. For example, they traced to the "responding to customer account inquiry" activity: (1) the cost of toll-free telephone lines at the customer service call center, and (2) depreciation on other equipment and facilities the call center personnel use. Similarly, the ABC team estimated the percentage of time the bank's information system was used for check processing and providing teller services (vs. other uses such as compiling periodic financial statements), to determine how much of the equipment's depreciation to assign to the activities "paying checks" and "providing teller services."

To complete the pilot study in a timely fashion, the ABC team based their estimated activity costs on last year's actual data, which were already available. If the pilot study succeeded, then the ABC team planned to develop *budgeted indirect cost rates* for each activity the following year. The advantage of budgeted rates over actual rates based on the prior year's data is that budgeted rates (budgeted cost associated with the activity divided by the budgeted quantity of the activity's cost driver) can incorporate expected changes in costs and operations.

After examining the three branch banks' indirect costs (that is, the cost items making up the branch banks' noninterest operating expenses), the ABC team classified the annual costs in each activity's cost pool (hereafter, all numbers are in thousands)[1] as shown in Exhibit B.

---

[1] An activity's cost pool is simply a grouping, or aggregation, of all the individual costs associated with that activity. The bank's ABC team created separate activity cost pools for the costs associated with each of the three activities: (1) paying checks, (2) providing teller services, and (3) responding to customer account inquiries.

The team identified the following cost drivers[2] for each activity cost pool:

EXHIBIT B
Assignment of Indirect (Noninterest Expense) Costs to Activity Cost Pools[a]

Total Indirect Cost	Activity Cost Pool to which Indirect Cost is Assigned	Estimated Annual Costs (in $1,000s)
Salaries of check-processing personnel	Paying checks	$ 700
Depreciation of equipment and facilities used in check processing	Paying checks	440
Teller salaries	Providing teller services	1,000
Depreciation of equipment and facilities used in teller operations	Providing teller services	200
Salaries of customer representatives at call center	Responding to customer account inquiries	450
Toll-free phone lines plus depreciation of equipment and facilities in customer call center	Responding to customer account inquiries	60
Total indirect costs		$2,850

[a] These indirect costs are part of the $3,805 "noninterest expenses" in the bank's 20x5 Income Statement in Exhibit A. The rest of the noninterest expenses in the Income Statement shown in Exhibit A pertain to other operating costs that are excluded from the pilot ABC study, such as the CEO's salary. (The costs listed in Exhibit B are indirect with respect to the retail customers and business account customers.)

EXHIBIT C Activity Cost Drivers by Customer Line

Activity Cost Driver	Annual Number of Units of Activity-Cost Driver Used by Retail Customers (in 1,000s)	Annual Number of Units of Activity-Cost Driver Used by Business Customers (in 1,000s)	Total
Checks processed	570	2,280	2,850
Teller transactions	160	40	200
Account inquiry calls to customer service call center	95	5	100

Activity Cost Pool	Activity Cost Driver
Paying checks	Number of checks processed
Providing teller services	Number of teller transactions
Responding to customer account inquiries	Number of account inquiry calls to customer service call center

The ABC team estimated that for the three pilot-test bank branches, the retail and business customer lines experienced the annual activity levels (in thousands) as shown in Exhibit C. For example, Exhibit C reveals that retail customers had 160,000 teller transactions and made 95,000 account inquiry calls to the customer service call center.

Buckeye National Bank currently services 150,000 retail customer checking accounts and 50,000 business customer checking accounts. The bank earns net interest revenue on the balances that customers keep in their checking accounts.[3] On average, the bank earns the following annual revenue from each type of account:

Average annual revenue per retail customer account	$10
Average annual revenue per business customer account	$40

---

[2] A cost driver is a factor, such as the number of checks processed, that causally affects costs. For example, the costs associated with the activity "paying checks" rise and fall as the quantity of the cost driver (the number of checks processed) rises and falls.

[3] The bank earns net interest revenue by managing the "interest rate spread." This spread is the difference between the interest rate the bank earns on customer deposits (say 8 percent), less the interest rate the bank pays the customer on the average checking account balance (say 4 percent).

Blocher, Stout, Cokins, Chen: *Cost Management, 4e*

©The McGraw-Hill Companies, Inc 2008

REQUIRED:

Your task is to assist Erik Larsen and his ABC team by providing the following information:

1) Under the *original* (old) cost system:
    A) Compute the *single* indirect cost allocation rate that the bank would use to allocate the total indirect costs presented in Exhibit B.
    B) Use your answer to part A to determine the total annual indirect cost assigned to:
        (i) the retail customer line, and
        (ii) the business customer line. What drives these allocations?
    C) What proportion of the total indirect cost is assigned to:
        (i) the retail customer line, and
        (ii) the business customer line? Why? That is, what is the underlying rationale for indirect cost allocation under the old system? What assumption must hold approximately true for the original cost allocation procedure to generate "accurate" customer cost information?
    D) Use your answer to part B and data on the number of retail and business accounts to determine:
        (i) the indirect cost per retail account, and
        (ii) the indirect cost per business account.
    E) Assuming there are no direct costs or other indirect costs, compute the average contribution to profit per account for retail customers and for business customers. What business strategy would a manager using the original cost allocation system likely adopt? Why?

2) What are the signs that Buckeye's original cost system is "broken," such that it needs refinement or improvement?

3) Under the new activity-based costing (ABC) system, compute the indirect cost allocation rates for each of the three activities:
    A) Paying checks
    B) Providing teller services
    C) Responding to customer account inquiries

4) Use the following schedule to compute the total indirect cost allocated to each customer line (show your computations beside the activity description):

Activity	Total Indirect Cost Assigned to Retail Customer Line	Total Indirect Cost Assigned to Business Customer Line
Paying checks		
Providing teller services		
Responding to customer account inquiries		
Total Indirect Costs		

5) What proportion of each activity is attributable to:
    (i) the retail customer line, and
    (ii) the business customer line?

6) Using the ABC data from Requirement 4, compute
    (i) the indirect cost per retail customer account and
    (ii) the indirect cost per business customer account.

7) Explain why the results in Requirement 1, Part D, and Requirement 6 differ. Be specific.

8) Using the ABC data, compute the average contribution to profit per account for both retail and business customers. What business strategy would a manager using the ABC cost system likely adopt? How does this result compare to your response to Requirement 1, Part E?

9) Recall Buckeye National Bank's bonus-based incentive plan to increase the number of customers. Do you believe this strategy is wise? Would you suggest any change in strategy based on the ABC analysis?

10) Activity-based management (ABM) refers to managers' use of ABC data in making business decisions. How can Buckeye's managers use the ABC data to plan more profitable marketing strategies? How can Buckeye's managers use ABC information to identify opportunities to trim costs while still satisfying customers' needs?

11) Why might Erik Larsen have suspected that the benefits of ABC would likely outweigh the costs of implementation at Buckeye National Bank?

12) Why do you think it is important for a CEO or a bank branch manager to understand ABC?

Readings

5.1: Activity-Based Costing and Predatory Pricing: The Case of the Petroleum Retail Industry

ABC Analysis Helped Settle a Lawsuit against a Gasoline Retailer, Proving the Company had not Committed Predatory Pricing.

By Thomas L. Bar Ton and John B. Macarthur

EXECUTIVE SUMMARY: The assignment of indirect costs in a traditional costing system can lead to product-cost subsidization. This is where excessive costs are charged to high-volume products and insufficient costs are charged to low-volume products. The result can lead to increased consumer demand for the undercosted—and underpriced—products and reduced customer demand for the overcosted—and thus overpriced—high-volume product. One way to deal with this problem is to employ activity-based costing (ABC). Product-cost subsidization also may have legal consequences, which ABC can help address. Undercosted products can lead to the appearance of predatory pricing where it actually does not exist. This article focuses on a lawsuit brought against a major chain of retail motor fuel (gasoline) service centers for allegedly selling regular-grade gasoline below cost, as defined by state statutes. The defendant employed ABC analysis to support its position that it was not selling its regular gasoline below cost. After the ABC analysis was presented, the case was settled, and the judge lifted the initial injunction

Activity-based costing (ABC) was originally developed by companies to deal with the problem of product-cost subsidization in traditional costing systems.[1] This is where the assignment of indirect costs leads to excessive costs being charged to high-volume products and insufficient costs being charged to low-volume products. The result can lead to increased consumer demand for the undercosted—and underpriced—products and reduced customer demand for the overcosted—and thus overpriced—high-volume product.[2] Subsequently, ABC has been found useful for several other purposes, such as costing nonvalue-added activities, long-term pricing, and capacity management.[3]

When prices are based on cost, product-cost subsidization can lead to increased demand for undercosted and underpriced low-volume products, which are probably being sold at unprofitable prices. Conversely, companies experience reduced customer demand for overcosted, overpriced high-volume products and services. These are unwanted economic consequences from product-cost subsidization that ABC seeks to correct by assigning indirect costs to products and services using appropriate unit-level and nonunit-level activity drivers that reflect resource consumption by the cost objects. ABC can also help address any legal consequences of the product-cost subsidization problem.

LEGAL CONSEQUENCES FROM PRODUCT-COST SUBSIDIZATION

State and federal laws have been enacted against predatory pricing, which is the selling of products below cost as a deliberate action to drive out the competition.[4] Alternatively, products may appear to be priced below cost because of the use of unrealistic, unit-based traditional costing systems, which results in the appearance of predatory pricing where it does not exist. This occurred in a case brought under the "Motor Fuel Marketing Practices Act" of Florida.

COST ASSIGNMENT USING ABC IN A RETAIL GASOLINE SERVICE CENTER

The lawsuit was brought against a major chain of retail motor fuel (gasoline) service centers, alleging that the chain was selling regular-grade gasoline below cost, as defined under state statutes. The plaintiff's expert used a unit-based approach to assign the gasoline service center's average monthly costs (as defined by statute) to the three grades of gasoline: regular (87 octane), plus (89 octane), and premium (93 octane). When these monthly costs were added to the purchase costs of the gasoline, this approach supported the allegation of predatory pricing. See Table 1A for the results.

On the other hand, the defendant's original expert used a simple average-cost approach to assign the average monthly gasoline service center costs equally to the three grades of gasoline (see Table 1B), which supported the defendant's position that regular gasoline was not being sold below cost. The judge in the case made a preliminary ruling that rejected the defendant's analysis and accepted the plaintiff's. The judge then issued an injunction prohibiting the defendant from selling regular gasoline below cost as determined in the plaintiff's analysis.

The defendant engaged an accounting professor as an expert witness to review the cost-assignment process and make his own recommendation as to the most reasonable determination of cost in applying state statutes. The expert witness used ABC as a third approach to cost assignment (see Table 1C), which involved performing activity analysis and selecting activity drivers.

ACTIVITY ANALYSIS

The purchase, storage, dispensing, and sale of gasoline at the retail level can be divided into activities grouped according to their cost hierarchy level:

♦ *Unit-level activities* are undertaken for each gallon of gasoline sold (such as electricity to power pumps when dispensing gasoline);

♦ *Batch-level activities* are the same for each gasoline transaction irrespective of the volume of gasoline purchased (for example, transactions to process customer payments for gasoline by cash, check, or debit/credit card);

♦ *Product-level activities* are conducted for specific gasoline products such as regular, plus, and premium gasoline and motor oil (for instance, gasoline tanks that are dedicated to specific gasoline grades); (Customer-level activities are conducted for specific gasoline customers (such as using billboard advertisements to promote the benefits of premium gasoline); and Organizational-supporting activities are for the gasoline dispensing organization as a whole and cannot be causally identified with units, batches, or individual products (including payroll and many other centralized activities).

Activities at the same hierarchy level that share a common activity driver could further be grouped into homogeneous activity cost pools.

The defendant's retail stores consisted of two main activities: the sale of gasoline and the sale of convenience store merchandise, such as bread and milk. With limited data, the expert witness developed a straightforward ABC model that identified three distinct overhead activities involved in selling gasoline in a retail outlet. First, it is necessary to have at least one attendant to receive payments for the gasoline sales transactions. Second, it is necessary to have a facility to house the gasoline attendant(s). This

does not require a space the size of a convenience store, so the expert assumed that a small kiosk would be used if there were no store. Third, it is necessary to have gasoline storage and dispensing assets.

Activity Cost Pool 1: Gasoline Sales Attendants (Labor). Attendants are needed to receive payments from customers who do not pay electronically at the gasoline pump. Attendants also can deal with malfunctioning gasoline pumps, security issues, and other problems as they arise. This is a batch-level activity because payment transactions occur only once for each purchase of gasoline, regardless of the volume of gasoline purchased.

Each service center has a convenience store with attendants who handle payments from the customers for gasoline and for any purchase of food, drink, and other products sold in the store. For the purpose of the case, it was necessary to estimate the labor cost including fringe benefits) of attendants, assuming that gasoline was the only product sold. It was decided that only one attendant would be required for the gasoline sales activity in the absence of a convenience store. Multiple regression analysis results confirmed that convenience store sales, not gasoline sales, were the major cost driver of labor cost above the base salary and benefits of one sales attendant.

Activity Cost Pool 2: Kiosk Facility and Activity Cost Pool 3: Gasoline-Dispensing Facility. Under state statutes, it was necessary to determine a "reasonable rental value" for the retail gasoline facility.[5] In the absence of a separate convenience store, it would be the rental value of the kiosk. It can be argued that this is a batch-level activity, following labor, as it facilitates the payment transactions that occur once per gasoline purchase.

Also, it was necessary to determine a "reasonable rental value" for the gasoline-dispensing facility, which, in general, can be classified as a product-level activity.[6] This activity cost pool includes assets that are specific to a particular gasoline grade and common gasoline dispensing assets. In a more comprehensive activity analysis, this cost pool could be divided into two or more activity cost pools that would be more homogeneous in nature.

In determining a reasonable rental value, lease information was obtained for the assumed rental of a kiosk and gasoline-dispensing assets in comparable gasoline retail outlets in the surrounding geographical market area.[7] The actual cost of insurance and average cost of repairs and maintenance, utilities, and real/property taxes was added to the reasonable rental value.[8] The total cost was divided between the kiosk facility and gasoline-dispensing facility in proportion to the estimated kiosk and actual gasoline-delivery assets

Table 1: Comparative Cost Assignment Bases in a Gasoline Service Center [1]

FACILITY-WIDE COST	TOTAL	ACTIVITY DRIVER	REGULAR	PLUS	PREMIUM
A. Unit-Based Approach:					
Average Monthly Cost	$26,300	Gas Sold2	$16,674	$5,129	$4,49?
Cost Per Gallon Sold			$ 0.058	$0.058	$0.058
B. Simple Average Approach:					
Average Monthly Cost	$26,300	1/3 each	$8,766	$8,767	$8,76?
Cost Per Gallon Sold			$0.030	$0.099	$0.113
C. ABC Approach:					
Pool 1-Labor	$ 9,300	Gas Sold[2]	$ 5,896	$1,814	$1,59?
Pool 2-Kiosk	2,737	Gas Sold[2]	1,735	534	46?
Pool 3-Gas Dispensing	14,263	1/3 each	4,754	4,754	4,75?
Total Cost	$26,300		$12,385	$7,102	$6,81?
Cost Per Gallon Sold			$ 0.043	$0.080	$0.08?

[1] The original information has been disguised.
[2] Gasoline Sold Proxy Transactional Cost Assignment Base Calculations:

	TOTAL	REGULAR	PLUS	PREMIUM
Average gallons of gas sold per month	454,000	288,000	88,500	77,50?
	(100.0%)	(63.4%)	(19.5%)	(17.1%

Table 2: Estimated Cost of Kiosk and Gasoline Dispensing[1]

Description		Percent
Cost of Gasoline-Dispensing Facilities[2]	$422,000	83.9%←
Cost of the Convenience Store Building[2]	$506,250	
Kiosk Cost Estimate versus Existing Convenience Store	16%	
Imputed Kiosk Cost[3]	81,000	16.1%←
Total Imputed Cost of Facility without Convenience Store (Excluding Land)	$503,000	100.0%
Rental[4] and Other Costs[5] Assigned to Gasoline Sales	$17,000	
Rental and Other Costs Assigned to Activity Cost Pool 2, Kiosk	2,737	16.1%←
Rental and Other Costs Assigned to Activity Cost Pool 3, Gasoline Dispensing	14,263	83.9%←
	$17,000	100.0%

[1] The original information has been disguised.
[2] Asset values were obtained from the company's fixed-asset master listing.
[3] If the location had mainly gasoline sales with no large, separate convenience store, this is the imputed cost of a "kiosk" to house an attendant to ring up gasoline sales.
[4] See endnote 7 for details of the sources of rental cost data.
[5] The actual cost of insurance and average cost of repairs and maintenance, utilities, and real/property taxes was added to the reasonable rental value of the kiosk and gasoline-dispensing facilities.

total value obtained from the company's fixed-asset master listing (see Table 2).

ACTIVITY DRIVERS

The volume of gasoline sold was readily available and was selected as the proxy activity driver for both the labor and kiosk activity cost pools. The average quantities of the three grades of gasoline sold over a 14- month period (October 1996-November 1997) were used to assign the activity costs. This was basically the same approach used by the plaintiff. The gasoline-dispensing activity cost pool was assigned equally to the three grades of gasoline because each grade of gasoline had exactly the same dispensing infrastructure.

Labor Activity Cost Pool. The volume of gasoline sold is a unit-level activity driver but can be justified for assigning labor activity costs to the gasoline grades as follows:

Blocher, Stout, Cokins, Chen: *Cost Management, 4e*

©The McGraw-Hill Companies, Inc 2008

Table 3: Gasoline-Dispensing Facilities

Facilities	Type of Asset
Gasoline Sign	Common Fixed Asset
Canopy	Common Fixed Asset
Cooler Vault	Common Fixed Asset
Gasoline Tanks	Gasoline Grade-Specific Fixed Asset
Pump & Tank Equipment	Common and Gasoline Grade-Specific Fixed Assets
Multi-Product Dispensers (MPDs)	Common Fixed Asset
Plumbing	Common and Gasoline Grade-Specific Fixed Assets
Electrical—Equipment	Common and Gasoline Grade-Specific Fixed Assets
Electrical—Canopy/MPDs	Common Fixed Asset
Lighting Fixtures	Common Fixed Asset
Area Lighting	Common Fixed Asset
Islands	Common Fixed Asset
Tank Excavation	Gasoline Grade-Specific Fixed Asset
Piping	Common and Gasoline Grade-Specific Fixed Assets

- The principal responsibility of a kiosk attendant would be to receive payments from customers for gasoline purchases, which is a batch-level activity. The volume of gasoline sold can be used as a proxy activity driver for these payment transactions if the average volume of gasoline sold to each customer is about the same, regardless of the gasoline grade, which appeared to be true in this case. The volume of gasoline sold is a better transaction proxy cost driver than the dollar sales because receiving payment from customers is not driven by the dollar amount of the purchases. In the case of credit/debit card payments made directly at the pump, an attendant is necessary to monitor these transactions, especially if the pump malfunctions, such as not printing a receipt. In any case, it can reasonably be assumed that sales transactions of each grade of gasoline that involve an attendant directly in processing customer payments are proportionate to the total gallons sold of each grade of gasoline.
- The number of gasoline sales transactions will be a major factor in determining the number of kiosk attendants and the hours a gasoline station is open, which directly affect the level of salary and benefits payments.

Kiosk Facility Activity Cost Pool. The volume of gasoline sold can be justified as an activity driver for the kiosk activity cost pool in the following ways:

- The entire purpose of the kiosk facility is to house the attendants who receive payments from customers for gasoline purchases. It is logical to use the same activity driver to assign both the labor and kiosk facility activity cost pools.
- The expected volume of gasoline sales will help determine the size of the kiosk necessary to house the number of attendants, which directly impacts the imputed rental payments.
- The volume of gasoline sales will determine the hours a gasoline station is open, which directly affects the level of repairs and maintenance, utilities costs, and so on.

Gasoline-Dispensing Activity Cost Pool. The facilities used for dispensing the three grades of gasoline are either common fixed assets (like the gasoline sign) or fixed assets that are identical in size and cost for each grade of gasoline irrespective of the volume of gasoline sold (for example, the gasoline tanks). Note that the gasoline tanks are identical in size and cost even though the demand is considerably higher for regular gasoline versus the other two grades. Table 3 identifies the major gasoline-dispensing fixed assets and whether they are common and/or gasoline grade-specific fixed assets.

This commonality of some gasoline-dispensing fixed assets with the cost equality of other, grade-specific gasoline-dispensing fixed assets means, for example, that if two grades of gasoline were sold instead of three, the reasonable rental and other long-run variable costs of the gasoline-dispensing facility would likely be one third less than is the case when three grades are sold. For example, one less tank excavation and gasoline tank would be required. Also, one-third fewer pump and tank equipment items would be needed, assuming each pump serves one grade of gasoline only. In terms of common assets, this would likely result in one-third fewer islands, a smaller canopy, and so on. In the case of multipurpose pumps that provide each grade of gasoline, the complexity and cost should be lower for pumps that serve two versus three grades of gasoline. Therefore, an equal assignment of the gasoline dispensing activity costs among the three grades of gasoline is a reasonable activity cost-driver measure.

ABC ANALYSIS RESULTS

The results from this straightforward ABC analysis can be considered from both the legal and cost management points of view.

Legal Outcome. According to the ABC analysis, the cost per gallon sold actually fell in between the amounts derived from the plaintiff's unit-level approach and the defendant's equal split of labor and overhead costs. In essence, the ABC approach split the difference between the costs per gallon sold obtained from the two extreme approaches. After this analysis was presented, the case was settled and the injunction lifted.

Cost Management Outcome. From a cost management perspective, the ABC model obtained a result that helped to correct the problem of product-cost subsidization of low-volume products by high-volume products, which often occurs when a pure unit-level cost assignment base is used. In this case, the low-volume products (plus and premium gasoline) were undercosted by the volume-based approach, whereas the high-volume product (regular gasoline) was overcosted. Thus the regular gasoline appeared to be more costly and priced under cost because of the use of the inappropriate unit based cost assignment method.

FURTHER REFINEMENT

Clearly, an ABC approach improves costing in a gasoline dispensing retail facility, but this model could be further refined. The use of practical capacity rather than expected or budgeted capacity may avoid charging the grades of gasoline for the costs of unused capacity.[9] A likely refinement would be the identification and measurement of nonunit-based activity drivers for the labor and kiosk facility costs. It is important to realize that more driver refinement away from unit-based activity drivers would only continue to strengthen the defendant's case by further lowering the cost of regular gasoline per gallon. Also, greater costing refinement usually entails greater information processing costs. It is important to ensure that the costs of ABC models are justified by the benefits obtained.

ENDNOTES

[1] See "John Deere Component Works (A)," *Harvard Business School Case Series 9-187-107* (Rev. November 1987).

[2] For a numerical example of overcosting and undercosting products, see John B. MacArthur, "Activity-Based Costing and Activity-Based Management: An Introduction," in *Guide to Cost Management*, Barry J. Brinker, editor, John Wiley & Sons, New York, N.Y., 2000, pp. 397-410.

[3] For discussion on ABC and capacity management, see Robin Cooper and Robert S. Kaplan, "Activity-Based Systems: Measuring the Costs of Resource Usage," *Accounting Horizons*, September 1992, pp. 1-13.

[4] For example, in Florida, the "Motor Fuel Marketing Practices Act" (526.302) states that: "Predatory practices and, under certain conditions, discriminatory practices, are unfair trade practices and restraints which adversely affect motor fuel competition." This legislation, in section 526.304, stipulates that: "(1)(a) It is unlawful for any refiner engaged in commerce in this state to sell any grade or quality of motor fuel at a retail outlet below refiner cost, where the effect is to injure competition" and "(b) It is unlawful for any nonrefiner engaged in commerce in this state to sell any grade or quality of motor fuel at a retail outlet below nonrefiner cost, where the effect is to injure competition."

[5] In Florida, the "Motor Fuel Marketing Practices Act" (526.303) states: "(9) 'Reasonable rental value' means the bona fide amount of rent which would reasonably be paid in an arm's length transaction for the use of the specific individual retail outlet, including land and improvements, utilized for the sale of motor fuel. The value of the land and improvements shall include the costs of equipment; signage; utilities, property taxes, and insurance, if paid by the owner; and environmental compliance, such as testing, detection, and containment systems; but does not include the costs of environmental cleanup and remediation. In determining the reasonable rental value of the specific retail outlet, the rental amount of comparable retail outlets in the relevant geographic market shall be considered. When motor fuel is sold at the retail level along with other products, the reasonable rental value attributable to the sale of motor fuel at the retail outlet shall be allocated by the percentage of gross sales attributable to motor fuel sales."

[6] *Ibid.*

[7] Comparable lease information was obtained from an outside appraisal service. This allowed the conversion of asset value into a reasonable rental value.

[8] The current actual cost of insurance was obtained from the defendant company, and the average cost of repairs and maintenance, utilities, and real/property taxes was calculated from monthly company data.

[9] See Cooper and Kaplan, September 1992.

Blocher, Stout, Cokins, Chen: *Cost Management, 4e*

5.2: Activity-Based Benchmarking and Process Management—Managing the Case of Cardiac Surgery

These techniques focus on in-depth identification of best processes and practices through a study of resource consumption. From them, hospitals can get a more accurate picture of how practices are linked to cost.

By Bea Chiang, Ph.D., CPA

The increasingly competitive nature of the healthcare market and the managed care system have put tremendous pressure on hospitals to control costs, manage service processes, improve quality of care, and market services competitively. Healthcare providers are now expected to manage economic resources prudently and need to be on top of their costs to ensure that revenues are sufficient for them to survive. Benchmarking is a strategic approach used widely in the manufacturing sector to monitor costs. It is a continuous process of measuring products, services, and activities against the best levels of performance.[1] This approach can also benefit healthcare organizations where the close monitoring of resources is critical to ensure the organization's effectiveness.

COSTING PROCESSES AND ACTIVITY-BASED BENCHMARKING

Healthcare organizations are increasingly sharing cost data on a per patient and per case basis for benchmarking the performance of individual units. There are several external industry benchmarks that a hospital can use to compare its operation to other healthcare providers. Examples include total margin, occupancy, cost per certain medical procedure, total cost per case, and cost per inpatient day. Some of these external benchmarks, however, confound direct cost comparisons, as costs may be aggregated in different ways by different hospitals. For instance, the selection of direct cost centers and the methods chosen to spread the indirect costs to other departments are hospital environment specific and affect the cost accumulation process for services delivered.

Generally, the hospital's costing system begins with the division of each general ledger account into cost types: variable direct cost, fixed direct cost, and fixed indirect cost. At the cost center or department level, each indirect cost center is assigned an allocation base (such as total cost, square feet, or gross revenue) to be used to spread the indirect costs to the direct cost centers. The departmental direct costs and allocated indirect costs become departmental total costs. The direct cost center or department is defined as a primary product/service unit. An example of a primary product/ service is a prescription, an injection, or a bed bath.

The next step is to calculate the standard unit cost of the primary product/service. This is done by first allocating the departmental total cost based on the relative value units (RVUs) multiplied by the budgeted volumes of each individual product/service to obtain the budgeted total cost of each basic product/service.[2]

Finally, the standard unit cost is calculated by dividing the total cost of the individual product/service by its budgeted volume. Once standard unit costs are established for primary products/services, they can be summed up into intermediate products, such as a surgical procedure. These, in turn, can be rolled up into final product/service, such as inpatient days or admissions. The hospital costing process is presented in Figure 1.

From the hospital's costing procedure, the unit cost of a product actually includes allocated indirect costs that are beyond the control of physicians and other medical personnel. Indirect cost is the cost that does not relate directly to the provision of medical services to patients. Examples include the salary of the administrative staff, the cost of the laundry department, cafeteria, and so forth. For pricing purposes, the accounting system needs to allocate these indirect costs to direct cost centers to account for each unit of product/service. The physicians or medical personnel, however, do not have control over the method or the amount of the indirect cost to be allocated to the department. Total unit cost, which includes both direct and indirect costs, does not reflect the efficiency of activities performed in the medical processes. Therefore, instead of total cost, activity-related measurements such as equipment setup time or surgery time tie in more to the resources consumption in the process and are more appropriate for benchmarking.

IMPROVING CARDIAC CARE PROCESSES BY ACTIVITY-BASED BENCHMARKING

In an economic sense, macro-level costs (like cost per certain diagnosis) are driven by numerous and complex micro-level decisions, such as procedures taken or equipment used by physicians and specialties. Macro cost control can be achieved only through reference to micro-level analysis.[3] Therefore, the benchmarking process should also use internal procedures data. This type of data is more activity specific and task related. It facilitates direct benchmark comparisons among physicians or staff so that these groups can see clearly how their practices need to be improved. The internal procedure level of performance may be identified in an organization through internal benchmarking. The internal benchmarks help the hospital ask why its costs differ from other hospitals, why costs differ among patients with the same diagnosis within the same hospital, and identify which practices can be transferred from less cost-effective to more cost-effective methods.

Studies have found that physicians do respond to benchmarking.[4] They also are more likely to be persuaded to change their practices if they see how they can use such data to improve their processes.[5] Activity-based benchmarking for medical-care processes involves three steps: (1) analyzing process flow and identifying major activities, (2) choosing the appropriate measurement of resource consumption for benchmarking, and (3) identifying the best process and practice as benchmarks.

ANALYZING PROCESS FLOW AND IDENTIFYING MAJOR ACTIVITIES

The first step in the benchmarking process is to perform an analysis of the activity across all operations and processes required to move the patient from admission to discharge. The case of a cardiac patient can be used to illustrate the benchmarking process. The patient is admitted on the scheduled date for an open-heart surgery. After going through the administration process, the patient will undergo many tests. Immediately before surgery, the patient will be given specific preoperative medications and will then be "prepped" for surgery. An intravenous (IV) line will be administered. The patient will then be given a sleep-inducing medication through the IV and anesthetic gas to breathe (general anesthesia). After the patient is asleep, the cardiac surgery procedure begins.

There are a variety of different types of open-heart surgeries, depending upon the condition being treated and the overall health of the patient. The surgery itself takes an average of five hours. After surgery, the patient is moved to a hospital bed in the cardiac surgical intensive care unit. The patient is carefully monitored in the cardiac intensive care unit for 12-24 hours and then on the general floor (step-down units). Throughout the process, from admission to discharge, major activities include general administration and patient education, lab procedure/test, medical equipment and supplies administration, setup, operation, nursing, and general services. The summary presented in Figure 2 details the process flow and activities engaged in providing the services. Costs incurred at each stage depend upon types of personnel, equipment, and supplies involved in the process. They are listed as cost inputs.

CHOOSING THE APPROPRIATE MEASUREMENT FOR BENCHMARKING

For different costs, there are different activity characteristics that drive the costs. For example, nursing costs are different when comparing the operating room to the cardiac intensive care unit because different types and numbers of nurses engage in different activities. To better capture cost incurrence in the case of a cardiac surgery patient, an activity-related measurement must be selected to measure the resource consumption.

Pre-Surgery

At the admission stage, the number of patients per registration staff or number of documents generated per staff hour can be used to measure the efficiency of the registration process. During the preparation for surgery (ambulatory care unit), medical staff explain the operation process to the patient, perform additional tests, and prepare the patient for surgery. At this stage, the preparation time, patient education time, number of tests performed by type, and the amount of medical supplies used can be drawn on to measure the performance.

Operating Room

The number of specialists and medical staff assigned to the operating room are defined by the hospital's surgery policy and remain consistent from patient to patient. Resource consumption among physicians and other medical personnel varies, however, in three significant ways: surgery time, operating room setup time, and medical supplies usage.

Surgery time is a critical indicator of cost. It relates to costs associated with the time for the operation, anesthesia, perfusion service, and nursing staff. Setup time is the time required to prepare equipment, tools, and medical supplies for the surgery. It is considered a major indicator of

Blocher, Stout, Cokins, Chen: *Cost Management, 4e*

efficiency.[6] Reducing setup time shortens the lead-time of service delivery and helps to keep it at a reasonable level. Medical supplies and equipment represent a significant part of hospital expenditures and are one of the major factors that drive healthcare costs.[7] Finding the best practices in using the facilities and supplies will help healthcare providers manage their costs. Benchmarks can be established to measure the performance of an operating room in terms of operation time, setup time, and medical supplies usage.

Post-Surgery

After the surgery, most of the resources and time are spent on monitoring surgery results, providing patient education, performing additional tests, taking vital signs, assessing post-surgery outcome, and providing general and dietary services. Major cost inputs in this stage include nursing staff, cardiologist, lab technician, general service staff, and medical supplies. Benchmarks such as results-assessment time, nursing care time by nurse type, medical supply usage, and patient education hours can be established to measure the performance.

NURSING-CARE SERVICES

Nursing services count as a significant part of activities in every stage of the process. The essence of the problem with nursing services is that the costs usually are averaged into room and board in most hospitals. As a result, all patients in a given unit of the hospital will receive the same daily charge for nursing-care services. It is presumed that all patients consume exactly the same amount of nursing resources. The fact that different patients have different nursing needs does not enter into consideration. For the purpose of improving the process through benchmarking, this approach provides very poor information. The most accurate method would be to measure the time each nurse spent with each patient. This, however, is an impractical, costly, and time-consuming way to account for the cost. One alternative, suggested by B. Dieter and J. Moorhead, is assigning each nursing procedure a predetermined relative value unit (RVU) based on the time taken to perform that task.[8] Initially, the relative value might be determined according to prior experience or by polling full-time staff nurses on the amount of time it takes them to complete each procedure. Thus, instead of counting nursing time spent on each activity with each patient, nursing care will be benchmarked based on RVU for procedures or tasks performed.

Figure 3 summarizes a set of benchmarks established to measure the performance of major activities in the care process. Benchmarks can be established at a detailed activity level as well as at the case level.

FIGURE 1
Costs of Primary Products/Services

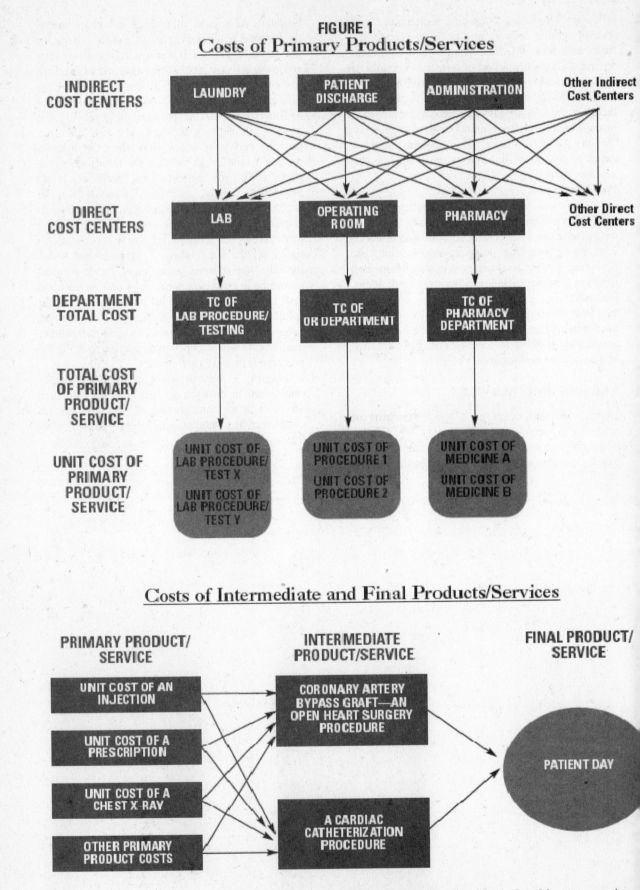

Costs of Intermediate and Final Products/Services

Blocher, Stout, Cokins, Chen: *Cost Management, 4e*

©The McGraw-Hill Companies, Inc 2008

FIGURE 2: Process Flow, Activities, and Cost Inputs for Cardiac Surgery Patient

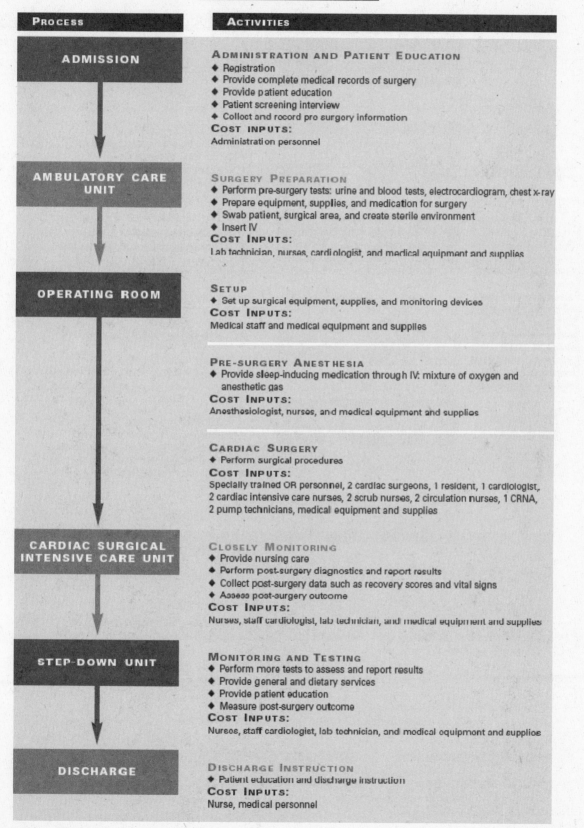

PROCESS	ACTIVITIES
ADMISSION	**ADMINISTRATION AND PATIENT EDUCATION** ♦ Registration ♦ Provide complete medical records of surgery ♦ Provide patient education ♦ Patient screening interview ♦ Collect and record pre surgery information **COST INPUTS:** Administration personnel
AMBULATORY CARE UNIT	**SURGERY PREPARATION** ♦ Perform pre-surgery tests: urine and blood tests, electrocardiogram, chest x-ray ♦ Prepare equipment, supplies, and medication for surgery ♦ Swab patient, surgical area, and create sterile environment ♦ Insert IV **COST INPUTS:** Lab technician, nurses, cardiologist, and medical equipment and supplies
OPERATING ROOM	**SETUP** ♦ Set up surgical equipment, supplies, and monitoring devices **COST INPUTS:** Medical staff and medical equipment and supplies **PRE-SURGERY ANESTHESIA** ♦ Provide sleep-inducing medication through IV: mixture of oxygen and anesthetic gas **COST INPUTS:** Anesthesiologist, nurses, and medical equipment and supplies **CARDIAC SURGERY** ♦ Perform surgical procedures **COST INPUTS:** Specially trained OR personnel, 2 cardiac surgeons, 1 resident, 1 cardiologist, 2 cardiac intensive care nurses, 2 scrub nurses, 2 circulation nurses, 1 CRNA, 2 pump technicians, medical equipment and supplies
CARDIAC SURGICAL INTENSIVE CARE UNIT	**CLOSELY MONITORING** ♦ Provide nursing care ♦ Perform post-surgery diagnostics and report results ♦ Collect post-surgery data such as recovery scores and vital signs ♦ Assess post-surgery outcome **COST INPUTS:** Nurses, staff cardiologist, lab technician, and medical equipment and supplies
STEP-DOWN UNIT	**MONITORING AND TESTING** ♦ Perform more tests to assess and report results ♦ Provide general and dietary services ♦ Provide patient education ♦ Measure post-surgery outcome **COST INPUTS:** Nurses, staff cardiologist, lab technician, and medical equipment and supplies
DISCHARGE	**DISCHARGE INSTRUCTION** ♦ Patient education and discharge instruction **COST INPUTS:** Nurse, medical personnel

FIGURE 3: <u>Activity-Based Benchmarking</u>

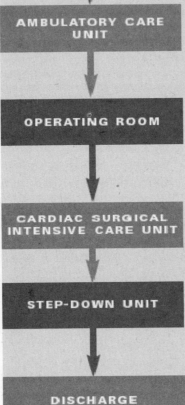

PROCESS	BENCHMARKS
ADMISSION	◆ Number of patients per registration staff hour ◆ Number of documents generated per staff hour
AMBULATORY CARE UNIT	◆ Number of tests by type ◆ Nursing care by relative value unit ◆ Medical equipment and supply usage ◆ Number of tests by type ◆ Surgery preparation time ◆ Patient transportation time
OPERATING ROOM	◆ Surgery time ◆ Medical equipment and supply usage ◆ Operating room setup time ◆ Surgical team combination ◆ Patient transport time ◆ Nursing care by relative value unit
CARDIAC SURGICAL INTENSIVE CARE UNIT	◆ Number of procedures by type ◆ Number of tests by type ◆ Nursing care by relative value unit ◆ Medical equipment and supply usage
STEP-DOWN UNIT	◆ Number of procedures by type ◆ Number of tests by type ◆ Nursing care by relative value unit ◆ Medical equipment and supply usage ◆ Patient education hours ◆ Results assessment time
DISCHARGE	◆ Discharge instruction and patient education hours

BENCHMARKS FOR ENTIRE PROCESS AT CASE LEVEL: Length of stay by diagnosis, total medical equipment and supply usage, total nursing time by nurse type, total medical records recording and handling time, total setup time, total surgery time, total patient education and instruction time

Blocher, Stout, Cokins, Chen: *Cost Management, 4e*

TABLE 1: Benchmarking Report—A Case of Cardiac Surgery

1. BENCHMARKING DATA: CARDIAC OPERATING ROOM (ACTIVITY LEVEL)

DRG: 107—Coronary Bypass with Cardiac Catheterization
Principal Procedure Code: 36.11   Severity Level: 2
Attending MD: # 11111

SEVERITY LEVEL:	PATIENT ENCOUNTER NO.: 00000100 SEVERITY LEVEL 2			PATIENT ENCOUNTER NO.: 00000500 SEVERITY LEVEL 3		
	PHYSICIAN #11111	AVERAGE	BEST PRACTICE	PHYSICIAN #11111	AVERAGE	BEST PRACTICE
1. Cardiac Surgery Time (minutes per surgery)	300	281.35	225	345	300.63	228
Perfusion Service (minutes)	300	281.35	225	345	300.63	228
Anesthesia (minutes)	300	281.35	225	345	300.63	228
2. Operating Room Total Setup Time (minutes per surgery)	65	53.2	38	66	49.72	40
Anesthesia Setup Time (minutes)	31	26.01	22	35	27.21	25
3. Equipment and Medical Supplies (number of units used)						
Aortic Punch	1	1	1	1	1	1
Bovie Pencil	3	2.74	2	2	2.57	2
Bulb Syringe	1	1	0	1	1.11	0
Bifur Blood Infusion Set	0	0.31	0	0	0.1	0
Breathing Circuits	1	1	1	1	1	1
Cable Ven	2	1.95	1	2	1.95	1
Cautery Electro Unit	1	1.62	1	1	1.48	1
Chest Tube	2	2	2	2	2	2
CO_2 Coupling	1	1	1	1	1	1
CVP Tray Arrow	1	0.8	0	1	1	0
Ioban Drape	2	1.19	1	1	1.15	0
Mayo Cover	2	1.24	0	1	1.22	0
Scapel Blade	6	5.19	4	4	4.86	4
Saphenous Vein Adaptor	2	2.19	1	2	2.33	2
Stopcocks 3 Ways	1	1	0	1	1	0
Sutures Cabg Pack	2	1.05	1	1	1	1
Y-Adaptor	0	0.2	0	2	0	0
Temp Sensing Foley	1	1	1	1	1	1
Blood Warmer Set	1	1	1	1	1	1
Imed Cassette	3	3.62	3	4	4.5	2
Hemaclip	4	3.2	2	3	3.2	2
Skin Prep	3	2.81	2	1	1.5	1
Transducer	1	0.4	0	3	2.77	0
Transducer Triple	1	1	1	1	1	1
Disposable Gown	3	3.43	2	3	3.9	2
Clip Applier	9	3.52	2	7	3.75	2
Extra Pressure Transducer	0	0.4	0	1	1	0

TABLE 1 (*continued*): Benchmarking Report—A Case of Cardiac Surgery

2. BENCHMARKING DATA: PRE- AND POST-SURGERY (ACTIVITY LEVEL)

	PATIENT 00000100	AVERAGE	BEST PRACTICE
1. NURSING CARE[1] (RVU)[2]			
Vital Signs (*Registered nurse, Licensed nurse, Unlicensed assistant*)			
Registered nurses	40	38.44	32
Licensed nurses	25	30.12	32
Unlicensed assistants	18	18.20	17
Patient Education and General Service (*Registered nurse, Licensed nurse, Unlicensed assistant*)	40	40.51	35
Medical Records Assessment (*Registered nurse*)	62	60.21	50
Administration of Medications (*Registered or Licensed nurse*)	81	70.21	50
Surgery Preparation (*Unlicensed assistant or Apprentice nurse*)	22	30.21	25
IV, Diagnostic Tests (*Registered nurse*)	75	70.21	66
2. LAB (RVU)			
Blood Tests	98	78.21	75
Pathological Tests	45	50.30	38
Other Tests and Procedures[3]	39	36.12	34
Radiology Films	40	42.69	39
3. CARDIAC CATHETERIZATION			
Cardiac Catheterization Time (*minutes*)	45	35.78	30
Cardiac Catheterization Setup Time (*minutes*)	20	18.23	16
4. RESPIRATORY THERAPY			
Setup Time (*minutes*)	17	18.20	15
Cont Oxygen Therapy (*units*)	114	96.25	38
Pause Oximeter (*units*)	3	4.55	3
5. TOTAL PATIENT TRANSPORTATION AND PREPARATION (*minutes*)	55	47.33	45

3. BENCHMARKING DATA: CASE LEVEL[4]

	PATIENT 00000100	AVERAGE	BEST PRACTICE
1. Length of Stay (*days*)	7	8.20	5
2. Total Actual Costs	$24,188	$22,521.20	$19,838
3. Total Surgery Time (*minutes*)	630	561.25	450
4. Total Cardiac Catheterization Time (*minutes*)	890	897.30	750
5. Total Nursing Costs[5]	1,419	1,410.42	952
6. Total RVU of Lab Test	1,418	1,082.52	899
7. Total RVU of Radiology	101	81.33	57
8. Total Medical Records Handling and Assessment Time (*RVU*)	772	630.55	521
9. Total Medical Supplies and Sterile (*units*)	250	225.17	155
10. Total Respiratory Therapy Time (*minutes*)	387	301.22	230

1 To simplify the illustration, only vital signs are reported by nurse type. Total RVUs are shown for the rest of the activities.

2 In the lab-testing and nursing-care areas, RVU represents the amount of time to complete a certain task or procedure.

3 A detailed benchmarking report will be sorted by test types.

4 The average and benchmarking data are based on patients with the same diagnosis and level of severity.

5 Total nursing costs are determined as follows: (nursing hours) x (nurse-patient ratio) x (hour rate). The hour rate will depend on the type of nurse.

Blocher, Stout, Cokins, Chen: *Cost Management, 4e*

IDENTIFYING BEST PROCESS AND BEST PRACTICE AS BENCHMARKS

Table 1 shows an internal benchmarking report of a hospital. The hospital combined clinical records, nursing logs, and surgery logs with the financial accounting records to benchmark performance. The data were sorted by Diagnosis Related Group (DRG), primary procedure code, and severity level.[9] Benchmarks are the cases that have the lowest-quantity usage in terms of surgery time, setup time, nursing-care time, lab tests/procedures time, and consumption of medical equipment and supplies. The benchmarks were determined by data collected from 259 patients admitted to the hospital for heart surgery in 1998 and 1999. The benchmarking report compares individual information to the overall average of the 259 cases and to the best practice. The first part of the report presents the comparative benchmarking data of two cardiac surgeries in the operating room (cardiac primary procedure code 36.12), performed by physician #11111, one at severity level 2 and the other at level 3 (Note: The report is shown as a subset of the results, so it does not include all benchmarking items).

The report shows that the surgery time taken by physician #11111 for a principal procedure code 36.11 at severity level 2 was 300 minutes, compared to an average time of 281 minutes and 225 minutes for the best practice. The same comparisons are made for anesthesia and perfusion service. The benchmarking also shows medical equipment and supply usage. It reveals that some equipment items were required for the surgery, such as a blood warmer set (individual, average, and best practice all show one unit). Some items, such as clip applier, however, could be used in a more cost effective way: Nine units of clip appliers were actually used, compared to an average of 3.52 units in all cases and two units for the best practice. Some items, such as transducers, were used on average in 104 cases out of 260 (an average of 0.4 usage) but were not used at all by the best practice. This raises the question of whether or not this procedure can be performed without the use of transducers.

The report provides a general internal profile of practices in the operating room. Physicians could review such a report to determine exactly how their consumption of supplies compares to the average consumption level in all cases and to the consumption level of the best performer. The report also is useful to physicians and other clinical personnel because it highlights the usage differences in a principal cardiac procedure and shows what supplies were not used in the best practices.

The second part of the benchmarking report shows pre- and post-surgery data. In the interest of providing a simple illustration, the report only shows a subset of benchmarking data. For nursing care, different types of nurses and nursing assistants, such as registered nurses, licensed nurses, unlicensed assistants, and apprentice nurses, are employed to provide services. Each of them has a different hour rate and skill set. Some tasks require a specific type of nurse for a specific task; for example, the operating room requires cardiac registered nurses for assistance. In the step-down unit, only registered nurses can perform certain tasks, such as an IV or any injection. Others, such as a bed bath, however, can be performed by licensed nurses. The benchmark report shows the time (measured by RVU) spent on each type of nursing activity. Detailed nursing activities can be reported by nurse type. For example, vital signs took 40 RVUs of a registered nurse's time, 25 RVUs of a licensed nurse's time, and 18 RVUs of an unlicensed assistant's time. In the best practice, 32 RVUs of a registered nurse's time, 32 RVUs of a licensed nurse's time, and 17 RVUs of an unlicensed assistant's time were devoted to taking vital signs. In this instance, the best practice utilizes more licensed nurses instead of registered nurses to take vital signs. Having licensed nurses take vital signs instead of registered nurses, therefore, can lower costs. The use of unlicensed assistants is about the same because of restrictions on the use of unlicensed assistants for quality considerations. These benchmarking data help the hospital monitor nursing services to ensure the quality of nursing care. In addition, the nursing department manager is able to assign the lowest-cost combination of nursing staff to provide the required services at the desired level of quality care.

The lab tests are also measured and benchmarked by RVU. The performance of the cardiac catheterization lab and respiratory therapy are benchmarked by setup time, procedure time, and medical supplies usage. Section three of the report presents the benchmarking data at case level. This information facilitates comparisons of cardiac surgery cases at a broader level. If the case and benchmarks show significant differences (for example, total RVUs of lab tests are 1,418 compared to 899 of the best practice), the case can be traced down to the activity level in order to explore the factors responsible for the high cost.

FOCUSING ON PROCESS IMPROVEMENT

Activity-based benchmarking focuses on in-depth identification of best processes and practices. The best practices can be found through the use of internal benchmarking. One of the benefits is that we can obtain specific and detailed information with which to facilitate process improvement. Hospitals can use benchmarking data to identify critical success factors and appropriate measures in the service process. Benchmarking also enables us to use both clinical and accounting information more effectively. When applied along with external benchmarking measures, internal procedure benchmarking helps the organization to determine major areas for improvement.

Information provided by the internal activity benchmarking process benefits hospitals by highlighting the resource consumption of particular procedures in the process flow so that physicians and staff have a more accurate picture of how practices are linked to cost. More important, activity benchmarking provides specific direction for the continual improvement of the care process and provides an explicit means of communication among various departments.

ENDNOTES:

[1] Charles T. Horngren, George Foster, and Srikant M. Datar, *Cost Accounting: A Managerial Emphasis*, Prentice Hall, 2000, pp. 236.

[2] The relative value unit (RVU) is a measure of resource consumption in the healthcare organization. It is defined as the amount of time to complete one unit or the amount of supplies for one unit.

[3] Ron Eden and Colin Lay, "Benchmarking on costs in healthcare," *Management Accounting*, March 1998, pp. 28-31.

[4] J. Evans, III, Y. Hwang, and N. Nagarajan, "Physicians' response to length-of-stay profiling," *Medical Care*, Vol. 33, No. 11, 1995, p. 1106.5 Girard Senn, "Clinical buy-in is key to benchmarking success," *Healthcare Financial Management*, Vol. 52, No. 5, May 1998, p. 46.

[6] Horngren, Foster, *et al.*, p. 726.

[7] *Material Management in Healthcare*, April 2000, Vol. 9, No. 4, pp. 6-9.

[8] B. Dieter, "Determining the Cost of Emergency Department Services," *Hospital Cost Accounting Advisor*, Vol. 2, No. 1, February 1987, pp.1, 5-7; J. Moorhead, "Costing Accounting for Emergency Services," *Hospital Cost Management and Accounting*, Vol. 1, No. 2, May 1999, pp. 1-7.

[9] DRG is a system used for classification of inpatient hospital services based on principal diagnosis, secondary diagnosis, surgical procedures, age, sex, and presence of complications. This system of classification is used as a financing mechanism to reimburse hospitals and selected other providers for services rendered.

5.3: Using Activity Based Costing To Assess Channel/Customer Profitability

Better understanding of your customers' profitability picture is imperative for survival in today's competitive environment. Here the CFO of an employment services company used ABC to analyze the company's profitability picture at the customer-channel and individual customer-level.

By Dewayne L.Searcy, Ph.D., Cma, Cpa

"With better information and accounting systems, firms are beginning to disaggregate revenues and costs to customer or account level. This analysis often reveals previously hidden subsidies across customers, products, and markets."[1]

Most firms are well aware of the 80/20 rule in which a small fraction of customers accounts for a large share of revenues and most of a firm's profits. As the above quote states, that small fraction of profitable customers subsidizes the firm's other unprofitable or, at best, breakeven customers. Instead of accepting the 80/20 rule, firms should strive to identify those subsidized customers and work with them in either altering the servicing of those customers (including pricing) to a more equitable arrangement or outsourcing the servicing of those customers altogether. Temp Employment Company, Inc. (TEC), a firm in the employment services industry, used Activity-Based Costing (ABC) in assessing the profitability picture in order to better understand which customers were profitable and which were subsidized. This article describes the journey of TEC's chief financial officer through the ABC implementation and subsequent analysis. (Note: The name of the actual company has been changed and the financial data altered to protect the company's confidentiality.)

ABC AND THE FIRM

TEC is a multi-office employment services firm offering temporary employment and permanent placements. The temporary employment division represents over 70% of TEC's business and is the focus of this article. Before covering how TEC used ABC information to assess its profitability picture, TEC's ABC implementation will be briefly discussed. Table 1 summarizes the four-step process TEC completed in transforming its cost management system.

Step 1. Develop the activity dictionary.

In the first step, TEC was divided into activities. It would have been possible to divide TEC into several activities, but it was important to develop a simple, yet meaningful, system. Three activities were defined as relevant to the operations of the firm: 1) filling work orders, 2) hiring temporary employees, and 3) processing payroll/billing. The *filling work orders* activity begins once an order is received from a customer and ends when the customer is provided with the name(s) of the temporary employee(s) assigned to work for them. The *hiring temporary employees* activity involves the process of hiring employees for temporary assignments. This activity begins when an application is completed and ends once the employee is debriefed on company polices and entered in the system. The last activity, *processing payroll/billing*, involves the weekly payroll and customer billing process.

Step 2. Determine how much the organization is spending on each of its activities.

Once the activities were identified, the CFO assigned the direct costs associated with each one. Any resource that could not be directly traced to an activity was initially assigned to a general overhead account. Once the directly traceable resources were assigned to each activity, the general overhead was allocated. Table 2 summarizes the results of assigning the costs to the three activities of TEC. The general overhead was allocated to each activity on the basis of the directly traceable costs of each activity to total directly traceable costs.

Step 3. Identify the organization's products, services, and customers.

As mentioned earlier, TEC offers two services, temporary employment and permanent placements. Within each service offering, TEC's customers are separated between two channels, industrial and clerical, depending upon the job classification of the position they are seeking to fill. Industrial customers hire temporary employees to fill touch-labor positions (such as assembly, machine operator). On the other hand, clerical customers seek to hire office positions (such as receptionist or secretarial).

Step 4. Select activity cost drivers that link activity costs to the organization's products, services, and customers.

The goal of identifying a cost driver for an activity is to determine the source that causes the consumption of that activity—what drives the activity. The cost driver identified must be quantifiable and reasonably accessible. The three activities and the related cost drivers are discussed next.

FILLING WORK ORDERS

The first activity identified was "filling work orders." As stated earlier, customer service coordinators begin to fill work orders once a customer calls in a request for a temporary employee. If a customer does not call in an order, there is no work order to fill. It makes sense then that the cost driver for the "filling work orders" activity is the number of temporaries ordered by customers. This is used as the cost driver instead of the number of orders generated because an individual order can be for more than one temporary

employee. The more temporaries on an order, the more servicing of the account is required. Thus, the number of temporaries ordered is a better indicator of resources consumed by the activity than the number of orders.

HIRING TEMPORARY EMPLOYEES

The company cannot hire temporaries unless someone comes in seeking employment. The cost driver used for "hiring temporary employees" is the number of applicants seeking employment. Each person seeking employment at TEC requires significant resources and time before he/she is eligible for a job assignment.

Table 1: Four Steps in Developing an ABC System

1. Develop the activity dictionary.

2. Determine how much the organization is spending on each of its activities.

3. Identify the organization's products, services, and customers.

4. Select activity cost drivers that link activity costs to the organization's products, services, and customers.

R. S. Kaplan and R. Cooper, Cost & Effect: Using Integrated Cost Systems to Drive Profitability and Performance, Harvard Business School Press, Boston, Mass, 1998.

PROCESSING PAYROLL/BILLING

Processing a paycheck for each employee and generating an invoice for each customer is performed weekly and is based on the number of hours worked. Because each hour worked requires this activity, the number of hours worked during the period in question appears to be the best cost driver for the "processing payroll/ billing" activity.

Step 5. Calculate activity rates for each activity identified.

TEC added another step, which was to calculate the activity rate for each activity identified. The following activity rates were calculated (see Table 2):

Filling work orders $48.2390

Hiring temporary employees $26.5710

Processing payroll/billing $ 0.1655

The information collected from these five steps was used to assess TEC's profitability at the customer level. Customer profitability analysis was conducted

in three stages. The first stage assessed customer-channel profitability (industrial and clerical channels). In the second stage, the information obtained from the first stage was used to assess classes of customers within each channel. Finally, the third stage involved assessing the profitability of individual customers.

CHANNEL PROFITABILITY

Table 3 displays the profitability picture by customer channel. When the gross margins are examined, major differences between the channels become apparent. TEC's margin in the industrial channel is significantly less than its margin in the clerical channel. The industrial customers demand lower rates for temporary employees, but the tight labor market prevents TEC from lowering wage rates.

Blocher, Stout, Cokins, Chen: *Cost Management, 4e*

Table 2: Temp Employment Company, Inc. Activity-Rate Calculations

ACCOUNT NAME	TOTAL	FILLING WORK ORDERS	HIRING TEMPORARIES	PROCESSING PAYROLL	GENERAL OVERHEAD	TOTAL ALLOCATED
Salaries & wages	$ 125,638	$ 57,501	$ 16,197	$ 12,308	$ 39,632	$ 125,638
Payroll taxes	11,192	5,118	1,442	1,095	3,537	11,192
Advertising	55,896	25,494	30,402	—	—	55,896
Automotive	15,718	7,722	—	—	7,996	15,718
Telephone	11,746	7,048	2,349	2,349	—	11,746
Rent	9,600	2,400	2,400	4,800	—	9,600
Other Operating Expenses	91,144	10,760	1,961	4,305	74,118	91,144
Total Operating Expenses	$ 320,934	$ 116,043	$ 54,751	$ 24,857	$ 125,283	$ 320,934
Allocation of General Overhead		74,307	35,059	15,917	(125,283)	$ —
	$ 320,934	$ 190,350	$ 89,810	$ 40,774	$ —	$ 320,934
Cost drivers						
# of temporaries ordered		3,948				
# of applicants			3,380			
# of hours worked				246,370		
Activity rates		$ 48.239	$26.571	$ 0.1655		

Also, industrial customers have significantly higher workers' compensation rates than clerical customers, which we will discuss later. Customers in the clerical channel demand quality over price, so a higher bill-to-pay rate is permissible. In allocating activity cost between channels for the "hiring temporary employees" activity, the CFO discovered there was no easily accessible procedure for determining if an applicant applied for clerical or industrial employment. That information is documented only if the applicant is hired by TEC. For the initial analysis, the CFO decided to use the ratio of the number of temporaries ordered by channel to total temporaries ordered across both channels multiplying this ratio by the total number of applicants provided the number of applicants for each channel.

There is some logic with the formula. The number of temporaries ordered determines the types of temporaries needed; this, in turn, forces the firm to focus its energies on hiring those types of temporaries. In other words, there is a close relationship between the number of temporaries ordered and the type of individuals applying for employment at TEC. Procedures were instituted to capture the relevant information during the application process to assign "hiring temporary employees" costs more accurately to the appropriate channel in the future. As shown in Table 3, the industrial channel comprises only 16% of total company profits, while its sales are over 86% of total company sales. The channel's net profit is only 0.3% of sales. In sharp contrast, the clerical side shows profits of 8.2% of sales. From the initial analysis of Table 3, the CFO began to see potential signs of trouble. TEC's largest customer channel is on the verge of going into the red. The clerical channel does not have enough sales to support the entire company for any length of time. Conclusion: The industrial channel must be an income producer for the overall success of the company. The initial analysis shows overall signs of weakness, but the CFO decided to analyze the industrial channel in more detail by applying ABC to the three classes of customers in the industrial channel to identify problems better.

Table 3: Temp Employment Company, Inc. Profitability Analysis by Customer Channels

	CLERICAL	%	INDUSTRIAL	%	TOTAL	%
Sales	$ 294,714	100.0%	$ 1,859,952	100.0%	$2,154,566	100.0%
Cost of Sales						
Wages–Temporary employees	200,377	68.0%	1,323,827	71.2%	1,524,204	70.7%
Payroll taxes & fees	28,629	9.7%	251,879	13.5%	280,508	13.0%
Total cost of sales	229,006	77.7%	1,575,706	84.7%	1,804,712	83.8%
Gross margin	65,708	22.3%	284,146	15.3%	349,854	16.2%
OVERHEAD ALLOCATIONS						
Filling work orders:						
Number of Temporaries ordered	508		3,438		3,946	
X						
Activity rate	$ 48.239		$ 48.239		$ 48.239	
	24,505	8.3%	165,846	8.9%	190,351	8.8%
Hiring temporary employees:						
Number of applicants	3,380		3,380		3,380	
X						
% of orders to total	12.9%		87.1%		100%	
Applicants by channel	436		2,944		3,380	
X						
Activity rate	$ 26.571		$ 26.571		$ 26.571	
	11,595	3.9%	78,225	4.2%	89,810	4.2%
Processing payroll/billing:						
Hours worked	32,890		213,480		246,370	
X						
Activity rate	$ 0.1655		$ 0.1655		$ 0.1655	
	5,443	1.8%	35,331	1.9%	40,774	1.9%
Total overhead allocation	41,534	14.1%	279,402	15.0%	320,936	14.9%
Net profit	$ 24,174	8.2%	$ 4,744	0.3%	$ 28,918	1.3%

INDUSTRIAL CLASS PROFITABILITY

By examining the composition of the industrial channel, the CFO discovered it was possible to divide the channel into three classifications by workers' compensation (WC) rates. As previously stated, the industrial customers are charged a much higher workers' compensation rate than clerical customers. In addition, there is a wide range of rates charged within the industrial channel. The industrial customers are divided into three classes by workers' compensation rates: Low WC class (WC rates under $5.00/$1,000 of wages paid), Average WC class (WC rates $5.00 to $8.99/$1,000 of wages paid), and High WC class (WC rates $9.00 and over/$1,000 of wages paid). Table 4 displays the cost allocation of the industrial channel by workers' compensation rates.

Low WC class

The Low WC rate class is 20% of the total industrial channel, but it is responsible for over 400% of the industrial channel profits. An obvious conclusion is that the company is incurring losses elsewhere (i.e., the Low WC rate class is subsidizing other unprofitable customers). TEC budgeted an 18% gross margin for the industrial channel; the Low WC

Blocher, Stout, Cokins, Chen: *Cost Management, 4e*

©The McGraw-Hill Companies, Inc 2008

class's gross margin is in line with the budget. From this analysis, the Low WC class appears to be contributing to the overall success and profits of the company. The goal of TEC should be to maintain the current pricing arrangements for these customers. The company also should look into targeting industries that would fall into this class to increase the sales volume and, in turn, the net profits of the company.

High WC class

As expected, the gross margin is lower in the High WC class than in the other classes due to the large increase in the WC rate. What is surprising, however, is that the wages paid to the temporary employees are over 73% of sales as compared to just over 70% for Low WC class employees. Ideally, higher rates should be charged to customers with higher variable costs, but the company is unable to do so because of the competitive nature of the industry. The low gross margin is partly attributable to one customer who accounts for nearly 70% of the total sales generated in this class. The customer, a trailer manufacturer, is a consistent user of long-term temporaries. TEC conceded a price break to the customer due to the high-volume use of temporaries. The High WC class generates a net profit even with the low gross margin. The overhead allocation is significantly less than with the other two classes because of the long-term nature of the assignments of the temporary employees in this class. Only 165 temporaries were ordered during the period of analysis. The low number of temporaries ordered (the cost driver for the "filling work orders" activity) results in the class being allocated less cost for the "filling work orders" activity.

Average WC Class

The last class in the industrial channel to examine, the Average WC class, is suffering from a net loss. The largest class in relation to total sales volume, it is also allocated over 77% of the overhead costs based on the activity analysis and is responsible for only 69% of the industrial sales. Is the Average WC class being penalized with excessive overhead allocation? No. The customers in the Average WC class consume considerable time and effort to service. The typical job assignments within this class vary from one day to several weeks. Customers order from one to more than 20 temporaries for these assignments, and customer service coordinators are continually searching for temporaries to fill these jobs. The firm's classified advertisements heavily recruit for employees in this class, and the heavy recruitment means more individuals apply for employment. The Average WC class should be allocated a large portion of overhead. The activity analysis accomplishes that task. Examining the net profits shown in Table 4 demonstrates the classic whale-curve effect. The Low WC class generates over 400% of total profits while the Average WC class loses over 400% of total profits. This leaves the profits generated by the High WC class comprising nearly 100% of the industrial channel profits. Even at this second stage of analysis, areas that need further investigation are revealed.

Table 4: Temp Employment Company, Inc.
Profitability Analysis by Industrial Channel Classes

	LOW WC RATES	%	AVERAGE WC RATES	%	HIGH WC RATES	%	TOTAL	%
Sales	$ 369,911	100.0%	$ 1,290,194	100.0%	$ 209,757	100.0%	$ 1,859,852	100.0%
Cost of Sales								
Wages–Temporary employees	260,019	70.3%	909,247	71.0%	154,561	73.7%	1,323,827	71.2%
Payroll taxes & fees	43,284	11.7%	174,037	13.6%	34,558	16.5%	251,879	13.5%
Total cost of sales	303,303	82.0%	1,083,284	84.6%	189,119	90.2%	1,575,708	84.7%
Gross margin	$ 66,608	18.0%	$ 196,900	15.4%	$ 20,638	9.8%	$ 284,146	15.3%
OVERHEAD ALLOCATIONS								
Filling work orders:								
Number of Temporaries ordered	554		2,719		165		3,438	
X								
Activity rate	$ 48.239		$ 48.239		$ 48.239		$ 48.239	
	26,724	7.2%	131,162	10.2%	7,959	3.8%	165,848	8.9%
Hiring temporary employees:								
Number of applicants	2,944		2,944		2,944		2,944	
X								
% of orders to total	16.1%		79.1%		4.8%		100%	
Applicants by channel	474		2,329		141		2,944	
X								
Activity rate	$ 26.571		$ 26.571		$ 26.571		$ 26.571	
	12,594	3.4%	61,876	4.8%	3,755	1.8%	78,225	4.2%
Processing payroll/billing:								
Hours worked	45,140		146,023		22,317		213,490	
X								
Activity rate	$ 0.1655		$ 0.1655		$ 0.1655		$ 0.1655	
	7,471	2.0%	24,167	1.9%	3,693	1.8%	35,331	1.9%
Total overhead allocation	46,789	12.6%	217,205	17.0%	15,408	7.3%	279,402	15.0%
Net profit	$ 19,819	5.4%	$ (20,305)	-1.6%	$ 5,230	2.5%	$ 4,744	0.3%

CUSTOMER PROFITABILITY

Table 5 summarizes the activity analysis of the four largest customers of TEC according to sales volume. The four customers account for almost 42% of the total sales volume of the company and over 48% of the industrial channel sales. Using activity-based costing, an analysis of these four customers was undertaken to uncover problem areas with them.

Chemical Company

TEC supplies 100% of the chemical company's production and supervisory personnel. Initial results indicate a net profit of 9.8%, much higher than even the clerical channel net-profit percentage. One reason for this is the low overhead allocation to this customer. For example, under the "filling work orders" activity, only 86 temporaries were ordered, a relatively low number. One of the reasons for this is the long-term nature of the assignments. Another reason is the hiring practices of the company. The chemical company has one person on-site to recruit employees. Once the chemical company hires a recruit, TEC is notified about the new employee, and the application is sent to him or her. For these two reasons, the overhead consumed by the chemical company is minimal as compared to other customers. As long as the company continues the use of an on-

Blocher, Stout, Cokins, Chen: *Cost Management, 4e*

site coordinator to recruit, it should continue to generate profits for TEC.

Trailer Manufacturer

Similar to the chemical company, the trailer manufacturer requests long-term employees. Orders for the trailer manufacturer are for normal turnover and peak periods of production. For the period under examination, only 56 temporaries were ordered, normal for the time of year. The gross margin for the customer is uncomfortably low due to the billing arrangement with the customer and the high WC rates incurred. Because the customer does not consume a large portion of the activities identified, however, it is not burdened with a high overhead allocation and is generating just over 3% net profit. As long as the trailer manufacturer maintains the low consumption of activities, TEC should be able to maintain the current profit level.

Newspaper Publisher

The newspaper company is a good example of the typical customer in the Average WC class. It manages its temporary employment needs differently from the other two customers discussed. The customer calls daily to order the number of temporaries needed that night, usually ranging from 10 to 40 individuals. Customer service coordinators are constantly searching for temporaries to fill the needs of this customer. The newspaper publisher consumes a significantly higher proportion of activities than the other two customers. One of the peculiar situations regarding this company is the standing request by a few of the temporary employees themselves to work at the newspaper publisher. As a result, the customer service coordinators only have to call the temporaries and ask what shift they want to work. Even though the company requested 928 temporaries during the time period investigated, some of those requests were filled rather easily. How was the situation handled by the activity-based costing model? Basically, the situation was ignored. The newspaper company was allocated the same rate no matter how easy or difficult it was for TEC to fill the orders. This was one of the deficiencies of the activity analysis performed by the CFO. Table 5 illustrates some startling results for the newspaper publisher, the first being the low gross margin. The culprit is the low ratio of bill-to-pay rates. TEC was required to lower its rates to retain the customer. The low bill rates along with the high overhead allocation result in a large net-loss situation. The company is allocated 27% of the "filling work orders" activity while accounting for just over 6% of the industrial channel's revenue. A similar pattern holds true for the "hiring temporaries" activity. Some tough decisions must be addressed regarding the future of servicing the newspaper publisher.

Food Processing Company

The company uses temporary employees for its production line on a consistent basis throughout the year, with a mix of long- and short-term assignments. As displayed in Table 5, the company generated higher sales than the newspaper publisher, but it only had requests for 332 temporaries as compared to 928. The gross margin for the food processor is the highest among the customers examined, but the high gross margin does not offset the activities consumed by the customer. The bottom-line result is a net loss. As with the newspaper publisher, TEC must address the net-loss situation.

Table 5: Temp Employment Company, Inc.
Profitability Analysis by Selected Customers

	CHEMICAL COMPANY	%	TRAILER MANUFACTURER	%	NEWSPAPER PUBLISHER	%	FOOD PROCESSOR	%
Sales	$ 466,733	100.0%	$ 145,764	100.0%	$ 122,604	100.0%	$ 167,327	100.0%
Cost of Sales								
Wages--Temporary employees	341,620	73.2%	110,473	75.8%	92,205	75.2%	120,451	72.0%
Payroll taxes & fees	65,366	14.0%	24,350	16.7%	18,621	15.2%	23,411	14.0%
Total cost of sales	406,986	87.2%	134,823	92.5%	110,826	90.4%	143,862	86.0%
Gross margin	$ 59,747	12.8%	$ 10,941	7.5%	$ 11,778	9.6%	$ 23,465	14.0%
OVERHEAD ALLOCATIONS								
Filling work orders:								
Number of Temporaries ordered X	86		56		928		332	
Activity rate	$ 48.239		$ 48.239		$ 48.239		$ 48.239	
	4,149	0.9%	2,701	1.9%	44,766	36.5%	16,015	9.6%
Hiring temporary employees:								
Number of applicants X	2,944		2,944		2,944		2,944	
% of orders to total	2.5%		1.6%		27.0%		9.7%	
Applicants by channel X	74		47		794		285	
Activity rate	$ 26.571		$ 26.571		$ 26.571		$ 26.571	
	1,954	0.4%	1,250	0.9%	21,099	17.2%	7,580	4.5%
Processing payroll/billing:								
Hours worked X	47,371		15,113		13,000		22,762	
Activity rate	$ 0.1655		$ 0.1655		$ 0.1655		$ 0.1655	
	7,840	1.7%	2,501	1.7%	2,152	1.8%	3,767	2.3%
Total overhead allocation	13,942	3.0%	6,453	4.4%	68,017	55.5%	27,363	16.4%
Net profit	$ 45,805	9.8%	$ 4,488	3.1%	$ (56,239)	-45.9%	$ (3,898)	-2.3%

Blocher, Stout, Cokins, Chen: *Cost Management, 4e*

©The McGraw-Hill Companies, Inc 2008

FINAL ANALYSIS

The activity analysis conducted by the CFO generated some startling results. It reaffirmed some beliefs and destroyed others held by TEC's management. The company held to the notion that the sales composition of the company was 60% industrial and 40% clerical. Table 3 clearly indicates the composition as 85% industrial and 15% clerical. This is one explanation for the overall weak profit. As explained earlier, the industrial customers traditionally generate lower profits. Driving the analysis to the industrial channel class provides a richer description of TEC's profitability picture. Table 4 shows that the largest industrial class, the Average WC class, is generating significant losses. In other words, almost 70% of the company's business is generating losses. What can be done to reverse this situation? An immediate response might be to attempt to increase the bill rates charged, but the industrial temporary employment industry is very elastic, and any attempt at increasing rates will produce an immediate decrease in demand. Another area of concern is the pay rates. TEC has been forced to increase the pay rates due to the low unemployment rate. The pool of temporary employees is small, so they demand a higher rate. Because the company cannot raise billing rates or lower pay rates, the only area available for improvement is overhead reduction. Some revealing results are encountered in Table 5. TEC's first problem is with the newspaper publisher. The bill rates and pay rates are fixed, so can the overhead allocated to this customer be lowered? One way is to change the way the customer requests and uses temporaries. As mentioned earlier, the customer calls daily with an order for temporaries and is unconcerned whether the temporaries are new or repeats. A preferred method would have the customer call, or be called, once a week with an order for the entire week. The temporaries could be assigned on a weekly basis. Also, an analysis of the number of temporaries usually ordered would be helpful to determine if a small core of long-term assignments could be employed. This method would reduce the consumption of activities by the customer and turn it into a profitable venture for TEC. A key point: A reduction in the overhead allocated to a customer will not, in and of itself, reduce the overhead incurred by the company. Activity-based costing does not reduce costs—it only reallocates them based on the consumption of activities identified. As a result, a customer who begins to consume fewer activities without the simultaneous reduction in overhead by the company will only result in a shifting of overhead allocation to another customer, creating a possible death spiral effect. Once a customer consumes fewer activities, the company must either permanently remove the associated overhead to benefit from the reduction in costs consumed by the customer or utilize the freed capacity to generate additional revenue. Overall, the activity analysis described here has shown that activity-based costing can be used as a strategic tool. It produced useful information to provide management with direction for costing and marketing strategies. The ABC model used will allow for better informed decision making at TEC. Traditionally, TEC used gross margin analysis to set prices and develop budgets. Now it can use ABC for setting prices and developing budgets. This case study also demonstrates that ABC information can be used for more than just costing products and services: It can be used to develop a firm's profitability picture. Developing strategic initiatives designed to transform TEC's unprofitable customers into profitable customers is the CFO's next challenge. In addition, the activity analysis will assist in bidding for contracts in the future. Before the ABC analysis, a bid was prepared without understanding the true cost of servicing the contract. As a result, the company was awarded contracts in the past that did not generate profits. By using ABC, the company can better understand the costs associated with servicing a contract and provide a competitive bid that, if won, will be profitably serviced.

ENDNOTES

1 J. N. Sheth, R. S. Sisodia, and A. Sharma, "The Antecedents and Consequences of Customer-Centric Marketing," *Journal of the Academy of Marketing Science*, Vol. 28, No. 1, 2000, pp. 55-66.

Chapter 6
Cost Estimation

Cases

Readings

"Applying Overhead: How to Find the Right Bases and Rates"
This article shows an actual application of regression analysis for determining multiple overhead rates using spreadsheet software. The steps and the results are very similar to EXCEL which has regression under TOOLS/ADD-INS/DATA ANALYSIS. The article explains the interpretation of the R-squared and t-values and provides a good discussion of when regression analysis is useful.

Discussion Questions:
1. What is regression analysis used to accomplish in this article?
2. What are the steps to perform a simple regression analysis?
3. What does Table 7 tell you? Which cost driver would you pick for each cost type—maintenance, packaging, materials handling, storage, and production scheduling?

Cases

6-1 The High-Low Method and Regression Analysis

The Brenham General Hospital was approached by Health Food, Inc. (HFI) which specializes in the preparation of meals for institutional patients. HFI stated that it would prepare all inpatient meals to provider specifications and deliver them on time for $11.50 per meal. The hospital was facing a steady decline in bed occupancy and was determined to hold the line on costs wherever possible.

Hospital management did not have a clear idea what the present system of providing meals to patients was costing. Hospital staff gathered the information below, which covered expenses for the dietary department for the past year.

The hospital has 120 beds. It is open year-round and has a 33% percent occupancy rate. Patients are served an average of 2.8 meals per occupancy day.

It was determined that the dietitian provided valuable counseling and advising services. Should the hospital eliminate in house meal preparation, it would want to retain her services. Also, the administration wanted to keep and maintain the kitchen and equipment.

REQUIRED:

1. Using the high-low method and regression analysis, determine the variable and fixed costs of the in-house meal service.
2. Which cost estimation method would you choose and why?
3. Should the hospital administration accept the offer of the outside company? Why or why not?

	Dietitian	Other staff	Food Costs	Maintenance	Patient Equipment	Days
January	$2,875	$ 3,122	$ 9,674	$ 1,401	$ 1,649	1,382
February	$2,875	$ 2,908	$ 9,184	$ 1,322	$ 1,415	1,312
March	$2,875	$ 2,655	$ 8,302	$ 1,322	$ 1,313	1,186
April	$2,875	$ 2,600	$ 7,084	$ 1,288	$ 1,105	1,012
May	$2,875	$ 2,433	$ 6,398	$ 1,200	$ 1,089	914
June	$2,875	$ 2,083	$ 4,338	$ 1,133	$ 1,011	604
July	$2,875	$ 1,809	$ 3,612	$ 1,093	$ 900	516
August	$2,875	$ 2,322	$ 6,275	$ 1,122	$ 1,112	896
September	$2,875	$ 1,434	$ 6,734	$ 1,235	$ 1,103	962
October	$2,875	$ 2,700	$ 9,002	$ 1,302	$ 1,300	1,286
November	$2,875	$ 2,798	$ 8,456	$ 1,300	$ 1,442	1,208
December	$2,875	$ 2,600	$ 7,798	$ 1,322	$ 1,396	1,114
TOTAL	$34,500	$29,464	$86,857	$15,040	$14,835	12,392

Blocher, Stout, Cokins, Chen: *Cost Management, 4e*

6-2 The Pump Division

The Pump Division has one plant dedicated to the design and manufacture of large, highly technical, customized pumps. Typically the contract life (production cycle) is one to three years. Most original equipment (OE) orders are obtained by preparing and submitting a bid proposal from a cost estimate analysis and conducting negotiating sessions with the customer. Sometimes orders are accepted as loss leaders in order to establish a position in the more profitable aftermarket business.

The contracts generally are fixed price. When coupled with the highly technical specifications and the length of the "in process" time, there is a high risk of job cost overruns. Company policy is to record revenue and costs on a completed contract basis, rather than as a percent of completion.

After a major decline in profitability, combined with several unfavorable year-end surprise inventory adjustments, new plant management decided to undertake a review of the operation to identify the key factors that affect inventory control. Management analysis revealed the following:

- The cost estimating function reported to the sales department.
- Final job costs varied significantly from original cost estimates. It was difficult to determine the source of variances until analyses were made upon completion of the jobs.
- The negotiated pricing of a contract was almost always on the basis of "whatever it takes to get the order," particularly when there was excess productive capacity in the industry.
- Progress payments/advanced payments were secured on some contracts, but such payments often were dropped if pricing competition was severe.
- When inflation was at double-digit levels, the company attempted to insert escalation clauses into contracts based on government indexes. However, most often, this resulted in fixed-price contracts with some estimate of inflation included.
- During the audit at the end of each year, a lower-of-cost-or-market analysis was made on major jobs in process. It was this exercise that revealed unfavorable inventory adjustments in recent years. Two examples are shown below:

(In Thousands)	Job 1	Job 2
Original cost Estimate	$2,113	$1,800
Costs Incurred to Date:		
Manufacturing	2,100	—
Engineering	373	100
Estimate to Complete	367	2,500
Total Current Estimate	2,840	2,600
Lower-of-cost-or-market: Contract Sales Price	2,520	2,000
Less 10% Allowance for Normal Profit Margin	(252)	(200)
Inventory Value	2,268	1,800
Inventory Reserve Adjustment (loss)	$ (572)	$ (800)

On job 2, the engineering department determined that the pump would not meet specifications in accordance with the original cost estimate and re-engineered the pump. This led to an increased estimate before the job entered the manufacturing stage.

REQUIRED:

1. What courses of action might be appropriate for the plant manager and his controller relating to (a) estimating costs, and (b) application of the lower of cost or market rule?
2. What is the significance of progress payments/advanced payments and escalation clauses on the performance of the operation?

6-3 Laurent Products

Laurent Products is a manufacturer of plastic packaging products with plants located throughout Europe and customers worldwide. "There is no doubt that the need to continue to grow sales is an important corporate objective and one which we need to always have in mind," remarked Arnoud Baynard, managing director. "Not only is this important in terms of continuing to increase sales revenue overall but it is an essential part of our commitment for next year's budget. Resisting group pressure and allowing ourselves this time to test the market for other new segments has brought some order into this phase of our development. The segment penetration achieved so far and the opportunity to build on this most successful initiative augers well for the future. Thank you, George, for a comprehensive summary of the market result to date" concluded Arnoud. "It seems as though this initiative is one which will help us meet out short and longer-term objectives." Arnoud Baynard's summary concerned a strategy overview provided by George St. Marc, marketing director of the company.

MARKETING STRATEGY

During the past ten years Laurent Products has successfully developed a line of packaging materials and a unique bagging system which present an important opportunity to increase the productivity of checkout counters in grocery stores. The plastic bags manufactured by Laurent are produced in several sizes, different plastic film colors, and may have attractive multi-color printed designs on one or both sides to meet the specification of a particular grocery store. The company concentrated its efforts in selling to the top twenty grocery market chains in Europe. By limiting its marketing efforts to a relatively few, very large multi-outlet grocery chains (which have centralized purchasing groups), the company achieved low marketing and selling costs but high market penetration. Last year the company reached a market share of 65% in the large grocery chain market and, in turn, relatively large customer order sizes. Two market segments are evident in the large grocery chain market. In the first (called the value added segment) customers buy the company's product primarily because of its advantage in reducing operating costs at checkout counters. The advantages provided by the Laurent bagging system include the lower cost of bags and labor costs of running the checkout counter as well as improved customer service. Frequently, the store operations personnel in this segment are active in making the buying decision. The second segment is referred to as being price sensitive as the customers purchase these products primarily on the basis of price. For these customers, purchasing managers are the key decision-makers in the buying decision.

RECENT COMPETITION

Laurent's success in the grocery chain market has attracted an increasing number of competitors into the market. While the company had been very successful in bringing out a series of new product types with innovative labor-saving features for the grocery stores, the competitors have eventually been able to develop quite similar products. The result has been increased competition with a substantial reduction in Laurent's prices (dropping 26% last year), and a major decline in the firms' profit margin. The size of the price sensitive segment is growing rapidly while the value added market segment is shrinking in size. The company faces an increasingly competitive market situation characterized by significant excess producer capacity.

WHOLESALE MARKET INITIATIVE

As a result of the increased competition in the grocery chain market, George has proposed to begin to a focus on the small independent grocery stores who purchase bags from large wholesale distributors. The potential sales for this wholesaler segment is about the same size as the grocery chain market (20 billion bags per year versus 25 billion bags per year), but includes a much larger number of independent store customers. At this time less than 15% of the bags sold in the wholesaler market are made of plastic. The independent grocery stores differ from the large grocery chains in that they purchase their grocery bags from wholesalers and distributors. Compared to the grocery chains, there are many more independent grocery store outlets widely dispersed over a large geographical area. The pilot marketing studies run last year by Laurent indicate that the customer order sizes for the wholesaler segment tend to be relatively small, and that the number of different product variations (in terms for example of print color, film color, and print type) tend to be relatively large in comparison with the

Blocher, Stout, Cokins, Chen: *Cost Management, 4e*

grocery chain market. These studies also indicate that prices (and corresponding profit margins) are much higher than in the price sensitive segment currently served by the company.

MANUFACTURING

To support domestic and export sales, the company has located a number of plants throughout Europe to best support the geographical spread of the supermarket and hypermarket outlets of its various customers. "In the early years," explained Marcel Ray, manufacturing director, "capacity had, by necessity, always chased demand. The rapid growth in sales during the past few years and the need to make major decisions concerning new plant locations and process investments had understandably contributed to this capacity following the demand situation. However, with sales starting to level off this problem of capacity has now corrected itself."

Investments in manufacturing had been to support two principal objectives; to increase capacity and to reduce costs. The cost reduction initiatives principally concerned material costs and reduced processing times. "Current initiatives," explained Marcel "are continuing these themes. Our capacity uplifts will take the form of equipment similar to our existing machines. Over the years we have deliberately chosen to invest in machines which are similar to existing equipment in order to capitalize on the fact that the process is relatively simple and that products can, with relatively few exceptions, be processed on any machine in the plant. The only major restriction is the number of colors which a machine can accommodate on a single pass. Future investment proposals now being considered are based on this rationale."

In order to make best use of total capacity at all sites, customer orders are collated at the head office site in Lyon. They are then allocated to plants to take account of current plant loading, available capacity, customer lead times, and transport distances between the plant and a customer's required delivery location. As a result, forward loading on a plant is only two or, at most three days ahead. Plants then schedule these orders into their production processes in order to meet customer call-offs and individual equipment loading rules.

Once the printing details are agreed with a customer, a plate is produced and checked. In line with a call-off schedule, the plates are allocated to machines. Color changes (where necessary) are also part of the setup details. Table 1 provides an actual schedule of orders for four different bagging lines which is representative of the operations in the Paris Plant (and also for the company's other plants).

CONCLUDING REMARKS

In reviewing the proposed marketing initiatives regarding the wholesaler market, Arnoud Baynard, commented, "Since sales in our traditional markets are leveling off, the new marketing initiative appears to be an important step in giving us a fresh impetus to sales volume growth. We have now reached a point in our company where we do not have to endure capacity shortage problems. In fact, with the drop in sales last year, the company currently has excess capacity with which to pursue the wholesaler market. So, our main concern is to improve the decline in the profit performance that has occurred during the past year, and the new marketing initiatives should help to restore the profit margins and hence to secure this necessary, overall improvement."

REQUIRED

1. Discuss briefly Laurent's competitive position and strategy.
2. What are the implications of the marketing and manufacturing initiatives undertaken by Laurent?
3. How does Laurent's strategy deal effectively with global competition in its business. How should it?
4. Using the data in Table 1 and appropriate methods of analysis such as regression, analyze the effect of order size and product variety on the productivity and cost structure of the Paris plant.

TABLE 1

Machine Number	Prod. Order Quantity	Print Type Complexity	Per unit Downtime & Setup	Per Unit Runtime	Total Setup & Downtime	Total Runtime	Total Variable Cost/Unit
2	480	1	0.0023	0.0423	1.10	20.30	7.04
2	489	1	0.0001	0.0434	0.07	21.20	6.99
2	480	1	0.0054	0.0419	2.60	20.10	6.99
4	180	1	0.0039	0.0400	0.70	7.20	6.97
4	2160	2	0.0022	0.0355	4.70	76.60	6.94
4	1377	2	0.0023	0.0405	3.10	55.70	6.95
4	120	2	0.0042	0.0400	0.50	4.80	6.97
4	540	2	0.0026	0.0413	1.40	22.30	6.97
4	360	2	0.0142	0.0411	5.10	14.80	6.98
4	1080	2	0.0111	0.0376	12.00	40.60	7.01
4	300	2	0.0037	0.0430	1.10	12.90	7.03
4	2400	2	0.0046	0.0345	11.00	82.90	7.05
4	81	2	0.0457	0.0407	3.70	3.30	7.09
8	360	1	0.0022	0.0425	0.80	15.30	7.82
8	120	1	0.0017	0.0433	0.20	5.20	7.83
8	120	1	0.0067	0.0417	0.80	5.00	8.17
8	60	1	0.0083	0.0417	0.50	2.50	8.83
8	240	1	0.0079	0.0425	1.90	10.20	7.94
8	60	1	0.0050	0.0467	0.30	2.80	7.97
8	240	1	0.0008	0.0583	0.20	14.00	8.2
8	120	1	0.0183	0.0433	2.20	5.20	8.09
8	60	1	0.0183	0.0433	1.10	2.60	7.93
8	480	1	0.0106	0.0435	5.10	20.90	8.23
8	240	2	0.0054	0.0413	1.30	9.90	7.91
8	537	2	0.0047	0.0423	2.50	22.70	7.87
8	420	2	0.0060	0.0421	2.50	17.70	7.89
8	1182	2	0.0150	0.0416	17.70	49.20	7.89
8	60	2	0.0550	0.0483	3.30	2.90	8.83
8	180	2	0.0122	0.0422	2.20	7.60	7.9
8	60	2	0.0417	0.0400	2.50	2.40	7.9
8	240	2	0.0067	0.0429	1.60	10.30	7.86
8	60	2	0.0083	0.0417	0.50	2.50	7.93
8	41	2	0.0293	0.0463	1.20	1.90	7.96
8	60	2	0.0417	0.0467	2.50	2.80	8
8	120	2	0.0117	0.0467	1.40	5.60	8.08
8	60	2	0.0617	0.0417	3.70	2.50	7.9
8	60	2	0.0433	0.0433	2.60	2.60	8
8	360	2	0.0108	0.0428	3.90	15.40	8.01
8	120	2	0.0200	0.0467	2.40	5.60	7.97
8	180	2	0.0144	0.0494	2.60	8.90	8.15
8	60	2	0.0233	0.0433	1.40	2.60	8.27
8	60	2	0.0400	0.0400	2.40	2.40	8.55
8	60	2	0.0417	0.0433	2.50	2.60	8.66
8	60	2	0.0467	0.0467	2.80	2.80	8.17
8	60	4	0.0483	0.0417	2.90	2.50	8.06
8	60	4	0.0150	0.0417	0.90	2.50	8.55
8	60	4	0.0583	0.0417	3.50	2.50	8.11
8	120	4	0.0167	0.0450	2.00	5.40	8.17
8	60	4	0.0567	0.0400	3.40	2.40	8.06
13	120	1	0.0050	0.0392	0.60	4.70	6.98
13	717	1	0.0043	0.0411	3.10	29.50	7
13	1500	1	0.0063	0.0427	9.50	64.10	7.08
13	2475	1	0.0091	0.0335	22.50	83.00	7.2
13	240	1	0.0100	0.0475	2.40	11.40	7.25
13	882	2	0.0178	0.0302	15.70	26.60	6.47
13	1677	2	0.0111	0.0361	18.60	60.50	7.04
13	243	2	0.0021	0.0457	0.50	11.10	7.05

Blocher, Stout, Cokins, Chen: *Cost Management, 4e*

©The McGraw-Hill Companies, Inc 2008

6-4 Regression Analysis

Custom Photography is a small company that provides photography services primarily for medium to large size local businesses. Most of the work is special assignments involving professional models, displays, and sets. At the end of 2006, Janice Glass, the owner of Custom Photography is interested in predicting the average hourly payroll cost of the professional models and others who work in the set-up and design of the photo sessions in 2007. In order to do this, she has taken the payroll costs for each of the prior 20 quarters and the approximate number of hours devoted to these photo sessions during the quarter.

The independent variable in this application is the number of hours for the sessions and the dependent variable is the payroll expense.

QU/YR	Hours	Payroll Expense
1/2002	145	5,122
2	90	3,011
3	25	1,203
4	175	5,188
1/2003	112	3,877
2	267	8,712
3	212	7,355
4	132	4,123
1/2004	289	9,938
2	235	7,327
3	156	5,592
4	277	9,387
1/2005	302	10,993
2	72	2,761
3	88	2,766
4	212	8,246
1/2006	155	5,499
2	222	7,729
3	116	3,892
4	250	8,473

Projected Data for hours:

QU/YR	Hours	Payroll Expense
1/2007	188	?
2	233	?
3	145	?
4	298	?

REQUIRED:

1. Develop a regression analysis to predict payroll costs, using Excel or equivalent regression software and the first 20 quarters of data. Evaluate the precision and reliability of the regression.
2. Predict payroll expense for each quarter of 2007.

Readings

6.1: Applying Overhead: How to Find the Right Bases and Rates

Determine the relationship between overhead costs and various cost drivers with the help of regression analysis.

By Adel M. Novin

Direct labor no longer may be the most effective base for applying factory overhead costs to various jobs and products. With today's highly automated systems, labor-related costs constitute only a small portion of total manufacturing costs, and overhead costs now correlate more with factors such as machine hours and material quantities. Accordingly, many companies are beginning to identify application bases that better reflect the causes of overhead costs in their unique manufacturing environments.

Selection of proper application bases also has received a boost from the recent growth in activity-based costing (ABC), ABC applies accumulated costs for each activity to products and jobs using a separate base for each activity. Thus, it is crucial to select the right bases (cost drivers) for applying the costs of various activities to products and jobs.

SEARCHING FOR A PROPER BASE

Theoretically, the factory overhead cost application base should be a principal cost driver—an activity (or activities) that causes factory overhead costs to be incurred. In other words, there should be a strong cause-and-effect relationship between the factory overhead costs incurred and the base chosen for their application. Selecting the proper base requires knowledge of the relationships between the overhead costs and various cost drivers such as machine hours, direct labor hours, direct labor costs, space occupied, pounds handled, invoices processed, number of component parts, number of setups, units produced, and material costs or material quantities.

Using an objective technique, regression analysis, rather than experience or observation of activities can be helpful in ascertaining the relationship between the overhead costs and various cost drivers. Regression analysis has not been explored fully in practice, possibly due to its computational complexities coupled with a lack of easily accessible computer software. With the widespread use of spreadsheet programs, however, regression analysis now can be performed rather easily. The regression analysis described below was done using a computer spreadsheet.

Regression analysis is one of the few quantitative techniques available for: (1) determining and analyzing the extent of the relationship between overhead costs and various cost drivers and (2) estimating the linear or curvilinear relationship between overhead costs and cost drivers. One of the values provided by regression analysis, the coefficient of determination or R Squared, measures the extent of the relationship between the two variables. More specifically, the value of R Squared indicates the percentage of variation in the dependent variable (overhead costs in this case) that is explained by variation in the independent variable (the cost driver). The value of R Squared is always between zero and 100%. The closer its value is to 100%, the stronger the relationship between the two variables.

Regression analysis can help us investigate the strength of the relationship between the overhead cost and various cost drivers. In simple terms, the cost driver that receives an R-Squared value closest to 100% will be the most accurate predictor of overhead costs. The following section will illustrate this concept.

To find the proper application base, the first step is to identify the various cost drivers that might explain changes in overhead costs. Suppose that in searching for an application base for overhead costs, we have found three possible cost drivers—direct labor hours, machine hours, and number of production setups.

Regression analysis requires actual data on selected variables for several periods. Suppose we have data from 12 consecutive months (with outliers excluded) on overhead costs, direct labor hours, machine hours, and number of production setups, as shown in Table 1.

With three possible cost drivers, three different regression analyses should be performed. Of course, a different output-range should be selected for each variable.

Table 2 presents the regression output obtained for the three regression analyses. According to the R-Squared values, machine hours explain about 77% of changes in variable overhead costs, while the number of set-ups and direct labor hours explain 39% and 29%, respectively. Thus, it appears that the most proper base for application of overhead costs in our example is machine hours because it has the strongest relationship with overhead costs.

CONSTRUCTION OF A SINGLE OVERHEAD RATE

Referring to the regression results in Table 2, "Constant" represents an estimate of the fixed portion of the overhead cost, while "X Coefficient(s)" represents an estimate of the variable rate of the overhead costs. For example, based on the regression results for machine hours, the estimated linear relationship between monthly overhead costs (OH) and machine hours (MH) can be presented by the following simple regression line: OH = \$72,794 + \$74.72 MH, where \$72,794 is an estimate of total monthly fixed overhead costs and \$74.72 is the rate for the application of variable overhead costs (i.e., \$74.72 per machine hour).

We then come to the question of how to assign the fixed portion of overhead costs to products and jobs. Often, a separate base that reflects the demands made by products and jobs on a firm's fixed resources is used to apply fixed costs to products and jobs. This base may be determined by engineering methods such as time and motion studies. In this case, there would be two rates based on two different bases for the application of overhead costs, one for fixed overhead and one for variable overhead costs.

TABLE 1			
DATA FOR REGRESSION ANALYSIS			
	A	B	C	D
1	FOH	DIR LABOR	MACHINE	NO. OF
2	COSTS	HOURS	HOURS	SETUPS
3	155,000	985	1,060	200
4	160,000	1,068	1,080	225
5	170,000	1,095	1,100	250
6	165,000	1,105	1,200	202
7	185,000	1,200	1,600	210
8	135,000	1,160	1,100	150
9	145,000	1,145	1,080	165
10	150,000	1,025	1,090	180
11	180,000	1,115	1,300	204
12	175,000	1,136	1,400	206
13	190,000	1,185	1,500	208
14	200,000	1,220	1,700	212

TABLE 2
REGRESSION OUTPUT

REGRESSION RESULTS FOR OVERHEAD COSTS WITH DL HOURS
Regression Output:

Constant		919.02
Std Err of Y Est		17,267.60
R Squared		0.29
No. of Observations		12
Degrees of Freedom		10
X Coefficient(s)	148.74	
Std Err of Coef.	74.35	

REGRESSION RESULTS FOR OVERHEAD COSTS WITH MACHINE HOURS
Regression Output:

Constant		72,793.81
Std Err of Y Est		9,799.08
R Squared		0.77
No. of Observations		12
Degrees of Freedom		10
X Coefficient(s)	74.72	
Std Err of Coef.	12.91	

REGRESSION RESULTS FOR OVERHEAD COSTS WITH NUMBER OF SETUPS
Regression Output:

Constant		74,033.14
Std Err of Y Est		15,909.72
R Squared		0.39
No. of Observations		12
Degrees of Freedom		10
X Coefficient(s)	465.00	
Std Err of Coef.	182.47	

CONSTRUCTION OF MULTIPLE OVERHEAD RATES

In a complex manufacturing environment, variable overhead costs may be driven by several equally important factors. Under such circumstances, the use of more than one base for the application of variable overhead costs to products and jobs results in a more accurate cost estimate. For example, the cost of one activity, material handling, may be applied to products based upon both the number of material requisitions and the number of parts per material requisition. To accommodate the use of more than one independent variable, we would need to perform a multiple regression. Thus, we can construct more than one overhead rate.

Continuing our prior example, suppose that we want to apply overhead costs based on the two cost drivers with the strongest relationship to overhead cost—machine hours and number of setups. To perform multiple regression analysis, follow the same steps as for performance of simple regression, except that the "X-Range" will consist of the range of observations for both machine hours and number of setups.

Table 3 presents the results for the multiple regression. "Constant" represents an estimate of the fixed overhead cost, while "X Coefficients" represent an estimate of the variable rates of the overhead costs. For example, the estimated relationship between the overhead costs (OH) and the two driving factors, machine hours (MH) and number of setups (NS), can be expressed by the following multiple regression line: OH = $19,796.43 + $65.44 MH + $322.21 NS, where $19,796.43 is an estimate of the total monthly fixed overhead costs, and $65.44 and $322.21 are the estimated variable overhead costs per machine hour and per setup, respectively. The value of R Squared for the multiple regression line is 95%, which is greater than that of the simple regression line based solely on machine hours (77%). This fact implies that the application of variable overhead costs based on both machine hours and number of setups would result in more accurate cost estimates.

Here, again, total fixed overhead costs may be applied to jobs and products either using a different base determined by engineering methods such as time and motion studies or using the same base as for variable overhead (machine hours and number

TABLE 3
MULTIPLE REGRESSION RESULTS FOR OVERHEAD COSTS WITH MACHINE HOURS AND NUMBER OF SETUPS

Regression Output:

Constant		19,796.43
Std Err of Y Est		4,951.11
R Squared		0.95
No. of Observations		12
Degrees of Freedom		9
X Coefficient(s)	65.44	322.21
Std Err of Coef.	6.74	58.66

of setups). Use of a separate base for the application of fixed costs would result in a total of three overhead rates, one for fixed overhead and two for variable overheads.

It is important to remember that the variable overhead rates computed by regression analysis (the "X Coefficients") are estimates derived from our 12 observations. The reliability of the estimated variable overhead rates can and should be determined by computing the t-test value for each rate. The t-test value equals the "X Coefficients" over the "Std Err of Coef." As a general rule, if the absolute value of the t-test for any variable rate is greater than two, then the estimated overhead rate is considered highly reliable. Referring to Table 3, for example, the value of the t-test for the variable overhead based on machine hours is about 5.8 (74.72/12.91), which tells us that the rate can be relied upon. The overhead sites determined from regression analysis, after adjusting for expected future inflation, would be usable as long as no major change in the cost structure and manufacturing process has occurred.

RATES FOR ACTIVITY-BASED COSTING

For more accurate product costing, firms are beginning to use activity-based costing for computing overhead costs. under this system, accumulated costs for each activity are applied to products and jobs using a separate base for each activity. in a manner similar to that described above, regression analysis can be used to investigate the strength of the relationship between various activities and cost drivers in order to determine the proper base(s) and rate(s) for applying the cost of each activity to products and jobs.

We also may use regression analysis to classify a large number of activities into a few groups (cost pools) based on common bases. Suppose that through use of simple regression analysis, we have computed the R-Squared values for the pairs of activities and cost drivers shown in Table 4. Based on the R-Squared values, we may group the five activities into two cost pools. It

appears that the principal cause of the packaging, materials handling and storage activities costs is pounds of materials. a few groups (cost pools) based on common bases. Suppose that through use of simple regression analysis, we have computed the R-Squared values for the pairs of activities and cost drivers shown in Thus, the cost pool consisting of the accumulated costs of these three activities can be applied to products and jobs based on number of pounds of materials used. Similarly, the accumulated costs of maintenance and production scheduling, which have a high correlation with machine hours, can be applied to products and jobs based on machine hours. In this way, all costs included in each cost pool will have the same cause-and-effect relationship with the chosen cost allocation base.

As business becomes increasingly more competitive, decision makers are demanding more accurate cost figures from cost accounting systems. For accurate costing, it is crucial that factory overhead and activity costs be applied to various products and jobs using bases that reflect principal causes of the overhead costs. Regression analysis has proved to be a practical, effective, and objective method for selecting proper cost application bases.

In addition to its usefulness for determining proper application bases, regression analysis is a practical method for developing single or multiple overhead rates for the application of overhead costs to products and jobs. With the widespread use of spreadsheet programs, regression analysis can be performed easily.

Note: The article was edited with the author's permission to use generic spreadsheet references.

TABLE 4 R-SQUARED VALUES FOR VARIOUS PAIRS OF ACTIVITIES AND COST DRIVERS					
	Maintenance	Packaging	Materials Handling	Storage	Production Scheduling
Machine Hours	.85	.46	.68	.45	.82
Pounds of Material	.38	.88	.90	.75	.43
Labor Hours	.30	.28	.38	.22	.43

Chapter 7
Cost-Volume-Profit Analysis

Cases

Readings

7-1: "Tools for Dealing with Uncertainty" by David R. Fordham, CMA, CPA, Ph.D and S. Brooks Marshall, CFA. DBA

This article explains how to use simulation methods within a spreadsheet program such as Excel to perform sensitivity analysis for a given decision context. The available spreadsheet simulation software systems include the programs Crystal Ball and @Risk, among others. These software systems allow the user to analyze the effect of uncertainty on the potential outcomes of a decision. These tools can be applied directly to CVP analysis. The tools allow the user to see the potential effect on the breakeven level or total profit of potential variations in the key uncertain factors in the analysis. The uncertain factors affecting breakeven might be the unknown level of unit variable cost, price or fixed cost. Also, in determining total profit, the unknown level of demand might be a key uncertain factor.

EXERCISE: Use a spreadsheet simulation tool such as Crystal Ball or @Risk to analyze the uncertain factors in given case situation. Cases 7-1,2 and 3 could be used for this exercise.

Cases

7-1 Cost-Volume-Profit Analysis and Strategy

Mr. Carter is the manager of Simmons Farm and Seed Company, a wholesaler of fertilizer, seed, and other farm supplies. The company has been successful in recent years primarily because of great customer service—flexible credit terms, customized orders (quantities, seed mix, etc), and on-time delivery, among others. Global Agricultural Products, Inc., Simmons' parent corporation, has informed Mr. Carter that his budgeted net income for the coming year will be $120,000. The budget was based on data for the prior year and Mr. Carter's belief that there would be no significant changes in revenues and expenses for the coming period.

After the determination of the budget, Carter received notice from Simmons' principal shipping agent that it was about to increase its rates by 10%. This carrier handles 90% of Simmons' total shipping volume. Paying the increased rate will result in failure to meet the budgeted income level, and Mr. Carter is understandably reluctant to allow that to happen. He is considering two alternatives. First, it is possible to use another carrier whose rates are 5% less than the old carrier's original rate. The old carrier, however, is a subsidiary of a major customer; shifting to a new carrier will almost certainly result in loss of that customer and sales amounting to $70,000.

Assume that prior to the recent rate increase, the shipping costs of the principal carrier and the other carriers were the same, and that costs of the other carriers are not expected to change.

As a second alternative, Simmons can purchase its own trucks thereby reducing its shipping costs to 85% of the original rate. The new trucks would have an expected life of 10 years, no salvage value and would be depreciated on a straight line basis. Related fixed costs excluding depreciation would be $2,000. Assume that if Simmons purchases the trucks, Simmons will replace the principal shipper and the other shippers.

Following are data from the prior year:

Sales	$1,500,000
Variable costs (excluding shipping)	1,095,000
Shipping costs	135,000
Fixed costs	150,000

REQUIRED:

1. Using cost-volume-profit analysis and the data provided, determine the maximum amount that Mr. Carter can pay for the trucks and still expect to attain budgeted net income.
2. At what price for the truck would Mr. Carter be indifferent between purchasing the new trucks and using a new carrier?
3. Mr. Carter has decided to use a new carrier, but now is worried its apparent lack of reliability may adversely affect sales volume. Determine the dollar amount of sales that Simmons can lose because of lack of reliability before any benefit from switching carriers is lost completely.
4. Describe what you think is the competitive strategy of Simmons Farm and Seed Company. What should be the strategy? How would the use of a new carrier affect the strategy?
5. Can Mr. Carter use value chain analysis to improve the profits of Simmons Farm and Seed Company? If so, explain how briefly.

7-2 Cost-Volume-Profit Analysis and Cost Estimation

The following requirement is based on information in the Atlantic City Casino case, case 2-33 at the end of Chapter 2. Re-read the case and complete the requirements below.

REQUIRED:

1. Using the data provided in the case, build a cost estimation model to predict net income based on total revenues. Then, use this model to determine an estimate of the industry-wide breakeven point in sales revenue. Evaluate the reliability and precision of the estimation method you have chosen.
2. Develop a cost estimation model to predict casino revenues based on square feet of casino floor space. Use this model to determine the expected full-year revenue for casino number nine. Evaluate the precision and reliability of the method you have chosen.
3. Repeat part (2) above, using number of rooms to predict room revenues, and number of restaurants to predict food and beverage revenues for the full year for casino number nine.

7-3 Cost-Volume-Profit Analysis and Strategy

Melford Hospital operates a general hospital, but rents space and beds to separately-owned entities rendering specialized services such as pediatrics and psychiatric care. Melford charges each separate entity for common services such as patients' meals and laundry, and for administrative services such as billings and collections. Space and bed rentals are fixed charges for the year, based on bed capacity rented to each entity.

Melford charged the following costs to pediatrics for the year ended June 30, 2006:

	Patient Days (variable)	Bed Capacity (fixed)
Dietary	$ 600,000	—
Janitorial	—	$ 70,000
Laundry	300,000	—
Laboratory	450,000	—
Pharmacy	350,000	—
Repairs and maintenance	—	30,000
General and administrative	—	1,300,000
Rent..	—	1,500,000
Billings and collections..................	300,000	—
Total..	$2,000,000	$2,900,000

During the year ended June 30, 2006, pediatrics charged each patient an average of $300 per day, had a capacity of 60 beds, and had revenue of $6,000,000 for 365 days. In addition, pediatrics directly employed the following personnel:

	Annual Salaries
Supervising nurses	$25,000
Nurses	20,000
Aides	9,000

Melford has the following minimum departmental personnel requirements based on total annual patients days:

Annual Patient Days	Aides	Nurses	Supervising Nurses
Up to 21,900	20	10	4
21,900 to 26,000	26	13	4
26,001 to 29,200	30	15	4

These staffing levels represent full-time equivalents. Pediatrics always employs only the minimum number of required full-time personnel. Salaries of supervising nurses, nurses, and aides are therefor fixed within ranges of annual patient days.

Pediatrics operated at 100% capacity on 90 days during the year ended June 30, 2006. It is estimated that during these 90 days the demand exceeded 20 patients more than capacity. Melford has an additional 20 beds available for rent for the year ending June 30, 2007. Such additional rental would increase pediatrics' fixed charges based on bed capacity.

REQUIRED:

1. What is the strategic role of CVP analysis for the pediatrics unit of Melford hospital?
2. Determine the minimum number of patient days required for pediatrics to breakeven for the year ending June 30, 2007, if the additional 20 beds are not rented. Patient demand is unknown, but assume that revenue per patient day, cost per patient day, cost per bed, and salary rates will remain the same as for the year ended June 30, 2006.
3. Assume that patient demand, revenue, revenue per patient day, cost per patient day, cost per bed, and salary rates for the year ending June 30, 2007 remain the same as for the year ended June 30, 2006. Prepare a schedule of increase in revenue and increase in costs for the year ending June 30, 2007, in order to determine the net increase or decrease in earnings from the additional 20 beds if pediatrics rents this extra capacity from Melford.

Blocher, Stout, Cokins, Chen: *Cost Management, 4e*

©The McGraw-Hill Companies, Inc 2008

7-4   Cost Volume Profit Analysis and Strategy:
The ALLTEL Pavilion

The ALLTEL Pavilion in Raleigh, North Carolina is an outdoor amphitheater that provides live concerts to the public from April through October each year. The seven-month season usually hosts an average of 40 concerts with 12 year-round staff planning and managing each season. SFX Entertainment Inc. operates the pavilion. SFX is the largest diversified promoter, producer, and venue operator for live entertainment events in the United States. Upon completion of pending acquisitions, it will have 71 venues either directly owned or operated under lease or exclusive booking arrangements in 29 of the top 50 U.S. markets, including 14 amphitheaters in nine of top 10 markets.

HISTORY/DEVELOPMENT

The ALLTEL pavilion was built in 1991 by the City of Raleigh and Pace Entertainment Company of Houston, Texas. The management of the pavilion was contracted to Pace Entertainment and Cellar Door Inc. of Raleigh, NC. Hardee's Food Systems, Inc. of Rocky Mount, NC, the original sponsor of the amphitheater, paid an annual fee to carry their name and logo on all signs and ads regarding the amphitheater. On February 3, 1999 the title sponsor for the amphitheater became ALLTEL Corp.

    The demand for the outdoor facility came about because the rapidly growing city of Raleigh lacked a major entertainment complex. So, in the mid to late 80's and early 90's Pace Entertainment and the City of Raleigh came to an agreement to build the facility. The City of Raleigh would own the land while Pace Entertainment would assume sole operations of the facility and Cellar Door would do the booking for all the concerts.

    In 1998, SFX Entertainment Inc. acquired Pace Entertainment Inc. The amphitheater facility and its employees became part of SFX Entertainment Inc. Also, in 1999 SFX Entertainment Inc. acquired Cellar Door Inc. and merged with Clear Channel Communications Inc., the largest owner of radio stations in the country. This move brought together both worlds of the entertainment business. While the company has diverse holdings, the philosophy of SFX is *"One Company, One Mission."* Many companies that are now owned by SFX were at one time hard-nosed bitter rivals in the concert promoting business. These companies now maintain good working relationships within SFX.

PERSONNEL

    When the marketing department plans a promotion for an up-coming event, it coordinates with sales to see if there is a conflict in sponsorship. Marketing also coordinates with operations to effectively manage the activities in preparation for and on show days. Finally, the budgets of each department (sales, marketing, and operations) are reviewed by the accounting department and head of finance for the overall financial management of the project.

BRINGING CONCERTS TO REALITY

A concert becomes reality in many steps. First, a group or performer with an interest in performing at ALLTEL will discuss with Cellar Door, Inc the possibility of performing at the pavilion, and look at the open dates. When agreement is reached, Cellar Door and the booking agent for the performer sign a contract. A time is specified for gate openings and once the gate is opened the show is underway. The job of the staff during a concert is to make sure every patron of the ALLTEL Pavilion has a pleasant experience and that the mission of the company is clearly seen by everyone that "a concert…*it's better live.*" After a show, Clean Sweep Inc. of Raleigh handles the clean up.

KEY BUSINESS ISSUES

    Marketing has an important role in the success of ALLTEL Pavilion, but marketing expenditures are carefully watched. For every show, the marketing budget is limited to $20,000. For many shows it is difficult to stay within the budget, since the Pavilion serves a 5-market region consisting of Raleigh-Durham, Fayetteville, Wilmington, Greensboro, and the Carolina Coast. Most of the marketing budget is spent on advertising with radio, TV, and print media in the designated regions. Prior to developing advertising plans, the marketing staff analyzes ticket sales geographically over the five-market region. It is important to know the demographics of the five regions and compare them with the profile for each performer. The more ALLTEL

Pavilion can know about the fans, the more they know about where to spend the $20,000.

While the different advertising media were viewed initially as cost-based strategic business units, SFX now considers them to be profit-based SBUs and develops measures of performance and profitability for each advertising media, by region. This type of analysis is important to the ALLTEL Pavilion because increased ticket sales, through effective advertising, not only affects ticket revenues but also revenue from parking, merchandise, and concessions. It is also important because of the increased cost of advertising. The advertising rates in the Raleigh-Durham region are comparable to the rates in Washington, D.C. The rates are up two hundred percent over the last five years while the budgets per show are only up fifteen percent over this time.

Other areas where costs have increased dramatically include the cost of the performing artist. The average cost for an artist is approximately $160,000. Some of the artists are paid on a fixed-fee basis, and others are paid on a per capita basis. Generally, the most popular artists seek a per capita contract because they are confident of a high level of attendance. In contrast, the artist paid on fixed base is guaranteed the same fee whether 100 or 20,000 people attend (the capacity of the Pavilion is approximately 20,000 attendance). The fixed-fee shows often have a projected attendance under 10,000. These artists do not have the "draw' of the other artists. In these types of shows, the role of marketing is especially important, as the Pavilion must work hard to attract attendance for the artist. As noted above, lower ticket sales also mean less money spent on parking, concessions, and merchandise, so effective marketing is critical. One method the Pavilion uses in addition to advertising is to distribute "comp" tickets (comp tickets are free tickets distributed throughout the community) to build interest in the Pavilion that will later be realized in paying customers, and because the comp customers will spend on parking, concessions, and merchandise.

This cost of the performing artists grows annually, so that it is very important for the ALLTEL Pavilion to reduce non-artist costs. There are a number of operating costs at ALLTEL Pavilion, including expenses for parking, security, concessions, and merchandise. Also, there are a number of other methods used to make the concerts more profitable. For example, the parking service passes out flyers for upcoming events. Also, the pavilion trade "comp" tickets for online spots in the radio industry and gives local businesses tickets in exchange for advertising on their premises.

FUNDING AND FLASH REPORT

The sources of funding for the Pavilion are ticket revenues, concession (food) revenues, merchandising revenues, parking revenues, sponsorship revenues, and other. Exhibit A is a mock flash report for an example show, the KFBS Allstars. A flash report is a projection of what a concert will cost and what revenues will be received. The guaranteed talent costs ($160,635) is the amount the KFBS Allstars are guaranteed for the show. Attendance is the number of projected **paying** ticket holders, while the "drop count" is total attendance, both for paid tickets and comp tickets. The drop count is usually projected to be about 125% of paying attendance. The Flash Report then projects total revenues including parking, food, and merchandise based on per capita (drop count) rates. Also, other revenues include per capita facility charges and service charges paid by the performer. The parking, food concession, and merchandise operations are outsourced to other service providers, so the direct costs for parking, merchandise and concessions are determined based on contracts with the service providers which include both a percentage (10%) of applicable (parking, merchandise or concession) revenues and a fixed fee. Operating expenses include an allocation of the total of fixed production and operations costs for the season, the advertising expenses for the KFBS Allstars event, and other variable expenses. These are then added to the direct costs for concessions, merchandise, parking, and insurance to determine total operating expenses.

REQUIRED:

1) How would you describe the competitive strategy of the ALLTEL Pavilion? What do you think it should be?

2) For the show illustrated in Exhibit A, the KFBS Allstars, how many tickets must ALLTEL Pavilion sell to break even?

3) For which type of performer (fixed fee or per capita) is breakeven analysis particularly important, and why? Which type of performer is preferred by the Pavilion, and why?

4) Explain how sensitivity analysis could be used to better understand the uncertainty surrounding the KFBS Allstars event.

Blocher, Stout, Cokins, Chen: *Cost Management, 4e*

©The McGraw-Hill Companies, Inc 2008

7-5 Sensitivity Analysis; Regression Analysis

Fast Shop, Inc is a chain of 10 convenience stores located in and around Houston, Texas. Selected operating data for the 10 stores for the most recent month is shown below. All but two of Fast Shop's stores sell gasoline as well as convenience items, primarily food, beverage, and household products. Because of zoning and other restrictions, the other stores sell only convenience items. Jim Sacco, the chief financial officer for Fast Shop, plans to utilize multiple regression analysis to determine which stores are most effective in generating sales, given differences in size (square feet) among the stores, differences in advertising and promotion costs for the stores, and whether or not the store sells gasoline. Jim knows that stores which sell gasoline typically have better than average sales because gasoline sales bring in sales for other convenience items.

Jim also knows that if regression analysis can be used to develop a sensitivity analysis of the effect of advertising and store size on sales. If he prepares a multiple regression analysis in which all the numerical variables are transformed by their natural logarithm, then the coefficients for each independent variable in the resulting regression equation will represent the percentage effect on sales for a given percentage change in the independent variable.

Selected Operating Information for the 10 Locations of Fast Shop Inc

Store	Sales	Advertising	Square Feet	Gas Sales
1	$ 56,034	$ 5,540	2,200	No
2	23,045	3,310	1,200	Yes
3	89,337	8,837	2,800	No
4	66,073	11,200	2,000	No
5	18,993	1,879	1,500	No
6	64,926	6,648	2,300	No
7	28,773	3,756	1,500	No
8	46,294	5,899	1,800	No
9	73,546	6,899	2,400	Yes
10	36,968	5,100	1,600	No
	$ 503,989	$ 59,068		

REQUIRED:

1.   Using regression analysis, determine which store(s) seem to be operating below their potential, given advertising expenses, gasoline sales, and size?

2.   Using regression analysis and log transforms, determine the sensitivity of sales to advertising and store size.

Readings

7.1: Tools for Dealing with Uncertainty

Sophisticated spreadsheet software incorporating probability functions can help you forecast more accurately.

BY DAVID R. FORDHAM, CMA, AND S. BROOKS MARSHALL

Aside from the proverbial death and taxes, there is little in life that is certain. As management accountants, we recognize that one of our most crucial uncertainties involves capital investments. Why, then, are so many of us still using analysis tools designed for fixed numbers?

Let's take a simple example. Your company is considering a $1 million capital investment. The project is expected to return 12% per year, with the annual profits reinvested annually. What will be your final compounded return at the end of 20 years?

If you are like most management accountants, you will use the traditional compounding formula (multiplying your initial investment times one plus the rate of return raised to the 20th power). This time-honored analysis approach tells you that your final compounded return should be $9,646,293. But is this the best answer?

Unfortunately, it is not—at least for most capital investment projects. The compounding formula works well for investments in which the annual rate of return is fixed. But this is not the situation with most capital investments. While the initial outlay may be a fairly firm number, the annual rate of return most likely will vary from year to year.

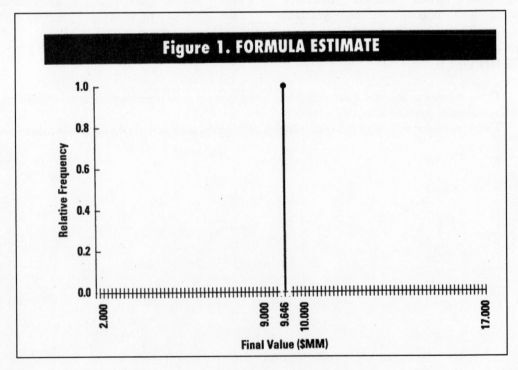

Figure 1. FORMULA ESTIMATE

Blocher, Stout, Cokins, Chen: *Cost Management, 4e*

Thus, this project might yield a 25% (or higher) return in a good year and a 0% return (or even a loss) in another year. Even a relatively safe capital investment (say, a market-rate financial instrument) can involve variable rates of return.

But the compounding formula operates as though the rate of return is exactly 12% for all 20 years, with no variability. Because the formula has no way of recognizing the uncertainty in the annual rates of return, it may not be providing the best answer.

The most popular capital budgeting tools (the compounding formula, the internal rate of return, and net present value calculations) are simple to use and can be handled with little more than a pocket calculator. But they all suffer from a major drawback: They provide a single-number answer by assuming that their input is a set of fixed or known numbers, with no provision for variability.

A POPULAR WAY OF DEALING WITH UNCERTAINTY: SENSITIVITY ANALYSIS

One way of providing for uncertainty is to rerun the calculations several times using different fixed values. Today's computerized spreadsheets make it easy to play "what-if" games. By changing the numbers and re-performing the calculations, we can generate various possible outcomes. Comparing these different outcomes generally provides a better analysis than merely looking at a single point estimate.

Continuing our example above, a modern analyst would use the compounding formula to arrive at the $9,646,293 figure and also to provide alternative possibilities from the what-if analyses, showing the effect of changing the estimated rate of return from 12% to, say, 10% or 14%. By reporting multiple possible final values, the analyst is providing more and better information than by reporting a single point estimate. The name for this technique is "sensitivity analysis."

This approach provides a much more realistic means of analyzing uncertain situations than simply using the compounding formula alone, but it still uses analysis tools that operate on only one set of numbers at a time. The fact remains that no matter how many times we rerun the calculations, the formula still operates as though the rate of return is constant throughout all 20 years of the project's life. Ideally, our analysis should employ a tool that incorporates the possible changes from year to year in the annual rate of return. Even more important, we need to know the probability of earning different amounts from our project, not just a list of some possible amounts.

A BETTER WAY: PROBABILITY DISTRIBUTION

Statisticians tell us that the law of large numbers applies to most situations involving uncertainty and that variable numbers tend to cluster around a central value or mean. Financial research has shown that annual rates of return on most modern investments do indeed form a "normal distribution" around a mean.

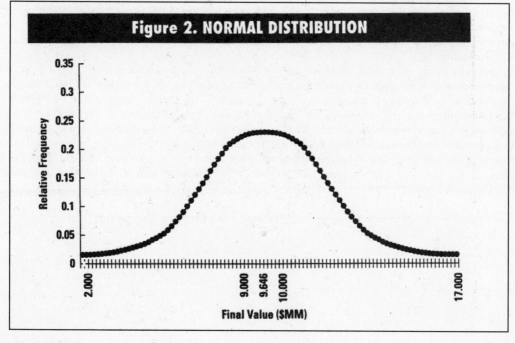

Figure 2. NORMAL DISTRIBUTION

Values close to the mean occur with greater frequency than values farther away from the mean. If you can establish a reasonable estimate of the mean and have some idea of the range of possible realistic values, you generally can get by with handling your uncertainty as a probability distribution.

Traditional analysis tools (the compounding formula in our example) yield a single point estimate of the project's final value (see Figure 1). If we were to use the formula by itself, our analysis would show that the project will return exactly $9,646,293. Most management accountants, however, recognize the uncertainty and report several different possible outcomes, assuming that the most likely final values will center around $9,646,293. Values far away from this figure will be unlikely, while values close to it will be more likely. The analyst even may illustrate the relative likelihood of the different outcomes with such a probability distribution as that in Figure 2.

Figure 2 is superior to Figure 1 in that it shows relative likelihoods of many possible final values ranging from a very unlikely $2 million figure all the way up to an equally unlikely $17 million. The most likely values, however, are close to $9,646,293. And most analysts assume that the probability curve is symmetric, as shown in Figure 2. In other words, they assume the chances of earning slightly less than the projected amount are about the same as the chances of earning slightly more than the projected amount.

But is this the case? Assuming the rate of return does average 12% over the life of the project, are the chances of slightly underperforming the estimate the same as the chances of slightly outperforming it? It might surprise you to learn that Figure 3 is actually a more accurate illustration of the likely final values of our project!

Some Surprising Statistics

When using analysis models that approximate reality surprising results sometimes emerge. Take the probability distribution of our compound investment's final value. Most people, including many financial analysts, would assume that if the annual rate of return varies in a normal (and symmetric) fashion across the 20-year life of the project, then the possible final values also should vary in a symmetric pattern. This makes intuitive sense. But it isn't what actually happens.

Consider closely the value of the investment at the end of the first year. The exact rate of return during that year is unknown, but it will vary around a 12% expected value. If we expect the rate of return to vary in a normal fashion, at the end of the first year we will have a range of possible final values that will be centered around $1.12 million (for our $1 million original investment). This probability distribution is symmetric because it is the product of a fixed amount (the original investment) multiplied by a normal probability distribution (the rate of return).

Most things change in the second year, though. This time, we are not multiplying a constant by a normal distribution. We are multiplying one normal distribution (the final value at the end of the first year) by another normal distribution. It yields a skewed, asymmetric distribution known in statistical circles as a log-normal distribution.

The skewness of the probability distribution becomes even more pronounced in the third year, and the symmetry continues to degrade as more and more compounding periods are added. By the 20th year, you have the noticeably asymmetric distribution shown in Figure 3. The unusual shape of the distribution curve and the probabilities associated with each of the possible outcomes of the project derive directly from the compounding of the investment. Once the initial investment is made, all future values are unknown figures. Using probability distributions to illustrate these unknown values is a more accurate approach than simply treating them as fixed estimates. Therefore, the asymmetric probability of the project's final value is a better predictor of the project's performance than a perfectly symmetric curve fitted around the traditional financial formula's output.

Blocher, Stout, Cokins, Chen: *Cost Management, 4e*

SURPRISES FROM MODERN ANALYSIS TOOLS

Figure 3 reveals some startling new information about our project. First, the most probable final value (represented by the peak of the probability curve) is not the $9,646,293 predicted by the traditional analysis formula! Rather, it is somewhat less. From looking at Figure 3, you see that it is more likely that our project's final value will be approximately $9 million rather than the approximately $9.6 million reported by the traditional analysis approach.

Management accountants and financial analysts who have for years relied on the formulas are astounded to see this increase in the likelihood of underperforming the formula estimate. But even more surprising is the fact that the probability distribution is not symmetric. For example, the chances of the project yielding half a million dollars less than the $9,646,293 are actually much greater (perhaps two or three times as great) than the chances of earning half a million dollars more than that amount. In other words, while the chance of slightly underperforming the formula's prediction has increased, the chance of outperforming the formula's prediction by the same amount has gone down quite dramatically. Also, the probability of "losing one's shirt" has diminished somewhat, while the probability of making much more than the formula estimate has increased.

What causes these surprising results? The answer lies in the fact that the rate of return can vary from year to year. Each year's earnings are dependent not only on that single year's rate of return, but also on all previous years' rates, because the project involves compounding reinvestment. Thus, if you assume that the rate of return averages 12% annually over the course of the 20-year project, and you assume that the changes occur in accordance with the law of large numbers (specifically, in accordance with a normal probability distribution from year to year), you still come up with the skewed probability curve for the final value of the project shown in Figure 3 because of the changing rates of return. (For an explanation of this phenomenon, see the sidebar, "Some Surprising Statistics.")

SOPHISTICATED TOOLS, BUT EASY TO USE

Probability curves such as Figure 3 can give a much more accurate picture of the likely outcome of projects under uncertainty. These analyses can be generated by a little-used analysis tool that is included in most of today's modern spreadsheet software.

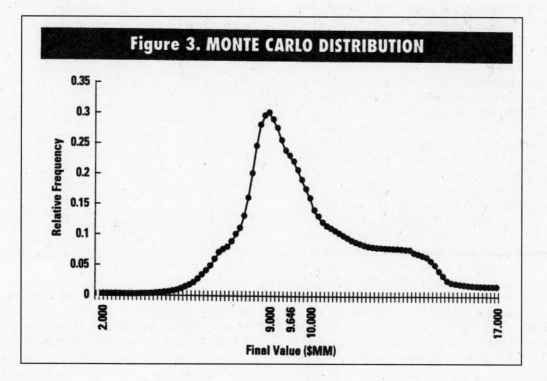

Figure 3. MONTE CARLO DISTRIBUTION

This tool enables us to create mathematical models that more closely approximate real-life situations involving uncertainty.

As our capital budgeting problem involves an uncertain annual rate of return that varies from year to year, we must develop an analysis model with a rate of return that varies from year to year. In addition, we need to analyze many different combinations of these varying annual rates of return.

Until a few years ago, creating such a model required extensive computer programming, weeks of effort, and significant time on a large mainframe or minicomputer. Today, though, with the recent advances in personal computers, including larger memory capacities, faster and more powerful numerical processors, and advanced software, we now have the ability to build such mathematical models on our desktops in a matter of minutes.

The tools necessary to construct probability distributions can be found on all of the popular Windows-based spread-sheets—Lotus 1-2-3, Excel, Supercalc, and Quattro-Pro. Specific instructions vary from package to package, but they are contained in the On-Line Help features. Look for Help topics involving random number generators, probability distributions, and statistical tools.

To analyze our sample problem properly, we begin by constructing a spreadsheet showing how the project's returns will be reinvested (Figure 4). But instead of the 12% annual rate of return for all 20 years, we want to substitute a variable rate of return, one that is expected to average 12% over the 20 years.

Because we assume the rates of return will average 12% and might vary between 0% and 25%, we can say that, in any one year, the rate of return will come from a normal distribution with a mean of 12% and a standard deviation of about 6%. We use the computer's random number generator to draw 20 values from a distribution with a mean of 12 and a standard deviation of 6. Then we incorporate these values as the assumed rate of return for each of our 20 years. This approach gives us one possible outcome of our capital project. In other words, if it just so happens that the annual rates of return come out as shown in Figure 5, then our project's final value will be $9,595,504.[1]

The particular combination of annual rates of return shown in Figure 5 is only one of many possible combinations. We also must look at others. In fact, we need to duplicate the scenario many times (a technique known as Monte Carlo analysis) to represent the many different combinations of annual rates of return.

Figure 4

Year	Rate of Return	Final Value
1	12.00%	$1,120,000
2	12.00%	$1,254,400
3	12.00%	$1,404,928
4	12.00%	$1,573,519
5	12.00%	$1,762,342
6	12.00%	$1,973,823
7	12.00%	$2,210,681
8	12.00%	$2,475,963
9	12.00%	$2,773,079
10	12.00%	$3,105,848
11	12.00%	$3,478,550
12	12.00%	$3,895,976
13	12.00%	$4,363,493
14	12.00%	$4,887,112
15	12.00%	$5,473,566
16	12.00%	$6,130,394
17	12.00%	$6,866,041
18	12.00%	$7,689,966
19	12.00%	$8,612,762
20	12.00%	$9,646,293

Figure 5

Year	Rate of Return	Final Value
1	11.30%	$1,113,000
2	12.10%	$1,247,673
3	13.30%	$1,413,614
4	14.10%	$1,612,933
5	9.00%	$1,758,097
6	10.00%	$1,933,907
7	13.00%	$2,185,315
8	15.50%	$2,524,038
9	16.50%	$2,940,505
10	14.00%	$3,352,175
11	14.50%	$3,838,241
12	8.00%	$4,145,300
13	11.00%	$4,601,283
14	7.00%	$4,923,373
15	10.30%	$5,430,480
16	13.10%	$6,141,873
17	11.50%	$6,848,188
18	9.50%	$7,498,766
19	14.20%	$8,563,591
20	12.05%	$9,595,504

By constructing hundreds, or even thousands, of possible combinations and then displaying a histogram of the final outcomes, we begin to get a feel for the likely performance of our project.

There are numerous add-in products on the market that enhance the major spreadsheet packages, making it easy to perform thousands of Monte

Blocher, Stout, Cokins, Chen: *Cost Management, 4e*

Carlo scenarios. These software products are surprisingly easy to learn and operate, especially for users already familiar with the Windows point-and-click system. One such package, known as @RISK, is able to perform 1,000 iterations of the above scenario with only a few keystrokes. Therefore, the calculation of 2,000 scenarios of our capital budgeting problem can be performed in less than three minutes on a 486 computer. Furthermore, most of the packages automatically display the histogram upon completion of their calculations, giving you an instant picture of the likely outcomes of your investment.

MORE PROBLEM SOLVING

This same technique (drawing numbers from a probability distribution and constructing a histogram of the final outcomes) can be used to simulate the uncertainty of discount rates for net present value analysis. It also can be used to simulate the uncertainty surrounding cash flow amounts, future revenues, and expenses. Yet another use for it might involve modeling possible

changes in tax rates or inflation rates—or almost any uncertain figure. All that is needed is some idea (or assumption) about the possible behavior of the uncertain value, such as its expected average and likely variability. Often the assumption can be simply the one that would have been used in the formula analysis, coupled with the estimated rate of variability over time. By constructing a model that resembles the real situation more closely, you can see that the likely outcome of a capital project may be very different from what you normally would expect, based on the traditional analysis output. The likelihood of doing very poorly, fairly well, or extremely well on a given project may surprise you and other decision makers. A realistic probability distribution requires additional information, which cannot be provided by the traditional analysis tools. This information even may affect management's decision in some situations (see the sidebar, "Good News, Bad News.") Regardless, it always is better to provide management with the best information possible.

Good News, Bad News: What the Picture Tells Us

Figure 3 is a much more accurate portrayal of our project's expected performance. Most important, it presents some new information that might make a difference in the decision as to whether to accept or reject the project. Let's take a close look at exactly what this new tool is telling us that we didn't know before. To make the comparison, we will use the compounding formula's predicted value ($9,646,293) as a base because it is the figure that most analysts would have presented to management.

First, as mentioned in the text, the probability of the project's value coming in slightly under the base is much higher than the probability of hitting the base or of hitting any other possible value. Some managers may consider it misleading to say that the project likely will return $9,646,293 when, in fact, the most probable return is less than this amount.

More significant, the chance of slightly outperforming the base by a given amount is much less than the probability of slightly underperforming the base by the same amount. Again, managers may consider it misleading to quote the $9,646,293 figure when the chances of making a million less than this figure may be two or three times the likelihood of making a million more than the figure.

The bad news, then, is that the project probably will slightly underperform the base estimate and probably will not slightly overperform the base estimate. But wait! There is some good news, too.

Look at the ends of the curve. The possibility of losing your shirt on the investment has almost disappeared compared with the chance of making a killing. In other words, the possibility of coming out far under the base prediction is extremely low, compared with the chance of outperforming the base by the same large amount. Managers who don't mind the risk of slightly underperforming the base prediction but who want to avoid an extremely low final value—especially if it means a chance at yielding an extremely high final value—might be more inclined to accept the project if they had access to this probability distribution. In short, decision makers find the probability distribution analysis a much richer source of information than the traditional sensitivity analysis using common capital budgeting techniques.

THERE IS STILL UNCERTAINTY

Of course, any time we try to predict the future; we are dealing with unknown information. Modem analysis tools are only as good as the input with which they are provided. We will continue to

encounter problems trying to estimate future returns' means and their variability. But for a given set of input information, these sophisticated tools can greatly expand the richness of information provided as output.

Remember: The traditional capital budgeting tools may be providing your decision makers with misleading figures regarding the likely performance of your investment projects. A much better tool would be one that enables you to construct a mathematical model that depicts the actual situation more accurately, including year-to-year variations. With the advent of powerful spreadsheet software incorporating statistical probability functions, it now is feasible to perform analyses that portray the real situation more accurately. By using these more sophisticated models, you can do a much better job of forecasting the likelihood of possible outcomes, which can lead to your making better decisions for your company.

David R. Fordham, CMA, CPA, Ph.D, is an assistant professor at James Madison University's School of Accounting. He is a member of the Virginia Skyline Chapter, through which this article was submitted. He can be reached at (540) 568-3024, phone, or e-mail, fordhadr@jmu.edu.
S. Brooks Marshall, CFA. DBA, is an associate professor of finance at James Madison University's College of Business. He can be reached at (540) 568-3075, phone, or e-mail, marshasb@jmu.edu.

---

[1] Note that the annual rates of return in Figure 5 do indeed average 12% across the 20-year life of the project and that the final value is less than the $9,648,293 predicted by the formula. This is in line with the probability curve shown in Figure 3, which predicts that final values slightly less than the $9,646,293 will occur with greater frequency than amounts slightly above it.

Blocher, Stout, Cokins, Chen: *Cost Management, 4e*

Chapter 8
Strategy and the Master Budget

Cases

8-1 **Emerson Electric Company** © Joseph San Miguel, reprinted with permission.

8-2 **Letsgo Travel Trailers** (Source: "Letsgo Travel Trailers: A Case for Incorporating the New Model of the Organization into the Teaching of Budgeting," by Sally Wright, *Cases from Management Accounting Practice*, Vol. 14, Montvale, NJ: Institute of Management Accountants, 1998). Note that part 2 of this case requires the use of **Excel**.

Readings

8-1: "How to Set Up a Budgeting and Planning System" by Robert N. West and Amy M. Snyder, *Management Accounting* (January 1997), pp. 18-20, 22, 24.

This article demonstrates the setting up of a budgeting and planning system for Penn Fuel Gas Inc., a public utility holding company that provides natural gas storage and transportation services. It stresses the need to review the chart of accounts, account classification and the reporting system of the firm. The discussion includes factors to be considered in the budgeting process and moves to update its current accounting information system.

Discussion Questions:
1. What motivates PFG to install a budgeting and planning system?
2. Why is flexibility very important for PFG's budgeting system to be effective?
3. What problems that the budget manager at PFG had to resolve before setting up a budgeting system? Do you find these problems unique to PFG?
4. Why the authors suggest that a thorough review of the firm's chart of accounts, account classifications, and reporting systems is a must before initiating a budgeting and planning system?
5. Describe budgetary games that people play. What are the reasons for PFG to experience minimal budgetary gamesmanship?

8-2: "Strategic Budgeting: A Case Study and Proposed Framework" by Audrey G. Taylor and Savya Rafai, *Management Accounting Quarterly* (Fall 2003), pp. 1-10.

This reading applies the Critical Chain technique proposed by Eliyahu Goldratt to budget preparations. All department budgets are reduced by 50%. The savings are grouped in a Group Budget Buffer. Department heads can request additional funds from the buffer but the request would be discussed openly with other department heads. This reduction method allows costs to be cut where the cuts will not negatively impact performance of the service departments. At the same time, it identifies areas of bloat where cost reduction can be significant increases communication between departments, lowers overall spending levels, and assures output integrity.

Discussion Questions:
1. What is the lawnmower method of cost reduction?
2. What will be the size of a division's total budgeted amount after 4 years if the division includes 10% slack each year? After 10 years?
3. What is the strategic budgeting model?
4. What are the strengths of strategic budgeting?

8-3: "How Challenging Should Profit Budget Targets Be?" by Kenneth A. Merchant, *Management Accounting* (November 1990), pp. 46-48.

The article argues for using highly achievable budget targets, and explains six key advantages for doing so, including the favorable effect on the managers' commitment and confidence. The article also explains some of the risks of using highly achievable budget targets. The concept of risk is illustrated with probability distributions and with a relatively low-risk environment having a probability distribution with lower variance.

Discussion Questions:
1. Explain each of the six advantages of highly achievable budget targets mentioned in the article. Can you think of any in addition?
2. What are the risks of highly achievable budget targets mentioned in the article? Can you think of any in addition?

Blocher, Stout, Cokins, Chen: *Cost Management, 4e*
©The McGraw-Hill Companies, Inc 2008

Cases

8-1 Emerson Electric Company[1]

Emerson Electric Company was founded in 1890 as a manufacturer of motors and fans. In 1993, Emerson marked its thirty-sixth consecutive year of improved earnings per share. On $8.2 billion sales, the diversified St. Louis based company reported a 1993 profit of $708 million. In addition, the company had $2 billion in unconsolidated sales in international joint ventures. It manufactures a broad range of electric, electromechanical, and electronic products for industry and consumers. Brand names include Fisher Control Valves, Skil, Dremel, and Craftsman power tools, In-Sink-Erator waste disposals, Copeland compressors, Rosemount instruments, Automatic Switch valves, and U.S. Electric Motors in the power transmission market. Since 1956, Emerson's annual return to shareholders averaged 18 percent. Sales, earnings per share, and dividends per share grew at a compound rate of 9 percent, 8 percent, and 7 percent, respectively, over the 1983-93 period. Inter-national sales have grown to 40 percent of total sales and present a growth area for the company.

Emerson is a major domestic electrical manufacturer. Its U.S. based competitors include companies such as General Electric, Westinghouse, and Honeywell. Its foreign competitors include companies such as Siemens and Hitachi. Emerson has had the narrowest focus as a broadly diversified manufacturing company among its primary competitors. Other manufacturers, such as GE and Westinghouse, are diversified into financial services, broadcasting, aircraft engines, plastics, furniture, etc. Emerson follows a growth-through-acquisition strategy, but no one acquisition has been very large. There are periodic divestitures as management seeks the appropriate or complementary mix of products.

In 1973, Charles F. Knight was elected Chief Executive Officer, after joining the company the prior year. Under Knight's leadership, Emerson analyzed historical records as well as data on a set of "peer companies" the investment community valued highly over time. From this analysis, top management concluded that Emerson needed to achieve growth and strong financial results on a consistent basis reflecting constant improvements. The company set growth rate targets based on revenue growth above and beyond economy-driven expectations.

During the 1980s, the company maintained a very conservative balance sheet rather than using leverage. Top management felt that this was a competitive weapon because it permitted flexibility to borrow when an attractive business investment became available. In the economic downtown of the 1990s, Emerson, unlike a number of companies, was not burdened by heavy debt and interest payments.

ORGANIZATION

Historically, Emerson was organized into 40 decentralized divisions consisting of separate product lines. A president ran each division. The goal was to be number one or two in the market for each product line. The company resisted forming groups, sectors, or other combinations of divisions as found in other large companies until 1990, when Emerson organized its divisions into eight business segments: fractional horsepower electric motors; industrial motors; tools; industrial machinery and components; components for heating and air conditioning; process control equipment; appliance components; and electronics and computer support products and systems. This new structure exploits common distribution channels, organizational capabilities, and technologies.

The Office of the Chief Executive (OCE), which consists of the Chief Executive Officer, the President, two Vice Chairmen, seven business leaders, and three other corporate officers, directs management of the company. The OCE meets 10 to 12 times a year to review division performance; and discuss issues facing individual divisions or the corporation as a whole.

Each division also has a board of directors, which consists of a member of the OCE who serves as chairman, the division president, and the division's key managers. The division boards meet monthly to review and monitor performance.

Corporate staff in 1993 consisted of 311 people; the same number as in 1975, when the company was one-sixth its current size in terms of sales. Staff is kept to a minimum because top management believes that a large staff creates more work for the divisions. To encourage open communication and interaction among all levels of employees, Emerson does not publish an organization chart.

---

[1]This case was written and copyrighted by Joseph G. San Miguel, Naval Postgraduate School.

In the early 1980s, the company was not globally competitive in all of its major product lines, and recognized that its quality levels in some product areas did not match levels available from some non-U.S. competitors, particularly the Japanese. Therefore, top management changed its twenty-year strategy of being the "low cost producer" to being the "best cost producer." There were six elements to this strategy:

1. Commitment to total quality and customer satisfaction.
2. Knowledge of the competition and the basis on which they compete.
3. Focused manufacturing strategy, competing on process as well as product design.
4. Effective employee communications and involvement.
5. Formalized cost-reduction programs, in good times and bad.
6. Commitment to support the strategy through capital expenditures.

Since the 1950s, the low cost producer strategy required the divisions to set cost-reduction goals at every level and required plant personnel to identify specific actions to achieve those goals. Improvements of 6 percent to 7 percent a year, in terms of cost of goods sold, were targeted. With the best-cost producer strategy, Emerson now aims for higher levels of cost reduction through its planning process. For example, machine tools were used to streamline a process to save labor costs, and design changes saved five ounces of aluminum per unit. Sometimes a competitor's products were disassembled and studied for cost improvements. Products and cost structures of competitors were used to assess Emerson's performance. Factors such as regional labor rates and freight costs were also included in the analyses. For example, before investing millions of dollars in a new plant to make circular saws, top management wanted to know what competitors, domestic and global, were planning.

In the period 1983 to 1993, capital investments of $1.8 billion were made to improve process technology, increase productivity, gain product leadership, and achieve critical mass in support of the best-cost producer strategy. Division and plant management report every quarter on progress against detailed cost reduction targets.

Quality was an important factor in Emerson's best-cost producer strategy. Improvements were such that Emerson was counting defects in parts per million. For example, in one electric motor line, employees consistently reached less than 100 rejects per one million motors.

PLANNING PROCESS

CEO Knight made the following comments on Emerson's planning process:

> "Once we fix our goals, we do not consider it acceptable to miss them. These targets drive our strategy and determine what we have to do: the kinds of businesses we are in, how we organize and manage them, and how we pay management. At Emerson this means planning. In the process of planning, we focus on specific opportunities that will meet our criteria for growth and returns and create value for our stockholders. In other words, we "identify business investment opportunities."[2]

Emerson's fiscal year starts October 1. To initiate the planning process, top management sets sales growth and return on total capital targets for the divisions. Each fiscal year, from November to July, the CEO and several corporate officers meet with the management of each division at a one or two day division planning conference. Knight spends 60 percent of his time at these division-planning conferences. The meetings are designed to be confrontational in order to challenge assumptions and conventional thinking. Top management wants the division to stretch to reach its goals. It also wants to review the detailed actions that division management believes will lead to improved results.

Prior to its division planning conference, the division president submits four standard exhibits to top management. Developing these four exhibits requires months of teamwork and discipline among each division's operating managers.

The "Value Measurement Chart" compares the division's actual performance five years ago (1989), the current year's expected results (1994), and the long-range forecast for the fifth year (1999). See **Exhibit 1** (Note: the numbers in all exhibits are disguised). The Value Measurement Chart contains the type, amount, and growth rates of capital investment, net operating profit after tax (NOPAT), return on average operating capital, and "economic profit" (NOPAT less a capital charge based on the cost of capital). To create shareholder value, the goal is to determine the extent to which a division's return on total capital (ROTC) exceeds Emerson's cost of capital. Use of

---

2 Knight, C. F., "Emerson Electric: Consistent Profits, Consistently," *Harvard Business Review,* January-February 1992, p. 59.

Blocher, Stout, Cokins, Chen: *Cost Management, 4e*

the cost of capital rate (Line 3000 on **Exhibit 1**) is required in all division plans.

The next two exhibits contain sales data. The "Sales Gap Chart" and "Sales Gap Line Chart" show the current year's expected sales (1994) and five-year sales projections (1995-1999). See **Exhibits 2** and **3**. These are based on an analysis of sources of growth, the market's natural growth rate, market penetration, price changes, new products, product line extensions, and international growth. The "gap" represents the difference between the division's long-range sales forecast and top management's target rate for sales growth (Line 19 in **Exhibit 2**). Exhibit 2 shows the five-year sources of sales growth in Column H. These are illustrated in the Sales Gap Line Chart in Exhibit 3 for one of the divisions for the 1995-99 periods. The division president must explain what specific steps are being taken to close the gap.

The "5-Back by 5-Forward P&L in **Exhibit 4** contrasts detailed division data for the current year (1994) with five prior years of historical data and five years of forecast data (1995-99). This comprises 11 years of profit statements including sales; cost of sales; selling, general and administrative expenses; interest; taxes; and return on total capital (ROTC). This statement is used to detect trends. Division management must be prepared with actions to reverse unfavorable movements or trends.

Beyond the review and discussion of the four required exhibits, the division planning conference belongs to the division president. Top management listens to division management's view of customers, markets, plans for new products, analyses of competition, and reviews of cost reductions, quality, capacity, productivity, inventory levels, and compensation. Any resulting changes in the division plan must be submitted for approval by top management. The logic and underlying assumptions of the plan are challenged so that managers who are confident of their strategies can defend their proposals. CEO Knight views the test of a good planning conference is whether it results in manager actions that significantly impact the business. According to Knight:

> Since operating managers carry out the planning, we effectively establish ownership and eliminate the artificial distinction between strategic and operating decisions. Managers on the line do not-and must never-delegate the understanding of the business. To develop a plan, operating managers work together for months. They often tell me that the greatest value of the planning cycle lies in the teamwork and discipline that the preparation phase requires.[3]

Late in the fiscal year, the division president and appropriate division staff meet with top management to present a detailed forecast for the coming year and conduct a financial review of the current year's actual performance versus forecast. The forecast is expected to match the data in the plan resulting from the division planning conference, but top management also requests contingency plans for several lower levels of activity. A thorough set of actions to protect profitability at lower sales levels is presented. These are known as contingency plans. Changes to the division's forecast are not likely unless significant changes occurred in the environment or in the underlying assumptions. Top management must approve changes in the forecast. It is not Emerson's practice to aggregate financial reports for planning and controlling profits between the division and corporation as a whole.

In August, the information generated for and during the division planning conferences and financial reviews is consolidated and reviewed at corporate headquarters by top management. The objective is to examine the total data and prepare for a corporate wide planning conference. In September, before the start of the next fiscal year, top management and top officers of each division attend an annual corporate planning conference. At this meeting, top management presents the corporate and division forecasts for the next year as well as the strategic plan for the next five years. The conference is viewed as a vehicle for communication. There is open and frank discussion of success stories, missed opportunities, and future challenges.

REPORTING

At its meetings the CEO uses the President's Operating Report (POR) to review division performance. Each division president submits the POR (see **Exhibit 5**), on a monthly basis. This reporting system is different from budget reports found in other companies.

First, the POR contains three columns of data for the "current year." The third column of data (Forecast) reflects the plan agreed to by the division president and top corporate management at the beginning of the fiscal year. The forecast data is not changed during the fiscal year and the division president's performance is measured using the

---

[3] Knight, p. 63.

fiscal year's forecast. The first column reports the actual results for completed quarters or expected amounts for the current and future quarters. The division president may update expected quarterly results each month. The second column reports the "prior expected" results so that each month's updated expectations can be compared with data submitted in the prior month's POR. Updated expectations are also compared with the forecast data.

Second, in addition to current year data, the POR lists the prior year's actual results. This permits a comparison with the current year's actual results for completed quarters (or expected results for subsequent quarters) and over (0) or under (U) percentages are reported. Midway through the fiscal year, expected data for the first quarter of the next fiscal year is added to the POR.

Corporate top management meets quarterly with each division president and his or her chief financial officer to review the most recent POR and monitor overall division performance. The meetings are taken very seriously by all concerned and any deviations from forecast get close attention. When a division's reported results and expectations are weak, a shift to contingency plans is sometimes ordered by top management, Emerson does not allocate corporate overhead to the divisions but does allocate interest and taxes to divisions at the end of the fiscal year.

COMPENSATION

During the year, each division assesses all department heads and higher-level managers against specific performance criteria. Those with high potential are offered a series of assignments to develop their skills. Human resources are identified as part of the strategy implementation. In addition, personnel charts on management team are kept at corporate headquarters. The charts include each manager's photo, function, experience, and career path. About 85 percent of promotions involve internal managers.

Each executive in a division earns a base salary and is eligible for "extra salary," based on division performance according to measurable objectives (primarily sales, profits, and return on capital). An extra salary amount, established at the beginning of the year, is multiplied by "1" if the division hits targeted performance. The multiplier ranges from .35 to 2.0. Doing better than target increases the multiplier. In recent years, sales and profit margin, as identified in the POR forecast column, have had a 50 percent weighting in computing compensation targets. Other factors include inventory turnover, international sales, new product introductions, and an accounts receivable factor. In addition, stock options and a five-year performance share plan are available to top executives.

COMMUNICATION

Top management strongly encourages open communication. Division presidents and plant managers meet regularly with all employees to discuss the specifics of the business and the competition. As a measure of communication, top management feels that each employee should be able to answer four essential questions about his or her job:

1. What cost reduction are you currently working on?
2. Who is the competition?
3. Have you met with your management in the past six months?
4. Do you understand the economics of your job?

The company also conducts opinion surveys of every employee. The analysis uncovers trends. Some plants have survey data for the prior twenty years. The CEO receives a summary of every opinion survey from every plant.

RECENT EVENTS

As a result of a $2 billion investment in technology during the past 10 years, new products as a percent of sales increased from 13 percent in 1983 to 24 percent in 1993. A new product is defined as a product introduced within the past five years. About 87 percent of total U.S. sales are generated from products that are either first or second in domestic position. Still, some in the investment community do not view Emerson as a technology leader, but as a very efficient world-class manufacturer. Although internally generated new products are part of the planning process, Emerson is sometimes a late entrant in the marketplace. For example, in 1989, a competitor introduced a low-cost, hand-held ultra-sonic gauge. Within 72 days, Emerson introduced its own version at 20 percent less cost than its competitor's gauge. Emerson's gauge was also easier to use and more reliable. It was a bestseller within a year.

To some Wall Street observers, it seems that Emerson is attempting to reduce its dependence on supplying

Blocher, Stout, Cokins, Chen: *Cost Management, 4e*

©The McGraw-Hill Companies, Inc 2008

commodity-type products, such as motors and valves, to U.S. based appliance and other consumer-durables manufacturers by moving into faster growing global markets, such as process controls. As the economy recovers, Emerson is likely to continue its acquisition strategy, with an emphasis on foreign acquisitions, and international joint ventures.

The impact of the recent business segment organization structure on the planning and control process is not clear. The added layer of management between the division managers and top management might change the previous relationship between them.

QUESTIONS

1. Evaluate Chief Executive Officer Knight's strategy for the Emerson Electric Company. In view of the strategy, evaluate the planning and control system described in the case. What are its strong and weak points?
2. What changes, if any, would you recommend to the CEO?
3. What role should the eight business segment managers have in Emerson's planning and control system?

EXHIBIT 1 The Value Measurement Chart Assesses Value Creation at a Glance*

| | | 5th Prior Year | | Current Year | | 5th Year | | 5-Year Increment | | | | 10-Year Increment | |
| | | Actual FY 1989 | | Expected FY 1994 | | Forecast FY 1999 | | Historical CY vs 5th PY | | Forecast 5th Yr vs. CY | | 5th Yr vs. 5th PY | |
		Amt.	% Sales	Amt.	% Sales	Amt.	% Sales	Amt.	% Sales	Amt.	% Sales	Amt.	% Sales
Growth Rate and Capital Requirements	Line No.	A	B	C	D	E	F	G	H	I	J	K	L
Working capital operating-Y/E	1127	117.1	29.8%	120.2	21.8%	153.3	18.5%	3.1	1.9%	33.1	12.0%	36.2	8.3%
Net noncurrent assets-Y/E	1128	92.9	23.6%	150.0	27.2%	221.6	26.8%	57.1	35.9%	71.6	26.0%	128.7	29.6%
Total operating capital-Y/E	1129	210.0	53.4%	270.2	48.9%	374.9	45.3%	60.2	37.9%	104.7	38.0%	164.9	37.9%
Average operating capital	1130	201.1	51.1%	267.1	48.4%	370.4	44.7%						
Incremental investment	1584							66.0		103.3		169.3	
Net oper. prof. aft. tax (NOPAT)	1119	33.4		49.5		79.0		16.1		29.5		45.6	
Return on incremental investment								24.4%		28.6%		26.9%	
NOPAT growth rate								8.2%		9.8%		9.0%	
Capital growth rate								5.8%		6.8%		6.3%	
Rate of Return													
Return on total capital = NOPAT / Avg. oper. cap.		16.6%		18.5%		21.3%							
Net sales	0001	393.2		552.2		827.9		159.0		275.7		434.7	
Sales growth rate								7.0%		8.4%		7.7%	
NOPAT margin		8.5%		9.0%		9.5%		10.1%		10.7%		10.5%	
Operating capital turnover (T/O)		1.96		2.07		2.24		2.41		2.67		2.57	
Cost of capital	3000	12.0%		12.0%		12.0%							
Capital charge (L1130 X L3000)	3001	24.1		32.1		44.4		8.0		12.3		20.3	
Economic profit (L1119-L3001)		9.3		17.4		34.6		8.1		17.2		25.3	

*In millions of dollars (all numbers in the exhibit are disguised).
Source: Charles F. Knight, "Emerson Electric: Consistent Profits, Consistently," *Harvard Business Review*, January–February 1992, p. 63. Used with permission of the Emerson Electric Company. All numbers are disguised.

Exhibit 2   The Sales Gap Chart Forecasts Five-Year Plans*

| | | | | Forecast | | | | | |
| | Line No. | Prior Year Actual FY 93 | Current Year Expected FY 94 | FY 95 | FY 96 | FY 97 | FY 98 | FY 99 | 5-Year Source of Growth (%) | 5-Year Company Annual Growth (%) |
		A	B	C	D	E	F	G	H	I
Domestic Excluding Exports										
Current year domestic sales base @ 10/1 prices	1		305.7	305.7	305.7	305.7	305.7	305.7		
Served industry-growth/(decline)	2			3.0	24.6	39.0	49.6	58.3	21.1%	3.6%
Penetration-increase/(decrease) (Including-new line extension/buyouts)	3			6.3	14.1	21.0	29.8	37.8	13.6	2.0
Price increases-current year through 5th year	4		3.3	7.6	14.7	21.6	29.5	38.0	12.6	1.7
Incremental new products: Prior 5 year introduction	5		16.1	16.4	17.7	17.4	17.5	19.0	1.1	
Current year through 5th year	6		1.4	5.6	11.8	18.5	25.9	34.2	11.9	
Other	7		3.1	1.4	1.6	2.3	2.5	2.8	-0.1	
Total Domestic	8	363.7	329.6	346.0	390.0	425.5	460.5	495.6		8.5
International Excluding Sales to U.S.										
Current year international sales base @ 10/1 prices	9		202.9	202.9	202.9	202.9	202.9	202.9		
Served industry-growth/(decline)	10			(0.1)	8.8	17.0	24.8	35.4	12.9	3.3
Penetration-increase/(decrease) (Including-new line extensions/buyouts)	11			(0.5)	18.8	27.2	36.2	45.1	16.4	3.6
Price increases-current year through 5th year	12		2.0	4.9	8.5	12.5	16.9	21.7	7.1	1.4
Incremental new products: Prior 5 year introduction	13		6.9	7.1	6.7	7.1	8.0	9.2	0.8	
Current year through 5th year	14		1.1	4.5	6.3	10.1	14.3	16.9	5.7	

Exhibit 2   The Sales Gap Chart Forecasts Five-Year Plans* (continued)

	Line No.	Prior Year Actual FY 93 — A	Current Year Expected FY 94 — B	Forecast FY 95 — C	FY 96 — D	FY 97 — E	FY 98 — F	FY 99 — G	5-Year Source of Growth (%) — H	5-Year Company Annual Growth (%) — I
Currency	15		9.3	–	–	–	–	–	– 3.4	
Other	16		0.4	0.8	0.7	0.9	1.0	1.1	0.3	
Total international	17	204.3	222.6	219.6	252.7	277.7	304.1	332.3		8.3
Total consolidated	18	568.0	552.2	565.6	642.7	703.2	764.6	827.9	100.0	8.4
Annual growth %—nominal			–2.8%	2.4%	13.6%	9.4%	8.7%	8.3%		
Gap:										
15% Target—nominal	19			635.0	730.2	839.8	965.7	1,110.6		15.0
Sales gap—over(under)	20			(69.4)	(87.5)	(136.6)	(201.1)	(282.7)		
U.S. exports (excluding to foreign subsidiaries)	21	35.3	31.3	33.7	35.9	39.9	43.9	47.6		8.7
Foreign subsidiaries (excluding sales to U.S.)	22	169.1	191.4	185.8	216.8	237.8	260.3	284.7		8.3

*In millions of dollars (all numbers in the exhibit are disguised).

Source: Charles F. Knight, "Emerson Electric: Consistent Profits, Consistently," *Harvard Business Review*, January–February 1992, p. 64. Used with permission of the Emerson Electric Company.

EXHIBIT 3

The sales gap line chart projects sales growth against other targets

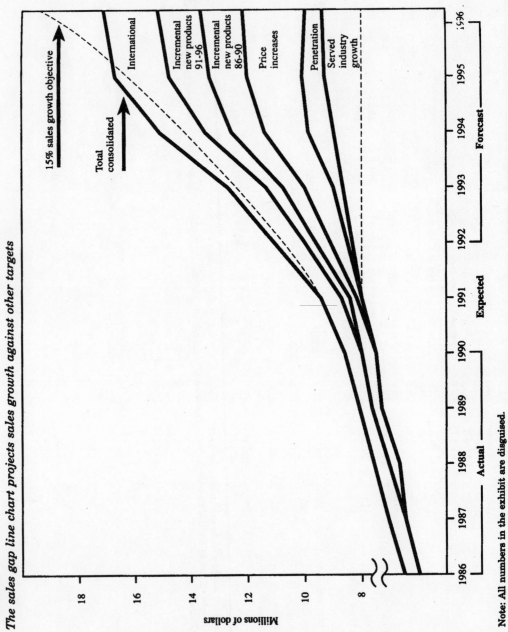

Note: All numbers in the exhibit are disguised.

Source: Charles F. Knight, "Emerson Electric: Consistent Profits, Consistently," *Harvard Business Review*, J1992, p. February 19⁶⁰, p. 65. Used with permission of the Emerson Electric Company.

ЕХНІВІТ 4 The 5-Back-by-5-Forward Chart Provides 11 Years of P&L Measures*

	Line No.	Actual/Restated					Current Year	Forecast				
		5th PY FY 89 A	4th PY FY 90 B	3rd PY FY 91 C	2nd PY FY 92 D	Prior Year FY 93 E	Expected FY 94 F	Next Yr FY 95 G	2nd Yr FY 96 H	3rd Yr FY 97 I	4th Yr FY 98 J	5th Yr FY 99 K
Order entries	1143	71,363	77,057	92,716	100,164	126,591	128,247	142,612	157,972	173,743	189,856	207,133
Sales backlog (year end)	1144	13,310	14,051	17,098	16,534	29,334	29,842	31,509	33,082	34,805	36,591	38,363
Net sales	0001	71,163	76,316	89,669	100,728	113,791	127,739	140,945	156,399	172,020	188,070	205,361
Annual growth %-nominal			7.2%	17.5%	12.3%	13.0%	12.3%	10.3%	11.0%	10.0%	9.3%	9.2%
-real							11.3%	7.8%	8.4%	6.7%	6.8%	6.1%
Cost of sales	0009	36,802	39,382	46,487	51,593	60,003	67,651	74,432	82,109	89,966	98,173	106,997
% to sales		51.7%	51.6%	51.8%	51.2%	52.7%	53.0%	52.8%	52.5%	52.3%	52.2%	52.1%
Gross profit	0010	34,361	36,934	43,182	49,135	53,788	60,088	66,513	74,290	82,054	89,897	98,364
% to sales		48.3%	48.4%	48.2%	48.8%	47.3%	47.0%	47.2%	47.5%	47.7%	47.8%	47.9%
SG&A expenses	0011	21,773	22,558	26,246	29,941	32,163	36,150	40,169	44,887	49,714	54,366	59,555
% to sales		30.6%	29.6%	29.3%	29.7%	28.3%	28.3%	28.5%	28.7%	28.9%	28.9%	29.0%
Operating profit	0012	12,588	14,376	16,936	19,194	21,625	23,938	26,344	29,403	32,340	35,531	38,809
% to sales		17.7%	18.8%	18.9%	19.1%	19.0%	18.7%	18.7%	18.8%	18.8%	18.9%	18.9%
Other (inc.)/ded. (excl. int.)	0235	423	1,090	1,395	1,232	1,488	1,764	1,766	1,794	1,530	1,438	1,423
Earnings before interest & taxes	0240	12,165	13,286	15,541	17,962	20,137	22,174	24,578	27,609	30,810	34,093	37,386
% to sales		17.1%	17.4%	17.3%	17.8%	17.7%	17.4%	17.4%	17.7%	17.9%	18.1%	18.2%

Exhibit 4   The 5-Back-by-5-Forward Chart Provides 11 Years of P&L Measures* (continued)

	Line No.	Actual/Restated					Current Year			Forecast			
		5th PY FY 89	4th PY FY 90	3rd PY FY 91	2nd PY FY 92	Prior Year FY 93	Expected FY 94	Next Yr FY 95	2nd Yr FY 96	3rd Yr FY 97	4th Yr FY 98	5th Yr FY 99
		A	B	C	D	E	F	G	H	I	J	K
Interest (income)/ expense, net	0230	(771)	(1,041)	(1,127)	(1,326)	(1,781)	(2,224)	(2,330)	(2,576)	(2,734)	(2,903)	(3,070)
Pretax earnings	0015	12,936	14,327	16,668	19,288	21,918	24,398	26,908	30,185	33,544	36,996	40,456
% to sales		18.2%	18.8%	18.6%	19.1%	19.3%	19.1%	19.1%	19.3%	19.5%	19.7%	19.7%
Income taxes	0016	5,445	6,785	7,788	8,447	9,668	10,551	11,753	13,101	14,497	15,948	17,387
Effective tax rate		42.1%	47.4%	46.7%	43.8%	44.1%	43.2%	43.7%	43.4%	43.2%	43.1%	43.0%
Net earnings	0017	7,491	7,542	8,880	10,841	12,250	13,847	15,155	17,084	19,047	21,048	23,069
% to sales		10.5%	9.9%	9.9%	10.8%	10.8%	10.8%	10.8%	10.9%	11.1%	11.2%	11.2%
Return on total capital	1324	20.4%	19.7%	20.3%	23.6%	23.8%	25.1%	26.1%	28.0%	30.1%	32.0%	33.9%
ROTC excluding goodwill	1323	27.3%	28.0%	27.2%	30.6%	31.5%	32.5%	32.9%	34.7%	36.6%	38.3%	40.2%

*In thousands of dollars (all numbers in the exhibit are disguised).

Source: Charles F. Knight, "Emerson Electric: Consistent Profits, Consistently," *Harvard Business Review*, January–February 1992, p. 66. Used with permission of the Emerson Electric Company.

EXHIBIT 5   President's Operating Report Division—Fiscal Year by Quarters/Actual and Expected

(Thousands of Dollars)

Line No.		Current Year						Prior Year		% Act/ Exp O/(U) PY
		Actual/ Expected	% Sales	Prior Expected	% Sales	Forecast	% Sales	Actual	% Sales	
1st Quarter Ending December 31										
1	Intercompany Sales	36		36		34		37		-2.7%
2	Net Sales	29,613		29,613		29,463		25,932		14.2%
3	Gross Profit	14,065	47.5%	14,065	47.5%	13,790	46.8%	12,384	47.8%	13.6%
4	SG&A Expenses	8,312	28.1%	8,312	28.1%	8,281	28.1%	7,650	29.5%	8.7%
5	Operating Profit	5,753	19.4%	5,753	19.4%	5,509	18.7%	4,734	18.3%	21.5%
6	Earnings Before Interest & Tax	5,280	17.8%	5,280	17.8%	5,048	17.1%	4,343	16.7%	21.6%
2nd Quarter Ending March 31										
7	Intercompany Sales	5		5		9		56		-91.1%
8	Net Sales	33,324		33,324		31,765		22,661		25.0%
9	Gross Profit	15,283	45.9%	15,283	45.9%	14,612	46.6%	12,518	47.0%	22.1%
10	SG&A Expenses	9,301	27.9%	9,301	27.9%	8,937	28.1%	7,393	27.8%	25.8%
11	Operating Profit	5,982	18.0%	5,982	18.0%	5,875	18.5%	5,123	19.2%	16.8%
12	Earnings Before Interest & Tax	5,785	17.4%	5,785	17.4%	5,612	17.7%	4,918	18.4%	17.6%
3rd Quarter Ending June 30										
13	Intercompany Sales	25		25		39		146		-82.9%
14	Net Sales	32,845		32,845		33,424		30,678		7.1%
15	Gross Profit	15,353	46.7%	15,353	46.7%	15,664	46.9%	14,310	46.6%	7.3%
16	SG&A Expenses	8,916	27.1%	8,916	27.1%	9,389	28.2%	8,424	27.4%	5.8%
17	Operating Profit	6,437	19.6%	6,437	19.6%	6,265	18.7%	5,886	19.2%	9.4%
18	Earnings Before Interest & Tax	6,126	18.7%	6,126	18.7%	5,646	16.9%	5,378	17.5%	13.9%
4th Quarter Ending September 30										
19	Intercompany Sales	94		94		94		25		276.0%
20	Net Sales	36,611		36,611		35,722		30,521		20.0%
21	Gross Profit	17,109	46.7%	17,109	46.7%	16,833	47.1%	14,576	47.8%	17.4%

EXHIBIT 5 **President's Operating Report Division—Fiscal Year by Quarters/Actual and Expected (continued)**

(Thousands of Dollars)

Line No.		Current Year						Prior Year		% Act / Exp O/(U) PY
		Actual/ Expected	% Sales	Prior Expected	% Sales	Forecast	% Sales	Actual	% Sales	
22	SG&A Expenses	10,537	28.7%	10,537	28.7%	10,029	28.1%	8,695	28.5%	21.2%
23	Operating Profit	6,572	18.0%	6,572	18.0%	6,803	19.0%	5,881	19.3%	11.7%
24	Earnings Before Interest & Tax	6,122	16.7%	6,122	16.7%	8,146	22.8%	5,498	18.0%	11.3%
	Fiscal Year Ending September 30									
25	Intercompany Sales	160		160		176		264		−39.4%
26	Net Sales	132,393		132,393		130,374		113,792		16.3%
27	Gross Profit	61,810	46.7%	61,810	46.7%	61,098	46.9%	53,788	47.3%	14.9%
28	SG&A Expenses	37,066	28.0%	37,066	28.0%	36,646	28.1%	32,164	28.3%	15.2%
29	Operating Profit	24,744	18.7%	24,744	18.7%	24,452	18.8%	21,624	19.0%	14.4%
30	Earnings Before Interest & Tax	23,313	17.6%	23,313	17.6%	24,451	18.8%	20,137	17.7%	15.8%
31	Pre-Tax Earnings	25,154	19.0%	25,154	19.0%	24,771	19.0%	21,918	19.3%	14.8%
32	Net Earnings	14,361	10.8%	14,361	10.8%	14,024	10.8%	12,250	10.8%	17.2%
	Expected First Quarter Next Fiscal Year									
33	Intercompany Sales	67		65				36		86.1%
34	Net Sales	32,830		32,311				29,613		10.9%
35	Gross Profit	15,142	46.1%	15,143	46.9%			14,065	47.5%	7.7%
36	SG&A Expenses	9,179	27.9%	9,217	28.6%			8,312	28.1%	10.4%
37	Operating Profit	5,963	18.2%	5,926	18.3%			5,753	19.4%	3.7%
38	Earnings Before Interest & Tax	5,628	17.1%	5,619	17.4%			5,280	17.8%	6.6%

Used with permission of the Emerson Electric Company. All numbers are disguised.

8-2: LETSGO TRAVEL TRAILERS

Letsgo manufactures travel trailers bought primarily by young families and retirees interested in a light, low-cost trailer that can easily by pulled by a mid-sized family car. The market for travel trailers has expanded nicely over the past few years due to the number of families seeking a relatively low-cost, outdoor vacation experience. But in the view of Letsgo's president, Mark Newman, the real growth in the future is in the retiree market. Newman believes the vigorous health of the average retiree, couple with the national trend toward a return to nature, will translate into continuing sales growth for Letsgo. As Newman loves to say, "camping recently moved from number seven to number six on the top-10 leisure activities in the United States, and the baby boomers are getting older every day."

The Retiree Market

Baby boomers (born between 1/1/46 and 12/31/64) carry a lot of consumer clout. Research indicates that for an organization to meet the needs of the senior market, including baby boomers, the following must be addressed:

- Independence and control
- Intellectual stimulation and self-expression
- Security and peace of mind
- Quality and value

According to the National Opinion Research Center at the University of Chicago, 78% of boomers (aged 33-51) own their own home, 45% are satisfied with their financial situation, 67% have not been hospitalized in the past five years, 73% are married, and 69% of their households have two wage earners. By the year 2000, boomers are expected to have an estimated $1 trillion to spend.[1] By 2010, the United States will be home to 53 million people aged 55 or older, with eight states expected to double their elderly population: Alaska, Arizona, California, Colorado, Georgia, Nevada, Utah, and Washington. Seniors respond to benefit-driven messages; to attract them, advertising has to communicate tangible benefits rather than features and amenities.

Marketing and Sales

The forecasted increase in Letsgo's sales can be seen in the company's sales projections presented in Exhibit 1 (actual for the years 1992 through 1997 and projected for the years 1998 through 2002). Although the weather can have a significant impact on the travel trailer industry (i.e., hurricane season, flooding, and even droughts have had negative effects on the sales and rentals of travel trailers), Letsgo's management believes these problems will be mitigated in the future by global warming. All sales projections are done by Mark Newman in his role as Letsgo's president.

To keep from losing sales, the company maintains finished goods inventory on had at the end of each month equal to 300 trailers plus 20% of the next month's projected sales. The finished goods inventory on December 31, 1997 was budgeted to be 1,000 trailers. Jim West, Letsgo's vice-president of marketing and sales, would rather see a minimum finished goods inventory of no less than 1,500 trailers. Jim refuses to talk to Tom Sloan, Letsgo's production manager. Tom is always trying to get Jim to consider adopting flexible inventory levels, which Jim is certain would affect his yearly bonus. The vice-president of sales and marketing is eligible for a 20% bonus based on sales. Unfortunately, Jim did not receive a bonus in 1997. Sales were up, but Mark refused to give Jim the bonus, although it was earned, due to the high number of customer complaints. Jim was really steamed when he heard "no bonus." Didn't Mark know those complaints were for poor quality? All of Jim's efforts to grow sales and attract customers were, once again, destroyed by Tom Sloan and his production failures.

Trailer Production

Sheet aluminum represents the company's single most expensive raw material. Each travel trailer requires 30 square yards of sheet aluminum. The wholesale cost of sheet aluminum varies dramatically by time of year. The cost per square yard can vary from $13 in the Spring, when new construction tends to start, to $6 in December and January, when demand is lowest. In September 1997, the Department of Energy and the aluminum industry launched a collaboration to pursue technologies to improve energy efficiency and production processes. "The pact will increase

---

[1]Note that this case was published in 1997.

global competitiveness and enhance the environmental performances of a key manufacturing sector by applying advanced scientific know-how to day-to-day industry needs" (Secretary of Energy Hazel R. O'Leary, September 1997). This collaboration will increase the aluminum industry's competitiveness and thus help businesses that rely on aluminum to reduce costs. Manufacturers requiring aluminum as a raw material potentially should be able to negotiate better purchase prices from suppliers.

Aluminum promises to be the construction material of the future. The use of aluminum in vehicles, including travel trailers, is increasing rapidly due to a heightened need for fuel-efficient, environmentally friendly vehicles. Aluminum can provide a weight savings of up to 55% compared to an equivalent steel structure, improving gas mileage significantly. The aluminum industry and suppliers are dispersed across four-fifths of the country, yet they are largely concentrated in four regions: the Pacific Northwest, industrial Midwest, northeastern seaboard, and mid-South. Although this is a broad geographic presence, Letsgo Travel Trailers will be affected by distribution costs.

Vicky Draper, Letsgo's vice-president of purchasing and materials handling, is eager to implement just-in-time (JIT) as a way of lowering Letsgo's aluminum cost, to offset the expense of distribution--Letsgo is located in Pennsylvania. Vicky's projected 20% bonus, recently announced by Mark and effect for the year-end 1998, is based on her ability to lower total material costs. Initially enthusiastic about her job and ability to earn a significant bonus, Vicky has become discouraged and angry. She is unable to convince Letsgo's current aluminum supplier to sign a prime vendor contract, and her efforts to locate an alternative vendor willing to accept the conditions of a JIT contract have similarly failed. She blames Tom Sloan. Letsgo's current aluminum vendor refuses to sign a JIT prime vendor contract due to Tom's uneven production schedule and his refusal to pay on time. Tom has been seen reading the Help Wanted ads, and Vicky overheard him talking to an employment agency.

In keeping with the policy set by Tom as Letsgo's production manager, the amount of sheet aluminum on hand at the end of each month must be equal to one-half of the following month's production needs for sheet aluminum. The raw materials inventory on December 31, 1997, was budgeted to be 39,000 square yards. The company does not keep track of work-in-process (WIP) inventories. Total budgeted merchandise purchases (of which the sheet aluminum is a significant part) and budgeted expenses for wages, heat, light and power, equipment rental, equipment purchases, depreciation, and selling and administrative for the first six months of 1998 are given below:

	January	February	March
Merchandise purchases	$870,000	$1,320,000	$1,110,000
Wages	624,000	1,008,000	1,104,000
Heat, light, & power	130,000	195,000	220,000
Equipment rental	390,000	390,000	390,000
Equipment purchases	300,000	300,000	300,000
Depreciation	250,000	250,000	250,000
Selling & administrative	400,000	400,000	400,000

	April	May	June
Merchandise purchases	$690,000	$420,000	$330,000
Wages	672,000	432,000	240,000
Heat, light, & power	135,000	110,000	110,000
Equipment rental	340,000	340,000	340,000
Equipment purchases	300,000	300,000	300,000
Depreciation	275,000	275,000	275,000
Selling & administrative	400,000	400,000	400,000

Merchandise purchases are paid in full during the month following purchase. Accounts payable for merchandise purchases on December 31, 1997, which will be paid during January, total $850,000.

Competition

All forms of vacation and leisure activities, including theme parks, beach or cabin rentals, health spas, resorts, and cruise vacations compete with Letsgo Travel Trailers for the consumer dollar. Other recreational purchases such as automobiles, snowmobiles, boats, and jet-skis are indirect competitors.

Travel trailer manufacturers such as Rexhall Industries, Coachman Industries, Winnebago Industries, Foremost Corporation of America, and Thor Sales Industries also offer a moderate-to-low-priced trailer. Manufacturers that

Blocher, Stout, Cokins, Chen: *Cost Management, 4e*

©The McGraw-Hill Companies, Inc 2008

offer more diverse product lines such as high-end trailers with luxury accommodations could compete for the fairly affluent senior market.

Coachman Industries, a direct Letsgo competitor, has become a leader in the recreational vehicle, motor home, and travel trailer industry through a commitment to quality and value based on excellence in engineering and attention to detail. Creative engineering, combined with high-accuracy analysis, reduced material costs at Coachman by more than 60% and labor costs by 78%.

Budget Preparation

To minimize company time lost on clerical work, Letsgo's accounting department prepares and distributes all budgets to the various departments every six months. Per Mark Newman, "Freeing departmental managers from the budgeting process allows them to concentrate on more pressing matters." In keeping with the recently announced bonus plan for the vice-president of purchasing and materials handling, Newman has instructed the accounting department to budget aluminum at $6 per square foot. The accounting manager recently received a 20% bonus for having prepared the budgets on time with little or no help from the other functional areas.

Cash

Letsgo's vice-president of finance, Becky Newman, has requested an $800,000, 90-day loan from the bank at a yet-to-be-determined interest rate. Since Letsgo has experienced difficulty in paying off its loans in the past, the loan officer at the bank has asked the company to prepare a cash budget for the six months ending June 30, 1998, to support the requested loan amount. The cash balance on January 1, 1998, is budgeted at $100,000 (the minimum cash balance required by Letsgo's Board of Directors).

Human Resources

To accomplish the company's corporate strategic goals, Letsgo Travel Trailers encourages upward communication among all its employees, from senior management to line employees. Decision-making, although not an entirely democratic process, is based on a team approach. Newman, as Letsgo's president, encourages managers to think in terms of the marketplace and to look at the business of travel trailers as a whole rather than as functional department successes and decisions. In fact, Newman is so committed to the idea of cooperative management and teamwork that he has hired three separate human resource consultants in the past six months to lead the company's managers through team-building exercises.

REQUIRED:
1. Discuss the validity and reasonableness of Letsgo's sales projections.
2. Prepare production, purchasing, and cash budgets for Letsgo for the fist six months of 1998. Discuss the advantages and disadvantages of the budgets you prepared. Who in the company does the budget help and whom, potentially, does it hurt? Does the budget help or hurt the sales department? What about production and finance? How are the various functional areas affected, and why?
3. Andy Baxter, newly hired by Letsgo from a competitor, suggests preparing the production budget assuming stable production. Prepare a second and third set of production, material purchases, and cash budgets with production held constant at 3,000 trailers per month for the second set of budgets and 3,500 trailers per month for the third set of budgets, using the following approach for the production budget (the purchasing and cash budget formats remain as presented above in question 2)--*note*: please see the tabs at the bottom of the spreadsheet template presented above:

	Jan	Feb	March	April	May	June	Six-Month Total
Production	3,000	3,000	3,000	3,000	3,000	3,000	18,000
Add: Beg inventory							
Total Available							
Less: Est. sales							
Ending inventory							

Assumptions: You will have to make some assumptions in order to complete the materials purchases (and cash payments) budget and for the budget for wages (labor) expense.

1) Assume that the labor cost per unit produced = average wage cost per unit, January - June in the original data set. As before, assume that wages are paid in the month incurred.

2) In terms of materials, note that the total amount purchased each month = purchases of aluminum (sheet metal) + purchases of other materials. As before, assume that all purchases are paid in the month following the month of purchase (i.e., there is a one-month payment lag). Assume that the beginning-of-year balance for total purchases payable is $850,000 (the same as before). To estimate total purchases PAYMENTS in a given month, use the following percentage obtained from the original data, any of the months March through June: Total Purchases$_t$ /Aluminum Purchases$_{t-1}$. (**Hint:** this number should be 166.67 %.) Assume that the ALUMINUM purchases (from January) to be paid in February = $711,000 (same as before). This amount will have to be increased by estimated non-Aluminum materials purchased using the preceding rate.

Discuss the advantages and disadvantages of the second and third sets of production, material purchases, and cash budgets you've prepared. Who in the company do these budgets help and whom, potentially, do they hurt? Do these budgets help or hurt the sales department? What about production and finance? How are the various functional areas affected, and why?

4. What should Letsgo use to measure performance for each of the managers in the case? What bonus system would you suggest that incorporates these measures and also encourages the managers to work as a team?

Exhibit 1
Actual and Projected Sales, in Number of Trailers

	1992	1993	1994	1995	1996	1997
Actual sales	13,765	14,880	15,991	17,809	19,634	23,322

	1998	1999	2000	2001	2002
Projected sales	28,000	33,600	40,320	48,384	58,060

The detail sales for 1997 (actual) and 1998 (projected) by month are as follows:

	1997 Actual	1998 Projected
January	1,983	2,500
February	3,218	4,000
March	3,981	5,000
April	3,240	3,000
May	1,755	2,000
June	901	1,000
July	763	1,000
August	611	1,000
September	1,622	2,000
October	1,678	2,000
November	1,439	2,000
December	2,131	2,500
Total no. of trailers	23,322	28,000

Blocher, Stout, Cokins, Chen: *Cost Management, 4e*

©The McGraw-Hill Companies, Inc 2008

Actual sales in dollars for the last two months of 1997 and budgeted sales for the first six months of 1998 follow:

November 1997 (actual)	$1,439,000
December 1997 (actual)	2,131,000
January 1998 (budgeted)	2,500,000
February 1998 (budgeted)	4,000,000
March 1998 (budgeted)	5,000,000
April 1998 (budgeted)	3,000,000
May 1998 (budgeted)	2,200,000
June 1998 (budgeted)	1,100,000

Past experience shows that 25% of a month's sales are collected in the month of sale, 10% in the month following the month of sale, and 60% in the second month following the month of sale. The remainder is uncollectible.

Readings

8.1: HOW TO SET UP A BUDGETING AND PLANNING SYSTEM

By Robert N. West, CPA, and Amy M. Snyder CPA,
Certificate of Merit

Two years ago, Penn Fuel Gas, Inc. (PFG) initiated its first annual and long-range operating budget process. PFG is a public utility holding company with consolidated revenues of $125 million and 550 employees. In addition to selling natural gas, the company provides natural gas storage and transportation services, provides merchandise services, and has a propane business. PFG's utility operations are split between two subsidiaries, each with a number of locations.

The motivation for budgeting came jointly from PFG's bankers, its board of directors, and its management. The information needs of all three users were fairly similar. All three were interested in cash flow projections and future earnings potential. The board was interested in improving PFG's return on equity (ROE), and it wanted to analyze the prospects of reinstituting a common stock dividend. In addition, management wanted segment P&Ls and improved departmental (cost center) expense and cash flow tracking. PFG's segments are regions, lines of business (utility, propane, and merchandise, and type of customer commercial, industrial, residential).

WHERE TO START?

The first decision was whether to use existing in-house personnel, hire consultants, or hire a full-time budget manager. Consultants or a new hire would offer the benefit of an independent, fresh perspective with no biases. The disadvantage is that they wouldn't know the business as well as an insider. Penn Fuel Gas used consultants to set up its first budget and then hired a full-time, experienced professional to handle its budgeting. PFG wisely gave the position a manager title to assign appropriate status to the position. Once the staffing decision was resolved, the new budget director faced three primary tasks.

Learn the business. PFG hired a self-directed person (co-author Amy Snyder) who could understand the business quickly and get both long-range and operating budget processes up and running. Although the operations of PFG's business are relatively straightforward, the rules and regulations of the public utility industry are complex. PFG did two things to bring the budget manager up to speed. It sent her to a week-long technical program to learn the regulatory side of the business, and it extended her an open invitation to important meetings of operations vice presidents and top management so she could learn the operating side of the business.

Budgeting for natural gas and propane operations is difficult because a significant amount of demand for these products is dependent upon Mother Nature. Penn Fuel experienced two abnormal winters in its first two years of budgeting. In 1994, Pennsylvania had its coldest, iciest winter in history; in 1995, it had one of its warmest. But forecasting is difficult for many rapidly growing companies (one group for whom this article is intended). They must be flexible. For example, PFG prepares budgets using the normal weather forecast, but it also provides sensitivity analyses and budget reprojections at least quarterly. Company and budget personnel realize that capital spending is partially a function of the winter season's revenues, which won't be known until the first quarter is over. The first quarter is particularly important in the utility and propane business as it represents 40% of total annual product delivered.

Determine the users' information needs. Different users have different information needs, and users don't always know what information they "need." If managers or board members are not financially oriented, as is the case with many small businesses, they may need a little guidance. PFG's directors included several financially astute individuals who had a clear idea of what information they wanted. Costs were budgeted on both an accrual basis (for P&L reports) and cash basis (for cash flow reports).

Review and update the information system. All accounting information systems (AIS) face the daunting task of trying to provide the appropriate output for multiple sets of users. The reports needed from Penn Fuel's MS included:

1. External financial reports (GAAP),
2. Tax reporting,
3. Internal management segment reports,
4. Cash flow reports, and
5. Reports for regulators.

The budget manager analyzed the AI to determine whether data were classified and summarized in a manner useful for internal business plans and budget reports. Most accounting systems are geared toward external financial reports, and, in the case of regulated industries, for reports to regulators as well. Internal managers usually prefer information provided in a different format, such as results by division, product line, region, or customer group.

DECISIONS TO MAKE

PFG's budget manager faced some interesting information systems setups on which she had to make decisions when she started her work.

Different internal reporting systems. The Northern division, acquired several years ago, reported its results in different formats from the Southern division. Eventually a common reporting system will be attained, but the immediate task was to rearrange the data to assist with the consolidation and make the division data comparable. The underlying information systems differed as well. The two divisions used different accounting software, adding another challenge to the eventual merging of information systems.

Treatment of a different business segment. PFG's propane business segment seems similar to the natural gas business, but it has several key differences. Because it is unregulated, it has direct control over the pricing of its product. The utility's chart of accounts was not a perfect fit. PFG had to decide whether to maintain a uniform chart of accounts or create a separate general ledger account structure for its propane business segment. PFG adapted the propane business unit's account structure to the utility account structure. The tradeoff was ease of corporate reporting versus the individual business unit's desired view of the data. A slight edge was given to corporate reporting.

Management and the board of directors wanted segment information that was difficult to obtain. Total spending and spending by operating unit were easy to retrieve, but other views of the information had not been developed. For example, segregating operating expenses by business segment was provided partially by existing reports, but aggregation of all segments was tedious to reconcile to the general ledger due to corporate staff allocations. Most corporate personnel, from the president down to the fixed asset accountants, do not keep formal track of their time. Allocations were made to the various business segments on spreadsheets, requiring an audit trail and explanations to reconcile back to the results per the accounting records.

Review expense classifications. As a company grows, its chart of accounts should be reviewed periodically to determine if information is being captured in the most meaningful way. Introducing a budget system is an ideal time to modify the accounting system with a view toward future information needs. PFG's new budget manager reviewed the utility's accounting system with a fresh perspective and came up with a couple of suggestions to improve the precision of the accounting information system.

The first suggestion was to get rid of miscellaneous expense accounts with large balances. Most businesses prefer that almost nothing be recorded in miscellaneous accounts. PFG's state-mandated chart of accounts lent itself to this practice as the chart of accounts included many miscellaneous expense accounts. The challenge here was twofold:

1. Perform an account analysis to reclassify some of the charges to the miscellaneous expense account, and
2. Change the accounting system (add accounts and subaccounts) to ensure that future transactions are put into more descriptive accounts.

Lack of sufficient detail, such as the overuse of miscellaneous expense, is a common small business practice, so many new budget managers will face a housekeeping task similar to PFG's.

The next suggestion was to change the expense classification system. For example, the training & education account included charges for the training course fee, hotel, travel, meals, and the salary charge for the time at the training session, and so on. This system actually was an activity-based costing system in which training included all costs driven by the decision to send an employee to a training program. While this classification of costs is perfectly acceptable, some accountants would record these items in separate accounts to maintain more detail. PFG has several hundred active general ledger accounts, so transaction classification is not a trivial task.

Most companies initiating a budgeting and planning function should review thoroughly the chart of accounts, account classification (particularly expenses), and the reporting system. In many cases, the accounting system will not have kept pace with the changes in the company (for example, expanded product lines or changes in customers and geographical regions served. It is best if the budget manager resolves information classification and reporting issues up front so that future budgets are comparable. It is difficult to change a system once it has been developed, and budget systems are no different from any other information system in that respect.

Difficulty reconciling amounts back to the ledger. Using the example of training costs cited above, some salary costs were included in accounts other than salary expense. Reconciling accounts such as salaries between the ledger and the payroll register can be difficult. Other accounts are difficult to reconcile as well. The budget manager decided to reclassify some data, but verifying the accuracy of reclassified data was, and still is, a challenge.

Information timeliness/availability. Budgeting brought the desire for better and faster information. PFG uses a minicomputer-based accounting package for general ledger, human resources, and payables. Yet portions of the accounting system still are manual, and monthly closings can take up to three weeks. PFG responded to some of its information needs by installing a new billing system that computerizes cash receipts and provides excellent summary information. PFG also is looking into a computerized project tracking system (for its many construction projects) and improving the computerized fixed assets system by adding a budget feature.

DELIVERABLES

Management wanted a one-year business plan prior to year-end as well as monthly updates (for example, budget vs. actual results). In addition, the board of directors wanted a long-range (three-year) plan each year. To meet these needs, the budget manager developed packets for the directors and management.

The board wanted the financial and operational data reported by segment—some reports segmented geographically, some by product line, and others by customer type.

The monthly financial packet. The monthly financial packet includes the following schedules:

A. P&L and cash flow (by region and in total)
 1. Current month
  a. Actual vs. budget
  b. Actual vs. same month in prior year
 2. Year-to-date (YTD)
  a. YTD actual vs. YTD budget
  b. Budget projections for remainder of year
  c. YTD actual vs. prior YTD actual
 3. Two full-year monthly bar charts
  a. Actual vs. budgeted cash flow
  b. Actual vs. budgeted net income
 4. Capital structure and ROE

B. Selected five-year comparative data
 1. Current month and YTD units of product delivered
  a. Residential
  b. Commercial
  c. Industrial
  d. Resale
  e. Detail provided for 10 largest customers
 2. Gas and propane stored
 3. Comparative YTD income statements

The annual business plan. The annual business plan contains data similar to the monthly package by region and in total. Full-year budget data are compared with the current year estimated (10 months' actual plus estimates for November and December) results and prior year actual results. These data are shown in tabular and graphical form. The annual plan also contains:

A. Budgeted income statements for all 12 months.
B. Budgeted cash flow statements for all 12 months.
C. Budgeted ROE schedule for all 12 months.
D. Capital expenditures forecasts, including brief written descriptions of the projects, by segment.
 1. New business (line extensions)
 2. Replacements/betterments
 3. Meters
 4. Tools & equipment
F. Personnel data including projected new hiring, replacement hiring, and workforce reductions.

Explanations of significant variances from prior year actual results are provided in both the annual and monthly packages. Second-stage variance analysis (breaking the variance into its price and quantity components) is provided as needed.

Formatting tips. After completing the first budgeting exercises, the budget manager came to the conclusion that some formatting tips might help those persons who were not familiar with the budgeting

Blocher, Stout, Cokins, Chen: *Cost Management, 4e*

process. First, she suggests using graphs. Whoever is preparing a budget should consider displaying the information in graphical form rather than tables of numbers so it will appeal to all levels of readers.

Second, she suggests that a company consider the direct method for cash flow reports. PFG uses the direct method for its cash flow statement because it is more informative and is easier for readers to understand. The adjustments to net income with the indirect method are confusing and do not tell the reader where the money is coming from and to whom it is going. Reports for external parties still can use the indirect method if companies prefer. **Table 1** contains a sample direct method cash flow statement.

THE BUDGET CALENDAR

What does the budget group do throughout the year? **Table 2** shows the other functions performed by the budget manager each month. Notice that the annual budget data collection process begins five months before the packet is due to the board of directors. A four- to six-month lead time is fairly standard.

PFG decided to prepare its three-year forecast before doing the annual budget because the board wanted information on ROE and cash flow to analyze future earnings potential, for financing requirements, and for general business planning purposes. Once the three-year plan was reviewed, the first year's data were used as a guideline for the current year annual budget's operational and segment detail.

ONGOING CHALLENGES

We already highlighted the initial challenges faced by a new budget manager. Now let's look at some ongoing challenges.

Evolving mission. The budget function is formed with planning as its primary mission. In the early stages of its existence, however, it is expected to analyze company and segment performance. Variance analysis can be both interesting and challenging, challenging because no two years are ever the same. One obvious difference in the natural gas and propane business is the weather, which rarely is the same two years in a row. But other changes such as geographical growth, changes in product mix, and restructuring of divisions increase the challenge of reconciling operating results of two consecutive periods.

Gamesmanship. Budgeting also brings behavioral challenges such as lowballing revenues or padding expenses. PFG has experienced minimal budgeting gamesmanship for two reasons that are described next.

1. Budgets are developed with management, arriving at agreed-upon, reasonable expectations.
2. PFG has not used the budget as a "hammer" at year-end for employees or divisions who did not make budget.

Get people up to speed. The behavioral challenge at PFG has been to get people up to speed with budgeting. The budget manager came from a large company where budgeting was part of the culture. At PFG, she sent out schedules and written instructions on completing the budget requests the first time through. But not everyone understood how to complete the budget forms. Her goal the next year was to sit down with people and work through the forms with those who were unaccustomed to the budget process.

When formal budgeting is new to a company, the budget manager may end up doing the bulk of the budget preparation because people are new to the process. One unfortunate byproduct that can occur is that managers then think it's the budget manager's budget. The budget manager has to impress upon them that it is their department and their budget. It is important to determine up front who is responsible and accountable.

Top management support. All new systems require top management's support. To make budgeting effective, management must communicate the importance of well-thought-out input from departments and operating units. If preparing a well-thought-out budget is not included in managers' goals and objectives for the year, employees may not make the time for the process. Resistance may result, not because employees feel threatened by the new budget system, but, rather, because they lack time.

BENEFITS FROM BUDGETING

Budgeting has improved communication throughout Penn Fuel Gas, Inc., and has improved teamwork toward a common goal. It has helped the board of directors to represent shareholders better and has provided support to management on major decisions. PFG expects even better planning in the future to result in operational improvements, improved management of resources, better cost control, earnings growth, and improved responsibility resulting from managers' active participation in the planning process.

Robert N. West, CPA, Ph.D., is an assistant professor at Villanova University. He is the author of several articles and the text, *Microcomputer Accounting Systems.* He is a member of the Valley Forge Chapter, through which this article was submitted, and can be reached at (610) 519-4359.

Amy M. Snyder, CPA, was manager of budgeting and planning at Penn Fuel Gas, Inc., when this article was written. Now she is controller of Espe America, Inc. She is a member of the Valley Forge Chapter and can be reached at (610) 277-3800.

Table 1. DIRECT METHOD CASH FLOW STATEMENT						
	Current Month			**Year-to-Date**		
	Actual	Budget	Variance	Actual	Budget	Varianc
Cash Inflows						
Utility						
Propane						
Merchandise						
Total Cash Inflow						
Cash Outflow's						
Gas purchases						
Propane purchases						
Merchandise purchases						
Operating and maintenance expenses						
Labor and benefits						
Insurance						
Outside services						
Leases						
Storage						
Other						
Rate case preparation						
Other taxes						
Income taxes						
Interest on LTD						
Other interest						
Principal payments						
Common dividends						
Preferred dividends						
Total Cash Outflow						
Available funds						
Capital expenditures						
Net Change in Cash						

Blocher, Stout, Cokins, Chen: *Cost Management, 4e*

Table 2. THE BUDGET CALENDAR
PROCEDURES AND REPORTS DUE

December

Annual budget for coming year. Presentation to board of directors. Present current year results; 10 months of actual and projections for remaining two months (November's results would not be available at this point).

January

Issue approved budgets to managers and vice presidents. Set up monthly financial report for the new year.

February

Prepare actual P&Ls and cash flow by month for the prior year.

March

Clean-up work after year-end closing and audit.

April

1st quarter actual vs. budget to board of directors. Nine-month projections. Send out requests for long-range forecast.

May

Prepare long-range forecast.

June

Present long-range forecast to board of directors.

July

Requests for the upcoming year's capital spending, operating revenues, expenses, and cash flows sent to operating units and corporate departments. 2nd quarter actual vs. budget to board of directors. Six-month projections.

August

Follow up on July requests. Help employees unfamiliar with budget requests.

September

July budget requests due. Input, analyze, and summarize the data.

October

Top management reviews budgets. Have meetings, and negotiate final amounts with various vice presidents and managers. 3rd quarter actual vs. budget to board of directors. Three-month projections.

November

Prepare final budget.

8.2: Strategic Budgeting: A Case Study and Proposed Framework

by Audrey G. Taylor, Ph.D., and Savya Rafai

In 1999, a manager at one of the "Big 3" automotive companies in the Detroit area implemented a new budgeting process called strategic budgeting (SB) that reduced costs in his area by 37.6% without compromising the delivery of services or causing the layoff of personnel.

The budgeting method was based on the assumptions behind a project management technique developed by Eliyahu Goldratt in his 1997 book, Critical Chain. The technique was applied to a service department where the linkages between the "optimal level" of inputs for the outputs provided were unknown. As a project, by definition, embodies the development of a new product or process, the time needed for each task in the project is unknown. To deal with the uncertainty of each step within a project, estimates are made to ensure that milestones can be met. In a similar fashion, budgets are developed to ensure that targets can be met without going over the planned budget.

Traditionally, companies trying to reduce costs use "the lawnmower method" for cost reduction. In the lawnmower method, cost cutting does not discriminate on the basis of need or capacity. All departments are simply required to reduce costs by a given percentage. The assumption of many managers is that all budgets contain slack.[1] In his study of budgetary slack, Mohammed Onsi documented that 80% of the managers he interviewed admitted that they "bargain for slack."[2] Onsi also discovered that slack is created to ensure managers meet budget targets and to protect them from uncertainty. The problem for the upper-level manager is to identify how much slack exists in the budgets for the departments under his or her control and to remove it without jeopardizing the amount or the quality of the services provided.

In Critical Chain, Goldratt introduced a technique for removing unnecessary padding from time estimates for tasks in a project. Goldratt built his model on several observations. First, he recognized that forecasts for the timing of tasks or for cost estimation are relatively accurate in the aggregate but are much less accurate when used to estimate tasks and costs of subunits. Second, Goldratt states that managers tend to overestimate the time needed for individual tasks by a minimum of 100% (see **Figure**

1). Overestimation protects managers from missing "milestones" in projects. Finally, Goldratt states that

Figure 1: Developing Time Estimates for Project Completion

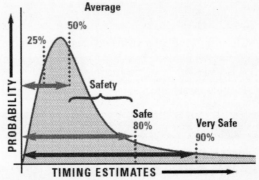

procrastination, labeled the Student Syndrome, causes estimates to be overrun and due dates to be missed.

In order to counteract the unnecessary padding of steps in a project, Goldratt recommended cutting time estimates for each project task in half and then grouping all of the time saved from individual tasks into one "project buffer" placed at the end of the project's estimated time sequence. The "project buffer" was hen reduced by one half in order to reduce the overall project time allowed by one third of its original estimate (**Figure 2**).

By following these simple steps, many companies experienced dramatic reductions in the time necessary to complete projects. Among those using the Critical Chain technique are DaimlerChrysler, Lucent Technologies, Israel Aircraft Industries, and Harris Semiconductor.

What Is The Strategic Budgeting Model?

Strategic budgeting bases cost reduction on the same assumptions and on the same techniques used in the Critical Chain method of reducing project time. The first assumption of SB is that service department budgets contain a great deal of slack. The slack multiplies exponentially over time.

In the example in **Table 1**, the amount of slack buildup after just four years in a budget with 10% slack added at each level is over 100% of the original

Blocher, Stout, Cokins, Chen: *Cost Management, 4e*

budget. By year 10 the slack has increased to almost five times the original amount. With so much potential for slack in even a modest increase of 10% over estimated needs, there is probably room to

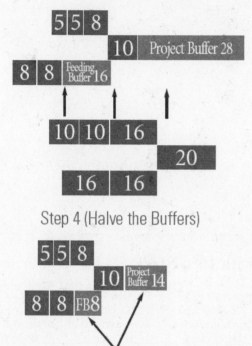

Figure 2: Step 1 (Identify), Step 2 (Halve Time), and Step 3 (Create the Project Buffer)

Step 4 (Halve the Buffers)

reduce most budgets in most service departments by significant amounts.

Even though, on average, budgets have large levels of slack, we cannot say that every budget has tremendous amounts of slack built into it. Therefore, SB allows departments to receive more funds when necessary. Kenton Walker and Eric Johnson discovered in their study of budgetary slack building in a sales division that lower-level managers built slack into their budgets in order to secure bonuses.[3] The authors also noted, however, that upper-level managers eliminated slack due to their knowledge of historical patterns of sales. It is worth mentioning that building slack is more difficult in areas with defined relationships between inputs and outputs. The department studied in this case is not a production or sales department and does not have a well-defined relationship between given inputs for a specific level of outputs.

SB also recognizes that forecasting in the aggregate is much more accurate than forecasting at the task level, an observation documented by David Otley in 1985.[4] SB allows for slack in one place only—the group budget buffer. Any department may draw funds from the group budget buffer if those funds are needed during the year. Providing the safety net of extra funds allows budgets to be drastically slashed at the lower levels without compromising performance of needed services.

A Specific Implementation of Strategic Budgeting

In this case study, SB was implemented at a major manufacturing firm using the following process:
1. Gathered budget estimates from department heads.
2. Reduced all department budgets by 50%.
3. Grouped all "savings" from department budgets in a Group Budget Buffer.
4. Told each department head that if he or she needed further funds, the funds would be available but the request would be discussed openly with other department heads.

The Implementation Process

In 1999, shortly after a new manager took over the Testing Department of 42 employees in three functional divisions (Service, Application Development, and System Integration), the edict came to reduce operating expenses by 10%. The operating expenses under review involved the cost of purchasing services for equipment repair and calibration, hardware and software for testing services, overtime payments, and miscellaneous supplies. Each manager adamantly fought against any reductions, stating that all of the funds were needed.

In order to achieve the required reduction, another approach was taken. The first step was to develop a holistic goal for the entire department. The consensus goal was, "*To offer superior-quality products and services to our customer with a focus on speed and flexibility*." The process of using the team to develop the goal follows Joshua Ronen and J.L. Livingstone's premise that intrinsic rewards are achieved through the process of participation in goal setting.[5] Once the goal was agreed upon, the measurements for the department had to be changed to align with the new goal of working as one unit rather than as three functions. Employees were now measured on their ability to find synergies between the three functions and cross-functional team-based ideas for improvement opportunities.

Next, training started on the new Critical Chain method of reducing cost by grouping the cost reductions taken from each department together in one departmental buffer while reducing each function's budget by one half.

Table 1a: Budget Year 1 without Slack

Department	Lowest Tier	Second Tier	Department Total + $200,000 for Administration of Department	Division Total + $200,000 for Administration of Division	Slack as a Percent of Original Budget
RESEARCH AND DEVELOPMENT				$5,600,000	0%
Design			$1,700,000		
Feature Engineering		$500,000			
Overall Manufacturing Engineering		$500,000			
Prototype Build		$500,000			
Testing			$3,700,000		
Prototype Testing		$500,000			
Advanced Prototype Testing		$500,000			
Individual Labs		$500,000			
Lab 1	$200,000				
Lab 2	$200,000				
Lab 3	$200,000				
Lab 4	$200,000				
Lab 5	$200,000				
Lab 6	$200,000				
Lab 7	$200,000				
Lab 8	$200,000				
Lab 9	$200,000				
Lab 10	$200,000				

Table 1b: Budget Year 1 with 10% Slack

Department	Lowest Tier	Second Tier	Department Total + $200,000 for Administration of Department	Division Total + $200,000 for Administration of Division	Slack as a Percent of Original Budget
RESEARCH AND DEVELOPMENT				$7,359,000	31%
Design			$2,035,000		
Feature Engineering		$550,000			
Overall Manufacturing Engineering		$550,000			
Prototype Build		$550,000			
Testing			$4,455,000		
Prototype Testing		$550,000			
Advanced Prototype Testing		$550,000			
Individual Labs		$550,000			
Lab 1	$220,000				
Lab 2	$220,000				
Lab 3	$220,000				
Lab 4	$220,000				
Lab 5	$220,000				
Lab 6	$220,000				
Lab 7	$220,000				
Lab 8	$220,000				
Lab 9	$220,000				
Lab 10	$220,000				

Blocher, Stout, Cokins, Chen: *Cost Management, 4e*

Table 1c: Budget Year 4 with 10% Slack

Department	Lowest Tier	Second Tier	Department Total + $200,000 for Administration of Department	Division Total + $200,000 for Administration of Division	Slack as a Percent of Original Budget
RESEARCH AND DEVELOPMENT				$11,880,978	112%
Design			$2,708,585		
Feature Engineering		$732,050			
Overall Manufacturing Engineering		$732,050			
Prototype Build		$732,050			
Testing			$5,929,605		
Prototype Testing		$732,050			
Advanced Prototype Testing		$732,050			
Individual Labs		$732,050			
Lab 1	$292,820				
Lab 2	$292,820				
Lab 3	$292,820				
Lab 4	$292,820				
Lab 5	$292,820				
Lab 6	$292,820				
Lab 7	$292,820				
Lab 8	$292,820				
Lab 9	$292,820				
Lab 10	$292,820				

Table 1d: Budget Year 10 with 10% Slack

Department	Lowest Tier	Second Tier	Department Total + $200,000 for Administration of Department	Division Total + $200,000 for Administration of Division	Slack as a Percent of Original Budget
RESEARCH AND DEVELOPMENT				$32,744,641	485%
Design			$4,798,424		
Feature Engineering		$1,296,871			
Overall Manufacturing Engineering		$1,296,871			
Prototype Build		$1,296,871			
Testing			$10,504,657		
Prototype Testing		$1,296,871			
Advanced Prototype Testing		$1,296,871			
Individual Labs		$1,296,871			
Lab 1	$518,748				
Lab 2	$518,748				
Lab 3	$518,748				
Lab 4	$518,748				
Lab 5	$518,748				
Lab 6	$518,748				
Lab 7	$518,748				
Lab 8	$518,748				
Lab 9	$518,748				
Lab 10	$518,748				

Table 1e: Budget Increases Using 10% Slack Compounded Annually

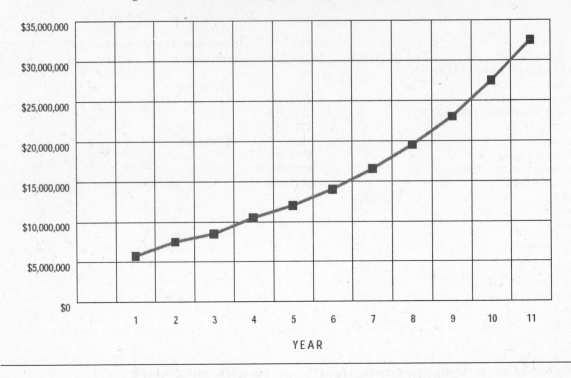

YEAR

The departmental buffer functioned to reduce the risk of the group having insufficient funds for vital tasks. Any funds needed over the approved amount had to be explained to the other function managers and to the departmental manager. Justification for extra funds from the buffer was presented in a business case using the Theory of Constraints Thinking Process Tools, including the Current Reality Tree, CRT, and the Evaporating Cloud.[6] The CRT documented current ripple effects from current processes including, especially, any negative effects of the loss of funds on other departments' products or services.

The manager and the supervisors created a priority-spending matrix (**Figure 3**), which was used by the entire organization to evaluate the importance of the extra spending. The spending matrix was inspired by Steven R. Covey's book, *The Seven Habits of Highly Effective People: Restoring the Character Ethic.*

Once a month, at a departmental meeting called the Town Hall Meeting, all 42 departmental employees were briefed on the state of the departmental buffer. Any collaborative cross-functional accomplishments and any customer compliments for the department's services and products were highlighted.

During one meeting of the function managers, the Service Department manager requested buffer funds to purchase the services of an outside company to track the expenses of the Service Department. Fortunately, the Application Group's manager volunteered to develop the database for the Services Department at no charge. Through this synergy, the company avoided dipping into the departmental buffer and fostered collaboration. The event was described in an article circulated to all of the 42 departmental employees and reviewed in a Town Hall Meeting.

The Results

1. Budget Depletion for Important Tasks

After the first year, almost the entire departmental pool was intact. Of the original $6,250,000 buffer, $1,550,000 was reallocated to the System Integration function, reducing the buffer to $4,700,000. System Integration requested the extra funds for the purchase of data acquisition equipment to be used to solve warranty related problems. The managers of the other two functions agreed that the purchase of the equipment served a compelling function and furthered the goals of the department as a whole. Due to the added funds from the budget buffer, the System Integration Department ended up with almost twice the level of its original funding prior to the reductions at the start of the SB process (see **Figure 4**).

Blocher, Stout, Cokins, Chen: *Cost Management, 4e*

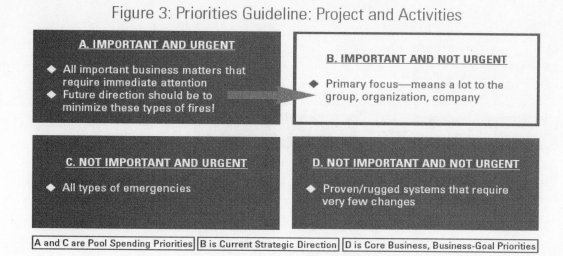

Figure 3: Priorities Guideline: Project and Activities

A. IMPORTANT AND URGENT	B. IMPORTANT AND NOT URGENT
◆ All important business matters that require immediate attention ◆ Future direction should be to minimize these types of fires!	◆ Primary focus—means a lot to the group, organization, company
C. NOT IMPORTANT AND URGENT	D. NOT IMPORTANT AND NOT URGENT
◆ All types of emergencies	◆ Proven/rugged systems that require very few changes

A and C are Pool Spending Priorities | B is Current Strategic Direction | D is Core Business, Business-Goal Priorities

2. Utilizing Synergies to Maintain the Budget Buffer

In order to maintain the buffer, the service manager reviewed his purchases of thermocouples. He observed that, in the past, the department had stockpiled the wire without regard for the utilization patterns. After researching the historical usage patterns, he discovered that the thermocouples were only heavily used in the summer months during "In-Vehicle Testing." In addition, management discovered that several times the inventoried thermocouples were not needed because the vehicle department requesting the testing had already purchased the parts. Eventually, the purchase of thermocouples was eliminated.

Probably the largest savings came from the change in the buying patterns for data acquisition equipment. The Testing Department would traditionally purchase this equipment for customer departments requesting specific tests. The equipment was then transferred to the customer department and maintained there. The equipment generally was used only once for specific testing needs. The customer department also would calibrate the equipment, but the calibration frequently was not accurate, so testing results were suspect.

To reduce the waste of a one-time equipment purchase, the departmental manager created a library of data acquisition equipment. As a result, the equipment now is used repetitively instead of just once. Another major benefit of the library was that the Testing Department also maintained the equipment, so the calibrations were more accurate. This step not only saved costs but also improved overall quality of the services provided.

3. Removing Redundancies

In the process of reviewing spending patterns, managers discovered that one costly function performed by the department also was being handled by another department. Once the double tasking was identified, the work was returned to the department originally assigned the task and was no longer also performed by the Testing Department.

Over the next two years, the department was thrice asked to reduce expenditures by 10%. The cuts were made from the departmental buffer without any loss of headcount or product or with any project termination. During this period, employee morale was very high.

4. An Unforeseen Negative Consequence of Success

Unfortunately, the divisional manager retired at the end of the first year's implementation. The new divisional manager immediately requested another 10% reduction. Due to the projected $6,250,000 in the budget buffer, the Testing Department manager was able to immediately comply with the request. Every other departmental manager fought the reduction.

Later on in the same year, the divisional manager again requested another 10% reduction in the budgets of all departments in the division. Again, the Testing manager easily complied. Due to the alacrity of the response, the divisional manager assumed that there must be high levels of excess capacity in Testing. Therefore, she dramatically downsized the department, eliminating personnel and reassigning them to other areas within the corporation. The successful team was split up, their success rewarded with dismissal from the project.

Although the initial response of upper management was devastating to the employees of the Testing Department, eventually, after seeing the innovation of the manager in this one department, the company asked the manager to spread the Theory of Constraints innovations corporate-wide.

Figure 4:
Original Group Budget — Year 1

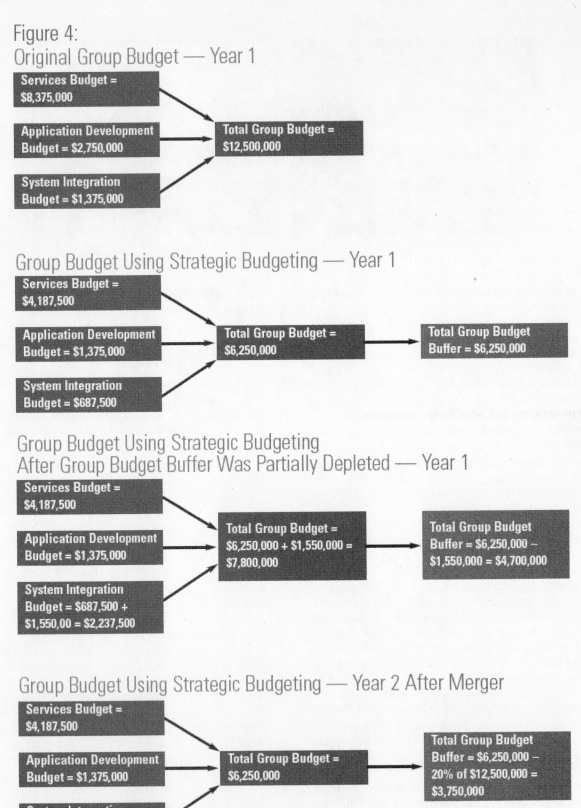

Group Budget Using Strategic Budgeting — Year 1

Group Budget Using Strategic Budgeting
After Group Budget Buffer Was Partially Depleted — Year 1

Group Budget Using Strategic Budgeting — Year 2 After Merger

Blocher, Stout, Cokins, Chen: *Cost Management, 4e*

The Strengths of Strategic Budgeting

1. Ease of Implementation
In contrast to zero based budgeting (ZBB), strategic budgeting does not require managers to rank tasks or to justify current expenditures in order to ferret out the slack within the budget.[7] Instead, strategic budgeting assumes that most budgets contain significant amounts of slack and can be cut in half without jeopardizing the output of any department. For those few departments with little or no slack, the safety provided is in the budget buffer for the entire company. Departments requiring extra expenditures can draw from the budget buffer once they have shared the need with the other affected departments.

In addition, SB can be implemented relatively quickly once the manager is determined to make the change. ZBB, on the other hand, takes a great deal of time to implement.[8] With SB, estimates of the amount of slack in each budget are not needed because all budgets are simply cut in half.

2. Increased Communication between Departments
According to the findings of Joseph Fisher, James Frederickson, and Sean Peffer, managers are more willing to accommodate the needs of other departments when information is readily available about the other departments.[9] Requiring department heads to share their needs for buffer spending with the other department heads ensures cooperation. In addition, this practice transmits a subtle message that any buffer expenditures must be valid.

3. Lower Overall Spending Levels
In many corporations, managers are held responsible for overspending the budget. Therefore, managers tend to overstate their needs[10] and to spend the entire budgeted amount, even if excesses are available to refund to the company at year-end.[11] Budgetary slack is also difficult if not impossible to detect. In strategic budgeting, however, managers are encouraged to spend half of their original budget and to spend more only if the expenditure is valid and can stand up to the scrutiny of the managers competing for the same buffer of dollars. Through the use of this technique, true slack is identified without penalizing those areas with minimum or no slack. In fact, in this case, one department ended up with almost twice the amount of its original allotment of funds before the 50% reduction.

4. Assurance of Output Integrity
The danger of many cost-cutting initiatives is the loss of quality and quantity in the pursuit of reduced expenditures. What SB seems capable of delivering is reduced expenditures only in areas of increased slack while providing sufficient resources for those areas needing additional dollars in order to meet the corporation's stated goals. Because any expenditure of the budget buffer requires communication with other department heads, managers are reminded of the overall goal of any subunit when requesting extra funding. Those seeking unnecessary funds should be reluctant to ask for them, given the scrutiny of the other department heads. Those needing funds for legitimate corporate purposes, however, should feel totally justified in appealing for the extra funding. In fact, after using SB, some departments may end up with extra funding while others end up with significantly less.

5. Intrinsic Rewards through Goal Achievement
By eliminating significant amounts of slack, the upper level manager has created a situation where achieving the budget is something that can be valued by the lower-level manager.[13] It is difficult to meet previous output levels with half of the original funds. Therefore, the achievement of the target-spending levels is something of which to be proud. In addition, the agreement on a departmental goal and the continual realignment of departmental actions in light of the goal provide the structure and motivation mentioned by Ronen and Livingstone.[14]

Concerns and Cautions

Budget reductions of 50% in the first year of implementing strategic budgeting are relatively straightforward, but trying to continue such dramatic reductions in budgets year after year should be avoided. Once SB is implemented in the first year, managers will "know the game" and adjust their projections for needed funding accordingly. In addition, reductions beyond the original 50% would most likely be excessive and harmful to the delivery of the final product or service.

Implementation in just one lower-level area without coordinating with upper-level managers and "educating" the upper-level managers on the new technique could be suicidal. Upper-level managers who see large unspent budget amounts at year-end could assume many harmful things about the performance of the department and/or of the departmental manager. It is critical, therefore, to win the approval of the upper-level managers for the "experiment" with SB before its implementation. This case study should help in soliciting and winning such approval.

Current performance measurements reward spending the entire amount of budgeted funds and penalize underspending the budgeted amounts. Any unspent funding is likely to be lost to the department in the next budgeting cycle. Unless the performance measurement system rewards managers for spending less, they will continue to spend as much as is allowed. Therefore, the performance measurement system must be modified to encourage the creation and maintenance of a budget buffer for the protection of the overall performance of the firm. Rather than focusing on a detailed budget, employees should be focusing on the overall strategy of the corporation. To foster this team effort, management should consider rewards or bonuses that encourage team behavior and high levels of cooperation among departments.

ENDNOTES

[1] Kari Lukka, "Budgetary Biasing in Organizations: Theoretical Framework and Empirical *Evidence,*" *Accounting, Organizations and Society,* 1988, vol. 13, no. 3, pp. 281-301. Kenneth Merchant and Jean-Francois Manzoni, "Achievability of Budget Targets in Profit Centers: A Field Study," *The Accounting Review,* July 1989, pp. 539-558.

[2] Mohammed Onsi, "Factor Analysis of Behavioral Variables Affecting Budgetary Slack," *The Accounting Review,* July 1973, pp. 535-548.

[3] Kenton B. Walker and Eric N. Johnson, "The Effects of a Budget-Based Incentive Compensation Scheme on the Budgeting Behavior of Managers and Subordinates," *Journal of Management Accounting Research,* vol. 11, 1999, pp. 1-28.

[4] David T. Otley, "The Accuracy of Budget Estimates: Some Statistical Evidence," *Journal of Business, Finance and Accounting,* 1985, vol. 12, pp. 415-428.

[5] Joshua Ronen and J. L. Livingstone, "An Expectancy Theory Approach to the Motivational Impacts of Budgets," *The Accounting Review,* October 1975, pp. 671-685.

[6] Eliyahu M. Goldratt, *It's Not Luck* (Great Barrington, MA: North River Press, 1994).

[7] Allen Schick, "The Road from ZBB," *Public Administration Review,* March/April 1978, pp. 177-180.

[8] Norton S. Beckerman, "The Missing Link: The Planning Portion of the Zero Base Approach," *The Government Accountants Journal,* Winter, 1978-1979, vol. 27, no. 4, pp. 24-31.

[9] Joseph G. Fisher, James R. Frederickson, and Sean A. Peffer, "Budgeting: An Experimental Investigation of the Effects of Negotiation," *The Accounting Review,* January 2000, pp. 93-114.

[10] Merchant and Manzoni, 1989.

[11] David T. Otley, "Budget Use and Managerial Performance," *Journal of Accounting Research,* Spring 1978, pp. 122-149.

[12] Onsi, 1973.

[13] Alan S. Dunk, "Budgetary Participation, Agreement on Evaluation Criteria and Managerial Performance: A Research Note," *Accounting, Organizations and Society,* vol. 15, no. 3, 1990, pp. 171-178.

[14] Ronen and Livingstone, 1975.

FURTHER READING

Christopher K. Bart, "Budgeting Gamesmanship," *The Academy of Management Executive,* November 1988, vol. 2, no. 4, pp. 285-294.

S. R. Covey, *The Seven Habits of Highly Effective People: Restoring the Character Ethic* (New York, N.Y: Simon and Schuster, 1989).

Joseph G. Fisher, L.A. Maines, S.A. Peffer, G.B. Sprinkle, "Using Budgets for Performance Evaluation: Effects of Resource Allocation and Horizontal Information Asymmetry on Budget Proposals, Budget Slack, and Performance," *The Accounting Review,* October 2002, pp. 847-865.

Eliyahu M. Goldratt, *Critical Chain* (Great Barrington, MA: North River Press, 1997).

Floyd G. Lawrence, *"Zero Base Budgeting: Cure or Curse?" Industry Week,* March 20, 1978, pp. 94-98.

William C. Letzkus, "Zero-Base Budgeting: Some Implications of Measuring Accomplishments," *The Government Accountants Journal,* Summer 1978, vol. 27, no. 2, pp. 34-42.

8.3: How Challenging Should Profit Budget Targets Be?

by Kenneth A. Merchant
Certificate of Merit, 1989-90

It is a basic axiom of management that budget targets should be set to be challenging but achievable. But to establish that target, managers must first determine what "challenging but achievable" really means. Should profits be targeted at some easily obtainable goal, a realistic middle ground, or at a point so high that hope of attainment is slim?

There is no one right answer, given the number of purposes for which budgets are used: planning, coordination, control, motivation, and performance evaluation. Some may argue that planning purposes are served best with a best-guess budget, one that is as likely to be exceeded as missed.[1] Others may propose that, for optimum motivation, budget targets should be highly challenging, with only a 25% to 40% chance of achievement.[2]

There is one target-level choice, however, that serves the combination of purposes for which budgets are used quite well in the vast majority of organizational situations. Therefore, it provides an effective compromise. That choice is to set budget targets with a high probability of achievement—achievable by most managers 80% to 90% of the time—and then to supplement these targets with promises of extra incentives for performance exceeding the target level.[3] This prescription for the optimal budget target level, which is nearest point A in **Figure 1**, is made assuming that **Figure 1** represents the probability distribution of forthcoming profits for an effective management team working at a consistently high level of effort.

These targets with an 80% to 90% probability of achievement are labeled properly "highly achievable" for most managers, but because of the assumption described in the preceding paragraph, the targets are at least somewhat challenging. They are not "easy." Even talented, experienced profit center managers must work hard and effectively to give themselves a good chance of achieving these targets.

THE ADVANTAGES OF USING HIGHLY ACHIEVABLE BUDGET TARGETS

Choosing budget targets with such a high probability of achievement provides many advantages to corporation, including the following:

1. *Managers commitment to achieve the budget targets is increased*. When targets are set to be highly achievable, the corporation can assess profit center managers high penalties for failing to achieve the targets at least many more years than not. These penalties can include loss of reputation, loss of autonomy, inability to get funding proposals approved, and sometimes even loss of job. Corporations can allow managers few or no excuses for not achieving the targets because the high achievability is designed to protect the managers to considerable circumstances that were unforeseen at the time performance targets were set.

Because profit center managers face the risk of high penalties for performance shortfalls and do not have the safety net of excuses, they become highly committed to achieve their targets. This commitment causes them to prepare their budget forecasts more carefully and to spend more of their time managing rather than inventing excuses to explain their failures.

Firms that switch their budgeting philosophy to using highly achievable targets instead of "stretch" or "best guess" targets note the increase in commitment quite quickly. Comments a profit center manager in a large U.S. chemical corporation which made the switch:

> "Two years ago, our budgets were just best-effort forecasts. Today they are commitments. There is a vast difference. It's better to run this way. We have discipline. People used to make projections, but they forgot about them until they had to make another projection. Nobody ever came back and slapped their hand. Now people are challenged to put the things in place that are required to make the projections happen. The plans have begun to have credibility. Our spending plans are based on realistic projections."

Conversely, when budget targets are set at highly challenging levels, the danger exists that managers will not be committed to try to achieve their targets. For example, in a small publicly held electronics firm, which until recently had used a stretch target budgeting philosophy, profit center managers had started earning bonuses when their division's reported profit exceeded 60% of the budgeted level. But all too often, the profit center and corporate budgets were not achieved. In the words of the chief financial officer: "The system had some fudge in it. The managers were still in bonus territory, so they didn't have to worry about meeting the budget. It was like a wish, too easily blown off."

The corporation now has changed to what is

known as "minimum performance standard" budget targets and its managers' commitment to these new targets has increased sharply. Since the change, the profit centers have achieved virtually all their budget targets every quarter.

The danger of lack of commitment to achieve targets is particularly acute if something goes wrong early in the year and loss of commitment leads to lower motivation. In the words of a manager whose entity had not achieved its budget targets for several years, "After the first few months of the year, we began to look at our goals as 'pie in the sky.' [The goals] didn't inspire us to do different things. They were just demoralizing."

2. *Managers' confidence remains high.* Regardless of the level of budget achievability, in the minds of most managers budget achievement defines the line between success and failure. Budget targets are the most specific and tangible goals managers are given, and most people define personal success in terms of their high degree of achievement of predetermined targets. As one manager put it, "If I were to miss my budget, I would feel like a failure. When I exceed my budget, I feel proud."

It is to the corporation's advantage to have its managers feel like winners. Managers who feel good about themselves and their abilities are more likely to work harder and to take prudent risks.

3. *Organizational control costs decrease.* Most corporations use a management-by-exception control philosophy where negative variances from budget signal the need for investigation and perhaps intervention in the affairs of the operating units. If budget targets are set to be highly achievable, negative variances are relatively rare, and top management or staff attention is directed to the few situations where the operating problems are most likely and most serious.

This point is illustrated in Figure 1. The probability distribution of profit outcomes shifts to the left (lower profit) for a lazy or ineffective manager. What was a highly achievable target for an

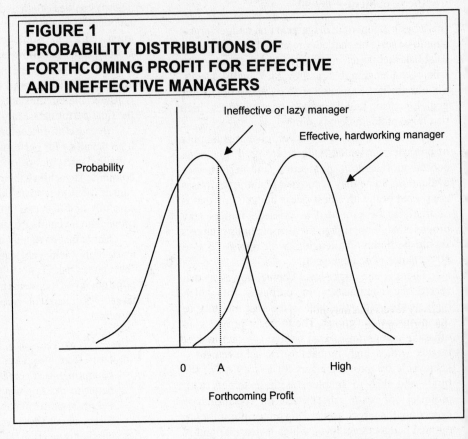

FIGURE 1
PROBABILITY DISTRIBUTIONS OF FORTHCOMING PROFIT FOR EFFECTIVE AND INEFFECTIVE MANAGERS

effective, hardworking manager (point A) is not as highly achievable for an ineffective or lazy manager. Budget misses of two or three years send a strong signal that something is wrong and that top management intervention is necessary. Budget misses also provide objective rationales for relieving poor managers of their jobs.

4. *The risk of managers engaging in harmful earnings management practices is reduced.* Managers who are likely to achieve their budget targets are less likely to engage in costly actions designed to boost earnings in the short term. These actions include making potentially risky operating decisions (such as delaying preventative maintenance) and engaging in deceptive accounting practices (such as altering judgments about reserves).

Highly achievable budget targets also lessen the incentives some managers have to reduce current period income. Those individuals who are facing stretch targets they consider nearly impossible to achieve may "take a bath"; they may take costly actions to position their entities for the subsequent

Blocher, Stout, Cokins, Chen: *Cost Management, 4e*

©The McGraw-Hill Companies, Inc 2008

accounting period. For example, they may defer sales and incur as many discretionary expenses as possible in the current period.

5. *Effective managers are allowed greater operating flexibility.* Highly achievable budget targets allow managers whose entities are performing well to accumulate some slack resources. Most managers will use this slack so that they do not have to respond to unforeseen, unfavorable short-term contingencies in costly ways, such as a suspension of productive long-term investments or a layoff. Some managers also will use the slack in productive, creative ways to fund "skunkworks" that may have high payoffs.

6. *The corporation is somewhat protected against the costs of optimistic revenue projections.* Budgets with optimistic revenue projections often induce managers to acquire resources in anticipation of activity levels that may not be forthcoming. Some of these resources, particularly people, can be difficult to eliminate when reality sets in. As one corporate president expressed it: "I think we ought to have a semi-aggressive plan, but one that is achievable." We want to make it every year. It's too hard to adjust on the downside, to slough off commitments of expenses or not launch something you're psychologically committed to."

7. *The predictability of corporate earnings is increased.* When budget targets are likely to be achieved, the consolidated budget provides a highly probably lower bound of forthcoming corporate profits. This earnings predictability is valuable, particularly to managers of publicly held corporations. Earnings are usually less predictable in corporations whose business units face similar business risks, so this earnings-predictability advantage of highly achievable budget targets is higher in undiversified rather than diversified, firms.

A RISK IN USING HIGHLY ACHIEVABLE BUDGET TARGETS

The primary risk in using highly achievable budget targets is that managers may not be challenged to perform at their maximum. They may be satisfied with mediocrity—their levels of aspiration may be too low—and their motivation may slack off after the budgeted profit targets are achieved.

This problem of lack of challenge is potentially more serious when planning uncertainty is relatively

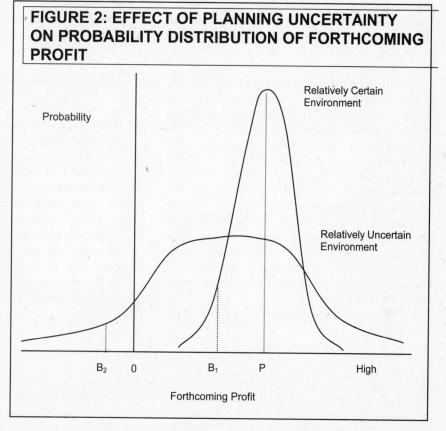

FIGURE 2: EFFECT OF PLANNING UNCERTAINTY ON PROBABILITY DISTRIBUTION OF FORTHCOMING PROFIT

high (and the inability to make adjustments for the effects of factors over which the managers had little or no control is relatively low). This is because the distance between the highly achievable target levels and the best-guess (or even higher) target levels is much greater than when planning uncertainty is low. This is shown in Figure 2. The tall curve shows a profit probability distribution in a relatively low uncertainty environment. The highly achievable budget level (B1) is not far from the most likely performance level (P). The shorter, flatter curve shows a distribution in a relatively uncertain environment. In this case, the highly achievable budget level (B2) is far below the most likely performance level.

Even in environments of high uncertainty, however, this lack-of-challenge problem is not inevitable. Most profit center managers have risen through the ranks because they are good performers with strong internal drives for competition and self-satisfaction. Furthermore, the "winning" feeling generated from budget achievement in prior periods is likely to increase, not decrease, the managers' levels of aspiration.

Furthermore, even when the risk of less than optimal challenge does exist, it can be minimized by giving managers incentives to strive for and to produce profits in excess of their budget targets. These incentives can be provided in combinations of many forms of rewards, including extra bonuses, recognition, autonomy, and command over resources, and increased prospects for career advancement.

Profit center managers also can be asked to turn in more profit than originally was budgeted. This is a common occurrence in U.S. corporations.[4] These orders, combined with the highly achievable original targets, make the budget somewhat flexible. The highly achievable targets protect the profit center managers from the effects of unfavorable influences not explicitly expounded in the budget forecasts. The requests for profits above budgeted levels can be used to adjust for the effects of unforeseen good fortune on the measures of operating results. They can protect the corporation from the negative effects of excessive easy performance targets, such as managers' lagging ambition and the creation of excessive slack.

Only in a few organizational situations is it not desirable to set highly achievable profit budget targets. One exception is caused by organizational need. A company in grave difficulty may want to set less achievable budget targets as a signal to its managers that a certain higher level of performance is necessary for the corporation to survive or for the profit center to stave off divestment.

A second exception occurs when it is desirable to correct for a profit center's windfall gain. Sometimes when managers have been lucky in a prior period, perhaps earning large and mostly undeserved bonuses, a more challenging budget target can be set as an effective way of making compensations more fair across the multiyear period. Here, though, care must be taken to guard against unwarranted management turnover because current period expected compensation probably will fall below competitive market levels.

In virtually all other situations, it is desirable to set highly achievable profit budget targets while allowing the managers few excuses for not achieving the targets. Setting targets that are highly achievable, but not too easy takes considerable managerial skill. Upper-level managers must know enough about the profit centers capabilities and business prospects to be able to judge the probability of budget success reasonably well in order to make this budget philosophy work properly. But when they implement this combination of mechanisms effectively, they will ensure that all the purposes for which budgets are used—planning, coordination, control, motivation, and performance evaluation—are served well.

---

[1] For example, see M. E. Barrett and L. B. Fraser III, "Conflicting Roles in Budgeting for Operations," *Harvard Business Review*, July-August 1977, pp. 137-146.

[2] For example, see R. L. M. Dunbar, "Budgeting for Control," *Administrative Science Quarterly*, March 1971, pp. 88-96.

[3] This finding emerged in a recent intensive study of 12 divisionalized corporations and some related fieldwork. Ten of the 12 corporations participating in the research study had used highly achievable budget targets for some time. One had recently changed its budgeting philosophy. It formerly used "stretch" budget targets but changed to have its targets reflect "minimum performance standards." One firm was still using stretch budget targets, but most of the managers in the firm were recommending that this philosophy of budgeting be changed. (For a detailed report of the findings of this study, see K Merchant, *Rewarding Results: Motivating Profit Center Managers*, Harvard Business School Press, 1989.)

[4] For example, Merchant (1989) found that profit center managers in seven of the 12 firms studied were sometimes given direct orders from upper management to turn in greater profits than were budgeted. In some of these firms, the orders were given virtually every quarter.

Chapter 9
Decision Making with Relevant Costs
and a Strategic Emphasis

Cases

Readings

9-1: "Relevance Added: Combining ABC with German Cost Accounting" by Gunther Friedl, PROF. DR., Hans-Ulrich Kupper, PROF. DR., and Buckhard Pedell, PD DR, *Strategic Finance* (June 2005), pp. 56-61.

This article describes ABC costing and German cost accounting (GPK) and provides a comparison of the two methods. GPK is presented as a superior method for relevant cost analysis. The authors encourage the use of both ABC and GPK.

Discussion Questions:
1. What is GPK?
2. How does GPK compare to ABC costing?
3. What are the key elements of GPK?
4. What are the two types of cost centers used in GPK? Explain the difference.

9-1 Decision Making Under Uncertainty

Exquisite Foods Incorporated (EFI) sells premium foods. Three independent strategies are being considered to promote a new product, *Soufflés for Microwaves*, to dual-career families. Currently the contribution margin ratio on EFI's foods is 65%, which is expected to apply to the new product. EFI's policy for promoting new products permits only one type of advertising campaign until the product has been established.

STRATEGY ONE

The first strategy concentrates on television and magazine advertising. EFI would hire a marketing consultant to prepare a 30-second video commercial and a magazine advertisement. The commercial would air during the evening to address the working market, while the magazine advertisement would be place in magazines read by career-minded individuals. This advertising campaign would provide EFI $230,000 expected contribution from sales.

STRATEGY TWO

The second strategy promotes the product by offering 25% off coupons in the Sunday newspaper supplements, with a projected 15 percent redemption rate on sales revenue. EFI would hire a marketing consultant for $5,000 to design a one-quarter page, two-color coupon advertisement. The coupon would be distributed in the Sunday newspaper supplements at a cost of $195,000. Based on prior experience, EFI expects the following additional sales from this form of advertisement.

Expected sales	Probability
$500,000	10%
600,000	25
700,000	35
800,000	20
900,000	10

STRATEGY THREE

The third strategy offers a $.50 mail-in rebate coupon attached to each box of *Soufflés for Microwaves*. EFI would hire a marketing consultant for $5,000 to create a one-sixth page, one-color rebate coupon. Printing and attaching costs for the rebate coupon are $.07 per package, and EFI is planning to include the rebate offer on 500,000 packages. Although 500,000 packages may be sold, only a 10 percent redemption rate is expected. EFI expects the following additional sales from this type of promotion:

Expected sales	Probability
$400,000	10%
450,000	30
500,000	35
550,000	20
600,000	5

REQUIRED:

1. Exquisite Foods Incorporated (EFI) wishes to select the most profitable marketing alternative to promote *Soufflés for Microwaves*. Recommend which of the three strategies presented above should be adopted by EFI. Support your recommendation with appropriate calculations and analysis.
2. What selection criteria, other than profitability, should be considered in arriving at a decision on the choice of promotion alternatives?

Blocher, Stout, Cokins, Chen: *Cost Management, 4e*

©The McGraw-Hill Companies, Inc 2008

9-2 Profitability Analysis

Sportway, Inc. is a wholesale distributor supplying a wide range of moderately priced sporting equipment to large chain stores. About 60 percent of Sportway's products are purchased from other companies while the remainder are manufactured by Sportway. The company has a Plastics Department that is currently manufacturing molded fishing tackle boxes. Sportway is able to manufacture and sell 8,000 tackle boxes annually, making full use of its direct labor capacity at available work stations. Presented below are the selling price and costs associated with Sportway's tackle boxes.

Selling price per box		$86.00
Costs per box		
Molded plastic	$ 8.00	
Hinges, latches, handle	9.00	
Direct labor ($15.00/hr.)	18.75	
Manufacturing overhead.................	12.50	
Selling and administrative cost	17.00	65.25
Profit per box.................................		$20.75

Because Sportway believes it could sell 12,000 tackle boxes if it had sufficient manufacturing capacity, the company has looked into the possibility of purchasing the tackle boxes for distribution. Maple Products, a steady supplier of quality products, would be able to provide up to 9,000 tackle boxes per year at a price of $68.00 per box delivered to Sportway's facility.

Bart Johnson, Sportway's product manager, has suggested that the company could make better use of its Plastics Department by manufacturing skateboards. To support his position, Johnson has a market study that indicates an expanding market for skateboards and a need for additional suppliers. Johnson believes that Sportway could expect to sell 17,500 skateboards annually at a price of $45.00 per skateboard. Johnson's estimate of the costs to manufacture the skateboards is presented below.

Selling price per skateboard		$45.00
Costs per box		
Molded plastic	$5.50	
Wheels, hardware	7.00	
Direct labor ($15.00/hr.)	7.50	
Manufacturing overhead....................	5.00	
Selling and administrative cost	9.00	34.00
Profit per box...................................		$11.00

In the Plastics Department, Sportway uses direct labor hours as the application base for manufacturing overhead. Included in total manufacturing overhead for the current year is $50,000 of factory-wide, fixed manufacturing overhead that has been allocated to the Plastics Department, and would not change irrespective of the option chosen. For each unit of product that Sportway sells, regardless of whether the product has been purchased or is manufactured by Sportway, there is an allocated $6.00 fixed overhead cost per unit for distribution that is included in the selling and administrative cost for all products. Total selling and administrative costs for the purchased tackle boxes would be $10.00 per unit.

REQUIRED:

1. Prepare an analysis based on the data presented that will show which product or products Sportway Inc. should manufacture and/or purchase to maximize profitability and show the associated financial impact. Support your answer with appropriate calculations.
2. Identify the strategic factors Sportway should consider in its product decisions.

(CMA adapted)

9-3   The Superior Valve Division

In 2001, the Superior Valve Division of the Able Corporation found itself in a position typical of fast-growing companies. Although sales revenues were increasing rapidly, capital equipment allocations from Able were less than desired, and profits were variable. Jerry Conrad, the general manager of the division, enrolled that year in a seminar on contribution margin income sponsored by the American Management Association (AMA). According to Conrad, "Before I went to that seminar, my knowledge of contribution margin income was limited to casual comments that I overheard at group general managers' meetings. A large acquisition in the automotive aftermarket industry had always used a contribution margin approach in its accounting systems. All other segments of the Able Corporation used the full costing method, but this company was allowed to keep its contribution margin cost system because a forced change of systems at the time of acquisition would have been too disruptive."

Jerry believed that the full cost reports used in his division were accurate. He and Frances Kardell, the Division Controller, were confident they knew the total manufacturing cost of each of their products. However, Jerry did not have the same confidence in his staff's ability to determine how volume changes would affect profits. He was convinced that better utilization of plant and equipment and a more effective pricing structure would lead to substantially improved earnings. The division was not as profitable as others in the industry or other similar-size divisions in the corporation that had comparable manufacturing processes.

A main point of the AMA seminar was that product lines do not produce profits; they produce contribution margin (sales revenue minus variable costs), which can become profits only after fixed costs are covered. The seminar also underscored not only the importance of cost behavior analysis but also the arbitrariness of many fixed cost allocations. Jerry immediately saw in contribution margin a new approach to solving Superior Valve's problems with both product mix and pricing decisions.

Jerry discussed the subject of contribution margin with Todd Talbott, the Group Controller. After hearing the advantages and disadvantages of the approach, Jerry recommended that his division's product costing system be overhauled for the third time since Able Corporation acquired Superior Valve 20 years ago. Todd agreed to support a change in the management reporting system, but he pointed out that the contribution margin approach was contrary to the reporting philosophy of the corporation and, for external purposes, did not comply with GAAP, S.E.C. reporting requirements, and Internal Revenue Service directives on inventory valuation.

When the decision to proceed was made, Frances and her accounting staff used regression analysis to classify manufacturing costs, other operating costs, and selling and general administration costs as either variable, fixed, or mixed. Mixed costs were separated into their variable and fixed components. Fixed costs then were identified as either discretionary (amounts to be expended based on decisions made annually or at shorter intervals) or committed (usually not subject to change in the short-run). A booklet on contribution margin which Jerry gave to his staff stated that fixed expenses are a function of time, and variable expenses (1) vary directly with changes in volume and (2) are usually expressed as a percentage of sales dollars or direct labor dollars.

SPECIAL ORDER

The Wadsworth Company, which was experimenting with various components of its product line, offered to purchase 6,000 Hydro-Con multi-function control valves from Superior for $160 each. Wadsworth would need 500 units per month with delivery commencing at the start of the new year. The special order would be in addition to the 80,000 units that Ralph Darwin, the division's Marketing Manager, expected to sell at the regular $200 price. Ralph considered the order to represent an excellent opportunity to increase long-term sales volume because it would be a new application for the product. He negotiated a flat $48,000 commission with the selling distributor.

Jerry was concerned that cutting the price of the valve would set an undesirable precedent. He pondered the special deal for several days before going to see Ralph. "The price is below our full cost of $175 per unit," he said. "If we accept the Wadsworth proposal, the firm can always expect favored treatment."

Jerry asked Daria Good, the Manufacturing Manager, and Frances to join this discussion in Darwin's office. When they arrived, he asked, "What is the division's capacity for making Hydro-Con Control?" Good's reply was "One hundred thousand (100,000) units per year, if we don't retool any machines dedicated to another product line."

Blocher, Stout, Cokins, Chen: *Cost Management, 4e*

Frances presented the following standard cost data for Hydro-Con valves:

Raw material	$ 35
Purchased components	30
Direct labor	12
Manufacturing overhead	44
Total standard cost	$121

After distributing copies of the budgeted income statement for the upcoming fiscal year (Table A), Frances revealed the variable overhead for the 80,000 unit Hydro-Con budget was $2,400,000. Of the budgeted fixed manufacturing costs, $400,000 was discretionary, with the remainder committed to basic capacity charges. Variable "other operating expenses" totaled $4 per unit; a 10% distributor commission ($20 per unit) comprised the variable portion of selling and general administration expenses. The Controller further indicated that manufacturing adjustments represented production variances and scrap, which she expected to vary with the number of valves produced. At the budgeted volume level, fixed other operating expenses would add an average of $16 to unit cost. Basic service costs such a production control, engineering administration, and accounting totaling $880,000 were allocated to Hydro-Con; the remaining fixed other operating expenses were directly related to the product line and were discretionary in nature.

As the discussion continued, Ralph reviewed next year's budget. Of the total fixed selling, general, and administrative expense, $160,000 was earmarked for future advertising space in several trade publications and an upcoming trade show. The remainder of the budget related to salaries and other firm commitments.

The Hydro-Con budget was designed to fully recover all costs at the 80,000 unit production level. The other product line budgets also were designed to fully recover costs at budgeted volume levels, and all fixed costs were expected to remain unchanged until the current maximum capacities were surpassed (Table B). Jerry asked his Division Controller what effect the Wadsworth offer would have on profits. But Daria had not yet studied the effects volume changes would have on division operations.

PRODUCT LINE ELIMINATION

Superior Valve's Marketing Department prepared a sales order plan by product line for each new year in both units and dollars. The Production Control Department then used the order plan to develop a sales shipment plan for each of the division's three plants. Ralph Darwin had very little marketing information to use in developing the Made to Order (MTO) Hydraulic Control product line plan. However, he knew that the line's compound growth pattern over the last three years had been quite disappointing, and he saw little prospect for substantial sales growth in the short-term future.

Ralph recommended the division consider eliminating the Made to Order line. Daria had assured him that the MTO-dedicated machinery could be retooled to produce either of the standard lines. Darwin was convinced he could develop a market for the additional standard product in a relatively short time, and he strongly believed the division should concentrate on its two basic product lines. "After all," he commented, "that's where we're most successful." However, until the additional market for the standard product was developed, the elimination of MTO would mean the elimination of 30 manufacturing jobs.

At the last staff meeting of the year, Jerry Conrad told Ralph he would study the product line elimination proposal after he made a decision on the Hydro-Con special order. He assigned the proposal top priority for the new year.

REQUIRED:
1. Assume that inventories will not change during the year. Prepare budgeted contribution approach product line income statements for the year ending 6/30/19X3. Categorize fixed costs as either discretionary or committed.
2. Should Jerry Conrad decide to accept the Wadsworth Company special order? If so, what will be the new Hydro-Con return on sales?
3. Should the Superior Valve Division eliminate the Made to Order product line if there were no alternative uses for its production capacity?
4. If all resulting standard products could be sold, how should the MTO capacity be allocated? (Assume only the capacity currently being used to produce 20,000 MTO units would be used to produce additional standard products.)
5. Identify the strategic factors that Superior Valve should consider.

6. What changes, if any, should be made to the division's cost system? Why?
7. What ethical issues, if any, should the division consider in connection with the decision to eliminate MTO?

TABLE A

Superior Valve Division
Budgeted Income Statement for the Year Ending 6/30/2002
($000)

	Hydro-Con	Pneu-trol	Made to Order	Total Division
Revenue	$16,000	$13,000	$ 5,000	$34,000
Material	5,200	3,900	1,300	10,400
Direct Labor	960	1,235	1,000	3,195
Overhead	3,520	2,990	1,531	8,041
Total Cost of Sales @ Standard	9,680	8,125	3,831	21,636
Gross Margin	6,320	4,875	1,169	12,364
Adjustments	800	520	554	1,874
Net Manufacturing Margin	5,520	4,355	615	10,490
Other Oper. Exp. Expenses	1,600	1,560	750	3,910
Selling & General Administration	1,920	1,560	600	4,080
Operating Income	$ 2,000	$ 1,235	$ (735)	$ 2,500

TABLE B

Superior Valve Division
Product Line Data

	Pneu-trol	MTO
Unit selling price	$ 50.00	$ 250.00
Variable overhead per unit	$ 6.50	$ 50.55
Total discretionary fixed overhead	$225,000	$100,000
Variable other operating cost per unit	$ 1.50	$ 5.00
Variable selling and general admin. per unit	$ 5.00	$ 25.00
Committed fixed other operating costs	$970,000	$550,000
Committed fixed selling & general admin.	$160,000	$ 75,000

Product Line	Present Max. Capacity in Units	Machine Hrs./Unit
Hydro-Con	100,000	6
Pneu-trol	350,000	2
MTO	50,000	5

Blocher, Stout, Cokins, Chen: *Cost Management, 4e*

©The McGraw-Hill Companies, Inc 2008

9-4 OmniSport Inc.

OmniSport Inc. is a wholesale distributor supplying a wide range of moderately priced sporting equipment to large chain stores. OmniSport has an enviable reputation for quality of its products. In fact, the demand for its products is so great that at times OmniSport cannot satisfy the demand and must delay or refuse some orders, in order to maintain its production quality. Additionally, OmniSport purchases some of its products from outside suppliers in order to meet the demand. These suppliers are carefully chosen so that their products maintain the quality image that OmniSport has attained. About 60 percent of OmniSport's products are purchased from other companies while the remainder of the products are manufactured by OmniSport. The company has a Plastics Department that is currently manufacturing the boot for in-line skates. OmniSport is able to manufacture and sell 5,000 pairs of skates annually, making full use of its machine capacity at available workstations. Presented below are the selling price and costs associated with OmniSport's skates.

Selling price per pair of skates		$98
Costs per pair		
Molded plastic	$8	
Other direct materials	12	
Machine time ($16 per hour)	24	
Manufacturing overhead	18	
Selling and administrative cost	15	77
Profit per pair		$21

Because OmniSport believes it could sell 8,000 pairs of skates annually if it had sufficient manufacturing capacity, the company has looked into the possibility of purchasing the skates for distribution. Colcott Inc., a steady supplier of quality products, would be able to provide 6.000 pairs of skates per year at a price of $75 per pair delivered to OmniSport's facility.

Jack Petrone, OmniSport's product manager, has suggested that the company could make better use of its Plastics Department by manufacturing snowboard bindings. To support his position, Petrone has a market study that indicates an expanding market for snowboards and a need for additional suppliers. Petrone believes that OmniSport could expect to sell 12,000 snowboard bindings annually at a price of $60 per binding. Petrone's estimate of the costs to manufacture the bindings is presented below.

Selling price per snowboard binding		$60
Costs per binding		
Molded plastic	$16	
Other direct materials	4	
Machine time ($16 per hour)	8	
Manufacturing overhead	6	
Selling and administrative cost	14	48
Profit per binding		$12

Other information pertinent to OmniSport's operations is presented below.

An allocated $6 fixed overhead cost per unit is included in the selling and administrative cost for all of the purchased and manufactured products. Total fixed and variable selling and administrative costs for the purchased skates would be $10 per pair.

In the Plastics Department, OmniSport uses machine hours as the application base for manufacturing overhead. Included in the manufacturing overhead for the current year is $30,000 of fixed, factory-wide manufacturing overhead that has been allocated to the Plastics Department.

REQUIRED:

In order to maximize OmniSport Inc.'s profitability, recommend which product or products should be manufactured and/ or purchased. Prepare an analysis based on the data presented that will show the associated financial impact. Support your answer with appropriate calculations and strategic considerations.

Readings

9.1: RELEVANCE ADDED: COMBINING ABC WITH GERMAN COST ACCOUNTING

Activity-based costing is better for long-term decision making while a leading German cost accounting method supports short-term decisions more effectively.

By Gunther Friedl Hans-Ulrich Kupper, and Buckhard Pedell

Are you familiar with Grenzplankostenrechnung? Translated from German, it roughly means "flexible margin costing." Flexible margin costing, or GPK, is a time tested cost accounting system used by many companies in German-speaking countries. GPK is about marginal costing instead of full costing, short-term decision support instead of long-term, and cost centers instead of activities and processes. And by combining activity-based costing (ABC) with GPK, you can add relevance to your cost accounting system. Management accounting has long been more important to companies in German-speaking countries, such as Germany, Austria, and Switzerland, than to companies in the United States. This perhaps can be attributed to the external accounting rules in German-speaking countries, which put the interests of creditors before those of shareowners. In contrast, financial accounting provides little guidance for management decision making. Thus the need for a sophisticated cost accounting system—explicitly for management decision making—is paramount. Meanwhile, in the U.S., the cost accounting system that has attracted the most attention since the mid-1980s has been ABC. In this article, we're going to describe the principles of both GPK and ABC and analyze the differences between the two. First, let's delve into the details of GPK.

GPK UNPACKED

GPK was developed in the 1950s and 1960s by Hans-Georg Plaut, a practitioner, and Wolfgang Kilger, a cost accounting researcher. Both Plaut and Kilger were focused on developing cost accounting methods to support decision making. After its development, GPK became arguably the most important cost accounting system for industrial firms in German-speaking countries. In the past 20 years, its success can be at least partly attributed to the advent of SAP's enterprise resource planning (ERP) software because SAP offers the conceptual framework of GPK for cost accounting as part of its management accounting module. Similar to direct costing, the most important idea behind GPK is that fixed costs aren't charged to products.

If they were, managers would be induced to make incorrect short-term decisions, such as for pricing and make- or-buy decisions. In practice, however, GPK can be combined with a multilevel allocation of fixed costs. The fundamental structure of GPK, shown in Figure 1, follows the structure of basic cost accounting systems taught in the business schools of universities in German speaking countries. GPK consists of four important elements: cost-type accounting, cost center accounting, product cost accounting, and contribution margin accounting for profitability analysis. Cost-type accounting, seen in Table 1, separates different cost types, such as labor, material, and depreciation. In contrast to most U.S. cost accounting systems, GPK and other German systems also include interest as a cost type. Each cost type is decomposed into variable and fixed costs along with the assignment of costs to cost centers. As linear cost functions are assumed, variable unit costs are constant with respect to output. Obviously, this decomposition can't be done for each cost type, but it has to be made for each accounting transaction. Cost-type accounting leads us to one of the most important elements of GPK: cost center accounting. A cost center is a relatively small entity with a robust and quantifiable relationship between its costs and a single activity, and it is typically composed of around 10 workers or less. Firms usually have multiple cost centers for such areas as manufacturing, material, administration, sales, and R&D. Cost centers usually have one or a few cost drivers, and they determine the relationship between variable costs and the output of the cost center. This simplicity allows for detailed cost planning of each cost center, with cost functions that describe the relationship between costs and output. Aggregating this data over all cost centers allows for flexible, output-dependent planning scenarios. This detailed planning procedure also has advantages for monitoring cost centers, something GPK emphasizes. Comparing planned and realized costs at the cost-center level provides early and detailed information about emerging problems. You can determine the causes and measures of those variations by using sophisticated variance analysis instruments, and human behavior can be influenced effectively at the cost-center level by tying a manager's compensation and advancement to the performance of his or her cost center. GPK uses two different types of cost centers: primary cost centers and final cost centers. Primary cost centers cover activities that are relatively far away from the manufacturing process, such as plant management. Final cost centers are closely connected to the manufacturing process. This distinction is necessary because it isn't possible to assign the costs of a primary cost center directly to products. Therefore, costs of primary cost centers are charged to final cost centers, which are connected more closely to products. This gradual assignment allows for a more precise calculation of product costs. Among the costs of the primary cost centers, only variable costs are charged to final cost centers. In Table 1, the variable costs of Maintenance, a primary cost center, are $77,000. This is charged to Manufacturing, a final cost center. Otherwise, the

distinction between variable and fixed costs would blur during the allocation process. After this cost assignment, there are no longer variable costs on primary cost centers, yet the variable costs of each final cost center can still be obtained easily by adding them together. Only the variable costs of the final cost centers are charged to cost objects in product cost accounting. Product cost accounting assigns to products the cost of direct labor and direct material as well as the variable costs of the final cost centers—the latter assigned using specific charge rates. As a result, only the variable costs of each product are shown in product cost accounting. Although this contradicts the basic principles of GPK, fixed costs can also be allocated to products in a parallel calculation for mid- and long-term purposes. To keep the distinction between variable and fixed costs, the fixed cost calculation is separate from the variable cost calculation. Fixed costs usually are allocated by a surcharge as a percentage of variable costs. The final element of GPK is contribution margin accounting, shown in Table 2. In the U.S., the contribution margin after accounting for fixed product costs is normally referred to as gross margin. This completes the cost accounting system by adding the revenues and the fixed costs to product cost accounting. Here the contribution margin of each product can be obtained by subtracting variable costs from product revenues.

Table 1: Cost Assignments to Primary and Final Cost Centers

Primary Cost Center: Maintenance

COST TYPE	UNIT OF MEASURE	QUANTITY	COST PER QUANTITY	TOTAL COSTS	VARIABLE COSTS	FIXED COSTS
Labor	hours	1,800	20	36,000	36,000	
Benefits	$	36,000	0.5	18,000	18,000	
Tools	$			12,000	8,000	4,000
Depreciation	$			40,000	15,000	25,000
Interest Costs	$			10,000		10,000
Total				116,000	77,000	39,000

Final Cost Center: Manufacturing I

COST TYPE	UNIT OF MEASURE	QUANTITY	COST PER QUANTITY	TOTAL COSTS	VARIABLE COSTS	FIXED COSTS
Labor	hours	3,600	20	72,000	72,000	
Benefits	$	72,000	0.5	36,000	36,000	
Tools	$			15,000	8,000	7,000
Depreciation	$			70,000	30,000	40,000
Interest Costs	$			22,000		22,000
Total				215,000	146,000	69,000
Assigned Costs from Maintenance				77,000	77,000	
Total				292,000	223,000	69,000

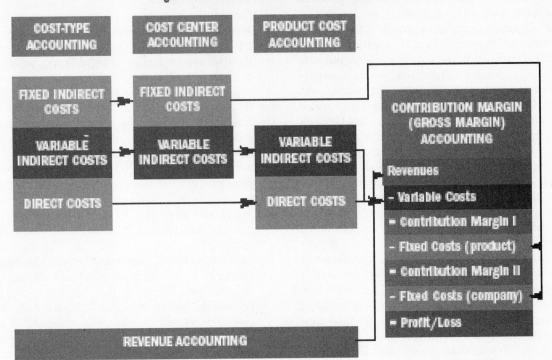

Figure 1: The Basic Structure of GPK

This supports many short-term management decisions because they are based on contribution margin rather than product costs. Moreover, the structure of GPK allows for more detailed analyses. By subsequently subtracting the relevant fixed costs from the contribution margin, different contribution margins on different layers can be obtained. For example, if there are fixed research and development or advertising costs for a small product group, these costs are subtracted from the product group's contribution margins. This type of layered contribution margin analysis not only supports short-term decision making, but it gives recommendations for long-term decisions. Based on the principles and structure described above, GPK is able to support many short-term management decisions, such as the optimal production plan, make or buy decisions, pricing decisions, or internal transfer pricing. Moreover, costs are highly transparent, which helps influence the behavior of employees and identify potential weaknesses. These advantages are a major reason for the prevalence of GPK in large industrial firms in German-speaking countries.

ACTIVITY-BASED COSTING

In the mid-1980s, significant changes made to the cost structures of U.S. companies left managers unhappy with traditional management accounting systems. According to two *Harvard Business Review* articles, written by Jeffrey G. Miller and Thomas E. Vollman and Robin Cooper and Robert S. Kaplan, respectively, these changes served as the impetus for the development of ABC. It's worth noting that Germany already had a range of fully developed cost accounting systems at the time, including GPK. But before ABC was developed, most companies in the U.S. used simple methods of overhead allocation and calculation. The most commonly used cost-allocation bases were direct labor hours, direct labor dollars, direct material, and machine hours (or a combination). With indirect activities such as production planning, quality control, maintenance, and R&D becoming more important, and, consequently, overhead costs capturing a larger share of total costs, overhead rates on direct labor would, in some instances, far exceed 1,000%. Because of these sharply higher direct labor overhead rates, minor errors in assessing direct labor costs of individual products resulted in large errors of total costs of these products. Furthermore, a systematic error in the calculation of costs of different products is made when total costs aren't proportional to the cost allocation base employed. In particular, cost allocation bias results when output drives the allocation base but the allocated costs aren't proportional to output. This was less of

Blocher, Stout, Cokins, Chen: *Cost Management, 4e*

a problem as long as direct labor and direct material represented the major part of costs and that products' cost structures remained relatively the same. But overhead costs don't depend predominantly on output. To a large extent, they depend on other cost drivers, such as number of product variants, product complexity, diversity of parts, and degree of automation. If overhead costs are allocated as a percentage surcharge on direct costs, the influence of these cost drivers isn't accounted for adequately. As a consequence, some products would be undercharged: those with product variants that are produced in small volumes; those that are very complex; those that are produced in highly automated, capital-intensive processes; or those that are marketed in small order sizes and distributed through expensive distribution channels. ABC addresses this problem by linking overhead allocation to the activities that are carried out to produce and sell a product instead of to output or output-related measures. The basic idea is that overhead costs are caused by activities directly, not by products. The process for implementing ABC comprises the following steps:

- **Assess and develop a hierarchy of activities.** This can be done by conducting interviews with employees, such as cost center or department managers.
- **Determine the cost drivers for the different activities.** A cost driver measures the process output and the use of an activity by a product. It serves as an allocation measure for products' process costs.

Table 2 Layered Contribution Margin Analysis

| | DIVISION I | | | DIVISION II | |
| | PRODUCT GROUP A | | PRODUCT GROUP B | PRODUCT GROUP C | |
	PRODUCT 1	PRODUCT 2	PRODUCT 3	PRODUCT 4	PRODUCT 5
Revenues	14,960	5,760	13,800	12,840	9,800
Variable Costs	10,259	2,257	9,278	8,021	4,791
Contribution Margin I	4,701	3,503	4,522	4,819	5,009
Fixed Costs, Product	0	0	100	0	0
Contribution Margin II	4,701	3,503	4,422	4,819	5,009
Fixed Costs, Product Group	150		0	250	
Contribution Margin III	8,054		4,422	9,578	
Fixed Costs, Division	4,295			4,795	
Contribution Margin IV	8,181			4,783	
Fixed Costs, Company	690				
Profit	12,274				

The assessment of activities and the identification of their cost drivers are practicable for standardized repeated processes.

- **Estimate the planned costs of activities.** The costs of cost centers or departments are allocated to the different activities within the cost centers. This can be done by analytical cost planning or dividing costs proportionally based on a particular measure, such as labor time. Adding up the planned costs of activities yields the costs of aggregated processes.

- **Activity cost control.** Planned and realized costs of business activities are compared. Deviations are analyzed together with the responsible process owners. The responsibility for processes across cost centers is supposed to improve the overhead cost management.
- **Determination of activity cost rates.** Before product costs can be calculated, activity cost rates are determined. These are computed by the costs of the activities over cost-driver volume, which, again, involves dividing costs proportionally

based on a particular measure. See Table 3.

- **Calculation of product costs.** Product costs are calculated by adding up direct costs, such as labor and material, and the process coefficients of a product—that is, the volume of a process used by a certain product—times the corresponding process cost rates. If one unit of a process is used by a single customer order of several products, the process coefficients are computed by one over the corresponding lot or order size: They are averaged. The activity-oriented calculation of product costs aims at displaying the long-term costs created by a product. See Table 4. ABC is used in Germany as well, though somewhat differently. In Germany, its application is concentrated on services and indirect processes though, even then, it is used infrequently. A 2002 study conducted by Klaus-Peter Franz and Peter Kajüter found that 47% of the large German companies used ABC in 2001, (compared to 52% in 1996), and half of these companies applied it only occasionally. There are also different ABC approaches in Germany. As originally proposed by Cooper and Kaplan, ABC doesn't link activities and products. Consequently, cost allocations based on activities might be misleading. An alternative approach to ABC—known in Germany as process cost accounting

(PCA)—only considers costs outside the manufacturing department. PCA pools activities with processes that produce some form of output, such as order fulfillment or procurement of raw material. And instead of single activities being assigned to products, the costs of these processes are assigned.

GPK AND ABC COMPARED

Since GPK applies the marginal costing principle and, accordingly, allocates only variable costs to products, it provides adequate information for short-term decisions, such as a decision to accept or reject an additional order based on contribution margin information. It's also common for GPK to be extended by an additional full-cost calculation to add a long-term perspective. ABC, on the other hand, aims at allocating all the costs required to produce and market a product in the long run. It focuses on long-term decisions such as product design and production, as shown in Table 5, and involves allocations of fixed costs that use assumptions about the proportionality of costs that normally won't be fulfilled, which makes ABC less suited for short-term decision making. Though GPK allocates overhead costs on products via cost centers and ABC does it via activities and processes, the underlying formal structure of cost pools and cost drivers is similar. In fact, some companies use the cost center module of SAP for implementing ABC.

Table 3: Determining Activity Cost Rates

PROCESS	COST DRIVER	COST-DRIVER VOLUME	ACTIVITY COSTS	ACTIVITY COST RATE
Production	Machine hours	5,000	200,000	40
Purchase order management	Number of purchase orders	1,200	9,600	8
Production planning	Number of production operations	2,000	10,000	5
Sales order management	Number of sales orders	1,500	22,500	15

Blocher, Stout, Cokins, Chen: *Cost Management, 4e*

Table 4: Activity-Oriented Calculation of Product Costs

COST ELEMENT	ACTIVITY COST RATE	ALLOCATED COEFFICIENT	ALLOCATED COSTS
Direct material	–	–	16
Production	40	2	80
Purchase order management	8	4 parts with purchase order size 16	2
		6 parts with purchase order size 12	4
Production planning	5	12 operations with lot size 10	6
Sales order management	15	1 product with sales order size 3	5
Product unit costs			113

This shows that the differences between GPK and ABC aren't about the structure of the systems but instead involve the types and number of cost drivers and the allocation of fixed costs. Both systems use direct cost drivers in production-related areas to measure the performance of cost centers and their activities, but ABC also employs nonoutput-related cost drivers such as product complexity and number of product variants, which is supposed to improve the manufacturing design and reduce the number of parts used. ABC also uses these cost drivers to allocate total costs on products. GPK, however, doesn't because charging fixed costs to products isn't in line with its principles. In practice, GPK can be expanded by a multilayered allocation of fixed costs, which it often is. For example, this could be done at the product variants level, which would account for this cost driver but wouldn't apportion fixed costs. If fixed costs are allocated in GPK for mid- and long-term purposes in a multilayered fashion, they are strictly separated from variable costs. Both management accounting systems stress the issue of cost and profitability control, such as through variance analysis. An important difference between GPK and ABC is the distinct focus of ABC on the process owners' responsibility for their processes across cost centers and departments. This implies a horizontal, process orientation compared to GPK's vertical, functional one.

SUPERIOR DECISION-SUPPORT ACCOUNTING?

All things considered, we think GPK is superior to ABC for making short-term decisions, primarily for short-run production decisions as well as short-run pricing, particularly for manufacturing companies. ABC's long-term perspective gives recommendations for product design and long-run production programs, yet long-term investment decisions actually require net present value analysis, restricting the relevance of ABC to a mid-term horizon. Combining GPK and ABC covers the short-term *and* the mid-term horizon. ABC emphasizes indirect areas of manufacturing and services. When it comes to cost control and cost management, GPK focuses on cost centers while ABC addresses process owners across functions. ABC has the advantage here because it ensures continuous responsibility across interdependent activities.

Table 5: Comparison of GPK and ABC

	GPK	ABC
Character of cost accounting system regarding cost separation	Marginal costing	Full costing
Decision relevance	Short-term decisions	Mid-term orientation
Allocation of overhead costs on products is via	Cost centers	Activities and processes
Cost drivers	Output-related	Also nonoutput related cost drivers such as product complexity and product variants
Cost responsibility/ cost consciousness	Cost center managers	Process owners across cost centers
Implied form of organization	Vertical	Horizontal

By combining GPK and ABC, cost control and cost management have a cost center *and* process perspective. There are advantages in combining GPK and ABC, especially as the importance of indirect costs increases. But a permanent ABC system that delivers detailed cost information of single activities on a monthly basis like GPK would be very expensive in most instances. An alternative solution for companies already using GPK could be to define cost centers in indirect areas in order to improve planning and control of the principal activities' costs. Yet another widely practiced alternative is to employ ABC on a case-by-case basis only, such as for the development of new products. For U.S. companies with an ABC-system in place, there would be substantial costs for adopting a new GPK system. ut having a look at the existing ERP system could bring a pleasant surprise. If its functionality already comprises elements of GPK, the necessary investment for a GPK system may be manageable.

Blocher, Stout, Cokins, Chen: *Cost Management, 4e*

Chapter 10
Cost Planning for the Product Life Cycle: Target Costing, Theory of Constraints, and Strategic Pricing

Cases

10-1   **California-Illini Manufacturing** (The Theory of Constraints)
10-2   **Blue Ridge Manufacturing (B)**
10-3   **Nebraska Toaster Company** (Target Costing)
10-4   **Mercedes-Benz All Activity Vehicle** (Target Costing)

Readings

10-1: "Target Costing at ITT Automotive" by George Schmelze, Rolf Geier, Thomas El Buttross, *Management Accounting* (December 1996).

This article provides a good example of an actual application of target costing. The example is of the production and sale of brake systems, an intensely competitive industry. The article explains how value engineering is used. Two important concepts of the article are (1) target costing is a moving target, and as prices fall in the industry, target costs and manufacturing costs are required to fall as well, and (2) target costing is a bottom-up, team-oriented process that requires cross-functional teams. Also, the article explains how ITT uses "tracking sheets" to manage the life cycle costs of the product.

Discussion Questions:
1. How are prices set at ITT Automotive?
2. How does ITT Automotive obtain information about a competitor's costs?
3. What are the target costing tools used at ITT Automotive?
4. How is the tracking sheet used in ITT Automotive's target costing system?

10-2: "Integrating Activity-Based Costing and the Theory of Constraints" by Robin Cooper and Regine Slagmulder, *Management Accounting* (February 1999).

The authors of this article show how ABC costing and the Theory of Constraints (TOC) methods can be compared and used in a complementary fashion.

Discussion Question: Explain how ABC and TOC can be viewed as complementary methods.

10-3: "Is TOC for You?" by Linda E. Holmes CMA, Ann B. Hendricks CMA, CPA, *Strategic Finance* (April 2005).

This article gives a good introduction to the objectives and techniques of the theory of constraints (TOC). There is also a discussion of key performance measures related to to the application of TOC in management accounting.

Discussion Questions:
1. What is meant by throughput?
2. What are the five steps of TOC?
3. List some ways to increase the capacity on a constraint.
4. What are the five management accounting truths related to TOC?

Cases

10-1 *California-Illini Manufacturing*

The California-Illini Manufacturing Company's (CI) plant operates in the rural central valley of California. It is family-owned and run. CI's plant manager, a grandson of the founder, went to school with many of the employees. Despite this family atmosphere, CI is the largest producer of plain and hard-faced replacement tillage tools in the United States. It averages annual sales of $13 million. Farmers use tillage tools to cultivate the land. Hard-facing, the application of brazed chromium carbide to leading edges, increases a tool's durability.

THE PRODUCTION PROCESS
Historically, CI grew from the founders' original blacksmith shop, and today the production process is still relatively simple. The plant manager described the process as "You simply take a piece of metal. And then you bang, heat, and shape it until it's a finished product. It really isn't a sophisticated process. We just do it better than anyone else." The production process is like a flow following a routing from one cost center to another in a sequence of move, wait, setup, and runtime for each process. Work-in-process inventories in the move and wait stage litter the plant. Economic lot size rules determine the size of each batch while production schedules push jobs onto the floor.

THE COST SYSTEM: MEASURING PERFORMANCE
CI uses standard unit costs to measure performance and profit potential. In this cost system, each materials and labor input is given a standard usage, and production managers are evaluated on their ability to meet or improve upon these standards. Differences from the standard were called "variances." For example, if a certain manufacturing operation required at standard 5 minutes, the operator would be expected to complete a lot of 100 parts in 500 minutes. If actually 550 minutes were required, there would be a 50 minute unfavorable variance. Also, using the operator's wage rate, the cost of the variance could be calculated.

CI'S IMPROVEMENT STRATEGY
The depressed market in the mid-1980s caused a 1986 net loss of close to $1.8 million. Inventory turns were down to one and a half, and cash flow was poor. Facing these conditions, management adopted a new strategy stressing improvements in accounting performance and reduction of inventories. Their strategies for improvement included: increasing productivity, cost cutting (overhead control), improving technology, and increasing prices.

1. **Productivity**. Productivity improvements centered on direct labor productivity measures. Output per direct labor hour was the crucial factor. Accordingly, improving efficiency, by definition, consisted of keeping direct labor busy producing as much product as possible during regular working hours. Actions supporting this strategy were 1) reducing idle manhours between jobs, 2) increasing batch sizes to maximize runtime, and 3) reducing setup times.

    The operational control system measured the "earned labor hours" for each department daily. While the plant manager only received these reports weekly, he was still aware of the daily figures. Budget reports, including variances, while processed monthly, were often two to three weeks late! Thus, they had little direct impact on day-to-day decisions. However, the plant manager knew what the accounting reports should be like from his daily earned labor hours information.

    The short-term results of these efforts were impressive because plant efficiency measures rose about 15%. There were, however, some negative, unanticipated side effects in work-in-process levels, scheduling, and overtime.

    First, work-in-process levels increased. In order to improve efficiency measures, departments kept processing large lots regardless of current demand. Once a machine had been set up, to economically justify large batches, the rationale was to provide for both current and future inventory needs. Consequently, finished goods grew from two to six-months' supply.

Blocher, Stout, Cokins, Chen: *Cost Management, 4e*

Second, the large batch sizes made scheduling difficult. They reduced plant flexibility by keeping machines on single jobs for long periods. Therefore, it was difficult to adjust for normal production problems and still maintain the production schedule. Machines were not readily available for special situations and expediting.

Finally, these large batches, while increasing productivity, created the need for overtime to maintain the schedule. Overtime in the finishing department, for example, increased by 15-20%, thus raising operating expenses. The larger lots reduced the variety of products produced each production period. This increased the lead time for custom orders could get stuck behind jobs with long runtimes. Overtime, then, became necessary to expedite out-of-stock orders. These factors combined with low sales volumes to create losses and more cash flow problems.

2. **Overhead.** Overhead improvement focused on two strategies. The first was direct cost reduction. The second concentrated on reducing unit costs by increasing volume. The higher volumes allowed overhead to be absorbed over more units. However, because CI's cost structure had large fixed obligations (like union contracted pension fund contribution), potential overhead savings were minimal.

The results of these strategies were unimpressive. The union didn't make many concessions, and few overhead savings occurred. Production volumes did increase, but the plant was producing to cover overhead rather than to satisfy immediate demand. Management hoped that increasing sales would eventually take care of the excess production. Unfortunately, this didn't happen. By 1989 inventories were 24% higher than in 1986. And, once again, there were cash flow and earnings problems.

3. **Technology.** CI considered the technology focus to be particularly troublesome. Concentrating on reducing unit costs through technology improvement often blocked out other aspects of the decision. Management's assumptions were that the savings from each decision flowed directly to the bottom line. However for CI this myopic view of unit costs encouraged mistakes.

Management's use of robots provided a vivid example of the problems. Robots were investigated as a means of decreasing the unit costs for the application knife. The anhydrous ammonia applicator knife was popular worldwide, to revitalize the soil with ammonia fertilizer after each harvest. Although CI led the industry in product quality, it was a high-cost producer. The primary reason was determined to be hand welding, using expensive piece rates, with manual electric arc welders.

After a unit-cost analysis, the savings in labor and applied overhead seemed to justify the introduction of welding robots (Tables 1,2,3). Subsequent price reductions increased sales from 20,000 to more than 60,000 units in the first. At the new, lower, price the company seemed to still realize savings of $1.25 per unit.

Unfortunately, these savings were illusory. During the second year, other manufacturers became price competitive and sales volume dropped to 40,000 units; however, management still believed the robots saved the company money. At a 10% discount rate the three-year net present value was $63,730. A major problem was that labor savings disappeared as manual welders found work in other areas of the plant. In fact, the robots required additional new hires and caused increases in utilities and maintenance costs. New operating expenses were greater than the increased throughput. Thus, management was misled by its focus on standard unit costs.

4. **Selling Prices.** Unfortunately, the market for the firm's products was very competitive. Due to such macroeconomic factors as government programs and foreign grain production, the domestic market was shrinking. Internationally, CI's high unit costs made foreign markets difficult to enter. Consequently, management perceived the marketplace to be mostly out of their control. Their main focus was on improving plant performance. Nonetheless, CI still tried to increase the sales volume in domestic markets and to find new foreign markets. As for the foreign markets they experienced some success and some failures.

In an attempt to find new international markets, the company successfully set up a working relationship with a John Deere distributor in Mexico and, unsuccessfully pursued a contract in Saudi Arabia. This failure was very revealing because Saudi Arabian soils were made to order for CI's product. The Saudi's cultivation process was particularly abrasive for tillage tools. Because of frequent breakdowns, crews with replacement parts had to constantly follow the field workers. But with CI's parts this practice wasn't necessary. Consequently, the Saudis were very enthusiastic about the company's products. Unfortunately, CI did not believe the 10% profit margins to be large enough. CI rejected the Saudi Arabia offer. This happened while at the same time the plant was having difficulty with operating expenses, overhead, and inventories. Thus, the accounting cost standards influenced market decisions as well as leading to questionable, limited improvements in manufacturing. All was not harmonious among management as well.

During this time, marketing and production meetings were frequent. Marketing pointed out that while quality was good, prices were too high and lead times were too inaccurate. On the other hand, production complained that marketing was constantly messing up their production schedules.

Using this combination of efficiency improvement, overhead reduction, unit-cost reductions and sales margins, management proceeded, over an 18-month period, to reduce domestic volume by 11.5% and to turn away significant foreign opportunities. Overall, decisions to improve the performance of the company using standard cost measurement failed. By February 1989, operating expenses were 20% greater than the disastrous 1986 figures. During the same period, inventories increased by 24%, and net profits continued to deteriorate.

At year-end CI hired a new Production Control/Inventory Control (PCIC) manager. However, the plant manager was suspicious when the PCIC manager came to him with revised schedules. The PCIC manager suggested processing job lots of 100 to 150 part rather than the current 6,000. The plant manager questioned the PCIC manager's ability. "Clearly he isn't very knowledgeable. How can we make any money running only small lots? The setup costs will kill us!

Finally the PCIC manager gave the plant manager a copy of The Goal by E. Goldratt and J. Cox. After reading the first few pages, the plant manager recognized many similarities between his plant and the one described in this book.

REQUIRED:

1. What is the firm's competitive strategy? Does the strategy seem appropriate?
2. What motivated the cost reduction strategy? Did the cost reduction strategy work? Why?
3. How did CI's standard cost system affect the cost reduction strategy?
4. What is the role of work-in-process in the cost reduction strategy?
5. Is the new Production control/Inventory Control (PCIC) manager on the right track with the smaller lot sizes?
6. What steps is the PCIC likely to take now?
7. What type of cost system should be used at CI?

(IMA adapted)

TABLE 1
IMPACT OF ROBOTICS ON STANDARD COST ANHYDROUS AMMONIA KNIVES

Department	Material: Before	After	Labor: Before	After	Overhead: Before	After	Total: Before	After
Cold Shear	$2.000	$2.000	$0.068	$0.068	$0.238	$0.238	$2.306	$2.306
Hot Forge			$0.127	$0.127	$0.445	$0.445	$0.572	$0.572
Heat Treat			$0.025	$0.025	$0.088	$0.088	$0.113	$0.113
Shot Blast			$0.025	$0.025	$0.088	$0.088	$0.113	$0.113
Arc Weld	$6.500	$6.500	$1.380	$0.250	$4.830	$0.875	$12.710	$7.625
Paint/Pack			$0.076	$0.076	$0.266	$0.266	$0.342	$0.342
Total	$8.500	$8.500	$1.701	$0.571	$5.954	$1.999	$16.155	$11.070
Selling Price							$18.150	$14.310
Gross Margin							12.353%	29.274%
Unit Profit							$1.995	$3.241

Note – OH/DL = 3.5/1

TABLE 2
IMPACT OF ROBOTICS ON STANDARD COST ANHYDROUS AMMONIA KNIVES

Year	Unit Savings	Unit Sales	+(–) Profits	Present Value (10%)
1	$1.245	6,000	$ 74,700	$ 67,909
2	$1.245	4,000	49,800	41,157
3	$1.245	4,000	49,800	37,415
Total			$174,300	$146,482
Initial investment				$ (60,000)
Net present value				$ 86,482

TABLE 3
IMPACT OF ROBOTICS ON STANDARD COST ANHYDROUS AMMONIA KNIVES

Actual Results:

Year	Net Additional: Labor	Maintenance	Utilities	Total Additional: Expenses	Net Additional: Throughput	+(-) Profits	Present Value (10%)
1	$52,000	$2,000	$4,000	$ 58,000	$155,600	$97,600	$88,727
2	$92,000	$2,000	$4,000	$ 98,000	$ 39,400	($58,600)	($48,430)
3	$92,000	$2,000	$4,000	$ 98,000	$ 39,400	($58,600)	($44,027)
Total				$254,000	$234,400	($19,600)	($3,730)
Initial Investment							($60,000)
Net Present Value							($63,730)

10-2 Blue Ridge Manufacturing (B)

Note: For the background information on this case, see Case 5-1. Case (B) is a continuation of Case 5-1

UPDATE OF RECENT DEVELOPMENTS

Blue Ridge Manufacturing (BRM) has found that the new non-toxic ink has stimulated sales substantially, so the firm has extended its markets both nationally and internationally. It has upgraded the quality of all its products and developed new products including bathrobes and bath towels for upscale hotels and resorts, bed and breakfasts, and some corporate clients. The majority of the new products also involve imprinting a logo or some form of embroidery.

At the same time BRM has been expanding its product line, significant new competition has developed, especially from non-U.S.-based manufacturers, particularly in Asian counties. These new competitors have caused BRM to lower its prices in some markets, and has reduced BRM's market share in many markets.

An important aspect of the new products for hotels and resorts is that these products sometimes involve a significant amount of design work. In contrast to BRM's other products which have logos and design that are standardized by license agreement, the hotel products fall into two categories. First, there are some well-established hotels and resorts that have a global logo and for which the design effort is negligible. The customer's logo or design is well specified and easy to work with in the production of the bathrobes, towels or other products. Second, there are some hotels and resorts that are not a part of a large chain, which may not have a well-designed logo for their towels and bathrobes. These customers require a significant amount of extra work in helping the customer develop a design that is workable for the desired products. The extra work can be as much as 18-26 hours per order, but is more often less than 10 hours. The bathrobes require more design time, roughly 2-16 hours per order, while the towels usually require 1-6 hours per order, when the additional design work is necessary. From recent months' results, it appears that the new products will become a significant part of BRM's overall business, especially the customers from smaller hotels and resorts that need design help. In view of the success of the new products, BRM is thinking of putting in place a product development team, a permanent activity within the firm, which would search out new product ideas and develop new products on an on-going basis.

REQUIRED:

1.   What is BRM's strategy now that it has developed the new products and become a global competitor? Has the strategy changed?
2.   How should BRM adapt to the new competitive environment?

10-3 Nebraska Toaster Company: Target Costing Case

Through market research and competitor analysis Nebraska Toaster Company has found a market for toaster oven new product that is not currently being produced by competitors. This new toaster can toast bagels or regular toast bread or grill sausages. It will be targeted for a consumer group of young family households. The customer requirements and important features to the consumer have been identified and the Nebraska Toaster Company will focus on these for the toaster oven design. The criteria are:

Toasts properly
Size
Speed of toasting
Toaster capacity
Appearance
Easy to clean

Nebraska Toaster Company wants to competitively match the price toaster oven to basic toasters; the competitive market price is $20.00. Nebraska Toaster Company wants to earn a profit of 20 % of sales price. Relevant cost information for the company follows in Table 1. Most of the life cycle activities are done inside the firm, but shipping is outsourced.

Table 1 Life Cycle and Value Chain Analysis

Value Chain	Inside			Outside			Total		
Life Cycle	Target	Current	Gap	Target	Current	Gap	Target	Current	Gap
R&D	$ 4.00 (25%)	$ 4.20	$ 0.20				$ 4.00 (25%)	$ 4.20	$0.20
Manufacturing	9.00 (56%)	12.00	3.00				9.00 (56%)	12.00	3.00
Selling	1.60 (10%)	1.80	0.20				1.60 (10%)	1.80	0.20
Shipping				$ 0.90 (6%)	$ 1.00	$ 0.10	0.90 (6%)	1.00	0.10
General Adm.	0.50 (3%)	0.70	0.20				0.50 (3%)	0.70	0.20
Total	$ 15.10 (94%)	$ 18.70	$ 3.60	$ 0.90 (6%)	$ 1.00	$ 0.10	$16.00	$19.70	$3.70

The toaster company through value engineering and continuous improvement plans to determine a way to reach the target cost by looking at the products life cycle and its value chain activities to determine where to reduce costs.

Step 1-- Product Functional Cost analysis
Nebraska Toaster Company plans to implement functional analysis to target areas of cost reduction. Here the company breakdowns the current $12.00 manufacturing costs (from Table 1 "Manufacturing" row and "Total Current" column) for the toaster oven by the components' estimated costs and functions performed. The result is in Table 2.

Blocher, Stout, Cokins, Chen: *Cost Management, 4e*

©The McGraw-Hill Companies, Inc 2008

Table 2 Product Functional Cost Analysis

Component	Function	Current Cost	% of Cost
Heating Unit	Toast bagels or grill sausages	$2.40	20
Display Light	Indicates the process of toasting or grilling	1.60	13
Lever	Lowers bagels or sausages into toaster & initiates toasting or grilling	0.60	5
Spring Coil	Pops up bagels or sausages when toasted or grilled	0.60	5
Temperature Control Timer	Controls degree of toasting or grilling	0.60	5
Body Design	Holds bagels or sausages	5.10	43
Crumb and Grease Catcher	Catches crumbs and greases & is removable for cleaning	1.10	9
TOTAL		$12.00	100%

The Nebraska Toaster Company plans to rank the features of the new bagel toaster according to customer preferences and requirements, in Step 2.

Step 2 -- Customer Requirement Analysis

Nebraska Toaster Company selected a customer focus group to rank the six most important characteristics or requirements as shown in Table 3.

Table 3 Customer Requirement Analysis

Customer Requirements	Customer Ranking	Relative Ranking	
	Ranking is from 1-5, 5 the most important	Raw Score	%
Toasts and grills properly	5	5	28
Size	3	3	17
Speed of toasting or grilling	3	3	17
Toaster oven capacity	2	2	11
Appearance	1	1	5
Easy to clean	4	4	22
TOTAL		18	100

The customers rank the criteria -- toast or grill properly, cleaning, and size -- as the most important relative to the other customer characteristics or requirements. The next process compares the customer requirement features to the component functions.

Step 3 -- Quality Function Development Analysis

Nebraska Toaster Company engineers assessed the new toaster oven product's functional performance as shown in Table 4.

Table 4 Quality Functional Performance Assessment

Components or Functions	Heating Unit	Display Light	Lever	Spring Coil	Temp. Control & Timer	Body Design	Crumb Catcher	
Customer Requirements								**Total**
Toasts properly	50 %		20 %	20%	10%			100%
Size	50 %					50 %		100%
Speed of toasting	70 %				10 %	20 %		100%
Toaster capacity	30 %		5 %			60 %	5 %	100%
Appearance		20 %				80 %		100%
Easy to clean	50 %					45 %	5 %	100%

REQUIRED:
1. Calculate the target cost for the toaster
2. Using the information above, develop a ranking of product functions that gives the company the importance and value of each component relative to the features that create value to the customer.

Blocher, Stout, Cokins, Chen: *Cost Management, 4e*
©The McGraw-Hill Companies, Inc 2008

10-4 Mercedes-Benz All Activity Vehicle (AAV)[1]

During the recession beginning in the early 1990s, Mercedes-Benz (MB) struggled with product development, cost efficiency, material purchasing and problems in adapting to changing markets. In 1993, these problems caused the worst sales slump in decades, and the luxury carmaker lost money for the first time in its history. Since then, MB has streamlined the core business, reduced parts and system complexity, and established simultaneous engineering programs with suppliers.

In their search for additional market share, new segments, and new niches, MB started developing a range of new products. New product introductions included the C-class in 1993, the E-class in 1995, the new sportster SLK in 1996, and the A-class and M-class All Activity Vehicle (AAV) in 1997. Perhaps the largest and most radical of MB's new projects was the AAV. In April 1993, MB announced it would build its first passenger vehicle-manufacturing facility in the United States. The decision emphasized the company's globalization strategy and desire to move closer to its customers and markets.

Mercedes-Benz United States International used function groups with representatives from every area of the company (marketing, development, engineering, purchasing, production, and controlling) to design the vehicle and production systems. A modular construction process was used to produce the AAV. First-tier suppliers provided systems, rather than individual parts or components, for production of approximately 65,000 vehicles annually.

THE AAV PROJECT PHASES

The AAV has moved from concept to production in a relatively short period of time. The first phase, the concept phase, was initiated in 1992. The concept phase resulted in a feasibility study that was approved by the board. Following board approval, the project realization phase began in 1993, with production commencing in 1997. Key elements of the various phases are described below.

CONCEPT PHASE, 1992-1993

Team members compared the existing production line with various market segments to discover opportunities for new vehicle introductions. The analysis revealed opportunities in the rapidly expanding sports utility vehicle market that was dominated by Jeep, Ford, and GM. Market research was conducted to estimate potential worldwide sales opportunities for a high-end AAV with the characteristics of a Mercedes-Benz. A rough cost estimate was developed that included materials, labor, overhead, and one-time development and project costs. Projected cash flows were analyzed over a 10-year period using net present value (NPV) analysis to acquire project approval from the board of directors. The sensitivity of the NPV was analyzed by calculating "what-if" scenarios involving risks and opportunities. For example, risk factors included monetary exchange rate fluctuations, different sales levels due to consumer substitution of the AAV for another MB product, and product and manufacturing cost that differed from projections.

Based on the economic feasibility study of the concept phase, the board approved the project and initiated a search for potential manufacturing locations. Sites located in Germany, other European countries, and the United States were evaluated. Consistent with the company's globalization strategy, the decisive factor that brought the plant to the United States was the desire to be close to the major market for sports utility vehicles.

PROJECT REALIZATION PHASE, 1993-1996

Regular customer clinics were held to view the prototype and to explain the new vehicle concept. These clinics produced important information about how the proposed vehicle would be received by potential customers and the press. Customers were asked to rank the importance of various characteristics including safety, comfort, economy, and styling. Engineers organized in function groups designed systems to deliver these essential characteristics. However, MB would not lower its internal standards for components, even if initial customer expectations might be lower than the MB standard. For example, many automotive experts believed the superior handling of MB products resulted from manufacturing the best automobile chassis in the world. Thus, each class within the MB line met strict standards for handling, even though these standards might exceed customer

---

[1] Prepared by Thomas L. Albright, © Institute of Management Accountants, 2000. Used with permission.

expectations for some classes. MB did not use target costing to produce the lowest-price vehicle in an automotive class. The company's strategic objective was to deliver products that were slightly more expensive than competitive models. However, the additional cost would have to translate into greater perceived value on the part of the customer.

Throughout the project realization phase, the vehicle (and vehicle target cost) remained alive because of changing dynamics. For example, the market moved toward the luxury end of the spectrum while the AAV was under development. In addition, crash test results were incorporated into the evolving AAV design. For these reasons, MB found it beneficial to place the design and testing team members in close physical proximity to other functions within the project to promote fast communication and decision making. Sometimes new technical features, such as side air bags, were developed by MB. The decision to include the new feature on all MB lines was made at the corporate level because experience had shown that customers' reactions to a vehicle class can affect the entire brand.

PRODUCTION PHASE, 1997

The project was monitored by annual updates of the NPV analysis. In addition, a three-year plan (including income statements) was prepared annually and reported to the headquarters in Germany. Monthly departmental meetings were held to discuss actual cost performance compared with standards developed during the cost estimation process. Thus, the accounting system served as a control mechanism to ensure that actual production costs would conform to target (or standard) costs.

TARGET COSTING AND THE AAV

The process of achieving target cost for the AAV began with an estimate of the existing cost for each function group. Next, components of each function group were identified, with their associated costs. Cost reduction targets were set by comparing the estimated existing cost with the target cost for each function group. These function groups included the following: doors, sidewall and roof, electrical system, bumpers, powertrain, seats, heating system, cockpit, and front end. Next, cost reduction targets were established for each component. As part of the competitive benchmark process, MB bought and tore down competitors' vehicles to help understand their costs and manufacturing processes.

The AAV manufacturing process relied on high value-added systems suppliers. For example, the entire cockpit was purchased as a unit from a systems supplier. Thus, systems suppliers were part of the development process from the beginning of the project. MB expected suppliers to meet established cost targets. To enhance function group effectiveness, suppliers were brought into the discussion at an early stage in the process. Decisions had to be made quickly in the early stages of development.

The target costing process was led by cost planners who were engineers, not accountants. Because the cost planners were engineers with manufacturing and design experience, they could make reasonable estimates of costs that suppliers would incur in providing various systems. Also, MB owned much of the tooling, such as dies to form sheet metal, used by suppliers to produce components. Tooling costs are a substantial part of the one-time costs in the project phase.

INDEX DEVELOPMENT TO SUPPORT TARGET COSTING ACTIVITIES I[2]

During the concept development phase, MB team members used various indexes to help them determine critical performance, design, and cost relationships for the AAV. To construct the indexes, various forms of information were gathered from customers, suppliers, and their own design team. Though the actual number of categories used by MB was much greater, Table 1 illustrates the calculations used to quantify customer responses to the AAV concept. For example, values shown in the importance column resulted from asking a sample of potential customers whether they consider each category extremely important when considering the purchase of a new MB product. Respondents could respond affirmatively to all categories that applied.

---

[2] All numbers have been altered for proprietary reasons; however, the tables illustrate the actual process used in the development of the AAV.

Blocher, Stout, Cokins, Chen: *Cost Management, 4e*

Table 1. Relative Importance Ranking by Category

Category	Importance	Relative Percentage
Safety	32	41%
Comfort	25	32
Economy	15	18
Styling	7	9
Total	79	100

To gain a better understanding of the various sources of costs, function groups were identified together with target cost estimates. (MB also organizes teams called function groups whose role is to develop specifications and cost projections.) As shown in Table 2, the relative target cost percentage of each function group was computed.

Table 2. Target Cost and Percentage by Function Group

Function Group	Target Cost	Percentage of Total
Chasis	$x,xxx	20%
Transmission	$x,xxx	25
Air conditioner	$x,xxx	5
Electrical System	$x,xxx	7
Other function groups	$x,xxx	43
Total	$xx,xxx	100%

Table 3 summarizes how each function group contributes to the consumer requirements identified in Table 1. For example, safety was identified by potential customers as an important characteristic of the AAV; some function groups contributed more to the safety category than others. MB engineers determined chassis quality was an important element of safety (50% of the total function group contribution).

Table 3. Function Group Contribution to Customer Requirements

Function Group/Category	Safety	Comfort	Economy	Styling
Chassis	50%	30%	10%	10%
Transmission	20	20	30	
Air conditioner		20		5
Electrical system	5		20	
Other systems	25	30	40	85
Total	100%	100%	100%	100%

Table 4 combines the category weighting percentages from Table 1 with the function group contribution from Table 3. The result is an importance index that measures the relative importance of each function group across all categories. For example, potential customers weighted the categories of safety, comfort, economy, and styling as .41, .32, .18, and .09, respectively. The rows in Table 4 represent the contribution of each function group to the various categories. The importance index for the chassis is calculated by multiplying each row value by its corresponding category value, and summing the results $((.50 \times .41) + (.30 \times .32) + (.10 \times .18) + (.10 \times .09) = .33$.

Table 4. Importance Index of Various Function Groups

Function Group/ Category	Safety .41	Comfort .32	Economy .18	Styling .09	Importance Index
Chassis	.50	.30	.10	.10	.33
Transmission	.20	.20			.20
Air conditioner		.20	.05	.05	.07
Electrical system	.05				.06
Other systems	.25	.40	.85	.85	.35
Total	1.00	1.00	1.00	1.00	

As shown in Table 5, the target cost index is calculated by dividing the importance index by the target cost percentage by function group. Managers at MB used indexes such as these during the concept design phase to understand the relationship of the importance of a function group to the target cost of a function group. Indexes less than one may indicate a cost in excess of the perceived value of the function group. Thus, opportunities for cost reduction, consistent with customer demands, may be identified and managed during the early stages of product development. Choices made during the project realization phase were largely irreversible during the production phase because approximately 80% of the production cost of the AAV was for materials and systems provided by external suppliers.

The AAV project used a streamlined management structure to facilitate efficient and rapid development. The streamlined MB organization produced an entirely new vehicle from concept to production in four years. Using the target costing process as a key management element, MB manufactured the first production AAV in 1997.

Table 5. Target Cost Index

Function Group/Index	(A) Importance Index	(B) % of Target Cost	(C) A/B Target Cost Index
Chassis	.33	.20	1.65
Transmission	.20	.25	.80
Air conditioner	.07	.05	1.40
Electrical Systems	.06	.07	.86
Other systems	.35	.43	.81
Total		1.00	

Questions for Discussion:

1. What is the competitive environment faced by MB?
2. How has MB reacted to the changing world market for luxury automobiles?
3. Using Cooper's cost, quality, and functionality chart, discuss the factors on which MB competes with other automobile producers such as Jeep, Ford, and GM.[3]
4. How does the AAV project link with MB strategy in terms of market coverage?
5. Explain the process of developing a component importance index. How can such an index guide managers in making cost reduction decisions?
6. How does MB approach cost reduction to achieve target costs?
7. How do suppliers factor into the target costing process? Why are they so critically important to the success of the MB AAV?
8. What role does the accounting department play in the target costing process?

---

[3] Robin Cooper, When Lean Enterprises Collide, Boston: Harvard Business School Press, 1995

Blocher, Stout, Cokins, Chen: *Cost Management, 4e*

10.1: TARGET COSTING AT ITT AUTOMOTIVE

By George Schmelze, CPA; Rolf Geir; and Thomas E. Buttross, CMA

Intense competition and pressure from customers to reduce prices has forced many companies to reduce their costs to survive. These companies have found that most costs are committed once production begins, and, therefore, the costs must be reduced earlier in the product life cycle, particularly while the product is in the planning and design stages. Target costing is a proven, effective method of reducing production costs throughout the product life cycle, without reducing quality or functionality and without increasing the time it takes to design and develop a product. At ITT Automotive, the brakes area has been using target costing for three to four years, and it provides an excellent model that other areas of the company are beginning to emulate.

Target costing is a proactive, strategic cost management philosophy that is price-driven, customer-focused, design-centered, and cross-functional. Unlike traditional cost control systems, which do not control costs until production has commenced, the target costing philosophy requires that aggressive cost management occur in the product planning stage, the product design stage, and the production stage. By designing lower costs into the product, companies realize the best sources of cost savings—before the product reaches the production stage. These cost savings cannot be realized, however, with traditional costing systems, such as standard costing systems and activity-based costing systems.

Target costing transcends the functional areas of a company. For target costing to be successful, integration is needed in the form of cross-functional teams comprising engineering, product design, production, purchasing, sales, finance, cost accounting, cost targeting, and, in many cases, customers and suppliers. Upper-level management support is crucial to the success of target costing because resources need to be allocated to the target costing area, and the cross-functional teams must be empowered to make many critical decisions.

Target costing differs from traditional "cost-plus" costing. Rather than the selling price being a function of estimated costs, the target cost is a function of the selling price and a desired profit. Furthermore, with target costing, the target cost is determined before the product is designed. The target costing equation is as follows:

$$\text{Target Price} - \text{Target Profit} = \text{Target Cost}$$

Various factors are considered when computing the future selling price of the proposed product including functionality of the product, projected sales volumes, and quality. For example, management strategy may call for a price that maintains or increases market share.

Due to intense competition, many companies have little flexibility when setting a price. When market conditions are extremely competitive, the price may be driven by the market. In other cases, the target cost of the downstream company is the target price of the upstream company. Where selling price and profit margin are fixed by competitive pressures and management policies, respectively, reducing the firm's production costs may be the only source of increased earnings.

Once the target cost is computed, it must be assigned to final assembly, subassemblies, and components before design can begin. After the product is designed, estimated costs of production are compared with target costs. If the estimated costs are higher than the target costs, value engineering is employed to help the company achieve its target. Value engineering is a process in which the cross-functional team attempts to reduce costs during the design and preproduction stages without compromising quality and functionality by determining the optimal processes, materials, and machinery needed for production.

Estimated costs are compared with the targets throughout the product life cycle. Once the product reaches production, however, cost maintenance (as opposed to cost reduction) generally becomes the objective.

TARGET COSTING AT ITT AUTOMOTIVE

To illustrate the process of target costing, let's look at the target costing practices at ITT Automotive. ITT Automotive, one of the world's largest suppliers of auto parts, produced sales of $4.8

billion in 1994, which represented an increase of more than 34% compared to 1993. In 1995, sales were approximately $5.7 billion. Products produced include brake systems and components, wiper handling systems and components, fluid handling systems and components, structural systems and components, electric motors, switches, and lamps. More than 35,000 employees work for the company, with the vast majority of these employees located in the United States and Germany.

The brakes area has used target costing extensively for the last few years because of an extremely competitive environment. For example, the price of anti-lock brake systems, which currently sell for about $200, is expected to drop to $100 by the year 2000. Furthermore, the functionality of the product is expected to increase.

ESTABLISHING THE TARGET PRICE AND TARGET MARGIN

At ITT Automotive, price is generally set externally, either by competitive pressure or by the customer's target costing system. For example, the price that Mercedes-Benz offers ITT Automotive for an anti-lock brake system (ABS) is Mercedes-Benz's target cost.

The first step in the process occurs when ITT Automotive receives an invitation to bid from the customer. Due to the competitive nature of this industry, ITT Automotive cannot use "cost-plus" pricing when setting the price. The price that the company generally will quote is a price that already has been set by market conditions. An analysis then is performed to determine if the product fits ITT Automotive's strategic goals and if the volume can be produced. Financial information including internal rate of return (IRR) and return on investment (ROI) also are calculated to ensure that ITT Automotive can earn a proper return. If productivity increases (reductions in price) are expected by the customer, the analysis must include an explanation concerning how the productivity increases will be achieved.

To determine whether the price is feasible, a permanent cost targeting group made up of employees with backgrounds in engineering, cost accounting, and sales receives the quote. Keeping in mind that the product being quoted will not be produced for several years, the ITT Automotive cost targeting group makes a determination concerning whether enough value engineering can be accomplished before the product is produced in order to meet the quoted price. Other factors considered by the cost targeting team when determining the feasibility of a price include

previous quotes issued, economic factors such as anticipated inflation and interest rates, competitor pricing, and cost structure.

Because ITT Automotive does not produce automobiles, it does not have information concerning prices (and costs) of competitors' component parts. Information from a tear-down analysis of a competitor's product, however, may provide ITT Automotive with information that is useful in determining a competitor's costs and, by adding a reasonable margin, the competitor's price. Tear-down analysis, sometimes referred to as reverse engineering, is an analytical process in which a company will examine in detail a competitor's product. During tear-down analysis, a competitor's product is torn apart by engineers, component by component. An indication of the competitor's design, estimated cost structure, quality, functionality, and possible processes used to build the product are garnered from this process. From this analysis, ITT Automotive may be able to improve designs or processes in order to reduce cost without losing functionality (or to increase functionality and quality without increasing costs). The information garnered from this study is recorded on a standardized document that compares each competitor's product with ITT Automotive's product. This information is useful for price setting because the tear-down analysis provides information concerning the estimated cost structure of the competitor.

Price setting is an iterative process. The cost targeting team will try to find ways to reduce costs in order to accept a bid without comprising ITT Automotive's expected return. For example, the cost targeting team may consult with the design engineers who may suggest that some new process or technology will be available when the produce is produced that will reduce the cost of the product.

ASSIGNING THE TARGET COST.

The target cost is the target price minus the target margin. Finding the target cost is a relatively straightforward calculation; the difficulty for most companies is reaching the target cost in order to meet the company's profit objectives. The target cost should include all costs related to the new product. At ITT Automotive, target costs include direct materials, direct labor, tooling costs, depreciation, promotion, service, and working capital.

Once the target cost has been computed, specific targets are assigned first to final assemblies, then to subassemblies, and then finally to individual components. This work is performed

Blocher, Stout, Cokins, Chen: *Cost Management, 4e*

by individuals in the permanent cost targeting group. Although the setting of the targets is a cross-functional procedure, the ITT Automotive team believes that it is critical for someone who is independent to first set the targets. Once the targets are set initially in cost targeting, feedback is given to the cost targeting area from various members of the cross-functional team, including purchasing and production, concerning targets that are considered unreasonable. This step allows the cross-functional team to be involved in the target-setting process without bogging down the process. Individual targets are set for each component that is purchased, along with targets for burden and labor. The target costs are tracked throughout the product's life cycle, beginning with the design of the product, continuing when tooling is released, and not concluding until the product is discontinued.

In many situations, the price that ITT Automotive will receive for the product will become lower each year. Thus, the target costs will have to be lower each year to provide the company with the same return from year to year. Eventually the margin will become too small, and new products will have to be developed. Figure 1 shows a typical target costing situation, where cost targets are lower each year fueled by productivity increases. The targets are met by using cross-functional teams, setting early cost targets, engaging in value engineering (including tear-down analysis of competitor products and concurrent engineering and production), and forming partnerships with suppliers.

Then these targets are compared with quotes (or estimated costs for items such as depreciation). If the targets are not met, costs are reduced through value engineering and value analysis.

SOME TARGET COSTING TOOLS USED AT ITT AUTOMOTIVE

Achieving the target cost requires companies to take a disciplined approach toward value improvement. Value improvement occurs when functionality and quality are held constant while costs are reduced or when quality and functionality are increased while price is held constant,[2008] At ITT Automotive, achieving the target cost is accomplished through several techniques including the use of cross-functional teams, setting early cost targets, value engineering, and forming partnerships with suppliers.

The target costing process, however, does not end in the early stages of the product life cycle. Once the product reaches production, cost maintenance is practiced through profit improvement planning and value analysis. These techniques help individuals in all of the functional

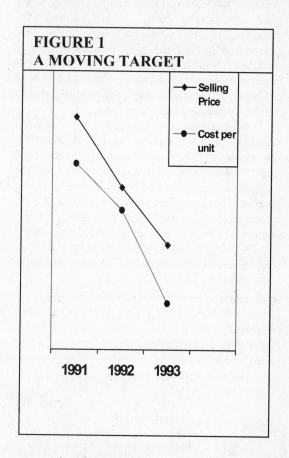

FIGURE 1
A MOVING TARGET

— Selling Price

— Cost per unit

1991   1992   1993

areas take ownership for meeting cost targets throughout the product's life cycle.

One byproduct of the use of cross functional teams is increased understanding of processes and product design by members of the cross-functional team. Members of the cross-functional team at ITT Automotive must have knowledge of processes and design to contribute in a meaningful way to the target costing process. For example, purchasing personnel must have a working knowledge of how the product is designed to make optimal decisions concerning the purchase of components and parts. Similarly, the cost targeting personnel must have a basic understanding of the prices of component parts and subassemblies in order to make decisions concerning the allocation of target costs.

Value engineering is another important component of target costing at ITT Automotive. The objective of value engineering is to reduce costs without reducing functionality or quality without increasing costs before the product reaches the production line. During value engineering, the cross-functional team will try to determine optimal processes, materials, and equipment for designing, engineering, and producing the product.[2008] The value engineering philosophy recognizes that decisions made early in the design process affect price and product costs. At ITT Automotive, members of the cross-functional team are empowered to find the most optimal processes, materials used, tooling and capital investment requirements and to decide whether to make or outsource the product. Tear-down analysis also is performed during value engineering.

Target costing should result in improved relationships with suppliers. At ITT Automotive, key suppliers are considered an integral part of the target costing team. This arrangement allows the suppliers to take "ownership" of the target costing process. These suppliers should be consulted early in the product life cycle, and they should play a significant role in product design and development.

Occasionally, a supplier may have a difficult time in meeting the target cost. In cases where the supplier is having this type of problem, ITT Automotive will ask for a detailed analysis of the supplier's cost to help the supplier reduce costs. This analysis is extremely detailed and provides the starting point for ITT Automotive to suggest some "value analysis" that will help the supplier reduce its costs.

Cost tracking sheets are used in the cost targeting area to keep track of the "targets" and to compare the targets with actual costs. At ITT Automotive, these sheets are used to assign the target cost from the final product to final assemblies, subassemblies, and components. Each tracking sheet becomes more specific until; finally, the individual components are tracked.

The tracking sheets track the cost of the product throughout the product life cycle: at the design stage (DS), when the tooling is in place (TS), and finally, when the product reaches production (PS). Setting early targets helps ITT Automotive investigate and try to remedy problem

FIGURE 2
COST TRACKING SHEETS

ABS System

Description	Design Stage		Tool Stage		Production Stage	
	Target	Quote	Target	Quote	Target	Quote
Control Unit	a	a + 1	a	a + 5	a	a − 1
Motor etc.	x	x	x	x	x	x
Production Cost	x	x	x	x	x	x
Other	x	x	x	x	x	x
Total Cost	x	x	x	x	x	X

Control Unit-Final Assembly

Description	Design Stage		Tool Stage		Production Stage	
	Target	Quote	Target	Quote	Target	Quote
Bracket	X	X	X	X	X	x
ECU	X	x	x	x	x	x
Piston Assembly	b	b + 2	b	b + 1	b	b − .1

Piston Assembly-Subassembly

Description	Design Stage		Tool Stage		Production Stage	
	Target	Quote	Target	Quote	Target	Quote
O-ring	x	x	x	x	x	x
Valve	x	x	x	x	x	x
Spring	x	x	x	x	x	x

Cost tracking sheets are prepared for the final product, final assemblies, and sub-assemblies, the latter includes tracking of individual

Blocher, Stout, Cokins, Chen: *Cost Management, 4e*

situations. For example, if the Quote of a certain supplier is higher than the target, the cross-functional team may decide to visit the supplier to determine why there is a difference between the target and the quote. Figure 2 shows a hypothetical example of this process. Investment in capital equipment, which can be quite substantial, also is tracked through the use of cost tracking sheets.

ITT Automotive periodically conducts meetings with the cross-functional team to hold them responsible for the targets that were set and to develop, through brainstorming, ways to further reduce costs. At these "profit improvement planning" meetings, a "checklist" of problems are discussed among the cross-functional team. Before the meeting, each member of the team is handed a document detailing each of the problem areas, the person(s) responsible for eliminating the problem, comments on why the problem is occurring, and a suggested completion date for solving the problem. During the meeting, the person responsible for the area where the problem is occurring will discuss the steps that are being taken to solve the problem and receive suggestions from members of the cross-functional team.

Value analysis at ITT Automotive is used on products that are not yielding an adequate return. The results of value analysis may not be as great as the results from value engineering because value analysis is performed during the production stage—after ITT Automotive is locked into a good portion of its costs. The results from value analysis, however, can be dramatic.

Readers interested in more information about target costing can look forward to the research monograph, *Target Costing and Value Engineering* by Robin Cooper and Regine Slagmulder, to be published by the IMA Foundation for Applied Research, Inc., in early 1997. It is the first in a series of five books by Cooper on Japanese cost management practices. CAM-1 (Consortium for Advanced Manufacturing-International) recently issued *Target Costing: The New Frontier in Strategic Cost Management*, which provides practical insights on how to use target costing for profit planning and cost management. It can be ordered (C1/$50) by calling (800) 638-4427, ext. 278, or faxing (201) 573-9507.

TARGET COSTING MARKET SHARE

ITT Automotive uses target costing to maintain its profitability and increase its market share during these extremely competitive times in the automotive industry. Although the process is difficult at times, and costly resources are needed to have an effective target costing system, companies such as ITT Automotive have found the investment critical to meeting their corporate objectives successfully.

Target costing basically is a bottom-up, team-oriented philosophy. It is a very structured method of setting and achieving goals. For target costing to be successful, setting up cross-functional teams is not enough. Most important, there must be senior management support for the process. Senior management must allocate the necessary resources to the project and must empower the cross-functional teams to make critical decisions. Other requirements include setting early cost targets, performing competitive analysis and value engineering, forming partnerships with suppliers, and applying pressure to everyone in the value chain to reduce costs.

George Schmelzle, CPA, is an assistant professor of accountancy at the University of Detroit, Mercy. He was a faculty intern at ITT Automotive in the summer of 1995. He is a member of the Detroit Chapter of the IMA, through which this article was submitted. He can be reached at (312) 993-3327.

Rolf Geier heads the target costing/value analysis team in the brakes department at ITT Automotive. Additional credits are given to Gerd Klostermann. He is head of the target costing/value analysis team in Europe with worldwide responsibilities.

Thomas E. Buttross, CMA, is an assistant professor of accountancy at Indiana University, Kokomo. He is a member of the Detroit Chapter of IMA. He can be reached at (317) 455-9471

10.2: INTEGRATING ACTIVITY-BASED COSTING AND THE THEORY OF CONSTRAINTS

By Robin Cooper and Regine Slagmulder

The profitability maps created by an activity-based costing system are powerful strategic tools designed to help firms become more profitable. But they are based on "general-purpose" costs designed to focus managerial attention, not to directly support decisions. For example, while an ABC system might indicate that a particular product is highly profitable and therefore a candidate for more aggressive selling, it cannot confirm that selling more of that product will indeed lead to higher profits. To make an informed decision, a company must undertake a special study to convert the ABC resource usage analysis into a resource supply one. These special studies are not failures of the ABC approach but are outcomes of a cascading cost benefit trade-off. Sometimes, these special studies are one-time events designed to answer a specific question (such as, "Should I sell more of this product?"), while other times, they are ongoing analyses designed to fine-tune the ability of the firm to generate profits.

The conversion from resource usage to resource supply is particularly important when the proposed change in resource usage predicted by the ABC system is not mirrored by an equivalent change in resource supply The underlying cause of this difference is the way that contracts for the acquisition of resources are structured. If the contract for a resource is on an "as-needed" basis, then resource supply and usage will be equal and the profitability

Map will be decision relevant. But if the contract is written on an "in-case" basis, then resource supply and usage are not necessarily equal. Here, resource supply will remain unchanged until a capacity limit established by the contract is reached. Then resource supply will change, not by the same amount as usage but by a contractually stipulated amount. Consequently, the ABC profitability maps lose their decision relevance, and special studies are required to understand the implications of decisions that involve these resources.

There are two ways in which capacity limits can be managed. Either management accepts that a capacity limit exists and the objective is to try to maximize the revenue (and hence profit) that can be generated given the constraint, or management

decides to change the level of resource supply and hence the capacity limit. When managers accept a capacity limit, they must be sensitive to bottlenecks and undertake a special study to optimize around them.

A bottleneck occurs when the demand for a resource, in a given time period, outstrips the firm's ability to deliver it. A pure ABC system is unable to acknowledge bottlenecks because it assumes that resource demand and usage always match. Consequently, a product that consumes a large quantity of the bottleneck resource is not penalized compared to a product that consumes only a small amount of that resource. This limitation of the ABC

Approach leads to poor decisions if the ABC profitability maps are used to manage the firm's short-term product mix when bottlenecks are present. In particular, decisions based upon an ABC analysis will not keep the bottleneck resources optimally loaded and hence will not lead to maximum profits.

To accommodate bottlenecks, the best solution is to use the theory of constraints (toc) to identify the optimal short-term mix of products that can be manufactured. The superiority of toc over abc for resolving the short-term implications of bottlenecks can be demonstrated using a simple numerical example. Assume that the firm has to choose among manufacturing three products: a, b, and c. The three products consume four different resources: material, labor, machining (the current bottleneck resource), and inspection. The cost of the supplied capacity for labor is \$50, for machining \$20, and for inspection \$50. All three products have the same selling price, but product a has the lowest abc costs (see table 1). Consequently, abc favors the manufacture of product a because it has the highest reported profits.

TOC takes a different approach; it splits resources into two categories. The first category incorporates all resources that are purchased on an "as needed" basis. These are the resources that vary directly with the changes in the level of production. The other category of resources is acquired on an "in-case" basis. The costs of these resources will be incurred irrespective of the level of usage. Under TOC, the costs of these "in-case" resources are grouped into the category "operating

Blocher, Stout, Cokins, Chen: *Cost Management, 4e*

expenses" and treated as fixed costs. For the purpose of the TOC analysis relating to product mix they are essentially ignored. Thus, TOC can be viewed as an extreme form of contribution analysis.

The objective under TOC is to maximize "throughput" defined as revenues minus the cost of the "as needed" resources. In the illustrative example, the only cost that is subtracted is material. Consequently, product A has the highest unit throughput and, on the surface, is the favored product under both TOC and ABC (see Table 2). Product A, however, consumes twice as much of the bottleneck resource "machining" as products B and C. Therefore, in a given time frame, the firm can manufacture two units of product B or C for every unit of product A. Despite the fact that product A has the higher unit throughput, product C generates the highest overall throughput and hence profits (see Table 3). Thus, the correct decision is to manufacture product C, not product A. Thus, the appropriate metric for such short-term decisions is not ABC profits but the throughput per unit of the constrained (or bottleneck) resource.

Initially, there is no apparent correspondence between the ABC and TOC reported profits. Under TOC, the reported profits include a charge for all of the unused nonbottleneck resources, so product C reports the highest profits. In contrast, under ABC only the consumed resources are included, and the initial ABC profitability report indicates that manufacturing and selling two units of product B generates almost double the profit compared to manufacturing and selling a single unit of product A or two units of product C (see Table 4-ABC Profit). The ABC profits will match those reported by the TOC once the unused labor and inspection costs are taken into account (see Table 4-Net Profit).

TOC outperforms ABC when bottlenecks are present because it can better match currently available resources to outputs and thus enables higher revenues and hence profits to be generated. The drawback to the TOC approach comes from ignoring operating expenses that can be managed over the long term. To illustrate this point we revisit the example. The ABC system indicates that product C is approximately half as profitable as products A and B (see Table 1), raising the question: Should product C be discontinued? A special study indicates that the inspection resource is dedicated to the production of product C. Therefore, if product C is discontinued, the inspection costs of $50 can be avoided and the overall profits of the firm will increase. A TOC analysis between products A and B now indicates that the best solution is to manufacture two units of product B, generating an overall profit of $60 (see Table 5), which is higher than the original TOC profit of $14.

The important point is that TOC and ABC are complementary, not competing, cost management techniques. They can coexist and be used together to identify the best short-term and long-term product mixes. TOC assumes that the existing infrastructure is a given and sets out to optimize throughput and hence short-term profits. As such, it is a tactical cost management technique. Alternatively, ABC assumes that the supply of most resources can be managed over the long-term; it sets out to identify the product mix that will lead to the highest long-term profits. As such, it is a strategic cost management technique. Thus, TOC can be viewed as a formal on-going special study that is used to render the ABC profitability maps more effective for a particular class of decisions -- those associated with short-term optimization of the use of capacity.

Table 1		Products		Supplied Capacity
	A	B	C	
Revenue	$70	$70	$70	
Material	2	5	3	N/A
Labor	6	20	17	50
Machining	20	10	10	20
Inspection	0	0	20	50
Total Cost	28	35	50	
ABC Profit	$42	$35	$20	

Table 2		Products	
	A	B	C
Revenue	$70	$70	$70
Material	2	5	3
Throughput	$68	$65	$67

Table 3		Products		Supplied Capacity
	A	B	C	
Revenue	$70	$140	$140	
Material	2	10	6	N/A
Throughput	68	130	134	
Labor	50	50	50	50
Machining	20	20	20	20
Inspection	50	50	50	50
Operating Expenses	120	120	120	
Net Profit	$ (52)	$10	$14	

Table 4		Products	
	A	B	C
Revenue	$70	$140	$140
Material	2	10	6
Labor	6	40	34
Machining	20	20	20
Inspection	0	0	40
Total Cost	28	70	100
ABC Profit	42	70	40
Unused Capacity	94	60	26
Net Profit	$(52)	$10	$14

Table 5		Products
	A	B
Revenue	$70	$140
Material	4	10
Throughput	$66	$130
Operating Expenses	$70	$70
Net Profit	$(4)	$60

Blocher, Stout, Cokins, Chen: *Cost Management, 4e*

©The McGraw-Hill Companies, Inc 2008

10.3: IS TOC FOR YOU?

By Linda E. Holmes, Cma and Ann B. Hendricks

Are you familiar with the Theory of Constraints (TOC)? Physicist Eliyahu M. Goldratt introduced this management technique in 1986 in the bestselling novel *The Goal*. TOC is another operation improvement technique centered on an innovative decision-making process. Just like ABM, BPR, CI, and TQM (Activity-Based Management, Business Process Reengineering, Continuous Improvement, and Total

Quality Management), TOC is founded on its own philosophy and has its own buzzwords. And like the other operation improvement programs, TOC considers speed, waste reduction, capacity, direct labor use, and the like according to its own unique perspective. But its foremost appeal is its simplicity. TOC is based on three logical, straightforward premises:
1. The only reason that companies do anything is to make *money*.
2. Anything that a company does to *speed up the processes that generate money is appropriate*.
3. Each business operation is *one big process* with many subprocesses.
According to TOC, companies that keep these three things in mind will prosper.

TOC TALK

TOC's basic vocabulary emphasizes its philosophy and its three performance measures. *Throughput* equals sales revenue minus direct materials cost—it measures the speed at which the company makes money. *Inventory* is the raw materials value tied up in work in process and finished goods. Large amounts of inventory are undesirable because it means that the company has spent money for production that hasn't generated revenue yet. *Operating expenses* are all of the costs of operations other than direct materials costs. Under the Theory of Constraints, operating expenses are fixed and therefore irrelevant to any TOC decision. Of the three terms, throughput is the most important. It tells the company that it is achieving its goal of making money. Moreover, increases in throughput mean that the rate at which the company is making money is increasing.

PROCESS IMPROVEMENT PROCEDURE

According to Goldratt, there are five basic steps to operations improvement:

1. Identify the system's constraint(s), and prioritize them according to importance.
2. Exploit the system's most critical constraint.
3. Subordinate everything else to the action taken in Step 2.
4. Elevate the system's constraint(s).
5. Repeat Steps 1-4, focusing on the new constraint.
(These are paraphrased from *The Goal*, p. 307.)

What these steps accomplish are incremental improvements in the operation as a whole. In Step 1, an assessment of the entire process identifies the slowest subprocess. This subprocess is called the constraint or the *bottleneck*. Identifying the constraint is very important because it sets the pace of the whole operation.

The Goal uses Boy Scouts on a hike to illustrate this concept. We learn that no matter how fast some of the boys walk, the boy who walks the slowest always sets the pace and determines when the whole troop will reach its destination. Faster boys in the front of the line will get far ahead, but faster boys at the end of the line won't be able to walk any faster than the slowest boy. Using this example, we can easily visualize the constraint in a production operation: Work in process is piled up in front of (or before) the constraint, and the processes behind (or after) the constraint sit idle waiting for something to do. In Step 2, the company determines how best to "exploit" the constraint. Exploiting means finding ways to get the maximum output possible from the constraint without overloading it and requires that the whole operation be slowed down to the pace of the constraint.

The most obvious way to exploit the constraint is by proper scheduling and control that favors the constraint's capacity. It's also important to improve quality control so that the constraint will work only on good inputs. Waste of time and effort incurred when the constraint spends its valuable time working on output that will eventually have to be scrapped or reworked should be avoided. In Step 3, the company subordinates all other operation improvement opportunities to exploiting the constraint. This may cause problems with managers and workers who have their own ideas about operation improvement. Glaring problems that everyone can see and that most know how to correct will always be present in any operation, but TOC requires that all operation improvement opportunities other than those dealing with the constraint be ignored. This may be very difficult for managers and employees to accept if they don't understand what's going on. Therefore, TOC recommends that the company discuss the Theory of Constraints and its rules with all employees involved so that they will understand what is going on, support it, and be willing to help. Step 4 calls for "elevating" the constraint. This means that the company finds ways to increase the capacity of the constraint.

Ways to increase the output of the constraint include:
1. Performing regular maintenance on the constraint to prevent breakdowns.
2. Running the constraint for extra shifts.
3. Automating the constraint.

Since the constraint sets the pace, making it faster will speed up the whole operation. This increases the rate of throughput (i.e., the rate at which it generates money), which is the company's overriding objective. By now you've probably guessed that after performing Steps 1-4 the original constraint is faster and no longer the constraint. Considering the value of continuous improvement, Step 5 says to find the new constraint and start the TOC process again.

WHAT ABOUT PERFORMANCE MEASURES?

So far, we've discussed increasing speed and output and improving quality, but we haven't mentioned any of the conventional management accounting performance measures (i.e., productivity, cost per unit, etc.). TOC won't suggest using any of them, either. Moreover, according to TOC, not only are conventional management accounting performance measures unnecessary, but focusing on them can make things worse. Of course, we still need management accounting—we just have to be very careful about what we believe is important, the measures we take, and how we use them. Here are five "truths" about management accounting to think about as they relate to TOC.

Management Accounting Truth #1: Process improvements work together to speed up the whole operation. We know that in Total Quality Management and Continuous Improvement the objective is to eliminate waste and speed up every process. The Theory of Constraints takes almost the opposite view. It requires that we focus on the constraint while leaving all other people, processes, and machines alone. Consider what would happen to TOC's inventory (i.e., work in process) if a process located before the constraint were sped up. This process would produce even more work in process that the already overloaded constraint couldn't handle. Likewise, if the newly improved, more efficient process were located after the constraint, it would still be sitting idle, waiting for the constraint to send it work. *Remember, increasing the speed of nonconstraint processes will only make things worse. Extra costs will be incurred with no increase in throughput.*

Management Accounting Truth #2: You have to spend money to make money. Under other operation improvement programs like Business Process Reengineering, a company is required to make radical process changes, usually by purchasing expensive machines, equipment, and/or technology. For example, in the landmark book *Re-Engineering the Corporation*, Michael Hammer and James Champy talk about the way that IBM Credit Corporation turned its step-by-step paper-based credit approval process into a one-step computerized process. Credit approval time went from seven days to four *hours*—an amazing improvement. But TOC discourages large expenditures for process improvements. It presumes that companies are already working at capacity and that all resources are running as efficiently as possible. According to TOC, all that a company needs to do is slow things down and work to the capacity of the constraint. Expensive improvements can be made, but only on the constraint. *Remember, be very careful that all money spent on new equipment, hardware, or software goes toward maximizing the capacity of the constraint.*

Management Accounting Truth #3: Operations can be made more efficient by improving labor efficiency variances. Who doesn't believe that keeping workers busy earning their pay benefits the firm? Well, TOC, for one. Just like any other nonconstraint, fully utilized labor will produce more work in process than the constraint can handle. This causes the same problems that happen when any other nonconstraint process becomes more efficient. Think what would happen if idle workers from processes located after the constraint were moved to processes located before the constraint to keep them busy. Let the workers spend their free time on machine maintenance, on learning new skills, or just having a rest. They will be happier, and the company will eventually have more money to spend. *Remember, increasing labor*

Blocher, Stout, Cokins, Chen: *Cost Management, 4e*

efficiency when labor isn't the constraint will only increase work-inprocess inventory and tie up money that could be used more effectively somewhere else.

Management Accounting Truth #4: Large production runs are desirable because they are an efficient use of setup time and fixed costs. Moreover, large production runs reduce per-unit costs, which will increase profit. Actually, the opposite is true for TOC. Large production runs overload the constraint and increase work in process without increasing throughput. Moreover, TOC views all costs other than direct materials as irrelevant fixed costs. It doesn't matter how they are arbitrarily allocated among individual products. *Remember, making production decisions based on reducing per-unit costs works against the objectives of TOC.*

Management Accounting Truth #5: Product mix should be determined based on maximizing total contribution margin. Traditional product mix decisions consider individual product profitability measured by contribution margin per unit. This makes sense in an operation with no constraint. But in operations with a constraint it's better to select among products based on the benefit (i.e., throughput) received per unit of capacity of the constraint. This is the same analysis used in traditional management accounting when the system is bound by a scarce resource. With TOC, the constraint is the scarce resource, so the benefit obtained from it should be maximized. *Remember, wise use of time at the constraint is the thing to consider in TOC product mix decisions.* The simplicity and logic of the Theory of Constraints make it very appealing. All that it requires is a thorough knowledge and understanding of the processes that are already in place. In addition, except for slowing things down (which can have its own benefits to work atmosphere and morale on all levels), no expensive or demoralizing changes will be needed. Finally, remember, you should adapt your performance measurement to your new understanding of processes and outcomes so that you can correctly gauge your performance and make effective decisions. Our five suggestions should help.

Chapter 11
Process Costing

Cases

11-1 **The Rossford Plant** (Two Production Processes with the Traditional Volume-Based Costing System)

11-2 **The United L/N Plant** (Scraps and Defects)

11-3 **Downstream Brewery (B)**

Readings

11-1: "How Boeing Tracks Costs, A to Z" by Robert J. Bowlby, *The Financial Executive*. Reprinted with permission.

This article explains the change in Boeing's costing approach, from one based on job - costing to a process costing approach.

Discussion Questions:
1. Explain what Boeing means by process accounting.
2. What are the advantages of the process accounting approach at Boeing?
3. How does the new process accounting approach affect each business unit's incentives and tools to control costs?

Cases

11-1 The Rossford Plant

Having heard Robert Kaplan speak on some of the shortcomings of current cost accounting systems, I decided to undertake a review of the cost accounting system at our Rossford Plant. I was particularly concerned whether the overhead costs were being allocated to products according to the resource demands of the products. Costing our products accurately has become more important for strategic purposes because of pressures to unbundle sets of original equipment windows for the automakers.

Mark MacGuidwin, Corporate Controller
Libbey-Owens-Ford Co.

BACKGROUND

Libbey-Owens-Ford Co. (L-O-F), one of the companies in the Pilkington Group, has been a major producer of glass in the United States since the turn of the century. Its Rossford Plant produces about 12 million "lites" of tempered glass per year. (A lite is a unit such as a rear window, which is called a "back lite," or a side window, which is called a "side lite.") The plant makes front door windows, quarter windows, back windows, and sunroofs. About 96 percent of the lites produced are sold to original equipment (OE) automotive customers; the remaining 4 percent are shipped to replacement depots for later sale to replacement glass wholesalers. Lite sizes range from .73 square feet for certain quarter windows to about 13 square feet for the back lite of a Camaro/Firebird. The average size is approximately four square feet.

The Rossford Plant is comprised of two production processes: float and fabrication ("fab"). The float process produces raw float glass, the raw material for automotive windows. Blocks of float glass are transferred to the fab facility, where lites are cut to size, edged, shaped, and strengthened. The final product is then inspected, packed, and shipped.

Parts of the Rossford Plant date to the founding of the company. Unlike other L-O-F plants, which were designed around the automated Pilkington float-tank process with computer controlled cutting and finishing operations, the Rossford Plant was designed for the older process of polishing plate glass to final products. Pilkington float-tanks were installed in the plant during the 1970s, and the cutting processes were substantially automated during the 1980s. However, the finishing processes have not yet been automated to the extent as at the other plants.

Mark MacGuidwin, Corporate Controller of L-O-F, and Ed Lackner, Rossford's Plant Controller, became concerned during 1987 about the cost allocation process at Rossford for several reasons. First, the process had not been critically evaluated since the automation of the cutting processes. Second, the overhead cost structure at Rossford differed dramatically from that of other L-O-F plants. A larger pool of indirect costs was allocated to equipment centers. Third, they had collected evidence that the cost alloca-tion process at Rossford was not accurately assigning costs to units of product. And fourth, changes in the company's competitive environment were raising strategic issues that demanded accurate product cost information for pricing, product mix, and production scheduling purposes.

RELATIONSHIP OF SIZE TO PROFIT

In his investigation, MacGuidwin discovered what he believed were two key observations made by the Vice Presidents of Engineering and Manufacturing. Historically in the automotive glass business, original equipment customers have purchased a complete set of windows for a car model from a single glass manufacturer. From the glass manufacturer's perspective it was therefore necessary that the markup on cost for the entire set, or bundle, of glass units be adequate for profitability. Despite the buying habits of these OE customers, firms in the industry quoted selling prices for individual units of glass within each set. As easy benchmarks, the selling prices were customarily set in proportion to the size in square feet of the units, with smaller lites priced lower than larger lites.

Blocher, Stout, Cokins, Chen: *Cost Management, 4e*

However, the cost of producing automotive glass is not related proportionately to the size of the unit produced. The production process involves two principal fabricating operations: cutting the unit from a larger block of glass, and then bending it to the necessary shape and strengthening it in a tempering furnace. Neither the cost of cutting nor the cost of tempering is proportional to the size of the unit produced. Only a limited number of units can be fed into either a cutting machine or a tempering furnace regardless of the size of the units, with little or no difference in feed rates or resource consumption related to size.

The joint effect of these two observations is an understanding in the glass industry of the average relationship between unit size and unit profit that is depicted in Figure 1. Margin percentages for passenger car lites are somewhat higher than the industry average.

Recent changes in the competitive structure of the OE automotive glass industry have led to the possibility of "unbundling" sets of windows. Major customers are considering not only allowing different manufacturers to supply units for the same car model (for example, windshields from one and rear windows from another) but also setting target prices based on the manufacturing costs of the units, a process already begun by General Motors. Under these circumstances, the costs reported by the accounting system for individual units of glass have strategic implications that were not relevant in the past.

CURRENT PRODUCT COSTING PROCESS

Figure 2 shows the cost center groupings for the production process. The float and fabricating operations report to the same plant manager and have a common support staff. Raw glass is transferred from float to fab at standard variable plus standard fixed cost. (Profits are measured only at the point of sale of the finished product to the customer.) Direct labor and overhead costs are assigned to units of final product as follows:

(1)   Direct labor costs are assigned to equipment centers (lines of machines in PC&E and furnaces in Tempering) based on standard crew sizes. Thus, a labor cost per equipment hour is developed for each of the several machines and furnaces based on crew sizes and standard wage and fringe benefit rates.

(2)   Overhead costs, both variable and fixed, that are directly traceable to a specific equipment center are pooled to develop a rate per equipment hour for that center.

(3)   A standard feed rate is established for each lite for each applicable cutting machine and furnace, and costs are applied to product based on costs per equipment hour/units fed per hour. (Feed rates to different tempering furnaces differ substantially.)

(4)   General (indirect) plant overhead costs are allocated in two steps:
   (i)   20 percent of the total is allocated to the float process and 80 percent to fabricating, then
   (ii)   the 80 percent allocated to fabricating is assigned to units of product at a flat rate per square foot (approximately $1.00 per square foot in 1987, adjusted for differing yield rates).

The costs classified as general plant overhead amount to 30 percent of the total indirect costs of the plant. General plant includes approximately 100 salaried employees involved in plant management, engineering, accounting, material control, pollution control, quality control, maintenance management, research and development, production management, and human resources. It also includes depreciation of equipment and buildings not assigned to operating departments, property taxes and insurance, general plant maintenance, and post retirement costs.

MacGuidwin decided to limit his initial analysis to the automotive glass fabricating facility at the Rossford Plant. He and Lackner were confident that the process of assigning costs to units of raw float glass was sufficiently accurate. They also believed that the direct costs of labor and overhead associated with the PC&E and Tempering Furnace equipment centers were being properly attached to units of product based on the units' standard feed rates per hour. The rates had been set with downtime assumptions intended to cover mechanical and electrical problems, stockouts, and part changeovers.

"On the whole, Ed Lackner and I felt pretty good about what we were discovering," commented MacGuidwin. "Over two-thirds of the costs of the plant were being assigned to units of product based on metered usage of our two constraining resources, machine time in the PC&E center and furnace time in the Tempering center."

"On the other hand," Lackner pointed out, "we had a potential problem with our general plant costs. For years we had been assigning them to units produced based on square footage. We knew that this allocation base didn't capture activities that were driving the overhead costs, but we didn't know whether the allocation process was substantially distorting the final product costs. Until recently it didn't matter how these costs were allocated because unit price/cost differentials did not enter into any strategic decisions."

ALTERNATIVE ALLOCATION METHOD

The allocation of general plant overhead costs between float and fab seemed reasonable to the two Controllers. They analyzed a number of factors that could have been driving the allocation, including the number of hourly employees, the space occupied, and the variable costs incurred. They also interviewed managers concerning where time was spent by employees in the overhead base. All indicators pointed to the appropriateness of assigning 20 percent of the general plant costs to float and 80 percent to fab.

"The principal outcome of our analysis was to propose and implement on a test basis an alternative method for re-allocating the 80 percent allocated to fab," explained MacGuidwin. "Under the old method we allocated a flat rate per square foot produced. This might be reasonable if each square foot of glass costs the same to make in the PC&E and Tempering departments. However, we knew from our production engineers and from our own tracking of direct costs in those cost centers that this was just not the case."

To test an alternative allocation method, MacGuidwin and Lackner chose four parts with the following characteristics:

(1) a small, high volume, low profit margin part (Truck Vent);

(2) a small, high volume, moderate profit margin part (Passenger Car Rear Quarter Window);

(3) a large, high volume, moderate profit margin part (Passenger Car Front Door); and

(4) a large, moderate volume, high profit margin part (Passenger Car Back Lite, Heated).

As indicated in the following table, the direct costs of fabricating these parts differ substantially:

Part	Square Feet Per Unit	Cost Per Cutting	Square Foot Furnace
Truck Vent	.77	$2.870	$1.676
Passenger Car Rear Quarter	.73	1.494	3.312
Passenger Car Front Door	5.03	.340	.634
Passenger Car Back Lite	7.07	.206	.682

The input measure selected as the basis for allocating general plant overhead costs to units of product was the most scarce (bottleneck) resource in the facility—time spent in the tempering furnaces. The production plan indicated a furnace capacity of 48,500 hours per year. Dividing the portion of the costs assigned to fab by the furnace capacity resulted in a rate of $503 per furnace hour.

Using the feed rates of the individual pieces, MacGuidwin was able to compute a new standard cost for each of the four products. Figure 3 shows the standard cost per square foot, the cost per lite, and the gross margin percentage of each product under both the old and new methods of allocating general plant overhead. The Corporate Controller was pleased with the results:

"Although the results shown for the four products are not as dramatic as I've seen for some manufacturers, they do indicate a need to rethink and reanalyze our cost allocation system. Basically, the new method of allocating general plant overhead represents more closely what the Engineering and Manufacturing Vice Presidents were telling me about cost incurrence. The old system allocated a large pool of indirect costs equally to output, whereas the new system makes some attempt to associate those costs with the resource demands placed on our productive capacity by individual products. The old method clearly distorted our product costs. The new method should work better as long as we produce at plant capacity."

REQUIRED:

1. What is the cost object before the change in the product costing system? After the change? Why did MacGuidwin and Lackner change the focus of the system?
2. What are the characteristics of a good product costing system?

Blocher, Stout, Cokins, Chen: *Cost Management, 4e*

©The McGraw-Hill Companies, Inc 2008

3. How do the process control and product costing functions of Rossford's cost accounting system interact? What conversion costs are treated as direct product costs in the system?

4. In your opinion, is the new allocation method for general plant costs better than the old method? Why or why not?

FIGURE 1

Unit Size/Profit Relationship

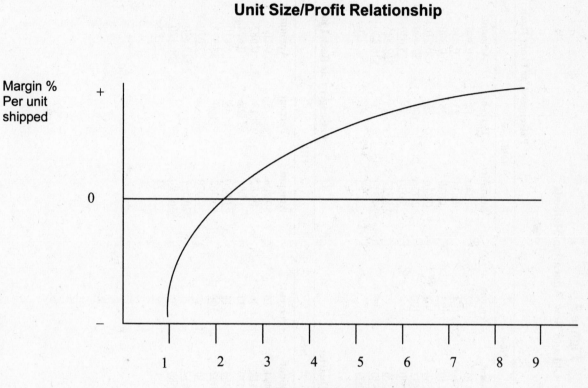

FIGURE 2

Production Cost Centers

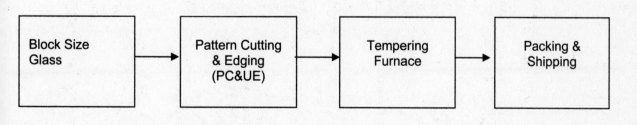

Figure 3
Unit Data Under Old and New Allocation Methods

Truck Vent

	Old		New	
	Amount	Percent	Amount	Percent
Cutting	$2.870	47	$2.870	42
Furnace	1.676	27	1.676	24
General Plant	1.020	17	1.740	25
All Other Costs	0.566	9	0.566	8
Std. Cost Per Sq. Ft.	$6.132	100	$6.852	100
Sq. Ft. Per Lite	0.770		0.770	
Cost Per Life	$4.722		$5.276	
Selling Price	$2.820		$2.820	
Gross Margin (Percent)	(67)		(87)	

Passenger Car Front Door

	Old		New	
	Amount	Percent	Amount	Percent
Cutting	$0.340	12	$ 0.340	14
Furnace	0.634	23	0.634	25
General Plant	1.036	38	0.800	32
All Other Costs	0.716	26	0.716	29
Std. Cost Per Sq. Ft.	2.726	100	$2.490	100
Sq. Ft. Per Lite	5.030		5.030	
Cost Per Life	$13.712		$12.525	
Selling Price	$16.820		$16.820	
Gross Margin (Percent)	18		26	

Passenger Car Rear Quarter

	Old		New	
	Amount	Percent	Amount	Percent
Cutting	$1.494	21	$1.494	16
Furnace	3.312	47	3.312	36
General Plant	1.022	14	3.020	33
All Other Costs	1.266	18	1.266	14
Std. Cost Per Sq. Ft.	$7.094	100	$9.092	100
Sq. Ft. Per Lite	0.730		0.730	
Cost Per Life	$5.179		$6.637	
Selling Price	$6.680		$6.680	
Gross Margin (Percent)	22		1	

Passenger Car Back Lite

	Old		New	
	Amount	Percent	Amount	Percent
Cutting	$0.206	5	$ 0.206	6
Furnace	0.682	18	0.682	20
General Plant	1.064	28	0.674	20
All Other Costs	1.810	48	1.810	54
Std. Cost Per Sq. Ft.	$3.762	100	$3.372	100
Sq. Ft. Per Lite	7.070		7.070	
Cost Per Life	$26.597		$23.840	
Selling Price	$56.120		$56.120	
Gross Margin (Percent)	53		58	

11-2 The United L/N Plant

We never imagined that we'd ever be looking at the type of costing issues at our United L/N Plant that have now become apparent. The plant design was engineered from the beginning as a state-of-the-art production process that would avoid most of the traditional problems. Now we're in the process of taking a second look.

> Ken Marvin
> Director, Planning and Control
> OE Business Unit
> Libbey-Owens-Ford Co.

BACKGROUND

Libbey-Owens-Ford Co. (L-O-F), one of the companies in the Pilkington Group, has been a major producer of glass in the United States since the turn of the century. Its newest plant, United L/N, began producing glass products in November 1987. Located in Kentucky, United L/N is a joint venture between L-O-F and a Japanese company, Nippon Sheet Glass.

Unlike the Rossford Plant, which produces the raw float glass used in its fabrication process, United L/N is a fabrication plant only. The organization of the plant reflects the just-in-time, pull through philosophy. The production process is fully automated, requiring no human intervention from beginning to end. Very high quality and minimal scrap were expected to be the norm.

L-O-F treats the Rossford Plant as a standard cost center, but United L/N is organized as a strategic business unit (SBU). SBUs are evaluated on profit as well as cost control and other goals. The company charges United L/N Rossford's standard manufacturing cost for raw glass transferred between the two plants, whereas transfer prices between SBUs are usually negotiated by their managements.

FABRICATION PROCESS AND PLANT DESIGN

The steps in the fabrication process are essentially the same as at other L-O-F facilities. First, the raw glass goes through pattern cutting where it is trimmed to the basic shape of the lite (window) it will become. Second, the cut pattern is edged. Third, the edged pattern goes through a furnace where it is formed (bent to shape) and tempered. Fourth, the final product is inspected, packed, and shipped.

The principal difference between United L/N's process and the fabrication process of traditional plants lies in the organization of these discrete steps. At the Rossford Plant, for example, pattern cutting and edging, tempering, and packing and shipping are treated as individual cost centers and are physically separated. Each department creates a work-in-process inventory, which is periodically moved to the next stage in the process. The next stage in most cases is located in a different section of the plant. Also, all processes at Rossford require human participation.

By contrast, United L/N's fabrication process is entirely in-line and automated. Raw glass from Rossford plant and other plants arrives packed on special racks that are designed for United L/N's automated loading process. (The racks are also designed to protect the raw glass from damage between the shipping plant and the receiving area.) The glass has been inspected at the shipping plant to determine that each piece meets the specifications of the fabrication process.

A forklift operator loads racks of glass at the beginning of one of United L/N's two production lines. From that point on, the entire process is operated through a numerical control computer system. Human intervention occurs only during planned downtime periods when the line undergoes preventive maintenance, when a problem stops the line's progress, and when finished pieces are inspected prior to packing. Glass is continuously pulled through the process, so that ideally there should be no idle work-in-process inventory.

A small team of operators monitors the process, performs regular preventive maintenance, changes the computer settings for different lites, and makes unscheduled repairs as needed.

PRODUCT COSTING SYSTEM

The product costing system at United L/N is very straightforward compared to those of less automated L-O-F plants. Overhead costs associated with handling, storing, protecting, and accounting for work-in-process inventories are dramatically lower. The major components of cost include short-term fixed operating costs, labor costs of the operating teams, and the transfer prices of raw glass from other plants.

Because the entire process is automated and in-line, the feed rate is constant across all sub-processes for each individual lite being fabricated. The costing system consequently was designed as one large pool, which is assigned to units based on standard input prices and standard feed rates. The system allows for standard levels of downtime and anticipated yields. Products are not charged for either planned downtime or planned scrap, which were expected to be minimal due to the care with which the plant was designed, engineered, and monitored.

PRODUCTION AND COSTING PROBLEMS

"It wasn't long before we began experiencing problems with our yields," commented Ken Marvin, Planning and Control Director of L-O-F's Original Equipment Business Unit. "At first we thought that the problems would be confined to adjusting and learning about the automated process. We thought that as we gained experience with it we could solve our difficulties without introducing more complicated costing mechanisms."

One of the first difficulties encountered was keeping the furnaces on the two lines working efficiently. Each one was designed to work perfectly when a certain number of glass pieces were being fired, a certain number were on the threshold entering the furnace, and a certain number were leaving it.

"In our traditional plants we stockpile pieces in front of the furnaces so that we can keep them filled to their optimal levels when forming and tempering," Marvin explained. "However, the United L/N lines were designed with no accumulators in front of the furnaces to keep them running efficiently at all times. For any number of reasons there might be gaps in the lines as they enter the furnaces. Partly because of these gaps and the resulting imperfect furnace operations, we have had unacceptably high scrap variances. Of course, scrap decreases the plant's yield."

"From the United L/N point of view the problem with scrap is caused by imperfections in the raw glass rather than by problems with the process. The plant's management therefore believes that the scrap variance should be charged to the shipping plants (including Rossford plant.) Shipping plant managers, on the other hand, believe that the charge-back, even if appropriate (which remains an issue), is much too high. United L/N's costing system costs every piece as if it goes through the entire process rather than dropping out at, for example, pattern cutting or edging stages."

Another factor contributing to furnace inefficiency and ineffectiveness is that a line sometimes goes down unexpectedly because of a problem in pattern cutting or edging. The plant then incurs the opportunity costs associated both with having an empty tempering furnace and with having to reset the furnace after it has been empty during periods of time when it was programmed to be full.

"We have been tracking all sorts of variances trying to get some insights into the effects on costs of the kinks in the process," continued Marvin. "We calculate a combined materials usage and spending variance, a downtime variance, a throughput variance, and a scrap (yield) variance. However, all of them are valued on the basis of costs of the entire production process rather than on the value added to the stages of production where problems occur. Now we're reevaluating the design of our costing system at United L/N, especially in light of the ongoing negotiations with Rossford plant and other shipping plants."

REQUIRED:

1. As a member of the Rossford Plant negotiating team, what would be your position regarding the proper treatment of the United L/N scrap variance? As a member of the United L/N team?
2. How could United L/N's management determine the specific causes of defects (for example, bad glass or defective cutting, edging, or tempering operations) in units that are scrapped at the plant? What are the implications for the product costing system?
3. What could be done to solve the problems with furnace inefficiency and ineffectiveness that Ken Marvin discussed? What are the probable effects of your suggestion(s)?

Blocher, Stout, Cokins, Chen: *Cost Management, 4e*

11-3 Downstream Brewery (B)

The small faucet to the right of your desk emitted a sputtering sound and bursts of white foam, rather than the liquid gold you'd become accustomed to. Well, I guess that means I can retire the Downstream Brewery file, kegs and all, you thought. You could not have been more wrong. Well, technically, yes, you could. But this was wrong enough, because as you turned off the tap you had installed in your office, you noticed a distraught C.D. Cervesa entering your office door.

It had been about six months since you had last seen C.D. Cervesa of Downstream Brewery fame. (See Case 12-3 Downstream Brewery (A) for a detailed description of C.D. Cervesa's previous problem). You had set up a system of job order costing, given C.D. a brief training session in how to keep it working, and taken delivery of the product you'd settled on as your fee. Sure, money would have been nicer. But once you'd installed the refrigerator and tap, entertaining prospective clients was much cheaper. Your business was picking up. Even you assistant was happy since your paychecks were showing less elasticity at the bank with the increase in business. You had figured the rest, as they say, would be history. But here was C.D., back again, and you could tell at once that this was not a social call.

———————

"Remember those contract negotiations I talked to you about?" C.D. asked. "Well, armed with the numbers from the accounting system you helped me set up, I went into negotiations feeling pretty good, but when I came out, my entire business had evaporated! When I figured out what it was costing me to fill the Lowerbrow contract, I jacked up the price to include a 40% profit. Not gouging certainly, when you consider that they turn around and get closer to 60%. But they did not see it that way, and cancelled the contract. They said I was 'too small to deal with.' Can you believe it? I bail them out when they're short, now I want a fair price and I'm too small to deal with!"

"What about Olde McIrish?" you asked.

"Oh yeah, that's even worse! Listen to this. Olde McIrish told me that they've decided *franchising* is the way to make big bucks. They're opening a series of franchises in the Rocky Mountain and Western regions, calling them McBreweries. Can you believe it!? McBreweries, for gosh sake! They offered me the Phoenix area franchise, but I'll be a rag picker before I do business under a golden spout with the notice "Billions of Gallons Sold."

"I decided to rely on my local reputation as a quality operation and to try cranking out my own brand of ale. So for the last three months, I've been making Froth, as I call it and selling it out of a friend's pub.

"Can you help me figure out what it costs me for each barrel I brew? I keep thinking that it should be just the same as when I was brewing for Lowerbrow and Olde McIrish. But things are a little different now. E.E. Phlunke and I just keep the production of Froth going constantly. We always have some brewing, some fermenting and some cooling. We don't have contracts to finish anymore. I'm baffled at how I can tell *exactly* what my costs are when there is always some brew in the process. I learned my lesson the last time around, and I want to keep track of my costs right along. I knew you were just the one to help me because you did such a great job last time, so I brought all my cost information in this box here."

["If you learned your lesson, C.D.," you wondered, "why did you vanish for six months, only to reappear three months after dramatically changing your business – with an orange crate full of little scraps of paper?"] C.D. left you a complimentary gallon jug of Froth and the pile of papers. You harkened back to Oliver Hardy's complaint "Another fine mess you've gotten me into!" But unlike Ollie, you did not have any Stan Laurel to serve as a contrapoint to your competence. Looking at the stack of receipts and other scraps of paper on your desk, you figured you understood how someone must feel when the pie lands SMACK on the old kisser – a mess indeed. The circus life still was unappealing, but the navy was beginning to look like a viable alternative to a career in accounting. After you got through C.D.'s information, you went by the brewery and filled in some blanks in your picture of what had been going on.

From the bits of flotsam in C.D.'s orange crate you were able to learn the following:

Cash Receipts

1944 half-kegs (972 barrels sold at $50 each)	$ 48,600

Cash Disbursements

Malted-Barley Extract (2,000 lbs @ $2.10/lb)	$ 4,200
Wheat Extract (1,000 lbs @ $2.75/lb)	2,750
Hops (240 bushels at $10/bushel)	2,400
Brewer's Yeast (50 bricks at $2.80/brick)	140
Water (116,667 @ $.0009/gal)	105
Half Kegs (200 @ $15)	3,000
Keg Washing Machine	12,000
Payroll (including taxes and benefits):	
C.D. Cervesa	8,000
E.E. Phlunke (520 hours)	5,200
Gas and Electricity (25% Gas)	160
Rent	3,000
Excise Taxes ($10 per barrel sold)	9,720
Miscellaneous Manufacturing Costs	130
Miscellaneous General & Administrative Expenses	2,285
Loan Payments:	
Principal	0
Interest	3,600
Total Cash Disbursements	$ 56,690

Beginning Inventories

Barley extract (500 lbs)	$ 1,050
Wheat extract (100 lbs)	275
Hops (4 bushels)	40
Yeast (5 bricks)	14

Blocher, Stout, Cokins, Chen: *Cost Management, 4e*
©The McGraw-Hill Companies, Inc 2008

Downstream Brewery had fulfilled its contracts with Lowerbrow and Olde McIrish at the end of last quarter. There was no work in process or finished goods on hand at the end of the last quarter. At the very beginning of this quarter, C.D. Cervesa had purchased an additional 200 half-kegs, making a total of 1000 half-kegs to hold the Froth production. Since Olde McIrish would no longer be cleaning and returning the empty half-kegs, C.D. also purchased a $12,000 machine to wash and sterilize the kegs. All equipment, including the half-kegs and the keg washing machine was depreciated on a straight line basis over 10 years with no salvage value.

The $12,000, one-year insurance policy that Downstream had prepaid remained in effect during the quarter. Ninety percent of C.D.'s time was still devoted directly to brewing ale, and the remainder was spent dealing with general and administrative duties.

You toured the warehouse and learned more about the brewing process, and about the stage that C.D.'s product was in at the end of the quarter. To keep things straight in your mind, you made a chart of the entire process.

THE BREWING PROCESS

Boiling Department		Fermenting Department			Shipping Department
Add extract, hops, water	Remove hops	Add yeast		Remove yeast	Ship
boil with gas (8 hrs.)	cool with elec. (16 hrs.) (15% elec.)	ferment with elec. (3 days) (50% elec.)		cool with elec. (4 days) (25% elec.)	clean kegs and refill (10% elec.)

C.D. estimated that about 30% of all labor was required for the Boiling operation, 60% for the Fermenting operation, and 10% for cleaning and refilling the half-kegs. You discussed the ins and outs of overhead allocation and decided that all overhead items should be allocated based on direct labor cost. You noted that other than the keg washing machine, no additions had been made to the $130,000 worth of brewing equipment you remembered from your previous engagement with Downstream. At the end of the quarter you did an inventory, and found that C.D. had one batch (12 barrels) that had just completed boiling and needed to have the hops strained out (virtually complete in the Boiling operation), and one batch in the middle of the Fermenting operation (the yeast had already been added). The recipe for each 12 barrel batch of Froth calls for 20 pounds of barley extract, ten pounds of wheat extract, one brick of yeast (each of which can be used in four batches), two bushels of hops, and 372 gallons of water. Ninety-six half kegs (48 barrels) that had just been filled and stabilized were in the refrigerator ready to be taken to the friend's pub where it would be sold.

Customer Needs

In answering the following questions, give C.D. sufficient details so that you can retire from this job in the near future and C.D. can continue without you.

1. Using three processes of Boiling, Fermenting, and Shipping, what journal entries should be made to record this period's activities?
2. What is Downstream's income statement for the period?
3. What is C.D.'s cost per barrel?
4. What is the value of the inventory?

Readings

11.1: HOW BOEING TRACKS COSTS, A to Z

When Boeing's internal customers clamored for better cost information, the company decided to empower its business units by giving them more responsibility for their own costs.

By Robert J. Bowlby

A few years ago, two of Boeing's internal customers, engineering and operations, told the finance department they weren't getting the cost information they needed to manage airplane design and production. They lacked relevant economic information on which to base their decisions.

When we heard that, we knew we had to do something to remedy the situation. Boeing's cost-accounting system worked for tax and financial accounting and could be used to determine product cost and profitability at an airplane model level. But we realized that at an operating level, we were giving our engineering and operations organizations budgets for only a few cost elements.

Further, the cost information we provided individual managers didn't align with their responsibilities or areas they could control or influence. Engineering and operations couldn't use the cost information they routinely received to perform reliable economic design trade studies or to make economically sound investment decisions. They had to generate such information almost exclusively by special analysis.

At Boeing, we've committed ourselves to continuously improving our processes so we can stay ahead of the competition and maintain or increase our long-term market share. We are rethinking and reshaping our corporate strategies, the cornerstone of which is "Customer In," a concept that means we continually seek input from our internal and external customers through internal feedback, customer-satisfaction surveys and market research.

With this type of strategy, finance must be a partner in all aspects of a business, from marketing and product design to production and customer support. One of finance's most important jobs is to help create a systematic framework of financial and nonfinancial information and measures that contribute to making the decisions that ensure the enterprise's success.

Therefore, to improve the cost-management process, Boeing finance, operations and engineering decided to team together to study and rethink our managers' real information needs with respect to unit costs. The team spent some time identifying and reviewing "best practices" by studying industry, academia and our own internal practices. We came up with several key concepts aimed at improving the relevancy of our cost-management information.

FRONT-END ALIGNMENT

First, we decided to align our accounting practices to support the way we manage the enterprise. This includes being flexible and responsive enough so that we can change or redirect the system to enhance continuous process improvement, even in the middle of an accounting period.

Also, we realized we had to routinely provide the financial data that management needs to improve our processes and ultimately our products. We agreed that this data, which includes the costs of such items as materials, labor and energy, should represent the sum of all the resources actually used to build the part or assembly and that the area building that part or assembly must assume the responsibility for generating and tracking the data. From these key concepts, along with others like activity-based analysis, Boeing finance has been progressing toward implementing a modified process cost-accounting system.

Using process accounting means significantly changing cost-management practices and cost-assignment techniques. Part of the problem is that our current system was designed when our primary business was producing military aircraft. Our production methods, the makeup of our costs and the information we need about them have changed a lot since then.

Over time, our traditional job-cost system and cost-accounting practices have caused more and more costs that we'd traditionally categorized as overhead to be unloaded onto an ever-smaller direct-labor base. This evolved to the point where between 70 percent to 80 percent of the costs assigned to the final cost objectives of a manufacturing or engineering line organization were allocations from common overhead pools. Building and equipment maintenance, depreciation costs and the costs of industrial-engineering support activities and other support functions were lumped together in general overhead pools.

In today's factory, it's not uncommon to find that depreciation, technology, energy and nondirect labor expenses are often individually more significant than direct-touch or shop labor. The 20 percent to 30 percent of our costs that were mostly direct-touch labor assigned to the final cost objectives were the only cost elements the manufacturing or engineering line organizations had responsibility for and could directly link to the products they make. This meant that any process-improvement or cost-reduction initiative made by the line organization that didn't involve direct-labor savings wasn't directly reflected, or maybe not reflected at all, in the costs allocated to it. In many cases, the line organization couldn't be sure if total company costs would decrease or increase as a result of its actions.

To better manage the other 70 percent to 80 percent of the costs, traditional cost accounting and cost management separately identified significant chunks of the overhead cost and managed them individually. But, identifying separate cost elements, such as depreciation computing and nondirect labor, and trying to budget and control each one separately, didn't show the ways in which these cost elements interacted with one another.

These old accounting practices meant the overhead the manufacturing or engineering line organization did receive was based on the direct-labor dollars it incurred. Because technology-related costs were buried in overhead, this approach tended to move the dollars from areas with higher technology costs into units with the larger direct-labor elements. What we needed were ways to better align more of our costs directly to what we really do—designing and assembling airplanes and manufacturing parts and assemblies for them.

THAT BILL HAS YOUR NAME ON IT

Aligning costs to operating decisions is an important component of the new management and operating philosophy we're striving to implement. The changes we're going through are substantial. We are moving from a functional enterprise to one organized around product processes, and from a company that allocates its resources by organization to one that aligns them to product processes. And we are replacing part/resource management with product-focused process management.

This new philosophy will allow us to match resources to small, focused product groups. These small business units will then contain one or more product-focused process units. Costs incurred at a broader level in the company will not become the responsibility of the product- or service-producing unit. Rather, these broader-level costs will be the responsibility of the general-purpose processes, such as the sales and marketing organization or the central tax staff. These groups will be accountable from the costs they are adding to the final product shipped to our customers.

By way of comparison, think about a typical activity-based costing model, which you could use to develop the cost drivers for overhead and manufacturing activities. The overhead drivers include the square footage, the headcount, direct-labor hours, and the number of products. Manufacturing's drivers are the unit volume, the number of shifts and the weighted unit volume. With an ABC model, you would use these drivers to link the overhead activities to the manufacturing processes and the manufacturing processes to products.

With process accounting, we trace the overhead costs to product-related manufacturing processes based on the business unit's responsibility for and ability to control and influence the costs that result from operating that process. This is important for several reasons. Under traditional accounting, a business unit can spend less money and thus help the company meet its overall cost-reduction targets. But it's the direct, measurable, cause-and-effect link back to the business unit's products that was missing. Reducing a few direct heads was about the only action the business-unit manager could take to actually see the business unit's costs, or rather the 20 percent to 30 percent of business-unit costs, go down.

Our new process-accounting approach has changed that situation dramatically. Today, the organization can exercise significant influence and control over the costs it incurs. In fact, the basic ground rule for assigning costs is the organization must be able to take some action on that cost element and see a predictable change in the overall costs being charged to it.

The costs the business unit is accountable for and can control now include those for detail and supplier parts, computing, depreciation, support labor and direct labor, and other nonlabor costs. The business manager has a much broader sphere of influence in which to exercise control and make improvements within the business unit.

But tracing this bigger bucket of costs to the business units is only part of the solution. The business units now need some tools with which cut costs, improve customer response time and so on. Our business units will use their unit cost targets and ad-hoc analysis techniques for the data they will track internally (see box on this page).

they can manage their costs. Once they identify the resources they consume, they must analyze them and learn to recognize their process and resource cost drivers and the relationship among them by continually asking why a certain item or process costs what it does. Business units need to understand their cost drivers to increase product quality,

As you can see from the example shown in the box, our basic approach is to compare and weight the individual parts produced in a product process, based on the differences between the parts or part families. We calculate

---

A FRACTION OF THE COSTS

Boeing's new cost-accounting system allows individual business units to portray their planned unit costs in today's environment and how they might compare to the unit costs upper management wants to achieve. The business units calculate their costs with the help of numerator and denominator charts like the ones below. The total dollar cost divided by good parts out equals the cost for good part shipped. Typical elements included under total costs are shown in the numerator chart. The denominator chart shows how we calculate our costs for good parts shipped.

In this example, the expected production, from the denominator table, is 13,439 units of output. The cost to product 13,439 units is estimated at $58.517 million (numerator table). Dividing 13,439 units into $58.517 million yields an expected average unit cost of $4,354.

Boeing's Cost Numerator...

Cost Element	Product Plan Costs (in $ thousands)
Touch Labor	12,150
Support Labor	9,223
Raw Materials	15,113
Equipment Depreciation	2,990
Equipment Maintenance	2,357
Tooling Depreciation	1,983
Tooling Maintenance	1,317
Distributed Material	503
Shop Supplies	915
Computing	6,662
Facilities Cost	3,552
Miscellaneous	1,752
Total	**$58,517**

...and Output Denominator

Part Number	Quantity	Product Weighting Factor	Units of Output
A	158	2.10	332
B	405	3.30	1,337
C	288	13.60	3,917

---

the relative differences in the resources required to produce the different parts. Then we multiply the result—the product weighting factor for each part or product—by the expected production quantity for each part. The result is the business unit's expected production expressed in equivalent output units.

IT'S ALL RELATIVE

The normal procedure for determining these factors is to first identify the typical or base part or part family. Often that turns out to be the part that is the simplest. We give the base part a value of 1, 10 or 100, depending on the scale we want to use.

Then we review the other parts we produce, compare their features' relative value to the base part and determine their values. Take airplane skin panels, for example. We might assign a simple panel a value of one. A panel with a window could have a value of five, while a panel with an unusual shape could be a nine, and so on. The method also allows us to calculate the relative value of adding to or modifying various features.

Determining the relative value is probably the most complicated part of the whole process, but it's an essential aspect of process accounting. It's important to understand what's driving out current production costs, as well as the relative value of the parts being produced and the impact of process improvements and future production plans.

Individual business units can now project their costs for expected future levels of production. The production-producing business units will now be able to better understand how they fit into the total company production and cost picture.

With this knowledge, Boeing can relate many aspects of the total business to one another in a manner that allows us to take actions at all levels of the company—actions with predictable results and a common focus. For example, we can now begin to trace the hidden costs of capacity to individual business units, and this brings up some different, interesting questions. What is the unit's excess capacity? What's the cost of holding inventory? Who's accountable for excess capacity and why?

Also, process accounting supports other concepts in our continuous process-improvement strategy, including total accountability, responsibility and control: flexibility; and total cost tied to customer value. With our process-accounting tools in hand, we can begin to answer the next round of questions we're asking ourselves in our continuing quest for quality.

Chapter 12
Cost Allocation: Service Departments
and Joint Product Costs

Cases

Readings

12-1: "Managing Shared Services with ABM" by Ann Triplett, Jon Scheumann, *Strategic Fnance* (February 2000).

This article outlines the benefits of using shared services (i.e., finance and accounting services) in large companies such as Ford Motor Company, Sun Microsystems and Marriott. There is also a discussion of how activity-based management (ref: chapter 4) is used to manage the costs of these shared services.

Discussion Question:
How do concepts for cost management of shared services differ from the concepts and methods presented in Chapter 12? Who are the customers referred to in the article? What do you think is the best way to manage the costs of shared services such as finance and accounting?

Cases

12-1 Southwestern Bell Telephone

In the fall of 1989, the Texas Division of Southwestern Bell Telephone Company (SWBT) was facing considerable earnings uncertainty. Nine months had passed since the Texas Public Utilities Commission (PUC) had initiated an inquiry into SWBT's earnings in Texas. The Company was trying to negotiate a settlement but was having difficulty reaching an agreement with the commission staff and other interested parties. One group was proposing a decrease in SWBT revenues that would result in a 76% reduction in the company's Texas revenues and adversely affect Southwestern Bell Corporation's stock price.

At the same time that the PUC was investigating alleged overearnings related to SWBT's Texas intrastate operations, company officers in Texas were trying to meet budgeted net income objectives. These targets were necessary to keep earnings growing at a conservative yet steady rate. With actual data already available for much of the year, it was apparent that the overall target for 1989 might not be met. One of the main causes of this probable shortfall was the decrease SWBT was experiencing in revenues from long distance telephone calls. This decrease was due largely to increased payments in the form of settlements to other local exchange telephone companies in Texas. SWBT's management was searching for alternatives to the settlement process that would allow the company to retain its fair share of long distance revenues without financially ruining smaller telephone companies operating in the state.

INDUSTRY BACKGROUND

In January 1984, SWBT and six other regional telephone companies were divested from American Telephone and Telegraph Company (AT&T). In addition to retaining ownership of Western Electric (manufacturing), Bell Labs (research and development), and AT&T Information Systems, AT&T was allowed to retain ownership of interstate long distance services and a portion of intrastate long distance. Under the provisions of the Justice Department's Modified Final Judgment decree, each state was divided into Local Access Transport Areas (LATAs). Texas was divided into seventeen LATAs in addition to the standard metropolitan statistical area of San Angelo, which belongs solely to General Telephone (GTE).

Long distance calling between LATAs (interLATA) may be provided only by interexchange carriers (IXCs) such as AT&T, MCI, and Sprint. Local exchange carriers (LECs) such as SWBT and GTE provide basic telephone service and long distance calling within each LATA (intraLATA). In Texas, there are 59 LECs. SWBT is by far the largest, serving approximately 6.6 million telephone lines.

Because IXCs access their customers through LEC facilities, LECs charge IXCs for using their local networks. Theoretically, these per-minute-of-use charges are based on LEC costs. However, state commissions often inflate the rates to subsidize basic telephone rates, thus keeping them priced below cost.

INTERSTATE INTRALATA LONG DISTANCE

When a customer of an LEC makes an intrastate intraLATA long distance (toll) call, completion of the call often requires the use of another LEC's facilities. For example, a call from Dallas to Denton is an intraLATA toll call that originates in a Southwestern Bell area (Dallas) but terminates in a GTE area (Denton). The originator of the call is billed by Southwestern Bell, which must reimburse GTE for costs incurred in assisting in the call. In Texas, this reimbursement is currently handled through a toll revenue pooling agreement among the LECs.

The pooling of intraLATA toll revenues is administered by the Texas Exchange Carrier Association (TECA). Each LEC reports monthly to the TECA administrator not only its billed toll revenues but also its expenses and investment incurred in providing toll service. TECA combines the revenue, expense, and investment information for all 59 LECs and calculates a rate of return equal to billed revenues less expenses (including

Blocher, Stout, Cokins, Chen: *Cost Management, 4e*

taxes) divided by investment. Each LEC is allowed to recover its expenses plus the pool rate of return on its investment.

In 1987 the pool rate of return was approximately 19%. Although SWBT billed $555.3 million in toll revenues, it was allowed to retain only the total of its expenses ($285.4 million) and return ($147.9 million). The $122 million difference between what SWBT billed and what it was allowed to keep was paid to the pool administrator for disbursement to those companies whose costs exceeded their billed revenues.

CONCERNS WITH THE POOLING PROCESS

Southwestern Bell's managers have several concerns with the current pooling process. One of their major concerns is that few incentives exist for companies to control costs. IntraLATA toll service is a much larger portion of the total operations of many of the smaller LECs than of SWBT. Consequently, each dollar of additional cost incurred by the smaller companies results in approximately one dollar of additional settlements. On the other hand, Southwestern Bell's retained toll revenues (after settlement with other LECs) decrease by approximately $1 million for each one percent reduction in its costs. This situation is not conducive to the efficient provision of telephone service and therefore is not in the best interest of the public.

The company's managers also are concerned about the manner in which total expenses and investment related to intraLATA toll service are calculated. Each company's accountants computes these amounts using procedures developed by the Federal Communications Commission (FCC). The very complex procedures, referred to in the industry as "separations," allocate monthly journalized expense and investment amounts to various categories of telephone service based on factors developed from studies of call traffic patterns and studies showing how telephone plant resources are utilized. The separations process was developed to provide a means of dividing expenses and investment amounts between state and interstate jurisdictions to facilitate rate setting by regulatory agencies. It never was intended to represent an accurate allocation system.

The first step in separations is to divide expense and investment amounts into traffic-sensitive and non-traffic-sensitive (NTS) categories. Traffic-sensitive expenses are primarily variable and are relatively easy to trace to specific categories of service. NTS expenses are primarily fixed. These amounts (over half the total SWBT reports to the pool) are incurred to provide and service connections between customers' premises and company's central offices. The same investment is required whether a customer makes no calls, a few calls, or hundreds of calls, and also whether those calls are intrastate or interstate.

NTS amounts are separated into three categories: interstate, intrastate toll, and intrastate local. In 1982, the FCC froze at approximately 20% the portion of Southwestern Bell's NTS expenses and investment allocated to intrastate toll operations. Thus, the initial separation of NTS amounts does not represent the current usage of the telephone network's resources. However, the interLATA toll and intraLATA toll components of the 20% factor are determined monthly based on relative actual usage. Therefore, if interLATA toll usage is increasing at a faster rate than intraLATA toll usage, less will be allocated to the intraLATA toll category. IntraLATA toll expenses and related investment could be increasing, but due to the separations process fewer dollars would be assigned to the category and thus recoverable through the pooling process. SWBT's intraLATA toll NTS factor is approximately 8%, whereas the factors of several smaller telephone companies are in the 30% to 50% range.

A third concern of Southwestern Bell managers is that revenues from non-joint-provided toll calls are included in the pooling process. For example, consider that the largest intraLATA toll market in Texas is between Dallas and Ft. Worth. Most toll calls between the two cities use only SWBT facilities, but through the pooling process revenues from the calls are shared with the state's other LECs. Company officials believe both revenues and costs of single-company toll calls should be excluded from the pool, but currently there is no means to isolate those amounts.

A final concern relates to the telecommunications industry goal of providing adequate telephone service to all U. S. citizens at reasonable rates. All telephone companies as well as the entire nation have benefited from the subsidies that higher cost companies have received from lower-cost companies. If local telephone service, especially in rural areas, were priced to cover its costs, the number of residences with service would be substantially lower. The concern at Southwestern Bell is that subsidization of high-cost companies has exceeded its historical intent; publications of the Texas PUC show that many high-cost LECs are earning well over their authorized rates of return.

After reviewing the situation, Southwestern Bell's senior managers realized they had their work cut out for them. They know that the course of action they recommended would have to effectively address both the concerns of SWBT and the financial needs of the other companies.

REQUIRED:

1. Assuming toll revenue sharing will continue to be administered by the TECA, what is the most important modification that could be made to the pooling procedures to produce a more equitable distribution of revenues from the perspective of Southwestern Bell?

2. Should SWBT officials negotiate changes in the subsidization procedures directly with the other Texas LECs or take their concerns to the state Public Utilities Commission and seek mandated changes?

3. What strategy would you recommend to Southwestern Bell managers? How would your recommendation address the four concerns expressed in the case?

(IMA adapted)

Blocher, Stout, Cokins, Chen: *Cost Management, 4e*

©The McGraw-Hill Companies, Inc 2008

12-2 Brookwood Medical Center[1]

"In 1990, a major insurer asked us to bid on performing all of their open-heart surgeries in the Southeast United States. We prepared a bid by pulling charges on all (not just Medicare) patients we had treated in the four diagnostic related groups (DRGs) and applying the hospital-wide cost-to-charge ratio. We did not get the bid and had *no idea* whether to be disappointed or relieved. From talks with third-party payers and major employers, we believed that by the mid-1990s we would be bidding for portions of business, like open-heart surgeries, on a regular basis. We realized that we needed a much better understanding of costs at the DRG and individual patient levels if we're to be able to compete effectively."

—Carolyn Johnson, Vice President of finance

INTRODUCTION

By the end of the 1980s, cost management had become one of the most important issues faced by Brookwood Medical Center (BMC) administrators. BMC faced pressure from managed care providers such as health maintenance organizations (HMOs) and preferred provider organizations (PPOs) to keep medical costs low while continuing to provide high-quality health care services. For the first time, BMC was asked to bid on specific health care services for members of managed care insurance plans. To provide bids that were competitive yet profitable, hospital administrators needed detailed cost information about specific health care procedures. In addition, Medicare and other insurance providers moved to fixed fee reimbursement schedules, paying a defined fixed rate depending on a patient's diagnostic related group (DRG) and severity level. The use of fixed payment rates provided incentives for BMC to identify costs associated with providing health care to specific patients in each DRG. Health care providers realized that reductions in the average length of stay (ALOS) as a result of shorter inpatient hospital stays and increased outpatient services could decrease costs without decreasing the quality of care.

THE NEW COST SYSTEM

As more payers moved to a fixed fee form of reimbursement, BMC administrators determined the existing cost system was not providing sufficiently accurate or detailed cost information. The old methodology provided aggregated cost data by department; but no reliable method existed to trace costs to individual patients or diagnostic groups. The new health care environment required hospitals to compete for managed care contracts and to make strategic decisions based on a solid understanding of costs.

Jan Kelly, Director of cost accounting, identified the following issues to support the need for a new cost management system:

- *Unexplained variation in practice patterns.* Physicians largely drove the health care delivery process through treatment protocols and medical orders that determined patient charges and length of stay. A new cost system could help identify costs associated with specific physician practice patterns.
- *Concern with costs and more appropriate care.* BMC recognized the opportunity to reduce tests and procedures for patients (e.g., ordering a component test rather than a whole profile on blood work). Some inpatient testing and care could be effectively done on an outpatient basis due to advances in medications and other technology. Many diagnostic tests and longer inpatient stays may not result in better patient outcomes.
- *Questions regarding effectiveness.* Questions concerning the effectiveness of care, especially when evaluating new technology or treatments, were becoming increasingly commonplace. Thus, BMC required more sophisticated cost management tools.
- *Beliefs regarding cost vs. value of care.* Balancing the quality of care with the costs of providing care was a fundamental concern for BMC. For example, if a new surgical procedure allows early discharge or little scarring but costs 10 times more than an old procedure, is it necessary for the hospital to offer the new procedure and incur additional costs? Executives had to identify a strategy for new technology

---

[1] Prepared by Thomas L. Albright and Robin Cooper, © Institute of Management Accountants, 1998. Used with permission.

and the existing methodology, management began to explore alternatives to the old cost accounting methodology. They required a cost system that would provide a product-line focus, i.e., open heart surgery, diabetes care, rehabilitation, or respiratory therapy, and that would permit segmentation of the patient population. Details of Mason's oncological study were reviewed, and the results reinforced the belief that costs calculated on a facility-wide basis were not helpful for making decisions that were DRG-specific.

In March 1991, BMC executives hired an Atlanta-based CPA firm to work with Kelly to gain an understanding of departmental operating costs and to build cost standards. They backloaded cost data for 20 months and identified two types of costs, direct and indirect. Meetings were held twice a week with key hospital administrators and clinicians to determine activities that caused costs.

BMC used a computerized information system known as Transition I (TSI) to assist with standard costing, financial modeling, and forecasting. The software allowed cost managers at BMC to identify activities, link activities to costs, and categorize costs based on predetermined or specific allocation bases. The system also generated simultaneous algebraic equations used to allocate indirect costs to revenue-generating departments. TSI allowed the creation of a database with cost and demographic information that could be sorted by both traditional and nontraditional demographic elements. Detailed information allowed BMC to obtain more accurate measurements of costs to provide care and to monitor and improve the quality of care provided to patients. For example, the patient number, length of stay, total charges, direct costs, and indirect costs for all appendectomy patients treated during a specific time period were summarized by the TSI system (see Table 1).

DIRECT COSTS

Direct costs could be traced to a patient or procedure and included resources consumed in providing testing services, supplies, pharmaceuticals, and nursing care. Costs for patient testing and procedures (including X-ray, laboratory services, operating room costs, labor and delivery room costs) were associated with each patient, using the internally calculated direct cost for each test or procedure. Major supplies and pharmaceuticals were individually assigned to the patient based on the actual cost of the supply or drug.

Nursing care costs were driven to the patient level through daily patient classification and room rate charges. These charges were based on the nursing skill level required to care for patients in each specialty area, as well as the average acuity levels in each specialty area. Nursing staff skill levels were divided into three classifications as follows: registered nurse (RN), licensed practical nurse (LPN), and aide. Examples of specialty areas were obstetrics, surgical, psychiatric, and cardiovascular. BMC divided six acuity levels according to the level of clinical attention required by the patient. For example, a direct cost of $123 per day was incurred in the Nursing-MED/SURG department acuity level 1 (see Table 2).

The cost system produced departmental reports identifying the daily rate by acuity level and the underlying assumptions of the allocation routine (see Table 3). Because the number of minutes required to attend patients varied across acuity levels, the estimated (budgeted) volume of patient days was adjusted for daily service levels, expressed in minutes. The department's budgeted cost was allocated to each acuity level as a percentage of total budgeted minutes. Finally, a daily rate for each acuity level was calculated by dividing the allocated costs by the budgeted volume of days within each acuity level.

INDIRECT COSTS

Indirect costs such as depreciation, administrative, and general were allocated to revenue-producing activities using simultaneous algebraic equations. The calculations were performed by BMC's computerized accounting system using allocation percentages based on the amount of services provided to other departments. The system allocated costs among several departments with reciprocal service relationships. For example, assume an organization has two support departments, housekeeping, information systems (IS), and two revenue-producing departments, operating room (OR) and emergency room (ER). The IS department manager estimated the housekeeping department consumed 10% of the IS department's activities, while the ER and OR required 40% and 50%, respectively. Thus, the IS department's direct costs of $100,000 were allocated to housekeeping, OR, and ER consistent with the resources demanded (see Table 4). Next, the housekeeping department's direct ($60,000) and allocated ($10,000) costs of $70,000 were allocated to IS, OR, and ER using 30%, 40%, and 30%, respectively. Though the IS department had allocated all costs total $100,000 in the first step, the housekeeping department transferred costs ($21,000) back into the department that had to be reallocated in the second iteration.

Blocher, Stout, Cokins, Chen: *Cost Management, 4e*

Iterations continued until the costs remaining in the support departments were too small to be significant. Thus, after multiple iterations, all support department costs were transferred to the OR and ER (see Table 4).

The cost system used by BMC simultaneously allocated costs associated with all indirect activities to revenue-producing activities based on cost drivers identified by BMC. For example, the education department allocated its costs to various departments including pain management, diabetic services, and emergency room using the percentage of paid hours within each department as the allocation base. Though the process required multiple iterations (see Table 4), the cost management system produced reports after each allocation iteration (see Table 5). When the allocation procedure had completed the final iteration, all costs for support-related departments were contained in the accounts of revenue-producing departments. Thus, education costs were included in the emergency room indirect cost per hour of $142 (see Table 2).

As the health care environment changed, new information demands were placed on the cost reporting system. The Mason study (discussed in the BMC Introduction) added length of stay as well as direct costs within DRG categories to the cost-to-charge ratio. According to Kelly, "TSI represented a significant step toward understanding and managing the costs of delivering health care services at BMC."

REQUIRED:
1. Why didn't the cost data make any sense?
2. What motivated the managers to build a new cost system?
3. How does the TSI system attach costs to a patient or procedure? What are the major design issues?
4. How is the daily rate determined for the Nursing Med/Surg department acuity level 1?
5. How does the reciprocal method allocate indirect costs to revenue-producing departments?
6. Given your understanding of the manner in which TSI allocates costs to patients, would you classify Brookwood's cost system as activity based?

Table 1 Brookwood Medical Center: Appendectomy Patient Listing

Patient Number	Length of Stay	Total Charges	Direct Cost Variable	Direct Cost Fixed	Indirect Cost	Total Cost
1	3	$8,486	751	164	1,187	2,102
2	4	18,394	2,960	566	3,106	6,631
3	2	7,297	926	245	1,280	2,451
4	2	12,350	2,069	258	1,556	3,884
5	2	5,854	765	210	1,152	2,126
6	3	14,574	1,966	395	2,160	4,522
7	2	14,289	2,440	332	1,577	4,349
8	1	5,772	856	102	661	1,619
9	2	11,589	1,404	325	1,553	3,282
10	2	8,398	1,192	365	2,045	3,601
11	2	8,771	1,033	225	901	2,159
12	3	14,920	2,626	295	2,546	5,466
13	3	10,320	1,751	487	2,644	4,882
14	3	8,871	1,097	178	1,460	2,735
15	1	9,103	1,998	221	1,647	3,865
16	2	8,365	1,563	168	1,050	2,781
17	5	13,355	2,195	687	3,237	6,119
18	2	11,235	2,414	258	2,195	4,867
19	1	8,976	1,170	201	1,067	2,438
20	5	18,033	3,123	563	3,457	7,143
21	4	11,756	1,739	229	1,279	3,247
22	1	8,068	1,698	210	1,350	3,258
23	1	8,133	1,669	247	1,257	3,174
24	1	7,396	1,232	160	825	2,217
25	1	6,926	911	147	637	1,695
26	1	7,558	1,268	188	1,141	2,598
27	5	20,140	3,151	468	3,419	7,037
28	2	6,211	718	167	843	1,728
29	2	8,740	1,324	189	1,212	2,724
30	1	6,931	779	140	736	1,656
31	1	8,493	1,345	152	1,013	2,510
32	1	6,580	1,041	153	863	2,056
33	2	8,646	1,328	195	1,200	2,723
34	2	11,319	1,214	247	1,424	2,885
35	1	7,435	1,042	161	817	2,020
36	2	11,765	1,564	267	1,647	3,478
37	1	9,822	1,443	165	1,143	2,752
38	2	10,354	1,929	184	1,669	3,782
39	3	9,117	1,117	126	1,309	2,552
40	1	11,097	1,623	348	1,847	3,818
41	1	9,030	900	141	859	1,901
42	1	7,659	1,558	112	1,045	2,716
43	2	9,943	1,619	174	1,217	3,010
44	2	11,238	1,177	202	1,273	2,651
Total	91	$443,309	67,688	11,017	66,506	145,210

Source: sample of appendectomy patients from TSI data.

Blocher, Stout, Cokins, Chen: *Cost Management, 4e*

©The McGraw-Hill Companies, Inc 2008

Table 2. DRG 470 - Appendectomy Utilization Report

Department Description	Product Description	Direct Cost	Indirect Cost	Quantity	Total Cost
NURSING - MED/SURG	Acuity level 1 -- daily rate	$123.00	$190.00	1	$313.00
	Acuity level 2 -- daily rate	140.00	229.00	2	738.00
OPERATING ROOM	Major surgery -- 1 hour	174.00	170.00	1	344.00
OPERATING ROOM SUPPLIES	Sutures	17.00	7.00	5	120.00
	Basic surgical pack	17.00	6.00	1	23.00
	Additional OR supplies*	118.00	50.00	1	168.00
RECOVERY	Recovery level II -- 1/4 hours	24.00	11.00	3	105.00
CENTRAL STORES	Central store supplies*	25.50	58.00	1	83.50
LABORATORY SERVICES	Blood profile, potassium, renal profile	29.50	11.00	2	81.00
CARDIOLOGY / EKG	EKG 3 channel w/o physician in	13.00	12.00	1	25.00
PHARMACY	Pharmaceuticals*	163.50	133.00	1	296.50
RESPIRATORY THERAPY	Incentive spirometer	4.00	3.00	5	35.00
	New start spirometer & oxygen	6.00	4.00	1	10.00
EMERGENCY ROOM	ER visit level II -- intensive	80.00	142.00	1	222.00
DIETARY	Daily hospital service	24.00	18.00	3	126.00
LAUNDRY / LINEN	Daily hospital service	9.00	6.00	3	45.00
					2,735.00

* Detail of specific items charged collapsed into one line item.

Table 3. Brookwood Medical Center, Department 6103, Nursing MED/SURG

Budget $95,759

Description	Budgeted Volume in Days	Minutes Daily Service	Budgeted Minutes	Percent Allocation	Allocation	Daily Rate
Acuity level 1	18	346	?	?	?	?
Acuity level 2	264	394	?	?	?	?
Acuity level 3	199	464	92,336	0.343	$32,864	$165
Acuity level 4	25	547	13,675	0.051	4,867	195
Observation	165	40	6,600	0.025	2,349	14
Observation	133	30	3,990	0.015	1,420	11
All others	211	200	42,200	0.157	15,020	71
Total			269,045	1.000	95,759	

Table 4. Calculations for Reciprocal Service Department Allocation

	Service Departments		Revenue Departments	
	IS	Housekeeping	OR	ER
Beginning balance	100,000	60,000	0	0
IS allocation (100,000)	10,000[1]	50,000[2]	40,000[3]	
Balance after allocation	0	70,000	50,000	40,000
Housekeeping allocation	21,000[4]	(70,000)	28,000[5]	21,000[6]
Balance after allocation	21,000	0	78,000	61,000
2nd IS allocation	(21,000)	2,100	10,500	8,400
Balance after allocation	0	2,100	88,500	69,400
2nd housekeeping allocation	630	(2,100)	840	630
Balance after allocation	630	0	89,340	70,030
3rd IS allocation	(630)	63	315	252
Balance after allocation	0	63	89,655	70,282
3rd housekeeping allocation	19	(63)	25	19
Balance after allocation	19	0	89,680	70,301
Transfer minimal balances	(19)	0	10	9
Ending balance	0	0	89,690	70,310

[1]$100,000 * 10%   [3]$100,000 * 40%   [5]$70,000 * 40%

[2]$100,000 * 50%   [4]$70,000 * 30%   [6]$70,000 * 30%

Blocher, Stout, Cokins, Chen: *Cost Management, 4e*

Table 5. Brookwood Medical Center, Education Allocation to Emergency Room

Allocation base: paid hours

Budget -- $500,000

Department	Paid Hours	Percentage of paid hours by department	Amount allocated
Pain Management	2,083	?	?
Diabetic Services	8,993	?	?
Emergency Room	124,212	?	?
Monitoring Services	40,634	?	?
Quality Assurance	21,314	?	?
Dietary	167,411	?	?
Collections	13,650	0.279320	$1,396.60
Outpatient Registration	19,776	0.404677	$2,023.39
All others	4,488,783	91.854210	$459,271.05
Total	4,886,856	100.00%	$500,000.00

12.1: MANAGING SHARED SERVICES WITH ABM

By Ann Triplett and Jon Scheumann

Shared service operations combine the efficiency and leverage of centralization (standardization, economies of scale, and a single base for improvement) with the superior customer service usually associated with decentralization.

Companies try to achieve this balance by drawing together activities performed similarly in various locations across the business (often focusing on transaction processes), standardizing on a common process design that emphasizes high quality and customer responsiveness, and putting in place measurement tools to monitor performance and guide improvement efforts.

Companies choose shared services for various reasons, but lower costs are a primary benefit, as are improvements in productivity and customer service. In addition, some companies see shared services as a platform for growing their business without growing administrative costs at the same rate.

Ford has been operating a shared services center (SSC) for finance in Europe since the early 1980s, and DuPont, Digital Equipment, and General Electric established shared services organizations in the United States in the late 1980s. A second wave of companies, including Hewlett-Packard, Dow Chemical, Dun & Bradstreet, IBM, and Allied Signal, followed that lead in the early 1990s, and today many of the top 500 companies in the United States have implemented some form of shared services.

Regardless of the services they provide—Payroll, Payables, Receivables, Fixed Asset Accounting, etc.—all SSCs are faced with the same three cost-related questions:

- What causes costs in our operation, and how can we manage them?
- How do we determine how much to charge each customer for the services we provide?
- How do our costs compare to those of others, in particular the costs of outsourcers who can provide the same services?

SSC managers are discovering that activity-based management (ABM) can be used to create a framework that provides the cost information required to answer these questions. Gunn Partners found that 16% of the service centers in its 1999 Global Shared Services Research project have completed their ABM implementation. But even more interesting is that 30% of the companies are in the process of implementing ABM, and an additional 21% expect to implement within the next three years. This means that by the end of 2002 nearly 70% of the research companies will have implemented ABM. These results clearly show the expected use of ABM as an important management tool.

HOW DO WE MANAGE SSC COSTS?

Critical to the success of any shared service center is a thorough understanding of costs and the ability to impact those costs. After all, most SSCs were founded on the premise of saving money for the corporation. Cost management is key—possibly more so than for any other part of the business. SSC managers must understand what activities are performed and how each activity contributes to total cost. They need to understand the drivers of cost—especially the drivers that are completely under their control. For example, an internal driver might be the number of internal approval levels required for a particular transaction.

A methodology to identify and evaluate the potential of improvement opportunities, on an ongoing basis, also should be in place. In operating shared service centers, managers strive to continually reduce the cost for existing services and to free resources for providing other services that customers may want. This information has to be developed and maintained with minimum complexity and cost.

In recent years, many companies have learned that an activity-based model of operations provides all of the information required to effectively understand and manage costs. Through use of this ABM model on an ongoing basis, they manage the business and answer the first question, "What causes costs in our operation, and how can we manage

Blocher, Stout, Cokins, Chen: *Cost Management, 4e*

them?"

The success of an SSC depends on cost management, but the ability to understand how customer requirements, actions, and demands for various types of services drive costs also is critical. It's absolutely necessary for managers to identify which activities are required to provide specific services and understand the external drivers of SSC cost—that is, those factors controlled by customers. The percentage of errors in customer-provided information is an example of an external driver. From this cost information, service prices can be developed, and a center should be able to develop and maintain the information with minimum complexity and cost.

If you need to explain cost information to customers, what language do you use? Answer: The activity-based model of operations can be used and expanded with the information required to determine the cost of providing each service. This process, known as service level costing, involves identifying the activities and costs associated with providing services, using that information to support discussions with customers, and then providing the level of service for which each customer is willing to pay. Customers can relate to this language when you discuss costs in terms of how they are caused by activities.

It's also possible, with additional detail, to establish differential pricing, that is, to charge customers different prices for the same service. These prices can be determined by identifying the specific impact that each customer has on cost, based on behavior as measured by cost drivers. A model to support differential pricing takes more time to develop and is larger and more complex to maintain, but some SSCs feel that it's worth the effort.

For many SSCs, service level costing supports the actual charge-out of appropriate costs to customers based on the types of services they receive. For SSCs whose cost is absorbed at a corporate level, the information is equally valuable and can be used to justify and explain decisions made about the services that will be provided. Approximately 60% of corporations who have implemented shared services charge out shared service costs, according to Gunn Partners research.

Furthermore, the research has shown that charging customers a differential rate based on ease or complexity of the transaction hasn't led to a position of cost or productivity leadership. While charging differential rates in an attempt to influence behaviors is emotionally appealing to the SSC leadership, this isn't yet a leading practice according to the data.

Ideally, a shared service center should regularly compare its cost of providing a service to the cost at which others can provide the service. But this isn't always easily accomplished. In some cases, a center can compare service costs with others in a group benchmarking study. For some services it may be possible to obtain information about how much an outsourcing provider would charge.

Here, again, the activity-based model of operations can provide the required information. The center's cost per output of a service is often the piece of information required to benchmark. It's also important to know whether this cost has increased or decreased over time, and a well-maintained model will facilitate this comparison.

One of the challenges is to ensure a valid comparison; the model provides detailed information about which activities are required to provide any given service. Activity costs can be combined in varying ways, if necessary, to arrive at an "apples to apples" comparison for benchmarking.

HOW DO YOU DEVELOP AN ACTIVITY BASED FRAMEWORK?

Companies go through three phases in the development of an activity-based framework to support a shared service center:

- Initial model building effort,
- Customer education and service-level review process, and
- Ongoing maintenance and use of the activity-based framework.

Typically, an ABM modeling software package is used to ensure that the SSC model can be easily sustained over time.

INITIAL MODEL BUILDING

The steps in this phase, illustrated in Figure 1, are those traditionally required to build an activity-based model. Actual implementation of this phase should begin with a much more detailed work plan.

These steps encompass all of the effort required to gather activity and cost information, define the relationships among activities, costs, and services provided, then build the information and relationships into a model. The amount of time it takes to do this will vary according to a number of factors including, but not limited to, resource commitment, size, and scope of center to be modeled, project leadership, and prior experience with ABM.

CUSTOMER EDUCATION AND SERVICE LEVEL REVIEWS

Once the model has been built, the center can begin to use the information to communicate with customers. Typically, the first step in this process is for the center to develop a proposed Service Level Agreement (SLA) for each customer. This document consists of information about which services are being provided, the activity-based cost of each service, and historical information about past service levels. The proposed SLA is the starting point for discussions with your clients.

The client reviews should begin with an introduction to the basic concepts of ABM. Accordingly, initial customer education is critical to the successful, ongoing use of an ABM framework. The rest of the session is spent reviewing the services provided, the level of service provided in the past, the basis for costing, and the actual cost of each service.

The detailed information about the activities required to provide each service should be available but used only if the additional detail is necessary. As each service is reviewed, determine whether or not that service will be provided in the future and, if so, at what level. Remember that the types of services, as described above, will impact these reviews. Some of the services are required for all customers, and others are provided based on customer needs and requirements.

Based on the results from each customer negotiating session, the center can prepare a final SLA for signature. Details about how required information will be gathered and reported over time should be included (for example, number of occurrences). The center should also cover agreements about how billing will be accomplished, whether review is allowed periodically, and so on.

ONGOING MAINTENANCE AND USE

A completed and signed SLA doesn't signify the end of the process, but rather the beginning of an ongoing mutually beneficial relationship between a service center and customer. The three key elements of the ongoing process are:

- Continuous improvement efforts,
- SLA maintenance, and
- Benchmarking.

All of these are linked through the ongoing maintenance of the original ABM model, as illustrated in Figure 2.

Continuous improvement efforts, especially with customer participation, can result in lower costs of services to be incorporated in each ensuing SLA. Information about service cost and customer requirements can support benchmarking efforts. Comparisons can be internal, as in customer to customer, or external comparison can be made to the cost of other service centers or outsourcing service providers. Benchmarking results, in turn, can provide ideas and goals for continuous improvement efforts.

Our work with many clients has demonstrated that a service center goes through three phases during its creation: *installation* (the "birth" of a center), *start-up* (the period of bringing a new center under control), and *steady state* (the ongoing movement into a mode of continuous improvement). It's in the last of these phases that the benefits of ABM can be realized. In earlier phases, activities aren't necessarily well defined, and processes aren't stable. The priorities of a center, then, should be more basic. Each center's situation is unique, and some may move through the phases more quickly than others. A general rule of thumb for when to consider implementing ABM is the second to fourth year of a center's existence.

And you can achieve impressive results by using an activity-based framework to manage a shared service center. First, it supports a new way of management. The activity-based cost model provides a more effective means of managing service center operations than can traditional cost statements and cost accounting analyses.

Service level costing results in more satisfied customers because they understand and have impacted exactly what services they will receive for their payments.

An improved understanding of costs and drivers by both service center providers and customers can result in a lower total cost to the corporation as a whole.

Finally, this effort can provide an improved ability to assess outsourcing, or even insourcing, opportunities. A thorough understanding of processes, activities, and costs results in the information required to make cost-effective and correct decisions.

As a point of reference, the Gunn Partners research data show that the leaders in cost and productivity are more likely to be using ABM as a management tool than their peers. But these leaders almost certainly would tell you it isn't a simple exercise and isn't a "project" to be done once and forgotten. The adoption of an activity-based framework for an SSC requires an ongoing commitment. Your rewards, though, will be great!

FIGURE 1

PROCESS MAPPING AND ACTIVITY IDENTIFICATION

What are the activities performed, and how are they linked together via inputs and outputs?

ACTIVITY AND COST INFORMATION COLLECTION

How much time is spent on various activities? Is the cost information readily available?

ACITIVITY COSTING

Which activities caused which costs to occur? What, then, is each activity's cost?

SERVICE INDENTIFICATION

What are the services provided, and how will these services be measured and costed?

SERVICE COSTING

Which services, for which customers required which activities? How will they be charged?

FIGURE 2

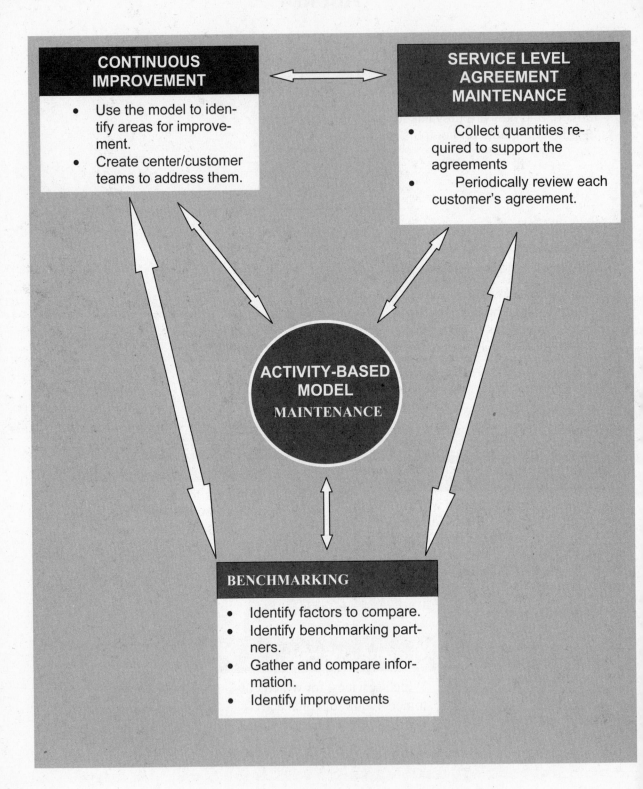

Blocher, Stout, Cokins, Chen: *Cost Management, 4e*

©The McGraw-Hill Companies, Inc 2008

Chapter 13
The Flexible Budget and Standard Costing: Direct Materials and Direct Labor

Cases

13-1   Hoof and Fin Restaurants

Readings

13-1: "Standard Costing Is Alive and Well at Parker Brass" by D. Johnsen and P. Sopariwala, *Management Accounting Quarterly* (Winter 2000), pp. 12-20.

The Brass Products Division of the Parker Hannifin Corporation is a world-class manufacturer of tube and brass fittings, valves, hose, and hose fittings. Despite the introduction of popular new costing systems, the Brass Product Division operates a well-functioning standard costing system.

Discussion Questions:
1. What features in the firm's standard costing that make it a success?
2. In addition to variances seen in the textbook Parker Brass created several new variances. Describe these variances. Why are these variance added at Parker Brass?

13-2: "Redesigning Cost Systems: Is Standard Costing Obsolete?" by Carole B. Cheatham and Leo B. Cheatham, *Accounting Horizons* (December 1996), pp. 23-31.

The article shows some new ways to analyze standard cost data, going beyond the traditional emphasis on production costs variances that focus on price and efficiency. Variances for product quality are developed and explained, as well as sales variances based on sales orders received and orders actually shipped. There is also a discussion of how to incorporate activity-based costing, and continuous standard improvement, including benchmarking and target costing.

The main premise of the article is that standard cost systems are the most common cost systems in use, and while there are a number of limitations to these systems, a careful and creative effort can transform them into more useful cost systems.

Discussion Questions:
1. What are the main criticisms of traditional standard cost systems?
2. What is meant by "push through" production? Is it preferred to "pull through" production, and why?
3. What are the best ways to make standard cost systems more dynamic?
4. Considering the suggestions make in this article, in contrast to the chapter presentation of standard costing, which ideas make the most sense to you and why?

13-3: Can Variance Analysis Make Media Marketing Managers More Accountable? by Ted Mitchell, Ph.D., and Mike Thomas, Ph.D., *Management Accounting Quarterly* (Fall 2005), pp. 51-61.

This article discusses, within the context of a marketing application, an alternative method for decomposing a total standard cost variance. The authors posit that in such applications the joint variance (that in conventional practice is assumed to be small) can be significant in amount and therefore invalidate conventional methods that include the joint price-cost variance as part of the price variance. However, the treatment proposed by the authors for the joint price-quantity variance differs from the "three-variance" solution found in some cost/managerial accounting texts.

Discussion Questions:

1. Explain what is meant by the term "joint variance" as this term is used in standard cost systems used for control purposes.
2. Explain what the authors of this article mean when they describe their proposed approach for standard cost variance decomposition as a "geometric solution."
3. Explain the term "Minimum Potential Performance Budget" model. How is this concept employed in the variance decomposition process recommended by the authors?
4. What are the primary advantages and primary disadvantages of the variance decomposition model recommended by the authors of this paper?

13.1: STANDARD COSTING IS ALIVE AND WELL AT PARKER BRASS

by David Johnsen and Parvez Sopariwala

Many people have condemned standard costing, saying it is irrelevant to the current just-in-time based, fast-paced business environment. Yet surveys consistently show that most industrial companies in the United States and abroad[1] still use it. Apparently, these companies have successfully adapted their standard costing systems to their particular business environments. In addition, many academics have contributed ideas on how the standard costing system could be and has been made more responsive to the needs of companies operating in this new economy.[2]

The Brass Products Division at Parker Hannifin Corporation (hereafter, Parker Brass), a world-class manufacturer of tube and brass fittings, valves, hose and hose fittings, is one of the standard costing success stories. It operates a well-functioning standard costing system of which we will show you some highlights.

WHAT'S SPECIAL ABOUT THE STANDARD COSTING SYSTEM AT PARKER BRASS?

Parker Brass uses its standard costing system and variance analyses as important business tools to target problem areas so it can develop solutions for continuous improvement. Here are some examples of these standard costing-related tools:

- **Disaggregated product line information.** Parker Brass has been divided into Focus Business Units (FBUs) along product lines. Earnings statements are developed for each FBU, and variances are shown as a percentage of sales. If production variances exceed 5% of sales, the FBU managers are required to provide an explanation for the variances and to put together a plan of action to correct the detected problems. To help the process, a plant accountant has been assigned to each FBU. As a result of these steps, each unit is able to take a much more proactive approach to variance analysis.
- **Timely product cost information.** In the past, variances were reported only at month-end, but

often a particular job already would have been off the shop floor for three or more weeks. Hence, when management questioned the variances, it was too late to review the job. Now exception reports are generated the day after a job is closed (in other words, the day after the last part has been manufactured). Any jobs with variances greater than $1,000 are displayed on this report. These reports are distributed to the managers, planners or schedulers, and plant accountants, which permits people to ask questions while the job is still fresh in everyone's mind.

- **Timely corrective action**. Because each job is costed (in other words, transferred out of Work-in-Process and into Finished Goods) 10 days after the job has closed, there is adequate time for necessary corrective action. For example, investigating a large material quantity variance might reveal that certain defective finished parts were not included in the final tally of finished parts. Such timely information would allow management to decide whether to rework these parts or to increase the size of the next job. This kind of corrective action was not possible when variances were provided at the end of each month.
- **An effective control system.** Summary reports are run weekly, beginning the second week of each month, to show each variance in total dollars as well as each variance by product line and each batch within the product line. In addition, at the end of each month, the database is updated with all variance-related information. As a result, FBU managers can review variances by part number, by job, or by high dollar volume.
- **Employee Training and Empowerment.** Meetings are held with the hourly employees to explain variances and earnings statements for their FBU, thereby creating a more positive atmosphere in which the FBU team can work. These meetings help employees understand that management decisions are based on the

Employee training and empowerment. Meetings are held with the hourly employees to explain

PANEL A: THE FACTS

Standard production in 1 hour (units)	50
Standard batch quantity (units)	2,000
Standard hours needed for 2,000 units	40
Standard time needed for 1 setup (hours)	4
Standard labor rate per hour	$10
Actual quantity produced (units)	1,200
Actual setup hours for 1 setup	4
Actual productive labor hours to make 1,200 units	24
Actual labor cost for 28 hours at $10 per hour	$280

PANEL B: WORKINGS

	Setups	Production	Total
Standard time per unit:			
Standard setup time (hours)	4		
Standard production time (hours)		40	
Standard batch size (units)	2,000	2,000	
Hence, standard time per unit (hours)	0.002	0.020	0.022
Standard time charged for 1,200 units:			
Standard time per unit (hours)	0.002	0.020	0.022
# of units actually produced	1,200	1,200	1,200
Standard time charged (hours)	2.40	24.00	26.40

PANEL C: SOLUTION

If SRQV is determined, the journal entry would be:		
Work in process [(26.40)($10)]	$264	
SRQV [(4.00 - 2.40)($10)]	$16	
Accrued payroll		$280
If SRQV is not determined, the journal entry would be:		
Work in process [(26.40)($10)]	$264	
LEV [{28.00 - (1 .200)(0.022)} {$10}]	$16	
Accrued payroll		$280

numbers discussed and that if erroneous data are put into the system, then erroneous decisions may be made. For example, a machine may not be running efficiently. An operator may clock off of the job so that his or her efficiency does not look bad. Because the machine's efficiency is not adversely impacted, no maintenance is done done to that machine, and the inefficiency continues. In addition, because the operator is not charging his/her cost to a job, the cost is being included in indirect labor, and manufacturing costs increase. If the operator had reported the hours correctly, management would have questioned the problem, and the machine would have been fixed or replaced based on how severe the problems were.

WHAT NEW VARIANCES HAS PARKER BRASS DESIGNED?

In addition to the aforementioned innovations that Parker Brass has made to adapt its standard costing system to its particular business environment, the company has created the following new variances:

- The *standard-run quantity variance* to explain situations where the size of a lot is less than the optimal batch quantity.
- The *material substitution variance* to evaluate the feasibility of alternative raw materials.
- The *method variance* to assess situations where different machines can be used for the same job.

Blocher, Stout, Cokins, Chen: *Cost Management, 4e*

©The McGraw-Hill Companies, Inc 2008

THE STANDARD RUN QUANTITY VARIANCE

The standard run quantity variance (SRQV) represents the amount of setup cost that was not recovered because the batch size was smaller than the earlier determined optimal batch size. Because setup costs are included in the standard labor hours for a standard batch quantity is likely to create an unfavorable labor efficiency variance (LEV). Unless, however, the impact of actual production

FIGURE 2

PANEL A: THE FACTS

Standard price per pound of material M1	$10
Standard price per pound of material M2	$11
Standard material quantity (M1 & M2) to make 100 units (lbs.)	2
Actual quantity produced (units)	2,000
Actual pounds of M2 purchased and used	43

PANEL B: WORKINGS

Standard quantity to produce 2,000 units:	
Standard material quantity to make 100 units (lbs.)	2
Actual quantity produced (units)	2.000
Hence, standard quantity to produce 2,000 units	40

PANEL C: SOLUTION

If MSV is determined, the journal entry would be:	
Work in process [(40.00)($10)]	$400
MEV [(43.00 - 40.00)($11)]	$33
MSV [(40.00)($11 - $10)]	$40
Material—M2 [(43.00)($11)1	$473

If MSV is not determined, the journal entry might be:	
Work in process [(40.00)($11)]	$440
MEV [(43.00 - 40.00)($11)]	$33
Material—M2 [(43.00)($11)]	$473

inefficiencies is separated from setup-related inefficiencies, the LEV reflects the combined impact of these two causes of inefficiencies and is not really useful for taking the necessary corrective action.

See **Figure 1** for an illustration of this issue. Panel A shows that standard batch quantity is 2,000 units, the standard production during one hour is 50 units, and, hence, 40 standard hours are needed to produce 2,000 units. In addition, it takes four standard and actual hours to set up one batch. Panel B reveals that standard hours for setup and production labor are 0.002 and 0.020 per unit, respectively, for a total of 0.022 per unit. In addition, because actual quantity produced is 1,200 units, the total standard hours chargeable to these 1,200 units is 26.40 [(0.002 + 0.020)(1,200)].

Finally, Panel C shows the recommended journal entry whereby an SRQV is created. This SRQV represents the unrecovered setup costs because 1,200 units were manufactured instead of the standard batch quantity of 2,000 units. Thus, because the company expected to spend $40 [(4 hours)($10 per hour)] on each setup, the setup cost relating to the 800 (2,000 - 1,200) units not produced, or $16 U, is considered an unfavorable SRQV or the cost of producing small lots. On the other hand, using traditional standard costing, this amount of $16 U would most likely have been categorized as an LEV. Yet there really is no LEV,[3] and the variance of $16 U attributed to labor efficiency is merely the unabsorbed portion of the setup cost attributable to the 800 units that were not produced.

The advantages of extracting the standard run quantity variance are many. First, the SRQV ordinarily would be included in the LEV and could provide a misleading impression of labor's efficiency. Second, because just-in-time practices recommend smaller lots and minimal finished goods inventory the SRQV is essentially the cost of adopting JIT Third, to the extent that setup cost and the cost of carrying inventory are competing undesirables, a determination of the cost of small lots could be used in the trade-off analysis against the cost of holding and carrying inventories. Finally, to the extent that this variance can be separated for each customer, it would reveal how much of a loss was suffered by allowing that customer to purchase in small lots. Such information could be used in future bids. If a customer's schedule required a smaller lot, then that customer's job cost could be enhanced appropriately.

THE MATERIAL SUBSTITUTION VARIANCE

The material substitution variance (MSV) assumes perfect or near perfect substitutability of raw materials and measures the loss or gain in material costs when a different raw material is substituted for the material designated in the job sheet. Substitutions may be made for many reasons. For example, the designated material may not be available or may not be available in small-enough quantities, or the company may want to use up material it purchased for a product that it has since discontinued.

The usefulness of MSV is discussed in Figure 2. Panel A shows that both materials, M1 and M2, can be used to manufacture a product, and it is assumed that two pounds is the standard input per unit for both materials. Material M1 is the material designated in the job sheet, but material M2 can be substituted for M1. The standard cost of M2 ($11 per lb.) is higher than that for M1 ($10 per lb.), and M2 is used because M1 is currently not available and a valued customer needs a rush job.[4] Panel B reveals that the standard quantity needed to manufacture 2,000 units is 40 lbs.

For the purposes of this illustration, we assume that material price variance (MPV) is detected when material is purchased (in other words, the material account is maintained at standard cost). Hence, Panel C reveals the recommended journal entry whereby MSV is created. The MSV represents the benefit obtained by substituting a more expensive material (M2) for the less expensive material (M1) and hence represents the loss through substitution. The MSV is $40 U because (1) 40 lbs. is the standard quantity of M1 and M2 needed to manufacture 2,000 units, and (2) M2 costs $1 more per lb. than M1. In addition, the material efficiency variance (MEV) is $33 U because 43 lbs. instead of the standard quantity of 40 lbs. were used to manufacture 2,000 units.

In contrast, the traditional standard costing system might ignore the substitution, and the job

might be charged with the standard cost of using 40 lbs. of M2. In that scenario, the job would cost $40 more and could have an impact on customer profitability analysis even though the customer did not request the substitution.

Now Parker Brass is evaluating an extension that would be to relax the simplifying assumption that both materials require the same standard input. See Figure 3. It adopts the facts from Figure 2 except that 1.9 lbs. of material M2 are required for 100 units instead of 2 lbs. for both materials in Figure 2. In this situation, we have two MSVs, one for the price impact called "MSV-Price" and the other for the efficiency impact, called "MSV-Efficiency."

Panel C shows the recommended journal entry whereby two MSV variances are created. First, MSV-Price is unfavorable because M2, a more expensive material, is being substituted for M1. As a result, MSV-Price is $40 U as material M2 costs $1 more per lb. than material M1. On the other hand, as you might expect, the MSV-Efficiency is favorable because only 1.9 lbs. of M2 are required to make 100 units as compared to 2 lbs. required for M1. Thus, MSV-Efficiency is $22 F because each batch of 100 units requires 38 lbs. of M2 against 40 lbs. of M1. The net result of the MSV variances is $18 U [(38 lbs.)($11) - (40 lbs.)($10)], suggesting that, barring any other complications, the substitution of M2 for M1 is not likely to be profitable under existing circumstances.

Finally, the MEV using material M2 is $55 U, reflecting the fact that 43 lbs. of material M2 actually were used whereas only 38 lbs. of material M2 should have been used. This variance could have been caused by the fact that M2 was a new material and required initial learning and other nonrecurring costs. In such a case, the standard quantity of 38 lbs. for 2,000 units may not need to be changed. On the other hand, the MEV variance may have been caused because of the inherent difficulty in working with material M2. In such a case, the standard of 38 lbs. for 2,000 units may need to be amended. In contrast, as was shown in Panel C of Figure 2, the journal entry that is likely to be made using traditional standard costing would completely ignore the impact of material substitution and would likely inflate the cost of this particular job.

The advantages of extracting the MSV are as follows. First, determining MSV lets the company assign the MSV cost to a customer whose rush job may have required using a more expensive material like M2. On the other hand, the MSV could be written off if the substitution were made to benefit the company. Also, creating an MSV and breaking it up into its price and efficiency components allows the company to evaluate whether the substitution of M2 for M1 is a profitable one. While all these calculations can also be performed off the accounting system, creating the MSV makes the process a part of the system so a history of such evaluations is available for future reference.

METHOD VARIANCE

A method variance occurs when more than one machine can be used to manufacture a product.[5]

For example, a plant may have newer machines that it normally would expect to use to manufacture a product, so its standards would be based on such new machines. Yet the same plant may also keep, as backups, older and less efficient machines that also could manufacture the same product but would require more inputs in the form of machine and/or labor hours. For this example, we assume that labor hours and machine hours have a 1:1 relationship.[6] As a result, the method variance becomes pertinent because the traditional LEV from operating the older machines could potentially include the

FIGURE 3
PANEL A: THE FACTS

Standard price per pound of material M1	$10
Standard price per pound of material M2	$11
Standard material quantity of M1 to make 100 units (lbs.)	2
Standard material quantity of M2 to make 100 units (lbs.)	1.9
Actual quantity produced (units)	2,000
Actual pounds of M2 used	43

PANEL B: WORKINGS

	Material M1	Material M2
Standard quantity to produce 2,000 units:		
Standard material quantity for 100 units (lbs.)	2	1.9
Actual quantity produced (units)	2,000	2,000
Hence, standard quantity to produce 2.000 units	40	38

PANEL C: SOLUTION

If MSV is determined, the journal entry would be:

Work in process [(40.00)($10)]	$400	
MEV [(43.00 - 38.00)($11)]	$ 55	
MSV-Price [(40.00)($11 - $10)]	$ 40	
MSV-Efficiency [(40.00 - 38.00)($11)]		$ 22
Material—M2 [(43.00)($11)]		$473

If MSV is not determined, the journal entry might be:

Work in process [(38.00)($11)]	$418	
MEV [(43.00 - 38.00)($11)]	$55	
Material—M2 [(43.00)($11)]		$473

following two impacts. First, an older machine may need additional labor hours to perform the same task, and the additional hours would be reflected in the LEV. Second, the LEV would include the workers' efficiency or lack thereof on the older machine.

We evaluate the usefulness of the method variance in Figure 4. Panel A shows that both

machines, A and B, can be used to manufacture a product. Machine A is the more efficient machine and the one used for setting the standard time. Machine B is the backup. Panel B shows that the standard machine hours needed to produce 1,800 units are 30 on machine A and 36 on machine B, which can be compared to the 35 hours actually used to manufacture 1,800 units on machine B.

Panel C of Figure 4 reveals the recommended journal entry whereby a method variance is created. This method variance represents the loss incurred by substituting the backup machine B for machine A. Because machine B's standard of 36 labor hours is greater than machine A's standard of 30 hours, there is an unfavorable method variance of $120. On the other hand, because machine B took 35 hours to manufacture 1,800 units instead of its standard of 36 machine hours, there is a favorable LEV of $20. As you can see, while there was a loss incurred by using machine B instead of machine A, the actual usage of machine B was efficient. In contrast, assuming the traditional costing system recognizes that machine B was used, it is likely to charge the job $720 [(36 hours) x ($20 per hour)] instead of the $600 [(30 hours) x ($20 per hour)] that would have been charged if machine A had been used.

Here are the advantages of extracting the method variance. First, the impact of the method variance ordinarily would be included in the LEV and would provide a misleading impression of labor's productivity. Second, the method variance could be used to isolate the additional cost that was incurred during the year by operating machine M2. This could permit a trade-off between purchasing a new machine and continuing to maintain the older

FIGURE 4
PANEL A: THE FACTS

Machine A: standard time needed for one unit (minutes)	1.0
Machine B: standard time needed for one unit (minutes)	1.2
Labor rate per hour	$20
Actual quantity produced (units)	1,800
Actual labor hours used to make 1,800 units using machine B	35
Actual labor cost	$700

PANEL B: WORKINGS

	Machine A	Machine B
Standard hours needed for 1.800 units on:		
Standard time needed for one unit (minutes)	1.0	1.2
Actual quantity produced (units)	1,800	1,800
Hence, the standard hours needed	30	36

PANEL C: SOLUTION

If method variance is determined, the journal entry would be:

Work in process [(30.00)($20)]	$600	
Method variance [(36.00 - 30.00)($20)]	$120	
LEV [(36.00 - 35.00)($20)]		$ 20
Accrued Payroll		$700

If method variance is not determined, the journal entry might be:

Work in process [(36.00)($20)]	$720	
LEV [(36.00 - 35.00)($20)]		$ 20
Accrued Payroll		$700

Blocher, Stout, Cokins, Chen: *Cost Management, 4e*

machine, especially if tight delivery schedules are not the norm. Finally, the product cost would still be based on the standards for the more efficient new machine, and the job would not be charged a higher cost merely because a less efficient machine was used. That means a job that was completed on the older machine would not be penalized.[7]

RELEVANT, NOT IRRELEVANT

As you can see from the Parker Brass examples, standard costing has not become irrelevant in the new rapid-paced business environment. Parker Brass not only has managed to modify its standard costing system to achieve disaggregated and timely cost information for timely corrective action, but it has also designed additional variances to determine how setup time relating to small batches should be absorbed, whether an alternative raw material is economically feasible, and how a product's cost might reflect the use of alternate production facilities.

ENDNOTES:

[1] Studies reporting on the widespread use of standard costing in the U.S., the U.K., Ireland, Japan, and Sweden are summarized by Horngren, Foster, and Datar on page 225 of the 9th edition of their cost accounting text published by Prentice-Hall in 1997.

[2] C. Cheatham, "Updating Standard Cost Systems," *Journal of Accountancy,* December 1990, pp. 57-60; C. Cheatham, "Reporting the Effects of Excess Inventories," *Journal of Accountancy,* November 1989, pp. 131-140; C. Cheatham and L.R. Cheatham, "Redesigning Cost Systems: Is Standard Costing Obsolete," *Accounting Horizons,* December 1996, pp. 23-31; H. Harrell, "Materials Variance Analysis and JIT: A New Approach," *Management Accounting,* May 1992, pp. 33-38.

[3] The standard production hours needed for 1,200 units were 24 [(1,200) x (0.020)], whereas the actual labor hours used have been intentionally set at 24. In addition, the standard and actual labor hours for one setup have been intentionally set at four.

[4] An alternative scenario could have the cost per pound of M2 ($9 per lb.) being lower than that for M1 ($10 per lb.) because M2 is used to manufacture other products as well and the company obtains quantity discounts for large purchases of M2.

[5] To a limited extent, the rationale behind the method variance is similar to that for the material substitution variance (MSV) discussed earlier.

[6] That is, the machine does not work independent of the worker. Hence, the labor hours spent on the machine are the same as the number of hours the machine was operated.

[7] A similar reasoning is applied in situations wherein the routing for the manufacture of a product is amended during the year, possibly because the customer wants an additional processing step. In such a case, the resulting process variance could be charged to the customer.

13.2: Redesigning Cost Systems: Is Standard Costing Obsolete?

By Carole B. Cheatham and Leo B. Cheatham,
Professors at Northeast Louisana University.

SYNOPSIS: *Since the early 1980s standard cost systems (SCSs) have been under attack as not providing the information needed for advanced manufacturers. In spite of its critics, SCSs are still the system of choice in some 86 percent of U.S. manufacturing firms.*

This paper discusses the criticisms of SCSs that (1) the variances are obsolete, (2) there is not provision for continuous improvement, and (3) use of the variances for responsibility accounting result in internal conflict rather than cooperation. Updates for SCSs in the form of redesigned variances, suggestions for dynamic standards, and refocused responsibility and reporting systems are presented.

The compatibility of SCSs and its main competitor as a cost system, activity-based costing (ABC), is examined. The authors discuss when it is appropriate to use ABC or SCS or some combination of the two.

Since Eli Goldratt's (1983) charge that cost accounting is the number one enemy of productivity in the early 1980s, traditional cost systems have been under attack. Although Goldratt subsequently softened his stand to say that *cost* rather than accounting was the culprit (Jayson 1987), others were quick to jump on the bandwagon to condemn the cost systems in use. New systems were proposed of which the most popular was activity-based costing (ABC).

In spite of all the criticism, a 1988 survey shows 86 percent of U.S. manufacturers using standard cost systems (Cornick et al. 1988). A survey by Schiff (1993) indicates that 36 percent of companies use activity-based costing, but only 25 percent of those use it to replace their traditional cost system. It would seem that only about 9 percent (25 percent of the 36 percent) of companies are using ABC as their main system while the vast majority use a standard cost system (SCS).

This is not to say that traditional SCSs could not benefit from being updated. However, accountants in industry (as well as academia) seem unaware that a redesigned SCS can provide the information they need, and that updating their present system is an easier process than adopting a new system. The SCS is one vehicle of articulation among managerial, financial and operations accounting, and it is a *control* system while the candidates for its replacement typically are only cost *accumulation* systems.

In this article the major criticisms of SCSs are examined along with ways that the weaknesses can be remedied or ameliorated. The criticisms relate to the use of specific variances, the lack of provision for continuous improvement, and the fact that administration of the system results in internal competition rather than cooperation. The appropriate use of ABC systems in conjunction with SCSs is also discussed.

UPDATING THE VARIANCES IN AN SCS

Concerning the variables analyzed in an SCS, most criticisms center on the overemphasis on price and efficiency to the exclusion of quality. Other criticisms center on the use of the volume variance to measure utilization of capacity while ignoring overproduction and unnecessary buildups of inventory. In making such charges, critics fail to realize variance analysis is not "locked-in" to a particular set of variables. Standards are only benchmarks of what performance should be. The particular variables used can be changed as the need arises.

The following discussion focuses on concerns of the new manufacturing environment—raw material ordering and inventory levels, quality, production levels, finished goods inventory levels and completion of sales orders.

VARIANCES PERTAINING TO RAW MATERIALS

The set of variances in **Figure 1** centers on the function of raw material ordering and inventory levels (Harrell 1992). The Raw Material Ordering Variance gives information about the effectiveness of suppliers. It contrasts the raw materials ordered with the raw materials delivered (purchased). Any variation may be considered unfavorable because the goal is to have orders delivered as placed. Too much delivered will result in unnecessary buildups of raw material stocks. Too little delivered is unfavorable because production delays may result.

The Price Variance in **Figure 1** is the traditional price variance computed on materials

FIGURE 1
VARIANCES RELATING TO MATERIAL PURCHASING

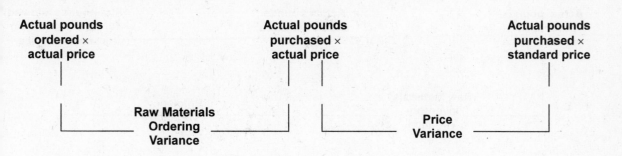

purchased. This variance has been criticized on the grounds that over-emphasis on price leads purchasing managers to ignore quality. However, price is a legitimate concern that should not be overlooked. This system also uses a Quality Variance (presented in a following section). If low quality materials are purchased in order to gain a low price, this will result in an unfavorable Quality Variance.

VARIANCES PERTAINING TO MATERIAL INVENTORIES AND EFFICIENT USE

The set of variances in **Figure 2** focuses on raw material inventory levels and quantity or efficiency of material use.

The Raw Materials Inventory Variance (Harrell 1992) shows either more material purchased than used (an inventory buildup) or more material used than purchased (an inventory decrease). With the JIT philosophy, purchasing more than used causes an unfavorable variance, while decreasing previous buildups causes a favorable variance.

The Efficiency Variance in **Figure 2** is based on the difference between the actual pounds of material used and the standard amount for *total* production. The traditional Efficiency or Quantity Variance is the difference between the actual pounds of material used and the standard amount for *good* production. The traditional variance is actually as combination of quality and efficiency factors. As can be seen in the next section, quality is better treated in a separate variance.

VARIANCES PERTAINING TO PRODUCTION LEVELS AND QUALITY

The next set of variances (**Figure 3**) turns from input analysis to output analysis and relates to

production levels and quality. All cost factors are included in the "standard cost per unit" including labor and overhead.

The Quality Variance is the standard cost of units produced that did not meet specifications (the difference between total units produced and good units produced). In traditional variance analysis, this variance is buried in the efficiency variances of the various inputs.

Ignoring labor and overhead, suppose a company used two pounds of material per finished unit at a standard cost of $1.00 per pound. Further assume they used 4,900 pounds in the production of 2,500 total units, of which 100 were defective. Traditional variance analysis would show an unfavorable Efficiency Variance of $100 computed on the difference between the standard cost of the 4,800 pounds that should have been used to produce the 2,400 good units and the 4,900 pounds actually used.

A better breakdown of the traditional variance shows a favorable Efficiency Variance of $100 and an unfavorable Quality Variance of $200. The Production Department did use only 4,800 pounds to produce 2,500 units that should have taken 5,000 pounds. The fact that some of these units were defective should appear as a Quality Variance, as it does in this analysis. The Quality Variance is $200 unfavorable representing $2.00 per unit invested in 100 defective units.

This analysis also yields a Production Variance based on the difference between the standard cost of good units produced and the scheduled amount of production. The goal in advanced manufacturing environments is to produce exactly what is needed for sales orders (scheduled production). A variance from scheduled production either way is unfavorable because too much production results in unnecessary buildups of inventory while too little results in sales orders not

FIGURE 2
VARIANCES RELATED TO MATERIAL USAGE

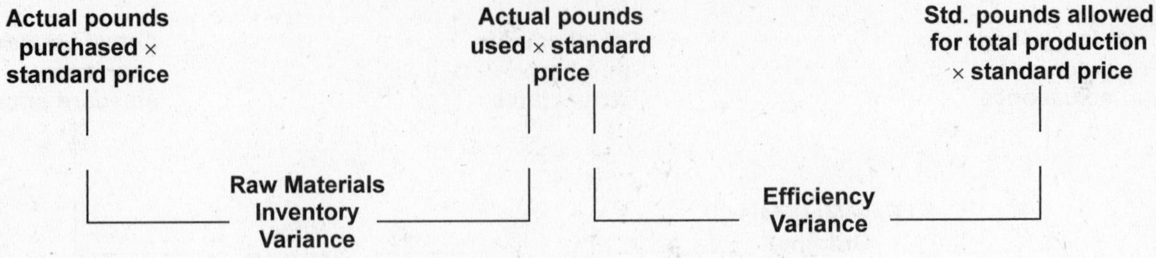

Actual pounds purchased × standard price		Actual pounds used × standard price		Std. pounds allowed for total production × standard price
	Raw Materials Inventory Variance		Efficiency Variance	

FIGURE 3
VARIANCES RELATED TO QUALITY AND PRODUCTION LEVELS

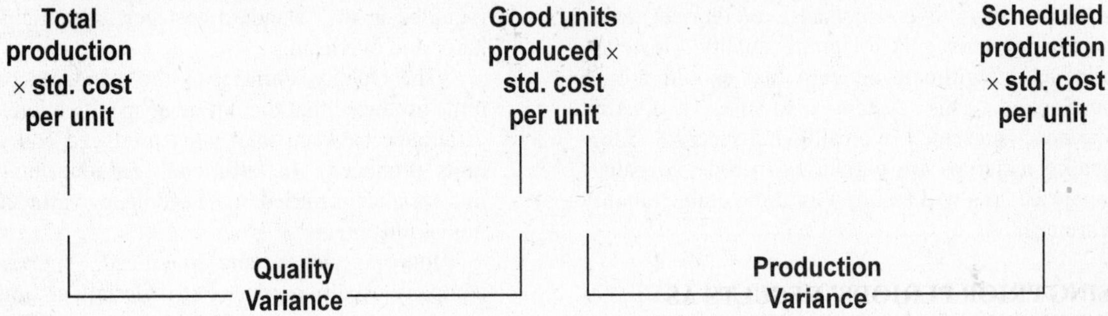

Total production × std. cost per unit		Good units produced × std. cost per unit		Scheduled production × std. cost per unit
	Quality Variance		Production Variance	

filled. As is the case with the Raw Material Inventory variance, the critical factor is the cost of the capital invested in excess inventories. It is desirable to highlight this cost in responsibility reports by applying a cost of capital figure. to the excess (Cheatham 1989).

For simplicity's sake, the above illustrations of input analysis pertain to materials. Labor and volume-related variable overhead can be analyzed in a similar manner. Since there is no difference between labor purchased and labor used in production, the labor input variances would include the traditional Rate Variance and the updated Efficiency Variance.

Other than showing a budget variance for the various elements of fixed overhead, there is no point in further analysis in terms of a Volume Variance. The updated Production Variance serves the same purpose in a far better fashion.

VARIANCES PERTAINING TO SALES ANALYSIS

There are various ways to analyze sales. One method is to use price, mix and volume variances. A further analysis is to break down the volume variance into market size and market share variances. The analysis in **Figure 4** is presented because it articulates well with the output analysis for production.

The sales variances indicate customer service as well as the cost of lost sales. The variances use budgeted contribution margin as a measure of opportunity cost. The Finished Goods Variance indicates the opportunity cost associated with orders completed but not shipped. A delay in shipment causes a loss because of subsequent delay in receiving payment. The Sales Order Variance represents the opportunity cost associated with sales orders that could not be filled during the time period for whatever reason—lack of capacity, scheduling problems, etc.

The above discussion presents a variety of variances that are not used in a traditional standard cost system. The variances can be used for control purposes alone or can be integrated into the financial accounting records (Cheatham and Cheatham 1993).

The system is not intended to be a generic solution for any company's needs. It is intended to demonstrate that, with a little creativity, it is possible to redesign SCSs to measure variables that are important to a particular company in today's manufacturing environment.

FIGURE 4
VARIANCES RELATED TO SALES

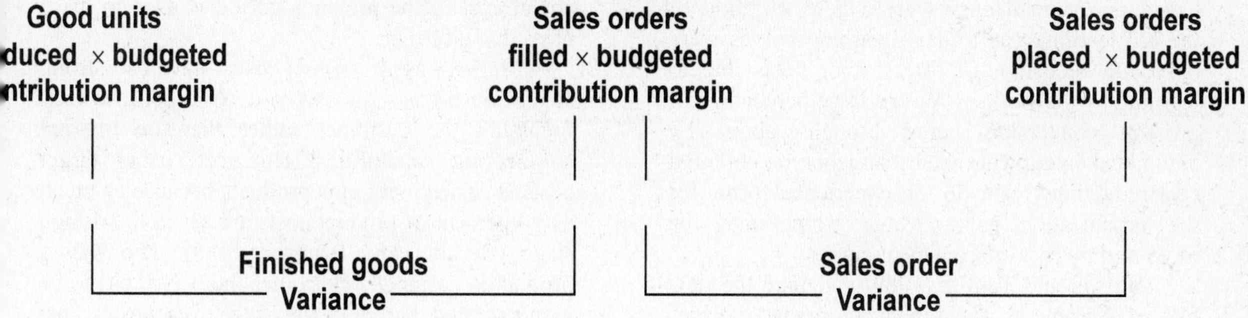

Good units produced × budgeted contribution margin	Sales orders filled × budgeted contribution margin	Sales orders placed × budgeted contribution margin

Finished goods Variance

Sales order Variance

UPDATING THE SCS FOR CONTINUOUS IMPROVEMENT

In a manufacturing environment in which continuous improvement is a goal of most companies, the charge has been made that SCSs do not encourage positive change. However, static standards based on engineering studies or historical data are not an essential part of an SCS. Standards can be adjusted to be dynamic, or changing, by any of several methods.

USING PRIOR PERIODS' RESULTS AS STANDARDS

One way to have dynamic standards is to use last period's results as standards. This idea has been advocated in the past as a way for small business to have the benefits of standards without the expense of engineering studies (Lawler and Livingstone 1986; Cheatham 1987). The objection can be made that last period's results may not make very good standards if last period was unrepresentative for whatever reason. If this is the case, last period's results can be modified.

Another variation on using past performances as standards is the use of a base period. Comparisons can be made with the base period and all subsequent periods, if desired. Boer (1991, 40) describes a system of using a base year as a "pseudo flexible budget" from which unit costs are developed. He comments that the system "encourages continuous improvement and never implies that a level of performance is adequate. Instead, it encourages managers to improve continuously."

Still another variation on using prior periods' results as standards is the use of best performance-to-date (BP). BP is a rigorous standard for self-improvement because it motivates workers as well as managers to exceed all past performance.

USING BENCHMARKING

Although past performance costs may be used in a variety of ways to formulate dynamic standards, any such system has an inward focus. Benchmarking looks outside the firm to the performance of industry leaders or competitors. Benchmarking typically is applied to performance measures rather than standard costs. However, using the performance of industry leaders as a standard provides motivation to become world-class in much the same fashion.

The primary barrier to use of benchmarking standards is, of course, lack of information. Edward S. Finein (1990), former vice president and chief engineer of Xerox, lists the following sources of information when using benchmarking for performance measures: (1) external reports and trade publications; (2) professional associations; (3) market research and surveys; (4) industry experts; (5) consultants' studies; (6) company visits; and (7) competitive labs. In the absence of hard information, an approach may be taken to estimate the performance of industry leaders. Trying to meet the supposed standards of industry leaders (or other competitors) can have results that are useful as long as the company is striving toward beneficial goals.

USING MOVING COSTS REDUCTIONS

Still another way to have dynamic standards is through use of predetermined cost reductions. Horngren et al. (1994) describe a system of what they call a "continuous improvement standard cost" or a "moving cost reduction standard cost." This system reduces the standard cost by a predetermined percentage each time period, such as a one percent reduction in standard cost per month computed by setting the new standard at 99 percent of the previous month's standard.

The question that their system raises is how to

determine the amount of the cost reduction. One possibility is the use of cost improvement curves. Cost improvement curves are a new variation of the old learning curve idea. Learning curves were based on reduction of direct labor costs due to learning by the workers. With a large percentage of product conversion being brought about by automated equipment rather than laborers, potential cost reductions relate to the experience factor for the organization as a whole which may be measured by cost improvement curves.

Pattison and Teplitz (1989) calculate the new rate of learning for an organization that replaces labor with automated equipment as:

$$Rate_{new} = Rate_{old} + (1 - Rate_{old}) \times L \times R$$

where $Rate_{old}$ is the rate of learning for the old system, L is the proportion of learning attributed solely to direct labor stated as a percentage, and R is the proportion of direct labor being replaced. The formula actually reduces the learning rate applicable to labor only, the assumption being that workers can learn but not machinery. An updated version of the formula is needed which encompasses factors such as managers', supervisors' and engineers' experience.

The Japanese stress the formula $2V=2/3C$, or if volume is doubled, the cost should be two-thirds of what it was originally. This formula equates to a 67 percent learning curve which represents a high degree of learning. However, their attitude is that learning does not just happen—it should be made to happen.

USING TARGET COSTS

Another idea borrowed from the Japanese is the use of target costs based on the market. Target costs are used in Japan primarily for new products that are still in the design stage. The idea is to set a cost that is low enough to permit a selling price that is viable on the market. The price is the starting point for calculating costs, and the various costs are backed out from the price. Typically, the target cost is very low. Hiromoto (1988) describes the use of target costs at the Daihatsu Motor Company. First, a product development order is issued. Then an "allowable cost" per car is calculated by taking the difference between the target selling price and the profit margin. Then each department calculates an "accumulated cost" based on the standard cost achievable with current technology. Finally, a target cost is set somewhere between the allowable and accumulated cost. All this takes place before the product is designed. The design stage typically takes three years. When the

product is finally in production, the target cost is gradually tightened on a monthly basis. Later the actual cost of the previous period is used to drive costs down further.

Market-based target costs have a strong appeal on a basis for standard costs because they focus on the customer rather than on internal engineering capabilities. However, using target costs is easiest with new products because as much as 90 percent of product costs are set in the design stage (Berliner and Brimson 1988). The way a product is designed determines the way it has to be manufactured and sets the stage for further cost reductions.

Standard costs do not have to be static. Dynamic standards can be formulated using a variety of methods including past performance, industry leader's performance, or target costs based on predetermined reductions or the market. Market-based target costs have the most intuitive appeal because the focus is on the future and on the customer. However, they may work better for new products rather than for established products.

UPDATING MANAGEMENT RESPONSIBILITY AND REPORTING

Besides revamping the SCS to better reflect today's concerns in terms of variables to be measured and continuous improvement, there needs to be improved reporting of variances. Old reporting systems tended to foster internal competition and arguments about whose department was to blame for unfavorable variances. There needs to be an attitude of cooperation among workers, managers and departments.

Revised lines of responsibility used with new plant layouts are improving some of the competitive attitudes that once prevailed in manufacturing organizations. Plants that used to feature "push through" production with large masses of raw materials and semi-finished product moving from one process to another are changing to work cells or similar arrangements. The work cell arrangement features equipment that can process a product from start to finish. Workers in the work cell typically can operate all or several types of machinery. This leaner "pull through" approach allows a sales order to be rapidly processed within the work cell which decreases cycle time and holds work in process and finished goods inventories to a minimum.

The work cell arrangement allows a team of workers to be responsible for the entire product and reduces the likelihood that defects will be passed along to the next department. Along with the work

FIGURE 5

WORK CELL A

VARIANCE TRADE-OFF REPORT FOR MONTH OF JULY 19X6

Raw Materials:

	Price	Quantity	Total
Material X	100 F	200 U	100 U
Material Y	50 F	100 U	50 U
Material Z	200 F	150 F	350 F
Total	350 F	150 U	200 F

Labor:

	Rate	Efficiency	Total
Type A	400 F	200 F	600 F
Type B	550 U	250 F	300 U
Total	150 U	450 F	300 F

Traceable Overhead Variances:

	Spending	Efficiency	Total
Power	150 F	50 U	100 F
Supplies	100 U	10 U	110 U
Other	50 F	10 F	60 F
Total	100 F	50 U	50 F

Quality Variance on Dept. A Contribution to Product Cost	
100 Defective Units @ $7.00	700 U
Total	150 U

cell arrangement many companies are decentralizing functions such as engineering and making these personnel responsible for a particular work area or product line. With the decentralization, there is more focused responsibility. Decentralization and a team approach to production eliminate many conflicts that once existed.

In addition to the new attitudes about responsibility, there needs to be improved reporting. The variances outlined in this paper can be reported in two types of management reports. The report illustrated in Fig. 5 shows the trade-offs between price, efficiency and quality. This type of report can be done on a plant level or department level as well as a work cell level. The price variance for work cells or departments should be computed on material used rather than purchased because this gives a better picture of the trade-offs involved. Upper-level management reports should probably show both types of price variances if there are significant differences between purchases and use.

The report illustrated in Fig. 6 shows the effects of variances related to inventories. Raw material excesses at cost, related to both current and past purchases, are listed along with the related cost of capital. In this case it is assumed the excess

was held the entire month and the cost of capital was one percent. Work-in-Process excesses are measured in terms of the Production Variance. This variance measures the difference between scheduled and actual production. Presumably if there were excesses from the previous month, there was an adjustment made in the scheduled production. Cost of capital figures show the effect of holding these excess inventories.

In the case of Finished Goods, the crucial factor is the opportunity cost of sales orders not filled measured by the lost contribution margins. Therefore, if orders are completed but not shipped or there is an inability to fill a sales order because of lack of capacity, this is indicated by the Finished Goods Variance or the Sales Order Variance. The illustration assumes a favorable Finished Goods Variance because more sales orders were filled than units produced, indicating a decrease in previous finished goods stock.

Although a reporting system such as that illustrated in **Figures 5** and **6** may not eliminate all conflicts, it is certainly helpful to recognize that trade-offs occur. It is also beneficial for upper-level managers to see the cost of excesses or deficiencies in inventories measured in terms of lost contribution margins and cost of capital.

Cases and Readings

13-17

FIGURE 6
PROFITABLE MANUFACTURING COMPANY
EXCESS INVENTORY REPORT FOR MONTH OF JULY 19X6

	Cost	Cost of Capital
Raw Materials		
Excess from previous month	$5,000	$ 50
Current inventory variance	3,000 F	($ 30)
Total	$2,000	$ 20
Work in Process		
Cell A Production variance	$4,000 U	$ 40
Cell B Production variance	$1,000 U	$ 10
Total	$5,000 U	$ 50
Total Excess and Cost of Capital	$7,000 U	$ 70

Finished Goods:

	Cost	Contribution
Finished goods variance	$ 5,000 F	$(1,500)
Sales order variance	8,000 U	2,400
Total	$ 3,000 U	$ 900

| **Total Cost of Capital and Lost Contribution Margins** | | $ 970 |

STANDARD COST SYSTEMS AND ABC

A final consideration in updating SCSs is how an SCS relates to ABC. Although ABC potentially has broader uses, it primarily has been used for manufacturing overhead.

When a company has a significant amount of indirect product cost, ABC results in better product costing because ABC is superior for allocating these costs among products. This permits company managers to more knowledgeably price products. However, ABC is a cost *accumulation* system rather than a cost *control* system. When used with process value analysis (PVA) or activity based management (ABM), ABC can have a cost *management* feature, but there is no day-to-day monitoring system to assure that costs are within certain parameters.

Most companies can benefit from some combination of ABC and an SCS. One possibility is use of ABC for indirect costs and an updated SCS for direct costs. Another possibility is use of an SCS for financial records and ABC for analysis of indirect costs outside the main record-keeping system. A combination of the two systems retains the advantages of the superior control features of an SCS with the benefits of better overhead analysis from ABC.

CONCLUSION

SCSs are not really the dinosaurs of cost systems, but they may benefit from a little evolution. Updated variances along with dynamic standards will vastly improve the usefulness of most SCSs. ABC can coexist with an SCS and bring some order to the general area of indirect costs. Improvements in the reporting of variances can allow managers to assess trade-offs and inventory stocks and their impact on profits.

REFERENCES

Berliner, C., and J. Brimson, eds. 1988. *Cost Management for Today's Advanced Manufacturing: The CAM-I Conceptual Design*. Boston: Harvard Business School Press.

Boer, G.B. 1991. Making accounting a value-added activity. *Management Accounting*, 73 (August): 36–41.

Cheatham, C. 1987. Profit and productivity analysis revisited. *Journal of Accountancy*, 164 (July): 123–130.

———. 1989. Reporting the effects of excess inventories. *Journal of Accountancy*, 168 (November): 131–140.

———, and L. Cheatham. 1993. *Updating Standard Cost Systems*. Westport, CT: Quorum Books.

Cornick, M., W. Cooper, and S. Wilson. 1988. How do companies analyze overhead? *Management Accounting*, 69 (June): 41–43.

Finein, E.S. 1990. Benchmarking for superior quality and performance. Performance Measurement for Manufacturers Seminar, Institutes for International Research (October).

Goldratt, E.M. 1983. Cost accounting is enemy number one of productivity. International Conference Proceedings, American Production and Inventory Control Society (October).

Harrell, H. 1992. Materials variance analysis and JIT: A new approach. *Management Accounting*, 73 (May): 33–38.

Hiromoto, T. 1988. Another hidden edge—Japanese management accounting. *Harvard Business Review*, 69 (July-August): 22–26.

Horngren, C. et al. 1994. *Cost Accounting: A Managerial Approach*, 8th ed. Englewood Cliffs, NJ: Prentice Hall: 246.

Jayson, S. 1987. Goldratt & Fox: Revolutionizing the factory floor. *Management Accounting* 68 (May): 18–22.

Lawler, W., and J. Livingstone. 1986. Profit and productivity analysis for small business. *Journal of Accountancy*, 163 (December): 190–196.

Noreen, E. 1991. Conditions under which activity-based cost systems provide relevant costs. *Journal of Management Accounting Research*, 3 (Fall): 159–168.

Pattison, D., and C. Teplitz 1989. Are learning curves still relevant? *Management Accounting*, 71 (February): 37–40.

Schiff, J. 1993. ABC on the rise. Cost Management Update Issue No. 24 (February). In *Cost Accounting: A Managerial Emphasis*, 1991, cited by C. Horngren, G. Foster, and S. Datar, 161. Englewood Cliffs, NJ: Prentice Hall, Inc.

13.3: Can Variance Analysis Make Media Marketing Managers More Accountable?

by Ted Mitchell, Ph.D., and Mike Thomas, Ph.D.

Arguments and assumptions made more than 50 years ago essentially established how we calculate cost variances today. It is time to review the accuracy and relevance of our traditional calculations, especially as variance analysis moves into new fields, such as marketing, and new applications, such as using nonfinancial performance measures. Indeed, models appropriate for the paper and pencil world of a hands-on analyst in 1950 may be ready for improvements, especially given the widespread use of computers and database control systems today.

We will demonstrate the errors in the traditional cost variance formulas and propose a new set of equations for calculating variances using the Minimum Potential Performance Budget (MPPB) model. After showing how this new model correctly calculates cost variances in all four economic situations, we will apply it to an advertising campaign using the nonfinancial performance measures of reach and frequency. First, though, we will provide background information on the assumptions and explain why they have been generally accepted.

BACKGROUND

More than 75 years ago, Henry Maynard wrote about variance analysis, "Its essential value lies in the fact that it is a control system."[1] Fifty years ago, detailed discussions arose concerning the algebra, formulas, and calculations to use in practice when evaluating financial performance.[2] In 1997, Josef Kloock and Ulf Schiller revisited some of the criticisms regarding variance analysis when companies used it to help improve decision making and in assigning responsibility for performance evaluations.[3]

Assumptions in Variance Analysis

The basic premise of variance analysis is that larger variances are symptoms of larger control problems.

The accuracy of variance calculations, however, hinges on two basic assumptions.[4] First, small errors due to the allocation of small joint variances should be of little concern, and, second, the conventional two-variance model (a price and quantity variance) provides the correct calculations in most practical cases.

Considering the first assumption, marketing settings are plagued with large joint variances and thus large potential calculation errors not often expected in traditional manufacturing cost applications. As for the second assumption, we will demonstrate that the conventional two-variance analysis (price and quantity) inflates variances in three of the four possible economic situations. We will also show that the normative three variance solution (price, quantity, and joint variances) is equally flawed. The traditional debate about the efficacy of the three-variance solution over the practical simplicity of the two-variance solution is made moot when we realize both are inaccurate.

To provide accurate, unbiased measures of the primary variances (price and quantity), we need a new method. The solution lies in the economic geometry behind variance analysis and is found in the Minimum Potential Performance Budget.

Reasons for the General Acceptance of the Two-Variance Solution

Apparently, two related causes led to the general acceptance of the traditional two-variance algebraic model taught in current management and cost accounting texts as well as in practice. One was the first Industrial Revolution and the Scientific Management strategy that organized work in the new capital-intensive factories. The other was the emphasis on external financial reporting in the United States.

To support the development of large, capital-intensive factories during the first Industrial Revolution, companies needed significant investment capital, so top management desired information about investment efficiency. Because these investments were directed toward converting materials and labor into manufactured products, cost accounting systems evolved to provide detailed information about the manufacturing costs of products.

Due in part to the labor environment (i.e., a force that was not highly educated, that was willing to work for low wages, and that was highly motivated to work), Scientific Management became the dominant strategy for organizing work.

Blocher, Stout, Cokins, Chen: *Cost Management, 4e*

Specifically, a company broke down value chain activities into tasks that were quickly and easily taught (e.g., shoveling coal) and created departments for controlling similar activities (e.g., welding or painting departments).

Through techniques such as time and motion studies, industrial engineers developed the "one best way" to perform each task, with performance standards (standard times and quantities) and measured variances from them logically following. Because each department was a functional silo operating independently from other departments, measuring efficiency through department cost variance reports dominated the cost accounting system (e.g., G.C. Harrison's 1918 set of equations for analyzing cost variances). Using cost variances to evaluate performance and motivate efficiency gains, the cost accounting system became the company's management accounting system.[5] Thus, the algebraic approach to variance analysis became the accepted pedagogy and practice, and its underlying geometric reality disappeared from our texts.

Through the interaction with a related cause (i.e., the U.S. emphasis on external financial reporting), the algebraic approach became entrenched. To raise the financial capital needed during the first Industrial Revolution, investors purchased stock in the manufacturing companies. Especially since the late 1920s and the American stock market crash, the investing public has demanded accountability for management's stewardship role, which came in the form of publicly available financial reports. Certified public accountants ensured report reliability through audits. To ensure that the financial statements were accurate, auditors required report articulation through a transaction-based financial accounting system following generally accepted accounting principles.

The result was the need for a product's "cost" to be verified objectively through a transaction--based journal entry recording system and, therefore, algebraic equations to calculate and journalize resource cost variances. Through journalized cost attaching, financial accountants could provide a fully absorbed product cost within a system that was simple to install and operate and that also was simple to understand.[6] Using the standard cost systems developed with Scientific Management, a simple two-variance solution and journalized cost variances became the accepted model.

To this day, traditional cost variance analysis supports Scientific Management and external financial reporting, reconciling budgeted and actual monthly earnings reports within an articulated set of external financial reports generated by a journal-entry-driven recording system.

The errors that result when standards are "loose" and joint variances are large, though, force a reconsideration of the two and three-variance models. When one reviews the geometry of budgeted and actual costs and their resulting variances, these errors become obvious, as does a new set of calculations solving this problem.

THE GEOMETRY OF VARIANCE ANALYSIS

The logic of variance analysis is to explore the impact from changes in one variable while holding the other variable constant. **Figure 1** illustrates the geometry. To understand the primary variances, imagine a rectangular clay tablet, A, with the length of one side representing the actual price and the length of the other representing the actual quantity. Tablet A's area represents the total actual cost and includes Areas 1 and 3 in **Figure 1**. A second clay tablet, B, represents the total budgeted cost (Areas 1 and 2).

Figure 1: Areas of Primary Variance

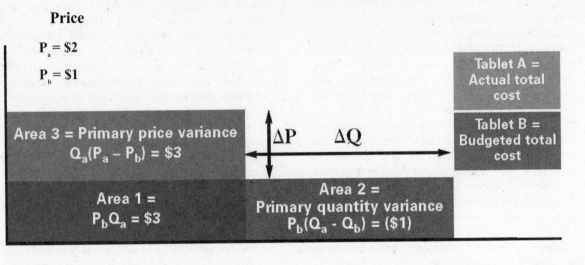

Figure 2: The Geometry of a Joint Variance

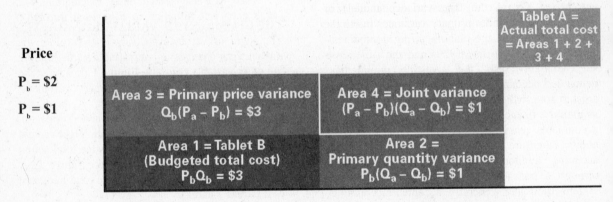

The two tablets overlap (Area 1). Area 2 is the primary quantity variance, and Area 3 is the primary price variance. In Figure 1, there is no residual or joint variance. The difference between the actual cost and the budgeted cost is equal to the sum of the two primary variances.

In Figure 2, actual cost is greater than budgeted cost. Area 1 represents the budgeted cost ($C_b = P_bQ_b$) and is like a tablet resting upon another tablet representing the actual cost. The sum of Areas 1, 2, 3, and 4 represents the actual cost, $C_a = P_aQ_a$. The difference between the two total costs, $C_a - C_b$, is the sum of areas 2, 3, and 4.

Area 2 represents the primary quantity variance, which is the change in cost caused by the change in quantity while holding price constant at $P_b = \$1$. Area 3 represents the primary price variance, which is the change in cost caused by a change in the purchase price when holding quantity constant at $Q_b = 3$.

In both Figures 1 and 2, Area 2 is the same primary quantity variance with the same magnitude, while Area 3 is the same price variance with the same magnitude. There is no difference in absolute values or primary variances. The primary variances provide the same magnitude of symptoms in Figures 1 and 2, and the only difference between the total variances is the joint or residual variance.

Blocher, Stout, Cokins, Chen: *Cost Management, 4e*

There is no joint variance in Figure 1, but, in Figure 2, Area 4 is needed to calculate the difference between actual and budgeted cost. It represents the joint variance and reflects the impact on cost of simultaneous or joint changes in both price and quantity. It is sometimes called the unexplained variance because it cannot be explained solely in terms of changes in a single attribute.

From a managerial point of view, the relative sizes of the primary variances are the diagnostic focus of variance analysis because they identify the impact of one change at a time. Of less interest is the joint or residual variance because it cannot be attributed to the change in a single variable.

The geometry in Figures 1 and 2 provides the basic logic and definitions used in the theory of variance analysis. An important feature of this geometry is that the size of each area remains constant regardless of a change in labels. That is to say, if the budgeted price, Pb, is relabeled to be the actual price, Pa, and vice versa, the size of the primary price variance remains the same, which we will explain later.

It is obvious from Figure 1 that there are situations in which a joint variance should not be calculated (as in the three-variance model) or included in one of the primary variances (as in the two-variance model). But there are some situations, as in Figure 2, in which a joint variance must be calculated when explaining the difference between budgeted and actual cost. Note that the geometrical definitions of the primary variances do not include the joint or residual variance.

ILLUSTRATIONS OF THE FOUR ECONOMIC SITUATIONS

Four situations are possible. **Figures 4** through **7** illustrate each by beginning with the geometric solution followed by a three-variance solution, then the two-variance solution used in practice and taught in all texts. To solve the calculation errors the two and three-variance models create, we propose a new set of variance calculations, the Minimum Potential Performance Budget model. These calculations mimic the geometry of each economic situation (labeled as Cases 1 through 4 in **Figures 4** through **7**). To calculate the primary variances correctly, the multiplier in each primary variance formula must be the minimum value for the other variable. The formulas for each variance are as follows:

$$\text{Price variance: } Q_{min}(P_a - P_b)$$
$$\text{Quantity variance: } P_{min}(Q_a - Q_b)$$

$$\text{Residual variance:}$$
$$(C_a - C_b) - [Q_{min}(P_a - P_b)] - [P_{min}(Q_a - Q_b)]$$

We will also present these calculations with each economic situation in **Figures 4** through **7**. **Figure 3** summarizes the four economic situations and the errors resulting from the three and two-variance models. Each of the incorrectly calculated variances in **Figures 4** through **7** appears in bold, and an * follows them.

Figure 3: Algebraic Variance Models' Errors

	$P_a > P_b$	$P_a < P_b$
$Q_a > Q_b$	**CASE 1** 3-variance model: None 2-variance model: Price variance	**CASE 3** 3-variance model: Quantity & Joint 2-variance model: Price & Quantity
$Q_a < Q_b$	**CASE 2** 3-variance model: Price & Joint 2-variance model: None	**CASE 4** 3-variance model: Price, Quantity, & Joint 2-variance model: Quantity

Figure 4: Case 1
$P_a > P_b$ and $Q_a > Q_b$

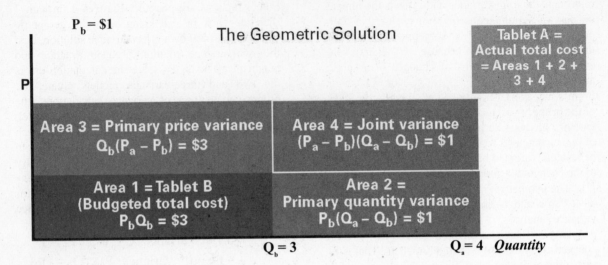

The Geometric Solution

$P_b = \$1$

P

Tablet A = Actual total cost = Areas 1 + 2 + 3 + 4

Area 3 = Primary price variance
$Q_b(P_a - P_b) = \$3$

Area 4 = Joint variance
$(P_a - P_b)(Q_a - Q_b) = \$1$

Area 1 = Tablet B
(Budgeted total cost)
$P_bQ_b = \$3$

Area 2 =
Primary quantity variance
$P_b(Q_a - Q_b) = \$1$

$Q_b = 3$ $Q_a = 4$ *Quantity*

The Three-Variance Solution

Price variance: $Q_b(P_a - P_b) = 3(\$2 - \$1) = \$3$
Quantity variance: $P_b(Q_a - Q_b) = \$1(4 - 3) = \$1$
Residual variance: $(Q_a - Q_b)(P_a - P_b) = (4 - 3)(\$2 - \$1) = \$1$

The Two-Variance Solution

Price variance: $Q_a(P_a - P_b) = 4(\$2 - \$1) = \$4*$
Quantity variance: $P_b(Q_a - Q_b) = \$1(4 - 3) = \$1$

The Minimum Potential Performance Budget Solution

Price variance: $Q_{min}(P_a - P_b) = 3(\$2 - \$1) = \$3$
Quantity variance: $P_{min}(Q_a - Q_b) = \$1(4 - 3) = \$1$
Residual variance: $(C_a - C_b) - [Q_{min}(P_a - P_b)] - [P_{min}(Q_a - Q_b)] = \$1$

THE NEED FOR A NEW VARIANCE MODEL

In all four cases, the traditional equations ensure that the sum of the individual variances equals the total variance, but a correct sum is not sufficient for an accurate solution. To provide a correct solution, the primary price and quantity variances must equal the absolute values found in the geometry of the situation.

Because the numbers are the same in all four cases, the sizes of the primary variances represented by Areas 2 and 3 remain constant. Only the labels of actual and budget change from case to case. That is to say, the absolute size of the two primary variances must remain $1 and $3, respectively, if a solution is to be correct.

Blocher, Stout, Cokins, Chen: *Cost Management, 4e*

Figure 5: Case 2: $P_a > P_b$ and $Q_b > Q_a$

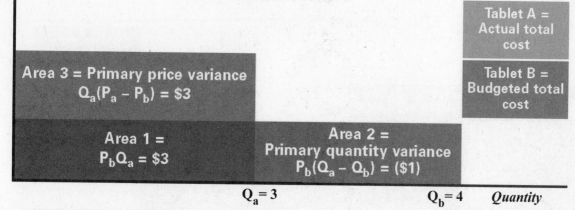

The Geometric Solution

Area 3 = Primary price variance
$Q_a(P_a - P_b) = \$3$

Area 1 =
$P_bQ_a = \$3$

Area 2 =
Primary quantity variance
$P_b(Q_a - Q_b) = (\$1)$

Tablet A =
Actual total cost

Tablet B =
Budgeted total cost

$Q_a = 3$ $Q_b = 4$ *Quantity*

The Three-Variance Solution
Price variance: $Q_b(P_a - P_b) = 4(\$2 - \$1) = \$4*$
Quantity variance: $P_b(Q_a - Q_b) = \$1(3 - 4) = (\$1)$
Residual variance: $(Q_a - Q_b)(P_a - P_b) = (3 - 4)(\$2 - \$1) = (\$1)*$

The Two-Variance Solution
Price variance: $Q_a(P_a - P_b) = 3(\$2 - \$1) = \$3$
Quantity variance: $P_b(Q_a - Q_b) = \$1(3 - 4) = (\$1)$

The Minimum Potential Performance Budget Solution
Price variance: $Q_{min}(P_a - P_b) = 3(\$2 - \$1) = \$3$
Quantity variance: $P_{min}(Q_a - Q_b) = \$1(3 - 4) = (\$1)$
Residual variance: $(C_a - C_b) - [Q_{min}(P_a - P_b)] - [P_{min}(Q_a - Q_b)] = \$0$

Errors Resulting from the Two and Three Variance Models

The three-variance solution inflates at least one of the primary variances in three of the four cases. Case 1 is the only case in which the three variance model provides a correct solution. Case 2 inflates the price variance, Case 3 inflates the quantity variance, and Case 4 inflates both primary variances. The geometry demonstrates that the source of the inflated variances is the inclusion of the joint variance. The three-variance model always generates a joint variance, and, in Cases 2 and 3, must be considered wrong because there is not joint variance (Area 4).

The two-variance solution arbitrarily allocates the joint variance to the primary price variance, which has no theoretical justification.[7] Only in Case 2 does this model provide the correct values found in the geometry of the situation.

Applications in Non-production Environments
If variance analysis is to be widely adopted outside the world of production control and cost accounting, we need a new procedure for calculating unbiased variances. In marketing environments, the standards and forecasts in budgets are not as tight as in production, so the inaccurate standards imply large variances. Large variances imply large joint variances, and large joint variances imply large potential errors due to inflated variances.

When the traditional two-and three-variance models inflate variances in three of four situations, the traditional assumption of small joint variances is crucial. In marketing control we cannot assume the forecasts and standards will be current and the variances will be small.[8] If the standards are not accurate and the variances are large, then Robert Watson's warnings of a potential for biased measurements and distorted decision-making must be taken seriously.[9]

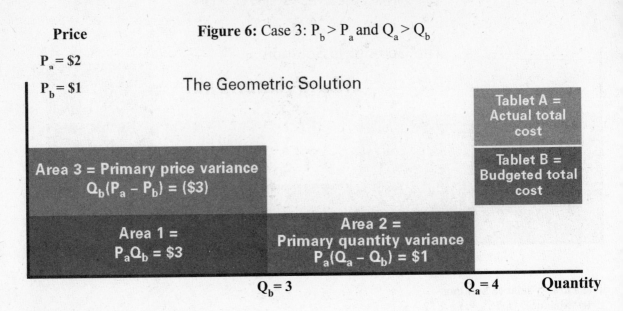

Figure 6: Case 3: $P_b > P_a$ and $Q_a > Q_b$

Price

$P_a = \$2$

$P_b = \$1$

The Geometric Solution

Tablet A = Actual total cost

Tablet B = Budgeted total cost

Area 3 = Primary price variance
$Q_b(P_a - P_b) = (\$3)$

Area 1 = $P_aQ_b = \$3$

Area 2 = Primary quantity variance
$P_a(Q_a - Q_b) = \$1$

$Q_b = 3$ $Q_a = 4$ Quantity

The Three-Variance Solution
Price variance: $Q_b(P_a - P_b) = 3(\$1 - \$2) = (\$3)$
Quantity variance: $P_b(Q_a - Q_b) = \$2(4 - 3) = \mathbf{\$2^*}$
Residual variance: $(Q_a - Q_b)(P_a - P_b) = (4 - 3)(\$1 - \$2) = \mathbf{(\$1)^*}$

The Two-Variance Solution
Price variance: $Q_a(P_a - P_b) = 4(\$1 - \$2) = \mathbf{(\$4)^*}$
Quantity variance: $P_b(Q_a - Q_b) = \$2(4 - 3) = \mathbf{\$2^*}$

The Minimum Potential Performance Budget Solution
Price variance: $Q_{min}(P_a - P_b) = 3(\$1 - \$2) = (\$3)$
Quantity variance: $P_{min}(Q_a - Q_b) = \$1(4 - 3) = \$1$
Residual variance: $(C_a - C_b) - [Q_{min}(P_a - P_b)] - [P_{min}(Q_a - Q_b)] = \$0$

The goal of variance analysis should be to calculate the primary variances in a way that ensures excluding the joint variance when it exists. This means the new focal point should be on the minimum potential performance level, $P_{min}Q_{min}$ (Area 1), which the following marketing example illustrates.

EVALUATING MEDIA MANAGERS USING THE MPPB MODEL

This example presents a new model of variance analysis designed to produce accurate measures of deviation impacts to control advertising plans. In the field of media planning, the term variance means the magnitude of impact on an overall advertising goal due to a change in advertising activities.

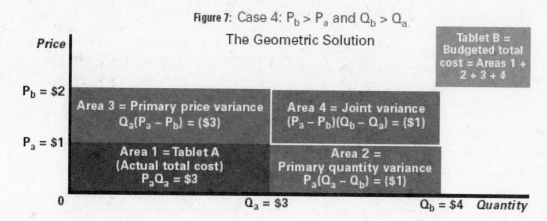

Figure 7: Case 4: $P_b > P_a$ and $Q_b > Q_a$
The Geometric Solution

The Three-Variance Solution

Price variance: $Q_b(P_a - P_b) = 4(\$1 - \$2) = (\$4)*$
Quantity variance: $P_b(Q_a - Qb) = \$2(3 - 4) = (\$2)*$
Residual variance: $(Q_a - Qb)(P_a - P_b) = (3 - 4)(\$1 - \$2) = \$1*$

The Two-Variance Solution

Price variance: $Q_a(P_a - P_b) = 3(\$1 - \$2) = (\$3)$
Quantity variance: $P_b(Q_a - Q_b) = \$2(3 - 4) = (\$2)*$

The Minimum Potential Performance Budget Solution

Price variance: $Q_{min}(P_a - P_b) = 3(\$1 - \$2) = (\$3)$
Quantity variance: $P_{min}(Q_a - Q_b) = \$1(3 - 4) = (\$1)$
Residual variance: $(C_a - C_b) - [Q_{min}(P_a - P_b)] - [P_{min}(Q_a - Q_b)] = (\$1)$

The new MPPB model we propose applies to two-variant planning models used in advertising. That is, if we express overall advertising performance, Z, as the product of two advertising activities, X and Y, then the impacts on the overall goal due to the deviations in each activity (X or Y) can be isolated, measured, and compared. In more formal terms:

Equation #1: $Z_a - Z_b = X_a Y_a - X_b Y_b = X_m (Y_a - Y_b) + Y_m (X_a - X_b) + r$

where: $Z_a - Z_b$ = the difference between the performance goal and the actual results, and

Equation #2: $X_m (Y_a - Y_b) = Y$ variance or the impact due to the deviation in activity Y,

Equation #3: $Y_m (X_a - X_b) = X$ variance or the impact due to the deviation in activity X,

Equation #4: $r = Z_a - Z_b - X_m (Y_a - Y_b) - Y_m (X_a - X_b) =$ joint variance or residual impact due to the simultaneous deviations in X and Y

(Subscripts: **a** = actual result, **b** = planned result, **m** = the minimum of a or b).

To evaluate media advertising campaigns, most companies use gross rating points (GRP), which media planners calculate by multiplying frequency by reach. For example, an advertising plan could call for 240 gross rating points by achieving a frequency of four exposures per household and reaching 60% of households. At the end of the campaign, the media planning results show advertising frequency has deviated from plan by 25% and the reach by 30%. The actual reach was 78%, and the actual exposure frequency was three, which resulted in a total of 234 gross rating points.

Table 1 summarizes this performance.

Table 1: Deviations in Advertising Plan

	Actual Results	Budgeted Values	Deviations from Plan
Gross rating points	Ga = 234	Gb = 240	– 6 GRP
Frequency = number of exposures per household (F)	Fa = Fm = 3*	Fb = 4	- 1 exposure per household (25%)
Reach = percentage of households reached (R)	Ra = 78	Rb = Rm = 60*	+18 (30%)
* Minimum level of each activity is labeled with subscript m			

Which of the two deviations from plan is having the greatest impact on the change in advertising performance? Observation leads us to believe it is reach because its variance is 30% compared to the frequency variance of only 25%. This is incorrect. The deviation from the planned frequency is the correct answer because it has the largest impact on the overall GRP performance (60 GRP, shown in **Table 2**). Using the MPPB model, the media planner can accurately identify which of the two deviations in the advertising plan is having the greater impact on GRP, as **Table 2** shows.

Because variance analysis is an alien concept to most media planners, they rely on experience and judgment in determining what to focus on to improve performance. Media planners have not had a model of variance analysis that is accurate enough to test their judgments across the full range of possible media situations. The full range of situations includes differences that can exceed or be short of budget for either reach or frequency.

Table 2: Variance Report—Reach and Frequency

Actual GRPs	234
Planned GRPs	240
Change in GRPs to be explained by deviations in reach and frequency activities	(6)
Impact on GRP due to the 30% increase in reach: $Fm (Ra – Rb) = 3(78 – 60)$	54
Impact on GRP due to the 25% decrease in frequency: $Rm (Fa – Fb) = 60(3 – 4)$	(60)
Residual impact on GRP due to the simultaneous changes in reach and frequency (r)	0

Thus, each media situation is analogous to the four economic situations (Cases 1 through 4 in Figures 4 through 7). In the Table 2 situation, the report conveys to the media planner that the 25% decrease in frequency lowered overall performance by 60 gross rating points. The 30% improvement in the number of households reached increased overall performance by 54 gross rating points. The net effect of the two deviations was a decrease of six gross rating points. On the basis of the variance report, the media planner now knows to focus on finding the cause behind the decrease in the frequency of exposures per household rather than the reasons behind the increase in households reached. If the media planner can increase frequency while maintaining the current reach, overall gross rating points will increase more than with the converse strategy.

PROS AND CONS

Accountants identified the miscalculations resulting from the two and three-variance models many years ago, but they dismissed the potential inaccuracies due to residual variances as offering "no reason for undue concern."[10] In more recent years, these models have been criticized for creating information that leads to inappropriate performance evaluations.[11] The alternative MPPB proposed here is based on the geometry of the four possible economic situations when comparing budgeted and actual results, so it does not produce primary variance errors. Here are some advantages and disadvantages of the MPPB solution.

Blocher, Stout, Cokins, Chen: *Cost Management, 4e*

Advantages

1. It is easier to apply in non-production environments where outcomes are not measured in terms of price and quantities.
2. The procedure produces unbiased measurements of the primary variances. That is, the measurement of the impact due solely to changes in the primary variables is isolated from the impact of the joint movement in several variables. The conventional two-variance solution adds the joint variance to the price variance.
3. It can be applied to a wider range of situations than the conventional flexible budget procedure. For example, it can produce accurate measures in situations with inaccurate forecasts and large variances. Conventional analysis assumes that standards are current and variances are small.
4. The residual joint variances that are unexplained by the changes in the individual variances are reported separately.
5. The proposed procedure eliminates the difficulty of explaining the arbitrary assignment of joint variances to the responsible managers. The conventional system results in the arbitrary allocation of joint variances to one manager or another, and this is perceived as an unfair practice.

Disadvantages

1. The concept of a minimum potential performance budget, $P_{min}Q_{min}$, is more abstract than the concept of the flexible budget, P_bQ_a. The minimum potential performance budget is not a rigid standard but varies with forecasts and performances.
2. The residual variance adds to the variance report's complexity but provides no managerial insights for control. There is very little managerial interpretation that can be given to the size of the residual variance caused by the joint changes in variables.
3. From a pedagogical point of view, the proposed solution makes it almost impossible to teach variance analysis using the traditional columnar format. The ability to assign a constant amount, such as the flexible-budget value, is lost for all four cases. The conventional columnar system based on flexible budgeting is simpler, but, in new fields of application, accuracy is more important than simplicity. If the proposed MPPB model is adopted for

textbooks, authors will have to rely on algebraic and geometric presentations.

ISSUES TO DISCUSS

1. While the concept of a minimum level of potential performance (Area 1) makes sense in marketing applications, does it make sense in production applications?
2. Are joint variances taught in cost accounting courses? If not, why not? Are they somehow not important in production applications but important in marketing applications?
3. If the MPPB model is rejected in favor of either the traditional two or three-variance model, how can we refine them so that they produce accurate performance evaluation measures?
4. If the two-variance model is to be applied in situations using nonfinancial performance measures, which measure should be held constant at its actual value, and which measure should be held constant at its budgeted value?

We presented the inaccuracies in current variance models. Both the two and three-variance models produce incorrect variances in three of the four possible economic situations that can result from comparing budgeted and actual performance. The correct analysis for each situation is demonstrated geometrically along with the MPPB equations derived from it.

Current cost accounting pedagogy and practice ignore the joint variance, which results in its inclusion in the price variance. Theoretical problems identified a half century ago are now resurfacing as real practical problems in performance evaluations. When applied outside cost accounting environments, such as in marketing, the need to calculate unbiased measures of the primary variances and isolate the joint variance are even more important. We hope the proposed MPPB model can be easily adapted to situations in which unbiased measures are needed, such as in nonfinancial marketing performance evaluations.

Ted Mitchell is a marketing professor at the University of Nevada, Reno. Ted's expertise is in marketing management. He can be reached at mitchjt@unr.nevada.edu.

Mike Thomas is a professor at Humboldt State University. His expertise is in management and cost accounting systems. Mike can be reached at mft5@humboldt.edu.

ENDNOTES

[1] Henry Maynard, "The Accounting Technique for Standard Costs," *NACA Bulletin*, February 1927, p. 562.

[2] L. L. Vance, "The Fundamental Logic of Primary Variance Analysis," *NACA Bulletin*, January 1950, p. 627; Gilbert Amerman, "The Mathematics of Variance Analysis," *The Accounting Review*, July 1953, pp. 258-269; K.C. Banerjee, "The Mathematics of Variance Analysis and the Possibilities of its Application," *The Accounting Review*, October 1953, pp. 351-363; R. H. Watson, "Two-Variate Analysis," *The Accounting Review*, January 1960, pp. 9699; C. Weber, "The Mathematics of Variance Analysis," *The Accounting Review*, July 1963, pp. 534-539.

[3] J. Kloock and U. Schiller, "Marginal Costing: Cost Budgeting and Cost Variance Analysis," *Management Accounting Research*, September 1997, pp. 299-323.

[4] Amerman, op. cit.

[5] H. T. Johnson and R. S. Kaplan, *Relevance Lost: The Rise and Fall of Management Accounting*, Harvard Business School Press, Boston, Mass., 1987.

[6] Ibid.

[7] Kloock and Schiller.

[8] J. M. Hulbert and N. E. Toy, "A Strategic Framework for Marketing Control," *Journal of Marketing*, April 1977, pp. 12-20; M. M. Weber, "A Framework for Analyzing Sources of Variance in the Supplier Buyer Relationship: Determining the Contribution of Buyer Planning and Supplier Performance to Total Variance," *Journal of Marketing Theory & Practice*, Spring 1996, pp. 61-71; D. R. Lehman, "What's On Marketers' Minds?" *Marketing Management*, November/December 2002, pp. 17-20; T. Mitchell and H. Olsen, "Marketing Control: Exogenous Aspects of Price Variance," *Journal of Business & Economics Research*, December 2003.

[9] Watson.

[10] Amerman, p. 266.

[11] W. F. Bentz and R. F. Lusch, "Now You Can Control Your Product's Market Performance," *Management Accounting*, January 1980, pp. 1725; Kloock and Schiller

Blocher, Stout, Cokins, Chen: *Cost Management, 4e*

Chapter 14
The Flexible Budget: Factory Overhead

Cases

14-1 **Berkshire Toy Company** (*Source*: Dean Crawford and Eleanor G. Henry, "Budgeting and Performance Evaluation at the Berkshire Toy Company," *Issues in Accounting Education,* 15 (2) (May 2000), pp. 283-309.)

14-2 **The Mesa Corporation** (*Source*: Robert Capettini, C. W. Chow, and J. E. Williamson, "Instructional case: the Proper Use of Feedback Information," *Issues in Accounting Education,* 7 (1) (Spring 1992) pp. 48-56.)

Readings

14-1: "Using Enhanced Cost Models in Variance Analysis for Better Control and Decision Making," by Kennard T. Wing, *Management Accounting Quarterly* (Winter 2000), pp. 1-9.

This article points out that oversimplifications of fixed and variable costs can result in the standard costing system not being used or, if used, can lead to bad decisions. That is, misclassifications of cost behavior patterns make variance analyses "paper tigers." For variance reporting to be useful, financial managers need to develop cost models that reflect how costs actually behave.

Discussion Questions:
1. Describe the implications for variance analysis of analyzing a semi-variable cost as either a variable or fixed cost.
2. Describe the implications for variance analysis of analyzing a step-fixed cost as either a variable or fixed cost.
3. Describe the implications on operating decisions of analyzing an operation with mixed costs as either a variable or fixed cost.

14-2: "Variance Analysis Refines Overhead Cost Control," by J. C. Cooper and J. D. Suver, *Healthcare Financial Management* (February 1992).

This article attempts to analyze the full costs of selected medical procedures using examples from a healthcare organization. A key feature of the analysis is how the overhead variances are handled, and in particular how to develop an understanding of the volume variance and how it affects profitability. Standard costs are determined for a hypothetical "Procedure 101" and there is an illustration of how variances can be obtained and interpreted, given example actual results for the procedure over a year's time. The analysis shows the effect of volume changes on overhead recovery and on profit contribution.

Discussion Questions:
1. Based on the analysis in this article, what is the key driver of profitability in the discussion example?

2. Explain how the two variances included in **Exhibit 3** are developed and interpreted.
3. Consider the example in **Exhibit 4**. Why are expenses improperly matched and reported income overstated?

14-3: "Overhead Control Implications of Activity Costing," by Robert E. Malcom, *Accounting Horizons* (December 1991), pp. 69-78.

This articles shows limitations of the traditional treatment of standard cost overhead variances. Using a problem from a CMA exam the authors solved the problem both in a traditional format and again using ABC drivers. Regression is used to identify the cost drivers, and a revised solution is derived.

Discussion Questions:
1. What are the limitations of traditional standard cost overhead analysis?
2. How does the activity approach improve upon the traditional analysis of overhead cost variances?

14-1: Berkshire Toy Company[1]

Janet McKinley is employed by the Quality Products Corporation, a publicly traded conglomerate. The corporation manufactures and sells many different kinds of products, including luggage, music synthesizers, breakfast cereals, peanut butter, and children's toys. McKinley is Vice President in charge of the Berkshire Toy Company, a division of Quality Products.

It is late July 2002 and McKinley has just received the preliminary income statement for her division for the year ended June 30, 2002 (see **Table 1**). The master (static) budget and master budget variances for the same period are included for comparison purposes. McKinley looks at the bottom line, a loss approaching a million dollars, then picks up the phone to call you. You are an accountant in the controller's office at the headquarters of Quality Products Corporation. You worked with McKinley when her company was acquired by Quality Products, and now she has called you for advice.

"I know the bottom line looks pretty bad," she says. "But we made great strides this year. Sales are higher than ever. Customers love our product and respect our quality. There must be a way to make this business work and turn a profit, too. The budget variances should provide some insights. Could you do an analysis of the budget variances?"

BACKGROUND

The Berkshire Toy Company was founded by Franklin Berkshire, Janet McKinley's father, in 1974. Berkshire was an industrial artist who enjoyed making stuffed animals in his spare time. His first creation, a teddy bear that he presented to Janet on her seventh birthday, occupies a place of honor at Berkshire Toy Company's headquarters. In 1974, Frank Berkshire acquired an old pneumatic pump that had been used to fill life-jackets for the Navy during World War II. He modified the machine to mass produce stuffed animals, and the Berkshire Toy Company was born.

The company started small at first, but grew quickly as Berkshire's reputation for quality spread. By 1986, annual sales exceeded a million dollars for the first time. Janet McKinley had learned the business from the bottom up. She had started out with the company in the mailroom as a part-time summer employee. As a college student, she had spent summers and Christmas vacations working on the production floor, in the sales department, and finally in the accounting department. She was named Assistant to the President in 1988 after receiving her M.B.A.

In 1991, at her urging, the company launched an initial public offering (IPO) of common stock and became publicly traded on the NASDAQ. Janet McKinley became CEO of the company on July 1, 1993 when her father retired. On March 17, 1995, Berkshire Toys was acquired by the Quality Products Corporation in a friendly exchange of common stock valued at $23.2 million.[2] The terms of the acquisition included an agreement to employ McKinley for no fewer than five years at an annual salary of $120,000.

The Berkshire Toy Company produces the Berkshire Bear, a fifteen-inch teddy bear enjoyed by children and adult toy collectors around the world. The company touts the handcrafted features of the bear and advertises its product as the only teddy bear made in America. The bears are fully jointed, constructed of washable acrylic pile fabric, and stuffed with a polyester fiber filling. The toys are dressed in various accessories, such as bow ties, sports jerseys, or character and occupational costumes. Thus, the product can be personalized for numerous occasions. The Berkshire Bear is sold with an unconditional lifetime guarantee. In communicating with customers, the company refers to its repair center as the "bear hospital." A damaged bear may be returned by

---

[1] This case is based on field research at an existing toy company. The essential facts relating to production and sales have been retained. However, all names, dates, actual events, and identifying details have been concealed to protect the privacy and identity of the company. Thus, if any names used in this case are those of actual firms or individuals, then it is purely coincidental.

[2] In a friendly acquisition, the terms of the exchange are negotiated by the acquiring company and the incumbent management of the target (acquired) firm. This method of merging two companies is quite different from a "hostile takeover," which is initiated by the acquiring company over the objections of the target's incumbent management.

the customer and repaired (or replaced, at the company's discretion) free of charge.

The Berkshire Toy Company's 241 employees are organized into three departments: purchasing, production, and marketing. The purchasing department consists of David Hall, the purchasing manager, and a staff of ten. The department is responsible for acquiring and maintaining the supply of production materials. Bill Wilford manages 174 employees in the production department, where the manufacture and assembly of the product takes place. The marketing department is headed by Rita Smith. She is responsible for all aspects of marketing and she supervises the nine sales clerks and 42 sales representatives that make up Berkshire's sales force. The remaining three employees are McKinley, her secretary, and her secretary's assistant.

TABLE 1

Berkshire Toy Company
A Division of Quality Products Corporation

Preliminary Statement of Divisional Operating Income
for the Year Ended June 30, 2002

	Actual	Master (Static) Budget	Master-Budget Variance	
Units sold	325,556	280,000	45,556	F
Retail and catalog (174,965 units)	$8,573,285	$11,662,000	$3,088,715	U
Internet (105,429 units)	4,428,018	0	4,428,018	F
Wholesale (45,162 units)	1,445,184	1,344,000	101,184	F
Total revenue	14,446,487	13,006,000	1,440,487	F
Variable production costs:				
Direct materials				
Acrylic pile fabric	256,422	233,324	23,098	U
10-mm acrylic eyes	125,637	106,400	19,237	U
45-mm plastic joints	246,002	196,000	50,002	U
Polyester fiber filling	450,856	365,400	85,456	U
Woven label	16,422	14,000	2,422	U
Designer Box	69,488	67,200	2,288	U
Accessories	66,013	33,600	32,413	U
Total direct materials	1,230,840	1,015,924	214,916	U
Direct labor	3,668,305	2,688,000	980,305	U
Variable overhead	1,725,665	1,046,304	679,361	U
Total variable production costs	6,624,810	4,750,228	1,874,582	U
Variable selling expenses	1,859,594	1,218,280	641,314	U
Total variable expenses	8,484,404	5,968,508	2,515,896	U
Contribution margin	5,962,083	7,037,492	1,075,409	U
Fixed costs:				
Manufacturing overhead	658,897	661,920	3,023	F
Selling expenses	5,023,192	4,463,000	560,192	U
Administrative expenses	1,123,739	1,124,000	261	F
Total fixed costs	6,805,828	6,248,920	556,908	U
Operating income[a]	$(843,745)	$788,572	$1,632,317	U

[a] The actual operating income reported in **Table 1** is a preliminary figure that has not been adjusted for fiscal 1998 bonuses, if any.

Blocher, Stout, Cokins, Chen: *Cost Management, 4e*

©The McGraw-Hill Companies, Inc 2008

Production

Production begins with a large press that cuts the acrylic pile fabric into the required pattern pieces. The press-cutter machine applies 23,000 pounds per square inch of pressure to a tray of pattern stainless steel dies[3] that are stamped into the fabric. The bolts[4] of fabric are rolled out and layered on the cutting table. The fabric is measured at this time for length and width and inspected for fabric flaws, tears, and soiled areas. Fabric flaws create waste. Shortages in length or width may require a different cutting set-up and increase fabric waste. Additional cutting set-ups increase production time. The press-cutter machine cuts 14 layered bolts at a time, enough for 588 units. The machine produces a clean, crisp, cut edge that will not fray or ravel.

The fabric is also inspected for trueness of color. The Berkshire Bear is advertised as a honey bear. Thus, fabric dye lots are important for matching shades of brown. The toy animal is available also in off-white and dark brown. Off-color fabric must be scrapped or returned to the supplier. Because the toy is designed to be washable, the fabric must be colorfast. Berkshire obtains the most economical price for specified colors by timing its fabric orders with the production runs of its suppliers. Rush orders almost always increase substantially the price of the required fabric.

In the next stage of production, operators of industrial sewing machines construct the six parts of the finished unit: two arms, two legs, the head, and the torso. Each piece is sewn inside-out and then turned right-side-out for assembly. Sewing is the most labor-intensive phase of the production process. Any additional sewing steps, such as appliqués[5] or monograms, require additional production time.

In the next step, two optical-grade, acrylic eyes are attached to the head with plastic rivets. If the rivet posts are too short, the eyes may fall off later. If the rivet posts are too long, the eyes will stand out from the head, giving a nonstandard appearance. Eye color is also somewhat important. Acrylic eyes are purchased from vendors in "dark brown," but the exact shade may vary from supplier to supplier. Defects are not discovered until the eyes are used in production. At that point, defective eyes are discarded and replaced with ones that meet specifications.

After the cut pieces have been sewn together and eyes attached, the company's unique pneumatic stuffing machine[6] is used to blow the polyester fiber filling into the unassembled parts. Except for two replacements of the electric motor and a new power cord, this is the same machine that Franklin Berkshire acquired from Navy surplus in 1974. Bags of filling are loaded into the machine hopper and mechanically fluffed to the proper loft.[7] An operator places the empty arm, leg, body, or head over a stationary nozzle and uses a foot pedal to control the flow of filling. The machine operator judges whether the part has been filled correctly. Too little filling affects the firmness of the bear; too much filling is unnecessary and expensive. Inferior grade fiber filling is less expensive but can cause clumping and clogging in the hopper. When this happens, production is interrupted and the operator must unclog the vacuum hose and reset the machine.

Next, the arms, legs, and head are attached to the torso using three-part, snap-on, hard plastic disc joints. The disc joints allow the head and limbs to rotate and eliminate the need for sewn attachment. The plastic joints are designed to be foolproof in production and dependable for the life of the product. However, the joints cannot be removed without destroying them. Occasionally, after initial joint insertion, the parts do not fit together properly and they must be removed and replaced.

At the end of the construction process, a woven satin label that states "Made in America by the Berkshire Toy Company" is attached to the back of each bear. More polyester filling is stuffed into the torso and the back seam is hand-stitched, using essentially the same "shoelace" procedure practiced by surgeons. Each seam is brushed by hand to give the bear a seamless look.

The production process is a continuous source of airborne polyester and acrylic fibers that must be controlled, both to protect the health and safety of the employees and to safeguard the production equipment. The company has taken several steps to control the fibers. First, an air filtration system works constantly to

---

[3] Dies are heavy-duty, three-dimensional patterns used to cut the fabric into parts for the bear. Dies function in a manner similar to cookie cutters.

[4] Fabric is shipped from the manufacturer wrapped around a cylindrical core or "bolt." A standard bolt of fabric is ten yards long and 72 inches wide.

[5] Appliqués are descriptive or ornamental features made from contrasting materials that are applied to the outside surface of the bear. The alligator emblem used by Izod on sweaters and polo shirts is a common example of an appliqué. Another example is an identifying patch applied to pockets of uniforms bearing the employer's name and logo.

[6] Berkshire Toy Company adapted technology used by the Navy. The stuffing machine is not patented.

[7] Fiber filling is a loose material. Two pounds of bagged filling occupy approximately one cubic foot of space. The filling is loaded manually into a metal bin or "hopper." Rotating sets of fork-like tines separate the strands of filling and increase the volume by incorporating air. The proper mixture of air and filling is the "loft."

remove dust and fibers from the factory. Second, production employees wear dust masks while they are working with fabric or filling. Finally, regular cleaning and maintenance of the sewing, cutting, and stuffing machines is performed to prevent the fibers from building up.

Maintenance is especially important for the sewing machines. Machine oil and static electricity attract pile fabric lint. Lint buildup can cause lines of stitches that are uneven and seams that do not hold. The Berkshire Bear workmanship is guaranteed for life. Burst seams require rework during the production phase and during the lifetime of the product.

All production employees are paid a regular wage for a 40-hour work week. They receive their regular wage plus an overtime premium of one-half the regular wage rate for overtime. The cost of fringe benefits and employer taxes, such as social security, health insurance, and vacation time, adds 20.55 percent to the cost of labor. The employees' regular wages are charged to direct labor. The overtime premium and the fringe benefits are carried as variable overhead costs.

MARKETING

Marketing of the product takes place at the retail level via catalogue sales and in the company's retail store adjacent to the factory. Retail Internet sales are a new addition to the overall marketing effort. The company also sells wholesale to department stores, toy boutiques, and other specialty retailers. The product can be delivered by two-to-five-day ground service, next-day air, or holiday express. The customer pays the insurance and delivery charges. Berkshire promises same or next-day shipment. Most orders are shipped the same day as received.

When the company receives a customer's order, an employee takes a bear of the requested color and dresses it according to the customer's wishes. Then the bear is packaged with a protective air bag and complimentary piece of chocolate candy, and shipped in a designer box. The designer box contributes to the product image. It is reminiscent of the packaging used for a famous-name cologne and intended to lend an air of status and exclusivity to the product. The box is also important to toy collectors who expect to pay or receive a price premium in the secondary market for items that are in "mint-in-box" condition. Producing the box is a custom job involving a box manufacturer and a printing company. The unit cost of the box decreases with the size of the order that the company places with the manufacturer. Rush orders are more costly than normal orders. In July 1997, the purchasing manager placed an order for enough boxes to cover budgeted sales in the coming year.

Berkshire's policy on sales commissions has remained stable over the past several years. Commissions of 3 percent are paid on retail store sales and sales to wholesale buyers. No commissions are paid on catalog sales. The company-owned retail outlets have proved unprofitable, so all of them, except for the factory store, have been closed in previous years.

THE ACCOUNTING PROBLEM

"I think I know what some of the problems are, but I would like a detailed analysis that provides confirmation from our accounting data," McKinley continues.

"Did inventory change much?" you ask.

"It's pretty negligible. Our peak selling time is from Christmas to Mothers Day, so we don't have much on hand at the June 30 year-end. We started last year with almost nothing and it was all we could do to keep up with demand, so we ended up with almost nothing as well." You jot down a note to ignore changes in raw materials and finished goods inventories and to assume that production volume equals sales volume.

"Didn't you put a new incentive compensation plan in place this year?"

"As a matter of fact, we did. Perhaps it was a factor in what happened this year."

The new incentive compensation plan was adopted effective July 1, 1997. Under this plan, each of the three department heads is rewarded based on the performance of his or her responsibility center. Performance is measured against the company's master budget and its standard cost system. The plan was the result of several meetings with McKinley and her managers who argued and bargained for a plan that rewarded the managers fairly for individual contributions and achievements. McKinley's plan was intended to promote participation and teamwork and the managers accepted the new program enthusiastically. The plan provides for the following:

- David Hall, the purchasing manager, will receive a bonus equal to 20 percent of the net materials price variance, assuming the net variance is favorable. Otherwise, the bonus is zero.

Blocher, Stout, Cokins, Chen: *Cost Management, 4e*

©The McGraw-Hill Companies, Inc 2008

- Rita Smith, the marketing manager, will receive a bonus equal to 10 percent of the excess, if any, of actual net revenues (revenues minus both variable and fixed selling expenses) over master budget net revenues.
- Bill Wilford, the production manager, will receive a bonus equal to 3 percent of the net of several variances: the efficiency (usage or quantity) variances for materials, labor, and variable overhead; the labor rate variance; and the variable and fixed overhead spending variances. Wilford receives no bonus if his net variance is unfavorable.

INTERNET SALES PROGRAM

"It seems that the incentive plan produced results," continues McKinley. "Smith had a terrific year this year. Unit sales were more than 16 percent above budget (**Table 1**). She says one of the principal factors was the new Internet sales policy she instituted and the advertising campaign to support it. We've never had that kind of year in sales before."

The Berkshire Toy Company began selling over the Internet in November 1997. At the same time, the company launched a nationwide radio advertising campaign. All radio advertisements are tagged with a reference to the web site that, in turn, provides visual support for the radio advertising and an opportunity for customers to order online. As an additional incentive to attract Internet customers, Rita Smith proposed that Berkshire offer a substantial discount to customers who ordered over the Internet. Because the discounted Internet price ($42.00) was still greater than the price that Berkshire was charging its wholesale customers ($32.00), McKinley approved the price change.

To boost its Internet sales, the company held special holiday sales. The Christmas and Valentine's Day sales featured the Berkshire Bear in special seasonal costumes. Both events were immediate successes not only with Internet customers, but also with retail and wholesale customers who paid the customary prices. The greatest success was the Mother's Day campaign. For this event, the web site displayed an image of "Mama's Boy," a bear sporting sunglasses, jeans and T-shirt, and an appliquéd tattoo on its upper arm that said "Mom."

The 15-inch bears produced by the Berkshire Toy Company are identical except for their color and their accessories. Although the bears may be purchased with differing accessories, the unit cost of the accessories per bear has been relatively stable over time. The average historical cost of accessories has been a very small part of the total cost of the bear, and the standard cost of accessories is computed as an average. The price differences in the product reflect the company's discounting practices and not differences in accessories.

The master (static) budget for the year ended June 30, 1998 was prepared before the Internet program and price change were adopted. It called for the sale of 280,000 units, allocated as follows:

Retail and mail order	238,000 units	x	$49.00	=	$11,662,000
Wholesale	42,000 units	x	$32.00	=	1,344,000
Total	280,000				$13,006,000

The expected distribution of 85 percent retail and 15 percent wholesale was based on the company's experience in prior years. Thus, the budgeted average selling price was $46.45. Actual sales for the year were as follows:

Retail and catalog	174,965 units	x	$49.00	=	$8,573,285
Internet	105,429 units	x	$42.00	=	4,428,018
Wholesale	45,162 units	x	$32.00	=	1,445,184
Total	325,556 units				$14,446,487

MATERIALS AND PRODUCTION

"Hall had a few triumphs of his own this year," said McKinley. "He managed to get some substantial price discounts on acrylic pile fabric, plastic joints, and polyester fiber-filling. Price discounts of 7 to 10 percent on our three main inputs add up to some real savings." Berkshire Toy Company's schedule of standard manufacturing costs is reproduced in **Table 2**. The schedule of actual manufacturing costs for the year ended June 30, 2002 is in **Table 3**.

"So," McKinley continues, "at least on the surface, it looks like marketing and purchasing had a good year, but production is another story. Bill Wilford was not part of the original Berkshire team. Headquarters sent him here from Hercules (the luggage division) to learn the ropes after Jack Johnson left. Jack joined a competitor last July."

"During Bill's first week on the job, we had a freak thunderstorm and the storm drain backed up, ruining a large amount of fiber filling. The loss was uninsured. Since then, I have gotten plenty of feedback from Bill who has been struggling to keep up with production. He has complained about the substandard direct materials, deviations from standard production plans, and the amount of overtime required to meet sales demand. The plant has been operating at near to maximum capacity of 350,000 units. His people are tired. Some of them quit and had to be replaced at higher-than-standard wage rates. Bill also said that extra maintenance was required on the machinery and that, even so, they've experienced frequent breakdowns. He's been vehement about stock-outs of some of the imported accessories. At one point, sales commitments made it necessary to schedule overtime to copy some of the bear outfits and make them in-house. But he tries to be fair and responsible. He admitted that he was the person who moved some of the plastic parts to an empty box marked 'refuse' that was hauled away later by the trash collectors. This is a small place and I hear almost everything that goes on."

"By the way," McKinley winds up, "did you get the information I faxed you?"

"Let's see," you reply. "I have the 2001-02 income statement (prior to bonus calculations), the breakdown of budgeted and actual revenues, and schedules of standard and actual direct production costs. I do need some more detailed information about manufacturing overhead and selling costs. After that, I'll get back to you as soon as I can." McKinley agrees to send you details of actual overhead expenditures for the last five years and actual selling expenses for 2001 and 2002. These are shown in **Tables 4** and **5**.

REQUIRED

1. a. Using the information in the case and **Tables 1-5**, prepare a flexible budget[8] for the Berkshire Toy Company for the year ended June 30, 2002. Analyze the company's total master (static) budget variance for the year. Compare the flexible and master (static) budgets and prepare a schedule showing the sales volume variance. Compare the actual results and the flexible budget, and prepare a schedule showing the flexible budget variance. Subdivide the flexible budget variances into the appropriate price (rate or spending) and efficiency (usage or quantity) variances for materials, labor, and variable overhead.

   b. Compute the bonuses earned in fiscal 1998, if any, by David Hall of the purchasing department, Rita Smith of the marketing department, and Bill Wilford of the production department.

2. a. You will be assisting in the investigation of certain variances. Using the information provided, formulate some likely explanations for the observed variances.

   b. Comment on the advantages and disadvantages of the incentive compensation plan as it applies to department heads. What is the appropriate role of the budget in performance evaluation? What modifications to the incentive plan would you recommend? Why?

3. (Optional) Suppose that Berkshire Toy Company adopts a balanced scorecard (BSC) to measure its performance. What performance dimensions are typically included in a BSC? What specific performance measures (indicators) might be included in the scorecard? For useful background information on BSCs, see Chapter 2 of *Cost Management: A Strategic Emphasis*, 4th edition, by Blocher, Stout, Cokins, and Chen (McGraw Hill, 2008).

---

[8] For the sales revenue categories shown in **Table 1**, prepare a flexible budget based on actual units sold multiplied by the master (static) budget prices. For Internet sales, use a "revised" budget price of $42. To analyze sales-volume effects, also prepare a second flexible budget for the sales revenue categories based on the total of 325,556 units sold, multiplied by the budgeted mix (85 percent for retail, 0 percent for Internet, and 15 percent for wholesale). Multiply these quantities by the respective budgeted sales prices. The difference between the two flexible budget amounts is generally termed a "sales-mix variance," which quantifies the effect on income that results because the actual mix of distribution channels deviates from the budgeted mix. A comparison between the master (static) budget and the flexible budget prepared on the basis of the budgeted mix is the "sales-volume variance." This variance measures the effect on operating income of selling more or fewer units than planned. The net of the sales mix variance and the sales volume variance equals the "sales activity variance."

Blocher, Stout, Cokins, Chen: *Cost Management, 4e*

TABLE 2
Berkshire Toy Company
A Division of Quality Products Corporation

Schedule of Standard Costs: Fifteen-Inch Berkshire Bear

Normal Capacity: 280,000 units

	Quantity Allowed Per Unit	Input Price	Standard Cost Per Unit
Direct materials			
Acrylic pile fabric[a]	0.02381 bolts	$35.00/bolt	0.8333
10-mm acrylic eyes	2 eyes	$0.19/eye	0.3800
45-mm plastic joints	5 joints	$0.14/joint	0.7000
Polyester fiber filling	0.90 lbs.	$1.45/lb.	1.3050
Woven label	1 label	$0.05/each	0.0500
Designer box	1 box	$0.24/each	0.2400
Accessories[b]	various		0.1200
Total direct materials			3.6283
Direct labor			
Sewing	0.50 hours		
Stuffing and cutting[c]	0.30 hours		
Assembly	0.30 hours		
Dressing and packaging	0.10 hours		
Total direct labor	1.20 hours	$8.00/hour	9.6000
Variable manufacturing overhead[d]	1.20 DLH	$3.1140/DLH	3.7368
			16.9651
Fixed manufacturing overhead	1.20 DLH	$1.9700/DLH	2.364
			$19.3291

[a] One bolt of fabric is 10 yards long by 72 inches wide. Fabric for 42 finished units can be cut from one bolt.

[b] The cost of accessories varies from 7 cents per unit for a bow tie to 45 cents per unit for fisherman's gear. The standard of 12 cents per unit reflects the historical assortment of accessories chosen by customers.

[c] Less than 0.01 hour per unit is spent cutting the fabric. Therefore, hours spent in the cutting operation are not separately recorded. They are included with hours spent operating the pneumatic stuffing machine because both operations are usually performed by the same employees.

[d] Variable and fixed overhead are allocated to production on the basis of standard direct labor hours allowed. Standard amounts are computed at normal capacity of 280,000 units. Maximum practical capacity is 350,000 units of production attainable in consideration of planned maintenance and scheduled down time for holidays. Normal capacity is the long-run average productive output that smoothes out seasonal, cyclical, and other variations in customer demand.

TABLE 3
Berkshire Toy Company
A Division of Quality Products Corporation

Schedule of Actual Manufacturing Costs
for the Year Ended June 30, 2002

	Quantity Used	Input Price	Total Cost	
Direct materials				
Acrylic pile fabric	7,910 bolts	$32.4174/bolt	$256,422	
10-mm acrylic eyes	661,248 eyes	$0.1900/eye	125,637	
45-mm plastic joints	1,937,023 joints	$0.1270/joint	246,002	
Polyester fiber filling	344,165 lbs.	$1.3100/lb.	450,856	
Woven label	328,447 labels	$0.0500 each	16,422	
Designer box	315,854 boxes	$0.2200 each	69,488	
Accessories		various	66,013	a
Total direct materials			1,230,840	
Direct labor				
Sewing	189,211 hours			
Stuffing and cutting	104,117 hours			
Assembly	121,054 hours			
Dressing and packaging	34,615 hours			
Total direct labor	448,997 hours	$8.1700/hour	3,668,305	
Overtime premium	103,787 hours	$4.0850/hour	423,970	
Other variable manufacturing overhead			1,301,695	b
Fixed manufacturing overhead			658,897	
			$7,283,707	

a The actual input price for accessories is derived by dividing the actual cost of $66,013 by units sold (325,556), yielding an average accessories cost of $0.20277 per bear.

b The actual input price for variable overhead is obtained by dividing the total variable overhead ($1,301,695 + $423,970) by actual direct labor hours worked, yielding a price or rate of $3.843377 per direct labor hour.

Blocher, Stout, Cokins, Chen: *Cost Management, 4e*
©The McGraw-Hill Companies, Inc 2008

TABLE 4

Berkshire Toy Company
A Division of Quality Products Corporation

Schedule of Actual Manufacturing Overhead Expenditures
for the Years Ended June 30, 1998 through 2002

	2002	2001	2000	1999	1998
Units produced	325,556	271,971	252,114	227,546	201,763
Variable overhead:					
Payroll taxes and fringes	$840,963	$524,846	$467,967	$413,937	$356,150
Overtime premiums	423,970	24,665	2,136	1,874	1,965
Cleaning supplies	4,993	6,842	6,119	5,485	4,996
Maintenance labor	415,224	256,883	232,798	244,037	216,142
Maintenance supplies	27,373	15,944	12,851	15,917	14,323
Miscellaneous	13,142	11,244	9,921	8,906	7,794
Total	$1,725,665	$840,424	$731,792	$690,156	$601,370
Fixed overhead:					
Utilities	$121,417	$119,786	$117,243	$116,554	$113,229
Depreciation-machinery	28,500	28,500	28,500	28,500	28,500
Depreciation-building	88,750	88,750	88,750	88,750	88,750
Insurance	62,976	61,716	57,211	55,544	54,988
Property taxes	70,101	70,101	68,243	68,243	66,114
Supervisory salaries	287,153	274,538	275,198	269,018	254,469
Total	$658,897	$643,391	$635,145	$626,609	$606,050

TABLE 5

Berkshire Toy Company
A Division of Quality Products Corporation

Schedule of Actual Selling Expenses
for the Years Ended June 30, 2002 and 2001

	2002	2001
Units sold:	325,556	271,971
Variable expenses:		
Packing and shipping	$1,580,089	$1,015,913
Commissions	129,080	216,116
Catalogs, brochures, and samples	150,425	65,658
Total	$1,859,594	$1,297,687
Fixed expenses:		
Salaries	$2,734,868	$2,345,121
Advertising and promotion	2,288,324	2,086,021
Total	$5,023,192	$4,431,142

14-2 The Mesa Corporation

The Mesa Corporation, a medium-sized manufacturing firm, uses injection molding machines to produce a variety of custom-ordered products for the airline and automotive industries. Recent recessionary pressures in the economy have negatively affected both the airline and the automotive industries. The major airline and auto firms are "squeezing" their suppliers, including Mesa. Consequently, there is a lot of pressure to control costs.

Adrian Bates is the production superintendent for Mesa (see the partial organization chart for Mesa in **Figure 1**). Her job includes aiding managers in solving production problems, in using management accounting information, and in using techniques to control production costs.

One of Ms. Bates's subordinates, Chris Kenyon, manages the Molding Department of Mesa Corporation. Mr. Kenyon has asked Ms. Bates' opinion about some perceived problems in his department and a potential solution which he is considering. Based on his rudimentary knowledge of cost control and some feedback data from recent production reports, Mr. Kenyon thinks that one of the standards in his department may be outdated. As a proposed solution, he is considering revising the standard usage of plastic which is used as a benchmark to signal an out-of-control machine.

The Molding Department has twelve identical molding machines (Machines A through L) which produce subassemblies for various products. When a machine is properly adjusted, it uses an average of 100 pounds of plastic (with a standard deviation of 3 pounds) to produce a subassembly. When a machine is not properly adjusted, it uses an average of 110 pounds of plastic (with a standard deviation of 5 pounds) to produce a subassembly. Since it is quite costly to adjust the machines, adjustments are made only when variances indicate that a machine might be out-of-control.

Mr. Kenyon's responsibilities include determining which variances should be investigated and whether the existing standard is correct or should be revised. The primary criterion underlying his decisions is to minimize the department's production costs per subassembly and to meet quality expectations. **Figure 2** illustrates the situation in Mr. Kenyon's department. The bell-shaped curve on the left represents the distribution of the material usage per unit of output when a machine is in-control. The mean of this distribution, $C_i = 100$, is used as the performance standard. The bell-shaped curve on the right is the distribution of material usage when a machine is out-of-control. The mean of this distribution, C_O, is 110. Since performance is typically subject to a multitude of random factors, actual material usage may be lower (a favorable variance) or higher (an unfavorable variance) than C_i or C_O.

Table I illustrates the two basic types of decision errors which increase the cost of producing the subassemblies. The rows of the table indicate the two alternative actions which Chris may take, while the columns indicate the two alternative states of nature which can occur. A Type I error results in the cost of an unnecessary investigation when a machine is actually in-control and does not need adjustment. A Type II error results in the cost of continuing to use too much plastic by not adjusting a machine which is actually out-of-control. Type I errors are caused by large random unfavorable variances from the in-control distribution. Type II errors are caused by large random favorable variances from the out-of-control distribution.

Recently, Mr. Kenyon received the variance report (shown in **Table 2**) for the twelve machines in his department. The observations from these twelve machines also are shown in **Figure 2**. The report shows usage variances, from the standard quantity of 100 pounds, ranging from a favorable 8 pounds to an unfavorable 17 pounds. Because Mr. Kenyon did not want to incur excessive and unnecessary investigation costs, he decided to have the firm's mechanic inspect and adjust only those machines with unfavorable variances two or more standard deviations from the standard (machines G, H, I, J, K, and Q. From his investigations the mechanic found machines G and H to be in-control while machines L J, K, and L were out-of-control (see **Table 3**).

Mr. Kenyon feels that knowing the means of both the in-control distribution and the out-of-control distribution is necessary to making sound investigation decisions. Based upon the mechanic's findings, Mr. Kenyon was considering revising the standard quantity allowed for production of the subassemblies from 100 to 108 (the amount used by machine H) pounds of plastic per unit; this is the standard which would have prevented the Type I errors resulting in the unnecessary investigation costs associated with machines G and H. He also was considering revising the expected mean usage of an out-of-control machine from 110 to 113 pounds of plastic per unit (the average usage of the four out-of-control machines).

Adrian Bates is concerned that Chris might be wasting resources by doing unnecessary investigations. However, Ms. Bates also is concerned that if Chris does not do enough investigations, the resultant lower quality may cause the product to be rejected by the airline and automotive firms. This may lead to expensive rework or loss of profitable contracts with these industries.

Blocher, Stout, Cokins, Chen: *Cost Management, 4e*

QUESTIONS:

Suppose that you are Adrian Bates who has been asked to evaluate Chris Kenyon.

1. Has Chris Kenyon performed his job well?
2. Which of the twelve machines would you have investigated (i.e., which cost variances do you think were caused by a machine NOT being in proper adjustment)? Why?
3. Why were the means of the two distributions (when a machine is properly adjusted and when a machine is not properly adjusted), based on the variances selected for investigation, higher than what Chris Kenyon thought they were?
4. Re-estimate the means of the two distributions. Is the mean plastic usage of 100 pounds when a machine is in proper adjustment still an appropriate standard or is 108 or some other number a better standard? Is the existing mean plastic usage of 110 pounds when a machine is not in proper adjustment still an appropriate estimate of the mean of that distribution or is 113 or some other number a better estimate?
5. What methods can you suggest to improve Chris Kenyon's ability to update, in the future, the means of the two distributions?
6. Do you agree with Chris is raising the standard to 108 pounds? Why? How often should a standard be reviewed for revisions?

FIGURE I
Mesa Corporation Organization Chart

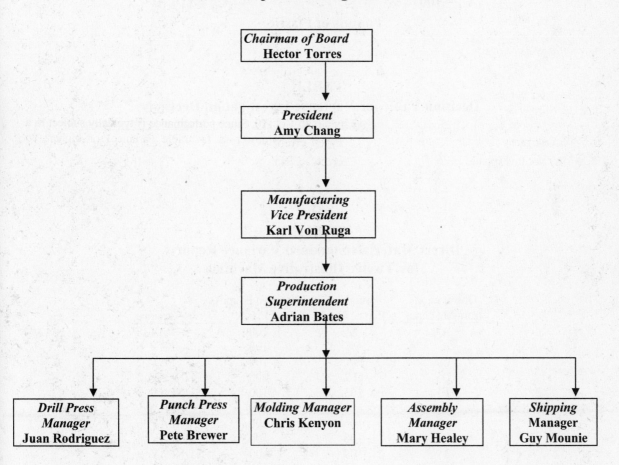

©The McGraw-Hill Companies, Inc 2008

FIGURE 2
Distribution of In-Control and Out-of-Control Costs with the Twelve Machines

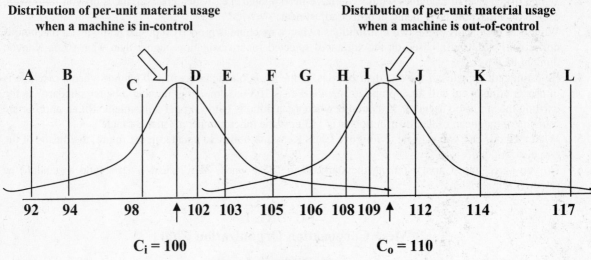

Distribution of per-unit material usage when a machine is in-control

Distribution of per-unit material usage when a machine is out-of-control

$C_i = 100$

$C_o = 110$

Pounds of Plastic

TABLE 1
Decision Table for Variance Investigation Decision

	Machine Is In-Control	Machine Is Out-of-Control
Investigate	Type I Error	Correct Decision
Do Not Investigate	Correct Decision	Type II Error

TABLE 2
Direct Materials Standard Variance Reports
for Twelve Illustrative Machines

Observation from Machine	Pounds of Plastic Used	Standard Pounds of Plastic	Variance
A	92	100	FAV 8
B	94	100	FAV 6
C	98	100	FAV 2
D	102	100	UNFAV 2
E	103	100	UNFAV 3
F	105	100	UNFAV 5
G	106	100	UNFAV 6
H	108	100	UNFAV 8
I	109	100	UNFAV 9
J	112	100	UNFAV 12
K	114	100	UNFAV 14
L	117	100	UNFAV 17

Blocher, Stout, Cokins, Chen: *Cost Management, 4e*

TABLE 3
Mechanic's Report of the Physical Inspection of Six Machines

In-Control Machines	Lbs. Used		Out-of-control Machines	Lbs. Used
G	106		I	109
H	108		J	112
			K	114
			L	117
Total Usage	214		Total Usage	214
Average Usage	107		Average Usage	113

14.1: USING ENHANCED COST MODELS IN VARIANCE ANALYSIS FOR BETTER CONTROL AND DECISION MAKING

by Kennard T. Wing, CMA

The budget and the analysis of variance between budget and actual are two of the most fundamental financial management tools. Yet in many organizations, these tools are "paper tigers" that can encourage or foster a lack of budget discipline. Managers who are called to account for their numbers in these organizations attack the budget variance report rather than going after the problems in their units. Their criticism might go something like this: "That report doesn't take into account the fact that once we pass 100,000 units per month, our preventive maintenance expenses go up. It only looks like we spent too much this month. Following recommended PM schedules is a key to successful financial performance long term." It sounds plausible. The result is that the managers are "off the hook" for their whole variance because no one knows how much of the budget variance for the month the increased maintenance activity should or actually does account for.

The reality is that the typical variance report is not particularly helpful even if managers want to use it to identify meaningful exceptions, which leads to a comment such as: "I can't tell which of those line-item variances are just noise in the accounting system and which ones are something I should he doing something about."

Worse still, bad decisions can result when managers do not understand the limitations of the reports. For example, someone might offer: "The report says labor is a variable cost. Volume's down, so people ought to be laid off."

Here's the basic problem. Variance analysis is based on overly simplistic cost models in which every cost has to he treated as either fixed or variable. In the real world, however, many costs do not behave according to those idealized models, which means that managers can always legitimately point to shortcomings in the variance analysis. The reports either do not help them identify cost issues, or managers can use the limitations to reduce their own financial accountability.

Let's take a simple example. XYZ Organization has a cost that is semi-variable. That is, the cost is fixed up to a certain level of volume and variable beyond that point. Suppose the cost is treated as fixed in the variance reporting system. When volume is high and the unit is over budget, the manager can indicate that the variance is from the increased volume (not controllable), the report is no good, and the cost is what it ought to be. Now suppose the cost is treated as variable. When volume is low and the unit is over budget, the manager can say that the variance is due to decreased volume (not controllable), the report is no good, and the cost is what it should be. It does not take too many of these experiences before the budget variance report carries little weight in the organization.

Does every cost need to be treated as fixed or variable? No. We have merely relied on what we were taught in Management Accounting 101 or on whatever capabilities were built into the reporting software we happened to have available. The time has come for financial managers to develop:

- Models of cost reflecting how costs actually behave, and
- Variance reporting using enhanced cost models.

Sidebar: Using EXCEL to Calculate a Volume Variance with Semi-Variable Costs

Let   BVOL be the address of the cell containing budgeted volume.

AVOL be the address of the cell containing actual volume.

BKPT be the address of the cell containing the breakpoint between fixed and variable.

ICU be the address of the cell containing the budgeted (or standard) incremental cost per unit for volumes above the breakpoint.

Then the volume variance is equal to the expression:

= (IF(BVOL>BKPT, BVOL, BKPT)–IF(AVOL>BKPT, AVOL, BKPT))*
ICU

A sample is shown at right. The 50 units above breakpoint should have cost $55 each, implying semi-variable costs should have been $2,750 higher than budgeted. This is our volume variance.

	BUDGET	ACTUAL	VARIANCE
Unit Volume	2,000	2,100	(100)
Total Step-Fixed Costs	$70,000	$78,000	$(8,000)
Budgeted Incremental Unit Cost	$55		
Breakpoint	2,050		
Volume Variance			$(2,750)
Controllable Variance			$(5,250)

I'll explain how to handle variance calculations for semi-variable costs, for step-fixed costs, and for several situations where a shifting mix affects cost behavior. Developing other, more sophisticated cost models and variance reporting is an important direction for the management accounting and financial management profession that will lead to improved control and decision making.

CALCULATING VOLUME VARIANCE WITH SEMI-VARIABLE COSTS

Let's examine how to calculate volume variance with semi-variable costs. Semi-variable costs are fixed below a certain level of volume, called the breakpoint, and are variable above that level. As an example, consider the emergency department of a hospital with which I worked. The largest cost in the department was nursing labor. Because emergency departments must be ready to handle large increases in volume instantaneously, nurses are not sent home or reassigned when volume is low. The department is staffed at a level that is consistent with a wide range of volumes. Still, there is some level of patient volume at which staff must be added. Flexing up above the department's core staffing level in either small or large increments can be handled by overtime, on-call staff and staff pulled from other units. These characteristics suggested that the semi-variable cost

model would be appropriate for nursing labor in this department.

The question was: How much of the budget variance was due to uncontrollable changes in patient volume, and how much was attributable to factors the manager was supposed to control? To provide an answer, we need to decompose the budget variance into a volume variance and a controllable variance.

Because semi-variable costs act like fixed costs over part of the range of volume and like variable costs over the rest of the range of volume, the volume variance associated with semi-variable costs behaves similarly.

- In the fixed cost range, the volume variance is zero.
- In the variable cost range, the volume variance is the same as for a variable cost.

In total, there are four cases financial managers need to be concerned about, depending on how budgeted and actual volume compare to the breakpoint at which semi-variable costs change from fixed to variable:

Case 1. Budgeted and actual volumes are less than breakpoint. In this case, the department was budgeted to operate and actually operated in the fixed cost range. The volume variance is zero.

Sidebar: Calculating a Volume Variance with Step-Fixed Costs

Step-fixed costs are readily handled in Excel using the HLOOKUP function. Let VOL be the address of the cell containing unit volume for which a corresponding step-fixed cost is required. Let ARRAY be the range reference for a two-row section of the spreadsheet, the first row containing the list of unit volumes at which costs step up and the second row containing the amounts to which step-fixed costs are supposed to increase at those points. Then the expression =HLOOKUP(VOL, ARRAY, 2) will return the standard step-fixed cost corresponding to the unit volume at VOL. If AVOL is the address of the cell containing actual volume and BVOL is the address of the cell containing budgeted volume, then the volume variance is equal to the expression: =HLOOKUP(BVOL, ARRAY, 2) – HLOOKUP(AVOL, ARRAY, 2).

A sample is shown below. The additional 50 units above budget should not have led to any increase in cost, so the volume variance is zero.

STEP-FIXED COST FUNCTION

Volume		o	1,000	2,000	3,000
Cost at that Volume		$5,000	$10,000	$15,000	$20,000

	BUDGET	ACTUAL	VARIANCE
Unit Volume	1,900	1,950	(50)
Total Step-Fixed Costs	$10,000	$15,000	$(5,000)
Volume Variance			$ —
Controllable Variance			$(5,000)

Case 2. Budgeted volume is less than breakpoint, and actual volume is greater than breakpoint. Cost is fixed between budgeted volume and the breakpoint. This means that the volume variance for this portion of the difference between budgeted and actual volume is zero. Between the breakpoint and actual volume, semi-variable costs act just like variable costs. Therefore, the volume variance for this portion is calculated the same as for a variable cost.

Case 3. Budgeted volume is greater than breakpoint, and actual volume is less than breakpoint. Between budgeted volume and the breakpoint, semi-variable costs behave just like variable costs. The result is that the volume variance for this portion of the difference between budgeted and actual volume is calculated the same way as a traditional volume variance. Cost is fixed between the breakpoint and actual volume, which means that the volume variance for this portion of the difference between budgeted and actual volume is zero.

Case 4. Budgeted and actual volumes are greater than breakpoint. In this case, the department was budgeted to operate, and actually did operate, in the variable cost range. Therefore, the volume variance is the same as for a variable cost.

See the sidebar "Using Excel to Calculate a Volume Variance with Semi-Variable Costs" to learn how to use an Excel spreadsheet for this calculation.

CALCULATING VOLUME VARIANCE WITH STEP-FIXED COSTS

In the step-fixed cost model, costs are fixed tip to a certain level of volume. Then the costs suddenly jump to a higher level of cost that is fixed over a range of volumes until another point is reached at which costs jump suddenly to a higher level, and so on. To calculate the volume variance, we need to know at what points costs jump up and to what levels they jump. The volume variance is merely what the cost is sup-posed to be at budgeted volume minus what the cost is supposed to be at actual volume.

See the sidebar above on "Calculating a Volume Variance with Step-Fixed Costs" for some calculations.

CALCULATING VOLUME VARIANCE FOR COST CENTER WITH MIXED COSTS

Most cost centers contain several kinds of costs, some of which are best modeled as:
- Variable;
- Fixed;
- Semi-variable; and
- Step-fixed.

The volume variance for the entire cost center is simply the sum of the volume variances for each of these four types. Obviously the volume variance associated with fixed costs is zero.

When different semi-variable costs have

different breakpoints, variances may need to be calculated by line item and then totaled. If there are different step-fixed costs with different step-up points and amounts, it might be easier to calculate variances by line item and then sum as opposed to creating the aggregate step-fixed cost function required to treat them together.

CALCULATING A MIX VARIANCE

Let's examine the calculation of a mix variance using the same hospital I mentioned before. In that hospital, the radiology department performed a significant variety of procedures that required quite different quantities of labor, materials, and equipment. The mix of procedures was not under the control of the department manager. The idea was to separate the budget variances attributable to procedure volume and procedure mix from those considered under the managers control.

Mix variances have been calculated in other situations. For example, sales mix variances have been used to calculate the effect on a firm's profitability of changes in the mix of products it sold. These variances are not relevant here because revenues are generally not available for individual procedures in hospital billing. Materials mix variances have also been applied in manufacturing to calculate the effect of using a mix of raw materials different from that specified in the standard. This is also unlike the hospital case, where a mix variance can exist even when every procedure is performed in accordance with standards. In any case, the mix variance developed is analogous to those two. Note that all costs in the radiology department were classified as either fixed or variable.

The total variable cost variance was decomposed into volume variance, mix variance, and unit variable cost variance. See sidebar below, "Calculating a Mix Variance."

Sidebar: Calculating a Mix Variance

Let each row of the spreadsheet represent data for a different procedure. We'll need columns for actual volume for each procedure, budgeted volumes for each procedure, and budgeted unit variable cost for each procedure. To calculate the mix index, create a column in which each cell is the product of that procedure's actual volume and budgeted variable unit cost. Use the sum function to calculate the sum of all the values in the column you just created. The result is the mix index.

To calculate the flexible budget, create a column in which each cell is the product of that procedure's budgeted volume and budgeted variable unit cost Use the sum function to calculate the sum of all the values in the column you just created. Multiply that sum by total actual volume and divide by total budgeted volume. The result is the flexible budget.

The volume variance is total budgeted variable costs minus the flexible budget. The mix variance is the flexible budget minus the mix index. The unit variable cost variance is the mix index minus actual variable costs.

A sample is shown below.

PROCEDURE	ACTUAL VOLUME	BUDGETED VOLUME	BUDGETED VARIABLE UNIT COST	MIX INDEX	BUDGETED VARIABLE COSTS	FLEXIBLE BUDGET
A	200	150	$100	$20,000	$15,000	
B	1,800	2,000	$35	$63,000	$70,000	
C	2,700	3,000	$25	$67,500	$75,000	
Total	4,700	5,150		$150,500	$160,000	$146,01

	BUDGET	ACTUAL	VARIANCE
Volume	5,150	4,700	450
Variable Costs	$160,00	$155,000	$5,000

Volume Variance			$13,981
Mix Variance			$(4,481)
Unit Cost Variance			$(4,500)

Sidebar: Using Excel to Calculate a Mix Variance with Semi-Variable Costs

Let each row of the spreadsheet represent data for a particular visit type. We'll need columns for actual volume for each visit type, budgeted volume for each visit type, and budgeted incremental cost per visit above the breakpoint for each visit type. Let SV be the address of the cell containing budgeted semi-variable costs below the breakpoint and BKPT be the address of the cell containing breakpoint volume.

First, calculate the mix index. Create a column in which each cell is the product of that visit type's actual volume and budgeted incremental variable unit cost Use the sum function to calculate the total of the column you just created. Call the cell address of that total M. Call the cell address for total actual volume SUMA and the cell address for total budgeted volume SUMB. Then the following Excel expression is equivalent to the mix index: = IF(SUMA>BKPT, ((SUMA - BKPT)/SUMA)*M + SV, SV).

Next calculate the flexible budget. Create a column in which each cell is the product of that visit type's budgeted volume and budgeted incremental variable unit cost. Use the sum function to calculate the total of the column you just created. Divide that total by SUMB. Call the cell address of the result F. Then the following *Excel* expression is equivalent to the flexible budget:
= IF (SUMA>BKPT, (SUMA – BKPT)*F + SV, SV).

The volume variance is budgeted semi-variable costs minus the flexible budget. The mix variance is the flexible budget minus the mix index. The unit cost variance is the mix index minus actual semi-variable costs.

An example is shown below.

VISIT TYPE	ACTUAL VOLUME	BUDGETED VOLUME	BUDGETED INCREMENTAL VARIABLE UNIT COST	MIX INDEX	BUDGETED VARIABLE COSTS	FLEXIBLE BUDGET
A	200	50	$100	$20,000	$5,000	
B	1,900	1,925	$35	$66,500	$67,375	
C	2,950	2,975	$25	$73,750	$74,375	
Total	5,050	4,950	$30	$160.250	$146,750	$151,482
				$151,587		

Breakpoint Volume	5,000
Cost at Breakpoint	$150,000

	BUDGET	ACTUAL	VARIANCE
Volume	4,950	5,050	—100
Step-Fixed Costs	$150,00	$155,000	$(5,000)
Volume Variance			$(1,482)
Mix Variance			$(104)
Unit Cost Variance			$(3,413)

Creating "what-if" budgets. The basic approach to calculating these variances is to create a pair of "what- if" budgets. Budgeted variable costs are based on budgeted unit volume, budgeted procedure mix, and budgeted unit cost for each procedure. Actual variable costs are based on actual volumes, actual procedure mix and actual but unknown unit costs for each procedure.

The first "what-if" budget is based on budgeted procedure mix, budgeted unit cost per procedure and actual volume. It is comparable to the flexible budget of traditional variance analysis. Because it uses the same values as total budgeted variable cost for procedure mix and unit costs,

differing only in using actual instead of budgeted volume, the difference between budgeted variable cost and the flexible budget is the volume variance—how much variable costs should have differed from budget if the uncontrollable change in volume were the only change from budget that occurred.

The second "what-if" budget is called the mix index. It is based on actual procedure mix and actual volume but budgeted unit costs by procedure. As it differs from the flexible budget only in using actual mix rather than budgeted mix, the flexible budget minus the mix index is the impact of the shift in mix—how much costs should

Blocher, Stout, Cokins, Chen: *Cost Management, 4e*

©The McGraw-Hill Companies, Inc 2008

have differed from budget if only the mix had differed from budget.

The mix index differs from actual variable costs only in using budgeted unit costs instead of actual unit costs, so the mix index minus actual variable cost is the impact of departures from budgeted unit cost that usually are held to be controllable by the manager. The first time this mix variance was implemented, a problem developed in which the variances for individual months failed to sum to the variance as calculated on the year-to-date numbers. I investigated the problem to see under what conditions this would be the case. I concluded that as long as the budgeted mix was the same each month, the monthly variances would sum to the variance of the year-to-date. If the budgeted mix changes from month to month, then the monthly variances generally will not sum to the variance of the year- to-date. In that case, variances should he calculated from the individual months and then summed to create variances for aggregate time periods Although I have not investigated this, I suspect that analogous limitations would affect the sales mix and materials mix variances others have developed.

CALCULATING A MIX VARIANCE WITH SEMI-VARIABLE COSTS

The hospital's emergency department also had a mix issue. That department dealt with even-thing from sore throats to cardiac arrests, and it classified all cases into 16 visit types. You would expect some costs to be higher if the visit mix shifted toward more serious cases, even if overall visit volume was flat. The severity of cases was beyond the department manager's control. Unfortunately the mix variance developed above could not he applied directly to the emergency department because it assumed all costs could he classified as either fixed or variable. Thus, what the hospital needed was to extend the mix variance to cases including semi-variable costs.

For an example, see the sidebar on "Calculating a Mix Variance with Semi-Variable Costs." The method is similar to the mix variance created above. We need to calculate two "what-if" budgets that will allow a comparison of numbers that differ in only one respect. As before, the flexible budget is based on actual volume, budgeted mix, and budgeted unit cost. The mix index is based on actual volume and actual mix, but budgeted unit cost. The volume variance is budgeted semi-satiable costs minus the flexible budget. Mix variance is the flexible budget minus the mix index. The unit cost variance is the mix index minus actual semi-variable costs.

The situation is more complicated because semi-variable costs force us to deal with multiple cases. Fortunately the calculations for volume variance with a mix are identical to the case with no mix. Two cases are presented as a result of the mix variance, although the first is trivial. When actual volume is less than or equal to the breakpoint, the mix variance is zero. The calculation is as shown in the sidebar when actual volume exceeds the breakpoint.

It may seem counterintuitive that there is no mix variance when actual volume is less than the break-point but budgeted volume is greater than the breakpoint. Here is the explanation: Mix is irrelevant below the breakpoint. For actual volume below the breakpoint, any mix should generate the fixed portion of cost. Therefore, the variance is due solely to the fact that volume is below breakpoint and has nothing to do with possible variations in mix.

The unit cost variance also presents us with two cases, depending on whether actual volume is above breakpoint. See the sidebar for calculations. Given the difficulties with the original mix variance, it seemed appropriate to investigate whether these variances calculated on a monthly basis would sum to the variance on the year-to-date numbers. The answer generally is no. If some periods are above breakpoint but others are below it, the variance calculation on the year-to-date numbers will be erroneous.

When there is a mix variance with semi-variable costs, variances should not be calculated on data for aggregate periods. Rather, variances for the shortest reporting period ought to be aggregated in order to report variances for longer periods.

CALCULATING MIX VARIANCES WITH STEP-FIXED COSTS

Under the standard step-fixed cost model, it is assumed that each unit of output makes a uniform demand on the step-fixed resource. Obviously there is no mix variance under that assumption. A mix variance is possible only when different kinds of output make different demands on a resource.

For example, different diagnostic procedures might require different amounts of hours on a leased machine. Each machine is available for a fixed number of hours but may be augmented by additional leased machines. The method for calculating a mix variance for a step-fixed cost of this sort is shown in the sidebar below entitled, "Using *Excel* to Calculate Mix Variances with Step-Fixed Costs."

As before, a flexible budget is created based

on actual volume, budgeted mix, and the budgeted step-fixed-cost function. Also created is a mix index based on actual volume, actual mix, and the budgeted step-fixed-cost function. The volume variance is budgeted step-fixed costs minus the flexible budget. The mix variance is the flexible budget minus the mix index.

There is an additional wrinkle for this type of cost. Actual step-fixed costs could differ from the mix index for either of the following reasons:

Sidebar: Using *Excel* to Calculate Mix Variances with Step-Fixed Costs

Let each row of the spreadsheet represent data for a particular procedure type. We'll need columns for actual volume for each procedure type, budgeted volume for each procedure type, and budgeted or standard unit consumption by each procedure type of the step-fixed resource. Let AC be the address of the cell containing actual consumption of the step-fixed resource. Let ARRAY be the range reference for a two-row section of the spreadsheet the first row containing the level of resource consumption at which costs step up, and the second row containing the amounts to which step-fixed costs are supposed to increase at those points.

First calculate the mix index. Create a column in the spreadsheet in which each cell is the product of that procedure's actual volume and budgeted hours per procedure. Use the sum function to calculate the total of the column you just created. Call the cell address of that total M. Then the mix index is calculated by the following Excel expression: =HLOOKLUP(M, ARRAY, 2).

Next calculate the flexible budget. Create a column in which each cell is the product of that procedure's budgeted volume and budgeted hours per procedure. Use the sum function to total the column you just created. Call the cell address of that total BC. Call the cell address of total actual volume SUMA and of total budgeted volume SUMB. Then the flexible budget is calculated by the following Excel expression: =HLOOKUP(SUMA*BC/SUMB, ARRAY, 2).

Now calculate the consumption index. It is simply the expression =HLOOKUP(AC, ARRAY, 2).

The volume variance is budgeted step-fixed costs minus the flexible budget. The mix variance is the flexible budget minus the mix index. The unit consumption variance is the mix index minus the consumption index. The price variance is the consumption index minus actual step-fixed costs.

An example is shown below.

STEP-FIXED COST FUNCTION

Hours per Month	0	240	480	720
Cost at that Volume	$5,000	$10,000	$15,000	$20,000

PROCEDURE	ACTUAL VOLUME	BUDGETED VOLUME	HOURS PER PROCEDURE	MIX INDEX	FLEXIBLE BUDGET	CONSUMPTION INDEX
A	50	15	1.0	50	15	
B	275	200	0.5	138	100	
C	320	300	0.2	64	60	
Total	645	515		252	175	
				$10	$5,000	
Total Hours Used	270					$10,000

	BUDGET	ACTUAL	VARIANCE
Volume	515	645	-130
Step-Fixed Costs	$5,00	$12,000	$(7,000)
Volume Variance			$ —
Mix Variance			$(5,000)
Unit Consumption Variance			$ —
Price Variance			$(2,000)

Blocher, Stout, Cokins, Chen: *Cost Management, 4e*

©The McGraw-Hill Companies, Inc 2008

- Too much of the step-fixed resource was used for the amount of volume, or
- The proper amount was used, but the price was too high.

To separate out these two causes, calculate another "what-if" budget called the consumption index, which is based on actual consumption of the step-fixed resource and the budgeted step-fixed-cost function. The cost of using more of the step-fixed resource than budget or standard would be the mix index less the consumption index. Because these two "what-if" budgets differ only in that the mix index is based on the use of budgeted or standard amounts of the resource per unit of output, while the consumption index is based on the actual amount of the resource used per unit of output, the difference between them isolates the effect of consuming more of the step-fixed resource per unit of output than called for in the budget or standard. Call this the unit consumption variance.

The other element can be called the price variance. It is calculated by taking the consumption index minus actual step-fixed costs. As both are based on actual use of the step-fixed resource, they differ only in how much cost that use generates. Thus, this expression isolates the variance due to the price of the resource.

Again, we investigated whether variances in step-fixed costs can be calculated on data from aggregate time periods or if variances for aggregate time periods must be calculated by summing variances from the shortest reporting periods. Consider this: The cost associated with leasing a single machine month after month is likely to be much different from the cost of leasing multiple machines for a single month. Here is the impact of this difference: When calculating variances where there are both a mix variance and step-fixed costs, it is a mistake to calculate variances directly on data for aggregate time periods. Variances should be calculated on the shortest reporting period and summed to get variances for aggregate time periods.

CALCULATING VARIANCES FOR DEPARTMENTS WITH MIXED COSTS

I limited my analysis to semi-variable costs or step-fixed costs. In reality departments have a mix of costs. As long as all costs in a department are classified as one kind or another, the department's total budget variance will be equal to the sum of the variances of each different kind of cost. In some cases, multiple costs can be lumped together when their cost behavior is similar. When different semi-variable costs have different breakpoints, separate variance analyses will have to be run for different costs. For step-fixed costs, it is probably both easier and more useful to aggregate line-item variances than to create the aggregate cost function needed to calculate variances on aggregated costs. Obviously, the effort and cost involved in developing these analyses must be weighed against the materiality of the costs and the likely benefit of the better information.

APPLYING THE METHODS

I have shown how to decompose budget variances for several cost models more sophisticated than the traditional cases of fixed and variable costs. While the methods I reported grew out of work in the healthcare field, they have wider applicability in other industries.

Calling a cost semi-variable instead of fixed may seem like a small matter. Such is not the case. A large healthcare system, for example, decided to classify all costs as variable. When volume dropped, it laid off more than 1,000 people, and the workload of most of them had no direct relation to patient volume. The result was that morale of the survivors plummeted, and within a year the system was scrambling to replace not only those it had let go, but many others who had quit.

The point is, the accounting systems we design and implement really do affect management decisions in significant ways. A system built on a bad model of the business will either not be used or, if used, will lead to bad decisions. The assumed behavior of a cost— whether fixed, variable, semi-variable, step-fixed, or something else—is a basic assumption affecting any kind of planning, financial analysis, or control. The stakes today are high. We can no longer afford the over-simplification of fixed and variable. Significant costs must be modeled more accurately in order for management accounting systems to better support executive deliberation and decision making. The extensions of variance analysis developed here are merely a first step along that road.

Kennard T Wing, CMA, is a project director at the OMG Center for Collaborative Learning in Philadelphia, Pa., where he heads the practice that helps nonprofit and public sector organizations build their capacity for financial and performance management. Yon can reach him at Ken@omgcenter.org or (215) 732-2200.

14.2: Variance Analysis Refines Overhead Cost Control

by Jean C. Cooper, PHD, CPA, and James D. Suver, FHFMA, DBA

Many healthcare organizations may not fully realize the benefits of standard cost accounting techniques because they fail to routinely report volume variances in their internal reports. If overhead allocation is routinely reported on internal reports, managers can determine whether billing remains current or lost charges occur. Healthcare organizations' use of standard costing techniques can lead to more realistic performance measurements and information system improvements that alert management to losses from unrecovered overhead in time for corrective action.

Because of current cost reduction pressures from healthcare payers, healthcare decision makers need better cost information for performance measurement, pricing decisions, and management of activities. Like other service organizations, many healthcare facilities have adapted cost accounting systems and techniques developed for the manufacturing sector—such as standard costing and variance analysis—to generate necessary information. But healthcare managers may not realize all potential benefits from variance analysis.

Because of high fixed and indirect costs, estimated at 80 to 85 percent of total costs in most healthcare organizations, overhead control is challenging to healthcare managers.[91] Standard cost systems, such as overhead volume variance, can aid overhead cost control because they are based on predetermined measures of resource consumption. These measures help managers control operations and evaluate performance by giving them standards with which to compare actual results.[2]

PRICING DECISIONS

For effective management of pricing and budgeting decisions, full costs per unit must be determined in advance of providing a service. Determining a service's variable cost component is fairly straightforward because facilities use variable costs directly in the pricing process and can estimate them accordingly.

Most healthcare providers, however, have relatively few true variable costs—costs that vary directly with changes in volume of input or output. Although only fee-for-service and material-related costs such as food and inpatient supplies meet this definition, many healthcare providers treat nursing or other clinical labor costs as variable costs. But unless staff members are paid fee-for-service, their labor is not a true variable cost.

Since most caregivers are salaried, their pay does not change automatically with patient volume. Only their time allocation between patient and nonpatient activities will change as patient volume changes. To change total costs, administrators must decide to increase or decrease staff.

As a result, fixed costs present a more challenging pricing problem. A healthcare organization must estimate the total amount of fixed cost and the volume used as an allocation base. Because most organizations provide several products or services, using a common surrogate, such as labor hours, can be problematic. For example, when the amount of nursing time for a specific diagnosis related group (DRG) already is being recorded, it may be expedient to use nursing hours to allocate direct and indirect overhead costs. If more nursing hours are used than planned, more overhead would be allocated even if total overhead costs were not increased. This apparent change in overhead costs must be recognized in pricing and control decisions.

Estimated per-unit costs are unique, however, to the specific level of estimated fixed costs and the specific volume of estimated output. Whether fixed costs are direct fixed costs in a department or indirect fixed costs of general administration, both must be recovered through pricing.

Exhibit 1 presents standard costs for a healthcare procedure. The per-unit costs ($127) and desired profit margin (10 percent or $12.70) could be used to evaluate offers discounted from the full charge of $164.35. Standard costs also can provide useful planning data for budgeting and control purposes.

---

[9]Overhead costs in this article are defined as all general and administrative expenses. General expenses include indirect patient care costs and all direct patient care costs which are fixed in nature, such as equipment and personnel or salaries.

[10]Adapted from *Fundamentals of Management Accounting* by Anthony, Weber and Reece, 4th ed. (Richard D. Irwin, 1985), Problem 9-32, pp. 346–347.

EXHIBIT 1 STANDARDS FOR ABDOMINAL SCAN PROCEDURE 101

Variable costs

Labor (1/2 hour at $12.00)	$ 6.00
Materials (7 scans at $3.00 per scan)	21.00

Fixed costs

Overhead A (direct and indirect)	100.00
Total cost per procedure	$127.00
Profit margin B (10% of total cost)	12.70
Charge for procedure 101 before deductions	$139.70
Deductions from revenue C	$24.65
Charge to be established	$164.35
Estimated number of procedures to be completed	50,000

A. The per-unit overhead costs are determined in the following manner:

Estimated total overhead costs	$5,000,000
Estimated number of labor hours for next accounting period (50,000 procedures x 0.5 hours)	25,000
Overhead rate per labor hour ($5,000,000/25,000 labor hours)	$200
Overhead rate for procedure 101 per labor hour (0.5 x $200)	$100

B. The profit margin in this organization is determined by a 10% markup on full cost.

Note: The flexible budget equation for procedure 101 would be:

$$\text{Total costs} = \$5,000,000 + (\$27.00 \times \text{quantity of procedures})$$

C. Deductions from revenue for uncompensated care are estimated at 15% of charges.

A hospital department could develop an income statement to estimate the next month's profit for a certain procedure, assuming a forecast of 50,000 procedures. This income data also would determine the department's budget:

Gross revenues (50,000 × $164.35)	=	$8,217,500
Allowances for uncompensated care (50,000 × $24.65)	=	1,232,500
Net revenues (50,000 × $139.70)	=	6,985,000
Expenses: Standard cost of services (50,000 × $127.00)	=	6,350,000
Projected profit margin (10% of total cost)	=	$ 635,000

Projected profit of Procedure 101 for the next accounting period would be $635,000, assuming that:

50,000 procedures will be completed during the month and capacity in the department is sufficient to accomplish this level without additional costs (such as overtime) being incurred;

- All 50,000 procedures will be billed at the stated charge of $164.35 and allowances will equal 15 percent of charges;
- All cost figures (such as salary costs) occur as planned; and
- The organization achieves all productivity measures (0.5 labor hours per test).

If any assumption is incorrect, a variance from planned profit will occur. Administrators then must determine whether variance was controllable and by whom.

PERFORMANCE MEASUREMENT

If the results for Procedure 101 were achieved as shown in **Exhibit 2**, the 49,000 procedures actually performed would be expected to provide $622,300 in profits ($12.70 × 49,000). The actual profit ($522,300), however, is $100,000 less than the expected profit ($622,300) and $112,700 less than the projected profit in the original budget ($635,000).

To evaluate the actual results for Procedure 101, a variance analysis report (**Exhibit 3**) could be constructed from the data in Exhibit 1 and 2 to explain the difference in profits. A profit of $12.70 is lost on each of the 1,000 procedures not completed. In addition, the $5,000,000 in overhead is not fully allocated to the 49,000 procedures actually billed. Because the overhead rate of $100 assumes that 50,000 procedures will be performed ($5,000,000/ 50,000), completing only 49,000 procedures results in an under-recovery of $100,000 ($100 × 1000) in overhead never billed to clients.

EXHIBIT 2 ACTUAL RESULTS FOR PROCEDURE 101

Standards:

Procedures planned	50,000	
Planned profit (50,000 × $12.70)	$635,000	
Standard charge per procedure		$164.35
Standard costs per procedure		127.00
Standard profit per procedure		12.70
Standard discount from charges		24.65

Actuals:

Procedures completed	49,000	
Gross revenues (49,000 × $164.35)		$8,053,15
Discounts (49,000 × $24.65)		1,207,850
Net revenues (49,000 × $139.70)		6,845,300
Actual labor and material costs (49,000 × $27.00)		1,323,000
Actual overhead		5,000,000
Actual profit		$ 522,300

Variance between planned and actual profit for 49,000 procedures:

Expected profit (49,000 × $12.70)	$522,300
Actual profit	522,300
Variance	$100,000 under-recovery

Failure to achieve the planned volume used in developing the overhead allocation for pricing always will result in an under-recovery of overhead costs. Each examination *not* completed results in a loss of $100 in fixed overhead recovery in addition to the loss of $12.70 in profit margin.

Because the planned and actual overhead totals were the same ($5,000,000), no overhead variance would show on the income statement. The charge for a procedure was established using the planned volume ($5,000,000/50,000 or $100), but the actual rate for 49,000 procedures would be $5,000,000/ 49,000 or $102. The difference results in an under-recovery of overhead. Unless a manager is aware of potential under-recovery of overhead, corrective action such as an increase in charges or a reduction in actual overhead expenses will not be taken in time to alleviate the shortfall in profit.

In this example, timely identification of the volume decrease of 1,000 could have led to a recovery of the $100,000 loss through overhead cost reductions or price increases. Managers can always estimate the amount of overhead that will be over- or under-recovered by multiplying the planned overhead rate by the forecasted difference between the planned volume used to establish the rate and the actual volume estimated to be billed.

Effective performance evaluation requires differentiation of costs controllable by managers from those heavily influenced by external events. Most healthcare administrators and managers are not able to control volume of services or even prices set under prospective reimbursement agreements. Physicians admit patients and order

services. Only when lost volume is due to capacity constraints can management be held responsible. Assigning responsibility and planning dollar implications *before* a contract is signed are the keys to successful contracting. Penalty clauses for not achieving volume and incentives for overachieving need to be negotiated with managed care organizations.

One way to prevent under-recovery of overhead is to stipulate contractually that HMOs will pay the fixed costs per day for each patient day not delivered and only the variable costs per day for each patient day in excess of the agreed on volume. Because variable costs per patient day are lower than fixed costs per patient day, HMOs have an economic incentive to deliver more than the negotiated total, limited, of course, by the provider's current capacity.

Focusing on the bottom line without fully understanding why variances occur can lead to dysfunctional decision making. A flexible budget, as shown in **Exhibit 3**, separates the profit expected under the planned volume from the profit variance caused by under-recovery of fixed overhead. Due to their high fixed costs, healthcare providers are particularly vulnerable to overhead under-recovery.

MANAGEMENT CONTROL

Some managers eliminate overhead volume variances by treating overhead as a period expense and not allocating it to individual outputs as done above. Because direct expensing of overhead eliminates the potential for volume variances, it

Blocher, Stout, Cokins, Chen: *Cost Management, 4e*

©The McGraw-Hill Companies, Inc 2008

also eliminates two powerful management tools: identifying impacts of fixed overhead on per unit prices, and monitoring recovery of overhead expenses to determine if and when fixed expenses should be reduced.

EXHIBIT 3 VARIANCE ANALYSIS FOR PROCEDURE 101

	Projected budget (50,000 procedures)	(49,000 procedures)	Variances
Gross revenue	$8.217.500	$8.053.150	$164.350 Unfavorable
Discount	1,232,500	1,207,850	24,650 Favorable
Net Revenues	6,985,000	6,845,300	139,700 Unfavorable
Costs^A	6,350,000	6,323,000	27,000 Favorable
Profit	$ 635,000	$ 522,300	$112,700 Unfavorable
Volume variance^B		$ 100,000 Unfavorable	=$100,000 Unfavorable
Profit margin variance^C			=$ 12,700 Unfavorable
Net variance			$112,700 Unfavorable

A. Based on flexible budget costs of $5,000,000 fixed costs + $27 variable costs per procedure.
B. 50,000 procedures were used to determine $100 overhead rate. 1,000 shortfall in procedures × $100 overhead rate per procedure = $100,000 of fixed overhead costs not recovered through billing process.
C. Profit margin lost due to reduced volume. 1,000 reduction in procedures × $12.70 profit per procedure = $12,700 reduction in profit.

A standard cost system that allocates fixed cost on a per unit basis provides information on the amount of fixed costs over- or under-recovered with volume changes. By monitoring changes between actual and planned (standard) volume, managers can make necessary changes in budgeted fixed costs as required. Volume shortfalls are also critical to other management decisions such as cash-flow planning, hiring, and strategic planning. Effective management control requires understanding how volume changes help achieve planned levels of performance and profits.

HIDDEN INVENTORY

Many healthcare organizations do not report work in process or finished goods inventories in their financial statements, implicitly assuming that all services provided by various cost centers have been entered in the billing system for accounting purposes. However, anecdotal evidence indicates that most clinical departments do not carry interim in-process charges, such as estimating inpatient charges for patients not yet discharged, on year-end financial statements.

The quantity of services provided by various cost centers can differ from the quantity reported in revenue accounts and recognized in accounting statements because of the normal time lag required to complete billing. For example, services (such as radiology, laboratory, and surgical procedures) provided to hospital inpatients usually are not billed until the entire procedure is finished.

Also, work completed at the end of a day typically is not forwarded to the accounting system immediately because patient care has highest priority, while billing comes later. (Time lag does not exist for expense accounts, which usually are recorded promptly.) Lost charges tend to increase when output and billing are not monitored.

Many overhead expenses are incurred as functions of time passing rather than patient volume. For example, most salaried employees insist on being paid without waiting for patient or client billing to be completed or cash received. If revenues and costs are to be monitored by departments, and if a matching of revenues and expenses is to occur, some type of cost system must be implemented to measure output that is in process or completed but not billed.

In manufacturing, unbilled activities are captured in work-in-process and finished goods inventories. As noted above, most healthcare providers do not maintain this type of formal inventory account. As a result, a "hidden inventory" of unbilled output can exist, distorting financial statements and information for management decisions.

For example, **Exhibit 4** presents data for a healthcare organization providing routine physical examinations including EKG and blood tests. Three hundred and ten examinations are billed on the income statement for the current period:

Revenues		
(310 exams × $80)		$24,800
Expenses: standard cost of service billed		
310 × $52.00	$16,120	
Volume variance	800	
Administrative expenses	$2,000	18,920
Net profit		$ 5,880

EXHIBIT 4: STANDARDS FOR ROUTINE PHYSICAL EXAM

Standard charge per exam[A]	$ 80.00
Standard costs for the laboratories:	
Supplies per exam	$ 8.00
Labor per exam	6.00
Variable laboratory overhead	18.00
Fixed laboratory overhead per month[B]	10,000.00
Fixed general administrative expenses per month[C]	2,000.00
Planned volume of exams per month	500
Standard unit cost per exam:	
Supplies	$ 8.00
Labor	6.00
Variable overhead	18.00
Total variable cost per exam	32.00
Lab overhead costs [D]	20.00
Standard full cost per exam	$ 52.00
Standard profit per exam: $80–$52=$28	

A. All patients pay charges for this exam. There are no uncompensated care accounts.
B. Fixed laboratory overhead is considered a product cost and allocated to individual products for control purposes.
C. Fixed administrative costs are treated as a period cost and not allocated to individual exams.
D. The per-unit fixed overhead cost is determined in the following manner: $10,000 lab overhead cost divided by the 500 exams estimated to be com
for the month = $20 lab overhead per exam.

The 460 examinations completed in the reporting period are used in calculating the volume variance for the department. The shortfall of 40 exams (500 planned - 460 actual) times the overhead rate of $20 equals the $800 volume variance reported.

Management is concerned because the profit at 310 exams should be $2,880 as determined below:

Revenues 310 × $80		$24,800
Expenses		
Variable 310 × $32.00	$9,920	
Fixed	$12,000	
Total expenses		21,920
Expected profit		$ 2,800

The $800 unfavorable volume variance explains why the reported profit ($5,800) is $3,000 greater than planned ($2,800).

While only 310 examinations were billed, the reported volume variance indicates that 460 were completed. Accordingly, 150 examinations (460 - 310) were *completed by the laboratory but not yet billed.*

Whether the paper work is still in the laboratory or has been lost (intentionally or unintentionally), revenues and expenses are improperly matched and reported income is overstated.

Performance evaluation is difficult to assess if only the bottom line is stressed and actual output measures are not available. A reconciliation can be determined in the following manner:

Expected net profit	$2,880
Actual reported profit	5,880
Unbilled overhead (150 exams ×	$3,000
$20 fixed overhead)	
Actual net profit	$2,880

The difference between examinations completed and examinations billed (460 - 310 = 150) times laboratory overhead costs per examination ($20) equals the $3,000 profit overstatement. If only 310 examinations had been completed, the volume variance would have been $3,800 instead of $800 and profit would have been as planned. Most managers like to report a higher level of productivity for their performance evaluation. Unless performance reports are matched with financial reports, unbilled charges will not be known.

In-process inventories exist in healthcare organizations whenever completed services are not billed. Standard cost accounting allows administrators to monitor both production and billing. Reporting unbilled services on internal financial statements or management reports draws attention to potential problems. Accounts similar to work-in-process and finished goods inventories for external reporting can be used to properly match revenues and expenses and provide more appropriate data for cost management and performance evaluation.

Blocher, Stout, Cokins, Chen: *Cost Management, 4e*

©The McGraw-Hill Companies, Inc 2008

14.3: OVERHEAD CONTROL IMPLICATIONS OF ACTIVITY COSTING

By Robert E. Malcom

Management accountants' "overhead control" analysis has historically been a contradiction in terms. We have understood for some time that traditional overhead analysis gave us no really useful control information. Recent research on cost drivers for activity based product cost determination has given us a new perspective on overhead control.[1] In addition to overhead pools being too aggregated and allocation of overhead being based on a single, probably irrelevant base, variance formulas are also being misapplied. As a result, accounting performance reports may signal that no deeper investigation is needed when one is warranted or indicate that consumption is a problem when price changes are to blame, etc.

The objective of this article is to assist in changing accounting practice, management education, and the professional examinations away from traditional overhead analysis and toward cost driver based flexible budgets. At best, any time being spent on the usual meaningless reports is a waste and should be avoided. Additionally, the credibility of other accounting reports may suffer by being tarred with the same brush. At worst, any managers relying on current reports may be misled into costly, incorrect decisions.

THE PROBLEM

Garrison's *Managerial Accounting,* a leading text in the field, contains the following typical treatment. "The variable portion of manufacturing overhead can be analyzed and controlled using the same basic variance formulas that are used in analyzing direct materials and direct labor."[2] As is common, the results are labeled Spending Variance and Efficiency Variance. Garrison then notes, "Most firms consider the overhead spending variance to be highly useful..., feeling that the information it yields is sufficient for overhead cost control."[3] Garrison does warn, as do most other authors, that *"...efficiency variance* is a misnomer" as efficiencies are "... not in the use of overhead *but rather in the use of the base itself."*[4] The efficiency variance simply tells the overhead effect of the difference between planned labor use and actual labor use. In a similar vein, Horngren and Foster say, "The spending variance is really a composite of price and other factors....For this reason, most practitioners used the term 'spending'

variance rather than merely 'price variance.'"[5] As will be demonstrated later with a case problem, faith in the spending variance to provide useful information can be very misplaced. If it can be demonstrated that the traditional spending variance is potentially misleading, and if we can agree that the efficiency variance is really just a reconciling item between absorbed overhead and budgeted overhead, why do we put ourselves through these analyses?

INDUSTRIAL PRACTICE

The traditional overhead analysis method—calculation of spending and efficiency variances—is a common procedure of major American manufacturers. Surveys of overhead accounting practices of *Fortune 500 Industrial Companies* from about a decade ago found that virtually all firms using standard costing computed summary overhead variances. It was also found that the number of firms using both spending and efficiency variances exceeded those using just a spending variance.[6]

---

1 See, for example, R. Cooper and R. Kaplan, "How Cost Accounting Distorts Product Costs," *Management Accounting* (April 1988), pp. 20-27 or J. Shank, "Strategic Cost Management: New Wine or Just New Bottles?" *Journal of Management Accounting Research* (Fall 1989), pp. 47-65.
2 R. Garrison, *Managerial Accounting: Concepts for Planning, Control, Decision Making,* 6th ed. (Homewood, IL: Richard D. Irwin, Inc., 1991), p. 371. The views quoted from Garrison are deemed representative of many managerial and cost accounting texts, especially those oriented toward undergraduate majors.
3 Ibid., p. 416.
4 Ibid., p. 417.
5 C. Horngren and G. Foster, *Cost Accounting: A Managerial Emphasis,* 7th ed. (Englewood Cliffs, NJ: Prentice-Hall, Inc., 1991), p. 255.
6 See J. Chiu and Y. Lee, "A Survey of Current Practice in Overhead Accounting and Analysis," contained in *Proceedings of the Western Regional Meeting, American Accounting Association* (San Diego, CA: San Diego State University, 1980), p. 240; or, J. Chiu and J. Talbott, Factory Overhead Analysis," *Managerial Planning* (July/August 1978), pp. 36-39.

In a broader based survey reported in 1990 at the American Accounting Association annual meeting, Emore and Ness reported, "cost information...has not progressed very far over the past few years, [....despite...] considerable literary attention.... ...[M]ost companies are still using the same labor-focused costing systems that have characterized U.S. industry since the early 1900s.... Even though direct labor accounts for less than 10 percent of production costs for the majority of firms responding, alternative bases for attaching indirect manufacturing costs to products (e.g., machine hours, material value, cycle time, etc.) were being used by fewer than 25 percent of the companies....The majority of firms do not break down overhead into its major component cost elements. Sixty-five percent....maintain five or fewer manufacturing cost elements in their product cost buildups [including materials and labor].... [M]any companies placed greater weight on the computational accuracy of their cost systems than their conceptual integrity."[7]

PROFESSIONAL EXAMINATIONS

As would be expected, standard costing problems have been an important part of the Certified Management Accountant examination since its inception. Problems with an emphasis on overhead spending and efficiency variances have continued through 1990 (the latest available at the time of writing).[8] Such problems occur less often on the Certified Public Accountant examinations, but at least two occurred through the 1980s[9]. Such findings should be expected based on usage in practice.

EDUCATION

Emphasis on overhead variances in the classroom is more difficult to detect. Norvin et al. recently synthesized surveys regarding the cost/managerial accounting curriculum. In all four of the synthesized surveys from the 1980s, standard costing/variance analysis was included in the top ten of the most important topics to be covered.[10]

Textbooks being published in the 90s continue to accommodate this preference. In an ad hoc sampling of numerous basic cost/managerial texts oriented toward the undergraduate accounting major, all incorporated the spending and efficiency overhead variances with their standard costing presentations. It is interesting however that Usry and Hammer, another widely used text (in addition to Garrison and Horngren and Foster cited above), has additionally an especially rich development of flexible budget detail articulated into its presentation of standard costing processes."

Most interestingly, a survey in final stages by Bayou reveals that less than two percent of AAA academics teaching cost and/or managerial accounting object to these variances. Bayou's survey was focused toward obtaining terminology preferences. The study produced 600 responses, a rather remarkable 40 percent response rate. He found that 23.5 percent preferred "Price Variance," 74.8 percent preferred "Spending Variance," and a mere 1.6 percent objected to the calculation of variable overhead variances (including a few with strong comments).[12]

A CASE DEMONSTRATION

The deficiencies involved in current overhead control techniques are difficult to convey in abstract terms. A case demonstration is therefore provided. As noted earlier, equivalent CMA examination problems on overhead variances have continued through 1990.
However, a June 1983 CMA problem is unusually rich in detail and was selected for demonstration analysis here.[13] (This problem also appears in Horngren and Foster with the CMA recommended solution.[14]) Relevant data are given in **Exhibit 1**.
The requirements of the problem include the calculation of variable overhead spending and efficiency variances. Two components make up variable overhead, indirect labor and supplies, but as is typical, only a summary analysis is required. Indeed, in most professional examination and text problems, only the summary data are provided. The published solution is given in **Exhibit 2**, although in a format to emphasize the generic price and quantity variance formulas and to extend the analysis to the two components.

---

[7]J. Emore and J. Ness, "Advanced Cost Management: The Slow Pace of Change," *Collected Abstracts of the American Accounting Association's Annual Meeting* (Sarasota, FL: American Accounting Association, 1990—full papers are available from the presenters), pp. 4, 6, 9, 11, and 14. [Ness is a Cost Management Group partner with Price Waterhouse in St. Louis, which has also published overlapping material from this survey.]

[8]See, for example, the following CMA examinations: December 1990, Part 3, Question 1; December 1989, Part 4, Question 1; and December 1988, Part 4, Questions 17 and 18.

[9]For examples from the CPA examinations, see: November 1987 (Theory Number 1, Question 42 and Practice II, Question 4) and May 1984 (Practice II, Problem Number 5).

[10]A. Norvin, M. Pearson, and S. Senge, "Improving the Curriculum for Aspiring Management Accountants: The Practitioner's Point of View," *Journal of Accounting Education* (Fall 1990), pp. 210-211.

GENERIC EQUIVALENCES

As shown in **Exhibit 2**, the spending variance calculation is generically equivalent to the price variance for materials and labor. A difference in prices (standard and actual overhead rates in this case) is multiplied by an implicit "actual" base quantity. Here the analogy to labor and material price variance begins to break down, because the assumed actual is a very arbitrary base. As is common in most traditional systems, the arbitrary base here is direct labor. The actual overhead exceeds the calculated standard overhead and the calculation suggests an unfavorable variable overhead spending variance of $150.

The efficiency variance is calculated as the difference between the actual and expected bases (labor hours in the problem) multiplied by the standard rate. Again, the calculation follows the form for quantity variance for direct materials and labor. Actual direct labor hours are less than standard direct labor hours, and so a favorable overhead variance results. The calculated efficiency variance is $8,850 and the combined spending and efficiency variance for variable overhead is $8,700 favorable.

What are the implications of the above analysis? At best there is a signal to management that direct labor; the base, was efficiently used. If that is a fact, that knowledge would be more directly available to management from the direct labor variance analysis. Another message is that since spending is close to budget, activity is probably close to plan and that managers might be criticized lightly because the direction is unfavorable. At worst, managers might incorrectly be commended highly because their overhead usage is reported to be highly favorable. The latter two results might or might not be the case, but it will be demonstrated that the report in **Exhibit 2** is not the relevant basis for making this determination.

RESPECIFICATION OF VARIABLES

To know whether overhead is being controlled, in general a more disaggregated report should be used. The data given in the CMA examination are not sufficient for this purpose, so additional data (consistent with given totals) are provided by the author in **Exhibit 3**. The new data show prices and quantities for each of the overhead components. For simplicity, supplies are assumed to be barrels of lubricants.

---

[11] M. Usry, and L. Hammer, *Cost Accounting: Planning and Control,* 10th ed. (Cincinnati, OH: South-Western Publishing Co., 1991), pp. 562-592.

[12] M. Bayou, Technical Terminology of Management Accounting," research in progress, University of Michigan, Dearborn. Data were provided by personal communication with the author, March 1991.

[13] December 1983 CMA examination, Part 4, Section B, Question 7.

[14] Horngren and Foster, op. cit., p. 279.

Exhibit 1
NORTON PRODUCTS' MAY DATA

Variable Overhead	Standard Cost per Unit	Standard per Direct Labor Hour	Planned Costs for May	Actual Costs for May	Standard Costs for May
Indirect Labor	$1.25	$.25	$ 75,000	$ 75,000	$ 82,500
Supplies	1.70	.34	102,000	111,000	112,200
Total	$2.95		$177,000	$186,000	$194,700

Other Activity	Planned Data	Actual Data
Output Units	60,000	66,000
Direct Labor Hours per Output Unit	x 5.000	x 4.772
Total Direct Labor Hours	300,000	315,000

Source: Given or derivable from June 1983 Certificate in Management Accounting Examination, Part 4, Section B, Question 7.

Exhibit 2
PUBLISHED SOLUTION PLUS EXTENDED DETAIL

	Total		Indirect Labor		Supplies
Spending (or Price) Variance:					
Actual Rate ($ Actual / 315,000 DLH)	$ .590476		$ .238095		$ .352381
Standard Rate (Given)	− .590000		− .250000		− .340000
Rate Difference (direction may vary)	.000476	U	.0011905	F	.012381
Actual Direct Labor Hours	x 315,000		x 315,000		X 315,000
Spending Variance	$ 150	U	$ 3,750	F	$ 3,900
Efficiency (or Quantity) Variance:					
Actual Base (Direct Labor Hours)	315,000		315,000		315,000
Standard Base (5 DLH x 66,000#)	− 330,000		− 330,000		− 330,000
Quantity Difference (always same way, here F)	15,000	F	15,000	F	15,000
Standard Rate (Given)	x $ .590000		x $ .250000		x $ .340000
Favorable Efficiency Variances	$ 8,850	F	$ 3,750	F	$ 5,100
Total Variance	$ 8,700	F	$ 7,500	F	$ 1,200

Source: Institute of Certified Management Accountants, *Questions and Unofficial Answers for June 1983 CMA Examinat* (Montclair, NJ: National Association of Accountants, 1983), p. 62. [Data have been rearranged by the author to empha: the generic price and quantity aspects of the computations; Spending Variance may be viewed as a flexible budget ba: on actual direct labor.]

In **Exhibit 4** the same generic formulas are used for indirect labor and supplies per se as were used for aggregated overhead in **Exhibit 2**. Labels have been changed to price and quantity variances as now the calculations truly provide these results, i.e., they are not mixed results (except for the generally inconsequential joint portion).

COMPARISON OF ALTERNATIVES
Where before there was a large favorable overhead quantity variance reported, there are now large unfavorable quantity signals. Where before there was a modest unfavorable spending signal, highly favorable price variances are now indicated.

The problem highlighted by this analysis warrants further management attention. The problem is not masked by the offsets of similar favorable and unfavorable variances as was the case in the development of **Exhibit 2**. A review of **Exhibit 4** suggests that the traditional approach to analyzing overhead variances, as exemplified in **Exhibit 2**, is based on totally false premises.

In this model, actual overhead activity is much different than called for by the original plan. For indirect labor, the indication is that a lower quality or lesser-trained workforce was used, as the hourly rate paid was 20 percent less than standard ($10 versus $12.50). At the same time, much more time had to be spent to accomplish the task. Assuming a review shows that the task was appropriately accomplished, the tradeoff was well worthwhile, with a total favorable indirect labor variance of $7,500. Management should therefore be commended for this action. The variance directions and proportions are the same for supplies as for indirect labor. However, *Exhibit 2 indicates the opposite signal!*

The problems with the traditional approach are several: first, the summary spending variance is too much of an aggregation to provide any useful information for managers. But more importantly, the direct labor hours base for calculating usage (and spending) is at best a gross activity indicator; at worst it is simply irrelevant.

Blocher, Stout, Cokins, Chen: *Cost Management, 4e*
©The McGraw-Hill Companies, Inc 2008

Exhibit 3

ADDITIONAL DATA FOR ILLUSTRATION

	Indirect Labor	Supplies	Totals
Unit of Measure for Inputs	Hours (hr.)	Barrels (bbl.)	
Actual Input Units	7,500 hr.	1,000 bbl.	
Actual Cost per Input Unit	x $ 10 /hr.	x $ 111/bbl.	
Total Actual Cost (given)	$ 75,000	$111,000	$186,000
Standard Input Units	6,600 hr.	990 bbl.	
Standard Cost per Input Unit	x $ 12.50 /hr.	x $113.333 /bbl.	
Total Standard Cost (given)	$ 82,500	$112,200	$194,700
Total Variance (Total Actual less Standard Cost)	$ 7,500 F	$ 1,200 F	$ 8,700 F

Source: Data assumed by author to be consistent with Exhibit 1; details are needed for a complete solution.

HOMOGENEITY PROBLEM

As noted earlier, a simplifying assumption was made in the case of supplies by deeming the category to be all lubricants of the same type. A common characteristic of overhead is that it is a mixture of many different items, so there is often no applicable price or quantity per se. That is, supplies may be pounds of cleaning agents, gallons of solvents, boxes of computer ribbons, etc.

The price and quantity aspects of analysis are not totally intractable even then. Prices may be sampled for representative items as is done for the Consumer Price Index. Then quantities may be inferred as the remainder; albeit an abstract measure. This could become complex and the cost of developing that data must be weighed against the benefit obtained.

The crucial point is still that the traditional computations for overhead spending and efficiency variances yield meaningless outcomes. Appropriate signals from the traditional variances appear only by coincidence. There is a cost to produce that largely irrelevant, perhaps coincidentally correct data. Why not allocate that effort to the development of more useful information?

THE SOLUTION

An increasingly practical alternative to the traditional analysis is to use flexible budgets based on appropriate cost drivers for major components of overhead, as is illustrated in **Exhibit 5**. In this report the large component variances could then well be the basis for further analyses, just as was done earlier in **Exhibit 4**.

For a number of reasons it is time for us to redirect our standard cost practices and our standard cost teaching. First, overhead itself is a relatively larger cost. American manufacturing cost structures have changed over the years from labor being more than overhead to overhead being more than three times labor (and this is only on the average).[15] Second, the statistical tools necessary to implement the above are much more widely understood by managerial accountants than just a few years ago. Third, and perhaps most importantly, widespread computer processing has made it economical to do both the statistical analyses and maintain more detailed cost data bases. Variable budgeting has been around for a long time, although at best it has been practiced and taught as an adjunct to the traditional standard cost system. I suggest that it is time for us to switch the order of things and give most attention to the development of variable budgeting systems— because they have the most potential as control tools—and that we relegate the traditional standard cost overhead analysis to an appendix. That clerical analysis may tell us something about the relationship between our estimated product costs and the actual costs of our production, but it gives us very little information that might be useful for the management of our production activities.

---

[15]J. Miller, and T. Vollmann, "The Hidden Factory," *Harvard Business Review* (September-October 1985), Exhibit I, p. 143.

Exhibit 4
SOLUTION PER DETAIL DATA, VOLUME DRIVEN STANDARDS

	Indirect Labor		Supplies		Totals	
Price (Spending) Variance						
Actual Price of Input	$ 10.000	/hr.	$111.000	/bbl.		
Standard Price of Input	−12.500	/hr.	−113.333	/bbl.		
Price Difference (Favorable)	$ 2.500	/hr.	$ 2.333	/bbl.		
Actual Quantity of Input	x 7,500	hr.	x 1,000	bbl.		
Favorable Price Variance	$ 18,750	F	$ 2,333	F	$21,083	F
Quantity (Efficiency) Variance						
Actual Quantity of Input	7,500	hr.	1,000	bbl.		
Standard Quantity of Input	−6,600	hr.	−990	bbl.		
Quantity Difference (Unfavorable)	900	/hr.	10	bbl.		
Standard Price of Input	x $12.500	/hr.	x $113.333	/bbl.		
Unfavorable Quantity Variance	$11,250	U	$1,133	U	$12,383	U
Total Variance	$7,500	F	$1,200	F	$ 8,700	F

Source: Data from Exhibits 1 and 3.

COST-DRIVER IDENTIFICATION

Presaging Johnson and Kaplan by many years, B. Goetz wrote in 1949, "Traditional cost data tend to be irrelevant and mischievous" and he proposed that "...the systems should be discontinued to save the clerical costs of operating them." Goetz argued that each overhead account "... should be homogeneous with respect to every significant dimension of managerial problems of planning and control. Some of the major dimensions along which burden may vary are number of units of output, number of orders, number of operations, capacity of plant, number of catalogue items offered, and span of anticipation [life cycle]...These recommendations would tend vastly to increase the number of primary burden accounts..."[16] Such dimensions of variability are today being referred to as cost drivers, i.e., the activity that drives costs.

The identification of cost drivers was an important part of J. Dean's pioneering cost study work of 1936. Indeed, using regression analysis, Dean identified product variety (recently rediscovered) as an important element which influenced cost levels.[17] His nonelectronic computations must have been laborious and a National Association of Accountants research study of 1949-50 implied that the least squares method was little used by industry.[18]

REGRESSION UNDERSTANDING

For accounting students the least squares method was included as a brief appendix by both R. Anthony and C. Horngren in the respective first editions of their managerial accounting texts of 1956 and 1962. Horngren then commented that the method was "cumbersome... [and] not so often used."[19] He did not expand this material until his third edition in 1972. Such coverage is now standard, although often the emphasis is merely on cost separation rather than cost driver selection.

[16] See B. Goetz, *Management Planning and Control: A Managerial Approach to Industrial Accounting,* 1st ed. (New York: McGraw-Hill Book Co., 1949), pp. 162-163, and T. Johnson and R. Kaplan, *Relevance Lost: The Rise and Fall of Management Accounting* (Boston: Harvard Business School Press, 1987).

[17] J. Dean, "The Statistical Determination of Costs with Special Reference to Marginal Costs" in *The Studies of Business Administration,* 7:1 (Chicago: School of Business, University of Chicago, 1936), p. 103 (may possibly be found as a supplement to *Journal of Business);* Dean was not the first to apply the least-squares method to the analysis of business costs and he cites an application by R. Livingston, "Control of Operating Expenses," *Mechanical Engineering* (LIV, 1926), p. 18. A Compilation of Dean's cost studies can be found in his *Statistical Cost Estimation* (Bloomington: Indiana University Press, 1976).

[18] National Association of Accountants, *Research Reports 16-18,* "The Analysis of Cost-Volume-Profit Relationships" (New York: National Association of Accountants, 1949-50), p. 16.

In the meantime, Touche had distributed to academics a case based on practice which focused on using regression analysis to select between product units and pounds as the best cost driver for controlling indirect labor in a shipping department.[20] These foresights notwithstanding, there is very little evidence in practice or academe of an integrated treatment of regression analysis in a flexible budgeting cost control system.

AN ILLUSTRATION

In **Exhibit 5** it is assumed that machine hours has been found by regression analysis to be the appropriate cost driver for the supplies (here lubricants). Also it is assumed that while all models of the product have the same direct labor hour standard, the more complex models require many more machine hours than the basic high volume model.

Thus, since **Exhibit 5** implies a shift in mix from complex to basic models, less lubricant should be needed than otherwise and the previous positive variance has here been transformed into a large negative variance. The analysis method of **Exhibit 4** still applies, but now the standard quantity is 900 rather than 990 barrels. This might indicate that a time-based maintenance schedule should be changed to a use-based schedule for optimum cost control.

Too often, the valuable notion of flexible budgeting has been wasted because we have failed to look diligently for the cost driver. For a useful example, consider forklift operator costs. In general, as output rises, so will direct labor and forklift labor. All appear to be associated. Where the flexible budget is based on direct labor, the resultant spending variance can send a seriously misleading signal. If direct labor usage is inefficient, there is no reason at all to expect more forklift labor, but this is the traditional accounting result. Indeed, if direct labor is inefficient, material may have been used more carefully and less fork lift labor should be needed.

The most likely cost driver for forklift labor is number of pallets moved, with pallet density a secondary consideration. Material usage might be a surrogate for number of pallets. Output volume would not usually be the appropriate driver either, as it would be common for material usage to be above or below expectations due to raw material quality or specification changes or machine malfunctions, etc. The most probable cause for forklift use must be found if the variable budget is to send the correct variance signals.

STICKINESS OF COSTS

Not only has there been a long run trend for overhead to grow as a proportion of total operating costs, but many of these new costs tend to be somewhat nonvariable in character i.e., lumpy and not strictly proportional to changes in activity. A common example is materials ordering and handling costs. As production grows, additional employees are added to handle the additional load; but, if production decreases, these personnel are not immediately laid off. Thus these lumpy costs stick even if activity declines and such costs have therefore sometimes been labeled "sticky costs."

Sticky costs have sometimes been found to be driven by product variety rather than units of output. **Exhibit 5** assumes that in addition to the basic high volume product, two dozen other models have been offered and every model requires roughly $3,000 per month in labor support costs for materials purchasing and handling. For May, twenty models were produced, which should have required only $60,000 in indirect labor. Since $75,000 was actually spent, there is an unfavorable variance now of $15,000.

R. Beyer devoted considerable attention to the problem of such sticky costs in his 1963 book on profitability accounting. He labeled these items "long-range variable costs," seemingly another oxymoron. Beyer's solution was to create two budget figures. The longer-run figure was the responsibility of top management and the shorter-run figure was the responsibility of operational management. He termed the former the "management decision variance" and noted that layoffs from "this 'hard-line' approach... [would]...ultimately result in the most economical operation."[21]

---

[19]See R. Anthony, *Management Accounting: Text and Casts* (Homewood, IL: R. D. Irwin, 1956), pp. 316-19, and C. Horngren, *Cost Accounting: A Managerial Emphasis* (Englewood Cliffs, NJ: Prentice-Hall, 1962), pp. 215-16.
[20]Touche, Ross, Bailey & Smart (now Deloitte & Touche), "Ralston Electric Company," miscellaneous paper, c.1966.

Exhibit 5

NORTON PRODUCTS' ACTIVITY BASED FLEXIBLE BUDGET FOR MAY
VARIABLE AND STICKY COSTS

Overhead Item (Activity Base)	(1) Budget Cost Per Activity Unit	(2) Activity Units	(3) Flexible Budget	(4) Actual Cost	(5) Variance
Variable Cost:					
Supplies (Machine Hours)	$17 per Machine Hour	6,000 Machine Hours	$102,000	$ 111,000	$ 9,000 U
Sticky Cost:					
Indirect Labor (Number of Models)	$3,000 per Model	20 Models	$ 60,000	$ 75,000	$15,000
Totals			$162,000	$186,000	$24,000 U
	(assumed)	(assumed)	(1) x (2)	Exhibit 1	(3) — (4)

*Implicit Standard supply use is $102,000 + $113.333 = 900 barrels and standard indirect labor hours are $60,000 + $12.50 = 4,800 hours.

If it is assumed for the Norton Products' case that top management had approved for May operations the $75,000 indirect labor planning budget of **Exhibit 1** per longer-run expectations, then top management would be responsible for the difference between the planned $75,000 amount (6,000 hours at $12.50) and the activity based $60,000 budget (4,800 hours) of **Exhibit 5**, or for 1,200 hours. The rationale for the strategic-operational split is that skilled indirect labor cannot be turned off and on as is usual for materials, but must be maintained with at least an intermediate-run outlook. The staffing level is primarily a higher management level decision.

Operational management is then responsible for using approved staffing levels as efficiently as possible. Since they were authorized $75,000 and spent $75,000, they have a zero total variance for indirect labor, albeit in a different manner than anticipated ($18,750 U for quantity and $18,750 F for price). Other inputs could be acquired in a similar manner, e.g., take or pay contracts; these would be amenable to the same treatment. Control is a shared responsibility, of course, and various management levels must work together for optimum operations.

Since sticky, lumpy costs may not be strictly variable with activity, the most viable procedure

for their determination is likely by an observant "walking around" manager or accountant and/or an engineering study. It is not possible to generalize this process; each company will have to make that determination based on its own cost and production character.

SUMMARY

Accounting for overhead control is an area ripe for improvement. With overhead costs rising as a proportion of manufacturing activity, with better educated business persons, and with computational power readily available to maintain data on a more disaggregated basis and to perform statistical analyses, better reporting is now likely to be cost beneficial and may make the difference between profitable or unprofitable operations.

[21]R. Beyer, *Profitability Accounting for Planning and Control* (New York: Ronald Press Company, 1963), pp. 156-57. Beyer also described in the same book a cost driver index, called the Control Factor Unit, for measuring departmental workloads; see pp. 144-45. Beyer was then managing partner of Touche, Ross, Bailey & Smart.

Blocher, Stout, Cokins, Chen: *Cost Management, 4e*

Exhibit 6
SOLUTION PER DETAIL DATA, ACTIVITY DRIVEN STANDARDS

	Indirect Labor		Supplies		Totals	
Standard Quantity of Input (Exhibit 5)	4,800	hr.	900 bbl			
Longrun Approved Quantity of Input (Exhibits 1 and 3)	− 6,000	hr.				
Difference	1,200	hr.				
Standard Price of Input (Exhibit 3)	x $12.50	hr.				
Strategic Quantity Variance	$15,000	U				
Longrun Approved Quantity of Input	6,000	hr.				
Actual Quantity of Input (Exhibit 3)	− 7,500	hr.	− 1,000	bbl.		
Difference	1,500	hr.	100	bbl.		
Standard Price of Input	x $ 12.50	/hr		/bbl.		
			$113.333			
Operational Quantity Variance	$18,750	U	$ 11,333	U		
Total Quantity Variance	$33,750	U	$11,333	U	$45,083	U
Price Variance (Exhibit 4)	18,750	F	2,333	F	21,083	F
Total Variance (Exhibit 5)	$15,000	U	$ 9,000	U	$24,000	U

Source: Exhibits 1, 3, 4, and 5; adapted from R. Beyer (see text).

As demonstrated, at best the continuance of the traditional standard cost approach to overhead analysis in the CMA and CPA examinations, in textbooks and classrooms, and in accounting reports of manufacturers, is a waste of time. It should be abandoned. The traditional labor based, flexible budget approach is almost as dangerous. At worst, the traditional approaches may be counter-productive, resulting in dysfunctional decisions and in a loss of credibility for other accounting reports.

The groundwork for better overhead control through activity based flexible budgets has been in development over the last half-century. Indeed, the professional literature abounds with success stories of leading edge companies in implementing advanced cost techniques. Many of these advances have more to do with production changes, as with materials requirements planning systems, than they do with underlying cost system changes, however.[22]

Mainstream accountants still have quite a long way to go. "Despite major conceptual and technological developments, little of the new thought in the field of cost management has found its way into practical application…"[23] For homogeneous data, regression and other analyses should be used to identify the underlying cost drivers. For less homogeneous data, sampling may be used to establish the underlying causes for differences from cost expectations. Sticky and strictly variable costs should be identified and controlled, respectively, by strategic and tactical techniques. Whenever activity based costing is appropriate for product cost determination, the same drivers should be equally relevant for cost control applications. It is time to set aside our primary occupation with traditional overhead variance analysis and focus our attention on cost-driver based variable budget systems. It is time for us to put our effort where there is more promise of return.

---

[22] J. Emore, and J. Ness, op. cit., p. 8
[23] Ibid.

Chapter 15
The Flexible Budget: Further Analysis of Productivity and Sales

Cases

15-1   Dallas Consulting Group

Readings

15.1: "Profit Variance Analysis: A Strategic Focus" by Vijay Govindarajan, John K. Shank, *Issues in Accounting Education* (Fall 1989).

This article uses a fictitious case to demonstrate how variance analysis can be tied explicitly to the strategies of the firm. It expands the Shank and Churchill framework (explained in the article) for variance analysis to include explicitly the strategy and the competitive position of the firm in the analysis and interpretation of results.

Discussion Questions:
1. Why is it inadequate and may even be misleading to rely only on the analysis reported in Table 3?
2. Does a favorable variance imply favorable performance?
3. Table 4 shows a rather elaborate and detailed analysis of variances of operating results. The analysis provides us information on the effect of variations of relevant operating factors on the operating result. The analysis includes relevant and important operating factors such as total market size, market share of the firm, sales mix, selling price, and costs. The analysis considers almost all, if not all, the factors that are of interest and important to management. Why is the analysis incomplete?

15.2: "Examining the Relationships in Productivity Accounting" by Anthony J. Hayzen, James M. Reeve, *Management Accounting Quarterly* (Summer 2000).

Change in profit of a firm or business unit can be analyzed in terms of a change in productivity and a change in price recovery. Change in product quantities and change in resource quantity drive the change in productivity. Change in product prices and change in resource prices drive the change in price recovery. These relationships can be displayed to provide an instant visual analysis of the causes of profit change. Such visualization can provide a robust method for analyzing strategy and stakeholder relationships.

Discussion Questions:
1. What is productivity accounting?
2. How can productivity accounting guide the overall strategy of the firm?

3. Give an example showing that a traditional business performance indicator may give conflicting signals on a firm's performance.

4. What are the elements in using productivity accounting to evaluate changes in profits?

5. What grid diagrams are needed in order to have an overall picture of the business's performance?

15.3: "Lean Accounting: What's it All About?" by Frances A. Kennedy, and Peter C. Brewer, *Strategic Finance* (November 2005), pp.27-34.

This article provides and introduction and illustration of the concept of lean accounting. A key ideas is the role of value streams. The illustration is based on an actual company, which is given the disguised name MIP.

Discussion Questions:
1. Why lean accounting?
2. What are the five steps of the lean thinking model?
3. What is a value stream and what role does it play in lean accounting?
4. What four areas did MIP address in implementing lean accounting?
5. How is waste defined in lean accounting?

Cases

15-1 Dallas Consulting Group

"I just don't understand why you're worried about analyzing our profit variance," said Dave Lundberg to his partner, Adam Dixon. Both Lundberg and Dixon were partners in the Dallas Consulting Group (DCG). "Look, we made $800,000 more profit than we expected in 2001 (see Exhibit 1). That's great as far as I am concerned." Continued Lundberg. Adam Dixon agreed to come up with data that would help sort out the causes of DCG's $800,000 profit variance.

DCG is a professional services partnership of three established consultants who specialize in helping firms in cost reduction through time-motion studies, streamling production by optimizing physical layout, and re-engineering operations. For each project DCG consultants spent the bulk of the total project time studying customers' operations.

The three partners each received fixed salaries that represented the largest portion of operating expenses. All three used his or her home office for DCG business. DCG itself had only a post office box. All other DCG employees were also paid fixed salaries. No other significant operating costs were incurred by the partnership.

Revenues consisted solely of professional fees charged to customers for the two different types of services DCG offered. Charges were based on the number of hours actually worked on the job.

Following the conversation with Lundberg, Dixon gathered the data summarized in Exhibit 2. He took the data with him to Lundberg's office and said, "I think I can identify several reasons for our increased profits. First of all, we raised the price for re-engineering studies to $70 per hour. Also, if you remember, we originally estimated that the 10 consulting firms in the Dallas area would probably average about 15,000 hours of work each in 2001, so the total industry volume in Dallas would be 150,000 hours. However, a check with all of the local consulting firms indicates that the actual total co0nsulting market must have been around 112,000 hours."

"This is indeed interesting, Adam," replied Lundberg. "This new data leads me to believe that there are several causes for our increased profits, some of which may have been negative. . . . . Do you think you could quantify the effects of these factors in terms of dollars?"

EXHIBIT 1: 2005 BUDGET AND ACTUAL RESULT

	Budget	Actual	Variance
Revenues	$12,600	$13,400	$ 800
Expenses: Salaries	9,200	9,200	
Income	**$ 3,400**	**$ 4,200**	**$ 800**

EXHIBIT 2: DETAIL OF REVENUE CALCULATIONS

	Hours	Rate	Amount
Budget:			
Re-engineering	6,000	$ .60	$ 360,000
Streamlining production	9,000	1.00	900,000
	15,000		$1,260,000
Actual:			
Re-engineering	2,000	$ .70	$ 140,000
Streamlining production	12,000	1.00	1,200,000
	14,000		$1,340,000

REQUIRED:

Use your knowledge of profit variance analysis to quantify the performance of DCG for 2005 and explain the significance of each variance to Mr. Lundberg.

This case was written and copyrighted by Professor Joseph G. San Miguel, Naval Postgraduate School.

Readings

15.1: PROFIT VARIANCE ANALYSIS: A STRATEGIC FOCUS[*]

by Vijay Govindarajan and John K. Shank

ABSTRACT: This paper uses a disguised case to compare and contrast three different frame works in analyzing profit variances—two that are in common usage today and one that is not but, in our view, should be. The purpose of the paper is to demonstrate how variance analysis needs to be tied explicitly to the strategic context of the firm and its business units.

Profit variance analysis is the process of summarizing what happened to profits during the period to highlight the salient managerial issues. Variance analysis is the formal step leading to determining what corrective actions are called for by management. Thus it is a key link in the management control process. We believe this element is underutilized in many companies because of the lack of a meaningful analytical framework. It is handled by accountants in a way that is too technical. This paper proposes a different profit variance framework as a "new idea" in management control.

Historically, variance analysis involved a simple methodology where actual results were compared with the budget on a line-by-line basis. We call this Phase I thinking. Phase II thinking was provided by Shank and Churchill [1977] who proposed a management-oriented approach to variance analysis. Their approach was based on the dual ideas of profit impact as a unifying theme and a multilevel analysis in which complexity was added gradually, one level at a time. We believe that the Shank and Churchill approach needs to be modified in important ways to take explicit account of strategic issues. Our framework, which we call Phase III thinking, argues that variance analysis

becomes most meaningful when it is tied explicitly to strategic analysis.

This paper presents a short disguised case, United Instruments, Inc., to illustrate the three phases or generations of thinking about profit variance analysis. We believe it also demonstrates the superiority of integrating strategic planning and overall financial performance evaluation, which is the essence of Phase III thinking. The purpose of this paper is to emphasize how variance analysis can be, and should be, redirected to consider the strategic issues that have, during the past 15 years, become so widely accepted as a conceptual framework for decision making.[1]

---

[1] During the past 15 years, several books (e.g., Andews [1971], Henderson [1979], and Porter [1980]) as well as articles (e.g., Buzzell et al. [1975] and Govindarajan and Gupta [1985]) have been published in the field of strategic management. In addition, two new journals (*Strategic Management Journal* and *Journal of Business Strategy*) have been introduced in the strategy area during the past ten years. Also, traditional management journals such as *Administrative Science Quarterly, Academy of Management Journal*, and *Academy of Management Review* have, during the past decade, started to publish regularly articles on strategy formulation and implementation.

---

[*] *John K. Shank is Noble Professor of Managerial Control and Vijay Govindarajan is Associate Professor of Accounting, both at the Amos Tuck School of Business Administration, Dartmouth College. The authors wish to acknowledge helpful discussions with Ray Stephens*

TABLE 1
UNITED INSTRUMENTS, INC.

		Budget (1,000s)		Actual (1,000s)
Sales		$16,872		$17,061
Cost of goods sold		9,668		9,865
Gross margin		$ 7,204		$ 7,196
Less: Other operating expenses				
Marketing	$1,856		$1,440	
R&D	1,480		932	
Administration	1,340	4,676	1,674	4,046
Profit before taxes		$ 2,528		$ 3,150

UNITED INSTRUMENTS, INC.: AN INSTRUCTIONAL CASE[2]

Steve Park, president and principal stockholder of United Instruments, Inc., sat at his desk reflecting on the 1987 results (T-1). For the second year in succession, the company had exceeded the profit budget. Steve Park was obviously very happy with the 1987 results. All the same, he wanted to get a better feel for the relative contributions of the R&D, manufacturing, and marketing departments in this overall success. With this in mind, he called his assistant, a recent graduate of a well-known business school, into his office.

"Amy," he began, "as you can see from our recent financial results, we have exceeded our profit targets by $622,000. Can you prepare an analysis showing how much R&D, manufacturing, and marketing contributed to this overall favorable profit variance?"

Amy Shultz, with all the fervor of a recent convert to professional management, set to her task immediately. She collected the data in T-2 and was wondering what her next step should be.

United Instruments' products can be grouped into two main lines of business: electric meters (EM) and electronic instruments (EI). Both EM and EI are industrial measuring instruments and perform similar functions. However, these products differ in their manufacturing technology and their end-use characteristics. EM is based on mechanical and electrical technology, whereas EI is based on microchip technology. EM and EI are substitute products in the same sense that a mechanical watch and a digital watch are substitutes.

United Instruments uses a variable costing system for internal reporting purposes.

---
[2] This case is motivated by a similar case titled "Kinkead Equipment Ltd.," which appears in Shank [1982].

PHASE I THINKING: THE "ANNUAL REPORT APPROACH" TO VARIANCE ANALYSIS

A straightforward, simple-minded explanation of the difference between actual profit ($3,150) and the budgeted profit ($2,528) might proceed according to T-3. Incidently, this type of variance analysis is what one usually sees in published annual reports (where the comparison is typically between last year and this year). If we limit ourselves to this type of analysis, we will draw the following conclusions about United's performance:
1. Good sales performance (slightly above plan).
2. Good manufacturing cost control (margins as per plan).
3. Good control over marketing and R&D costs (costs down as percentage of sales).
4. Administration overspent a bit (slightly up as percentage of sales).
5. Overall Evaluation: Nothing of major significance; profit performance above plan.

How accurately does this summary reflect the actual performance of United? One objective of this paper is to demonstrate that the analysis is misleading. The plan for 1987 has embedded in it certain expectations about the state of the total industry and about United's market share, its selling prices, and its cost structure. Results from variance computations are more "actionable" if changes in actual results for 1987 are analyzed against each of these expectations. The Phase I analysis simply does not break down the overall favorable variance of $622,000 according to the key underlying causal factors.

TABLE 2
ADDITIONAL INFORMATION

	Electric Meters (EM)	Electronic Instruments (EI)
Selling prices per unit		
Average standard price	$40.00	$180.00
Average actual prices, 1987	30.00	206.00
Variable product costs per unit		
Average standard manufacturing cost	$20.00	$50.00
Average actual manufacturing cost	21.00	54.00
Volume information		
Units produced and sold–actual	141,770	62,172
Units produced and sold–planned	124,800	66,000
Total industry sales, 1987–actual	$44 million	$76 million
Total industry variable product costs, 1987–actual	$16 million	$32 million
United's share of the market (percent of physical units)		
Planned	10%	15%
Actual	16%	9%

	Planned	Actual
Firm-wide fixed expenses (1,000s)		
Fixed manufacturing expenses	$3,872	$3,530
Fixed marketing expenses	1,856	1,440
Fixed administrative expenses	1,340	1,674
Fixed R&D expenses		
(exclusively for electronic instruments)	1,480	932

PHASE II THINKING: A MANAGEMENT-ORIENTED APPROACH TO VARIANCE ANALYSIS

The analytical framework proposed by Shank and Churchill [1977] to conduct variance analysis incorporates the following key ideas:

1. Identify the key causal factors that affects profit.
2. Break down the overall profit variance by these key causal factors.
3. Focus always on the *profit* impact of variation in each causal factor.
4. Try to calculate the specific, separable impact of each causal factor by varying only that factor while holding all other factors constant ("spinning only one dial at a time").
5. Add complexity sequentially, one layer at a time, beginning at a very basic "common sense" level ("peel the onion").
6. Stop the process when the added complexity at a newly created level is not justified by added useful insights into the causal factors underlying the overall profit variance.

T-4 and 5 contain the explanation for the overall favorable profit variance of $622,000 using the above approach. In the interest of brevity, most of the calculational details are suppressed (detailed calculations are available from the authors).

What can we say about the performance of United if we now consider the variance analysis summarized in T-5? The following insights can be offered organized by functional area:

Marketing
Comments:

Market Share (SOM) increase benefited the firm	$1,443 F
But, unfortunately, sales mix was managed toward the lower margin product	921 U
Control over marketing expenditure benefited the firm (especially in the face of an increase in SOM)	416 F
Net effect	$938 F
Uncontrollables: Unfortunately, the overall market declined and cost the firm	$680 U
Overall evaluation: Very good performance	

Blocher, Stout, Cokins, Chen: *Cost Management, 4e*

Manufacturing

Comments:

Manufacturing cost control cost the firm $ 48 U

Overall evaluation: Satisfactory performance

R&D

Comments:

Savings in R& D budget $ 548 F

Overall evaluation: Good performance

Administration

Comments:

Administration budget overspent $ 334 U

Overall evaluation: Poor performance

Thus, the overall evaluation of the general manager under Phase II thinking would probably be "good," though specific areas (such as manufacturing cost control or administrative cost control) need attention. The above summary is quite different—and clearly superior —to the one presented under Phase I thinking. But, can we do better? We believe that Shank and Churchill's framework needs to be modified in important ways to accommodate the following ideas.

TABLE 3
THE "ANNUAL REPORT APPROACH" TO VARIANCE ANALYSIS

			Budget (1,000s)				Actual (1,000s)	
Sales			$16.872	(100%)			$17.061	(100%)
Cost of goods sold			9,668	(58%)			9,865	(58%)
Gross margin			$ 7.204	(42%)			$ 7.196	(42%)
Less: Other expenses								
Marketing	$1,856	(11%)			$1,440	(8%)		
R&D	1,480	(9%)			932	(6%)		
Administration	1,340	(8%)	4,676	(28%)	1,674	(10%)	4,046	(24%)
Profit before tax			$ 2,528	(14%)			$ 3,150	(18%)

Sales volume, share of market, and sales mix variances are calculated on the presumption that United is essentially competing in one industry (i.e., it is a single product firm with two different varieties of the product). That is to say, the target customers for EM and EI are the same and that they view the two products as substitutable. Is United a single product firm with two product offerings, or does the firm compete in two different markets? In other words, does United have a single strategy for EM and EI or does the firm have two different strategies for the two businesses? As we argue later, EM and EI have very different industry characteristics and compete in very different markets, thereby, requiring quite different strategies. It is, therefore, more useful to calculate market size and market share variances separately for EM and EI. Just introducing the concept of a *sales mix* variance implies that the average standard profit contribution across EM and EI together is meaningful.

For an ice cream manufacturer, for example, it is probably reasonable to assume that the firm operates in a single industry with multiple product offerings, all targeted at the same customer group.

It would, therefore, be meaningful to calculate a sales mix variance because vanilla ice cream and strawberry ice cream, for instance, are substitutable and more sales of one implies less sales of the other for the firm (for an elaboration on these ideas, refer to the Midwest Ice Cream Company case [Shank, 1982, pp. 157–173]). On the other hand, for a firm such as General Electric, it is much less clear whether a sales mix variance across jet engines, steam turbines, and light bulbs really makes any sense. This is more nearly the case for United because one unit of EM (which sells for $30) is not really fully substitutable for one unit of EI (which sells for $206).

An important issue in the history of many industries is to determine when product differentiation has progressed sufficiently that what *was* a single business with two varieties *is now* two businesses. Some examples include the growth of the electronic cash register for NCR, the growth of the digital watch for Bulova, or the growth of the industrial robot for General Electric.

Following Phase II thinking, performance evaluation did not relate the variances to the differing strategic contexts facing EM and EI.

TABLE 4
VARIANCE CALCULATIONS USING SHANK AND CHURCHILL'S MANAGEMENT-ORIENTED FRAMEWORK

Key Causal Factors:

Total Market	Expected	Actual	Actual	Actual	Actual	Actual
Market share	Expected	Expected	Actual	Actual	Actual	Actual
Sales mix	Expected	Expected	Expected	Actual	Actual	Actual
Selling price	Expected	Expected	Expected	Expected	Actual	Actual
Costs	Expected	Expected	Expected	Expected	Expected	Actual

Profit Calculation:

Sales	$16,872	$15,836	$18,034	$16,862	$17,060	$17,060
Variable costs	5,769	5,440	6,195	5,944	5,944	6,334
Contribution	$11,076	$10,396	$11,839	$10,918	$11,116	$10,726
Fixed costs	8,548	8,548	8,548	8,548	8,548	7,576
Profit	$ 2,528	$ 1,848	$ 3,291	$ 2,370	$ 2,568	$ 3,150

Variance Analysis:

Level 1   Overall variance=$622 F

Level 2   Sales volume and mix=$158 U   Sales prices and costs=$780 F

Level 3   Sales volume=$763 F   Sales mix =$921 U   Sales prices =$198 F   Costs =$582 F

Level 4

Market Size =$680 U	Market Share =$1,443F	EM $1,418 U	EI $1,616	Sales prices =$198 F	Variable costs of manufacturing EM $142 U EI $248 U	Fixed costs

Fixed costs
- Manufacturing $342 F
- Marketing $416 F
- Administration $334 U
- R&D $548 F

Note: F indicates a favorable variance and U indicates an unfavorable variance.

TABLE 5
VARIANCE SUMMARY FOR THE PHASE II APPROACH

Overall market decline		$ 680 U
Share of market increase		1,443 F
Sales mix change		921 U
Sales prices improved		198 F
EM	$1,418 U	
EI	$1,616 F	
Manufacturing cost control		48 U
Variable costs	$390 U	
Fixed costs	$342 F	
Other		
R&D		548 F
Administration		334 U
Marketing		416 F
Total		$ 622 F

PHASE III THINKING: VARIANCE ANALYSIS USING A STRATEGIC FRAMEWORK

We argue that performance evaluation, which is a critical component of the management control process, needs to be tailored to the strategy being followed by a firm or its business units. We offer the following set of arguments in support of our position: (1) different strategies imply different tasks and require different behaviors for effective performance [Andrews, 1971; Gupta and Govindarajan, 1984a; and Govindarajan, 1986a]; (2) different control systems induce different behaviors [Govindarajan, 1986b; Gupta and Govindarajan, 1984b]; (3) thus, superior performance can best be achieved by tailoring control systems to the requirements of particular strategies [Govindarajan, 1988; Gupta and Govindarajan, 1986].

We will first define and briefly elaborate the concept of strategy before illustrating how to link strategic considerations with variances for management control and evaluation. Strategy has been conceptualized by Andrews [1971], Ansoff [1965], Chandler [1962], Govindarajan [1989], Hofer and Schendel [1978], Miles and Snow [1978], and others as the process by which managers, using a three- to five-year time horizon, evaluate external environmental opportunities as well as internal strengths and resources in order to decide on *goals* as well as *a set of action plans* to accomplish these goals. Thus, a business unit's (or a firm's) strategy depends upon two interrelated aspects: (1) its strategic mission or goals, and (2) the way the business unit chooses to compete in its industry to accomplish its goals—the business unit's competitive strategy.

Turning first to strategic mission, consulting firms such as Boston Consulting Group [Henderson, 1979], Arthur D. Little[Wright, 1975], and A. T. Kearney [Hofer and Davoust, 1977], as well as academic researchers such as Hofer and Schendel [1978], Buzzell and Wiersema [1981], and Govindarajan and Shank [1986], have proposed the following three strategic missions that a business unit can adopt:

BUILD:
This mission implies a goal of increased market share, even at the expense of short-term earnings and cash flow. A business unit following this mission is expected to be a net user of cash in that the cash throw-off from its current operations would usually be insufficient to meet its capital investment needs. Business units with "low market share" in "high growth industries" typically pursue a "build" mission (e.g., Apple Computer's MacIntosh business, Monsanto's Bioechnology business).

HOLD:
This strategic mission is geared to the protection of the business unit's market share and competitive position. The cash outflows for a business unit following this mission would usually be more or less equal to cash inflows. Businesses with "high market share" in "high growth industries" typically pursue a "hold" mission (e.g., IBM in mainframe computers).

HARVEST:
This mission implies a goal of maximizing short-term earnings and cash flow, even at the expense of market share. A business unit following such a mission would be a net supplier of cash.

TABLE 6 STRATEGIC CONTEXTS OF THE TWO BUSINESSES

	Electric Meters (EM)	Electronic Instruments (EI)
Overall market (units):		
Plan	1,248,000	440,000
Actual	886,080	690,800
	Declining Market	Growth Market
	(29% Decrease)	(57% Increase)
United's share:		
Plan	10%	15%
Actual	16%	9%
United's prices:		
Plan	$40	$180
Actual	30	206
	We apparntly cut price to build	We apparently raised price to ration
United's margin:		
Plan	$20	$130
Actual	9	152
Industry prices:		
Actual	$50	$110
	We are well below "market."	We are well above "market."
Industry costs:		
Actual	$18	$46
Procuct/market characteristics:	Mature	Evolving
	Lower technology	Higher technology
	Declining market	Growth market
	Lower margins	Higher margins
	Low unit price	High unit price
	Industry prices holding up	Industry prices falling rapidly
United's apparent strategic mission	"Build"	"Skim" or "Harvest"
United's apparent competitive strategy	The low price implies we are trying for low cost position	The high price implies we are trying for a differentiation position.
A more plausible strategy	"Harvest"	"Build"
Key success factors (arising from the plausible strategy)	Hold sales prices vis-à-vis competition.	Competitively price to gain SOM.
	Do not focus on maintaining and improving SOM.	Product R&D top create differentiation
	Aggressive cost control	Lower cost through
	Process R&D to reduce unit	experience curve effects

Businesses with "high market share" in "low growth industries" typically pursue a "harvest" mission (e.g., American Brands in tobacco products).

In terms of competitive strategy, Porter [1980] has proposed the following two generic ways in which businesses can develop sustainable competitive advantage:

LOW COST:

The primary focus of this strategy is to achieve low cost relative to competitors. Cost leadership can be achieved through approaches such as economies of scale in production, learning curve effects, tight cost control, and cost minimization in areas such as R&D, service, sales force, or advertising. Examples of firms following this strategy include: Texas Instruments in consumer electronics, Emerson Electric in electric motors, Chevrolet in automobiles, Briggs and Stratton in gasoline engines, Black and Decker in machine tools, and Commodore in business machines.

DIFFERENTIATION:

The primary focus of this strategy is to differentiate the product offering of the business

Blocher, Stout, Cokins, Chen: *Cost Management, 4e*

TABLE 7 VARIANCE CALCULATIONS USING A STRATEGIC FRAMEWORK

Key Casual Factors:

Total market	Expected	Actual	Actual	Actual	Actual
Market share	Expected	Expected	Actual	Actual	Actual
Selling price	Expected	Expected	Expected	Actual	Actual
Variable costs	Expected	Expected	Expected	Expected	Actual

Electric Meters (EM)

Sales	$ 4,992	$ 3,544	$ 5,671	$ 4,253	$ 4,253
Variable costs	2,496	1,772	2,835	2,835	2,977
Contribution	$ 2,496	$ 1,772	$ 2,836	$ 1,418	$ 1,276

Market size	Market share	Sales price	Manufacturing Cost
=$724 U	=$1,064 F	=$1,418 U	=$142 U

Electronic Instruments (EI)

Sales	$11,880	$18,652	$11,191	$12,807	$12,807
Variable costs	3,300	5,181	3,109	3,109	3,357
Contribution	$ 8,580	$13,471	$ 8,082	$ 9,698	$ 9,450

Market size	Market share	Sales price	Manufacturing Cost
=$4,891 F	=$5,389 U	=$1,616 F	=$248 U

Firmwide Fixed Costs (by responsibility centers)

	Budget	**Actual**	**Variance**
Manufacturing	$3,872	$3,530	$342 F
Marketing	1,856	1,440	416 F
Administration	1,340	1,674	334 U
R&D	1,480	932	548 F

unit, creating something that is perceived by customers as being unique. Approaches to a product differentiation include brand loyalty (Coca-Cola in soft drinks), superior customer service (IBM in computers), dealer network (Caterpillar Tractors in construction equipment), product design and product features (Hewlett-Packard in electronics), and/or product technology (Coleman in camping equipment).

The above framework allows us to consider explicitly the strategic positioning of the two product groups: electric meters and electronic instruments. Though they both are industrial measuring instruments, they face very different competitive conditions that very probably call for different strategies. T-6 summarizes the differing environments and the resulting strategic issues.

How well did electric meters and electronics instruments perform, given their stratetic contexts? The relevant variance calculations are given in Tables 7 and 8. These calculations differ from Phase II analysis (given in T-4) in one important respect. T-4 treated EM and EI as two varieties of one product, competing as substitutes, with a single strategy. Thus, a sales mix variance was comptued. Tables 7 and 8 treat EM and EI as different products with dissimilar strategies. Therefore, no attempt is made to calculate a sales mix variance. The basic idea is that even though a sales mix variance can always be calculated, the concept is meaningful only when a single business framework is applicable. For the same reason, Tables 7 and 8 report the market size and market share variances for EM and EI separately, and T-4 reported these

TABLE 8 VARIANCE SUMMARY FOR THE PHASE III APPROACH

Electric Meters	
Market size	$ 724 U
Market share	1.064 F
Sales price	1.418 U
Variable manufacturing cost	142 U
Electronic Instruments	
Market size	4.891 F
Market share	5.389 U
Sales price	1.616 F
Variable manufacturing cost	248 U
R&D	548 F
Firmwide Fixed Costs	
Manufacturing	342 F
Marketing	416 F
Administration	334 U
TOTAL	$ 622 F

two variances for the instruments business as a whole. Obviously, a high degree of subjectivity is involved in deciding whether United is in one business or two. The fact that the judgment is to a large extent subjective does not negate its importance. T-9 summarizes the managerial performance evaluation that would result if we were to evaluate EM and EI against their plausible strategies, using the variances reported in T-7 and 8.

The overall performance of United would probably be judged as "unsatisfactory." The firm has not taken appropriate decisions in its functional areas (marketing, manufacturing, R&D, and administration) either for its harvest business (EM) or for its build business (EI). The summary in T-9 indicates a dramatically different picture of United's performance than the one presented under Phase II thinking. This is to be expected because Phase II thinking did not tie variance analysis to strategic objectives. Neither Phase I nor Phase II analysis explicitly focused on ways to improve performance en route to accomplishing strategic goals. This would then imply that management compensation and rewards ought not to be tied to performance assessment undertaken using Phase I or Phase II frameworks.

CONCLUSIONS

Variance analysis represents a key link in the management control process. It involves two steps. First, one needs to break down the overall profit variance by key causal factors. Second, one needs to put the pieces back together most meaningfully with a view to evaluating managerial performance. Putting the bits and pieces together most meaningfully is just as crucial as computing the pieces. This is a managerial function, not a computational one.

Phase I, Phase II, and Phase III thinking yield different implications for this first step. That is, the detailed variance calculations do differ across the three approaches. Their implications differ even more for the second step. The computational aspects identify the variance as either favorable or unfavorable. However, a favorable variance does not necessarily imply favorable performance; similarly, an unfavorable variance does not necessarily imply unfavorable performance. We argue that the link between a favorable or unfavorable variance, on the one hand, and favorable or unfavorable performance, on the other, depends upon the strategic context of the business under evaluation.

No doubt, judgments about managerial performance can be dramatically different under Phase I, Phase II, and Phase III thinking (as the United Instruments case illustrates). In our view, moving toward Phase III thinking (i.e., analyzing profit variances in terms of the strategic issues involved) represents progress in adapting cost analysis to the rise of strategic analysis as a major element in business thinking [Shank and Govindarajan, 1988a, 1988b, and 1988c].

Blocher, Stout, Cokins, Chen: *Cost Management, 4e*

TABLE 9
PERFORMANCE EVALUATION SUMMARY FOR PHASE III APPROACH

	Electric Meters "Harvest" vs. "Build"	Electronic Instruments "Build" vs. "Skim"
Marketing		
Comments	If we held prices and share, decline in this mature business would have cost us $ 724 U	We raised prices to maintain margins and to ration our scarce capacity (our price was $206 vs. The industry price of $110). In the process, we lost significant SOM which cost us (netted against $1,616 F from sales prices). $3,773 U
	But, we were further hurt by price cuts made in order to build our SOM (our prices was $30 vs. the industry price of $50). $1,418 U 1,064 F	
	Net effect $1,078 U	This is a booming market that grew 57 percent during this period. Then why did we decide to improve margins at the expense of SOM in this fast growing, higher margin business?
	This is a market that declined 29 percent. Why are we sacrificing margins to build market position in this mature, declining lower margin business?	Fortunately, growth in the total market improved our profit picture. $4,891 F
	We underspent the marketing budget. $ 416 F	We underspent the marketing budget. $416 F
	But why are we cutting back here in the face of our major marketing problems?	But why are we cutting back here in the face of our major marketing problems?
Overall evaluation	Poor performance	Poor performance
Manufacturing		
Comments	Manufacturing cost control was lousy and cost the firm $142 U	Variable Manufacturing costs showed an unfavorable variance of $248 U (industry costs of $46 vs. our costs of $54).
	If we are trying to be a cost leader, where are the benefits of our cumulative experience or our scale economies? (industry unit costs of $18 vs. our costs of $21)	Does the higher manufacturing cost result in a product perceived as better? Apparently not based on market share data.
Overall evaluation	Poor performance	Poor performance
R&D Comments	Not applicable	Why are we not spending sufficient dollars in product R&D? Could this explain our decline in SOM?
Overall evaluation		Poor performance
Administration Comments	Inadequate control over overhead costs, given the need to become the low cost producer ($334 U).	Administration budget overspent. $334 U How does this relate to cost control?
Overall evaluation	Poor performance	Not satisfactory

REFERENCES

Andrews, K.R., *The Concept of Corporate Strategy* (Homewood, IL: Dow-Jones Irwin, 1971).

Ansoff, H.I., *Corporate Strategy* (New York: McGraw-Hill, 1965).

Buzzell, R.D., B.T. Gale, and R.G.M. Sultan, "Market Share—A Key to Profitability," *Harvard Business Review* (January-February 1975), pp. 97–106.
_____, and F.D. Wiersema, "Modelling Changes in Market Share: A Cross-Sectional Analysis," *Strategic Management Journal* (January-March 1981), pp. 27–42.

Chandler, A.D., *Strategy and Structure* (Cambridge, MA: The MIT Press, 1962).

Govindarajan, V., "Implementing Competitive Strategies at the Business Unit Level: Implications of Matching Managers to Strategies," *Strategic Management Journal* (May-June 1989), pp. 251–269.

_____, "Decentralization, Strategy, and Effectiveness of Strategic Business Units in Multi-Business Organizations," *Academy of Management Review* (October 1986a), pp. 844–856.

_____, "Impact of Participation in the Budgetary Process on Managerial Attitudes and Performance: Universalistic and Contingency Perspectives," *Decision Sciences* (1986b), pp. 496–516.

_____, "A Contingency Approach to Strategy Implementation at the Business Unit Level: Integrating Management Systems with Strategy," *Academy of Management Journal* (September 1988).

_____, and A.K. Gupta, "Linking Control Systems to Business Unit Strategy: Impact on Performance," *Accounting, Organizations and Society* (1985), pp. 51–66.

_____, and J.K. Shank, "Cash Sufficiency: The Missing Link in Strategic Planning," *The Journal of Business Strategy* (Summer 1986), pp. 88–95.

Gupta, A.K., and V. Govindarajan, "Business Unit Strategy, Managerial Characteristics, and Business Unit Effectiveness at Strategy Implementation," *Academy of Management Journal* (March 1984a), pp. 25–41.

_____, and _____, "Build, Hold, Harvest: Converting Strategic Intentions into Reality," *Journal of Business Strategy* (Winter 1984b), pp. 34–47.

_____, and _____, "Resource Sharing Among SBUs: Strategic Antecedents and Administrative Implications," *Academy of Management Journal* (December 1986), pp. 695–714.

Henderson, B.D., *Henderson on Corporate Strategy* (Cambridge, MA: Abt Books, 1979).

Hofer, C.W., and M.J. Davoust, *Successful Strategic Management* (Chicago, IL: A.T. Kearney, 1977).

_____, and D.E. Schendel, *Strategy Formulation: Analytical Concepts* (St. Paul, MN: West Publishing, 1978).

"Midwest Ice Cream Company," in J.K. Shank, Ed., *Contemporary Management Accounting: A Casebook* (Englewood Cliffs, NJ: Prentice-Hall, 1982), pp. 157–173.

Miles, R.E., and C.C. Snow, *Organizational Strategy, Structure and Process* (New York: McGraw Hill, 1978).

Porter, M.E., *Competitive Strategy: Techniques for Analyzing Industries and Competitors* (New York: The Free Press, 1980).

Shank, J.K., *Contemporary Management Accounting: A Casebook* (Englewood Cliffs, NJ: Prentice-Hall, 1982).

_____, and N.C. Churchill, "Variance Analysis: A Management-Oriented Approach," *The Accounting Review* (October 1977), pp. 950–957.

_____, and V. Govindarajan, "Making Strategy Explicit in Cost Analysis: A Case Study, " *Sloan Management Review* (Spring 1988a), pp. 19–29.

_____, and _____, "Transaction-Based Costing for the Complex Product Line: A Field Study," *Journal of Cost Management* (Summer 1988b), pp. 31–38.

_____, and _____, "Strategic Cost Analysis—Differentiating Cost Analysis and Control According to the Strategy Being Followed," *Journal of Cost Management* (Fall 1988c).

Wright, R.V.L., *A System for Managing Diversity* (Cambridge, MA: Arthur D. Little, Inc., 1975).

15.2: EXAMINING THE RELATIONSHIPS IN PRODUCTIVITY ACCOUNTING

By Anthony J. Hayzen, Ph.D., and James M. Reeve, CPA, Ph.D.

Productivity measures an organization's ability to convert labor, capital, and material inputs into valued goods and services. This, of course, is not a new concept. The challenge is to turn the concept into useful measures management can use. Peter Drucker put the case for productivity measurement as follows: "Without productivity goals a business has no direction, and without productivity measurement a business has no control." The purpose of productivity measurement, therefore, is control. Linking changes in productivity to resource allocation facilitates control. Therefore, we believe a useful productivity measure will link productivity changes to resources and hence to profitability.

We will demonstrate this link through an analytical technique we term "productivity accounting."[1] This approach measures the change in total resource productivity (that is, the changes in labor productivity. in materials productivity, capital productivity, and energy productivity) and the effects of these changes, taken together or individually, on the corresponding change in business profitability.

With this approach, a business can:

♦ **monitor** historical productivity performance and measure how much, in dollars or percent return on investment (ROL), profits were affected by productivity growth or decline;

♦ **evaluate** business profit plans (budgets) to determine whether the productivity changes implied are overly ambitious, reasonable, or not sufficiently ambitious; and

♦ **measure** the extent to which productivity performance is strengthening or weakening its overall competitive position relative to its competitors.

SOURCES OF PROFIT CHANGE

Productivity accounting seeks to link the change in profit to its underlying causes. Thus, we want to provide a dynamic assessment of the profit-generating ability of a company by focusing on change in profit rather than static profit levels. The drivers of profit *changes* will provide much greater directional insight than will descriptions of profit *levels*.

With the same basic accounting information used to calculate revenues and costs, we can gain more insight into the precise drivers of profit. We know that change in product prices and change in product quantities drive the change in revenue. Likewise, change in resource prices and change in resource quantities drive the change in the cost of producing the products. All of this information is available in traditional accounting systems. Thus, the change in profit can be described as the sum of two elements: the change in productivity and change in price recovery.

$$\text{Change in Profit} = \text{Change in Productivity} + \text{Change in Price Recovery}$$

In the equation above, productivity can be expressed in the following familiar way:

$$\text{Productivi ty} = \frac{\text{Product Quanity (Output Quantity)}}{\text{Resource Quantity (Input Quantity)}}$$

Productivity is a measure of process execution, or the ability to efficiently turn inputs into outputs. A company with superior process execution has very little waste or process leakage. Often this is the only way to successfully compete in hypercompetitive markets, such as consumer electronics.

Similarly, price recovery has the following relationship:

$$\text{Price Recovery} = \frac{\text{Product Price (Output Price)}}{\text{Resource Price (Input Price)}}$$

Price recovery is a measure of structural position, or the degree to which a firm is able to capture value it creates through pricing power. For example, a firm that has erected barriers to entry or captured markets through patent protection may be able to enjoy pricing power that would yield attractive price recovery. Examples of attractive price recovery can be found in firms in the aircraft repair and overhaul parts business, where barriers to entry due to customer-specific design and process knowledge make it difficult for new entrants to compete in the after-market parts sector. Some firms can compete on the basis of structural position (Microsoft or Coca-Cola), others on process execution (Nucor or Lincoln Electric), and a few others on both (Intel).

Table 1: CONVENTIONAL PRODUCTIVITY MEASUREMENT

	1998 Value	1998 Quantity	1998 Price	1999 Value	1999 Quantity	1999 Price
Sales	$99	11 units	$9	$110	11 units	$10
Rent	$52	26 sq. yards	$2	$78	26 sq. yards	$3
1. Profit	$47			$32		
2. Sates per sq. yard	$99/26 sq. yards = 3.8			$110/26 sq. yards = 4.2		
3. Productivity Quantity per sq.	11 units /26 sq. yards = 0.42			11 units /26 sq. yards = 0.42		

Firms without structural position and only average process execution will find it difficult to create and then capture value. More powerful supply chain participants will likely capture any value created. Examples abound in the automotive OEM parts business.

Productivity accounting decomposes these two sources of economic competitiveness—process execution and structural position—to guide the overall strategy of the firm.

TRADITIONAL MEASURES VS. PRODUCTIVITY ACCOUNTING

Traditional business performance indicators, such as sales per square yard, which is used in the retail industry; have the advantage of simplicity and familiarity Their main disadvantage, however, is that they can give conflicting signals because they do not isolate productivity from price recovery effects.

To illustrate this we will use the example of a simple retail business shown in Table 1. This business had revenue of $99 in 1998 from the sale of 11 items priced at $9 each. The revenue increased to $110 in 1999, generated from the sale of 11 items at $10 each. The rent paid for the store was $52 in 1998, which increased to $78 in 1999 for the same floor area of 26 square yards.

The first performance measure in Table 1 compares the profit of the business for the two years. Profitability decreased from $47 in 1998 to $32 in 1999.

The second approach uses the traditional ratio of sales per square yard. This method indicates that the performance of the business improved because the sales per square yard increased from $3.80 to $4.20.

The third method in Table 1 measures the performance of this business using productivity, As the table shows, productivity, and thus performance, has remained constant at 0.42 items per square yard.

We therefore have three conflicting measures of the business's performance. The second approach gives a conflicting signal as it uses revenue in the numerator, which contains both a quantity and a price effect.

The first and third methods (profit and productivity, respectively) give the correct signals. Profits have declined while productivity has remained constant. What would cause this? We must complete the picture by taking into consideration the effect the prices are having on the business. The productivity accounting method takes this into consideration and links both the effect of quantity changes (that is, productivity) and the price changes (that is, price recovery) to the change in profit, thus giving a complete picture of the performance of the business.

We can see from Table 1 what is happening in this business: Product prices have increased by 11% ($9 in 1998 to $10 in 1999) while the rent has increased by 50% ($2 per square yard in 1998 to $3 per square yard in 1999). Thus the decline in profit was due entirely to an inability to recover input price changes and had nothing to do with productivity, which remained constant.

NINE-BOX DIAGRAM

Profit, by itself, provides little managerial guidance. Rather, the manager needs information that identifies the causes for *change* in profit. Using the productivity accounting approach, one can take the *change in productivity* and the *change in price recovery* and relate them to the *change in profit*. If we now analyze the change in product quantities and change in resource quantities we get the change in productivity. If, in addition, we analyze the change in product prices and change in resource prices we get the change in price recovery. Price indexes may be used in situations where it is difficult to access detailed price and quantity information.

Together the measures give the manager a comprehensive analysis of how the changes in product quantity and resource quantity as well as the change in product price and resource price, are affecting the profitability of the business. Figure 1 shows a "nine-box diagram" summarizing these concepts.

Table2: QUANTITY AND PRICE INFORMATION FOR TWO PERIODS

	January 2000 (Reference Period)			February 2000 (Review Period)		
	Value	Quantity	Price	Value	Quantity	Price
Products						
Shirts	$150.00	10	$15.00	$216.00	12	$18.00
Cost Resources						
Linen (sq. yards)	$40.00	10	$4.00	$48.00	10	$4.80
Labor (staff-hours)	$48.00	6	$8.00	$60.00	5	$12.00
Total Cost Resources	$88.00			$108.00		
Capital Resources						
Machinery	$1,000.00	1	$1,000.00	$1,000.00	1	$1,000.00
% ROI	6.20			10.80		

The middle column of the figure explains the change in profit in the conventional way. But changes in revenues and costs include both price and quantity effects. Therefore, the change in profit also can be explained by the middle row, which explains the change in profitability as a function of the change in productivity and change in price recovery. The change in productivity, in turn, is explained by the change in output quantities over input quantities (the left-hand column). The change in price recovery is explained by the change in product prices over the change in resource (input) prices (the right-hand column).

AN EXAMPLE ILLUSTRATING PRODUCTIVITY AND PRICE RECOVERY COMPONENTS

Evaluating changes in profit using productivity accounting requires measures of productivity change and price recovery change over periods of time.

To illustrate changes in productivity and price recovery, we will use a simplified example of a business that manufactures shirts as the only product, using linen and labor as the cost resources and machinery as the capital resource. We ignore for the sake of simplicity buttons, cotton, thread, labels, wrapping, premises, and so on, which are also used to produce the shirts.

In our example we compare the performance of February 2000, the review period, with the performance of January 2000, the reference period, to arrive at the change in productivity and change in price recovery The data are shown in Table 2.

Using the basic definition of productivity and the data shown in Table 2, we can measure the change in productivity for each resource contributing to the business operation. Viewed in this context, labor productivity—by far the most commonly quoted productivity statistic—is but one of many aspects of a total resource productivity analysis. For example, the change in linen "productivity" can be measured as the change in the output/input ratio between shirts and square yards of linen across the two periods. The productivity of linen in January was 10 shirts/10 square yards, or 1.0, while it improved to 12 shirts/10 square yards, or 1.2, in February. The

Figure 1: NINE-BOX DIAGRAM

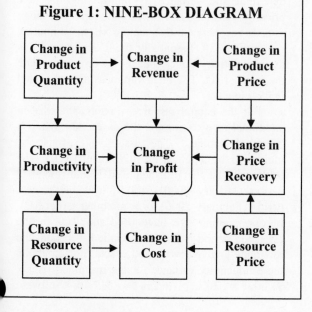

productivity change for linen shown in Table 3 is 20%, or (1.2 - 1.0)/1.0. A similar calculation can be performed for productivity change in labor [44% =(2.4 -1.67)/1.67]. Likewise, the productivity change in machinery must be 20% because the same number of machines produced 20% more output (see Table 3 for a summary of these results).

Table 3: CHANGES IN PRODUCTIVITY AND PRICE RECOVERY

| | Profit Variance | Productivity | | Price Recovery | |
		% Change	Variance	% Change	Variance
	A+B		A		B
Cost Resources					
Linen (sq. yards)	$ 9.60	20.00%	$ 9.60	0.00%	$ 0.00
Labor (staff-hours)	$ 9.10	44.00%	$26.40	(20.00%)	($17.30
Total Cost Resources	$18.70	(*) 33.33%	$36.00	(*) 9.09%	($17.30
Capital Resources					
Machinery	$27.30	20.00%	$12.40	20.0%	$14.90
Total Resources	**$46.00**	**(*) 28.47%**	**$48.40**	**(*) (1.100%)**	**($ 2.40)**

Similarly, there is also a unique price recovery relationship for each resource contributing to a business operation (that is, cost per unit of input). For example, the price recovery for labor can be measured as the change in the output/input ratio for shirt and labor prices across the two periods. The price recovery of labor in January was $15/$8, or 1.875, while it deteriorated to $18/$12, or 1.5, in February The price recovery change for labor shown in Table 3 is -20%, or (1.50- 1.875)/1.875. There was no change in the linen price recovery ($15/$4 = $18/$4.80).

The price recovery for the machine is calculated in the same way. The machine's value remained constant while output prices increased from $15 to $18, thus leading to a positive price recovery of 20% [($18/$1,000) - ($15/$1,000)]/($15/$1,000). This approach intuitively accounts for the opportunity cost of the machine. For example, if the machine's value increased by a hundredfold while the output prices remained steady a strong argument could be made for selling the machine instead of using it. Our approach shows the impact of consuming this opportunity cost.

PRODUCTIVITY ACCOUNTING CONTRIBUTIONS

The percentage changes in productivity and price recovery are in themselves informative to management but do not show the contribution these changes have on profit change, impacts that are far more important to management. The process for converting percentage changes to variances is rather complex as one must eliminate price recovery effects in the productivity variance

and productivity effects in the price recovery variance in order to achieve separation of the two effects.

To convert the percentage change in productivity into a dollar measure we take the new resource quantity (five staff—hours of labor) and multiply it by the new price ($12 per hour) and then by the percent change in productivity (44%), that is, 5 x $12 x 44% = $26.40. We have used the new price to show the current effect of the change in productivity. We determine the price recovery variance for labor by first establishing the resource input at assumed constant productivity. For labor, given that output increased by 20%, the assumed labor (at constant productivity) would also increase by 20%, or from 6 hours to 7.2 hours. Thus, we determine the variance by multiplying the new price by 7.2 hours and then by the percent change in price recovery (-20%), that is, $12 x 7.2 hours x -20% = $17.30. Essentially this calculation holds the productivity effect constant in order to isolate the price effect. The linen variances are calculated in the same way.

For the capital resources (assets) there is an additional step to convert the asset values into a "cost of capital." The asset value must be multiplied by a return on investment (ROI). The ROI could be the ROI achieved in the reference period (January 2000), the ROI in the review period (February 2000), or some other target ROI. In our example we have used the ROI in the reference period (6.2%) and applied it to both the reference and review period assets. For example, the productivity variance for the machinery is 1 x $1,000 x 20% x 6.2% = $12.40. Software

Blocher, Stout, Cokins, Chen: *Cost Management, 4e*

developed by one of the authors can be used to facilitate these calculations.[2]

For an illustration of the importance of measuring both productivity and price recovers notice in Table 3 that the financial benefit of the increase in labor productivity was $26.40 but that the unfavorable effect of price recovery of -$17.30 eroded this benefit. Therefore, the overall effect of labor on profit only amounted to a benefit of $9.10 ($26.40 - $17.30).

This simple example clearly illustrates the importance of measuring not only productivity but also price recovery so that the analyst can evaluate the effect of quantity and price changes on the profit of the business. The productivity accounting method of measuring productivity and price recovery shows that you can unambiguously evaluate each and every resource to find its productivity and price recovery impacts (that is, both change in index number and dollar effect) on the products produced. Next we will illustrate how this combined information can be displayed graphically for easier interpretation.

GRAPHICAL INTERPRETATION

In order to easily interpret a productivity accounting analysis for a business, the results should be presented in a visual form that is quick and easy to interpret. We will illustrate a grid format to visually represent the analysis. The "nine-box diagram" illustrated previously represents a large number of interactions, each having different implications for a business. A grid diagram helps to refine this information.

THE PROFIT GRID

The Profit Grid shown in Figure 2 is used to explain profit change in terms of a change in productivity and a change in price recovery. The productivity variance is plotted vertically and the price recovery variance is plotted horizontally. As the variances can be either positive or negative numbers, the grid is segmented into four quadrants with the origin in the center of the grid. The diagonal line connects all points where the productivity variance is offset by an exactly opposite price recovery variance. That is, there is no change in profit along this line. The segments above the diagonal (Segments 1, 2, and 3) signify an increase in profit while the segments below the diagonal (Segments 4, 5, and 6) signify a decrease in profit.

For example, assume that the business increased its profit by $20. This profit change arose from a $10 improvement in productivity and a $10 improvement in price recovery. Moving from the origin +10 in the vertical and horizontal directions places us in Segment 2. Segment 2 performance indicates the best of both worlds—the organization is improving productivity and price recovery. But excessive price recovery may create an opportunity for competitors to undercut the business's product prices and thereby reduce market share and profit.

Now assume that the $20 change in profit arose from a $25 productivity improvement, but the business lost $5 from price underrecovery. This is an example of a Segment 1 scenario. In Segment 1 the organization has strong competitive advantages from superior process execution while deterring competitors with price underrecovery

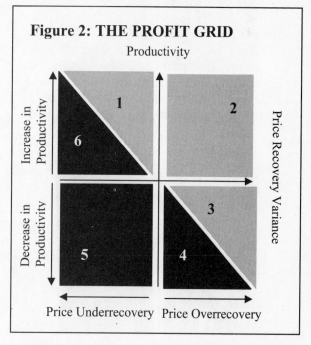

Figure 2: THE PROFIT GRID

(that is, the business has only partially recovered its resource price change through its product price change).

Continuing the example, assume that the $20 change in profit arose from a $10 decline in productivity, but there is a $30 price overrecovery. This places us in Segment 3. Profit in Segment 3 may be very temporary. It occurs primarily from very aggressive pricing relative to resource inputs. An organization will sustain such pricing power only in the face of sustainable competitive position. Without such position, competitors surely will be attracted to the business and erode the margin opportunities, leaving the firm to compete on weak process execution.

In each of these examples the same $20 change in profit had very different strategic interpretations. The favorable change in profit alone (that is, the difference between revenue and cost) does not give the insight necessary to evaluate business performance and competitive position in the marketplace.

Figure 3: FOUR-GRID FRAMEWORK

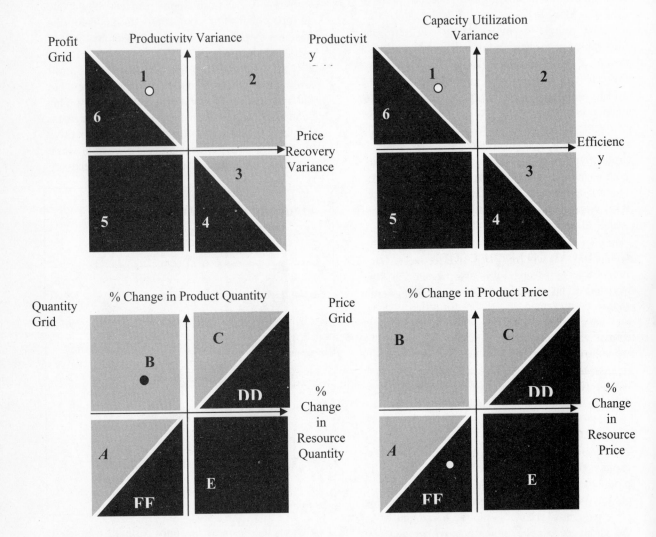

SUMMARY OF GRIDS

In order to have an overall picture of the business's performance, one needs to evaluate not only the Profit Grid but also the Quantity, Price, and Productivity Grids. Evaluation will clearly show the source of change in profit, productivity and price recovers, which are essential for understanding business performance. All four grids are shown in Figure 3.

The business appears in Segment 1 of the Profit Grid, indicating that the increase in profit arose from an increase in productivity which, however, was reduced by a price underrecovery. This places the business in a strong competitive position as competitors will require an even greater improvement in productivity to counter the price underrecovery. This segment is the classic position of the market leader in a hypercompetitive market. The Productivity Grid (Segment 1) shows that the increase in productivity arose from a large gain in capacity utilization, which was eroded by a decline in efficiency. In the short term, if the business

Blocher, Stout, Cokins, Chen: *Cost Management, 4e*

©The McGraw-Hill Companies, Inc 2008

improves its efficiency it will be able to increase productivity and thereby profits. The increase in utilization probably was due to increasing market penetration from the business's price leadership position.

We have introduced the concepts of efficiency and capacity utilization here for completeness. These concepts are used to distinguish between fixed and variable resources. Typically cost resources are regarded as variable and capital resources as fixed. In practice these resources fall somewhere between fixed and completely variable.

The Quantity Grid (Segment B) indicates that the business increased its production while discharging resources. In other words, it increased production and reduced resource use, clearly giving an increase in productivity.

The source of the price underrecovery, which placed the business in Segment 1 of the profit grid, is seen on the Price Grid. The decline of product prices exceeded the decline of resource prices, placing the business in Segment F.

Using this framework, it is clear that a business can generate profit growth through productivity growth or price overrecovery. The course that a business chooses, however, has important implications for its long-term competitive position.

STAKEHOLDER ANALYSIS

A simple value chain will link a company from the supplier to the customer. The impact of productivity and price recovery on suppliers and customers also can be evaluated using the grids, as the profit grid in Figure 4 shows.

In the segments to the right of the vertical axis the consumer pays a subsidy to the producer because of increasing product price relative to resource price (that is, product price is increasing faster than resource price). In the segments to the left of the vertical axis the producer is paying a subsidy to the consumer because of decreasing product price relative to resource price (that is, resource price is increasing faster than product price).

In the segments above the horizontal axis the resource supplier is harmed because of decreasing resource content per unit of product (that is, improved productivity). In the segments below the horizontal axis the resource supplier is favored because of increasing resource content per unit of product (that is, declining productivity).

This type of analysis also can be applied to the productivity, quantity and price grids. The expert analysis report generated by the FPM software automatically gives this analysis.

THE COMPLETE PICTURE

We have seen that a corporation or business unit can *analyze change in profit* in terms of a change in productivity and a change in price recovery. Change in product quantities and change in resource quantity drive the change in productivity. Change in product prices and change in resource prices drive the change in price recovery.

A corporation or business unit can achieve *productivity improvement* when product quantity increases at a faster rate than resource quantity but will experience *productivity decline* if resource quantity increases at a faster rate than product quantity. If all other factors are held constant, productivity improvement will translate directly into profit improvement.

When product price increases at a faster rate than resource price, the result is *price overrecovery*. If all other factors are held constant, price overrecovery will translate directly into increased profits in the short term. *Price underrecovery* occurs when resource price increases at a faster rate than product price. If all other factors are held constant, price underrecovery translates directly into a decrease in profits in the short term.

Instead of the conventional profit analysis represented by the middle column of the "nine-box diagram," many corporations and business units now analyze profit changes as a result of changes in productivity and price recovery, as represented by the middle row

These relationships then can be displayed to provide an instant visual analysis of the causes of profit change. Such visualization can provide a robust method for analyzing strategy and stakeholder relationships.

[1] As described by

[1] A.J. Hayzen, "Financial Productivity Management— An Overview;" WITS Industrial Engineering Conference, February 1988.

[2] B.J. van Loggerenberg, "Productivity Decoding of Financial Signals: A Primer for Management on Deterministic Productivity Accounting." PMA Monograph, 1988.

[2] Financial Productivity Management (FPM) software.

15.3: LEAN ACCOUNTING: WHAT'S IT ALL ABOUT?

by Francesa. Kennedy, CPA, and Peter C. Brewer, CPA

No, lean accounting has nothing to do with the South Beach Diet! Heck, you don't even need to count calories to become lean! But you *do* need to count what matters to the success of your business if you want to practice lean accounting. Though measuring what matters sounds intuitive, too many organizations are attempting to drive operational improvement with data that actually impedes the goals of improving customer satisfaction and financial results. Indeed, nonaccounting managers in numerous lean organizations across the globe would argue that their accountants are better off counting calories or carbohydrates rather than tracking performance indicators geared to the bygone era of mass production. The reason? Mass production metrics contradict lean thinking and often compel managers to make dysfunctional decisions. Lean thinking is about eliminating all forms of waste.

To be a lean thinker, or a lean accountant for that matter, you must relentlessly seek to view your organization through the eyes of your customers. Sounds simple enough, right? Yet a closer look at most "customerfocused" companies reveals that their employees myopically optimize functional performance, which results in enterprise-wide waste and unhappy customers. And, yes, in case you are wondering, the accountants often lose sight of the customer as well. Let's take a look at one company's experiences.

Figure 1: THE LEAN THINKING MODEL

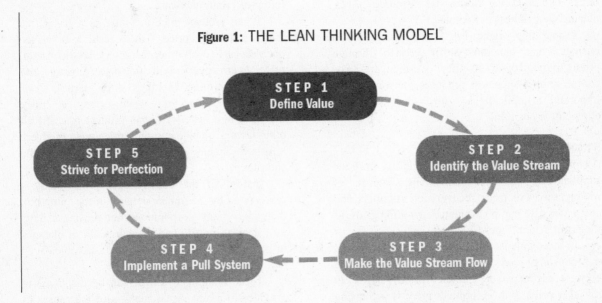

LEAN THINKING AT MIP

As the new millennium dawned, Midwest Industrial Products (MIP), a fictitious name for confidentiality purposes, didn't have cause for celebration. Bloated inventories, excessive waste, disgruntled customers, and unsatisfactory financial results were the order of the day for this *Fortune* 500 U.S. manufacturing company. In an effort to right the ship, MIP adopted the principles of lean thinking featured in Figure 1.

The first step of lean thinking is to Define Value. During this step it's critical to understand who's doing the defining and what they are valuing. The customers are the ones who define what they value in specific products and/or services.

The second step is to Identify the Value Streams—all the value-added activities that go into delivering specific products and services to customers. Inevitably, these value streams span functional boundaries, thereby requiring employees to see how their organization functions from the customer's viewpoint.

The third step, Make the Value Stream Flow, requires a departure from the mass production era approach of functionally organized batch-and-queue production that leads to inventory build-up, unsatisfactory order-to-delivery cycle times, and excessive rework and waste. Instead, lean uses cellular work arrangements that pull together people and equipment from physically separated and functionally specialized departments. The various pieces of equipment are sequenced in a manner that mirrors the steps of the manufacturing process, thereby enabling a continuous one-piece flow of production. Employees are cross-trained to perform all the steps within the cell.

The fourth step is to Implement a Pull System where customer demand dictates the production level. Visual controls are used to trigger upstream links in the value stream to initiate additional production. For example, when a point-of-use storage bin of component parts becomes empty, it automatically signals the upstream link in the value stream to replenish the parts without the need to prepare paperwork such as a materials requisition. Furthermore, establishing a takt time (the average production time allowed for each unit of demand), which is calculated by taking the total operating time available during a period and dividing it by the number of units demanded by the customer during that period, ensures that the pace of production remains in sync with customer demand.

The fifth step, Strive for Perfection, leverages the process knowledge of frontline workers. Rather than relying exclusively on management-level employees to generate ideas for improvement, management views all employees as intellectual assets capable of improving the flow of value to customers. To learn more about the principles of lean production, see Tom Greenwood, Marianne Bradford, and Brad Greene's "Becoming a Lean Enterprise: A Tale of Two Firms" in the November 2002 *Strategic Finance*.

GET OUT OF THE WAY!

With the transition to lean production under way, the nonaccounting managers at MIP had one clear message for their colleagues in accounting—add value or get out of the way! Three sources of discontent were underlying this message. First, the accountants were relying heavily on variance data that they tabulated in conjunction with the monthly financial accounting cycle. Variance data tabulated on March 5—five days after the month-end close—was totally useless when it came to helping managers make real-time operational decisions on February 5.

Second, the accountants were providing data that motivated managers to make decisions that contradicted MIP's lean production goals. For example, lot size variances and production volume variances motivated managers to maximize lot size and to keep workers busy making product to stock. Of course, these behaviors contradict the one-piece flow and make-to-order "pull" aspects of lean production where customer demand dictates the amount of production. Third, the financial accountants were inaccurately characterizing the financial impact of operational improvements. Most notably, the absorption costing income statement, which treats direct materials, direct labor, and variable and fixed overhead as product costs and all selling and administrative expenses as period costs, penalized managers' inventory-reduction efforts with a major hit to the bottom line.

The reason? In the illogical world of absorption costing, building up inventory increases income because of the fixed overhead deferral, while reducing inventory decreases income because of the need to expense previously deferred fixed overhead. To make matters worse, the absorption costing income statement was unintelligible to operations managers and frontline workers. Thanks to the concepts of closing out variances and fixed overhead deferrals, MIP's operations managers were confused—and frustrated—by an absorption costing income statement that didn't reflect the economics of the lean business model.

PROFITABLE GROWTH

Figure 2: LINKAGE BETWEEN STRATEGIC OBJECTIVES AND CELL MEASURES

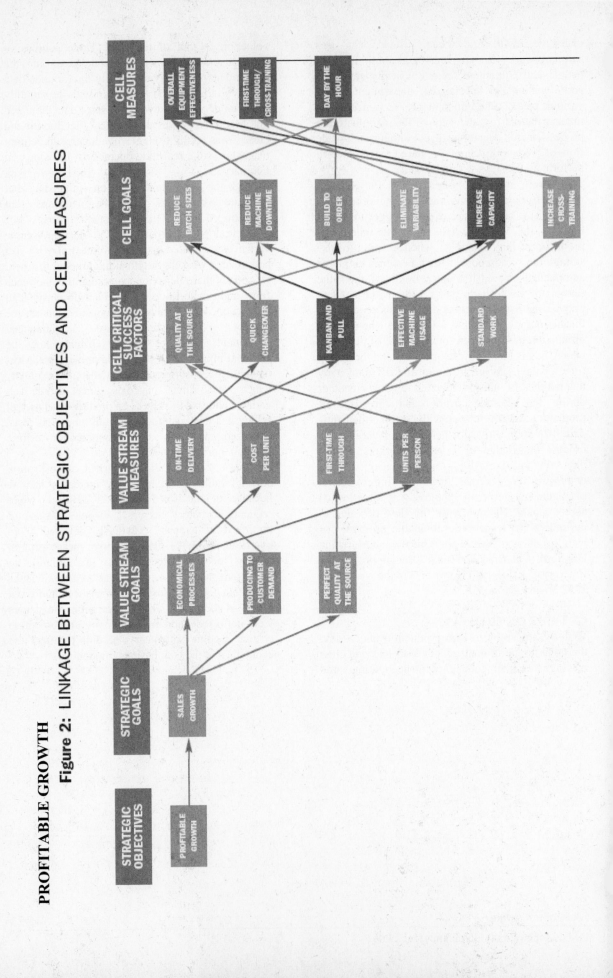

ENTER LEAN ACCOUNTING

In an effort to respond to what the accountants viewed as fair criticisms from their counterparts in operations, MIP initiated a transition to lean accounting in May 2002 by forming two cross-functional blitz teams that included members from operations, purchasing, engineering, and accounting to design lean accounting practices for one manufacturing cell. The cross-functional teams focused their efforts in four areas: (1) performance measurement, (2) transaction elimination, (3) calculating lean financial benefits, and (4) target costing.

PERFORMANCE MEASUREMENT

Historical financial measures that focused on functional efficiency were no longer going to get the job done. Instead, the team sought to create a cohesive set of linked strategic objectives and goals, value stream goals and measures, and cell goals and measures. Figure 2 shows a subset of what the value stream team developed. The strategic objective of profitable growth links to the strategic goal of sales growth, which is a function of three value stream goals: economical processes, producing to customer demand, and perfect quality at the source. These three value stream goals link to on-time delivery, cost per unit, first-time through, and units-per-person measures. These value stream measures are improved by focusing on five critical success factors at the cell level, namely quality at the source, quick changeover, kanban and pull, effective machine usage, and standard work processes. Finally, the cell critical success factors link to the six cell goals and three cell measures as shown. Notice that all measures link to the company's strategic objectives. In addition, frontline workers monitor the cell measures throughout the day to enable real-time response, and the operations managers monitor the value stream measures daily and weekly to drive the continuous improvement process.

TRANSACTION ELIMINATION

MIP's accountants realized that lean thinking applies to the information management side of the business as well as to making products. Therefore, as operations began to streamline its processes, the accounting department found that it was able to eliminate many of its transactions. For example, as materials requirements planning (MRP) was replaced with point-of-use visual controls (also called kanbans), material receipts were recorded by scanning bar codes rather than preparing receiving documents. As blanket purchase orders became more prevalent, the accountants authorized payment according to the terms of the purchase order when materials were received. This eliminated the need for accounts payable to perform the very time-consuming three-way match of purchase orders, invoices, and receiving documents that often required discrepancy investigation. MIP has reduced 18 labor categories to two, which is resulting in fewer errors and quicker processing. Furthermore, senior management is considering compensating its labor force on a salary basis, thereby eliminating the need to track labor hours altogether. Because manufacturing variance reporting has been eliminated and the value stream teams are using weekly value stream statements to make management decisions, MIP is considering closing the books on a quarterly basis rather than a monthly basis. Finally, as lean improvements have reduced inventory levels, cycle counts are becoming more accurate, and the time needed to perform these counts has declined. In fact, MIP believes it may be able to eliminate physical inventory counts altogether! Everything they need to verify inventory levels is readily in view.

CALCULATING LEAN FINANCIAL BENEFITS

The team created two tools to quantify the financial benefits of lean production. The first is a report called a value stream cost analysis that spans all functions directly involved in responding to customer orders for a particular product family. The second is an income statement format that complements lean production.

Value Stream Cost Analysis. Table 1 shows an example of a value stream cost analysis report. The top half of the report focuses on employees, and the bottom half focuses on machines. The table's top row shows employees' costs in total and for each link in the value stream. Employee time is broken down into four categories: productive, nonproductive, other, and available capacity. These four numbers sum to 100% for each column. So in Assembly, 40% of the employees' time is productively deployed, 25% is nonproductive, 4% is categorized as other, and 31% is currently idle. You interpret the data in the bottom portion of the table relating to the machines in the same fashion. The average conversion cost shown at the bottom of each column is calculated by dividing the total costs incurred as shown in each column by the total number of salable units actually produced during the period.

M

Table 1: VALUE STREAM COST ANALYSIS

	TOTALS	SALES & MARKETING	PRODUCTION CONTROL	MACHINING PARTS	QUALITY	ASSEMBLY	MFG. ENGINEERING	SHIPPING	MATERIAL HANDLING	PROD. ENGINEERING
EMPLOYEES										
Cost	$48,743	$11,000	$5,899	$9,100	$2,600	$4,550	$8,576	$2,275	$1,950	$2,793
Productive	27%	18%	8%	81%	0%	40%	10%	20%	0%	0%
Nonproductive	51%	60%	65%	16%	69%	25%	58%	42%	55%	76%
Other	5%	5%	5%	3%	6%	4%	6%	5%	5%	5%
Available Capacity	17%	17%	22%	0%	25%	31%	26%	33%	40%	19%
MACHINES										
Cost	$20,548			$15,000				$3,000	$2,548	
Productive	68%			71%				65%	55%	
Nonproductive	21%			20%				20%	24%	
Other	1%			0%				5%	6%	
Available Capacity	10%			9%				10%	15%	
Average Conversion Cost	$109.64	$17.41	$9.33	$38.13	$4.11	$7.20	$13.57	$8.35	$7.12	$4.42

ATERI

Table 2: THE LEAN INCOME STATEMENT FORMAT

	VALUE STREAM #1	VALUE STREAM #2	SUSTAINING COSTS	TOTAL PLANT
Sales	$1,500	$2,500		$4,000
Costs				
Material purchases	700	1,200		$1,900
Personnel costs	100	200	125	425
Equipment-related costs	200	300		500
Occupancy costs	75	125	50	250
Total Costs	1,075	1,825	175	3,075
Value stream profit before inventory change	425	675	(175)	925
Decrease (Increase) in inventory	50	75		125
Value stream profit	375	600	(175)	800
Shipping costs			300	300
Corporate allocation			75	75
Net operating income	$375	$600	$(550)	$425
Return on sales	25%	24%		11%

* The numbers are assumed and are for illustrative purposes only.

* The Shipping Department has not been entirely incorporated into the value streams at this point in time.

AL HANDLI

Blocher, Stout, Cokins, Chen: *Cost Management, 4e*

You can add material costs to this calculation's numerator to provide an actual average total cost per unit produced. If a particular value stream is characterized by product diversity, you can differentiate the costs assigned to products based on product features and characteristics. For simplicity, we won't explore this issue in detail. The benefits of this report are that it:

1. Shows where and how productively costs are incurred,
2. Is easy to understand,
3. Highlights areas of waste,
4. Shows actual costs rather than standard costs,
5. Identifies bottlenecks, and
6. Highlights opportunities to manage capacity more effectively.

For MIP, the value stream cost analysis highlighted the fact that the transition to lean production reduced waste and increased the amount of idle capacity. Consistent with the philosophy of lean thinking, MIP sought to redeploy its newfound idle capacity to grow sales rather than to reduce available capacity by cutting heads.

Income Statement Format. MIP's traditional absorption costing income statement suffered from three limitations. First, it obscured the impact of changes in inventory on profits by burying the "inventory effect" in cost of goods sold. Second, it included adjustments to income resulting from the use of standard costing that confused nonaccounting personnel. Third, it didn't depict costs from a value stream perspective. The product- vs. period-cost distinction satisfied financial reporting requirements, but it didn't offer useful insights to operations personnel. The lean income statement in Table 2 focuses on simplicity by attaching actual costs to each component of the value stream, isolating the impact of inventory fluctuations on profits, and separating organization-sustaining costs (costs that can't be traced to specific value streams) and corporate allocations from value stream profitability. Arbitrary cost allocations are avoided except in the case of occupancy costs, which are allocated to the value streams based on square footage to encourage minimizing space occupied. The profit for the total plant reconciles to the profit reported using an absorption format, but, unlike absorption costing, the underlying detail of the value stream statement is understandable to nonaccountants.

Target Costing

The lean team decided that traditional cost-plus pricing was no longer acceptable because it was based on the flawed assumption that customers would be willing to pay what MIP deemed appropriate based on its internal cost structure. MIP was taking its internal cost structure as a given and attempting to pass these costs on to customers rather than viewing its costs as a set of inputs that must be aligned profitably with the customer's expectations. Accordingly, the team turned its attention to target costing. The reason? Target costing is based on the premise that the pricing and continuous improvement processes begin by understanding customer needs.

As Figure 3 shows, MIP's target costing framework includes four main steps that break down into 11 smaller steps. The initial focus of the process clarifies customer needs and values followed by translating these insights into target costs that can drive the continuous improvement process. While MIP's transition to lean accounting is certainly not complete, the accountants have initiated the process of becoming a value-added partner to the organization's operations managers. The results of this partnership have been impressive. By May 2004, inventory levels had declined by 52%, waste and rework had decreased by 41%, and the timeliness of customer deliveries had increased by 27%. Now, instead of pleading with the accountants to move aside, the message from the shop floor has changed to welcome aboard!

HOW DO I BEGIN?

Implementing lean thinking within the accounting function is a journey that takes thoughtful consideration. Although changes in accounting can't outpace those in manufacturing, they should follow closely. The first step is to assess where in the lean journey your facility resides. Has production converted to a one-piece pull system?

Good. Then it's time to review performance metrics. Have you established value stream teams responsible for improvements? Good. Then it's time to look at value stream reporting. To assess your lean implementation progress read *Practical Lean Accounting* by Brian H. Maskell and Bruce Baggaley. It outlines a logical maturity process that matches accounting change with lean manufacturing changes (see a complete citation for this and other resources in "Resources at Your Fingertips" on p. 34). The second step on the path to lean accounting is to fully understand the length of the journey. For example, what will your lean accounting income statement look like? What does your income statement look like now? What steps must you take to make the transition? Who will be responsible for the change? What resources will be needed? Perform this analysis for each change in information accumulation and reporting. Relentlessly ask yourself the questions: Is this transaction still needed?

Does it add value to our business? The third step is to schedule dates to review implementation progress. The reviews should take place often enough to reinforce accountability and to communicate the importance of the lean transformation—and far enough apart to not drain resources. Include all stakeholders in these meetings, including value stream and cell leaders as well as key employees from purchasing, human resources, engineering, and accounting. Keep all implementation team members informed and on board.

Figure 3: TARGET COSTING

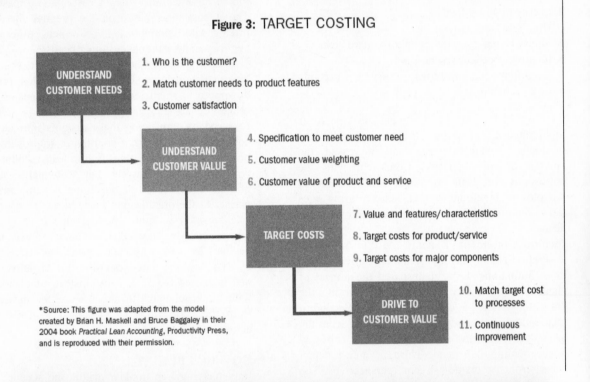

UNDERSTAND CUSTOMER NEEDS
1. Who is the customer?
2. Match customer needs to product features
3. Customer satisfaction

UNDERSTAND CUSTOMER VALUE
4. Specification to meet customer need
5. Customer value weighting
6. Customer value of product and service

TARGET COSTS
7. Value and features/characteristics
8. Target costs for product/service
9. Target costs for major components

DRIVE TO CUSTOMER VALUE
10. Match target cost to processes
11. Continuous improvement

*Source: This figure was adapted from the model created by Brian H. Maskell and Bruce Baggaley in their 2004 book *Practical Lean Accounting*, Productivity Press, and is reproduced with their permission.

RESOURCES AT YOUR FINGERTIPS

RESOURCE	DESCRIPTION
Lean Thinking by James Womack and Daniel Jones, Free Press Publishing, 2003.	Provides an in-depth look at lean principles and what it takes to achieve a responsive, customer-focused organization.
Real Numbers: Management Accounting in a Lean Organization by Jean Cunningham and Orest Fiume, Managing Times Press, 2003.	Introduces lean accounting concepts and discusses their impact on traditional reporting.
Practical Lean Accounting by Brian Maskell and Bruce Baggaley, Productivity Press, 2004.	Outlines step by step how to implement lean accounting, including a lean accounting assessment tool.
Who's Counting?: A Lean Accounting Business Novel by Jerrold Solomon, WCM Associates, 2003.	Chronicles the experiences of a plant controller as he gradually comes to understand why and how he and his department need to change.
The Complete Lean Enterprise: Value Stream Mapping for Administrative and Office Processes by Beau Keyte and Drew Locher, Productivity Press, 2004.	Describes how value stream maps can be created and used to improve administrative and office processes.

Blocher, Stout, Cokins, Chen: *Cost Management, 4e*

WHAT ABOUT SERVICE?

Lean thinking means identifying and eliminating waste in whatever form you find it. For manufacturers, such as MIP, it's easy to visualize the sources of waste—overproduction, waiting, defects, transportation, unnecessary inventory, unnecessary motion, and inappropriate processing. But how does waste manifest itself in a service business? The root cause often resides in the same type of functionally organized batch-and-queue processes that plague manufacturing. Hence, the logic of identifying value streams that span functional boundaries, building work processes that mirror those value streams, and using a pull approach to synchronize the level of output with customer demand is equally applicable to service businesses. Functionally organized service companies often find that it takes a piece of paper numerous days to route through two offices in the same building! The process view inherent in lean thinking is likely to reveal that this piece of paper could move through the system in minutes rather than days if you eliminate the time it spends sitting in somebody's inbox. Value stream maps are particularly useful in this type of situation. A "current state" map can be created that defines the flow of the current process and its performance levels. Then a "future state" map can be created to depict the desired flow of the process and its targeted performance levels. A modest number of specific improvement initiatives can be pinpointed on the "future state" map. Then a three-to-five-day improvement project, known as a kaizen event, can be scheduled and executed for each specific improvement initiative to make the "future state" map a reality. Whether you work in service or manufacturing, lean thinking can help your company improve its operations. The accounting function can either impede lean thinking by continuing to provide counterproductive information, or it can make the transition to lean accounting. If your company is making the lean transition, you can make the accounting department a part of the lean team.

Chapter 16
The Management and Control of Quality

Cases

16-1 **Precision Systems, Inc.,** by Suresh S. Kalgnanam and Ella Mae Matsumura (*Source*: Copyright © 1998 by the Institute of Management Accountants, Montvale, NJ).

16-2 **Kelsey Hospital** (*Source*: Arnold Schneider and John T. Large, *Global Perspectives in Accounting Education*, Vol. 1 (2004), pp. 17-24. The purpose of this case is to have students analyze and categorize costs of quality in a nonprofit health care setting. The case describes the need for a quality costing system in a hospital and the development of such a system for two primary treatments (intubation and bronchodilator treatments) performed in the respiratory therapy department of the hospital. A list of items pertaining to quality costs is presented and described for analysis, estimation, and categorization.

16-3 **Union Pacific Railroad: Using Cost of Quality in Environmental Management** (Source: *Cases from Management Accounting Practice* Volumes 10 and 11, Edited by Lawrence P. Carr, Copyright by Institute of Management Accountants, 1997). This case presents a good introduction to capital improvement justification as well as cost-of-quality (COQ) concepts. It can be used to reinforce the idea of justifying projects (and is therefore usable in conjunction with Chapter 20: *Capital Budgeting*) on the basis of not only cash savings but also based on "softer" savings such as cost avoidance, reducing future liabilities, efficiency savings, and the cost of non-compliance with the latest governmental regulations.

Readings

16-1: "GE Takes Six Sigma Beyond the Bottom Line" by G. T. Lucier and S. Seshadri, *Strategic Finance* (May 2001), pp. 40-46.

This article reports on the success of GE Medical Systems Inc.'s Six-Sigma effort. The article describes the training programs for employees in statistical process control and services and information offered by the Web site of the company to support the quality improvement efforts of more than 300,000 employees world-wide.

Discussion Questions:
1. What is a Six Sigma approach?
2. Describe the processes that GE used to implement its Six-Sigma program.
3. What are black belts? What roles do black belts play in GE's Six Sigma program?

16-2: "Accounting for Quality with Nonfinancial Measures: A Simple No-Cost Program for the Small Company" by Ronald C. Kettering, *Management Accounting Quarterly* (Spring 2001), pp. 14-19.

The author of this article argues that, to improve product/service quality, even small companies can develop and use nonfinancial, low-cost data to improve performance and customer satisfaction.

Discussion Questions:
1. In terms of a Cost of Quality (COQ) framework for managing and controlling quality costs, distinguish between cost of conformance and cost of non-conformance. Into what subdivisions can each of these two broad categories of quality-related costs be made? What is the definition of each of the four categories of quality cost in a typical COQ report?
2. Provide an overview of the three-step approach that the author of this paper recommends as a "no-cost" approach that can be used by smaller (i.e., more resource-constrained) organizations to monitor and control quality.
3. Provide at least two examples of non-financial quality indicators for each of the four categories of quality-related costs typically included in a COQ report.

Cases

16-1 Precision Systems, Inc.

Precision Systems, Inc. (PSD) has been in business for more than 25 years and has generally reported a positive net income. The company manufactures and sells high-technology instruments (systems). Each product line at PSI has only a handful of standard products, but configuration changes and add-ons can be accommodated as long as they are not radically different from the standard systems.

Faced with rising competition and increasing customer demand for quality, PSI adopted total quality management (TQM) in 1989. Many employees received training, and several quality initiatives were launched. Like most businesses, PSI concentrated on improvements in the manufacturing function and achieved significant improvements. However, little was done in other departments.

In early 1992, PSI decided to extend TQM to its order entry department, which handles the critical functions of preparing quotes for potential customers and processing orders. Order processing is the first process in the chain of operations after the order is received from a customer. High-quality output from the order entry department improves quality later in the process and allows PSI to deliver higher-quality systems both faster and cheaper, thus meeting the goals of timely delivery and lower cost.

As a first step, PSI commissioned a cost of quality (COQ) study in its order entry department. The study had two objectives:

- To develop a system for identifying order entry errors,
- To determine how much an order entry error costs.

PSI'S ORDER ENTRY DEPARTMENT

PSI's domestic order entry department is responsible for preparing quotations for potential customers and taking actual sales orders. PSI's sales representatives forward requests for quotations to the order entry department, though actual orders for systems are received directly from customers. Orders for parts are also received directly from customers. Service-related orders (for parts or repairs), however, are generally placed by service representatives. When PSI undertook the COQ study, the order-entry department consisted of nine employees and two supervisors, who reported to the order entry manager. Three of the nine employees dealt exclusively with taking parts orders, while the other six were responsible for system orders. Before August 1992, the other six were split equally into two groups: One was responsible for preparing quotations, and the other was responsible for taking orders.

The final outputs of the order entry department are the quote and the order acknowledgment or "green sheet." The manufacturing department and the stockroom use the green sheet for further processing of the order.

The order entry department's major suppliers are: (1) sales or service representatives; (2) the final customers who provide them with the basic information to process further; and (3) technical information and marketing departments, which provide configuration guides, price masters, and similar documents (some in printed form and others on-line) as supplementary information. Sometimes there are discrepancies in the information available to order entry staff and sales representatives with respect to price, part number, or configuration. These discrepancies often cause communication gaps between the order entry staff, sales representatives, and manufacturing.

An order-entry staff member provided the following example of lack of communication between a sales representative and manufacturing with respect to one order.

> If the sales reps have spoken to the customer and determined that our standard configuration is not what they require, they may leave a part off the order. [In one such instance] I got a call from manufacturing saying when this system is configured like this, it must have this part added.... It is basically a no charge part and so I added it (change order #1) and called the sales rep and said to him, "Manufacturing told me to add it." The sales rep. called back and said, "No [the customer] doesn't need that part, they are going to be using another option ... so they don't need this." Then I did another change order (#2) to take it off because the sales rep said they don't need it. Then manufacturing called me back and said "We really need [to add that part] (change order #3). If the

sales rep. does not want it then we will have to do an engineering special and it is going to be another 45 days lead time...." So, the sales rep and manufacturing not having direct communication required me to do three change orders on that order; two of them were probably unnecessary.

A typical sequence of events might begin with a sales representative meeting with a customer to discuss the type of system desired. The sales representative then fills out a paper form and faxes it or phones it in to an order entry employee, who might make several subsequent phone calls to the sales representative, the potential customer, or the manufacturing department to prepare the quote properly. These phone calls deal with such questions as exchangeability of parts, part numbers, current prices for parts, or allowable sales discounts. Order entry staff then keys in the configuration of the desired system, including part numbers, and informs the sales representative of the quoted price. Each quote is assigned a quotation number. To smooth production, manufacturing often produces systems with standard configurations in anticipation of obtaining orders from recent quotes for systems. The systems usually involve adding on special features to the standard configuration. Production in advance of orders sometimes results in duplication in manufacturing, however, because customers often fail to put their quotation numbers on their orders. When order entry receives an order, the information on the order is reentered into the computer to produce an order acknowledgment. When the order acknowledgment is sent to the invoicing department, the information is reviewed again to generate an invoice to send to the customer.

Many departments in PSI use information directly from the order entry department *(these are the internal customers of order entry)*. The users include manufacturing, service (repair), stockroom, invoicing, and sales administration. The sales administration department prepares commission payments and tracks sales performance. The shipping, customer support (technical support), and collections departments (also internal customers) indirectly use order entry information. After a system is shipped, related paperwork is sent to customer support to maintain a service-installed database in anticipation of technical support questions that may arise. Customer support is also responsible for installations of systems. A good order acknowledgment (i.e., one with no errors of any kind) can greatly reduce errors downstream within the process and prevent later non-value-added costs.

COST OF QUALITY

Quality costs arise because poor quality may—or does—exist. For PSI's order entry department, poor quality or nonconforming "products" refer to poor information for further processing of an order or quotation (see **Exhibit 1-1** for examples). Costs of poor quality here pertain to the time spent by the order entry staff and concerned employees in other departments (providers of information, such as sales or technical information) to rectify the errors.

CLASS I FAILURES

Class I failure costs are incurred when nonconforming products (incorrect quotes or orders) are identified as nonconforming before they leave the order entry department. The incorrect quotes or orders may be identified by order entry staff or supervisors during inspection of the document. An important cause of Class I failures is lack of communication. Sample data collected from the order-entry staff show that they encountered more than 10 different types of problems during order processing (see **Exhibit 1-1** for examples). Analysis of the sample data suggests that, on average, it takes 2.3 hours (including waiting time) to rectify errors on quotes and 2.7 working days for corrections on orders. In determining costs, the COQ study accounted only for the time it actually takes to solve the problem (i.e., excluding waiting time). Waiting time was excluded because employees use this time to perform other activities or work on other orders. The total Class I failure costs, which include only salary and fringe benefits for the time it takes to correct errors, amount to more than 4% of order entry's annual budget for salaries and fringe benefits (see **Exhibit 1-2**).

CLASS II FAILURES

Class II failure costs are incurred when nonconforming materials are transferred out of the order entry department. For PSI's order entry department, "nonconforming" refers to an incorrect order acknowledgment as specified by its users within PSI. The impact of order entry errors on final *(external)* customers is low because order acknowledgments are inspected in several departments, so most errors are corrected before the invoice (which contains some information available on the order acknowledgment) is sent to the final customer.

Blocher, Stout, Cokins, Chen: *Cost Management, 4e*

Corrections of the order entry errors does not guarantee that the customer receives a good quality system, but order entry's initial errors do not then affect the final customer. Mistakes that affect the final customer can be made by employees in other departments (e.g., manufacturing or shipping).

Exhibit 1-1: Examples of Failures

1. Incomplete information on purchase order.
2. Transposition of prices on purchase order.
3. More than one part number on order acknowledgment when only one is required.
4. Incorrect business unit code (used for tracking product line profitability) on the order acknowledgment.
5. Freight terms missing on the purchase order.
6. Incorrect part number on order acknowledgment.
7. Incorrect shipping or billing address on the order acknowledgment.
8. Credit approval missing (all new customers have a credit approval before an order is processed).
9. Missing part number on order acknowledgment.
10. Customer number terminated on the computer's database (an order cannot be processed if customer number is missing).
11. Incorrect sales tax calculation on the order acknowledgment.
12. Part number mismatch on purchase order.

Exhibit 1-2: Estimated Annual Failure Costs (as a percentage of order entry's annual salary and fringe benefits budget)

	Order Entry	Other Department	Total Costs
Class I Failure Costs			
Quotations	1.1%	0.4%	1.5%
Orders	0.9%	1.7%	2.6%
Total Class I Failure	2.0%	2.1%	4.1%
Class II Failure Costs			
Order acknowledgments	2.6%	4.4%	7.0%
Change orders	2.6%	—	2.6%
Final customers	0.02%	0.1%	0.1%
Return authorizations	1.9%	—	1.9%
Total Class II Failure	7.12%	4.5%	11.6%
Total Failure Costs	9.1%	6.6%	15.7%

Sample data collected from PSI's users of order entry department information show that more than 20 types of errors can be found on the order acknowledgment (see **Exhibit 1-1** for examples). The cost of correcting these errors (salary and fringe benefits of order entry person and a concerned person from another PSI department) accounts for approximately 7% of order entry's annual budget for salaries and fringe benefits (see **Exhibit 1-2**).

In addition to the time spent on correcting the errors, the order entry staff must prepare a change order for several of the Class II failures. Moreover, a change order is required for several other reasons not necessarily controllable by order entry. Examples include: (1) changes in ship-to or bill-to address by customers or sales representatives, (2) canceled orders, and (3) changes in invoicing instructions. Regardless of the reason for a change order, the order entry department incurs some cost. The sample data suggest that for every 100 new orders, order entry prepares 71 change orders; this activity accounts for 2.6% of order entry's annual budget for salaries and fringe benefits (see **Exhibit 1-2**).

Although order entry's errors do not significantly affect final customers, customers who find errors on their invoices often use the errors as an excuse to delay payments. Correcting these errors involves the joint efforts of the order entry, collections, and invoicing departments; these costs account for about 0.12% of order entry's annual budget (see **Exhibit 1-2**).

The order entry staff also spends considerable time handling return authorizations when final customers send their shipment back to PSI. Interestingly, more than 17% of the goods are returned because of defective shipments, and more than 49% fall into the following two categories: (1) ordered in error and (2) 30-day return rights. An in-depth analysis of the latter categories suggests that a majority of these returns can be traced to sales or service errors. The order entry department incurs costs to process these return authorizations, which account for more than 1.9% of the annual budget (see **Exhibit 1-2**). The total Class I and Class II failure costs account for 15.7% of the order entry department's annual budget for salaries and fringe benefits. Although PSI users of order entry information were aware that problems in their departments were sometimes caused by errors in order entry, they provided little feedback to order entry about the existence or impact of the errors.

CHANGES IN PSI'S ORDER-ENTRY DEPARTMENT

In October 1992, preliminary results of the study were presented to three key persons who had initiated the study: the order entry manager, the vice president of manufacturing, and the vice president of service and quality. In March 1993, the final results were presented to PSI's executive council, the top decision-making body. Between October 1992 and March 1993, PSI began working toward obtaining the International Organization for Standardization's ISO 9002 registration for order entry and manufacturing practices, which it received in June 1993.

The effort to obtain the ISO 9002 registration suggests that PSI gave considerable importance to order entry and invested significant effort toward improving the order entry process. Nevertheless, as stated by the order entry manager, the changes would not have been so vigorously pursued if cost information had not been presented. COQ information functioned as a catalyst to accelerate the improvement effort. In actually making changes to the process, however, information pertaining to the different types of errors was more useful than the cost information.

REQUIRED QUESTIONS

1. Describe the role that assigning costs to order-entry errors played in quality improvement efforts at Precision Systems, Inc.
2. Prepare a diagram illustrating the flow of activities between the order-entry department and its suppliers, internal customers (those within PSI), and external customers (those external to PSI).
3. Classify the failure items in **Exhibit 1-1** into internal failure (identified as defective before delivery to internal or external customers) and external failure (nonconforming "products" delivered to internal or external customers) with respect to the order-entry department. For each external failure item, identify which of order entry's internal customers (i.e., other departments within PSI that use information from the order acknowledgment) will be affected.
4. For the order-entry process, how would you identify internal failures and external failures? Who would be involved in documenting these failures and their associated costs? Which individuals or departments should be involved in making improvements to the order entry process?
5. What costs, in addition to salary and fringe benefits, would you include in computing the cost of correcting errors?
6. Provide examples of incremental and breakthrough improvements that could be made in the order entry process. In particular, identify prevention activities that can be undertaken to reduce the number of errors. Describe how you would prioritize your suggestions for improvement.
7. What nonfinancial quality indicators might be useful for the order entry department? How frequently should data be collected or information be reported? Can you make statements about the usefulness of cost-of-quality (COQ) information in comparison to nonfinancial indicators of quality?

Blocher, Stout, Cokins, Chen: *Cost Management, 4e*

16-2: Kelsey Hospital

"We need a way to identify quality indicators and measure these on an on-going basis. We already have some indicators of quality relating to clinical operations, but we want to add measures relating to service, such as patient waiting time. Eventually, we want to have hundreds of indicators to allow us to track performance throughout the hospital."

Michael Hopkins, Quality Control Manager

BACKGROUND

Kelsey Hospital is a private, nonprofit hospital located in Pennsylvania. The hospital has an affiliation with a local university medical school, and as such, its staff has faculty physicians and medical student residents and interns. Kelsey Hospital was founded in 1922 and in 2003 had adjusted revenues of $132 million and expenses of $126 million. This margin is fairly typical for tertiary health care providers, i.e., institutions that provide most services of a traditional hospital. Kelsey serves a seven-county area within a radius of 45 miles. The vast majority of patients, however, live within 10 miles.

Like most other hospitals, Kelsey's in-patient numbers have been decreasing in recent years (currently averaging around 350 patients), while its out-patient numbers have been on the increase (an average of eight percent for the last three years). In 2003, there were 16 out-patient programs. Contracted physicians are generally working in these areas. The contracted physicians are not employed by Kelsey Hospital. In contrast, "house physicians" are those directly employed by Kelsey.

Kelsey Hospital's strategic goal is to provide as many services as possible in health care. The hospital provides the following major in-patient services: Cardiology, Obstetrics/Gynecology, Orthopedics, and Neurology. Open-heart surgery, in particular, is one of Kelsey's specialties for which it is renowned. Two significant services that Kelsey does not perform, and does not plan to offer, are Psychiatry and Pediatrics. Several years before, Kelsey attempted to provide pediatric services, but abandoned it because of strong competition from other hospitals in the area. Kelsey has responded to market trends by increasing its capacity to handle out-patient treatments.

QUEST FOR QUALITY

In 2001, Kelsey Hospital commissioned a task force to study the issues affecting long-run success. One of its findings was that quality management would become an increasingly important factor for health care institutions. The task force concluded that all health care payers, from insurance companies to individual patients, would become more attentive to the quality management of health care service. The task force also recommended that Kelsey institute a balanced scorecard performance measurement system using the four standard categories (financial, customer, internal business process, learning & growth) found in the literature on balanced scorecards. It envisioned that quality measures would be included within the balanced scorecard.

A sense of urgency for quality control was felt largely due to the phenomenon of managed care contracts. With managed care contracts representing approximately 35 percent of Kelsey's patients, the task force believed Kelsey would need to convince these managed care organizations that it can provide high quality services at a reasonable cost. The Medicare and Medicaid programs also have a significant influence on Kelsey's revenues. For the majority of Medicare patients, their bills are reimbursed based on a system known as DRGs (Diagnosis Related Groups). For patients that cost more to treat than the fee schedule allows, Kelsey suffers a loss. Conversely, if Kelsey can treat the patient for less than the DRG reimbursement, then Kelsey is permitted to keep the difference.

As a result of the task force study, Kelsey made quality management one of its top priorities. Michael Hopkins was appointed as Quality Control Manager and, together with the Management Services Department, was instructed to develop a system for the entire hospital that would identify and measure quality indicators to be used for all of Kelsey's customers. Hopkins had been reading and hearing about cost of quality (COQ) systems in manufacturing settings and was impressed with what he came across and heard, so his first decision was to initiate a COQ system for one specific area of the hospital as a pilot study. He chose the Respiratory Therapy Department because of its relative simplicity. If a feasible COQ system could be developed in Respiratory Therapy, it would be used as a basis to implement COQ systems elsewhere in the hospital.

Needing somebody with COQ expertise, Hopkins engaged the services of an experienced consultant, Norma Highlander. Highlander had developed COQ systems in several other service industries such as lodging and transportation. Hopkins arranged an introductory lunch meeting with Highlander, Morry Easton (Director of Respiratory Therapy Department) and Mildred Berger (Administrative Director of Respiratory Care Services). Easton was managing three different departments, the smallest one of them being Respiratory Therapy. Berger had over 20 years of experience as a therapist and was currently working directly for Easton. The following conversation took place at this first meeting:

Hopkins: Norma will look at your operations and try to develop indicators of quality. We want to look at both clinical and service indicators.

Easton: Well, we already have our clinical indicators identified. But, I don't see how you can measure our service level.

Berger: That's right. I mean, you perform the therapy and either it helps the patient or not. How do you determine after the fact how performance was?

Hopkins: The main reason for going through this exercise is to assign costs to what we are doing. We need to categorize our quality costs as being prevention, appraisal, or failure costs. Hopefully, from this, we can assess our performance.

Berger: I just don't see how you break down what we do into neat little categories. If we were actually making something, a product, then maybe. But we are working on people.

Easton: I'd like to see us do this, but I just don't think it can be done. If you and Ms. Highlander can come up with something, that would be great.

Highlander: I know I have my work cut out for me, but I'm sure we can come up with something useful.

Their lunch ended soon thereafter and a second meeting was scheduled for highlander to become acquainted with the procedures in the respiratory therapy department.

RESPIRATORY THERAPY

To make the project more manageable, Hopkins and Highlander decided to focus further study on only two of the nine primary treatments performed in Respiratory Therapy. The two chosen were intubation and bronchodilator treatments because these were felt to be most representative of all the primary treatments.[1]

Intubation is the process of placing a breathing tube down the patient's nose, or more typically, throat. This procedure can only be ordered by a physician. Usually, intubation is ordered as the result of an emergency call. A total of eight to ten doctors, nurses, and therapists typically respond to the call. Once on the scene, one or two therapists examine the patient and another one or two get the equipment ready for use. A therapist is given two attempts at correctly placing the tube. If unsuccessful, another therapist makes an attempt. The wrong size tube is occasionally placed in the patient and must be replaced when this happens. All of this information is recorded and delivered back to Respiratory Therapy for quality review purposes. **Exhibit 1** contains a flowchart for the intubation process.

Bronchodilator treatments are also ordered by physicians. A bronchodilator is anything that opens or expands the bronchi (that part of the body that conveys air to and from the lungs). Unlike intubation, however, bronchodilator treatments do not result from emergency conditions. Once the treatments begin, they are given every four to six hours thereafter. The treatments last for four days and then a written order must be received for continued treatments. Once Respiratory Therapy receives an order for bronchodilator treatment, a therapist examines the patient for at least one of five medically necessary criteria (e.g., reversible air flow obstruction). If the patient fails to meet any one of the criteria, the therapist notes this on the patient's chart. However, even if none of the five criteria are present, the therapist still provides the treatment unless he/she feels it would be harmful to the patient. **Exhibit 2** contains a flowchart for the bronchodilator process.

Sharon King serves as the Respiratory Therapy Department's quality coordinator. Her duties include the monitoring of clinical quality for all nine primary treatments performed in Respiratory Therapy and also providing training for those therapists identified as having clinical skills deficiencies such as performing

---

[1] Examples of other treatments are mechanical ventilation, oxygen treatment, and saline solution treatment

Blocher, Stout, Cokins, Chen: *Cost Management, 4e*

unneeded therapies[2] or installing tubes incorrectly. For example, King will make random spot checks of patients' charts to determine how many unneeded therapies were performed within a given time period (as evaluated and noted by a physician). Based on these checks, therapists with clinical skills deficiencies may be identified and then sent to obtain additional training. If retraining does not solve the problem, then the therapist's employment is usually terminated.

The department holds meetings on a monthly basis to discuss quality problems and to determine corrective courses of action. These meetings also serve to review the performance of therapists. If a therapist is continually being written up by physicians for improper procedures (e.g., intubation installation), then the therapist is given an opportunity to explain the circumstances. If deemed unsatisfactory by Mildred Berger, then Sharon King will be asked to provide retraining to that individual.

COSTS OF QUALITY

Norma Highlander came up with the following list of items pertaining to costs of quality after spending two months reviewing manuals and other documents, conducting interviews and surveys with employees (particularly Sharon King) and customer groups[3], and examining financial records (e.g., payroll, budgets):

a)   **Quality Planning and Procedures** -- involves tracking of quality and actions to improve quality; primarily performed during a monthly three hour meeting with the Director of the Respiratory Therapy Department, Administrative Director of Respiratory Care Services, three Supervisors, and three Lead Therapists; also includes costs associated with activities of a Program Instructor from a local university who also serves as Respiratory Therapy's quality coordinator (approximately one day per week of her time is spent on quality improvement).

b)   **Quality Audits** -- every time a therapy is ordered by a physician, a therapist must ascertain the appropriateness of the therapy (takes about five minutes per newly ordered therapy); also includes checking patient charts, generating quality reports, and developing indicators (performed by the quality coordinator one day per week).

c)   **Therapy Write-ups** -- after each therapy and procedure, the activity is written up by the therapist; typically takes five minutes, but for non-routine activities like intubation, the write-up will take about ten minutes.

d)   **Malpractice Lawsuits** – these are legal costs and losses resulting from malpractice lawsuits.

e)   **Training Procedures** -- involves maintenance of manuals (2.5 hours per month for one Supervisor), in-house educational programs, and monthly departmental awareness activities. These training procedures should help prevent problems like improper placing of tube, wrong size intubation, etc.

f)   **Incorrect Installations** -- primarily limited to intubation procedures; normally, two intubation attempts are allowed.

g)   **Performance Audits** -- consists of (1) time card reviews, where each of three Supervisors spends one-half hour per week reviewing time cards, and (2) order-entry reviews, where each therapist spends one-half hour per week reviewing the computerized order entries.

h)   **Forecast and Budget Generation** -- performed once a month by the Director, taking approximately one hour.

i)   **Overtime** -- if the number of required personnel has been underestimated for a given period, overtime cost is incurred for existing personnel.

j)   **Customer Relations** -- before starting a series of treatments, therapists spend about five minutes explaining the procedure and need for the therapy to the patient.

k)   **Rework** – this involves the additional cost of labor and supplies for a treatment already performed and then redone for any reason.

l)   **Retraining Current Employees** -- due to unsatisfactory performance (usually by the therapist). This involves time spent in sessions by both the employees being retrained as well as those doing the retraining.

---

[2] While intubation and bronchodilator treatments are ordered by physicians, other primary treatments performed in Respiratory Therapy are initiated by therapists.

[3] For a listing of key personnel, see **Exhibit 3**.

m) **Handling Complaints** – this involves the time spent handling and correcting specific complaints made by physicians and patients.

n) **Administrative Actions** -- actions taken by management resulting from unfavorable clinician practices (identified by therapy write-ups, complaints, rework, etc.); methodologies, practice guidelines, and procedures may be reviewed and changed; disciplinary action may ensue against the clinician or supervisor, or both; additional training may be required of the employees. This cost is measured by the time spent on these reviews and actions.

o) **Absenteeism/Turnover** – this is measured by the amount in excess of industry averages.

p) **Appraisal Support** -- two outside departments support Respiratory Therapy in its efforts to appraise quality: the Quality Assurance Department conducts monthly reviews of Respiratory Therapy's performance and a Quality Assurance Committee examines Respiratory Therapy's performance on both a monthly and quarterly basis. This cost is measured by the time spent on these reviews and examinations.

After compiling this COQ list and before submitting it to Hopkins, Highlander began thinking about categorizing and measuring these costs as her next step in developing a COQ system for Kelsey Hospital.

REQUIRED:

1. What groups and individuals are the "customers" of the respiratory therapy department? Describe the concerns and perceptions about quality that might differ across the different types of customer. Identify the problems that the different customers would want quality control to prevent, detect, or correct.

2. Categorize the list of quality costs into prevention, appraisal, internal failure and external failure. Justify your choices.

3. What additional costs of quality might you suggest? How would you categorize each of them?

4. Discuss how you would estimate (i.e., measure) the following costs for the Respiratory Therapy Department: Quality Planning and Procedures, Therapy Write-ups, and Incorrect Installation.

5. Which of Highlander's COQ measures (or similar ones) might you include in a balanced scorecard for Kelsey's Respiratory Therapy Department? What other performance measures would you suggest to include? Classify each of these measures into the four standard balanced scorecard categories (financial, customer, internal business process, learning & growth).

Blocher, Stout, Cokins, Chen: *Cost Management, 4e*

©The McGraw-Hill Companies, Inc 2008

Exhibit 1
INTUBATION FLOWCHART

Start

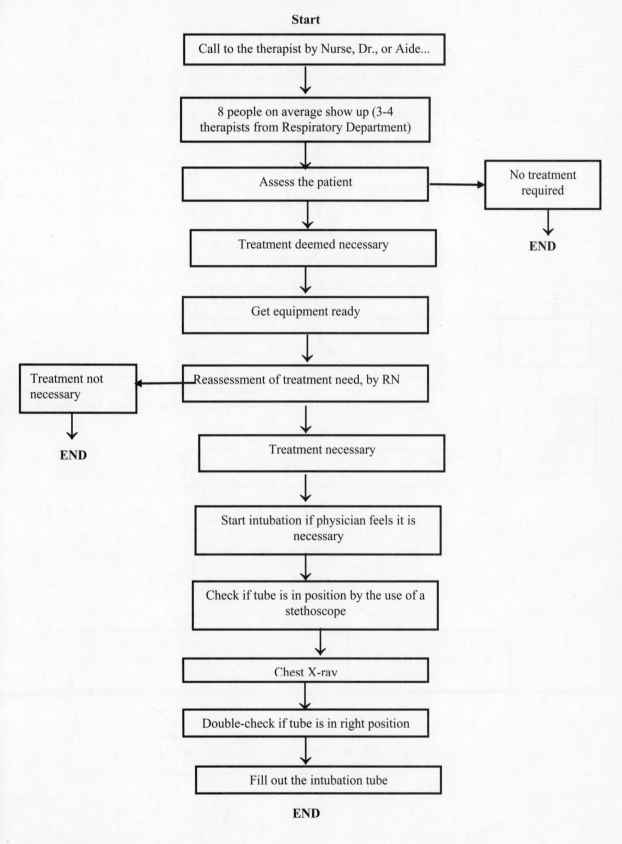

Call to the therapist by Nurse, Dr., or Aide...

8 people on average show up (3-4 therapists from Respiratory Department)

Assess the patient → No treatment required → **END**

Treatment deemed necessary

Get equipment ready

Treatment not necessary ← Reassessment of treatment need, by RN

END

Treatment necessary

Start intubation if physician feels it is necessary

Check if tube is in position by the use of a stethoscope

Chest X-ray

Double-check if tube is in right position

Fill out the intubation tube

END

Exhibit 2
BRONCHODILATOR FLOWCHART

Start for New Therapy

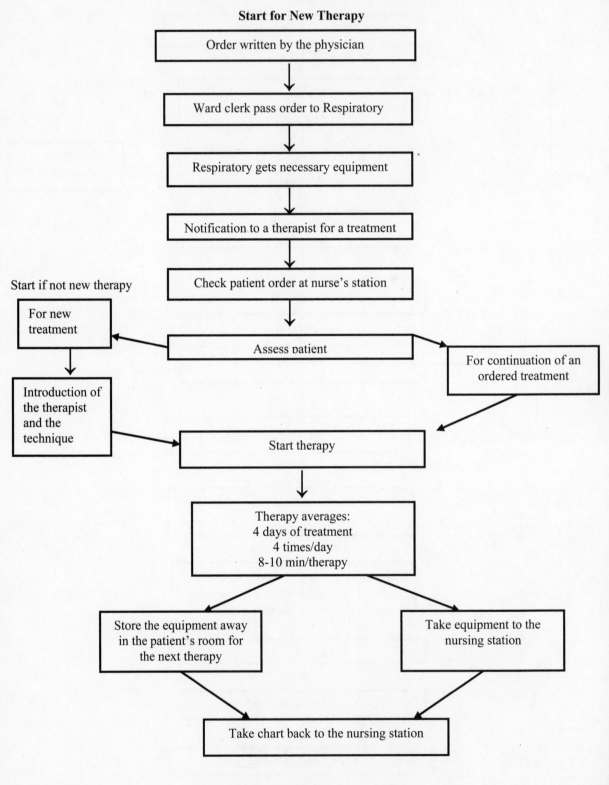

END

Exhibit 3

Personnel Listing

Name	Title
Michael Hopkins	Quality Control Manager
Morry Easton	Director of Respiratory Therapy Department
Mildred Berger	Administrative Director of Respiratory Care Services
Sharon king	Quality Coordinator for Respiratory Therapy Department

16-3: Union Pacific Railroad--Using Cost of Quality in Environmental Management

In 1989, the Union Pacific Corporation's Board of Directors relied on the expertise of USPCI, Inc. (a wholly-owned subsidiary in the environmental management industry) to review environmental management issues at each of the Corporation's subsidiaries. This move was motivated by several factors. First, the costs of complying with various Federal, state, and local environmental statutes was growing rapidly (see **Exhibit 1** for a summary of the primary Federal environmental acts). Further, the Corporation's directors were conscious of an increased societal awareness of and concern about environmental issues. The Board felt an obligation to the Corporation's shareholders, its employees, and to society at large to guarantee that Union Pacific was operating in an environmentally responsible manner.

After considering USPCI's review, the Board subsequently directed each of the subsidiaries to develop a comprehensive environmental management process. The Corporation's commitment to protect the environment is evidenced by a growing investment in environmental spending. For example, capital expenditures for prevention and control activities grew from $4 million in 1990 to $16 million in 1993, while capital expenditures for remediation activities grew from $24 million to $42 million. During this same period, the Corporation substantially increased its staff of full-time environmental managers and expanded its employee training and communication programs to include environmental issues.

The largest of the Corporation's subsidiaries is the Union Pacific Railroad Company (UPRR). UPRR owns over 19,000 miles of track; it owns or leases more than 3,000 locomotives and almost 70,000 freight cars. Headquartered in Omaha, Nebraska, the Railroad operates in 19 states and employs approximately 29,000 people. Financial highlights from 1993 for both the Corporation and the Railroad appear in **Exhibit 2**.

Exhibit 1
Primary Federal Environmental Acts

- *Resource Conservation and Recovery Act* (RCRA)--Enacted in 1976, RCRA regulates hazardous waste management from initial generation to ultimate disposal. It applies to generators and transporters of hazardous waste and to facilities that threat and dispose of hazardous waste.

- *Comprehensive Environmental Response Compensation and Liability Act* (CERCLA, also know as the Superfund Act) and Superfund Amendment a Reauthorization Act (SARA)--CERCLA was enacted in 1980 and was amended by SARA in 1986. These acts provide for the remediation of contaminated sites and impose liability for remediation on a broadly defined group of Potentially Responsible Parties (PRPs). PRPs include, for example, past and current site owners and operators, generators of the waste disposed at the site, and transporters of the waste to the site.

- *Clean Air Act* (CAA)--Originally enacted in 1955 and amended in 1970, 1977, and 1990, CAA establishes air quality standards and emissions limits.

- *Clean Water Act* (CWA)--Enacted in 1972 and amended in 1987, CWA regulates the release of pollutants into U.S. waterways.

Blocher, Stout, Cokins, Chen: *Cost Management, 4e*

©The McGraw-Hill Companies, Inc 2008

Exhibit 2
1993 Financial Highlights
(000,000's omitted)

	Union Pacific Corporation	Union Pacific Railroad
Operating revenues	$ 7,561	$ 4,987
Operating income	1,489	1,042
Income before accounting adjustments	766	669
Cash from operations	1,563	1,074
Assets (at end-of-year)	15,001	10,014
Capital expenditures	1,520	805

Source: *Union Pacific 1993 Annual Report*

UPRR'S RESPONSE TO THE CORPORATE ENVIRONMENTAL DIRECTIVE

In response to the Board's directive, UPRR adopted an environmental policy, which states in part:

> Union Pacific Railroad is committed to protecting the environment for our customers, our employees, and the communities in which we operate. Beyond compliance with laws and regulations, Union Pacific is committed to the development and use of new technologies to preserve the environment for future generations. Environmental protection is a primary management responsibility as well as the responsibility of every Union Pacific employee.

Exhibit 3 presents the remainder of the Railroad's policy.

In October, 1991, UPRR centralized most of the company's environmental personnel in a single department called the Environmental Management Group (EMG). The EMG is housed within the company's Risk Management function and is chartered to serve as "an environmentally proactive influence in the Company, to coordinate implementation of the Environmental Policy, and to assist UPRR employees in developing ways to perform their work in an environmentally sound manner."

By 1994, the EMG had over 40 employees. The group's Environmental Site Remediation team is charged with evaluating and remediating sites contaminated as a result of past operating practices. EMG's Environmental Operations team coordinates and oversees compliance activities throughout various parts of the Railroad. The EMG is also responsible for educating all UPRR employees on both the general need to care for the environment and the specific actions they can take to keep abreast of various regulations regarding the education of employees who handle hazardous materials and must develop appropriate training programs to satisfy or exceed these regulations.

ENVIRONMENTAL MANAGEMENT ACTIVITIES

UPRR actively pursues policies and practices that demonstrate its commitment to protecting the environment. The following paragraphs provide a brief overview of the some of the EMG's recent activities.

Cleanup. Like many companies, UPRR has numerous, decades-old facilities and processes that are in need of cleanup. In March 1993 UPRR initiated a comprehensive cleanup of all facilities in its system. By year-end, the Railroad had identified and recycled or disposed of a wide variety of hazardous and nonhazardous wastes, including over 1,200 drums of petroleum products, more than 2,500 drums of other materials (both hazardous and nonhazardous), over 500 pallets of used signal batteries, and almost 2,600 other miscellaneous containers (e.g., small drums, buckets, and paint cans).

Exhibit 3
Union Pacific Railroad Environmental Policy

Union Pacific and its employees will:

Comply with applicable environmental laws and regulations.

Establish measurable business objectives for environmental performance with the goal of achieving continuous improvement.

Develop employee awareness of environmental responsibilities and encourage adherence to sound environmental practices on and off the job.

Use environmentally sound treatment and disposal services for company waste.

Use sound environmental practices to address contaminated real property assets, including leased sites and right-of-ways.

Respond promptly to community and governmental inquiries about environmental issues and, where appropriate, initiate communications with customers and communities that might be affected.

Support and participate in governmental processes that seek to develop effective and balanced environmental laws and regulations.

Promote the conservation of resources through waste minimization and the recycling/reuse of materials.

Support community Emergency Response Planning groups by furnishing current information on potential community hazards associated with railroad operations and conduct joint planning and response activities.

Develop and implement a self-monitoring program to assure company facilities and operations adhere to our environmental policy.

Waste reduction. An investment of $140,000 at one rail yard resulted in a 90% reduction in waste water produced there. The Railroad is also making its painting operations more environmentally sound by switching to water-based paints at some of its paint shops. In Texas, the Railroad is testing the use of a special adaptor that allows rechargeable radio batteries to be used in railroad lanterns. If successful, UPRR will have fewer batteries to dispose of or recycle.

Conservation. UPRR's locomotives must be washed periodically to remove petroleum residues, mud, and exhaust from the exterior surfaces. The Railroad has numerous facilities where locomotives are manually washed. A recent investment of $3 million replaced one manual facility with a fully-automatic facility. The new facility uses 50% less water and 33% less soap to wash an average of 40 more locomotives per day. At another facility, locomotives are washed with a high pressure spray that mixes steam with cold water. This method uses 90% less water and significantly less energy that the traditional method.

Emissions reduction. UPRR has reduced the number of its fueling facilities by 40% and is currently replacing stationary fuel storage tanks with mobile tankers. UPRR is also in the process of retrofitting all its locomotives with retention tanks designed to collect oil and fuel that may otherwise leak into the soil. The estimated cost of this project is $6 million.

Equipment upgrading to reduce nitrogen and sulfur oxide emissions by locomotives is underway, and many methods aimed at reducing fuel consumption and, consequently, air emissions are being adopted. UPRR is currently experimenting with alternative fuels as a long-term approach to the reduction of those emissions.

Blocher, Stout, Cokins, Chen: *Cost Management, 4e*
©The McGraw-Hill Companies, Inc 2008

UPRR'S COST OF QUALITY SYSTEM AND THE EMG

Since 1988, UPRR has relied on a formalized, comprehensive quality cost reporting system as an integral part of its Total Quality Management System. By 1991, when the EMG was formed, cost of quality (COQ) had been identified as a major company-wide business objective and formally incorporated into the company's performance management system. As such, reporting units throughout the company were asked to identify COQ accounts for their areas, and managers were expected to develop formal action plans for quality cost improvement. The managerial responsibilities for COQ are described in the company's *Quality System Procedure 1002*, "Cost of Quality Control Process." **Exhibit 4** contains excerpts from this procedure.

Exhibit 4
Excerpts from Quality System Procedure 1002, Cost of Quality Control Process

Objective

To provide the management process for identifying, capturing, reporting, and controlling quality costs. This process will be used to reduce failure costs and improve the effectiveness of control activities.

Scope

Quality costs are divided into four categories;

- Internal Failure
- External Failure
- Prevention
- Appraisal

Costs in each category are defined by a set of assignable, measurable, and controllable accounts that reflect costs directly associated with business activities.

Definitions

Internal Failure Costs--Costs incurred as a result of failure activities that are transparent to the customer.

External Failure Costs--Costs incurred as a result of failure activities that are known by the customer.

Prevention Costs--Costs associated with the prevention of failure activities.

Appraisal Costs--Costs associated with measuring, evaluating, or reviewing processes, services, or products to assure conformance to quality standards.

The reaction of the newly-formed EMG to the task of identifying COQ accounts was to question the applicability of the system to the EMG. UPRR's COQ system focuses on measuring current failures that could have been controlled by appropriate managerial actions. Any failure account must therefore have an associated action plan for reducing that failure; similarly, no control account (i.e., prevention or appraisal) can be added to the system unless it relates to an existing failure account.

At first glance, the EMG did not appear to have any significant, readily identifiable accounts meeting these criteria because so many of its initial activities were concentrated on the correction of past environmental failures (i.e., remediation activities). The group did not see that action plans could be established to eliminate past occurrences, nor could any related controls be currently established to prevent those past failures. During EMG's second year of existence, the head of Risk Management (to whom the EMG reported) urged the group to reconsider these views concerning the primary nature of its activities. He observed that the company's environmental management practices were not perfect and could therefore be improved. He also pointed to the environmentally-related fines that the company was being assessed for current failures. (These fines were already being accumulated in COQ accounts for other departments.) In his opinion, COQ could help the EMG become more proactive, so he assigned a team the responsibility of identifying COQ accounts.

The team members identified several areas for investigation in their search for potential COQ accounts. First, the team members ascertained that an assessment of customer requirements could prove worthwhile, since failure to meet customer requirements could result in controllable failure costs. They also recognized that an identification of the group's largest expenditures could reveal opportunities for improvement in control activities. Additional COQ accounts might be revealed by a careful review of the figures routinely reported elsewhere for their applicability to the COQ reporting framework. Conceivably, some COQ-related measures were already in place, but had simply not been defined as such. Finally, the team determined that an evaluation and review of EMG's goals might suggest some new COQ accounts, since failure to properly specify and attain the goals could cause otherwise unnecessary expenses for the company. The following sections describe a few of the COQ accounts that were ultimately identified by the team.

COQ RELATED TO CUSTOMER REQUIREMENTS

The EMG has both external and internal customers. The external customers include the various city, state, and federal agencies overseeing environmental regulations. Internal customers include all the other company departments receiving EMG services.

External customers. External customers' requirements are specified in numerous (and regularly changing) regulations and laws applicable to the geographic are covered by the Union Pacific's system. If UPRR fails to meet the external customers' requirements, the customers' dissatisfaction is expressed in the form of citations or letter complaining about, or serving notice on, violations to the present standards. Improved performance by the EMG would materialize in the form of fewer citations and, ultimately, in fewer fines and penalties.

Applying COQ concepts, the team determined that failure costs for each current incident could be estimated based on past experience. A failure cost per incident was estimated by dividing the total number of incidents in a recent year into the total dollar amount paid out in fines and penalties in the same year.

In any given month, the current COQ is thus reported to be the current month's number of incidents multiplied by the historical rate per incident. The team recognizes that the measure is flawed in that the actual pay-outs in any given year may typically relate to failures that occurred in prior years. However, the figure is accepted as an acceptable, rough estimate; it can be refined over time to reflect what the net present value (NPV) of the actual payment will be when the incident is eventually settled (normally, in two or three years).

Internal customers. The internal customers' primary requirement is to minimize their own environmental costs. To these customers, sound environmental management practices (dictated to them by the EMG) sometimes seem to fail the cost-benefit criterion. For example, maintaining proper documentation of all 55-gallon drums is a time-consuming task that might not appear to have any payback. However, if a container's record is lost or if the label is destroyed, the contents must be analyzed to determine what was in the drum so that the contents can be disposed of properly.

For COQ reporting purposes, the team determined the cost of analyzing the contents of a 55-gallon drum to be the simple average derived from bills received over a 12-month period. In any given reporting period, the COQ is estimated as the number of drums analyzed times the historical average analysis cost per drum. Actual analysis costs cannot be used on a timely basis because the number of drums tested and the results of the tests are not linked in the accounting system.

COQ IN THE LARGE EXPENDITURE CATEGORIES

The EMG's largest expenditures are associated with the clean-up of old sites. As discussed earlier, these costs are being incurred to correct past failures and are, by definition, not appropriate for inclusion in UPRR's COQ system. In developing its COQ accounts, the EMG team took a proactive view, however, and asked whether the clean-ups were being done to "World Class" standards. For example, they questioned whether the costs incurred were appropriate given the amount of material handled. They also expressed concern that the clean-up activities should reflect the latest in technology and process control.

A resulting account that the team developed is one that measures the disposal of diesel fuel-contaminated soil (the largest category of soil disposal). Before developing the account, the team reviewed the literature and interviewed consultants and subcontractors to determine the most efficient operations, i.e., a "World Class" standard. The new COQ account would reflect any costs incurred above this standard. Initially, the cost of disposing of one ton of hydrocarbon-contaminated soil was in excess of $50 a ton. The best operation was processing it at $23 a ton.

Blocher, Stout, Cokins, Chen: *Cost Management, 4e*

The difference between the two costs times the tonnage handled is now reported as a failure account in the COQ system. Essentially, the account represents EMG's failure to meet an operating efficiency standard for disposal of the contaminated soil. This account focuses management attention on a significant environmental cost. It serves as a constant reminder to EMG management that the group can process larger quantities of soil and clean up sites faster if it can reduce the efficiency gaps.

Another large cost incurred by the EMG is the cost of treating water coming from various UPRR shops and fueling facilities. Because the Railroad consumes a million gallons of diesel fuel per day, even a slight spillage rate implies that many gallons of diesel fuel are deposited into waste-water treatment facilities each day. In addition, the use of non-biodegradable soaps and cleaning solvents increases the need for treatment chemicals and lowers the probability that the water can flow directly into local sewage facilities.

In defining a related COQ account, the EMG took an aggressive stance and viewed the cost of the company's waste-water treatments costs as a total failure cost. The EMG's position was simple: if the discharge water coming from the various shops and facilities always met the local standards, UPRR would incur no treatment costs. The COQ account was then defined as any actual costs incurred. This particular account motivates various groups within UPRR to work together to reduce spillage at the company's fueling facilities, decrease the use of non-biodegradable solvents and soaps, and ensure that waste engine oil is disposed of properly.

The EMG also focused on the large expenditures associated with retrofitting all locomotives with retention tanks, or "catch" pans. As mentioned earlier, these pans minimize the amount of hydrocarbons dropped on the ground. Based on a survey of "best" practices, the EMG determined that the average locomotive leaks one quart of oil products per day. The group used this rate to estimate the amount of soil an average locomotive contaminates while idling in a year and incorporated the measure into a COQ failure account. (The idle time is considered more important because the amount of oil products leaked by a moving locomotive is significantly less.)

The COQ is the estimated cost of removing and treating the soil that the leaking hydrocarbons would contaminate during normal operating conditions. The account helps management track improvements associated with the retrofitting project. It also encourages management to reduce future exposures by installing catch basins at all major yards where locomotives stand idling for extended periods.

Other COQ-Related Measures Available in the Company's Existing System

Another COQ account resulting directly from a review of the group's existing reports is the cost of cleaning up reportable, environmental spills that occur in the "normal" course of business. Such spills happen for a number of reasons, ranging from a customer's failure to secure a valve on a 30,000-gallon tank to a track maintenance crew's dropping a 5-gallon can of cleaning solvent at a siding. The cleanup costs associated with these incidents vary widely depending on the nature of the spill; further, there is typically a time delay between the incident date and the receipt of the final bill for cleanup. For these reasons, each period's COQ is estimated using an average historical cost per incident. The account allows the EMG Group to assess the potential magnitude the spillages on an ongoing basis. The managers use this account to detect the presence of patterns in the spills and to evaluate the effectiveness of the corrective action programs at specific locations.

COQ Accounts Related to the EMG's Goals

A major objective of the EMG is to prevent environmental contaminations. Recognizing the potential for small diesel fuel spills during routine refueling operations, the EMG established a COQ account to draw attention to the cumulative effects of these spills. This account assigned a dollar value to the amount of diesel fuel contained in a sample of the waste-oil recovery tank at major fueling facilities. The COQ was estimated as the difference between the price paid for a gallon of diesel fuel and the price per gallon received from the oil recovery company.

This account focuses attention on the cost of fueling-mishaps. The EMG is not responsible for fueling the locomotives, but is responsible for running the waste-water treatment facilities and for cleaning up any spills. EMG managers believe this account can help the Group improve its own practices regarding waste-water treatment; they also believe that the account will motivate managers in other departments to focus on the elimination of these fuel spillages.

Summary

The examples presented in this case demonstrate how UPRR relies on COQ as a management tool in the environmental area. Given that the Railroad has a long-standing commitment to total quality management (TQM) and has experienced tremendous success with its use of COQ in other departments, the application of COQ to the environmental area does not require much "stepping out of the box" thinking. In this instance, all that was necessary was for the COQ team to consider some relatively simple questions like:

- What do the customers require, and what costs are incurred when their requirements are not met?
- Where is most of the money being spent, and are the related activities being performed to "World Class" standards?
- What measurements are already in place that do not reflect a financial impact, and what is the associated cost of failure?
- What are the group's goals or objectives, and what is the cost of not achieving those goals or objectives?

Determining the cost of not meeting the standard or requirement in each of these four categories is actually a fairly straightforward cost accounting exercise.

The Railroad views COQ as a useful management tool for all of its reporting units. Once costs have been assigned to each failure, management attention is focused on the largest account. Reducing the failure rate on these accounts not only improves the process, but also leads management to focus on other failure activity-reductions. In many cases, failure reductions result in significant, immediate cash savings that can be applied to employee recognition programs as well as to the prevention of failures in other areas.

REQUIRED:
1. How valid is the cost of future cleanup of the soil contaminated by the locomotive dripping oil and grease onto the soil? What additional information would you require before including this cost in a "return on investment" (ROI) analysis for the installation of the collection pans under the locomotive?
2. Identify your criteria for failure costs and explain how you would classify the total cost of the waste-water facilities. Is it a failure or a prevention cost? What are the best arguments for and against using the cost of the waste-water facilities to justify the higher cost of biodegradable soaps and solvents?
3. Looking at the trend in waste water standards established by the Environmental Protection Agency (EPA), would you feel comfortable closing these facilities permanently? Why or why not?
4. How realistic is it to hold a manager responsible for reducing the company's operating costs to a "World Class" standard as indicated by the disposal of contaminated soil example? What additional information would you like to have before basing your salary increase on meeting such a target?
5. Put yourself in the place of an external auditor working for a public accounting firm. Looking at the four situations outlined in the questions above, would you feel obligated to require any notes, disclosures, or comments before issuing an opinion? Under what circumstances would you feel obligated to require a disclosure of the situation?
    a. What about the current liability of all the soil contaminated by past years' running of locomotives without drip pans?
    b. Assume that during the study of the waste-water treatment plants it was found that none of the plants could handle a five-year rain. The fine for each occurrence was $100,000 for each plant. Would you require a disclosure contained within the financial statements? Give reasons supporting your position.
6. Looking at the case, what failure costs can you identify...
    a. at your place of business?
    b. at this college or university?
    c. in the teaching of this course?
    d. what costs would you assign to each of the failures you identify?
7. As the Chief Financial Officer (CFO) of the company, when would you begin to feel uncomfortable assigning costs to these environmental failures? Discuss the ethical questions that would be involved in limited the generation of failure costs that are based upon noncompliance or continued contamination of the environment, resulting in possible violation of future regulations. During your discussion, address how you

Blocher, Stout, Cokins, Chen: *Cost Management, 4e*

©The McGraw-Hill Companies, Inc 2008

would minimize the financial liability of potential litigation associated with the production and distribution of asbestos and tobacco products.

8. Under what conditions could you see a cost of quality (COQ) system working? What are the key enablers of a such as system if attempted in your organization. Discuss the arguments you would use to start or "kill" a COQ system.

9. What are the major differences between a COQ system as presented in the case and an Activity-Based costing (ABC) system? What are the similarities?

Readings

16.1: GE Takes Six Sigma Beyond the Bottom Line

by Gregory T. Lucier and Sridhar Seshadri

Imagine working for a company where every employee is required to go through two weeks of intensive training in statistical process control. Then at the end of this training, participants are required to demonstrate proficiency by completing two projects that directly improve either company or customer performance.

On top of that, the company's website provides 24/7 access to the tools and methodology required to support the quality improvement efforts of more than 300,000 employees world-wide. The site is constantly and consistently measuring and quantifying thousands upon thousands of active projects.

Has your satellite TV system somehow mingled the contents of the business channel with a late-night science fiction film? No. You're experiencing GE's Six Sigma quality program, one that has netted the corporation such amazing results that now GE's customers are clamoring for help.

GETTING STARTED

Roll back to 1981, when Jack Welch first took the helm at GE and began to transform (or reshape) the company from a $25 billion bureaucratic quagmire into a well-run and highly respected $100 billion giant. Welch understood the "command and control" management approach had run its course and spent the next 20 years resolutely pursuing other options, borrowing best practices, and implementing winning strategies.

Through the remainder of the '80s, GE employed corporate-wide streamlining to get the fat out of its organization while maintaining the muscle. In 1989, as the tumult began to settle, Welch realized the need to empower employees and give them a greater level of participation in the decision-making process. Despite a decade of change, the level of hierarchy and top-down communication had remained an impediment. To solve this, Welch launched an initiative known as Work-Out™, which is designed to facilitate focused decision making, resolve issues, and improve processes. A Work-Out session is generally led by those closest to a process or issue, with the goal toward finding workable solutions and developing action plans. Work-Out can be used to eliminate unnecessary steps and streamline tasks or to remove barriers between different departments or reporting levels. Built into this process are mechanisms for ensuring management buy-in and follow-through.

Some Work-Out session examples are:

- Improving back-office processing with new financial systems,
- Improving internal paperwork flow, and
- Streamlining approval processes.

By the mid-'90s it was time to shake things up again, this time with a focus on quality. Not because GE wasn't performing well, but because feedback from employees convinced the CEO that, despite top- and bottom-line growth, quality wasn't where it should be.

Welch decided Six Sigma was the way to go. He had learned about Six Sigma from Larry Bossidy, a former GE executive who left to take the helm at Allied Signal, a company then implementing the program. Bossidy introduced Welch to Mikel Harry of the Six Sigma Academy and to this breakthrough strategy for statistical process control. Jack Welch had always maintained that GE must look outside itself to identify and adopt best practices wherever they could be found. So in the spring of 1995, Welch asked Bossidy to share his unique Six Sigma philosophy with GE's executive council.

They were impressed. Welch set targets out past five years and proclaimed Six Sigma the largest, most significant initiative ever undertaken at GE. Since that proclamation, Six Sigma has been implemented aggressively and has become deeply ingrained in the corporation's culture. The company has deployed the methodology more extensively than any other to date, and maintaining its vitality continues to be a top priority. Throughout GE, there's a commonly echoed phrase...Six Sigma is "The Way We Work." Acquiring and using Six Sigma skills is considered a core competency for leadership roles, and each year new "stretch" goals and projects are established.

Figure 1: GE's Results from Six Sigma

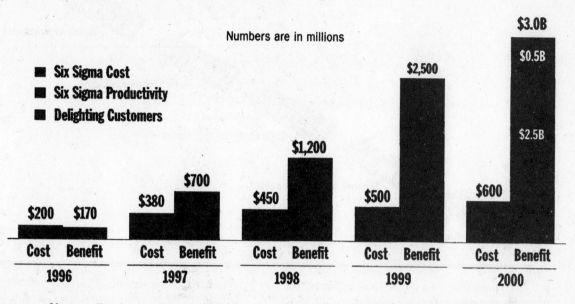

Numbers are in millions

- Six Sigma Cost
- Six Sigma Productivity
- Delighting Customers

	1996		1997		1998		1999		2000	
	Cost	Benefit	Cost	Benefit	Cost	Benefit	Cost	Benefit	Cost	Benefit
	$200	$170	$380	$700	$450	$1,200	$500	$2,500	$600	$3.0B ($0.5B / $2.5B)

In terms of bottom-line impact, payback, ROI, benefit—whatever you want to call it—GE has achieved it. During the first five years of the program, the company increased annual productivity gains by over 266% and improved operating margins from 14.4% to 18.4% (see **Figure 1**). The bottom line was enhanced tremendously, and stock-holders were rewarded handsomely and consistently.

Six Sigma wasn't invented by GE (Motorola initiated a version of Six Sigma in the late 1980s). But the results the corporation has achieved from its implementation have attracted attention from several fronts, especially a large segment of the international business community and GE's customers. In response, GE decided to offer customers high-level instruction in Six Sigma. For example, last year our group, GE Medical Systems, began taking Six Sigma to healthcare customers. That first effort resulted in over $94 million in benefits after touching only a fraction of the market. And as recognition grows, so will the numbers.

A CLOSER LOOK AT THE SIX SIGMA APPROACH

The name Six Sigma is derived from a statistical heritage and focus on measuring product or process defects. Sigma is the Greek letter assigned to represent standard deviation. Achieving a Six Sigma level of quality equates to nearly error-free performance—where a given process produces only 3.4 defects out of a million opportunities.

Here are some perspectives on levels of Sigma:

SIGMA	Defects Per Million Opportunities
2	308,537
3	66,807
4	6,210
5	233
6	3.4

Most organizations would probably rate their current quality at between Three and Four Sigma. When Jack Welch challenged GE to become a Six Sigma organization in four years, he was in effect calling for a reduction in defect levels of 84% per year. At stake was an estimated $8-$10 billion in costs consumed by lower levels of quality.

While the measure of quality is the cornerstone of the Six Sigma approach, it's the methodology and tools driving process change that translate to the difference between a simple quality campaign slogan and a rigorous management philosophy based on science. At the heart of the Six Sigma approach is a method summarized by the acronym DMAIC (see **Figure 2**).

Define. The GE process starts here. Teams work to clearly define problems related to the business or critical to customer satisfaction. CTQ (Critical to Quality) factors essential for customer satisfaction are correlated with the overall business process at issue. Project charters are established, required resources are identified, and leadership approvals are obtained to maximize project outcomes.

Figure 2: D M A I C

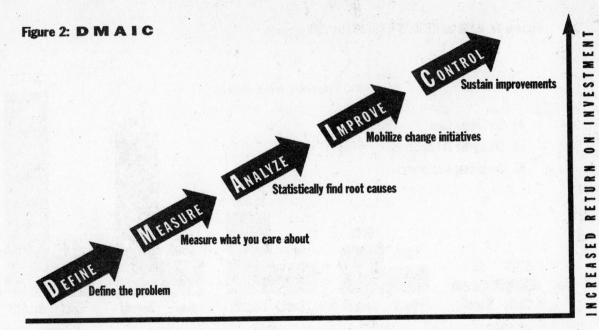

In preparation for this phase, employee training includes a review of process mapping techniques and orientation to online tools available to support teams.

Measure. The next stage is to establish base-level measures of defects inherent in the existing process. Customer expectations are defined to determine "out of specification" conditions. Training for this phase consists of basic probability and statistics, statistical analysis software, and measurement analysis.

While this heavy bombardment of statistics causes many participants to run for cover, GE makes it easier for employees to learn. It partners experienced Six Sigma practitioners with employees going through the training for the first time, which helps beginners overcome the challenge of mastering the concepts. And the use of automated tools minimizes the time required for complex calculations.

Analyze. In this phase, teams explore underlying reasons for defects. They use statistical analysis to examine potential variables affecting the outcome and seek to identify the most significant root causes. Then they develop a prioritized list of factors influencing the desired outcome.

Tools used for this phase include multivariate analysis, test for normality, ANOVA, correlation, and regression. Again, these tools aren't for those who have difficulty balancing a checkbook, but most participants succeed with help from their mentors.

Improve. During this phase, teams seek the optimal solution and develop and test a plan of action for implementing and confirming the solution. The process is modified and the outcome measured to determine whether the revised method produces results within customer expectations.

Additional statistical methods covering design of experiments and multiple linear regression are reviewed with trainees to support the final analysis of the problem and to test the proposed solutions.

Control. To ensure changes stick, ongoing measures are implemented to keep the problem from recurring. Control charting techniques are used as the basis for developing the ongoing measures.

The concept of control—taking concrete steps to make sure improvements don't unravel over time—has been missing from other process improvement initiatives. It's this phase of Six Sigma that leads to long-term payoffs—both in quality and monetary terms.

IMPLEMENTING THE PROGRAM

Training for GE employees takes about 10 classroom days spread over four sessions and 90 calendar days. Action teams are created in each class to attack an existing business problem. As each aspect of Six Sigma is taught, the team immediately applies the concepts to the chosen problem.

There's a progression of competency levels beginning with Green Belts—and all employees from clerical staff up are required to reach this level of proficiency. Green Belts must complete the required training and two projects to achieve certification. They must also complete one additional project and eight hours of post-

Blocher, Stout, Cokins, Chen: *Cost Management, 4e*

certification training each year. While Green Belts are trained in Six Sigma, they hold non-Six Sigma positions within the company. New employees are expected to obtain Green Belt certification within the first year of employment.

Taking Six Sigma to Customers

Once we had proof that the system really works, we decided to take Six Sigma beyond internal projects. Our group, GE Medical Systems, is offering its expertise to customers to enhance value and provide additional benefits.

The healthcare industry continues to experience monumental changes and tough challenges. Lower reimbursement, competition, and consolidation have transformed organizations from a 1980s' model—targeting quality at all costs—to today's approach where quality and efficiency must be the driving forces in the delivery of care.

In the 1990s, the industry saw a bevy of quality and reengineering consultants attempt to remedy the situation, but such efforts at cost cutting were quickly cancelled by the need to rehire personnel. Old operational habits also died hard for a lack of sustainable change management that should have included—among other elements—skills transfer.

The healthcare industry has quickly responded to the promise of Six Sigma. As of December 2000, GE Medical Systems reported 1,149 active Six Sigma projects for customers. GE even created a service unit expressly dedicated to providing Six Sigma management tools and processes to healthcare organizations requesting more extensive assistance in improving performance.

Is it working? Yes. Commonwealth Health Corporation, a 478-bed medical center in Kentucky, began its journey to implement a Six Sigma improvement culture over three years ago. Results have been overwhelming as the medical center reports a reinvigorated and transformed management culture. Within a mere 18 months, errors in one ordering process were reduced over 90%, overall operating expenses had been reduced by $800,000, and employee survey results had improved by 20%. These results were from a single division within the organization. Now the medical center has realized improvements in excess of $1.5 million and is expanding the program to other areas.

One of the main reasons the program is working is because customers determine project scope, acquire on-site training and tools, and verify the benefits they have received. During last year alone, 466 customer projects were completed that resulted in $91.2 million in customer benefits. Because it relies on rigorous statistical methods and puts control mechanisms in place, Six Sigma actually connects the dots among quality, cost, process, people, and accountability.

Some customers are using GE'S Six Sigma program to achieve even higher measures of success. As part of their Star Initiative, a system-wide performance improvement effort, Virtua Health of Marlton, N.J., saw the Six Sigma program as an opportunity to vault their system to the next level of clinical quality, patient satisfaction, and financial performance. Walter Ettinger, M.D., executive vice president at Virtua, credits the partnership with GE and the use of the Six Sigma program as helping to make vital changes in the organization. "The Six Sigma program has provided everyone in the organization with a common language and toolbox for achieving our objectives. The methodology is sound, and we have begun to get buy-in from our medical staff, who are very results oriented and turned off by initiatives du jour. Our goal is to use Six Sigma to create an outstanding experience for our patients, which is the first priority of our Trustees."

All other "Belts" are 100% Six-Sigma assignments and are selected from the top performers in our talent pipeline:

- Black Belts act as technical and cultural change agents for quality. They are leaders of small teams implementing/executing the Six Sigma method-ology in business-related projects, and they coach Green Belts on their projects. Today there are more than 4,500 Black Belts within GE.

- Master Black Belts teach, mentor, and develop Six Sigma tools and are full-time teachers of the Six Sigma process. Today there are over 800 Master Black Belts within GE.

- Champions back and promote the Six Sigma initiative and work with executives to help drive initiatives into daily operations and business metrics.

The mentoring structure behind Six Sigma training and the full-time dedication of the Black

Belts and Master Black Belts have provided the momentum necessary to complete thousands of projects at GE.

THE PAYBACK

To evaluate the payback of the significant commitment during the initial five-year implementation, we can look at individual projects and the cumulative results of thousands of projects.

One division recently reduced its annual expense for teleconferencing by $1.5 million encompassing a total of 19 million minutes. Another team cut customer order processing time in half. As a rule of thumb, GE managers expect that each project will save between $50,000 and $150,000.

Variations on a Theme

There are a couple of variations to the DMAIC process we mentioned. One involves the opportunity-to create a Six Sigma process where there are existing processes in place. In this case, participants use a variation of DMAIC called Design for Six Sigma (DFSS).

Here's an example of an actual DFSS project that author Sridhar Seshadri completed in working to-ward his Green Belt certification. In this project, one of GE'S businesses developed and implemented an entire business plan to provide professional services ranging from project management, systems integration, and consulting services regarding installation of complex medical imaging systems.

Prior to this project, GE typically installed such equipment with value-added services almost being an afterthought. The DFSS team—operating under the notion that the "whole solution" included hardware, software, and professional services—went through a formal DEFINE and MEASURE phase where customer requirements and analyses of the market were rigorously scrutinized.

The team then developed a business plan using a statistical modeling tool called Crystal Ball. The "stakeholders," including business leaders and other participants essential to making the project work, reviewed the business plan. Finally, the process was test-run at a few customer sites, then formalized and implemented.

So how is this different from a traditional rollout of a new project? First, DFSS applies a level of rigor not consistently seen in traditional business plans— consistent being the key word. Second, since Six Sigma is "institutionalized," everyone involved immediately understood the details of the project and could provide meaningful feedback and advice. Third, with project tracking the team was able to review similar projects across all of GE and learn from them. This set of services first implemented in the fall of 1999 is now routinely offered in over 90% of customer projects.

When talking about the payback associated with Six Sigma, think about popcorn. One kernel popping by itself (or one project completed) won't make much of a difference. But if you keep the heat on and thousands of kernels pop, you've multiplied the results exponentially. GE has kept the heat on now for five years, and the results are in. The following is a summary of some key performance measures at GE.

	SIX SIGMA BEGINS: 1995	FIVE YEARS LATER 2000
Annual Productivity Gain	1.5%	4.0%
Operating Margin	14.4%	18.4%
Inventory Turns	5.8%	9.2%

By internal calculations, the benefits of Six Sigma exceeded $2 billion in 2000. Certainly a four-to-one pay-back in quality and the associated savings resulting from reduced cycle times and defects would interest many considering similar options for their organizations.

The lesson we learned at GE is that there is definitely a payback. Complete dedication to the program and enterprise-wide implementation is attainable and rewarding in terms of quality, productivity, and the bottom line.

Blocher, Stout, Cokins, Chen: *Cost Management, 4e*

16.2: Accounting for Quality with Nonfinancial Measures: A Simple No-Cost Program for the Small Company

Executive Summary: Over the last two decades, large American firms competed in the global arena by applying traditional cost-cutting techniques to justify having to lower prices to match those of foreign firms. In order to make the extensive cost cuts to meet a competitor's price, product or service quality often was either sacrificed or ignored. As Japan and other countries continued to offer higher-quality goods and services at competitive prices, many large American companies met the challenge and achieved world-class status by adopting total quality management (TQM) programs. TQM programs, although expensive, are not reserved solely for large organizations. Many of the techniques can be easily adapted to fit the small firm.

Successful companies today rate customer satisfaction as priority number one, and they direct everything toward increasing it. Customers expect value. To meet this challenge, small firms must provide customers with exactly what they want—high quality at a low price. The small firm can achieve benefits similar to those achieved by large firms with their costly quality programs by using nonfinancial measures to identify and monitor quality. By following the procedures suggested with this simple no-cost program, small firms can increase product or service quality with a minimum of effort.

QUALITY COSTS

A company needs to understand quality costs before it starts any quality improvement program—especially with the suggested approach of using nonfinancial measures. The cost of quality is a cost classification that encompasses all costs involved in making a firm's product or delivering a service that meets a customer's specifications or expectations the first time. The costs include those specifically associated with the achievement (conformance) or non-achievement (nonconformance) of the quality of the product or service. Thus, the costs of quality have two components: (1) the costs of conformance, which are costs incurred to make sure the product or service is right the first time, and (2) the costs of nonconformance, which are costs incurred to correct a problem or irregularity. The components are inversely related. If a company spends money on the costs of conformance, the costs of nonconformance should be reduced. On the other hand, if the company pays little attention to the costs of conformance, the costs of nonconformance should escalate.

Most firms that account for quality costs further separate conformance costs into two subcategories: (1) prevention costs, which are costs to prevent defects and failures initially, and (2) appraisal costs, which are the costs to measure and evaluate products and services to ensure conformance to quality standards. Typically, nonconformance costs also are classified further into two subcategories: (1) internal failure costs, which are costs incurred when defects are discovered before the product is shipped or the service delivered to the customer,

and (2) external failure costs, which are costs incurred after delivery of defective goods or services. Examples of typical costs for each of the four subcategories are shown in **Table 1**.

As **Table 1** shows, the costs of quality are a significant portion of a product or service's total cost. Various studies have reported that these costs range anywhere from 25% for manufacturing firms to as high as 40% for service firms. Therefore, quality does have a sizable impact on profits. Although the simple approach presented does not account for costs, it is imperative that users of the approach understand the tremendous impact that quality costs have on profits as well as the inverse relationship of conformance and nonconformance categories.

NO-COST APPROACH

Measuring and accounting for the costs of quality are expensive, but the process is an essential step in TQM programs. The large firms that achieved world-class status committed the resources to accomplish these tasks, and the results speak for themselves. Most small firms do not have the resources to measure and account for the specific quality costs. If managers of small firms were able to see the importance of applying monetary amounts to their efforts to improve product or service quality, perhaps they might find additional resources. On the other hand, monetary amounts can always be applied to nonfinancial measures at a point in the future when and if resources become available to upgrade a simple quality program to full TQM status.

Because the essential key of TQM is to improve quality, the principle of this approach is to identify the activity that needs to be improved and monitor only the nonfinancial element(s) of the activity while not worrying about applying monetary amounts to the measures of the activity. The reasoning for this view is that as the activity is improved, the costs will take care of themselves.

Table 2: Sample Nonfinancial Quality Measures

CONFORMANCE COSTS

Prevention Costs	Appraisal Costs
Design review (number of hours)	Material inspection (number of inspections)
Preventive maintenance (number of hours)	WIP inspection (number of inspections)
Employee training (number of hours)	FG inspection (number of inspections)
Quality circles (number of hours)	Sample preparation (number of samples)
Quality engineering (number of hours)	Product simulation (number of simulations)

NONCONFORMANCE COSTS

Internal Failure Costs	External Failure Costs
Scrap (number of units)	Warranty claims (number of claims)
Rework (number of units)	Complaint processing (number of complaints)
Spoilage (number of units)	Loss of goodwill (return customers)
Quality-related downtime (number of hours)	Liability suits (number of suits)
Reinspection of rework (number of units)	Product recalls (number of recalls)

Therefore, this simple program for controlling quality is a three-step approach that can be used with any spreadsheet program: (1) identify the appropriate nonfinancial quality measures that should be monitored; (2) record the measures in a spreadsheet on a timely basis; and (3) prepare timely quality reports using the data recorded in the spreadsheet.

IDENTIFYING NONFINANCIAL QUALITY MEASURES

Nonfinancial measures represent information and analyses that are not expressed in monetary equivalents. Management accountants have always been responsible for analyzing nonfinancial data, but the majority of their time was spent on reporting these data in dollars and cents. The principle of this simple approach is to not waste time and effort to report the data in monetary equivalents but to simply report the nonfinancial data and look for trends in the measures. For example, if a small company found that the number of items requiring rework was increasing monthly, then it should take action immediately. If the number of reworked items can be reduced, then costs will be reduced and profits enhanced.

The appropriate nonfinancial measures that a manager or owner decides to monitor will be different for each firm and would be selected after a careful analysis of the complete product or service cycle. For example, some measures, such as customer complaints and warranty claims, will be appropriate for most companies. Other measures, such as trends in throughput time, would be appropriate for manufacturing firms.

Users must select those measures that will assist the company with its move toward producing a higher-quality product or service. Even though many firms will select only nonconformance measures to monitor and improve, they should also select conformance measures when possible because of the inverse relationship between the two categories as demonstrated earlier. The more effort expended toward conformance measures typically reduces the effort expended toward fixing a problem or irregularity. The inclusion of a conformance measure, such as preventive maintenance hours or the number of hours of employee training per week, will sometimes be used only to validate the fact that conformance tasks are being done and not necessarily to indicate that the measures should be fixed or improved. The nonconformance measures are those that must be improved and will probably comprise the bulk of a firm's measures.

Table 2 lists one of many possible nonfinancial quality measures for each of the cost categories listed in **Table 1**. Notice that each measure is in units, hours, or events.

Blocher, Stout, Cokins, Chen: *Cost Management, 4e*

Recording the Measures in a Spreadsheet

Once the appropriate nonfinancial measures of quality are selected, the measures must be recorded in a table so that the data can be analyzed. Any spreadsheet can be used for this purpose, even though the data could be easily tabulated by hand. A spreadsheet works best because it makes the next step of preparing the report very easy and allows for the presentation of the data in various graphical formats with a minimum of effort.

The time interval that is selected will depend on the situation and the size of the firm. Some larger firms probably will find that weekly recordings will be meaningful, while very small firms may find it better to use monthly data.

Preparing the Report

The report can take any form. Because the measures are already in a spreadsheet format, its printout makes for a simple report. It is also a good idea to supplement the printout with a presentation of some or all of the data in a graphical form, such as a line or bar graph, for emphasis.

ILLUSTRATIVE EXAMPLE

Now let's take a look at an example of a small firm such as a film processing establishment or other business that you might find at any mall. The firm used with this illustration has the owner, three employees, and declining profits over the last few years. The owner maintained a price structure that was competitive with the area and even lowered prices periodically in an attempt to increase profits. The owner found that he was spending a great deal of time handling complaints and learned that the quality of his service might be the problem.

Having just read about the aforementioned no-cost program to increase quality, the owner decided to give the program a try for 10 weeks. The first step was to select nonfinancial quality measures. The owner chose to use both conformance and non-conformance measures. Based on the nature of the business, he selected eight total measures to monitor and started to record the weekly results in a spreadsheet. He also decided to make no changes for two weeks until he was comfortable with the process.

Table 3 is a spreadsheet with the selected measures and 10 weeks of data. The same table also would serve as a simple quality report.

Table 3: Spreadsheet Illustration

Weeks	1	2	3	4	5	6	7	8	9	10
CONFORMANCE MEASURES										
Prevention Measures										
Maintenance Hours	0	0	1	1	2	2	3	3	3	2
Employee Training Hours	0	0	1	1	2	2	3	3	2	2
Appraisal Measures										
Material Inspections	0	0	1	1	2	2	3	3	2	1
Product Inspections	0	0	1	1	2	2	3	3	2	2
NONCONFORMANCE MEASURES										
Internal Failure Measures										
Units Scrapped	10	12	9	8	6	5	3	2	2	1
Reworked Units	20	22	19	18	14	12	9	6	5	4
External Failure Measures										
Number of Complaints	8	10	8	7	6	5	4	3	2	1
Warranty Claims	6	6	7	7	7	6	5	5	4	3

After two weeks of recording the data, and before he even thought of printing a report, the owner saw that the number of units that were scrapped and reworked were more than he had realized. He was further surprised by the number of complaints and warranty claims that were submitted. He thought there really was truth to the adage that you must see something in writing to believe it.

The owner made his first changes in the third week by requiring an hour of maintenance on the machines and an hour of training for all employees. He also mandated that one shipment each of incoming material and outgoing products would be inspected thoroughly. He noticed an almost instant decline in the number of scrapped and reworked units and complaints.

As the weeks stretched out, he increased maintenance, training, and inspections. The nonconformance measures continued to improve until the measures were within what he considered acceptable. By the 10th week he was able to adjust downward the maintenance and training hours required.

Step three of the program calls for a written report of the data. The owner did nothing more than print the spreadsheet in its present state with the 10 weeks of data. The report looked exactly like it appeared on his computer screen and thus, the same as **Table 3**. After defining four ranges of data, he printed a line graph of the four nonconformance measures for the 10 weeks to supplement the report. The supplement is shown as **Figure 1**.

Figure 1

Quality Report Illustration Using

All Nonconformance Measures

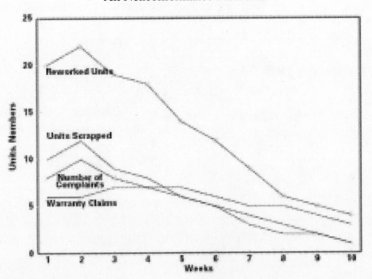

CUSTOMER SATISFACTION

Product or service quality is the top priority of successful businesses. Everything must be directed toward satisfying the customer. Most large companies have implemented TQM programs, and small businesses with limited resources must do the same. Accepting that quality is the key to survival, anything a company does to increase product or service quality is positive.

The no-cost approach to improve quality presented here is a simple alternative for any firm, especially the small one. Even the smallest firm should attempt to monitor nonfinancial quality measures over time. Monitoring and striving ti improve only a single measure, such as complaints, will improve product or service quality. The only requirement needed is a desire and commitment to improve.

Blocher, Stout, Cokins, Chen: *Cost Management, 4e*

Chapter 17
Management Control and Strategic Performance Measurement

Cases

Readings

17-1: "Transforming the Balanced Scorecard from Performance Measurement to Strategic Management: Part 1" by Robert S. Kaplan, David P. Norton," *Horizons,* (March 2001).

This article explains the emerging role of the balanced scorecard—a change from a focus only on performance evaluation to a concern also for strategic management. Through the use of strategy maps, the authors show how the balanced scorecard can be used to inform the development of the firm's strategy and improve shareholder value. This is accomplished through the linking of the scorecard perspectives: from the learning and growth perspective to the internal perspective, then to the customer perspective, and finally to the financial perspective and shareholder value.

Discussion Questions:
1. Give an example of a nonprofit or governmental organization that uses the balanced scorecard and explain how it links the scorecard to its overall strategy.
2. What is a Key Performance Indicator (KPI) scorecard and how does it differ from a balanced scorecard?
3. How can the balanced scorecard be used to supplement conventional financial reporting?
4. Explain the strategy map and how it is used.

17-2: "Strategy Maps" by Robert S. Kaplan, and David P. Norton, *Strategic Finance* (March 2004) pp.27-35.

This article expands Kaplan's and Norton's earlier work on the balanced scorecard and strategy maps (see Article 17-1 above) to the concepts of customer value propositions and the use of the strategy map to identify how the balanced scorecard can be used to facilitate achieving the desired value proposition.

Discussion Questions:

1. To achieve desired financial goals the organization focuses on which two levers of success?

2. What are the three strategic approaches through which a company can attempt to create sustainable value for the shareholder?

3. What are the four customer value propositions that a company can use to succeed?

4. What are the characteristics of firms that compete on the basis of the four customer value propositions identified above?

5. What are the four clusters of internal processes through which a company can succeed on the internal business value proposition:

6. What are the three components of the firm's use of learning and innovation as a value proposition?

Blocher, Stout, Cokins, Chen: *Cost Management, 4e*

Cases

17-1 Industrial Chemicals Company

In 2006, events which were thought about and planned for the past several years in the Industrial Chemicals Company (ICC) culminated in the most significant change in the company's 80-plus year history. A major corporate restructuring was announced including the purchase of a large U.S. based pharmaceutical company, for $2.8 billion. ICC is a large multinational manufacturer of industrial chemicals. The parent company is located in Amsterdam, and manufacturing plants and customers are located worldwide.

In February of 2007, the Chairman of the Board and Chief Executive Officer told a reporter of a major financial magazine: "We felt that if we were to build a strong technology base of biology and biotechnology that would simultaneously serve agriculture, animal nutrition, and health care, we could build a unique powerhouse backing it up in a way that companies in these individual businesses couldn't do; and we've built it." The changes initiated were thus not merely pruning and trimming, but changing the very direction of the company by getting out of commodity chemicals and into more innovative areas.

The magazine article made a key observation in its February 10, issue:

A major problem looms: Can ICC support the level of research needed to make a major impact in biotechnology? Earnings for the first three quarters of 2006 dropped and the company expects to show a loss for the fourth quarter, even before write-offs on closed chemical plants.

The chairman of the board was well aware of this major concern. In fact, as 2006 drew to a close, he commissioned a special subgroup of the Executive Management Committee (the EMC is the senior management group dealing with major strategic and operational issues) to review the company's overall R&D spending, its affordability and priorities, and bring back recommendations to the EMC in time for inclusion in the 2007 budgeting process.

RESEARCH AND DEVELOPMENT
From a total corporate perspective, the R&D effort falls into three classifications:

Class I—Maintain existing businesses—

This effort is associated with managing existing business assets, maintaining competitiveness of products in existing businesses, and supplying technical service.

Class II—Expand existing businesses—

R&D associated with expanding existing business assets, expanding markets of existing products, or substantially lowering costs of existing processes.

Class III—Create new businesses—

R&D associated with creating new business assets.

Organizationally, each of the operating units administers its own R&D efforts which cut across all three categories above. In very simple terms, the operating unit is relatively self-sufficient across all three categories where technology *already exists*. They "purchase" some support services from the corporate R&D group as described later. In terms of performance assessment for incentive compensation, the operating unit R&D groups are tied to the "bottom-line" results achieved by the respective units.

CORPORATE R&D
The corporate R&D group, in addition to providing support services to the operating unit's R&D efforts, is primarily responsible for required *new technology* in creating new businesses. At the point in time in the product invention time line when new-technology-based products reach a level of commercial viability, these programs are "handed-off" to an operating unit R&D group for eventual movement to commercialization. In the past several years, this corporate R&D group has been successful in "inventing" and "handing off" commercial leads despite some operating unit reluctance to fund the research costs. In these instances, funding sometimes remained with corporate R&D after the "hand-off."

A more detailed description of the corporate R&D group follows. The corporate research and development group is headed by a senior vice president reporting to the Chairman of the Board and CEO. The central research laboratory group consists of an information center (20 percent of its costs are charged to operating units on a fee for service basis), an MIS facility, bioprocess development and cell culture groups (which are essentially involved in devising production processes for biotechnology-based products),
a physical sciences center (a central analytical chemistry group providing very specialized and highly skilled

---

SUMMARY OF CORPORATE RESEARCH AND DEVELOPMENT

Research Laboratory Group
 Information Center
 MIS Facility
 Bioprocess Development and Cell Culture
 Physical Sciences Center
 Analytical Chemistry Group
 Chemistry Group

Biological Sciences Group

Patent Group

---

support to many users across the company—65 percent of this group's costs are charged out directly on a fee-for-service basis), a group called controlled delivery which develops vehicles for the transfer of pharmaceutical and animal science products into the living systems within which they must act, and a chemistry group providing very specialized skills in both conventional and biotechnology process chemistry (about 25 percent of this group's costs are charged directly on a fee-for-service basis). In addition to the direct fee-for-service chargeouts described above, a portion of the costs of this central laboratory group (primarily the bioprocess development and cell culture groups) is assigned to the biological sciences segment. The remaining costs, along with overall corporate R&D administrative costs, are allocated as a part of corporate charges.

The biological sciences group has been the major focal point for new technology in the pharmaceutical and animal sciences area. It supports plant sciences for the agricultural unit as well. The costs for the biological sciences group are reported as being for new direction basic research. Also controlled within corporate R&D and reported in this segment are costs of key university relationships supporting basic and applied biomedical, crop chemicals, and animal sciences research efforts.

The patent group has always been decentralized with a patent counsel and staff assigned to each operating unit reporting on a "dotted line" basis to the operating unit and administratively to the general patent counsel. Thus, about 80 percent of patent cost is already directly borne by operating units with the remainder allocated as part of corporate charges.

REQUIRED:

As the controller reflected on the information obtained and the important issues being addressed by the EMC subcommittee, the following questions surfaced in his mind. Develop a response for each question.

1. What is the role of R&D in the firm's overall strategy?
2. Would operating unit control of our key R&D growth programs enhance or mitigate our chances of meeting our goals? That is, should R&D be organized as cost SBUs within each of the operating units? What amount and type of R&D, if any at all, should be done at the corporate level?
3. I know there'll be pressure to level off our R&D spending across the company, including corporate R&D. We've got to make sure we get more for our money in terms of prioritizing those efforts to go after the most promising commercial opportunities if we're going to achieve our goals in biotechnology! How can we be sure we're prioritizing these efforts toward increased commercial success? That is, how do we evaluate the effectiveness of both the R&D cost SBUs in the operating units and corporate-level R&D?
4. How does the fact that ICC operates in several different countries affect the decisions the controller is facing?

Blocher, Stout, Cokins, Chen: *Cost Management, 4e*

17-2 Full Versus Variable Costing and Ethical Issues

HeadGear, Inc is a small manufacturer of headphones for use in commercial and personal applications. The HeadGear headphones are known for their outstanding sound quality and light weight, which makes them highly desirable especially in the commercial market for telemarketing firms and similar communication applications, despite the relatively high price. Although demand has grown steadily, profits have grown much more slowly, and John Hurley, the CEO, suspects productivity is falling, and costs are rising out of hand. John is concerned that the decline in profit growth will affect the stock price of the company and inhibit the firm's efforts to raise new investment capital, which will be needed to continue the firm's growth. While the firm is now operating at 68% of available production capacity, John thinks the market growth will soon exceed available capacity.

To improve profitability, John has decided to bring in a new COO with the objective of improving profitability very quickly. The new COO understands that profits must be improved within the coming 10-18 months. A bonus of 10% of profit improvement is promised the new COO if this goal is achieved. The following is the income statement for HeadGear for 2007, from the most recent annual report. Product costs for HeadGear include $25 per unit variable manufacturing costs and $1,920,000 per year fixed manufacturing overhead. Budgeted production was 120,000 units in 2007. Selling and administrative costs include a variable portion of $15 per unit and a fixed portion of $2,400,0000 per year. The same units costs and production level are also applicable for 2005.

HeadGear Inc.		
Income Statement for the Period Ended 12/31/2007		
Sales (125,000 @$75)		$ 9,375,000
Cost of Sales:		
Beginning Inv: 5,000 @ $41	$ 205,000	
Cost of Production: 120,000 @ $41	4,920,000	
Goods Available: 130,000	$5,125,000	
Less Ending Inv: 0 @ $41	-0-	$5,125,000
Gross Margin		$4,250,000
Selling and Administrative		
Variable Costs: 125,000 @ $15	$ 1,875,000	
Fixed Costs	2,400,000	$4,275,000
Net loss		$ <25,000>

The new COO is convinced that the problem is the need to aggressively market the product, and that the apparent decline in productivity is really due to underutilization of capacity. The COO increases fixed manufacturing costs to $2,100,000 and variable selling costs to $16 per unit and fixed selling costs to $2,750,000 to help achieve this goal. Budgeted sales and production for 2008 are set at 175,000 units.

Actual production was 175,000 as planned but sales for 2008 turned out to be only 140,000 units, short of the target. The new COO claims that profits have increased considerably, and is looking forward to the promised bonus.

REQUIRED:
1. Calculate the absorption cost net income for 2008, assuming the new selling costs, and that manufacturing costs remain the same as 2007.
2. Calculate the variable cost net income for 2008 and explain why it is different from the absorption cost net income.
3. Is the new COO due a bonus? Comment on the effectiveness of Hurley's plan to improve profits by hiring the new COO and promising the bonus.
4. Identify and explain any important ethical issues you see in this case.

17-3 Strategic Performance Measurement

Johnson Supply Company is a large retailer of office supplies. It is organized into six regional divisions, five within the United States, and one international division. The firm is growing steadily, with the greatest growth in the international division. Johnson evaluates each division as a profit SBU. Revenues and direct costs of the divisions are traced to each division using a centralized accounting system. The various support departments, including human resources, information technology, accounting, and marketing, are treated as cost SBUs and the costs are allocated to the divisions on the basis of sales revenues. The international division has cash, receivables, payables, and other investments in foreign currencies. As a result, this division experiences occasional significant losses and gains due to fluctuations in the value of foreign currencies. Based on the idea that these effects are uncontrollable, the effects of currency changes on the international division is retained in a single home-office account and is not traced to the division. Similarly, taxes paid by this division to other countries is pooled in a home office account and is not traced to it.

Because of rapidly increasing costs in the information technology (IT) department, Johnson's top management is considering changing this department to a profit SBU. IT would set prices for its services, and the user divisions could choose to purchase these services from IT or from a vendor outside the firm. The manager of IT is upset at the idea, and has told top management that this move would eventually create chaotic and ineffective information services within the firm.

REQUIRED:

1. Should Johnson's six divisions be treated as profit SBUs or some other type of strategic performance measurement system? Explain.
2. Comment on the firm's decision not to trace currency gains and losses and foreign tax expense to the international division.
3. Comment on the firm's consideration of changing the IT department from a cost SBU to a profit SBU. What are the likely effects on the firm and on the IT department?

Blocher, Stout, Cokins, Chen: *Cost Management, 4e*

©The McGraw-Hill Companies, Inc 2008

17-4 Strategic Performance Measurement: Employee Benefits

In its thirteen year of operations, Mount Drake Software is reviewing the methods it has used to evaluate its profit SBUs. Mount Drake has six product divisions, each of which is a profit SBU, and each markets specialized software products to specific customer groups. For example, one unit markets software systems to dental practices, and another provides software for real estate management firms. A critical factor in Mount Drake's success is the commitment and competence of its systems development and programming staff. While there is a relatively high turnover for these employees, Mount Drake has managed to retain the very best and to attract the very best. In recent months, as their business has grown, and as the software industry generally has grown significantly, it has become more and more difficult for Mount Drake to attract and to retain the best staff. Mount Drake is looking for ways to become more competitive in attracting and retaining these employees. One idea is to increase employee benefits by adding training opportunities, additional paid vacation, stock investment programs, and improved health insurance. The cost of some of these additional benefits could be traced directly to the divisions, while the cost of other benefits (such as improved group health coverage and company-wide training programs) could not be directly traced to the divisions.

REQUIRED:

How should Mount Drake handle employee benefits within its current performance measurement system? Should Mount Drake change the performance measurement system, and if so, how should it be changed?

17-5 Contribution Income Statement

Cathy's Classic Clothes is a retail organization that sells to professional women in the Northeast. The firm leases space for stores in upscale shopping centers, and the organizational structure consists of regions, districts, and stores. Each region consists of two or more districts; each district consists of three or more stores. Each store, district, and region has been established as a profit center. At all levels, the company uses a management by objective (MBO) system and a responsibility accounting system that focuses on information and knowledge rather than blame and control. Each year, managers, in consultation with their supervisors, establish goals which are not solely financial, and these goals are integrated into the budget. Actual performance is measured each month.

   The Northeast Region consists of Districts A and B. District A consists of three stores, 1, 2, and 3 with District B consisting of three stores, 4, 5, and 6. District A's performance has not been up to expectations in the past. For the month of May, the district manager has set performance goals with the managers of Stores 1 and 2 who will receive bonuses if certain performance measures are exceeded. The manager of Store 3 decided not to participate in the bonus scheme. Since the district manager is unsure what type of bonus will encourage better performance, the manager of Store 1 will receive a bonus based on sales in excess of budgeted sales of $570,000 while the manager of Store 2 will receive a bonus based on net income in excess of budgeted net income. The company's net income goal for each store is 12 percent of sales. The budgeted sales for Store 2 are $530,000.

   Other pertinent data for the month of May 2007 are given below.

- At Store 1, sales are 40 percent of District A sales while sales at Store 2 are 35 percent of District A sales. The cost of goods sold at both Stores 1 and 2 is 42 percent of sales.
- Variable selling expenses (sales commissions) are 6 percent of sales for all stores, districts, and regions.
- Variable administrative expenses are 2.5 percent of sales for all stores, districts, and regions.
- Maintenance cost includes janitorial and repair services and is a direct cost for each store. The store manager has complete control over this outlay; however, this cost should not be below one percent of sales.
- Advertising is considered a direct cost for each store and is completely under the control of the store manager. Store 1 spent two-thirds of District A's total outlay for advertising which was ten times more than Store 2 spent on advertising.
- The rental expenses at Store 1 are 40 percent of District A's total while Store 2 incurs 30 percent of District A's total.
- District expenses are allocated to the stores based on sales.

REQUIRED:
1. Complete the May 2007 performance report for District A and Stores 1 and 2.
2. Discuss the impact of the responsibility accounting system and bonus structure on the manager's behavior and the effect of this behavior on the financial results for Store 1 and Store 2.

Blocher, Stout, Cokins, Chen: *Cost Management, 4e*

©The McGraw-Hill Companies, Inc 2008

Readings

17.1: TRANSFORMING THE BALANCED SCORECARD FROM PERFORMANCE MEASUREMENT TO STRATEGIC MANAGEMENT: PART I

by Robert S. Kaplan and David P. Norton

Robert S. Kaplan is a Professor at Harvard University and David P. Norton is founder and president of the Balanced Scorecard Collaborative in Lincoln, Massachusetts.[1]

Several years ago we introduced the Balanced Scorecard (Kaplan and Norton 1992). We began with the premise that an exclusive reliance on financial measures in a management system is insufficient. Financial measures are lag indicators that report on the outcomes from past actions. Exclusive reliance on financial indicators could promote behavior that sacrifices long-term value creation for short-term performance (Porter 1992; AICPA 1994). The Balanced Scorecard approach retains measures of financial performance—the lagging outcome indicators—but supplements these with measures on the drivers, the lead indicators, of future financial performance.

THE BALANCED SCORECARD EMERGES

The limitations of managing solely with financial measures, however, have been known for decades.[2] What is different now? Why has the Balanced Scorecard concept been so widely adopted by manufacturing and service companies, nonprofit organizations, and government entities around the world since its introduction in 1992?

First, previous systems that incorporated nonfinancial measurements used *ad hoc* collections of such measures, more like checklists of measures

for managers to keep track of and improve than a comprehensive system of linked measurements. The Balanced Scorecard emphasizes the linkage of measurement to strategy (Kaplan and Norton 1993) and the cause-and-effect linkages that describe the hypotheses of the strategy (Kaplan and Norton 1996b). The tighter connection between the measurement system and strategy elevates the role for nonfinancial measures from an operational checklist to a comprehensive system for strategy implementation (Kaplan and Norton 1996a).

Second, the Balanced Scorecard reflects the changing nature of technology and competitive advantage in the latter decades of the 20th century. In the industrial-age competition of the 19th and much of the 20th centuries, companies achieved competitive advantage from their investment in and management of tangible assets such as inventory, property, plant, and equipment (Chandler 1990). In an economy dominated by tangible assets, financial measurements were adequate to record investments on companies' balance sheets. Income statements could also capture the expenses associated with the use of these tangible assets to produce revenues and profits. But by the end of the 20th century, intangible assets became the major source for competitive advantage. In 1982, tangible book values represented 62 percent of industrial organizations' market values; ten years later, the ratio had plummeted to 38 percent (Blair 1995). By the end of the 20th century, the book value of tangible assets accounted for less than 20 percent of companies' market values (Webber 2000, quoting research by Baruch Lev).

Clearly, strategies for creating value shifted from managing tangible assets to knowledge-based strategies that create and deploy an organization's intangible assets. These include customer relationships, innovative products and services, high-quality and responsive operating processes, skills and knowledge of the workforce, the information technology that supports the work force and links

---

[1] This article is adapted from R. S. Kaplan and D. P. Norton (2001a, 2000). © 2001 American Accounting Association, *Accounting Horizons*, Vol. 15 No.1, March 2001, pp. 87-104

[2] For example, General Electric attempted a system of nonfinancial measurements in the 1950s (Greenwood 1974), and the French developed the Tableaux de Bord decades ago (Lebas 1994; Epstein and Manzoni1998).

the firm to its customers and suppliers, and the organizational climate that encourages innovation, problem-solving, and improvement. But companies were unable to adequately measure their intangible assets (Johnson and Kaplan 1987, 201-202). Anecdotal data from management publications indicated that many companies could not implement their new strategies in this environment (Kiechel 1982; Charan and Colvin 1999). They could not manage what they could not describe or measure.

INTANGIBLE ASSETS: VALUATION VS. VALUE CREATION

Some call for accountants to make an organization's intangible assets more visible to managers and investors by placing them on a company's balance sheet. But several factors prevent valid valuation of intangible assets on balance sheets.

First, the value from intangible assets is indirect. Assets such as knowledge and technology seldom have a direct impact on revenue and profit. Improvements in intangible assets affect financial outcomes through chains of cause-and-effect relationships involving two or three intermediate stages (Huselid 1995; Becker and Huselid 1998). For example, consider the linkages in the service management profit chain (Heskett et al.1994):

- investments in employee training lead to improvements in service quality
- better service quality leads to higher customer satisfaction
- higher customer satisfaction leads to increased customer loyalty
- increased customer loyalty generates increased revenues and margins

Financial outcomes are separated causally and temporally from improving employees' capabilities. The complex linkages make it difficult, if not impossible, to place a financial value on an asset such as workforce capabilities or employee morale, much less to measure period-to-period changes in that financial value.

Second, the value from intangible assets depends on organizational context and strategy. This value cannot be separated from the organizational processes that transform intangibles into customer and financial outcomes. The balance sheet is a linear, additive model. It records each class of asset separately and calculates the total by adding up each asset's recorded value. The value created from investing in individual intangible assets, however, is neither linear nor additive.

Senior investment bankers in a firm such as Goldman Sachs are immensely valuable because of their knowledge about complex financial products and their capabilities for managing relationships and developing trust with sophisticated customers. People with the same knowledge, experience, and capabilities, however, are nearly worthless to a financial services company such as etrade.com that emphasizes operational efficiency, low cost, and technology-based trading. The value of an intangible asset depends critically on the context—the organization, the strategy, and other complementary assets—in which the intangible asset is deployed.

Intangible assets seldom have value by themselves.[3] Generally, they must be bundled with other intangible and tangible assets to create value. For example, a new growth-oriented sales strategy could require new knowledge about customers, new training for sales employees, new databases, new information systems, a new organization structure, and a new incentive compensation program. Investing in just one of these capabilities, or in all of them but one, could cause the new sales strategy to fail. The value does not reside in any individual intangible asset. It arises from creating the entire set of assets along with a strategy that links them together. The value-creation process is multiplicative, not additive.

THE BALANCED SCORECARD SUPPLEMENTS CONVENTIONAL FINANCIAL REPORTING

Companies' balance sheets report separately on tangible assets, such as raw material, land, and equipment, based on their historic cost—the traditional financial accounting method. This was adequate for industrial-age companies, which succeeded by combining and transforming their tangible resources into products whose value exceeded their acquisition and production costs. Financial accounting conventions relating to depreciation and cost of goods sold enabled an income statement to measure how much value was created beyond the costs incurred to acquire and transform tangible assets into finished products and services.

Some argue that companies should follow the same cost-based convention for their intangible assets—capitalize and subsequently amortize the expenditures on training employees, conducting research and development, purchasing and developing databases, and advertising that creates brand awareness. But such costs are poor approximations

---

[3] Brand names, which can be sold, are an exception.

Blocher, Stout, Cokins, Chen: *Cost Management, 4e*

©The McGraw-Hill Companies, Inc 2008

of the realizable value created by investing in these intangible assets. Intangible assets can create value for organizations, but that does not imply that they have separable market values. Many internal and linked organizational processes, such as design, delivery, and service, are required to transform the potential value of intangible assets into products and services that have tangible value.

We introduced the Balanced Scorecard to provide a new framework for describing value-creating strategies that link intangible and tangible assets. The scorecard does not attempt to "value" an organization's intangible assets, but it does measure these assets in units other than currency. The Balanced Scorecard describes how intangible assets get mobilized and combined with intangible and tangible assets to create differentiating customer-value propositions and superior financial outcomes.

STRATEGY MAPS

Since introducing the Balanced Scorecard in 1992, we have helped over 200 executive teams design their scorecard programs. Initially we started with a clean sheet of paper, asking, "what is the strategy," and allowed the strategy and the Balanced Scorecard to emerge from interviews and discussions with the senior executives. The scorecard provided a framework for organizing strategic objectives into the four perspectives displayed in Figure 1:

1. *Financial*—the strategy for growth, profitability, and risk viewed from the perspective of the shareholder.
2. *Customer*—the strategy for creating value and differentiation from the perspective of the customer.
3. *Internal Business Processes*—the strategic priorities for various business processes that create customer and shareholder satisfaction.
4. *Learning and Growth*—the priorities to create a climate that supports organizational change, innovation, and growth.

From this initial base of experience, we subsequently developed a general framework for describing and implementing strategy that we believe can be as useful as the traditional framework of income statement, balance sheet, and statement of cash flows for financial planning and reporting. The new framework, which we call a "Strategy Map," is a logical and comprehensive architecture for describing strategy, as illustrated in Figure 2. A strategy map specifies the critical elements and their linkages for an organization's strategy.

- Objectives for growth and productivity to enhance shareholder value.
- Market and account share, acquisition, and retention of targeted customers where profitable growth will occur.
- Value propositions that would lead customers to do more higher-margin business with the company.
- Innovation and excellence in products, services, and processes that deliver the value proposition to targeted customer segments, promote operational improvements, and meet community expectations and regulatory requirements.
- Investments required in people and systems to generate and sustain growth.

By translating their strategy into the logical architecture of a strategy map and Balanced Scorecard, organizations create a common and understandable point of reference for all organizational units and employees.

Organizations build strategy maps from the top down, starting with the destination and then charting the routes that lead there. Corporate executives first review their mission statement, why their company exists, and core values, what their company believes in. From that information, they develop their strategic vision, what their company wants to become. This vision creates a clear picture of the company's overall goal, which could be to become a top-quartile performer. The strategy identifies the path intended to reach that destination.

FINANCIAL PERSPECTIVE

The typical destination for profit-seeking enterprises is a significant increase in shareholder value (we will discuss the modifications for nonprofit and government organizations later in the paper). Companies increase economic value through two basic approaches—revenue *growth* and *productivity*.[4] A revenue growth strategy generally has two components: build the franchise with revenue from new markets, new products, and new customers; and increase sales to existing customers by deepening relationships with them, including cross-selling

---

[4] Shareholder value can also be increased through managing the right-hand side of the balance sheet, such as by repurchasing shares and choosing the low-cost mix among debt and equity instruments to lower the cost of capital. In this paper, we focus only on improved management of the organization's assets (tangible and intangible).

multiple products and services, and offering complete solutions. A productivity strategy also generally has two components: improve the cost structure by lowering direct and indirect expenses; and utilize assets more efficiently by reducing the working and fixed capital needed to support a given level of business.

CUSTOMER PERSPECTIVE

The core of any business strategy is the *customer-value proposition,* which describes the unique mix of product, price, service, relationship, and image that a company offers. It defines how the organization differentiates itself from competitors to attract, retain, and deepen relationships with targeted customers. The value proposition is crucial because it helps an organization connect its internal processes to improved outcomes with its customers.

Companies differentiate their value proposition by selecting among *operational excellence* (for example, McDonalds and Dell Computer), *customer intimacy* (Home Depot and IBM in the 1960s and 1970s), and *product leadership* (Intel and Sony) (Treacy and Wiersema 1997, 31-45). Sustainable strategies are based on excelling at one of the three while maintaining threshold standards with the other two. After identifying its value proposition, a company knows which classes and types of customers to target.

Specifically, companies that pursue a strategy of operational excellence need to excel at competitive pricing, product quality, product selection, lead time, and on-time delivery. For customer intimacy, an organization must stress the quality of its relationships with customers, including exceptional service, and the completeness and suitability of the solutions it offers individual customers. Companies that pursue a product-leadership strategy must concentrate on the functionality, features, and performance of their products and services.

The customer perspective also identifies the intended outcomes from delivering a differentiated value proposition. These would include market share in targeted customer segments, account share with targeted customers, acquisition and retention of customers in the targeted segments, and customer profitability.[5]

INTERNAL PROCESS PERSPECTIVE

Once an organization has a clear picture of its customer and financial perspectives, it can determine the means by which it will achieve the differentiated value proposition for customers and the productivity improvements for the financial objectives. The internal business perspective captures these critical organizational activities, which fall into four high-level processes:

1. *Build the franchise* by spurring innovation to develop new products and services and to penetrate new markets and customer segments.
2. *Increase customer value* by expanding and deepening relationships with existing customers.
3. *Achieve operational excellence* by improving supply-chain management, internal processes, asset utilization, resource-capacity management, and other processes.
4. *Become a good corporate citizen* by establishing effective relationships with external stakeholders.

Many companies that espouse a strategy calling for innovation or for developing value-adding customer relationships mistakenly choose to measure their internal business processes by focusing only on the cost and quality of their operations. These companies have a complete disconnect between their strategy and how they measure it. Not surprisingly, organizations encounter great difficulty implementing growth strategies when their primary internal measurements emphasize process improvements, not innovation or enhanced customer relationships.

The financial benefits from improvements to the different business processes typically occur in stages. Cost savings from increases in *operational efficiencies* and process improvements deliver short-term benefits. Revenue growth from enhancing *customer relationships* accrues in the intermediate term. Increased *innovation* generally produces long-term revenue and margin improvements. Thus, a complete strategy should generate returns from all three high-level internal processes.

---

[5] Measurement of customer profitability (Kaplan and Cooper 1998, 181-201) provides one of the connections between the Balanced Scorecard and activity-based costing.

FIGURE 1
The Balanced Scorecard Defines a Strategy's Cause-and-Effect Relationships

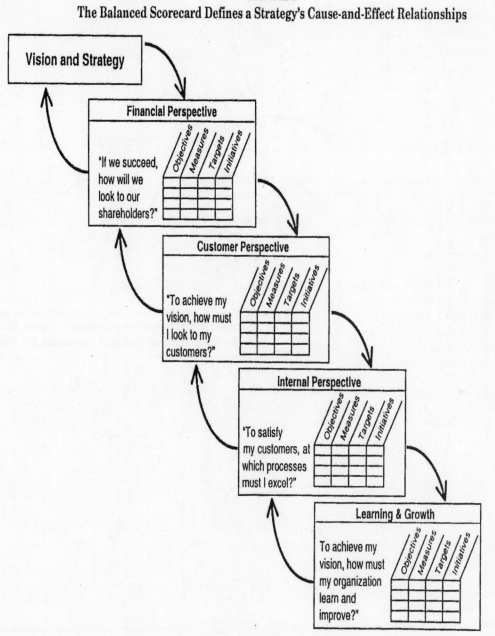

©The McGraw-Hill Companies, Inc 2008

FIGURE 2
The Balanced Scorecard Strategy Map

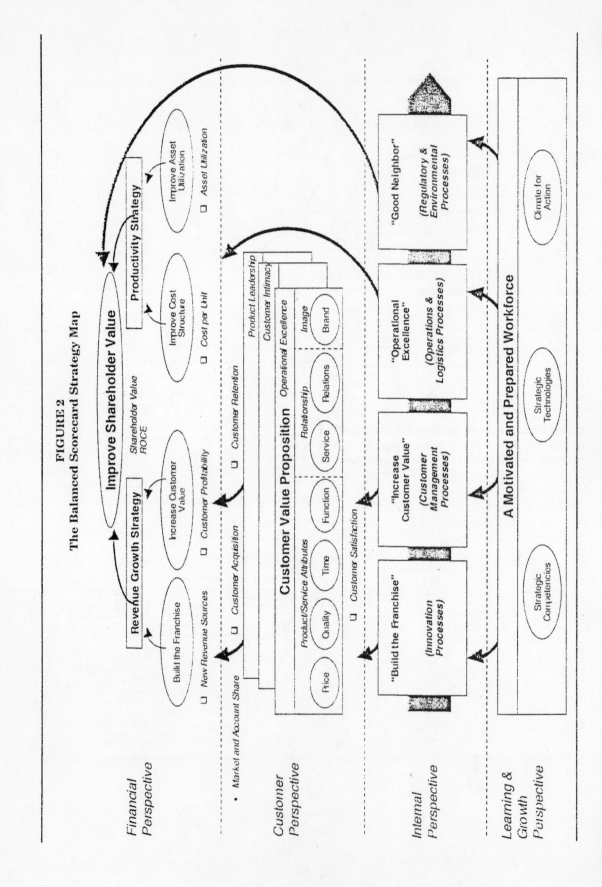

LEARNING AND GROWTH PERSPECTIVE

The final region of a strategy map is the learning and growth perspective, which is the foundation of any strategy. In the learning and growth perspective, managers define the employee capabilities and skills, technology, and corporate climate needed to support a strategy. These objectives enable a company to align its human resources and information technology with the strategic requirements from its critical internal business processes, differentiated value proposition, and customer relationships. After addressing the learning and growth perspective, companies have a complete strategy map with linkages across the four major perspectives.

Strategy maps, beyond providing a common framework for describing and building strategies, also are powerful diagnostic tools, capable of detecting flaws in organizations' Balanced Scorecards. For example, Figure 3 shows the strategy map for the Revenue Growth theme of Mobil North America Marketing & Refining. When senior management compared the scorecards being used by its business units to this template, it found one unit with no objective or measure for dealers, an omission immediately obvious from looking at its strategy map. Had this unit discovered how to bypass dealers and sell gasoline directly to end-use consumers? Were dealer relationships no longer strategic for this unit? The business unit shown in the lower right corner of Figure 3 did not mention quality on its scorecard. Again, had this unit already achieved six sigma quality levels so quality was no longer a strategic priority? Mobil's executive team used its divisional strategy map to identify and remedy gaps in the strategies being implemented at lower levels of the organization.

STAKEHOLDER AND KEY PERFORMANCE INDICATOR SCORECARDS

Many organizations claim to have a Balanced Scorecard because they use a mixture of financial and nonfinancial measures. Such measurement systems are certainly more "balanced" than ones that use financial measures alone. Yet, the assumptions and philosophies underlying these scorecards are quite different from those underlying the strategy scorecards and maps described above. We observe two other scorecard types frequently used in practice: the *stakeholder scorecard* and the *key performance indicator scorecard*.

STAKEHOLDER SCORECARDS

The *stakeholder scorecard* identifies the major constituents of the organization—shareholders, customers. and employees—and frequently other constituents such as suppliers and the community. The scorecard defines the organization's goals for these different constituents, or stakeholders, and develops an appropriate scorecard of measures and targets for them (Atkinson and Waterhouse 1997). For example, Sears built its initial scorecard around three themes:

- "a compelling place to shop"
- "a compelling place to work"
- "a compelling place to invest"

Citicorp used a similar structure for its initial scorecard—"a good place to work, to bank, and to invest." AT&T developed an elaborate internal measurement system based on financial value-added, customer value-added, and people value-added.

All these companies built their measurements around their three dominant constituents—customers, shareholders, and employees—emphasizing satisfaction measures for customers and employees, to ensure that these constituents felt well served by the company. In this sense, they were apparently *balanced*. Comparing these scorecards to the strategy map template in Figure 2 we can easily detect what is missing from such scorecards: no objectives or measures for *how* these balanced goals are to be achieved. A vision describes a desired outcome; a strategy, however, must describe *how* the outcome will be achieved, how employees, customers, and shareholders will be satisfied. Thus, a stakeholder scorecard is not adequate to describe the strategy of an organization and, therefore, is not an adequate foundation on which to build a management system.

Missing from the stakeholder card are the drivers to achieve the goals. Such drivers include an explicit value proposition such as innovation that generates new products and services or enhanced customer management processes, the deployment of technology, and the specific skills and competencies of employees required to implement the strategy. In a well-constructed *strategy scorecard,* the value proposition in the customer perspective, all the processes in the internal perspective, and the learning and growth perspective components of the scorecard define the "how" that is as fundamental to strategy as the outcomes that the strategy is expected to achieve.

Stakeholder scorecards are often a first step on the road to a strategy scorecard. But as organizations begin to work with stakeholder cards, they inevitably confront the question of "how." This leads to the next level of strategic thinking and scorecard design. Both Sears and Citicorp quickly moved beyond their stakeholder scorecards, developing an insightful set of internal process objectives to complete the description of their strategy and, ultimately, achieving a strategy Balanced Scorecard. The stakeholder scorecard can also be useful in organizations that do not have internal synergies across business units. Since each business has a different set of internal drivers, this "corporate" scorecard need only focus on the desired outcomes for the corporation's constituencies, including the community and suppliers. Each business unit then defines how it will achieve those goals with its business unit strategy scorecard and strategy map.

KEY PERFORMANCE INDICATOR SCORECARDS

Key Performance Indicator (KPI) scorecards are also common. The total quality management approach and variants such as the Malcolm Baldrige and European Foundation for Quality Management (EFQM) awards generate many measures to monitor internal processes. When migrating to a "Balanced Scorecard," organizations often build on the base already established by classifying their existing measurements into the four BSC categories. KPI scorecards also emerge when the organization's information technology group, which likes to put the company database at the heart of any change program, triggers the scorecard design. Consulting organizations that sell and install large systems, especially so-called executive information systems, also offer KPI scorecards.

As a simple example of a KPI scorecard, a financial service organization articulated the 4Ps for its "balanced scorecard:"

1. Profits
2. Portfolio (size of loan volume)
3. Process (percent processes ISO certified)
4. People (meeting diversity goals in hiring)

Although this scorecard is more balanced than one using financial measures alone, comparing the 4P measures to a strategy map like that in Figure 2 reveals the major gaps in the measurement set. The company has no customer measures and only a single internal-process measure, which focuses on an initiative not an outcome. This KPI scorecard has no role for information technology (strange for a financial service organization), no linkages from the internal measure (ISO process certification) to a customer-value proposition or to a customer outcome, and no linkage from the learning and growth measure (diverse work force) to improving an internal process, a customer outcome, or a financial outcome.

KPI scorecards are most helpful for departments and teams when a strategic program already exists at a higher level. In this way, the diverse indicators enable individuals and teams to define what they must do well to contribute to higher level goals. Unless, however, the link to strategy is clearly established, the KPI scorecard will lead to local but not global or strategic improvements.

Balanced Scorecards should not just be collections of financial and nonfinancial measures, organized into three to five perspectives. The best Balanced Scorecards reflect the strategy of the organization. A good test is whether you can understand the strategy by looking only at the scorecard and its strategy map. Many organizations fail this test, especially those that create stakeholder scorecards or key performance indicator scorecards.

Strategy scorecards along with their graphical representations on strategy maps provide a logical and comprehensive way to describe strategy. They communicate clearly the organization's desired outcomes and its hypotheses about how these outcomes can be achieved. For example, *if* we improve on-time delivery, *then* customer satisfaction will improve; *if* customer satisfaction improves, *then* customers will purchase more. The scorecards enable all organizational units and employees to understand the strategy and identify how they can contribute by becoming aligned to the strategy.

APPLYING THE BSC TO NONPROFITS AND GOVERNMENT ORGANIZATIONS

During the past five years, the Balanced Scorecard has also been applied by non-profit and government organizations (NPGOs). One of the barriers to applying the scorecard to these sectors is the considerable difficulty NPGOs have in clearly defining their strategy. We reviewed "strategy" documents of more than 50 pages. Most of the documents, once the mission and vision are articulated, consist of lists of programs and initiatives, not the outcomes the organization is trying to achieve. These organizations must understand Porter's (1996, 77) admonition that strategy is not only what the organization intends to do, but also what it decides *not* to do, a message that is particularly relevant for NPGOs.

FIGURE 3
Mobil Uses Reverse Engineering of a Strategy Map as a Strategy Diagnostic

The Template (Strategy Map: Partial)

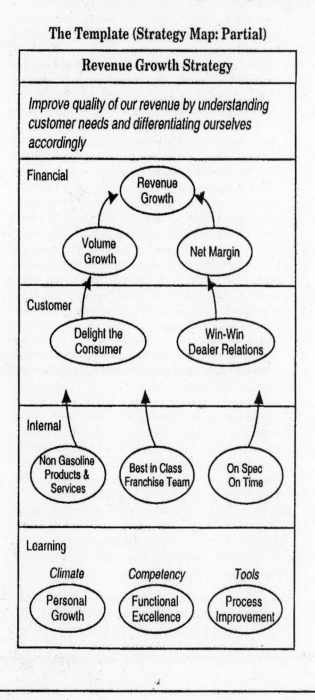

SBU A: "Did we eliminate the dealer?"

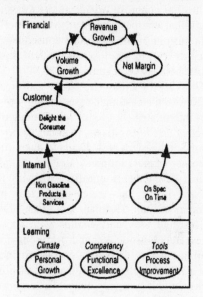

SBU B: "Have we achieved perfection?"

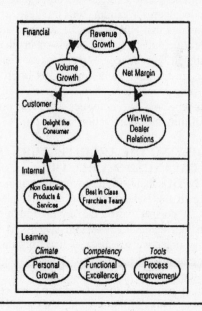

Most of the initial scorecards of NPGOs feature an operational excellence strategy. The organizations take their current mission as a given and try to do their work more efficiently—at lower cost, with fewer defects, and faster. Often the project builds off of a recently introduced quality initiative that emphasizes process improvements. It is unusual to find nonprofit organizations focusing on a strategy that can be thought of as product leadership or customer intimacy. As a consequence, their scorecards tend to be closer to the KPI scorecards than true strategy scorecards.

The City of Charlotte, North Carolina, however, followed a customer-based strategy by selecting an interrelated set of strategic themes to create distinct value for its citizens (Kaplan 199S). United Way of Southeastern New England also articulated a customer (donor) intimacy strategy (Kaplan and Kaplan 1996). Other nonprofits—the May Institute and New Profit Inc.—selected a clear product-leadership position (Kaplan and Elias 1999). The May Institute uses partnerships with universities and researchers to deliver the best behavioral and rehabilitation care delivery. New Profit Inc. introduces a new selection, monitoring, and governing process unique among nonprofit organizations. Montefiore Hospital uses a combination of product leadership in its centers of excellence, and excellent customer relationships—through its new patient-oriented care centers—to build market share in its local area (Kaplan 2001). These examples demonstrate that NPGOs can be strategic and build competitive advantage in ways other than pure operational excellence. But it takes vision and leadership to move from continuous improvement of existing processes to thinking strategically about which processes and activities are most important for fulfilling the organization's mission.

MODIFYING THE ARCHITECTURE OF THE BALANCED SCORECARD

Most NPGOs had difficulty with the original architecture of the Balanced Scorecard that placed the financial perspective at the top of the hierarchy. Given that achieving financial success is not the primary objective for most of these organizations, many rearrange the scorecard to place customers or constituents at the top of the hierarchy.

In a private-sector transaction, the customer plays two distinct roles—paying for the service and receiving the service—that are so complementary most people don't even think about them separately. But in a nonprofit organization, donors provide the financial resources—they pay for the service—while another group, the constituents, receives the service. Who is the customer—the one

paying or the one receiving? Rather than have to make such a Solomonic decision, organizations place both the donor perspective and the recipient perspective, in parallel, at the top of their Balanced Scorecards. They develop objectives for both donors and recipients, and then identify the internal processes that deliver desired value propositions for both groups of "customers."

In fact, nonprofit and government agencies should consider placing an over-arching objective at the top of their scorecard that represents their long-term objective such as a reduction in poverty or illiteracy, or improvements in the environment. Then the objectives within the scorecard can be oriented toward improving such a high-level objective. High-level financial measures provide private sector companies with an accountability measure to their owners, the shareholders. For a nonprofit or government agency, however, the financial measures are not the relevant indicators of whether the agency is delivering on its mission. The agency's mission should be featured and measured at the highest level of its scorecard. Placing an over-arching objective on the BSC for a nonprofit or government agency communicates clearly the long-term mission of the organization as portrayed in Figure 4.

Even the financial and customer objectives, however, may need to be re-examined for governmental organizations. Take the case of regulatory and enforcement agencies that monitor and punish violations of environmental, safety, and health regulations. These agencies, which detect transgressions, and fine or arrest those who violate the laws and regulations, cannot look to their "immediate customers" for satisfaction and loyalty measures. Clearly not the true "customers" for such organizations are the citizens at large who benefit from effective but not harsh or idiosyncratic enforcement of laws and regulations. Figure 5 shows a modified framework in which a government agency has three high-level perspectives:

1. *Cost Incurred:* This perspective emphasizes the importance of operational efficiency. The measured cost should include both the expenses of the agency and the social cost it imposes on citizens and other organizations through its operations. For example, an environmental agency imposes remediation costs on private-sector organizations. These are part of the costs of having the agency carry out its mission. The agency should minimize the direct and social costs required to achieve the benefits called for by its mission.

Blocher, Stout, Cokins, Chen: *Cost Management, 4e*

©The McGraw-Hill Companies, Inc 2008

2. *Value Created:* This perspective identifies the benefits being created by the agency to citizens and is the most problematic and difficult to measure. It is usually difficult to financially quantify the benefits from improved education, reduced pollution, better health, less congestion, and safer neighborhoods. But the balanced scorecard still enables organizations to identify the outputs, if not the outcomes, from its activities, and to measure these outputs. Surrogates for value created could include percentage of students acquiring specific skills and knowledge; density of pollutants in water, air, or land; improved morbidity and mortality in targeted populations; crime rates and perception of public safety; and transportation times. In general, public-sector organizations may find they use more output than outcome measures. The citizens and their representatives—elected officials and legislators—will eventually make the judgments about the benefits from these outputs vs. their costs.

3. *Legitimizing Support:* An important "customer" for any government agency will be its "donor," the organization—typically the legislature—that provides the funding for the agency. In order to assure continued funding for its activities, the agency must strive to meet the objectives of its funding source—the legislature and, ultimately, citizens and taxpayers.

After defining these three high-level perspectives, a public-sector agency can identify its objectives for internal processes, learning, and growth that enable objectives in the three high-level perspectives to be achieved.

BEYOND MEASUREMENT TO MANAGEMENT

Originally, we thought the Balanced Scorecard was about performance measurement (Kaplan and Norton 1992). Once organizations developed their basic system for measuring strategy, however, we quickly learned that *measurement* has consequences far beyond reporting on the past. Measurement creates focus for the future. The measures chosen by managers communicate important messages to all organizational units and employees. To take full advantage of this power, companies soon integrated their new measures into a *management system.* Thus the Balanced Scorecard concept evolved from a performance measurement system to become the organizing framework, the operating system, for a new strategic management system (Kaplan and Norton 1996c, Part II). The academic literature, rooted in the original performance measurement aspects of the scorecard, focuses on the BSC as a measurement system Ittner et al. 1997;

Ittner and Larcker 1998; Banker et al. 2000; Lipe and Salterio 2000) but has yet to examine its role as a management system.

Using this new strategic management system, we observed several organizations achieving performance breakthroughs within two to three years of implementation (Kaplan and Norton 2001a, 4-6, 17-22). The magnitude of the results achieved by the early adopters reveals the power of the Balanced Scorecard management system to focus the entire organization on strategy. The speed with which the new strategies deliver results indicates that the companies' successes are not due to a major new product or service launch, major new capital investments, or even the development of new intangible or "intellectual" assets. The companies, of course, develop new products and services, and invest in both hard, tangible assets, as well as softer, intangible assets. But they cannot benefit much in two years from such investments. To achieve their breakthrough performance, the companies capitalize on capabilities and assets—both tangible and intangible—that already exist within their organizations.[6] The companies' new strategies and the Balanced Scorecard unleash the capabilities and assets previously hidden (or frozen) within the old organization. In effect, the Balanced Scorecard provides the "recipe" that enables ingredients already existing in the organization to be combined for long-term value creation.

Part II of our commentary on the Balanced Scorecard (Kaplan and Norton 2001b) will describe how organizations use Balanced Scorecards and strategy maps to accomplish comprehensive and integrated transformations. These organizations redefine their relationships with customers, reengineer fundamental business processes, reskill the work force, and deploy new technology infrastructures. A new culture emerges, centered not on traditional functional silos, but on the team effort required to implement the strategy. By clearly defining the strategy, communicating it consistently, and linking it to the drivers of change, a performance-based culture emerges to link everyone and every unit to the unique features of the strategy. The simple act of describing strategy via strategy maps and scorecards makes a major contribution to the success of the transformation program.

---

[6] These observations indicate why attempts to value individual intangible assets almost surely is a quixotic search. The companies achieved breakthrough performance with essentially the same people, services, and technology that previously delivered dismal performance. The value creation came not from any individual asset—tangible or intangible. It came from the coherent combination and alignment of existing organizational resources.

FIGURE 4

Adapting the Balanced Scorecard Framework to Nonprofit Organizations

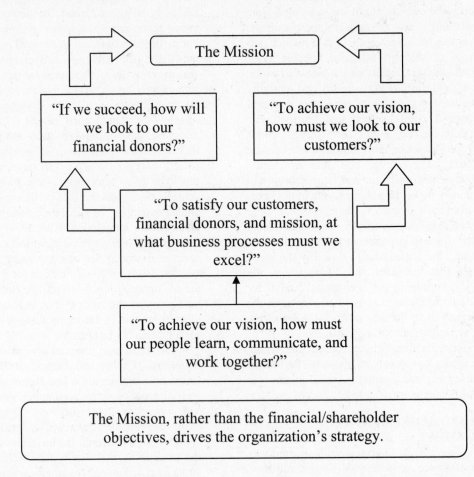

The Mission

"If we succeed, how will we look to our financial donors?"

"To achieve our vision, how must we look to our customers?"

"To satisfy our customers, financial donors, and mission, at what business processes must we excel?"

"To achieve our vision, how must our people learn, communicate, and work together?"

The Mission, rather than the financial/shareholder objectives, drives the organization's strategy.

Blocher, Stout, Cokins, Chen: *Cost Management, 4e*

FIGURE 5
The Financial/Customer Objectives for Public Sector Agencies
May Require Three Different Perspectives

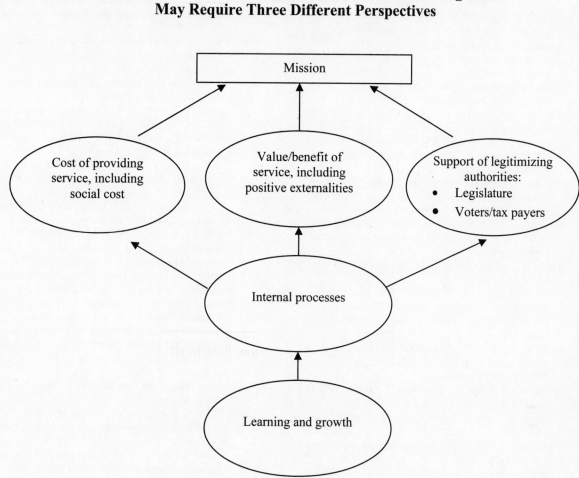

Professor Dutch Leonard, Kennedy School of Government, Harvard University, collaborated to develop this diagram.

REFERENCES

American Institute of Certified Public Accountants (AICPA), Special Committee on Financial Reporting. 1994. *Improving Business Reporting—A Customer Focus: Meeting the Information Needs of Investors and Creditors.* New York, NY: AICPA.

Atkinson, A. A., and J. H. Waterhouse. 1997. A stakeholder approach to strategic performance measurement. *Sloan Management Review* (Spring).

Banker, R., G. Potter, and D. Srinivasan. 2000. An empirical investigation of an incentive plan that includes nonfinancial performance measures. *The Accounting Review* (January): 65-92.

Becker, B., and M. Huselid. 1998. High performance work systems and firm performance: A synthesis of research and managerial implications. In *Research in Personnel and Human Resources Management,* 53-101. Greenwich, CT: JAI Press.

Blair, M. B. 1995. *Ownership and Control: Rethinking Corporate Governance for the Twenty-First Century.* Washington, D.C.: Brookings Institution.

Chandler, A. D. 1990. *Scale and Scope: The Dynamics of Industrial Capitalism.* Cambridge, MA: Harvard University Press.

Charan, R., and G. Colvin. 1999. Why CEOs fail. *Fortune* (June 21).

Epstein, M., and J. F. Manzoni. 1998. Implementing corporate strategy: From Tableaux de Bord to Balanced Scorecards. *European Management Journal* (April).

Greenwood, R. G. 1974. *Managerial Decentralization: A Study of the General Electric Philosophy.* Lexington, MA: D. C. Heath.

Heskett, J., T. Jones, G. Loveman, E. Sasser, and L. Schlesinger. 1994. Putting the service profit chain to work. *Harvard Business Review* (March-April): 164-174.

Huselid, M. A. 1995. The impact of human resource management practices on turnover, productivity, and corporate financial performance. *Academy of Management Journal:* 635-672.

Ittner, C., D. Larcker, and M. Meyer. 1997. Performance, compensation, and the Balanced Scorecard. Working paper, University of Pennsylvania.

_____, D. Larcker, and M. Rajan. 1997. The choice of performance measures in annual bonus contracts. *The Accounting Review* (April): 23 1-255.

_____, and D. Larcker. 1998. Innovations in performance measurement: Trends and research implications. *Journal of Management Accounting Research:* 205-238.

Johnson, H. T., and R. S. Kaplan. 1987. *Relevance Lost: The Rise and Fall of Management Accounting.* Boston, MA: Harvard Business School Press.

Kaplan, R. S., and D. P. Norton. 1992. The Balanced Scorecard: Measures that drive performance. *Harvard Business Review* (January-February): 71-79.

_____, and _____. 1993. Putting the Balanced Scorecard to work. *Harvard Business Review* (September-October): 134-147.

_____, and E. L. Kaplan. 1996. United Way of Southeastern New England. Harvard Business School Case 197-036. Boston, MA.

_____, and D. P. Norton.].996a. Using the Balanced Scorecard as a strategic management system. *Harvard Business Review* (January-February): 75-85.

_____, and _____. 1996b. Linking the Balanced Scorecard to strategy. *California Management Review* (Fall): 53-79.

_____, and _____. 1996c. *The Balanced Scorecard: Translating Strategy Into Action.* Boston, MA: Harvard Business School Publishing.

_____, 1998. City of Charlotte (A). Harvard Business School Case 199-036. Boston, MA.

_____, and R. Cooper. 1998. *Cost and Effect: Using Integrated Cost Systems to Drive Profitability and Performance.* Boston, MA: Harvard Business School Press.

_____, and J. Elias. 1999. New Profit, Inc.: Governing the nonprofit enterprise. Harvard Business School Case 100-052. Boston, MA.

_____. 2001. Montefiore Medical Center. Harvard Business School Case 101-067. Boston, MA.

_____, and D. P. Norton. 2000. Having trouble with your strategy? Then map it. *Harvard Business Review* (September-October): 167-176.

and . 2001a. *The Strategy-Focused Organization: How Balanced Scorecard companies Thrive in the New Business Environment.* Boston, MA: Harvard Business School Press.

_____, and . 200 lb. Transforming the Balanced Scorecard from performance measurement to strategic management. Part II. *Accounting Horizons.* (forthcoming).

Kiechel, W. 1982. Corporate strategists under fire. *Fortune* (December 27): 38.

Lebas, M. 1994. Managerial accounting in France: Overview of past tradition and current practice. *European Accounting Review* 3 (3): 471-487.

Lipe, M., and S. Salterio. 2000. The Balanced Scorecard: Judgmental effects of common and unique performance measures. *The Accounting Review* (July): 283-298.

Porter, M. E. 1992. Capital disadvantage: America's failing capital investment system. *Harvard Business Review* (September-October).

_____. 1996. What is strategy? *Harvard Business Review* (November-December).

Treacy, F., and M. Wierserma. 1997. *The Wisdom of Market Leaders.* New York, NY: Perseus Books.

Webber, A. M. 2000. New math for a new economy. *Fast Company* (January-February).

Blocher, Stout, Cokins, Chen: *Cost Management, 4e*

17.2: STRATEGY MAPS

by Robert S. Kaplan and David P. Norton

An organization's strategy describes how it intends to create value for its shareholders, customers, and citizens. In working with more than 300 organizations over the past dozen years, we have learned how to use the Balanced Scorecard (BSC) as a powerful management tool for describing and implementing strategy. The key is to design a scorecard to focus on the critical few parameters that represent a strategy for long-term value creation. With its multiple perspectives, the BSC framework allows an integrated view of strategic measurement:

Financial performance, a lag indicator, provides the ultimate definition of an organization's success. Its strategy describes how a company intends to create sustainable growth in shareholder value. (The strategies of public sector and non-profit organizations are designed to create sustainable value for citizens and constituents.)

☐ Success with targeted customers provides a principal component for improved financial performance. In addition to measuring the lagging outcome indicators of customer success, such as satisfaction, retention, and growth, the customer perspective defines the value proposition for targeted customer segments. Choosing the **customer value proposition** is the central element of strategy.

Internal processes create and deliver the value proposition for customers. The performance of internal processes is a leading indicator of subsequent improvements in customer and financial outcomes.

Intangible assets are the ultimate source of sustainable value creation. **Learning and growth** objectives describe how the people, technology, and organization climate combine to support the strategy. Improvements in learning and growth measures are lead indicators for internal process, customer, and financial performance. Enhancing and aligning intangible assets leads to improved process performance, which, in turn, drives success for customers and shareholders.

STRATEGY MAPS AND THE BALANCED SCORECARD

The strategy map provides the specificity needed to translate general statements about high-level direction and strategy into specific objectives that are more meaningful for all employees and that they can act on. We'll start by looking at the financial perspective of the balanced scorecard and work successively through the customer, internal, and learning and growth perspectives. Then we'll show how the strategy map puts all the pieces together.

FINANCIAL PERSPECTIVE: STRATEGY BALANCES LONG-TERM AND SHORT-TERM OBJECTIVES

The balanced scorecard retains the financial perspective as the ultimate objective for profit-maximizing companies. Financial performance measures indicate whether a company's strategy, including its implementation and execution, is contributing to bottom-line improvement. Financial objectives typically relate to profitability—measured, for example, by economic value added, operating income, or return on investment. Basically, financial strategies are simple: Companies increase shareholder value by (1) selling more and (2) spending less. Any program—customer intimacy, six sigma quality, knowledge management, disruptive technology, just-in-time— creates more value for the company only if it leads to selling more or spending less. Thus, a company's financial performance improves through two basic approaches: revenue growth and productivity. Companies can generate profitable revenue growth by deepening relationships with their existing customers. This enables them to sell more of their current product or service or to cross-sell additional products and services. For example, banks can attempt to get their checking account customers to also use a credit card issued by the bank and to borrow from the bank to purchase a home or car. Companies also generate revenue growth by selling entirely new products. For example, Amazon.com now sells CDs and electronic equipment as well as books, and Mobil encourages its customers to buy from its stations' convenience stores in addition to filling their cars with gasoline. And companies can expand revenue by selling to customers in new segments—for example, Staples now sells to small businesses as well as to retail customers—and in new markets, such as by expanding from domestic sales to international sales. Productivity improvements, the second dimension of a financial strategy, can also occur in two ways. First, a company can reduce costs by lowering direct and indirect expenses. Such cost reductions enable it to produce the same quantity of output while spending less on people, materials, energy, and supplies. Second, by using their financial and physical assets more efficiently, companies can reduce the working and fixed capital needed to support a given level of business. For example, through just-in-time approaches, companies can support a given level of sales with less inventory. By reducing unscheduled downtime on equipment, they can produce more without increasing their investments in plant and equipment. The link to strategy in the financial perspective occurs as organizations choose a balance between the often contradictory levers of growth and productivity. Actions to improve revenue growth generally take longer to create value than actions to improve productivity. Under the day-to-day pressure to show financial results to shareholders, the tendency is to favor the short term over the long term. Developing the first layer of a strategy map forces an organization to deal with this tension. The overarching financial objective is—and must be—to *sustain* growth in shareholder value. Thus, the financial component of the strategy must have *both* long-term (growth) and short-term (productivity) dimensions. The simultaneous balancing of these two forces is the organizing framework for the remainder of the strategy map.

CUSTOMER PERSPECTIVE: STRATEGY IS BASED ON A DIFFERENTIATED VALUE PROPOSITION

The revenue growth strategy requires a specific value proposition that describes how the organization will create differentiated, sustainable value to targeted segments. In the customer perspective, managers identify the targeted customer segments in which the business unit competes and the measures of the business unit's performance for customers in these targeted segments. Several common measures are customer satisfaction, retention, acquisition, profitability, market share, and account share. Market share refers to the percentage of a company's sales to total industry sales. Account share measures the company's proportion of a certain customer's or group of customers' purchases in a given category. For example, a retail clothing store can estimate that it supplies, on average, 13% of the clothing purchased by its customers. A fast food outlet might supply 40% of a family's fast food purchases or 2% of its total food consumption. These customer outcome measures can themselves be viewed as cause-and-effect relationships.

For example, customer satisfaction generally leads to customer retention and, through word of mouth, the acquisition of new customers. By retaining customers, a company can increase the share of business—the account share—it does with its loyal customers. Combining customer acquisition and increased business with existing customers, the company should increase its overall market share with targeted customers. Finally, retention of customers should lead to increases in customer profitability since retaining a customer typically costs much less than acquiring new or replacement customers. Virtually all organizations try to improve these measures, but merely satisfying and retaining customers is hardly a strategy. A strategy should identify specific customer *segments* that the company is targeting for growth and profitability. For example, Southwest Airlines offers low prices to satisfy and retain price-sensitive customers. Neiman Marcus, on the other hand, targets customers with high disposable incomes who are willing to pay more for high-end merchandise. Companies should measure satisfaction, retention, and market share with their targeted customers. Price-sensitive customers with low disposable incomes aren't likely to be satisfied with the shopping experience at Neiman Marcus, whereas business travelers with generous expense accounts typically don't seek out a Southwest Airlines flight because of its long lines and lack of reserved seats and first-class cabins.

VALUE PROPOSITIONS

Once a company understands who its targeted customers are, it can identify the objectives and measures for the *value proposition* it intends to offer. The value proposition defines the company's customer strategy by describing the unique mix of product, price, service, relationship, and image that a company offers its targeted group of customers. It should communicate what the company expects to do for its customers *better* or *differently* than its competitors. For example, companies as diverse as Southwest Airlines, Dell, Wal-Mart, McDonald's, and Toyota have been extremely successful by offering customers the *best buy* or *lowest total cost* in their categories. The objectives for a low-total-cost value proposition should emphasize attractive prices, excellent and consistent quality for the product attributes offered, good selection, short lead times, and ease of purchase (see the top row in Figure 1). Another value proposition, followed by companies such as Sony, Mercedes, and Intel, emphasizes *product innovation and leadership*. These companies command high prices, above the average in their category, because they offer products with superior functionality. The objectives for their

Blocher, Stout, Cokins, Chen: *Cost Management, 4e*

©The McGraw-Hill Companies, Inc 2008

value proposition would emphasize the features and functionalities of the products that leading-edge customers value and are willing to pay more to receive. The objectives could be measured by speed, accuracy, size, power consumption, or other performance characteristics that exceed the performance of competing products and that are valued by customers. Being the first to market with new features and functionality is another objective for such product leadership companies (see the second row in Figure 1). A third type of value proposition stresses the provision of *complete customer solutions*. Good examples here are Goldman Sachs and IBM (from 1960 to 1985). For this value proposition, customers should feel that the company understands them and is capable of providing them with customized products and services tailored to their needs. IBM, when it dominated the computer industry, didn't offer the lowest prices and only rarely delivered its new products on time. Nor were IBM's products the most advanced technologically, the most powerful, or the fastest. But IBM offered information technology executives, its targeted customers, complete solutions—hardware, software, installation, field service, training, education, and consulting—that were tailored to each organization's needs. Companies offering such a customer-solutions value proposition stress objectives relating to the completeness of the solution (selling multiple, bundled products and services), exceptional service before and after the sale, and the quality of the relationship (see the third row in Figure 1). A fourth generic strategy, called *lock-in*, arises when companies create high switching costs for their customers. Ideally, a proprietary product, such as a computer operating system or microchip hardware architecture, becomes the standard for an industry. In this case, both buyers and sellers want their products to be consistent with the standard so they can benefit from the large network of users and complementors. Complementors are the people or organizations who add value to the company's basic product. For example, Microsoft's complementors are the more than five million programmers who write application programs that run on Microsoft's operating systems and that make Microsoft's systems more useful for end-use consumers. Becoming a dominant exchange, such as eBay and the Yellow Pages, is another example of a successful lock-in strategy. Buyers will choose an exchange where the largest number of sellers is offering products or services, and sellers will offer their products and services on an exchange that exposes them to the largest number of potential buyers. In this situation, one or two companies will tend to be dominant suppliers of the exchange, and they will create large barriers to entry for other exchange providers and high switching costs to its buyers and sellers (see the bottom row in Figure 1). A company defines its strategy by the objectives and measures it chooses for its value proposition. By developing objectives and measures that are specific to its value proposition, the company translates its strategy into tangible measures that all employees can understand and work toward improving.

INTERNAL PERSPECTIVE: VALUE IS CREATED THROUGH INTERNAL BUSINESS PROCESSES

Objectives in the customer perspective describe the strategy—the targeted customers and value proposition— and the objectives in the financial perspective describe the economic consequences from a successful strategy—revenue and profit growth and productivity. Once an organization has a clear picture of these financial and customer objectives, it can develop objectives in the internal and learning and growth perspectives that describe how the strategy will be accomplished. Excellent performance in these two perspectives drives the strategy. Internal processes accomplish two vital components of strategy: They produce and deliver the value proposition for customers, and they improve processes and reduce costs for the productivity component in the financial perspective. We group organizations' myriad internal processes into four clusters (see Figure 2):
1. Operations management,
2. Customer management,
3. Innovation, and
4. Regulatory and social.

OPERATIONS MANAGEMENT PROCESSES

Operations management processes are the basic, day-today processes by which companies produce their existing products and services and deliver them to customers. Some examples in manufacturing companies are:

- Acquire raw materials from suppliers,
- Convert raw materials to finished goods,
- Distribute finished goods to customers, and
- Manage risk.

Operating processes for service companies produce and deliver the services customers use.

CUSTOMER MANAGEMENT PROCESSES

Customer management processes expand and deepen relationships with targeted customers. We can identify four customer management processes:

- Select targeted customers,
- Acquire the targeted customers,

- Retain customers, and
- Grow business with customers.

Customer *selection* involves identifying the target populations for which the company's value proposition is most desirable.

This process defines a set of customer characteristics that describes an attractive customer segment for the company.

For consumer companies, segments can be defined by income, wealth, age, family size, and lifestyle; typical business customer segments are price-sensitive, early adopting, and technically sophisticated. Customer *acquisition* relates to generating leads, communicating to potential customers, choosing entry-level products, pricing the products, and closing the sale. Customer *retention* is a result of excellent service and responsiveness to customer requests. Timely, knowledgeable service units are critical for maintaining customer loyalty and reducing the likelihood of customer defections. *Growing* a customer's business with the company involves managing the relationship effectively, cross-selling multiple products and services, and becoming known as a trusted adviser and supplier.

INNOVATION PROCESSES

Innovation processes develop new products, processes, and services, often enabling the company to penetrate new markets and customer segments. Managing innovation includes the following processes:

- Identify opportunities for new products and services,
- Manage the research and development portfolio,
- Design and develop the new products and services, and
- Bring the new products and services to market.

Product designers and managers generate new ideas by extending the capabilities of existing products and services, applying new discoveries and technologies, and learning from customers' suggestions. Once ideas for new products and services have been generated, managers must decide which projects to fund and whether they will be developed entirely with internal resources, collaboratively in a joint venture, licensed from another organization, and/or outsourced. The design and development process—the core of product development—brings new concepts to market. A successful design and development process culminates in a product that has the desired functionality, is attractive to the targeted market, and can be produced with consistent quality and at a satisfactory profit margin. At the conclusion of the product development cycle, the project team brings the new product to market. The innovation process for a particular project concludes when the company achieves targeted levels of sales and production at specified levels of product functionality, quality, and cost.

Blocher, Stout, Cokins, Chen: *Cost Management, 4e*

Figure 1: CUSTOMER OBJECTIVES FOR DIFFERENT VALUE PROPOSITIONS

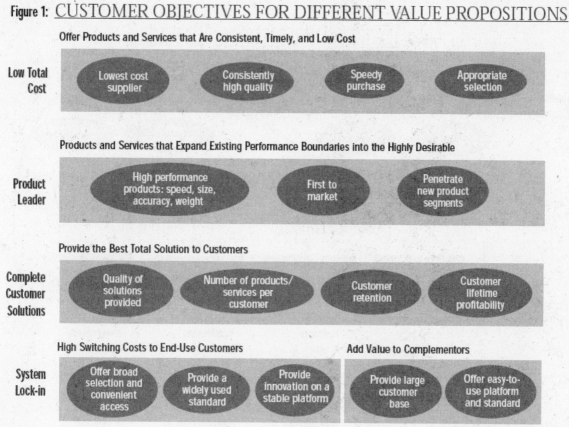

©2004 HBS Press, Boston, Mass.

Figure 2: INTERNAL PROCESS OBJECTIVES

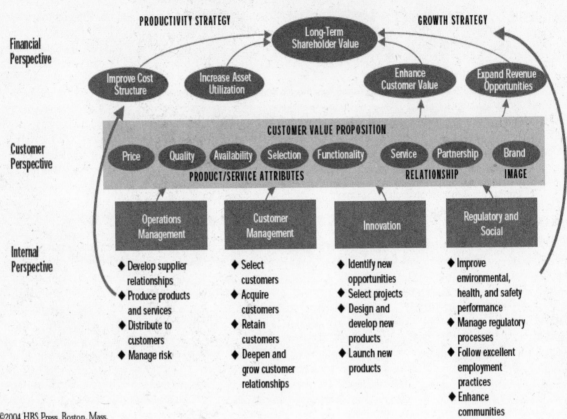

©2004 HBS Press, Boston, Mass.

Blocher, Stout, Cokins, Chen: *Cost Management, 4e*

THE DATEX-OHMEDA STRATEGY MAP

Datex-Ohmeda, the largest division of Instrumentarium Corporation (now owned by GE Medical Systems), is based in Helsinki, Finland, with manufacturing operations in Finland, Sweden, and the U.S. Datex-Ohmeda's product line includes patient monitors and networked systems for anesthesia, intensive-care units, and subacute care, as well as anesthesia machines, ventil tors, drug delivery systems, pulse oximeters, and supplies and accessories. Datex-Ohmeda had been a product leader since its founding in the early 1900s, but it faced tough competition from companies such as Philips, Siemens, and Drager. Organizational alignment was another growing challenge since most of the company's factories and business units had been acquired through mergers and continued to operate as mostly independent business units and sales channels with goals that would occasionally conflict or diverge. The executive team worked on developing a new, integrated strategy in the summer of 2001 and used the strategy map to crystallize its thinking. Planning sessions led to the company deciding to change from its historic value proposition based on product innovation to one that leveraged long-term customer relationships. This meant providing the right solution for customers based on thoroughly understanding their needs and operating customer-focused processes for ongoing support and ease of doing business. Datex-Ohmeda used its strategy map to describe these new directions. The financial perspective shows the goal of obtaining revenue growth from new customers (F2) and expanding relations with existing customers (F3). The key to achieving the F3 objective is delivering "team-designed solutions" (C1) based on product-line breadth. Objectives for two internal processes describe how this value proposition will be created and delivered: A customer management objective (P9) defines the process of teamwork across Datex-Ohmeda, as well as with its channel partners, and objective P4 defines the innovation required to "develop and manage platform-based solutions throughout their life cycle." These two internal process objectives, in turn, create the demand for organizational capabilities and culture that would promote the development of new human and informational capital, strong networking, and teamwork across lines of business and national boundaries. The learning and growth objectives, organized under the heading "Continuous Learning and Improvement," align the intangible assets with the strategic priorities. Objectives L1, L2, and L3 create organization readiness for implementing the new strategy. Objective L1 identifies the need for consistency in decision-making processes required for a platform-based product strategy. Objective L2 defines the need for teamwork required by the team-solutions strategy. Objective L3 focuses on the process of alignment with the strategy at the individual level. The strategy map addresses the human capital needs ("right skills, right place, right time") of the new strategy in objective L4. The details of these requirements will be described in lower-level human resources plans. Objectives L5 and L6 focus on the information capital requirements, with particular emphasis on knowledge sharing across the organization. The strategy map provided Datex-Ohmeda with a framework to align its human capital, information capital, and organization readiness to the strategy with sufficient specific detail to be meaningful, measurable, and actionable.

The Datex-Ohmeda Strategy Map is shown on the following page.

The Datex-Ohmeda Strategy Map

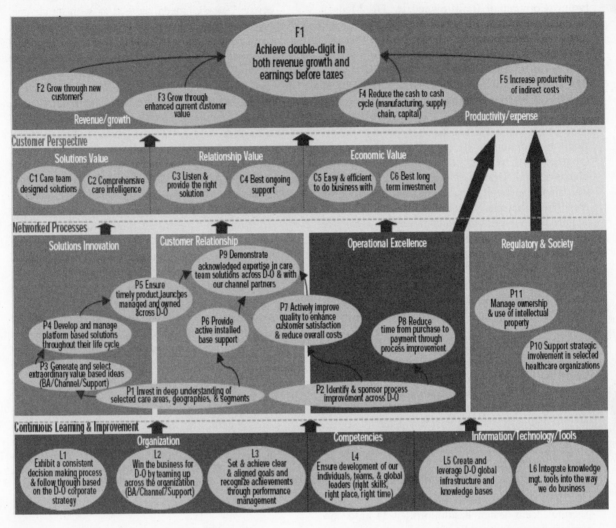

REGULATORY AND SOCIAL PROCESSES

Regulatory and social processes help organizations continually earn the right to operate in the communities and countries in which they produce and sell. National and local regulations—on the environment, on employee health and safety, and on hiring and employment practices—impose standards on companies' operations. But many companies seek to go beyond complying with these minimal standards. They want to perform better than the regulatory constraints so that they develop a reputation as an employer of choice in every community in which they operate. Companies manage and report their regulatory and social performance along a number of critical dimensions:

- Environment,
- Health and safety,
- Employment practices, and
- Community investment.

Investing in these needn't be for altruistic reasons alone. An excellent reputation for performance along regulatory and social dimensions assists companies in attracting and retaining high-quality employees, thereby making human resource processes more effective and efficient. Also, reducing environmental incidents and improving employee safety and health improves productivity and lowers operating costs. And companies with outstanding reputations generally enhance their images with customers and with socially conscious investors. All these linkages—to enhanced human resource, operations, customer, and financial processes—illustrate how effective management of regulatory and community performance can drive long-term shareholder value creation. There are literally hundreds of processes taking place simultaneously in an organization, each creating value in some way. The art of strategy is to identify and excel at the

Blocher, Stout, Cokins, Chen: *Cost Management, 4e*

critical few processes that are the most important to the customer value proposition. All processes should be managed well, but the few strategic processes must receive special attention and focus since they create the differentiation of the strategy. They should also be drawn from all four clusters: Every strategy should identify one or more processes within operations management, customer management, innovation, and regulatory and social. In this way, the value creation process is balanced between the short and long term. This ensures that the growth in shareholder value will be sustained over time.

Learning and Growth: Strategic Alignment of Intangible Assets

The fourth perspective, learning and growth, describes the organization's intangible assets and their role in strategy. We organize intangible assets into three categories (see bottom section of Figure 3):

Human capital: The availability of skills, talent, and know-how required to support the strategy.

Information capital: The availability of information systems, networks, and infrastructure required to support the strategy.

Organization capital: The ability of the organization to mobilize and sustain the process of change required to execute the strategy.

Whereas all organizations attempt to develop their people, technology, and culture, most do *not* align these intangible assets with their strategies. The key to creating this alignment is *granularity*— that is, to move beyond generalities such as "develop our people" or "live our core values" and focus on specific capabilities and attributes required by the critical internal processes of the strategy. The balanced scorecard strategy map enables executives to pinpoint the specific human, information, and organization capital required by the strategy (we wrote about this in "Measuring the Strategic Readiness of Intangible Assets," *Harvard Business Review*, February 2004).

TRANSLATING STRATEGY INTO ACTION

The strategy map describes the logic of the strategy, clearly showing the objectives for the critical internal processes that create value and the intangible assets required to support them. The balanced scorecard translates the strategy map objectives into measures and targets. But objectives and targets won't be achieved simply because they have been identified. The organization must launch a set of action programs (*strategic initiatives*) that will enable the targets for all the measures to be achieved, and it must supply scarce resources— people, funding, and capacity—for every program. For each measure on the balanced scorecard, man-

agers must identify the strategic initiatives needed to achieve the target because the initiatives create results. Hence, the execution of strategy is managed through the execution of initiatives. The action plans that define and provide resources for the strategic initiatives can be *aligned* around strategic themes that enable the initiatives to be viewed as an *integrated* bundle of investments instead of as a group of stand-alone projects. Each strategic theme represents a self-contained business case. Figure 4 illustrates an action plan and business case for the *fast ground turnaround* theme of a low-cost airline. This theme was core to the low-total-cost customer value proposition. It would contribute to on-time departures and arrivals that would increase satisfaction among customers, leading to future revenue increases. It also would enable the company to reduce costs by operating with fewer planes and flight crews than competitive airlines so that it could offer lower fares to attract price-sensitive customers while still earning profits and a return on investment above its cost of capital. The figure shows the intangible assets required to enable the strategy: new skills for the ramp agent, an improved information system, and the alignment of the ground crew to the strategy. The middle columns of the figure show the balanced scorecard of measures and targets for the strategic objectives in the strategy map. The right side of the figure identifies the strategic initiatives and the costs required to achieve the targets established in the scorecard. Eight initiatives have been identified—each affects one or two objectives—and all eight are necessary for the strategy to succeed. If one is deleted, a critical objective will be missed, and the chain of cause-andeffect relationships will be broken. For example, ground crew training and a new crew scheduling system might be introduced, but if the ground crew doesn't understand how it fits in (communications program) or doesn't have incentives to improve organizational performance (ESOP, an employee stock ownership plan), then the strategy will fail. Thus, the strategic theme for fast ground turnaround requires aligned capabilities for intangible assets and a complete set of strategic initiatives.

BRINGING IT TOGETHER: THE STRATEGY MAP

We have now worked systematically through the four balanced scorecard perspectives to determine the objectives and measures that describe the strategy. A strategy map (go back to Figure 3) is a visual representation of the strategy. It provides a single-page view of how objectives in the four BSC perspectives integrate and combine to describe the strategy. Each company must customize the strategy map to its particular set of strategic objectives. Typically, the objectives in the four perspectives of a strategy map lead to 20-30 measures being required in the associated balanced scorecard. Some people have criticized the balanced scorecard, believing that people can't focus on 25 different measures. If a scorecard is viewed as 25 independent measures, it *will* be too complicated for an organization and its employees to absorb. But this is the wrong way to think about it. The strategy map shows how the multiple measures on a properly constructed balanced scorecard provide the instrumentation for a *single* strategy. Companies can formulate and communicate their strategies with an integrated system of approximately two to three dozen measurements that identify the cause-and-effect relationships among the critical variables—including leads, lags, and feedback loops—that describe the trajectory, or the flight plan, of the strategy. Employees— in their day-to-day actions, decisions, and initiatives— should focus on the objectives and measures in the internal and learning and growth perspectives since these are where the strategy gets implemented and improved. If the theory of the strategy is valid, improvements in internal and learning and growth measures should soon translate into enhanced performance in the customer and financial outcome measures.

Figure 3: <u>THE STRATEGY MAP ALIGNS INTANGIBLE ASSETS WITH THE STRATEGY FOR VALUE CREATION</u>

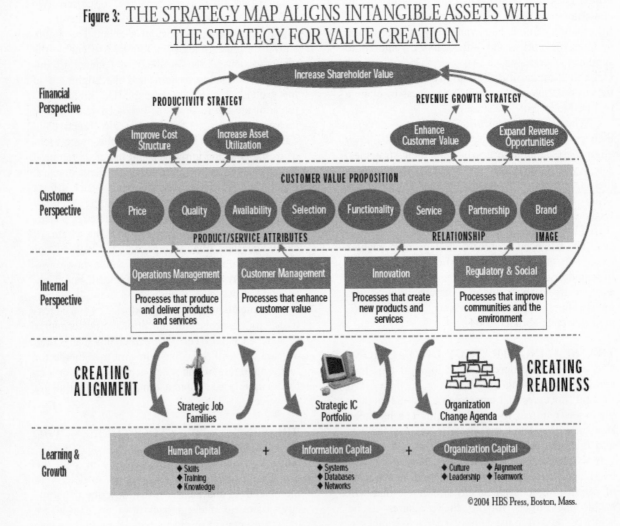

©2004 HBS Press, Boston, Mass.

Figure 4: THE STRATEGIC THEME DEFINES THE PROCESS, INTANGIBLE ASSETS, TARGETS, AND INITIATIVES REQUIRED TO EXECUTE PIECE OF STRATEGY

STRATEGY MAP		BALANCED SCORECARD		ACTION PLAN	
Process: Operations Management Theme: Fast Ground Turnaround	Objectives	Measurement	Target	Initiative	Budget
FINANCIAL Profits & RONA Grow Revenues — Fewer Planes	❑ Profitability ❑ Grow revenues ❑ Fewer planes	❑ Market Value ❑ Seat Revenue ❑ Plane Lease Cost	❑ 30% CAGR ❑ 20% CAGR ❑ 5% CAGR		
CUSTOMER Attract & Retain More Customers On-time Service — Lowest Prices	❑ Flight is on-time ❑ Lowest prices ❑ Attract and retain more customers	❑ FAA On-Time Arrival Rating ❑ Customer Ranking ❑ # Repeat Customers ❑ # Customers	❑ #1 ❑ #1 ❑ 70% ❑ Increase 12% annual	❑ Quality Management ❑ Customer Loyalty Program ❑ Implement CRM System	◆ $XXX ◆ $XXX ◆ $XXX
INTERNAL Fast Ground Turnaround	❑ Fast ground turnaround	❑ Time On Ground ❑ On-Time Departure	❑ 30 Minutes ❑ 90%	❑ Cycle Time Optimization	◆ $XXX
LEARNING Strategic Job Ramp Agent Strategic Systems Crew Scheduling Ground Crew Alignment	❑ Develop the necessary skills ❑ Develop the support system ❑ Ground crew aligned with strategy	❑ Strategic Job Readiness ❑ Info System Availability ❑ Strategic Awareness ❑ % Ground Crew Stockholders	❑ Yr 1 - 0% Yr 3 - 90% Yr 5 - 100% ❑ 100% ❑ 100% ❑ 100%	❑ Ground Crew Training ❑ Crew Scheduling System Rollout ❑ Communications Program ❑ ESOP	◆ $XXX ◆ $XXX ◆ $XXX ◆ $XXX
				Total Budget	$XXXX

©2004 HBS Press, Boston, Mass.

Chapter 18
Strategic Investment Units and Transfer Pricing

Cases

Readings

18-1: "Does ROI Apply to Robotic Factories?" by Gerald H. Lander, Mohamed E. Bayou, *Management Accounting*.

This article provides a useful summary of the limitations of ROI performance evaluation of investment SBUs. Three criteria for appropriate ROI measures are proposed: (1) the ROI measure must include long-term performance, (2) the ROI measure must consider cash flows, and (3) the ROI measure must consider the time value of money. Also, the authors argue that the ROI measure should be consistent with the phases of the project life:
• First: acquisition of the new investment
• Second: use of the new investment
• Third: disposition of the investment
Four methods are developed and illustrated for a hypothetical investment in robotics. The four methods are: (1) annual book ROI, (2) average ROI (over the project's life), (3) discounted book ROI, and (4) discounted cash flow ROI. The authors explain how the different methods are to be used at the different phases of the project's life.

Discussion Questions:
1. Which ROI method(s) should be used at each of the phases of the project's life?
2. What is the profitability index and how is it used?
3. What are the limitations of ROI, and how does the authors' proposed approach deal with these limitations?

Note: This article makes extensive use of the concept of the time value of money, and thus can also be used in Chapter 20: Capital Budgeting.

18-2: "Transfer Pricing with ABC" by Robert S. Kaplan, Dan Weiss, Eyal Desheh, *Management Accounting* (May 1997).

This article explains how Teva Pharmaceutical Industries Ltd adopted transfer pricing and ABC to enhance profits, to improve coordination between operations and marketing, and to reduce the proliferation of new product lines and small volume orders. The article explains why a marginal cost (based on materials cost only) approach and other traditional approaches to transfer pricing did not work for Teva. Teva introduced ABC costing in its plants, and used this cost information for transfer pricing. The article explains how the ABC based transfer pricing system incorporated batch level costs, product based costs, and plant based costs.

Discussion Questions:
1. Why did Teva introduce transfer pricing?
2. What were the goals of the transfer pricing system? How did top management, division managers, and financial staff differ about these goals?
3. Why did traditional approaches for transfer pricing not work at Teva, and why did the ABC approach work instead?
4. How did the ABC transfer pricing system incorporate batch level costs? Product level costs? Plant level costs?
5. What are some of the benefits of the ABC transfer pricing system at Teva?

Blocher, Stout, Cokins, Chen: *Cost Management, 4e*

©The McGraw-Hill Companies, Inc 2008

Cases

18-1 Investment SBUs; Strategy; International Issues

In 2000, the Polymer Products Company was a multinational company engaged in the manufacture of a widely diverse line of products including chemical and agricultural products, man-made fibers, electronic materials, health care, process controls, fabricated products, and oil and gas. Sales in 2000 were $6.7 billion with the following breakdown as to operating units and major markets:

Operating Unit	Percent	Major Markets	Percent
Agricultural products	18	Agriculture	20
		Construction and home	
Biological sciences	3	furnishings	19
Fibers & intermediates	18		
Industrial chemicals	14	Capital equipment	13
		Pharmaceuticals &	
Polymer products	28	personal products	13
Electronic materials &			
fabricated products	8	Motor vehicles	9
Baker controls	8	Apparel	7
		Chemicals and	
Oil & gas	3	hydrocarbons	7
		Other markets	12

For the past five years the firm has been restructuring its core businesses (industrial chemicals, fibers and intermediates, and polymer products) by withdrawing from those product lines that do not fit with the firm's long-term strategy or which are not expected to produce adequate long-term results.

Polymer's management has carefully examined each of the various business units and is prepared to fully support those that have the potential to compete successfully in selected markets. Businesses which cannot produce returns that exceed the company's cost of capital have been, or will be, disposed of or shut down.

As 2001 ended, the company realigned its financial reporting of operating unit segments to more closely align it with the restructuring and to better reflect the company's operations. These new operating unit segments are:

- Agricultural products
- Crop chemicals
- Animal sciences
- Chemicals
- Electronic materials
- Baker controls
- Pharmaceuticals
- Sweeteners
- Oil and gas (this business was sold during the 4th Quarter of 19X5.)

Fibers and intermediates, industrial chemicals, polymer products, and a portion of fabricated products have been combined to form a new segment—chemicals. Two new segments, pharmaceuticals and sweeteners, include the acquired operations of a pharmaceutical company. The electronics business, previously part of fabricated products, has been transferred to and combined with Baker controls, serving similar process control equipment markets. The former biological sciences segment has been eliminated and their animal nutrition products are now part of animal sciences. The health care division was merged with the acquired company and is included in the pharmaceuticals segment.

COMPANY PERFORMANCE MEASUREMENT PHILOSOPHY

Up until the start of the decade, Polymer focused on a performance income measure of an operating unit's performance; assigning only the directly controllable elements of sales, cost of goods sold, marketing, administrative, technical expenses, inventory, and receivables to the operating units for internal reporting purposes. Non-directly controllable elements, such as corporate staff support groups, interest expense/interest income and foreign currency gains and losses were pooled corporately and various formulae were used to assign these corporate charges to operating units for determining a pro-forma net income, return on investment, and cash flow. Such overall indicators of performance were thus only directionally representative at the operating unit level.

As some of the company's core businesses matured and declined, an awareness began to emerge of the need to shift business strategies thus requiring tougher decisions as to divestment/investment/acquisition activities. Top management recognized the need for more accurate measurement and understanding of worldwide operating unit results.

For example, currency gains and losses were treated as a component of corporate charges. Thus, if a U.S. produced product were sold to a French customer on 180-day terms, the selling business unit reflected the full sales value at the then current exchange rate; leaving the company exposed to devaluation of the French franc. If devaluation occurred, performance of the operating unit was not affected but the company results were.

As another example, all operating units applied an average worldwide tax rate to compute a pro-forma net income, return on capital, and cash flow. When an operating unit had a choice to source the same product from Belgium or the U.K., a dilemma was created. Although costs were nominally higher in the U.K., lowering a unit's performance income, the company was in a non-tax position there which drastically improved real net income. However, by reporting results using an average worldwide tax rate, all product sourcing from the U.K. appeared disadvantageous. Also, the company was not taking advantage of an entity's tax loss carry-forward situation in various pricing and sourcing decisions.

Top management wanted a reporting and performance measurement system which brought operating unit managements' attention to *all* the financial impacts of a business decision. To accomplish this, it was decided that as many of the income statement and balance sheet items as was practicable would be identified with each operating unit and charged out accordingly. Each operating unit would then be measured by the achievement against goals established for return on investment and cash flow as defined below.

cash flow = net income + depreciation and obsolescence – capital expenditures +/- (change in receivables, inventories, payables, net capitalized interest, deferred taxes, other assets, and other liabilities)

$$\text{return on investment} = \frac{\text{net income} + \text{after tax interest expense}}{\text{investment}}$$

(Where investment is defined as net long-lived investment, working capital, and deferred taxes)

The incentive compensation system employed for upper management positions is essentially based upon the relative success in achieving annual budgets established for the above measures. The total corporate annual incentive award is determined somewhat rigidly, based upon where earnings fall within a budget range determined at the beginning of each year. The award is apportioned to cascade down the organization. Thus a similar quantitative assessment of results is made to reward or penalize managers for their ultimate contribution to results. The incentive awards are then presented 2/3 in cash and 1/3 in restricted stock which is accessible only after 3 years and only if stock prices meet certain appreciation tests. This latter feature was recently employed to add a long-term dimension to the program in addition to near-term annual income/cash flow results.

Prior to the new reporting and measurement scheme (called asset management) the amount of corporately pooled costs allocated as a corporate charge was over 3 percent of worldwide sales. After the asset management program was instituted, along with selected decentralization of certain corporate staff groups, these corporately pooled costs were less than 2 percent of worldwide sales.

REQUIRED:
1. What type of performance measurement system did Polymer Products use prior to the recent change?
2. What type of performance measurement system is Polymer Products using now? Why did Polymer Products move to this new system? How does the change affect the firm's global competitiveness?
3. In the new performance measurement system, should managers be held responsible for foreign currency exchange gains and losses and income taxes.

(IMA adapted)

Blocher, Stout, Cokins, Chen: *Cost Management, 4e*

18-2 Transfer Pricing; Strategy

Robert Products Inc. consists of three decentralized divisions: Bayside Division, Cole Division, and Diamond Division. The president of Robert Products has given the managers of the three divisions authority to decide whether to sell outside the company or among themselves at an internal price determined by the division managers. Market conditions are such that sales made internally or externally will not affect market or transfer prices. Intermediate markets will always be available for Bayside, Cole, and Diamond to purchase their manufacturing needs or sell their product.

The manager of the Cole Division is currently considering the two alternative orders presented below.

- The Diamond Division is in need of 3,000 units of a motor that can be supplied by the Cole Division. To manufacture these motors, Cole would purchase components from the Bayside Division at a price of $600 per unit; Bayside's variable cost for these components is $300 per unit. Cole Division will further process these components at a variable cost of $500 per unit.

- If the Diamond Division cannot obtain the motors from Cole Division, it will purchase the motors from London Company which has offered to supply them to Diamond at a price of $1,500 per unit. London Company would also purchase 3,000 components from Bayside Division at a price of $400 for each of these motors; Bayside's variable cost for these components is $200 per unit.

- The Wales Company wants to place an order with the Cole Division for 3,500 similar motors at a price of $1,250 per unit. Cole would again purchase components from the Bayside Division at a price of $500 per unit; Bayside's variable cost for these components is $250 per unit. Cole Division will further process these components at a variable cost of $400 per unit.

The Cole Division's plant capacity is limited, and the division can accept either the Wales contract or the Diamond order, but not both. The president of Robert Products and the manager of the Cole Division agree that it would not be beneficial in the short or long run to increase capacity.

REQUIRED:

1. Determine whether the Cole Division should sell motors to the Diamond Division at the prevailing market price, or accept the Wales Company contract. Support your answer with appropriate calculations.
2. What strategic factors should Robert Products consider as the Cole and Diamond divisions make their respective decision?

(CMA adapted)

18-3 Transfer Pricing (Foreign Sales Corporations); Use of the Web

The Foreign Sales Corporation Act, enacted by the U.S. Congress in 1971 provides special tax advantages for U.S. based exporters. The foreign subsidiaries of U.S. corporations are allowed to act as agents for the company, so that the parent firm can exempt up to 15% of the export earnings from federal tax. This apparent subsidy has angered some countries in the European Union. To learn more about Foreign Sales Corporations, search the Web and use whatever other research resources available to you. As a start, you might want to look at web site of the United States Mission to the European Union: http://www.useu.be/ISSUES/FSCdossier.html.

REQUIRED:
1. Explain foreign sales corporations and the nature of the benefits to U.S. exporters. Why have countries in the European Union disputed the existence of these corporations.
2. What role do foreign sales corporations play in transfer pricing, and what is the management accountant's responsibility regarding these types of corporations?

18-4 Interior Systems, Inc.: The Decision To Adopt EVA®

by Robert M. Bowen and James S. Wallace

Our sales and profits are growing again but our investment bankers tell us we have to do even better to have a successful public offering. Despite dissatisfaction with our profitability, everyone received a bonus last year. Should we dump our current incentive compensation scheme in favor of one that provides better motivation? Now we're bickering about whether to add new products that everyone expects will be clearly profitable. Is it possible that profits are not the "bottom line" when it comes to making decisions and evaluating corporate performance?

> Bill Alberts
> President and CEO
> At lunch with the CFO
> Early 1996

BACKGROUND

Interior Systems, Inc. (ISI)[1] designs, manufactures and markets high- technology interior "furniture" for the passenger airline and corporate office markets. The Company's business strategy is to develop products that "help our customers become more productive and profitable." Founder and CEO Bill Alberts believes that the Company should stay close to its entrepreneurial roots by focusing its employees on the needs of customers. Excerpts of Mr. Alberts' remarks from a recent business luncheon include:

• "Mission and goal statements are just so much talk until you provide powerful incentives to guide management action."

• "Our ultimate goal is value creation. By delivering what our customers want before they ask for it, we will achieve superior value for ISI stockholders."

• "Hire talented people, give them incentives to act like owners, and get out of their way."

Mr. Alberts has long used incentive compensation to motivate his managers and employees. In order to empower his managers "to run the business as if it were their own," the Company is organized into two semiautonomous divisions. "Airline Interiors" serves the commercial airline business, and "Office Solutions" serves the corporate office furniture market. Given its decentralized, profit-center structure, the Company maintains only a small staff at ISI headquarters. An abbreviated organization chart for senior management is provided in figure 1. Selected consolidated financial data for ISI for 1991–1995 are presented in exhibit 1.

---

[1] Interior Systems, Inc. is a fictitious company used solely for illustrative purposes.

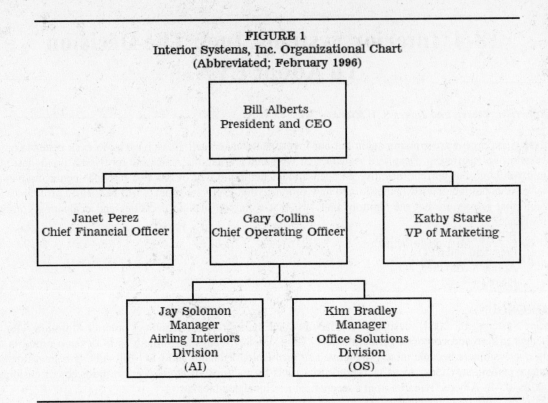

FIGURE 1
Interior Systems, Inc. Organizational Chart
(Abbreviated; February 1996)

Blocher, Stout, Cokins, Chen: *Cost Management, 4e*

©The McGraw-Hill Companies, Inc 2008

EXHIBIT 1
Interior Systems, Inc.
Consolidated Financial Data
(all financial amounts in thousands of dollars)

	Notes	1991	1992	1993	1994	1995
Sales revenue		$155,083	$164,423	$148,311	$141,114	$156,142
Variable operating expenses	1	42,216	46,370	37,660	38,101	42,663
Variable selling expenses	2	4,711	4,961	4,884	5,090	5,721
Contribution margin		$108,156	$113,092	$105,767	$ 97,923	$107,758
Fixed expenses:						
Production costs	3	51,107	51,129	48,580	46,659	50,606
Research and development	4	7,141	7,647	6,869	6,461	8,193
Fixed selling & admin	5	33,316	36,255	35,138	29,484	29,870
Common (corporate) expenses	6	1,432	1,503	1,348	1,372	1,464
Interest expense	7	3,215	3,311	3,388	3,407	3,541
Net income before tax		$ 11,945	$ 13,247	$ 10,444	$ 10,540	$ 14,084
Income taxes		3,584	3,974	3,133	3,162	4,225
Net income		$ 8,361	$ 9,273	$ 7,311	$ 7,378	$ 9,859
Assets traceable to the divisions		$ 95,712	$102,412	$110,297	$118,239	$127,816
Common assets		$ 1,875	$ 2,012	$ 2,044	$ 2,368	$ 2,467
Corporate cost of capital	8	9.0%	9.0%	9.0%	9.0%	9.0%

Notes:
1 Includes direct material, direct labor and variable overhead.
2 Includes primarily sales commissions.
3 Includes rent, salaries, depreciation, property taxes and other fixed overhead.
4 A period expense.
5 Includes advertising, salaries, rent and other costs.
6 Includes interest, salaries and rent of corporate headquarters.
7 Interest expense is not traced to divisions.
8 The corporate cost of capital is the overall weighted opportunity cost of debt and equity capital.

AIRLINE INTERIORS DIVISION
Airline Interiors (AI) designs and builds interior components (e.g., seats, partitions and overhead bins) that allow an aircraft manufacturer to outfit a plane with additional capacity while maintaining or even improving the comfort of airline passengers. AI uses a patented algorithm for seat spacing along with sophisticated market research (including direct observation of passengers' reactions) to allow airlines to configure their planes to trade off seating capacity and passenger comfort. For example, by using AI's interior design and products, United Airlines can order a new plane with a range of seating configurations that, at one extreme, has more seats but retains a similar level of passenger comfort or, at the other extreme, has the same number of seats and a noticeably higher level of comfort. Fierce price competition following deregulation of the airline industry in the late 1970s stimulated a trend toward denser seat configurations. Since the incremental cost of carrying an additional passenger on a flight is very low (e.g., food and beverage cost), extra seats are very profitable when the plane flies at full capacity—a common situation during peak times. Much of AI's success is due to innovative seating configurations that provide greater comfort during flights with smaller nonpeak loads, yet have extra seats that pay off during peak loads. To do this, they "steal" a few centimeters from each row, which,

over the entire length of most planes, can mean adding an extra row of seats. To offset the effects of tightening the spacing between rows, AI has designed a comfortable custom seat with adjustable lumbar support and assorted options. The seat design gives passengers in adjacent rows more freedom of movement, and thus more comfort, even though the rows are slightly closer together. The seat design has special support struts that reduce the depth of the seat bottom and back cushion. Changes to the seat bottom allow an optional shelf to be installed under each seat so that passengers can conveniently store items such as reading materials or a notebook computer.

Added storage is especially convenient during meal service. The AI seat also allows space for an optional adjustable footrest. AI expects that airlines will use these optional modules as another way to differentiate among classes of travel, e.g., first class would have more optional modules installed and economy would typically have none. AI engages in extensive R&D and market research in a continuous effort to stay ahead of the competition and maintain the loyalty of both airlines and aircraft manufacturers. Because of the partnership formed at the design stage between the airline (e.g., United), the manufacturer (e.g., Boeing) and its suppliers (e.g., AI), AI knows what its share will be of each consummated deal for new or retrofitted planes. To illustrate, when one of its aircraft manufacturing customers lands a new order for a passenger airline, AI management can predict with some confidence when and what they will be producing related to that order. This prediction is quantified in AI's "order backlog," which is expressed in dollars. While current period orders are the key driver of future success, the division's financial accounting system focuses on reporting current period sales and costs generated by the completion and delivery of past orders. Since sales lag orders potentially by years, traditional accounting measures may provide a distorted measure of AI's current performance. Exhibit 2 provides selected financial data for AI from 1991 through 1995.

OFFICE SOLUTIONS DIVISION

In late 1990, ISI acquired "Office Solutions" (OS), a company that manufactures and sells a line of high quality office furniture. It was hoped that the acquisition of OS would dampen the effects of normal, but sometimes large, swings in the demand for airline interiors. Exhibit 3 provides financial data for OS from 1991 through 1995. At the time of the acquisition, it was felt that some of the new seating ideas being developed at AI could be transferred to the high-end office furniture market.

Blocher, Stout, Cokins, Chen: *Cost Management, 4e*

©The McGraw-Hill Companies, Inc 2008

EXHIBIT 2
Interior Systems, Inc.
Airline Interiors Division—Selected Financial Data
(all financial amounts in thousands of dollars)

	Notes	1991	1992	1993	1994	1995
Sales revenue		$114,850	$120,665	$103,290	$92,459	$105,665
Variable operating expenses	1	32,158	34,993	26,855	24,964	28,529
Variable selling expenses	2	2,297	2,292	2,273	2,219	2,642
Division contribution margin		$ 80,395	$ 83,380	$ 74,162	$ 65,276	$ 74,494
Controllable fixed expenses						
Production costs	3	36,752	36,200	33,053	30,511	33,813
Research and development	4	6,940	7,384	6,644	6,218	7,688
Fixed selling & admin	5	24,889	26,609	24,461	18,698	19,477
Division fixed expenses		$ 68,581	$ 70,193	$ 64,158	$ 55,427	$ 60,978
Controllable profits		$ 11,814	$ 13,187	$ 10,004	$ 9,849	$ 13,516
Income taxes @ 30%		3,545	3,956	3,001	2,955	4,055
Division profit after taxes		$ 8,269	$ 9,231	$ 7,003	$ 6,894	$ 9,461
Net division assets, beginning of year	6	$ 63,857	$ 68,327	$ 73,588	$ 78,887	$ 85,276
Order backlog		$196,000	$171,000	$198,000	$202,000	$205,000
Division cost of capital	7	9.80%	9.80%	9.80%	9.80%	9.80%

Notes:
1 Includes direct material, direct labor and variable overhead.
2 Includes primarily sales commissions.
3 Includes rent, salaries, depreciation, property taxes and other fixed overhead.
4 A period expense.
5 Includes advertising, salaries, rent and other costs.
6 Assets traceable to the Division, net of depreciation and amortization, as of the beginning of the year.
7 Division cost of capital rates are set higher than the overall corporate cost of capital to cover costs not allocated to divisions.

While these technology transfers have been slow to reach fruition, OS's new "E-chair" proposal has generated excitement inside the Company.

THE PROPOSED "E-CHAIR"

OS management proposes to build an office version of AI's spacesaving "ergonomic chair" for the corporate workplace—the "E-chair." Marketing feels that the two lines of seating would eventually cross-sell themselves, i.e., that business travelers would ask to be booked on planes that have seating they were accustomed to in their offices and vice versa. A forecast of incremental revenues, expenses and investment related to the E-chair proposal is provided in exhibit 4. To keep the cost of the E-chair competitive, OS proposes to manufacture several variations of a base-model chair. Every chair comes standard with adjustable lumbar support and optional plug-in modules, including various swivel and stationary pedestals and different arm configurations.

EXHIBIT 3
Interior Systems, Inc.
Office Solutions Division—Selected Financial Data
(all financial amounts in thousands of dollars)

	Notes	1991	1992	1993	1994	1995
Sales revenue		$40,233	$43,758	$45,021	$48,655	$50,477
Variable operating expenses	1	10,058	11,377	10,805	13,137	14,134
Variable selling expenses	2	2,414	2,669	2,611	2,871	3,079
Division contribution margin		$27,761	$29,712	$31,605	$32,647	$33,264
Controllable fixed expenses						
Production costs	3	14,355	14,929	15,527	16,148	16,793
Research and development	4	201	263	225	243	505
Fixed selling & admin	5	8,427	9,646	10,677	10,786	10,393
Division fixed expenses		$22,983	$24,838	$26,429	$27,177	$27,691
Controllable profits		$ 4,778	$ 4,874	$ 5,176	$ 5,470	$ 5,573
Income taxes @ 30%		1,433	1,462	1,553	1,641	1,672
Division profit after taxes		$ 3,345	$ 3,412	$ 3,623	$ 3,829	$ 3,901
Net division assets, beginning of year	6	$31,855	$34,085	$36,709	$39,352	$42,540
Division cost of capital	7	9.30%	9.30%	9.30%	9.30%	9.30%

Notes:
1 Includes direct material, direct labor and variable overhead.
2 Includes primarily sales commissions.
3 Includes rent, salaries, depreciation, property taxes and other fixed overhead.
4 A period expense.
5 Includes advertising, salaries, rent and other costs.
6 Assets traceable to the Division, net of depreciation and amortization, as of the beginning of the year.
7 Division cost of capital rates are set higher than the overall corporate cost of capital to cover costs not allocated to divisions.

Each module is adjustable so that users can tailor the seating for their preferences. Perhaps more important, OS plans to market the ergonomics and comfort of these chairs as productivity enhancements in the workplace. Based on market research, the chairs will be advertised "to pay for themselves by adding (on average) the equivalent of three extra weeks of productive work each year." This estimate was determined by grossing up an estimated additional four minutes of productive time per hour (= 30 minutes per day, 2.5 hours per week and over 120 hours per year). These estimates were based on studies of the effects of introducing prototype chairs into the workplace at ISI headquarters as well as headquarters at both AI and OS.

EXHIBIT 4
Interior Systems, Inc.
Office Solutions Division—Pro Forma Data for "E-Chair" Proposal
(all financial amounts in thousands of dollars)

	Notes	Estimated Annual Amount
Incremental sales revenue		$8,000
Variable operating expenses	1	2,240
Variable selling expenses	2	800
Incremental contribution margin		$4,960
Incremental fixed expenses		
Production costs	3	3,450
Depreciation	4	400
Research and development	5	100
Selling & administrative	6	500
Incremental pretax profits		$ 510
Incremental income taxes at 30%		153
Incremental after-tax profits		$ 357
Incremental investment in depreciable assets	7	$4,000 or $4,500
Incremental working capital	8	$ 900

Notes:
1 Includes direct material, direct labor, variable overhead, variable selling and administrative.
2 Includes primarily sales commissions.
3 Includes rent, salaries, depreciation, property taxes and other fixed overhead.
4 Straight line; 10-year life; no salvage value.
5 A period expense.
6 Includes advertising, salaries, lease costs.
7 Either investment in depreciable assets is equally likely.
8 Working capital committed to the project is released at the end of the 10-year project life.

Because of the dramatic increases in productivity (especially at OS), OS management decided to give their office staff an additional week of paid vacation per year. OS management believes that the extra week's lost productivity was more than recovered by the overall increased productivity resulting from the use of the prototype E-chair.

MEETING TO DISCUSS OS'S E-CHAIR PROPOSAL

The following discussion between the CEO and the COO concerns the specific question of whether to approve the E-chair proposal, as well as a more general discussion about how best to use the cash that has been accumulating. The Company has been generating cash in excess of its operating needs and has had some difficulty identifying suitable new projects in which to invest.

Bill Alberts, CEO: I guess this is an enviable position to be in—trying to figure out what to do with the substantial cash reserves we've been accumulating. As I see it, we have several options, and I want to hear your opinion. I understand that Kim Bradley [Manager, OS] has submitted a capital request for the E-chair, but that Janet Perez [CFO] remains un-convinced. Janet feels that lacking superior investment opportunities, the proper course of action is to either pay out a special [one-time] dividend or repurchase some of our outstanding stock. Kathy Starke [VP, Marketing], in contrast, feels that we shouldn't be so hasty to pay out our hardearned cash. She feels it would be best to put the cash in short-term investments such as marketable securities so that it is available when we need it.

Gary Collins, COO: I like Starke's idea of keeping some money around for a rainy day. However, I think the E-chair proposal deserves to be funded now. If we delay, we could miss an opportunity to take advantage of the seating technology we've developed at AI.

Bill Alberts, CEO: I agree that we ought to have better things to do with our cash than simply invest in marketable securities. However I'm not sure that the capital budget requests I've reviewed are truly outstanding—even the E-chair proposal. The uncertainty about the initial investment is especially troubling. It's not clear whether the project will need $4 million or $4.5 million in new depreciable assets.

Gary Collins, COO: I still support the E-chair proposal. OS is experiencing some pretty stiff competition in the office furniture market. We really need to come up with some new products to bolster our reputation as a high-quality supplier of office chairs. The Echair can give us an edge on the competition, something that will bring attention to our entire line of office furniture. And since we can fund the whole project with retained cash, there won't be any additional interest expense. The entire profit margin after taxes goes straight to the bottom line. It also helps us meet our bonus plan targets, I might add!

Bill Alberts, CEO: While I understand that the E-chair project is projected to show a substantial annual pretax profit, Janet claims that we are not really seeing a complete picture. She argues that the proposal focuses on only "accounting" profits. Because there's no accounting expense associated with using internally generated funds, we're failing to burden the project with the division's average cost of funds.

Gary Collins, COO: That's just the point. This is *not* our average project. We can finance it with internally generated funds whether the initial investment in depreciable assets is $4 million or $4.5 million— and we avoid an accounting charge for interest expense on our income statement. Further, at either level of investment, the payback for this project is less than seven years,[2] and if we don't continue to come up with new products, we will lose market share and morale in the division. Besides, isn't it profits that drive the value of this firm? Why would our bonus be tied to profits if they didn't matter?

Bill Alberts, CEO: You bring up a good point, Gary. I've been giving our bonus scheme some serious thought and would like to meet with the rest of the management team in a few weeks to reconsider our incentive compensation plan. I'm not sure our current efforts are properly directed. We need incentives that align our interests with those of our shareholders; especially given we expect to go public in the next two years.

SUMMARY OF EXISTING INCENTIVE COMPENSATION PLAN

As 1996 unfolded, Mr. Alberts and the management team were considering ways to more closely align the interests of management and shareholders by modifying the incentive plan for senior management. Annual goals at ISI are currently a function of profitability and sales growth for each division[3]. Individual managers can earn cash bonuses of up to 50 percent of their base salary, depending on their level, their strategic importance to the Company and their performance. Factors that contributed to dissatisfaction with the existing plan include:
• bonus compensation that is focused on income statement numbers (sales and earnings) without considering the level of balance sheet investments;
• a general belief that the Company's new investment projects are less attractive than they used to be.
Investment bankers had been emphasizing the importance of creating shareholder value and suggested that Mr. Alberts read a book entitled *The Quest for Value* by G. Bennett Stewart (1991). In his book, Stewart discusses how a properly structured management incentive plan can tie the compensation of management directly to the firm's long-run creation of economic value.

MEETING TO DISCUSS POSSIBLE NEW PERFORMANCE MEASURE AND INCENTIVE COMPENSATION PLAN

In late February 1996, Mr. Alberts called a meeting to discuss a new incentive compensation plan he had been reading about. In attendance, in addition to Mr. Alberts were Gary Collins (COO), Janet Perez (CFO), Kathy Starke (VP, Marketing), Jay Solomon (Manager, AI) and Kim Bradley (Manager, OS).

---

[2] Payback is calculated to be the initial investment divided by the (assumed constant) annual after-tax cash flow.

[3] In addition, senior managers receive stock options in proportion to their annual cash bonus compensation.

Blocher, Stout, Cokins, Chen: *Cost Management, 4e*

Bill Alberts, CEO: As you all know, our plans are to take the company public in the spring of 1998. As part of that process, our current owners plan to sell a sizable portion of their stock. Thus, it's important that the next two years be good ones. We expect to end up with a pretty diffuse group of stockholders. We need a performance measure that rewards management for superior results that add value for our shareholders.

Gary Collins, COO: Isn't that exactly what our current bonus plan does?

Janet Perez, CFO: That's what we're here to discuss, In addition, senior managers receive stock options in proportion to their annual cash bonus compensation. Gary. Since recovering from the downturn that seriously hurt AI, our sales and profits have been growing. Because of this improved performance, bonus targets were met last year. On the other hand, our return on investment (ROI) is lower than it was three or four years ago. I doubt that this is what our shareholders want to see.

Kathy Starke, VP Marketing: We need to consider each division separately. OS faces intense competition in the office furniture market. There are already so many players that, if we don't continue to grow and innovate, we will be left behind. And at AI we're at the mercy of cycles in the airline business. The airlines have to be financially strong before we can expect to generate new orders, much less deliveries. Success is driven by *new* orders and is reflected in the order backlog.
The accounting numbers are old news.

Janet Perez, CFO: I agree that the root issues differ between the two divisions. Luckily margins are sufficient to allow us enough cash flow to continue to invest in new projects. The bad news is that, while our recent new projects have helped generate higher earnings, they seem to be pulling down our ROI.

Gary Collins, COO: What do you propose?

Bill Alberts, CEO: From my reading in *The Quest for Value*, they are pretty critical about accounting earnings as a benchmark for corporate performance. In the author's mind, net income suffers from at least two problems. First, it includes items as expense that we all would agree benefit the future and thus should properly be capitalized and amortized over their useful lives.

Jay Solomon, Manager AI (interrupting): This is what I've been arguing for years, Bill! R&D is an asset. It's the key driver of our future success, yet we ignore this fact in our accounting statements and expense it all as incurred! I've always disliked being penalized for my commitment to R&D. Even OS stands to benefit from our research with their E-chair project. Yet I'm forced to expense R&D, which artificially depresses AI's earnings, provides the wrong message to our managers and, frankly, unfairly decreases my annual bonus.

Bill Alberts, CEO (regaining control): Well, Jay, I believe Bennett Stewart [author of *The Quest for Value*] would be sympathetic to your position. Returning to my summary, the second drawback to earnings is that it fails to deduct an expense for the cost of equity capital. Thus a firm can be profitable and not cover its opportunity cost of capital. I've had Janet prepare a brief summary of how EVA® deals with these two issues. (Mr. Alberts hands out exhibits 5 and 6.)

Kim Bradley, Manager OS: That all sounds fine; however, I still don't understand what's wrong with basing our bonus on earnings. It's something I can understand; I have some control over it and after all, every other company in the capitalistic world seems to focus on earnings. I doubt that they are all misguided.

Bill Alberts, CEO: Those are good questions. Let's invite representatives from Stern Stewart, a financial consulting firm, to do a presentation of the benefits and costs of their plan.

Gary Collins, COO: Great idea, Bill, but since Stern Stewart has a vested interest in its products, I think we should also invite a neutral consultant to help us prepare for a meeting with Stern Stewart.

Bill Alberts, CEO: Okay, Gary, set it up. (See exhibit 7.)

EXHIBIT 5
Interior Systems, Inc.
Description of Economic Value Added (EVA®) [a]
Prepared by Janet Perez, CFO

This document describes the purpose, philosophy and mechanics of an EVA®-based incentive compensation system.

Purpose of EVA® Incentive Compensation

The objective underlying EVA® incentive compensation is to more closely link incentive awards to management decisions that add value for shareholders. In brief, the goal is to promote a corporate culture that rewards what our shareholders care most about—the value of their ownership in the Company.

What is EVA®?

Economic value for shareholders is created when a firm earns a rate of return on its investment in ISI that exceeds the current opportunity cost of capital. EVA® is calculated as follows:

$$EVA® = NOPAT - Capital\ Charge$$

$$Capital\ charge = Beginning\text{-}of\text{-}year\ Capital\ Employed - Cost\ of\ Capital$$

where:

NOPAT =	net operating profits after taxes. This is the equivalent of "division profit after tax" in exhibits 2 and 3 except that Stern Stewart recommends NOPAT be adjusted for "accounting distortions." Examples of accounting distortions include: • expensing R&D that benefits the future • treating long-term noncancelable leases as operating leases Note that NOPAT is *before* any deduction for interest expense since interest on debt is accounted for in the capital charge as discussed below.
Capital Employed =	beginning-of-year assets (net of depreciation and amortization) adjusted for accounting distortions as discussed above.
Cost of Capital =	a weighted average of the minimum return required by debt and equity holders, respectively, to compensate investors for the riskiness inherent in the Company's operations. The AI division is somewhat riskier and requires a higher after-tax cost of capital than the OS division. These rates are provided in each division's financial data (see exhibits 2 and 3). The division after-tax cost of capital rates are set somewhat higher than the overall corporate rate to implicitly cover costs incurred at the corporate level that are not allocated to the divisions.

Blocher, Stout, Cokins, Chen: *Cost Management, 4e*

©The McGraw-Hill Companies, Inc 2008

EXHIBIT 6
Interior Systems, Inc.
Potential Accounting "Distortions"
Prepared by Janet Perez, CFO

Potential Accounting Distortions:

- Jay Solomon (manager AI) believes that, despite financial accounting rules requiring R&D to be a period expense, R&D at AI benefits the future. Jay argues that the entire R&D budget is committed by the beginning of the year and should be treated as an asset at that point. He estimates that, on average, the benefit should last three years—two years beyond the end of the year the expenditure was incurred. AI's R&D expenditures (in thousands) for 1989 and 1990 were $6,768 and $6,842, respectively. There is general agreement among the management team that OS division R&D is less likely to benefit future periods. Thus, OS division R&D is treated as a period expense.

- The Company has substantial long-term noncancelable leases that are treated as operating leases under SFAS No. 13. For simplicity, assume each division has one major lease in this category and that each lease began at 1/1/90. Current rent expense (in thousands) associated with these leases is provided below:

Selected leases treated as operating leases for financial reporting, 1990–2004:

	AI	OS	ISI
Rent expense	$850	$380	$1,230

If these leases were capitalized, it would affect assets and amortization expense traceable to each division as follows:

Pro forma amounts as of 1/1/90, as if selected operating leases were capitalized as that date and related annual lease amortization for the period, 1990–2004:

	AI	OS	ISI
Capitalized lease asset, net of amortization to date	$8,125	$3,600	$11,725
Annual lease amortization expense	542	360	902

Lease amortization expense is estimated using the straight-line method. Interest expense related to these leases is not provided because interest expense is not allocated to divisions.

EXHIBIT 7
Interior Systems, Inc.
Engagement Letter

To: B.A. Consulting Teams
From: Bill Alberts, President and CEO
Re: Revised metric for Division Performance Evaluation and Senior Management
        Incentive Compensation
Date: April 9, 1996

As discussed earlier, the purpose of this engagement is to have you investigate several
issues surrounding our potential adoption of an EVA®-based scheme for division performance evaluation and senior management incentive compensation. We will be meeting soon with representatives of Stern Stewart, a consulting firm that has successfully
marketed EVA®, to a number of leading corporations including Briggs & Stratton,
Coca-Cola and Eli Lilly. These corporations seem happy with EVA® and feature it in
their annual reports to shareholders. Since Stern Stewart has a vested interest in their
product, we feel it prudent to seek independent advice to prepare for our meeting
with their representatives. We would like you to provide us with an overview of the
benefits and drawbacks of switching from our existing performance metric (division
earnings) to one based on division EVA®. On balance, is the proposed change to EVA®-
based performance evaluation a good idea? If yes, would it work equally well for each
of our divisions (Airline Interiors and Office Solutions)? We seek your assistance in
the following areas:

1. Calculate EVA® for each division and compare to our current reporting. Which do
    you prefer and why?
2. Holding other factors constant, how would implementation of EVA®-based incen-
    tive compensation likely affect our investment, financing and operating decisions?
    For example, if we adopt EVA®:

    a) What changes would likely occur in the general nature and number of projects
        adopted? Specifically, would you recommend that we accept or reject Office
        Solutions division's "E-chair" proposal?
    b) What would likely be the effect on the level of cash dividends, share repur-
        chases, debt and equity capital?
    c) What would be the likely effect on the firm's utilization of existing assets?

3. Will an EVA®-based bonus plan reduce (or eliminate) dysfunctional incentives to
    maximize short-run performance at the cost of hurting long-run performance? If
    so, how?
4a. Should we include EVA® numbers in our annual report?
4b. Should we consider having our auditors attest to the numbers to increase cred-
    ibility with shareholders?

If we decide to proceed with Stern Stewart's recommendations, you will likely be involved
in our presentation to the Board of Directors. Thank you for your prompt attention.

Supplemental Questions:

5. Since ISI shares will likely be publicly traded within the next few years, should all
    of our incentive compensation at the division level and above ultimately be tied to
    the performance of the Company's stock price?
6. Evaluate the CFO and VP marketing opinions on what to do with ISI's excess
    cash.

Blocher, Stout, Cokins, Chen: *Cost Management, 4e*

REFERENCES

Biddle, G., R. Bowen, and J. Wallace. 1997. Does EVA® beat earnings? Evidence on association with stock returns and firm values. *Journal of Accounting and Economics* (December): 301–336. Fisher, A. 1995. Creating stockholder wealth. *Fortune* (December 11): 105–116.

Hamilton, R. 1777. *An Introduction to Merchandize.* Edinburgh.

Kaplan, S., and D. Norton. 1992. The balanced scorecard—Measures that drive performance. *Harvard Business Review* (January-February): 72–79.

Lambert, R. 1993. The use of accounting and security price measures of performance in managerial compensation contracts: A discussion. *Journal of Accounting and Economics* (January/April/July): 101–123.

Marshall, A. 1890. *Principles of Economics.* New York, NY: The MacMillan Press Ltd.

Solomons, D. 1965. *Division Performance: Measurement and Control.* New York, NY: Financial Executives Research Foundation.

Stewart, G. B. 1991. *The Quest for Value.* New York, NY: Harper Business.

Tully, S. 1993. The real key to creating wealth. *Fortune* (September 20): 38–50.

———. 1998. America's greatest wealth creators. *Fortune* (November 9): 193–204.

Wallace, J. 1997. Adopting residual income-based compensation plans: Do you get what you pay for? *Journal of Accounting and Economics* (December): 275–300.

Zimmerman, J. 1997. EVA® and divisional performance: Capturing synergies and other issues. *Bank of America Journal of Applied Corporate Finance* (Summer): 98–108.

Readings

18.1: DOES ROI APPLY TO ROBOTIC FACTORIES?

By Gerald H. Lander and Mohamed E. Bayou

Return on investment (ROI) has been the most popular method of performance evaluation in most companies for the past 50 to 70 years. Many companies adopted a decentralized management philosophy along with the RO technique. Even though the decentralized structures in large corporations were very complex, the easily understandable ROI ratio offered top management a handy tool for comparing performances of numerous divisions. But ROI has come under increasing criticism, raising the question: Does the growing trend toward automation alter the validity of this criticism? In other words, is the traditional ROI still valid for managerial performance evaluation in the new robotic manufacturing environment?

MAJOR ATTACKS ON ROI

We evaluate various measures of ROI in the context of the three phases of the decision cycle: acquisition, utilization, and disposition of robotic equipment. Then we present an ROI measure that satisfies the other criteria of acceptance.

Several critics have questioned the validity of the ROI method of performance evaluation. Elements targeted by this criticism appear in the ROI model commonly known as the DuPont formula, shown in Table 1. Typically, the variables of earnings, sales, and investments in this formula are all measured annually. Cash flows, time-value of money, and analysis beyond one year are excluded from the ROI measurement. As machinery replaces labor, with the consequent shift to more fixed costs and fewer variable costs, this criticism becomes more cogent. For example, Dearden contends that while ROI is a valid measure of past performance, it is not valid for setting future objectives because the historical costs of assets used in the formula are meaningless in planning future actions.[1]

Another criticism is that ROI creates dysfunctional intercompany goals. For example, an investment project with an ROI higher than the firm's cost of capital may be acceptable, yet the divisional manager may reject it unless it exceeds the currently attained ROI rate. Acceptance would dilute the manager's current ROI level, so many acceptable projects probably never get proposed to top management.

Another dysfunctional type of behavior arises when the investment in the denominator of the ROI formula is evaluated at net book value. Thus, as assets get older, stable earnings augment ROI, which in turn, may lead to management reluctance to replace the old assets with new advanced technology. This criticism of ROI is especially to the point in a robotic factory—robot obsolescence is more significant than obsolescence gnificant than obsolescence in a labor-intensive factory.

Send argues that the use of ROI motivates management to operate near full capacity in order to maximize ROI,[2] Even worse, divisional management may manipulate short-term income, and the asset base to the point of long-term detriment to the earning power of the company.[3] Consider this scenario: An insecure manager would be unlikely to accept projects that generate negative ROI results during the earlier years and large positive ones during later periods. Recognizing this problem, the corporation may be obliged to centralize several strategic discretionary programs such as R&D in order to minimize these ROI manipulations. Such interference by corporate headquarters does not harmonize with the decentralization philosophy.

In spite of these criticisms, ROI still enjoys internal popularity in evaluating managerial performance, for several reasons:

- As a ratio, ROI is simpler to understand than other evaluation methods such as residual income.
- It is a single measure that combines the effects of three critical performance variables—sales, earnings, and investment.

Blocher, Stout, Cokins, Chen: *Cost Management, 4e*

- ROI is popular with financial analysts, investors, creditors, and other external information users, a fact that encourages corporate top management to tie divisional performance to the way the public views the corporation.[4]

So strong are these reasons that ROI gained popularity as attacks on it increased during the '70s.[5] Because the use of ROI as an evaluation method undoubtedly will continue in practice, managers and other business people need to understand the mechanics and limitations of ROI.

CRITERIA FOR AN ACCEPTABLE ROI MEASURE

Given the serious criticisms of ROI and the nature of machine-intensive environments, the following criteria become necessary for an acceptable ROI measure:

- An ROI measure must consider long-term performance. This criterion is particularly relevant to the robotic factory; automation decreases variable labor and variable overhead costs and increases fixed costs over several years.
- An ROI measure must consider cash flows, a corollary of the first criterion. In the long run, cash flows are more relevant than accrual income because most accrued revenues and expenses will be settled in cash. In addition, the use of cash flows instead of accrual income avoids the distortions caused by the latter, namely, discouragement of growth by the use of net book value in ROI computations[6] and the meaningless use of historical costs of assets for planning future actions.[7]
- An ROI measure must consider the time-value of money, a corollary of the first two criteria.

FIGURE 1: ROI AND CAPITAL BUDGETING MODELS APPLIED TO THE THREE PHASES OF THE DECISION CYCLE			
	Acquisition	Utilization	Disposition Replacement
Capital Budgeting	I Applied	II N/A	III Applied
ROI	IV N/A	V Applied	VI Applied

Because the ROI measure incorporates cash flows in long-run planning, discounting these flows in the ROI computations becomes natural.

To apply these criteria properly, managers need to understand the role of ROI in the various decision processes for acquisition, utilization, and disposition of robotic assets.

TABLE 1 THE DUPONT FORMULA
$\text{ROI} = \dfrac{\text{Earnings}}{\text{Sales}} \times \dfrac{\text{Sales}}{\text{Investment}} = \dfrac{\text{Earnings}}{\text{Investment}}$
$\qquad = \quad \text{Margin} \quad \times \quad \text{Turnover}$

THE DECISION CYCLE FOR ROBOTIC ASSETS

The life cycle of a robotic asset as an investment generally goes through three different phases. First, it is acquired, then used in operations, and finally disposed of by replacement, sale, or discarding. Each phase requires different decisions and information. Furthermore, each phase has a different impact on the goals of the manager making the investment decision and on the goals of the division as an economic entity.

For fairness and accuracy in performance measurement, the three phases have to be analyzed from the manager's viewpoint separately from that of the division. Dearden argues that the current performance evaluation system fail to distinguish between the financial performance of the manager and that of the organizational unit being managed.[8] The distinction is important because the manager's potential for success and failure often differs from the division's. Moreover, the extent of the manager's controllability of revenues and expenses is irrelevant to measuring a division's performance because the division's performance incorporates both controllable and uncontrollable income determinants.

Fig. 1 shows how ROI and capital budgeting techniques generally are applied in practice to the three phases of the decision cycle.

The acquisition phase includes all activities necessary for the purchase, installation, and preparation for use of a new robotic asset. Capital budgeting models such as the net present value, internal rate of return, profitability index, and payback period commonly are applied in practice for this phase (Box 1 in Fig. 1). ROI usually is not applied in the evaluation of the division's performance during this phase (Box IV in Fig. 1).

The utilization phase involves the actual use of the asset in operations, which normally affects the

TABLE 2
ROI ANALYSIS IN THE SHORT AND LONG RUN

		Year 1	Year 2	Year 3	Year 4	Year 5
Cost of robot and accessories	(a)	90,000	90,000	90,000	90,000	90,000
Installation	(b)	10,000	10,000	10,000	10,000	10,000
Total (a + b)	(c)	100,000	100,000	100,000	100,000	100,000
Annual Costs:						
Depreciation	(d)	20,000	20,000	20,000	20,000	20,000
Maintenance	(e)	1,000	2,000	3,000	4,000	5,000
Operating & program	(f)	3,000	3,000	3,000	3,000	3,000
Insurance	(g)	3,000	3,000	3,000	3,000	3,000
Total (d + e + f + g)	(h)	27,000	28,000	29,000	30,000	31,000
Annual Benefits:						
Quality effect:						
On sales & rework	(i)	20,000	20,000	20,000	20,000	20,000
Materials savings	(j)	12,000	12,000	12,000	12,000	12,000
Labor savings:						
$10/hour	(k_1)	20,000	20,000	20,000	20,000	20,000
$20/hour	(k_2)	30,000	30,000	30,000	30,000	30,000
$30/hour	(k_3)	40,000	40,000	40,000	40,000	40,000
Overhead savings (30% of labor cost):						
$3/hour	(l_1)	6,000	6,000	6,000	6,000	6,000
$6/hour	(l_2)	9,000	9,000	9,000	9,000	9,000
$9/hour	(l_3)	12,000	12,000	12,000	12,000	12,000
Annual Net Benefits $= (l + j + k_1 + l_1) - h = m_1$						
Labor = $10/hour	(m_1)	31,000	30,000	29,000	28,000	27,000
Labor = $20/hour	(m_2)	44,000	43,000	42,000	41,000	40,000
Labor = $30/hour	(m_3)	57,000	56,000	55,000	54,000	53,000

1. Annual Book ROI $= \dfrac{\text{Net Annual Benefits}}{\text{Initial Investment}} = \dfrac{m_i}{c}$

The term "net benefits" indicates the use of accrual income rather than cash flows in the computations.

Annual Book ROI:	Year 1	Year 2	Year 3	Year 4	Year 5
at $10/hour		31%	30%	29%	28%	27%
at $20/hour		44%	43%	42%	41%	40%
at $30/hour		57%	56%	55%	54%	53%

2. Average ROI $= \dfrac{\text{Average Net Benefits Over 5 Years}}{\text{Initial Investment}} = \dfrac{\sum m/5}{c}$

This ROI also is known as the accounting rate of return

Average ROI when labor is $10/hour = 29%
Average ROI when labor is $20/hour = 42%
Average ROI when labor is $30/hour = 55%

3. Discounted Book ROI $= \dfrac{\text{Present Value of Net Benefits}}{\text{Initial Investment}}$

(The discount rate, i.e., cost of capital used = 10%)

Discounted ROI when labor is $10/hour = 111%
Discounted ROI when labor is $20/hour = 160%
Discounted ROI when labor is $30/hour = 209%

4. Discounted-Cash-Flow ROI (DCF ROI) $= \dfrac{\text{Present Value of Net Cash Inflows}}{\text{Initial Investment}}$

Because depreciation expense (d) is not a cash item it is added back:

Net Cash Inflows $= m_{i + d - c} = n_i$ for year 1

$\qquad\qquad\qquad = m_{i + d} = n_i$ for each of years 2–5

		Year 1	Year 2	Year 3	Year 4	Year 5
$10/hour	(n_1)	(49,000)	50,000	49,000	48,000	47,000
$20/hour	(n_2)	(36,000)	63,000	62,000	61,000	60,000
$30/hour	(n_3)	(23,000)	76,000	75,000	74,000	73,000

The discount rate, i.e., cost of capital used = 10%: DCF ROI:

When labor is $10/hour = 0.86
When labor is $20/hour = 1.36
When labor is $30/hour = 1.85

Blocher, Stout, Cokins, Chen: *Cost Management, 4e*

manager's performance. Hence, ROI is applied frequently (Box V in Fig. 1), and capital budgeting models rarely are applied (Box V in Fig. 1), and capital budgeting models rarely are applied (Box II). This phase has two problems. First, with robotic assets, the manager's controllability decreases because of the large value of the assets, with costs that become sunk as soon as the assets are acquired. In addition, in some companies top management evaluates major investments in robots, reducing the divisional manager's influence over the investment base and

decreasing the applicability of ROI as a means to evaluate the manager's performance. Yet these limitations do not affect ROI's usefulness in evaluating the investment center's performance. Second, the apparent inconsistency of applying capital budgeting models for the acquisition phase (Box I) and ROI for the utilization phase (Box V) creates confusion and unfair reporting if only one performance report is issued for evaluation.

The disposition phase is, in effect, an acquisition phase if it leads to replacing the old asset with a new one. Thus, capital budgeting models usually are applied (Box III) but only as a secondary justification. That is, a manager rationally would apply ROI first to determine if the replacement improves the currently attained ROI level (Box VI). If it improves the ROI, the manager models to justify the replacement decision to senior management. On the other hand, if the replacement decision negatively affects the current ROI, the replacement issue may be suppressed and never be made known to superiors even if it is acceptable to the corporation.

SCREENING DIFFERENT ROI MODELS

To avoid these conflicts, a modified ROI model should be used in all of the six boxes of Fig. 1. Table 2 illustrates how to accomplish this consistency. A flexible robotic system with an economic life of five years is considered as a replacement for an older labor-intensive system. Flexible manufacturing systems are the new trend in manufacturing. They integrate machines and systems to produce a particular product or a major component from start to finish. A flexible manufacturing system can take different forms. It can be a series of interlocked electronic machining

centers, controlled by a computerized robot, which performs a set of prescribed operations or it can be one machine performing a complex series of mechanical tasks. These systems normally provide several benefits: reduced material handling and work-in-process and increased quality, flexibility, and throughput.[9] The example in Table 2 is designed to capture most of these features. In reality, precisely predicting benefits and costs beyond one year is difficult. Probability distributions can be applied to incorporate these uncertainties, but to simplify the analysis, Table 2 does not include probability assessments.

Table 2 shows four different measures of ROI:

1. The Annual Book ROI. This traditional ROI measure, which involves no discounting or averaging and ignores cash flows and the time-value of money, concentrates on a single year of performance. Notice in Table 2 that the ROI ratio increases as automation replaces labor costs. This measure is simple to understand.

2. The Average ROI. This method also is known as the accounting rate of return. The method improves upon the traditional annual ROI because it considers the entire life of the asset. (A moving average ROI may be employed. For example, when the first year of the planning period expires, the sixth year would be added at the end of the period. Thus, a new average for ROI will be calculated every year, giving the manager a continuous five-year planning horizon.) The average ROI method, however, ignores cash flows and the time-value of money.

3. Discounted-Book ROI. This method considers the time-value of money and the long-run

---

TABLE 3 THE CAPITAL BUDGETING MODEL OF PROFITABILITY INDEX

$$\text{Profitability Index} = \frac{\text{Present Value of Total Cash Inflows}}{\text{Initial Investment}}$$

$$\text{Since Net Cash Inflows} = \text{Total Cash Inflows} - \text{Initial Investment}$$

$$\text{Profitability Index} = \frac{\text{P.V. of Net Cash Inflows} + \text{Initial Investment}}{\text{Initial Investment}}$$

$$= \frac{\text{P.V. of Net Cash Inflows}}{\text{Initial Investment}} + \frac{\text{Initial Investment}}{\text{Initial Investment}}$$

$$= \text{DCF} + 1.00$$

$$\text{Thus...DCF ROI} = \text{Profitability Index} - 1.00$$

performance. Nevertheless, it includes accrual income (which we call net benefits) rather than cash flows in the computations. Accordingly, depreciation expense on line "d" in Table 2, which is not a cash item, is incorporated into the computation. Can the discounted-book ROI be used to evaluate a manager's performance? A manager's performance should be measured over a period longer than one year, a requirement for applying this method, using budgeted and actual data. Therefore, a good performance results when the actual discounted-book ROI ratio equals at least the budgeted ratio.

4. Discounted-Cash-Flows ROI (DCF ROI). This method satisfies all three criteria for acceptance, and it considers the time-value of cash flows over the life of the robotic asset. The mathematical format of this model is shown in the first line of section 4, Table 2. The DCF ROI measure relates to the capital budgeting model of the profitability index. This index is defined in the literatures of accounting and finance as shown in Table 3.

Table 2 shows DCF ROI ratios of .86, 1.36, and 1.85 when hourly labor wage rates are $10, $20, and $30, respectively. Thus, larger savings in labor costs increase the DCF ROI ratio. Generally, interpretation of DCF ROI ratios parallels that of the profitability index. For instance, if a project has a DCF ROI ratio of zero, it indicates that the project's internal rate of return (IRR) equals the interest rate (or cost of capital) used in the discounting process. Similarly, a positive DCF ROI ratio indicates an IRR greater than the cost of capital, and a negative DCF ROI means an IRR lower than the cost of capital. In general, the larger the DCF ROI ratio, the more profitable the project. Greater cost of capital used in discontinuing the cash flows also lowers the DCF ROI ratio.

The application of this DCF ROI model to the six cells of the decision cycle depicted in Fig. 1 eliminates the inconsistency problems caused by applying capital budgeting and the traditional ROI models to the decision cycle as discussed above. The DCF ROI model satisfies the three acceptance criteria of: (1) the emphasis on long-run performance, (2) cash flows, and (3) time-value of money. Finally, the DCF ROI can be used in conjunction with the traditional ROI. Probability distributions can be incorporated into the analysis to account for uncertainties of future cash flows. These computations can be made easily by using available software packages on present value applications.

[1] J. Dearden, "The Case Against ROI," *Harvard Business Review*, May-June 1969, pp. 124-135; his arguments on the subject are still valid today.

[2] A. H. Seed, III, "Cost Accounting in the Age of Robotics," MANAGEMENT ACCOUNTING®, October 1984, pp. 39-41.

[3] L. B. Hoshower and R. P. Crum, "Straightening the Tortuous—and Treacherous—ROI Path," MANAGEMENT ACCOUNTING®, December 1986, pp. 41-44.

[4] J. S. Reece and W. R. Cool, "Measuring Investment Center Performance," *Harvard Business Review*, May-June 1978, pp. 28-176.

[5] Ibid.

[6] J. J. Mauriel and R. N. Anthony, "Misevaluation of Investment Center Performance," *Harvard Business Review*, March-April 1966, pp. 98-105.

[7] J. Dearden, "Measuring Profit Center Managers," *Harvard Business Review*, September-October 1987, pp. 84-88.

[8] Ibid.

[9] R. A. Howell and S. R. Soucy, "The New Manufacturing Environment: Major Trends for Management Accounting," MANAGEMENT ACCOUNTING®, July 1987, pp. 21-27.

18.2: TRANSFER PRICING WITH ABC

By Robert S. Kaplan, Dan Weiss, and Eyal Desheh

In the mid-1980s, Teva Pharmaceutical Industries Ltd. decided to enter the generic drug market. Already a successful worldwide manufacturer of proprietary drugs, the Israel-based company wanted to vie globally in this competitive new market, particularly in the United States. The move has proved lucrative so far, as sales have been increasing at an annual rate of nearly 20%. In 1996, Teva's worldwide sales were $954 million and its after-tax net income, $73 million.

As part of its new strategy, Teva reorganized its pharmaceutical operations into decentralized cost and profit centers consisting of one operations division and three marketing divisions. The operations division is made up of four manufacturing plants in Israel, which are organized as cost centers because plant managers have no control over product mix or pricing. The plants produce to the orders placed by the marketing divisions, and plant managers are responsible for operational efficiency, quality, cost performance, and capacity management.

The marketing divisions are organized into the U.S. market (through Teva's Lemmon subsidiary), the local market (Israel), and the rest of the world. All three have substantially different sales characteristics. The Lemmon USA division handles about 30 products, each sold in large quantities. The Israel division handles 1,200 products in different packages and dosage forms, with many being sold in quite small quantities. The division handling sales to the rest of the world works on the basis of specific orders and tenders [a request from a customer for a price/bid to deliver a specified product or service], some of which are for relatively small quantities. All three divisions order and acquire most of their products from the operations division, although occasionally they turn to local suppliers. The marketing divisions are responsible for decisions about sales, product mix, pricing, and customer relationships.

Until the late 1980s, the marketing divisions were treated as revenue centers and were evaluated by sales, not profit, performance. Manufacturing plants in the operations division were measured by how well they met expense budgets and delivered the right orders on time. The company's cost system emphasized variable costs, principally materials expenses—ingredients and packaging—and direct labor. All other manufacturing costs were considered fixed.

Teva's managers decided to introduce a transfer pricing system, which they hoped would enhance profit consciousness and improve coordination between operations and marketing. They were concerned with excessive proliferation of the product line, acceptance of many low-volume orders, and associated large consumption of production capacity for changeovers. They proposed a transfer pricing system based on marginal costs, defined to be just materials cost. Direct labor would not be included in the transfer price because the company was not expecting to hire or fire employees based on short-term marketing decisions. High costs were associated with laying off workers in Israel, and, more important, pharmaceutical workers were highly skilled. With Teva's rapid growth, managers were reluctant to lay off workers during short-term volume declines because if new employees had to be hired later, they would need up to two years of training before they acquired the skills of the laid-off workers.

But the proposed transfer pricing system generated a storm of controversy. First, some executives observed that the marketing divisions would report extremely high profits because they were being charged for the materials costs only. Second, the operations division would get "credit" only for the expenses of purchased materials. There would be little pressure and motivation to control labor expenses and other so-called fixed expenses or for improving operational efficiency. Third, if Teva's plants were less efficient than outside manufacturers of the pharmaceutical products, the marginal cost transfer price would give the marketing divisions no incentive to shift their source of supply. Finally, the executives concluded that using only a short-run contribution margin approach would not solve the problems caused by treating the marketing divisions as revenue centers. Measuring profits as price less materials cost would continue to allow marketing and sales decisions to be made without regard to their implications for production capacity and long-run costs. An alternative approach had to be found.

WHAT EVERYONE WANTED

Teva senior management wanted a new transfer pricing system that would satisfy several important characteristics:

1. The system should encourage the marketing divisions to make decisions consistent with long-run profit maximization. The transfer price should not encourage actions that improved the profit or cost performance of a division at the expense of Teva's overall profitability.
2. The system should be transparent enough so that managers could distinguish costs relevant for short-run decisions—such as incremental, occasional bids for orders—from long-term decisions—such as acquiring a new product line, deleting product lines, and adding to existing product lines.
3. The transfer prices could be used to support decisions in both marketing and operating divisions, including:

Marketing	Operations
• Product mix	• Inventory levels
• New product introduction	• Batch sizes
• Product deletion	• Process improvements
• Pricing	• Capacity management
	• Outsourcing: make vs. buy

Division managers wanted a transfer pricing system with the following characteristics:

1. The transfer prices would report the financial performance of their divisions fairly.
2. Managers could influence the reported performance of their divisions by making business decisions within their scope of authority. That is, the reported performance should reflect changes in product mix, improved efficiency, investments in new equipment, and organizational changes.
3. The decisions made by managers of marketing divisions would reflect both sales revenue and associated expenses incurred in the operations division.
4. The system must anticipate that division managers would examine, in depth, the method for calculating transfer prices and would take actions that maximized the reported performance of their divisions.

Finally, the financial staff wanted a transfer pricing system such that:

1. The transfer prices and financial reports derived from them would be credible and could be relied upon for decision making at all levels of the organization without excessive arguments and controversy.
2. The transfer pricing system would be clear, easy to explain, and easy to use. Updating transfer prices should be easy, and the components of the transfer price calculation should promote good understanding of the underlying factors driving costs.
3. The system would be used for internal charging of costs from the operations division to the marketing divisions.

Table 1. PAIN RELIEVER 10 TABLETS, 250 mg.

Annual Sales 1996—$2.1 Million

ABC Cost per Package

Materials use	$1.50
Production costs	2.10
(The traditional production costs per package were only $1.50, 40% difference)	
Total	$3.60

Production Cost Analysis:

Resources

Salaries	$0.86
Energy	0.27
Utilities	0.34
Depreciation	0.41
Administrative	0.22
Total	$2.10

Main Activities

Storage	$0.25
Manufacturing	0.61
Packaging	0.71
Q.A.	0.42
Logistics	0.11
Total	$2.10

Cost Drivers

Number of materials	$0.55
Batches	0.24
Labor hours	0.71
Machine hours	0.47
Samples	0.13
Total	$2.10

TRADITIONAL TRANSFER PRICE APPROACHES WOULDN'T WORK

Teva's managers considered but rejected several traditional methods for establishing a new transfer pricing system: market price, full cost, marginal

Blocher, Stout, Cokins, Chen: *Cost Management, 4e*

cost, and negotiated price. Market price for the transferred product was not feasible because no market existed for Teva's manufactured and packaged pharmaceutical products that had not been distributed or marketed to customers. A full cost calculation including materials, labor, and manufacturing over-head was rejected because the traditional methods for allocating overhead (labor or machine hours) did not capture the actual cost structure in Teva's plants. Also, the accumulation of all factory costs into average overhead rates could encourage local optimization by each division that would lower Teva's overall profit. For example, manufacturing plants would be encouraged to overproduce in order to absorb more factory overhead into inventory, while marketing divisions might be discouraged from bidding aggressively for high-volume orders and encouraged to accept more low-volume custom orders. Also, this system would not reveal the incremental costs associated with short-run decisions or the relative use of capacity by different products and different order sizes.

Using short-run marginal cost, covering only ingredients and packaging materials, was the system proposed initially, which the managers already knew was inadequate for their purposes. And, finally, senior executives believed strongly that negotiated transfer prices would lead to endless arguments among managers in the different divisions, which would consume excessive time on nonproductive discussions.

ACTIVITY-BASED COSTING IS THE ANSWER

In December 1989, Teva's senior management attended a presentation on the fundamentals of activity-based costing and decided to implement ABC in its largest production plant. They wanted to investigate the use of ABC for calculating transfer prices between that plant and the marketing divisions. Teva put together a multidisciplinary project team consisting of managers from the production, finance, and marketing divisions. The team worked for about six months to develop an activity dictionary, drive factory costs to activities, identify cost drivers for each activity, collect data, and calculate ABC based product costs. It took the team several more weeks to analyze the results. Table 1 shows a sample calculation (updated to reflect 1996 data) of the costs to produce 10 tablets of a pain reliever. With this information, managers believed they now had a defensible, quantifiable answer to a question about how much it cost to manufacture a special small batch for a customer.

After seeing how ABC worked at the first plant, in subsequent years the project team rolled out the ABC analysis to the remaining production plants. The ABC models were retrospective, calculating the activity costs, activity cost driver rates, and product costs for the prior year. By the end of 1993, senior managers wanted to use ABC prospectively, to calculate transfer prices for the coming year. In November, Teva built its ABC production cost model for 1994 using data from the first three quarters 1993. But managers objected to calculating costs for 1994 based on 1993 historical data. The numbers would not incorporate the impact of new products, new machines, and expected changes in production processes. Also, the historical data contained volume and spending variances that occurred in 1993 but that were not expected to be representative of production operations in 1994.

The project team took this issue to the company's Financial Control Forum where representatives from the operations and marketing divisions and company headquarters met to discuss costing and financial reporting methodologies. After several meetings, the group decided to use the next year's (1994) forecasted costs—based on budgeted expense data, forecasted volume and mix of sales, and projected process utilization and efficiencies—to calculate the transfer prices.

THE ABC TRANSFER PRICE MODEL STRUCTURE

The structure of the early retrospective ABC models and the current prospective model recognizes the ABC hierarchy of unit, batch, product sustaining, and plant-level costs.[1] Unit-level costs represent all the direct expenses associated with producing individual product units such as tablets, capsules, and ampoules. These expenses principally include the cost of raw materials, packaging materials, and direct wages paid to production workers.

Batch-level costs include the expenses of resources used for each production or packaging batch, mainly the costs of preparation, setup, cleaning, quality control, laboratory testing, and computer and production management. The lot sizes for pharmaceutical production usually are predetermined based on the capacity of containers in the production line,[2] but a second batch process, determined by customer orders, occurs for packaging the tablets or syrup. The costs of a production or a packaging batch can vary among different products and, of course, among different plants. For example, a small customer order can trigger the production of a large batch of tablets or syrup of which only a small portion may be packaged for the particular customer order.[3] Thus, the batch costs assigned to a particular order include two components: a pro-rata share of the batch cost of the production setup and the full batch cost of the packaging setup. The calculation of batch-level costs for several different types of customer orders is shown in Table 2.

Product-specific costs include the expenses incurred in registering the products,[4] making changes to a product's production processes, and designing the package. Plant-level costs represent the cost of maintaining the capacity of production lines including depreciation, cost of safety inspections, and insurance, as well as the general expenses of the plant such as security and landscaping. In many ABC applications, machine appreciation would be included in the unit and batch costs associated with producing products and changing from one product to another. Teva decided to treat equipment depreciation as a plant-level cost so the calculated unit and batch costs could be used to estimate more closely the marginal costs associated with producing one more unit or batch of a product.

USING ABC COSTS FOR TRANSFER PRICING

Teva bases its transfer price system on a prospective ABC calculation. Prices are set for the coming year based on budgeted data. The company calculates standard activity cost driver rates for each activity. During the year these costs get charged to products based on the actual quantity of activities demanded during the year. The use of standard activity cost driver rates enables product costs to be calculated in a predictable manner throughout the year. It also eliminates monthly or quarterly fluctuations in product costs caused by variations in actual spending, resource usage, and activity levels.

Transfer prices are calculated in two different procedures. The first one assigns unit and batch-level costs, and the second assigns product-specific and plant-level costs. The marketing divisions are charged for unit-level costs (principally materials and labor) based on the actual quantities of each individual product they acquire. In addition, they are charged batch-level costs based on the actual number of production and packaging batches of each product they order (see examples in Table 2). Now that Teva has the ability to analyze the costs of different presentations, the trend of having a large number of presentations for each product has

slowed. For example, the marketing divisions realized that producing special sample packages of six tablets was very expensive and that it was cheaper to give physicians the regular packages of 20 tablets. In general, the procedure has given marketing managers the flexibility to decide when to accept a small order from a customer or how much of a discount to grant for large orders. Table 3 shows a sample calculation

---

Table 2. BATCH-LEVEL TRANSFER PRICE

The batch-level transfer price has two components: the production setup and the packaging setup. Consider the production and packaging process for a cough syrup. In the production process, the active ingredients, a syrup simplex, and flavors, are mixed together in a 600 liter container to produce the syrup solution. The cost of setup—labor, cleaning, maintenance, and quality control resources—is $300. The setup cost is assigned proportionally to the entire output.

Subsequently, bottles are filled with the syrup solution and packed into cardboard boxes. The entire packaging process is performed on an automatic filling and packing line. The setup of the line costs $500, which includes the cost of a skilled technician, cleaning, maintenance, and quality control. Packing the same syrup into two different presentations, such as different sized bottles (5O ml and 1OO ml), or different packaging materials requires two different setups.

The batch-level transfer price consists of the pro-rata share of the production setup and the full cost of the packaging setup. We illustrate the approach with three numerical examples:

Produce a full batch of 6,000 bottles of 1OO mI syrup for a large order from a customer in the local market

[$300/6,000] + [$500/6,000] = $.05 + $.083 = $.133/bottle
   mixing   packing

Produce a small order of 1,000 bottles of 1OO ml syrup, packed in special boxes, for a special tender in South America

[$300/6,000] + [$500/1,000] = $.05 + $.50 = $.55/bottle
   mixing   packing

Produce a full batch of 12,000 bottles of 5OmI syrup for a large order from a customer in the local market

[$300/12,000] + [$500/12,000] = $.025 + $.042 = $.067/bottle
   mixing   packing

Blocher, Stout, Cokins, Chen: *Cost Management, 4e*

Table 3. MONTHLY DEBIT — MAY 1995

From Plant A to Local Market Division

Product	Quantity Produced	Material (Per Package)	Unit Based Costs (Per Package)	Batch Based Costs (Per Package)	Total Costs [†] (Per Package)	Total Debit [‡]
Pain reliever 20 tablets, 500 mg.	1,000,000	$2.10	$0.22	$0.41	$2.73	$2,730,000
Pain reliever 30 Capsules	1,200,000	1.60	0.20	0.32	2.12	2,544,000
Syrup 200 cc.	200,000	0.81	0.43	0.11	1.35	270,000
• • •						• • •
Total						$15,100,200

[†] Total costs = material + unit based costs = batch based costs
[‡] Total debit = total costs per package x quantity produced

of the monthly unit and batch-level charges from a plant to a marketing division.

The product-specific and plant-level expenses are charged to marketing divisions annually based on budgeted information (see Table 4). The product-specific costs are easy to assign because each marketing division has specific products for its own markets. No individual product is sold to more than one marketing division. The plant-level (capacity-sustaining) expenses are charged to each marketing division based on the budgeted use of the capacity of the four manufacturing facilities.

Activity cost driver rates are calculated based on the practical capacity of each of the four plants. In this way, the rates reflect the underlying efficiency and productivity of the plants without being influenced by fluctuations in forecasted or actual usage. Analysts estimated the practical capacity by noting the maximum production quantities during past peak periods.

What about unused capacity? Unused capacity arises from two sources: (1) declines in demand for products manufactured on an existing line, and (2) partial usage when a new production line is added because existing production lines cannot produce the additional quantities requested by one of the marketing divisions. To foster a sense of responsibility among marketing managers for the cost of supplying capacity resources, Teva charges the marketing division that experienced the decline in demand a lump-sum assignment (see Table 4) for the cost of maintaining the unused production capacity in an existing line. When a marketing division initiates an increment in production

capacity or manufacturing technology, it bears the costs of all the additional resources supplied unless or until the increment begins to be used by one of the other marketing divisions. At that point, each marketing division would be charged based on its percentage of practical capacity used.

The assignment of the plant-level costs (still referred to as "fixed costs" at Teva because of its long history with the marginal costing approach) receives much attention, particularly from the managers of the marketing divisions. They want to verify that these costs do indeed stay "fixed" and don't creep upward each period. By separating the unit and batch-level costs from the product-sustaining and plant-level costs, the marketing managers can monitor closely the costs incurred in the manufacturing plants. In particular, the marketing managers make sure that increases in plant-level costs occur only when one or more of them requests a change in production capacity. The responsibility for the fixed cost increment is then clearly assignable to the requesting division.

The integrated budget process lets marketing managers plan their product mix with knowledge of the cost impact of their decisions. When they propose increases in variety and complexity, they know the added costs they will be charged because of their increased demands on manufacturing facilities. Active discussions occur between marketing and operations personnel about the impact of product mix and batch sizes.

Table 4. ANNUAL DEBIT — 1995

From Plant A to Lemmon Marketing Division (USA)

Product	Annual Budgeted Quantity	Product Based Costs (Per Package)	Plant Based Costs (Per Package)	Total Costs [†] (Per Package)	Total Debit [‡]
Pain reliever 20 tablets, 500 mg.	12,000,000	$0.10	$0.21	$0.31	$3,720,000
Pain reliever 30 Capsules	20,000,000	0.12	0.20	0.32	6,400,000
Syrup 200 cc.	3,500,000	0.14	0.12	0.26	860,000
	•				•
	•				•
	•				•
Cost of used capacity					141,900,000
Cost of unused capacity					1,300,000
Total					$143,200,000

[†] Total costs = product based costs + plant based costs
[‡] Total debit = total cost per package x annual budgeted quantity

Marketing managers now distinguish between products that cover all manufacturing costs versus those that cover only the unit and batch-level expenses but not their annual product-sustaining and plant-level expenses. Because of the assignment of unused capacity expenses to the responsible marketing division, the marketing managers incorporate information about available capacity when they make decisions about pricing, product mix, and product introduction.

One example illustrates the value of assigning product-sustaining and plant-level expenses to individual products in the new transfer pricing system. The initial and subsequent ABC analyses revealed that quite a few of Teva's products were unprofitable; that is, the revenues they earned were below the cost of the unit, batch, and product and plant-sustaining expenses associated with these products. But managers were reluctant to drop these products because many of the expenses assigned to them, including direct labor, would remain for some time even if production of the unprofitable products were to cease.

In the early 1990s, however, Teva's growing sales volume led to shortages in capacity. Teva eventually decided to sell 30 low-volume products to another company. These products were not central to Teva's strategy, yet they consumed a great number of resources and managers' attention.

By shifting the product mix away from the unprofitable products, Teva was able to use the freed-up capacity of people, machines, and facilities to handle the production of newly introduced products and the expanded sales of existing profitable products. While the debate about selling off the 30 products lasted three years, the ABC system contributed to the final decision by revealing that the cheapest source of new capacity was the capacity released by reducing the production and sales of currently unprofitable products.

ONGOING BENEFITS FROM ABC TRANSFER PRICING SYSTEM

With Teva's continued growth, requests for investments in new production capacity arise continually. ABC's highlighting of unused capacity often reveals where production can be expanded without spending additional money. A second source is the capacity released by ceasing production of unprofitable products—when feasible without disrupting customer relations. Beyond these two sources, investments in a new production line can be assessed by simulating production costs if the line were to be installed. For example, a new line can reduce batch-level costs because of less need for changeovers on both the

Blocher, Stout, Cokins, Chen: *Cost Management, 4e*

existing and the proposed production lines. These cost reductions could provide the justification for the investment decision. In addition, the investment decision for a new production line explicitly incorporates the cost and assignment of responsibility for the unused capacity in the early periods while market demand has not yet built to long-term expected levels. Teva executives say that the discipline of recognizing and assigning unused capacity costs of new production lines provides valuable realism to the demand forecasts provided by the marketing divisions.

The transfer pricing system also motivates cost reduction and production efficiencies in the manufacturing plants. Managers in the different divisions now work together to identify ways to reduce unit and batch-level expenses. Manufacturing, purchasing, and marketing employees conduct common searches for lower-cost, more reliable, and higher-quality suppliers to reduce variable materials costs. Marketing managers compare Teva's production costs with those of alternative suppliers around the world. They share this information with manufacturing managers who learn where process improvements are required and may concur with a decision to outsource products where the external suppliers' costs are lower than Teva could achieve in the foreseeable future. These actions contribute to increasing Teva's long-term profitability.

The activity-based cost information also helps managers determine which manufacturing facility is appropriate for different types of products. For example (see Figure 1), Plant A has a relatively inflexible (high capital-intensive) cost structure with a high percentage of plant-level costs and a low percentage of unit costs. This plant is most appropriate for high-volume production of standard products. Plant B, with a significantly lower percentage of plant-level costs and a relatively high percentage of unit costs, is much more flexible and is appropriate for producing small batch sizes and test runs of newly introduced products. Thus, ABC information also is being used to determine operating strategy.

Figure 1 Structure of Costs in Plants A and B

	Plant A	Plant B
Unit Based Cost	42%	45%
Batch Based Cost	32%	30%
Product Based Cost	20%	23%
Plant Based Cost	6%	2%

THE BEST NEWS: HARMONY IS GROWING

An unexpected benefit of the activity-based transfer price system is the ability to measure profit performance under changing organizational structures. Teva, like many other pharmaceutical companies, undergoes periodic organizational changes. By understanding cost behavior at the activity and product level, financial managers can forecast the potential performance of newly created profit centers and reconstruct what the past profit performance history would have been, assuming that the proposed profit center reorganization had existed for the past several years. The ABC system also enables senior executives to measure profit performance across organizational—cost and profit center—boundaries. For example, Table 5 shows the profitability of a significant product family whose individual products are manufactured in different plants and are sold by more than one marketing division.

Jacob Winter, Teva's vice president of pharmaceutical operations, commented on the benefits derived from the ABC transfer price system:

In our changing environment, it is important for us to be able to understand and forecast our cost behavior. Some products remain in certain stages of production for a long time. These stages require resources of professional production and quality assurance staff even when no direct labor is involved. On the other hand, since the supply of these resources is relatively fixed in the short run, we understand that we can use their capabilities for several small batch runs.

He also recognized that activity-based costs are not the primary information used for short-term operational decision making:

The ABC data provide an indication that must be sup-ported by other information and facts One cannot rely only on costing information when making operational decisions. Our short-term operational decisions focus on current bottlenecks and lead-time considerations. ABC provides guidance and insights about where we should be looking, but it is not the primary data for operational decisions.

Perhaps most important, the introduction of ABC-based transfer prices has led to a dramatic reduction in the conflicts among marketing and manufacturing managers. The managers now have confidence in the production cost economics reported by the transfer price system. Manufacturing managers who "sell" the product and marketing managers who "buy" the product concur with the reasonableness of the calculated transfer prices. Teva's senior executives interpret the sharp reduction in intraorganizational conflicts as one of the most important signs that the use of activity-based transfer prices is succeeding.

Table 5. 10 LEADING PRODUCTS (Segment A): 1995

	$ Million
Sales revenue	50
Marketing expenses	
USA Lemmon division	10
Local market division	9
Other export division	-
Total	19
Manufacturing expenses	
Plant A	11
Plant B	-
Plant C	9
Plant D	-
Total	20
Total expenses	39
Profit	11

ENDNOTES:

[1] R. Cooper, "Cost Classification in Unit-Based and Activity-Based Manufacturing Cost Systems," *Journal of Cost Management,* Fall 1990, pp. 4-14.

[2] Production lot sizes can be expanded, if demand increases to a higher, sustainable level, by making technical changes to the production process and performing a quality control procedure to verify and validate that the product characteristics and quality have not been altered by the larger production batch.

[3] At present, the Teva transfer price system does not charge the customer order for the full cost of setting up the production batch nor for the inventory carrying cost of the unused tablets or syrup. This is a refinement that could be added to the system in future years.

[4] Registration costs include the costs of gaining and maintaining approval from governmental agencies for the right to manufacture each product.

Blocher, Stout, Cokins, Chen: *Cost Management, 4e*

Chapter 19
Management Compensation, Business Analysis, and Business Valuation

Cases

19-1   **Midwest Petro-Chemical Company** (Evaluating a Firm)
19-2   **Evaluating a Firm**
19-3   **OutSource, Inc.** (Economic Value Added)

Readings

19-1: "Using Shareholder Value to Evaluate Strategic Choices" by Nick Fera, *Management Accounting* (November 1997).

The basic principle of the article is that performance evaluation based on accounting measures alone is not sufficient. The evaluation of a business unit or of the unit's manager must also consider the business unit's performance in creating shareholder value. Based on ideas from Alfred Rappaport's book, Creating Shareholder Value, the article develops the measures of cash flow and market risk. An illustration for a hypothetical firm is provided.

Discussion Questions
1.   Explain the differences between the two measurement methodologies presented in the article.
2.   Why is it important for firms and managers to consider shareholder value?
3.   What are the key factors in determining shareholder value?

19-2: "The Role of Strategy" by Priscilla O'Clock and Kevin Devine, *Management Accounting Quarterly* (Winter 2003).

This article presents a careful look at the role of local culture in the desirability of different management control systems. Local culture is defined in terms of Hofstede's research paradigm, including the measures: individualism, uncertainty avoidance, power distance, masculinity, and Confucianism. The culture of several major countries (including the U.S., U.K., Japan, Germany, and others) is considered and suggestions are provided for designing the management controls system for foreign SBUs. Companies should include both the firm's strategy and the culture of the foreign country in determining the most effective form of SBU and how it is to be implemented.

Discussion Questions
1. Identify and explain the meaning of each of the cultural factors (or "dimensions") used in Hofstede's research of cultures in various countries.
2. How should each of the cultural factors be used in developing effective SBU control systems?
3. For which countries do you think it would be most difficult to develop an effective management control system, and why?
4. For which countries do you think it would be easiest to develop an effective management control system, and why?

Cases

19-1 Midwest Petro-Chemical Company (Evaluating a Firm)[1]

Midwest Petro-Chemical, an industrial chemical distributor, was formed in 1960 by James Fletcher, a chemical engineer who had spent 10 years with the petrochemical division of a major oil company. His oil company experience which included a variety of technical, sales, and management positions, provided valuable business training. His final oil company position was regional marketing manager. He felt hindered by the slow-moving oil company bureaucracy, so he left a corporate career to begin Midwest Petro-Chemical.

The company began operation in Chicago in a rented warehouse with Fletcher as the only full-time employee. First-year sales totaled $113,000 and the company reported a loss of $6,200. Although first-year sales were less than planned and most of his initial capital was lost, Fletcher remained optimistic. Unable to obtain debt capital, he sought equity investors. He approached his college fraternity brothers and oil company colleagues to invest in the new venture. Six accepted, with each providing between $10,000 and $20,000 of much needed capital.

Sales exceeded $300,000 the second year of operations, but the company still reported a small loss of $4,000. The company reported its first profit of $14,000 in year three. Its first bulk distribution facility, capable of handling truck, rail, and barge transportation, was leased the next year.

Over the next 35 years, the company expanded operations beyond Chicago. New offices and plants were opened in five metropolitan cities: St. Louis, Kansas City, Louisville, Cincinnati, and Memphis. Plants were built in industrial areas on sites ranging from two to four acres. Each facility included a warehouse and tank farm with multiple-size tanks with capacities ranging from 1.5 million gallons (barge shipments) to 10,000 gallons (truck shipments). Chemical manufacturers and oil companies were the major supplier of chemicals. Midwest would purchase in bulk (barge, rail, or truck), blend chemicals as necessary, repackage, and ship product in smaller quantities (less than truckload, tote tanks, 55-gallon drums, and other smaller package sizes) to a variety of users.

CURRENT SITUATION

The company prospered and remains a privately held corporation. Annual sales exceeded $95 million in 2007, and a profit of $2,315 million was reported. Fletcher, now in his late 60s, is still CEO and the largest shareholder, owning 314,260 shares or 41.8% of the total shares outstanding. Three of the original investors (Stan Davis, Tom Williams, and Don Stewart) own another 326,216 shares (43.4%), and the company's pension fund owns 78,000 shares. Ron Allen, the company's chief financial officer, is the pension trustee and votes the shares. The remaining 32,524 shares are owned by 37 current or former employees.

There is not an active market for Midwest's stock. Sales or transfers of the stock occur infrequently between a buyer and seller, and Midwest does not participate in the exchange transaction. The sale price of stock is negotiated at arm's length between the buyer and seller. During 2007, approximately 18,000 shares were exchanged in 27 transactions at prices ranging from $21 to $24 per share.

Fletcher, the three remaining original investors (Davis, Williams, and Stewart) and Midwest's local counsel, Frank Armstrong, compose the Board of Directors. Despite Midwest's consistent growth and profitability, recent Board meetings have resulted in heated discussions concerning three issues.

1. *Succession plan*. Despite his age, Fletcher remains a more capable leader and has no desire to retire or even plan for retirement. The Board is concerned that no succession plan exists.
2. *Stock value and liquidity*. Stan Davis (age 72) wants to sell his Midwest stock (126,415 shares) but feels the stock is substantially undervalued at its recent trading range of $21 to $24. Like Fletcher, Davis has

---

[1] Prepared byDavid A. Kunz and Keith A. Russell, © Institute of Management Accountants, 1996. Used with permission.

Blocher, Stout, Cokins, Chen: *Cost Management, 4e*

started his own business—Western Solvents, Inc., a chemical distribution company on the West Coast. With the aid of an investment banking firm, he recently sold Western Solvents at a price that was 16 times earnings. He has been pressuring Fletcher to purchase his Midwest shares.

3. ***Offer to purchase the company***. Davis's interest in selling has been heightened due to an unsolicited purchase inquiry from Georgia Chemical, a chemical distributor in Atlanta. The inquiry was made via letter to Fletcher asking if there were any interest in selling Midwest. It is Fletcher's position that Midwest is not for sale, and he does not want to talk about the offer.

At the most recent Board meeting, Fletcher stated he was going to send a letter to Georgia Chemical indicating Midwest is not for sale. Davis objected and argued that it is their fiduciary responsibility as directors to consider all serious offers. Fletcher responded by saying, "Georgia Chemical's inquiry didn't even include a price, so how could it be considered an offer to buy?" Fletcher, Davis, and Allen offered their opinions as to what the stock was worth, but all agreed that their value estimates were not based on systematic or quantifiable processes. They also felt the current stock trading range was low. Stewart felt that without an established valuation of the stock, it would be very difficult, if not impossible, to evaluate objectively any offer to buy the firm. Frank Armstrong agreed with Stewart.

Before a response can be given to the Atlanta inquiry, a reasonable price must be determined. Don Stewart suggested an independent study be undertaken to determine the fair market value of Midwest's common stock. Stan Davis agreed and recommended using the investment banking firm of Warner and David, which recently valued his company. Ron Allen had worked with Warner and David with his previous employer and also thought highly of that firm's ability. Allen also commented that one of the hot new services offered by public accounting firms is business valuation. In fact, a partner in Midwest's auditing firm had mentioned this service in a recent meeting.

Despite his many years in business, Fletcher is unfamiliar with the procedures used to value a business. He is unwilling to bring in any outsider at this point. As a compromise, Tom Williams, a retired banker, suggested that Allen perform an in-house valuation by comparing Midwest's performance with industry norms. Analyses of ratios such as profit margin, return on assets, and return on equity were effective profit measures. Benchmarking Midwest's performance with industry data should be an indication of strength or weakness, which relates to value. Williams also mentioned the price-to-earnings ratio and the price-to-book-value ratio as other possible value indicators. He said that as a banker, he began evaluation of all loan requests with a detailed historic performance analysis using ratios. Sources such as Value Line Investment Survey and Robert Morris Associates Annual Statement Studies provide industry data. Allen agreed that financial analysis was beneficial but was skeptical about it yielding a usable value. Another approach Williams suggested was to perform a valuation using the market values of the firm's assets (appraisals were performed on all properties over the last two years for insurance purposes).

Allen thought a valuation process based on projected future cash flows might be a more accurate measure of the firm's value. Fletcher agreed with Allen because he feels the company is poised for considerable future growth. Davis suggested Allen use the sale of Western Solvents as a reference because the businesses were almost identical except for geographic location.

As the Board members began discussing the various proposals and the advantages and disadvantages of each, Frank Armstrong proposed yet another course of action: giving Ron Allen and his staff the assignment to (1) investigate valuation alternatives, (2) perform an in-house valuation, and (3) prepare a report for review at the next Board meeting (one month away). All Board members agreed, and Allen was given the assignment.

THE ASSIGNMENT

The next day, Ron Allen met with Linda Warren, Midwest's controller, to discuss the task. Warren mentioned that her previous employer used yet another valuation method—capitalization of earnings—to determine its worth. Allen said he planned to use all the methods suggested by the board members plus any other appropriate methods.

Together they reviewed each valuation method and prepared a description of each. They also listed information needed for each technique.

1. ***Financial Ratio Analysis***: Allen directed Warren to obtain industry comparative data and suggested starting with Value Line Investment Survey. Other sources of industry comparative data are Robert Morris Associates Annual Statement Studies and Standard and Poor's Industry Surveys.

2. ***Asset-Based or Market Value Method***: Although Tom Williams didn't refer specifically to this valuation method, Ron Allen thought he was describing it when he suggested using "market value of the assets." Linda Warren was to gather the most recent appraisals based on replacement values (see Table 1).

3. ***Market Comparison Method***: This approach suggested by Stan Davis is based on the assumptions that value of a privately held company can be estimated by comparing it to a similar company whose market values are known. As Davis's company recently sold at 16 times earnings, it can be used as the known market value.

4. ***Discounted Cash Flow***: Ron Allen and James Fletcher favor this approach based on expected future cash flows. Linda Warren pointed out that this technique requires forecasting future cash flows. Allen agreed and thought forecasting for five years would be appropriate. In preparing the forecasts, Allen suggested they project revenues to grow at 3.5% per year and forecast operating expenses (including depreciation) as a percentage of sales using an average of actual 2007 and 2006 percentages. As annual depreciation expense has been about $1.4 million the past two years, and no major acquisitions are expected, it was decided to use $800,000 for annual net cash from depreciation (assume $600,000 is reinvestment in existing operations). To keep it simple, Warren suggested forecasting interest expense of $900,000 in 2008 and reducing the amount by $50,000 each subsequent year. She also suggested projecting income tax expense at 30% of income before income taxes. Allen recognized this was an oversimplification, but agreed.

   Warren asked how she should handle working capital changes, dividends, and residual values. Allen commented that because the current relationship between revenues, current assets, and current liabilities was close to optimum, they should assume it is maintained. Dividends per share of $.35 should be projected for 2008 with a $.05 per share increase each year thereafter. Book value should be used for residual values.

   The rate of return that investors require on equity capital depends on the riskiness of the cash flow stream. The risk premium on equity frequently is regarded at 3% higher than debt capital. Further, the risk and liquidity premium on private small companies without a liquid market indicated an additional premium in the range of 20%.

5. ***Capitalization of Earnings***: The capitalization of earnings approach embodies the concept that an investor in a going business has in mind a desired or "target" return on capital. Warren thought it would be another good technique but that they should perform two calculations, one based on past earnings and another using projected earnings. Allen agreed. The target return is expressed as a percentage of after-tax earnings to invested capital or equity and is referred to as return on equity (ROE). Warren thought they should use a capitalization rate based on an average ROE for 2007 and 2006. Allen concurred but told her to use beginning-year equity to calculate ROE.

REQUIRED:

Assume the roles of Ron Allen, Midwest Petro-Chemical's chief financial officer, and Linda Warren, controller, and prepare the required report for the Board. The report should address the following:

1. What is Midwest's strategic competitive advantage, and what type of compensation plan is most consistent with this strategy?
2. Analyze company performance using financial ratio analysis and industry norms as a bench mark. What are the strengths and weaknesses of this evaluation process?
3. Why did financial ratio analysis serve as an effective tool for Tom Williams?
4. Discuss each valuation method. What are the strengths and weaknesses of each? What difficulties are encountered when applying each method?
   a. Asset-based or market value
   b. Market comparison
   c. Discounted cash flow
   d. Capitalization of earnings
      1. Historic earnings
      2. Projected earnings
5. Develop values for Midwest Petro-Chemical's stock using the four valuation methods discussed in requirement 4.
6. Based on your previous answers, develop a fair-market value for Midwest's common stock. Support your value.

Blocher, Stout, Cokins, Chen: *Cost Management, 4e*

©The McGraw-Hill Companies, Inc 2008

7. Recommend a negotiating strategy for dealing with the inquiry from the Atlanta company.
8. Once a price is agreed upon by a buyer and seller, sale terms must be structured.
   a. Will the price be paid in cash at closing? As an initial cash payment plus future payments? As stock or some combination of the aforementioned?
   b. Will stock or assets be sold? Will the sale terms affect price? If so, how? Explain your answer.
   (IMA adapted)

TABLE 1

	Acquisition Date	Land	Plant Prop.& Equip	Accumulated Depreciation	Net Book Value
Chicago	1963	$ 634	$ 4,415	$ 3,012	$ 2,037
St. Louis	1967	960	4,602	3,118	2,444
Louisville	1970	1,100	5,809	4,019	2,890
Cincinnati	1980	2,600	6,222	3,216	5,606
Memphis	1982	2,466	7,214	3,037	6,643
		$7,760	$28,262	$16,402	$19,620

	Appraisal Date	Land	Plant. Prop. & Equip	Total
Chicago	1994	$2,010	$2,050	$ 4,060
St. Louis	1991	1,580	1,738	3,318
Louisville	1992	1,720	1,612	3,332
Memphis	1989	2,910	3,702	6,612
Cincinnati	1990	2,700	4,313	7,013
				$24,335

		Shares	%
James Retcher	CEO/Director	314,260	41.8
Stan David	Director	126,415	16.8
Tom Williams	Director	105,060	14.0
Don Stewart	Director	94,741	12.6
Pension fund*		78,000	10.4
Other		32,524	4.4
	Total	751,000	100.4
*Shares voted by trustee Ron Allen			

Table 1 (Continued)

Balance Sheets (000s). December 31						
	2007	**2006**			**2007**	**2006**
Current assets			Current liabilities			
Cash	$ 510	$ 212	Accounts payable		$11,264	$8,944
Receivables	13,925	12,816	Accrued expenses		2,245	1,745
Inventories	9,310	10,463	Total current liabilities.		13,509	10,689
Prepaid expenses	745	413				
Total current assets	$24,490	$23,904	Long-term obligations		10,899	15,600
			Total liabilities		24,408	26,289
Property and equipment at cost			Shareholders'equity			
Land	7,760	7,760	Common stock $1 par value			
Plant, property and equipment ..	28,262	27,232	2,000,000 shares authorized			
Less accumulated depreciation .	(16,402)	(14,995)	751,000 shares outstanding		751	751
Total plant and property	19,620	19,997	Paid in capital		2,253	2,253
			Retained in earnings		16,198	14,608
			Total shareholders'equity		19,702	17,612
Total assets	$44,110	$43,901	Total liabilities and equity		$44,110	$43,901

Blocher, Stout, Cokins, Chen: *Cost Management, 4e*

©The McGraw-Hill Companies, Inc 2008

Table 1 (continued)

FINANCIAL STATEMENTS
MIDWEST PETRO-CHEMICAL, INC.
Statement of Income (000s)
For the Years Ending December 31

	2007	2006	2005	2004
Net Sales	$95,652	$92,333	$90,114	$86,414
Costs of Sales and Selling cost				
Cost of sales	77,719	74,882	74,374	70,859
Selling	13,712	13,388	13,049	12,703
Total costs	91,431	88,270	87,423	83,562
Operating income	4,221	4,063	2,691	2,852
Interest expense	914	1,214	1,612	1,728
Income before income	3,307	2,849	1,079	1,124
Income tax expense	992	854	270	259
Net Income	2,315	1,995	809	865
Earnings per share	$3.08	$2.66	$1.08	$1.15
Dividends per share	.30	.25	.22	.20

Statement of Cash Flows (000s)
For the Year Ending December 31, 2007

Operating activities	
Net income	$2,315
Additions (sources of cash)	
Depreciation	1,407
Decrease in inventory	1,153
Increase in accounts payable	2,320
Increase in accrued expense	500
Subtractions	
Increase in accounts receivable	(1,109)
Increase in prepaid assets	(332)
Net Cash provided by operating activities	6,254
Long-term investing activities	
Cash used to acquire fixed assets	(1,030)
Financing activities	
Decrease on long-term debt	(4,701)
Payment of dividends	(225)
Net cash provided by financing activities	(4,926)
Net increase in cash	298
Cash at beginning of year	212
Cash at end of year	$ 510

19-2 Evaluating a Firm

REQUIRED:

Consider the financial data below for the Example Company, and assess the value of the Company. Explain your choice(s) of valuation method(s). All figures are 000s except for share price

Example Company
Selected Financial Data

Account Description	2002	2003	2004	2005	2006	2007
Cash	25,141	25,639	32,977	34,009	49,851	30,943
Accounts Receivable	272,450	312,776	368,267	419,731	477,324	542,751
Prepaids	3,982	4,402	5,037	5,246	5,378	6,648
Inventories	183,722	208,623	222,128	260,492	298,696	399,533
Property & Equipment (net)	47,578	49,931	55,311	61,832	77,173	91,420
Other Assets	18,734	20,738	23,075	26,318	36,248	39,403
Total Assets	551,607	622,109	706,795	807,628	944,670	1,110,698
Accounts Payable	49,831	64,321	70,853	80,861	94,677	78,789
Accrued Expenses	86,087	102,650	113,732	131,899	143,159	164,243
Notes Payable	99,539	118,305	182,132	246,420	237,741	390,034
Long-term Debt	62,622	43,251	35,407	32,301	128,432	126,672
Deferred Taxes Payable	7,551	7,941	8,286	8,518	9,664	11,926
Other Liabilities	5,279	5,521	5,697	5,593	5,252	4,695
Total Liabilities	310,909	341,989	416,107	505,592	618,925	776,359
Capital Stock	73,253	87,851	79,009	71,601	81,238	73,186
Retained Earnings	167,445	192,539	211,679	230,435	244,507	261,153
Total Stockholders Equity	240,698	280,120	290,688	302,036	325,745	334,339
Total Liabilities & Equity	551,607	662,109	706,795	807,628	944,670	1,110,698
Net Sales	982,244	1,095,083	1,214,666	1,259,116	1,378,251	1,648,500
Cost of Goods Sold	669,560	739,459	817,671	843,192	931,237	1,125,261
Depreciation Expense	8,303	8,380	8,972	9,619	10,577	12,004
Interest Expense	11,248	13,146	14,919	18,874	16,562	21,128
Income Tax Expense	26,650	34,000	38,000	32,800	26,500	25,750
Dividends Paid	13,805	17,160	19,280	20,426	20,794	20,807
Net Income	32,563	37,895	41,809	39,577	35,212	37,787
Number of common shares outstanding at year-end	12,817	13,714	13,728	13,684	14,023	13,993
Market price per share	38	43	55	65	43	31

Blocher, Stout, Cokins, Chen: *Cost Management, 4e*

19-2 Economic Value Added;
Review of Chapter 18; Strategy[1]

"I've been hearing a lot lately about something called EVA, which stands for Economic Value Added, and I was curious whether it is something we can use at OSI," Keith Martin said as he finished his lunch. Keith is president and CEO of OutSource, Inc. His guest for lunch that day was a computer industry analyst from a local brokerage firm. Keith had invited him to lunch so he could get more information on EVA and its uses.

"Yes," the analyst replied, "I've heard a great deal about EVA. It's a residual income approach in which a firm's net operating profit after taxes—called NOPAT—is reduced by a minimum level of return a firm must earn on the total amount of capital placed at its disposal.

"Have you seen the recent articles on EVA? The after-tax operating profit, NOPAT as you called it, and the amount used for capital don't come directly off the financial statements. You have to analyze the footnotes to determine the adjustments that have to be made to come up with those amounts."

"The article sounds like interesting reading for me, especially at this point," Keith said. "Can you send me a copy?"

"Sure," said the analyst. "But tell me, what is it about EVA that piqued your interest in trying it at OSI?"

"In tracking our industry," Keith replied, "I see the stock prices of some of our key competitors, like Equifax, increasing. Yet, when I compare OSI's recent growth in sales and earnings, our return on equity and earnings per share compare well to those firms, but our stock price doesn't achieve nearly the same rate of increase, and I don't understand why."

The analyst suggested, "Some of those firms might be benefiting from using EVA already, and the market value of their stock probably reflects the results of their efforts. It has been shown that a higher level of correlation exists between EVA and a stock's market value than has been found with the traditional accounting performance measures like ROE or EPS."

"But will EVA work in a small service firm like OSI?"

"I've read about EVA being used at smaller firms," said the analyst. "I'm not an expert on EVA, but I don't see any reason why it wouldn't work at OSI."

"I'd like to find out more about EVA and how we can use it at OSI. For example, we've talked about a new incentive plan-will EVA work in that area? And, if so, will it help us in deciding how we should organize and manage our operations as we expand and grow? What can you do to get more information on these things to me?"

COMPANY INFORMATION

OutSource, Inc. (OSI) is a computer service bureau that provides basic data processing and general business support services to a number of business firms, including several large firms in the immediate local area. Its offices are in a large city in the mid-Atlantic region, and it serves client firms in several Mid-Atlantic States. OSI's revenues have grown rapidly in recent years as businesses have downsized and outsourced many of their basic support services.

The CorpInfo Data Service (CIDS) classifies OSI as an Information Services firm (SIC 7374). This group is composed, in large part, of smaller, independent entrepreneurs that provide a variety of often disparate services to both corporate and government clients. Market analysts feel a continuously healthy economy translates into strong potential for higher earnings by members of this group. A factor sustaining an extended period of growth is the increased attention of firms to control costs and to outsource their non-core functions, such as personnel placement, payroll, human resources, insurance, and data processing. This trend is expected to continue, probably at an increasing rate. Several firms in this industry have capitalized on their growth and geographic expansion to win lucrative contracts with large clients that previously had been awarded on a market-by-market basis.

Although OSI operates out of its own facilities, which include some computing equipment and furniture, the bulk of its computer processing power is obtained from excess computer capacity in the local area, primarily rented time during third-shift operations at a large local bank. To be successful in the long term, however, OSI management knows it must expand its business considerably, and, to ensure it has full control over its opera-

---

[1] Prepared by Paul A. Dierks, © Institute of Management Accountants, 1998. Used with permission.

tions, it must set up its own large-scale computing facility in-house. These items are included in OSI's strategic plan.

As OSI's reputation for accurate, reliable, and quick response service has spread, the firm has found new business coming its way in a variety of data processing and support services. The issue has been deciding which services to take on or to stay out of in light of the current limitations on OSI's computing resources and assurance it can continue to provide high-quality service to its customers. Things definitely are looking up for OSI, and industry market analysts recently have begun to look more favorably on its stock.

In 2005, OSI's board decided to pursue additional opportunities in payroll processing and tax filing services, and OSI purchased a medium-sized firm that had an established market providing payroll calculations, processing, and reporting services for several Fortune 500 firms on the East Coast. Now OSI is in the midst of developing a new payroll processing system, called PayNet, to replace the outmoded system that was originally created by the firm it acquired.

Once PayNet is developed, it will give users an integrated payroll solution with a simpler, more familiar graphic user interface. From an administrative perspective, it will allow OSI to reduce its manual data entry hiring, to speed data compilation and analysis, and to simplify administrative tasks and the updating of customer files for adds, moves, and changes. PayNet will serve as the backbone for OSI's service bureau payroll processing operations in the future, but developmental and programming costs have been higher than expected and will delay the roll out of the final version of the new payroll program. Beta testing of the production version of PayNet is being delayed from the second to the third quarter of 2008.

TABLE 1 OUTSOURCE INC.
Balance Sheet
December 31,

ASSETS	2007	2006
Current Assets:		
Cash	$144,724	$169,838
Trade and other receivables (net)	217,085	192,645
Inventories	15,829	23,750
Other current assets	61,047	49,239
Total current assets	438,685	435,472
Noncurrent Assets:		
Property, plant, equipment	123,135	109,600
Software and development costs	33,760	14,947
Data processing equipment & furniture	151,357	141,892
Other noncurrent assets	3,650	8,844
	311,902	275,283
Less: Accumulated depreciation	85,108	57,929
Total (net) noncurrent assets	226,884	217,354
Goodwill	88,200	96,600
	$753,769	$749,426

LIABILITIES AND SHAREHOLDERS' EQUITY

	2007	2006
Current liabilities		
Short-term debt & current portion of long-term note	$27,300	$31,438
Accounts payable	67,085	57,483
Deferred income	45,050	32,250
Income taxes payable	19,936	12,100
Employee compensation and benefits accrued	30,155	28,950
Other accrued expenses	28,458	27,553
Other current liabilities	17,192	29,769
Total current liabilities	235,176	219,543
Long-term note, less current portion	98,744	117,155
Deferred income taxes	6,784	4,850
Shareholders' Equity:		
Cumulative Nonconvertible Preferred Stock, $100 par value, authorized 5,000 shares, issued and outstanding 1,000 shares	100,000	100,000
Common stock, $1 par value; 300,000 shares authorized; 219,884 shares issued & outstanding	219,884	219,884
Additional paid-in capital	32,056	32,056
Retained earnings	61,125	55,938
Total shareholders' equity	413,065	407,878
	$753,769	$749,426

OutSource, Inc. - Statement of Income for
The Year Ended December 31, 2007

Operating revenue	$2,604,530
Less: Costs of services	1,466,350
Gross profit	1,138,180
Less: Operating expenses	
Selling, general and administrative	902,388
Research and development	89,089
Other expense (income)	59,288
Write-off of goodwill and other tangibles	13,511
Earnings (Loss) before interest and taxes	73,904
Interest income	1,009
Interest expense	12,427
Earnings (Loss) before income taxes	62,486
Income tax provision	21,870
Earnings (Loss)	$40,616

Blocher, Stout, Cokins, Chen: *Cost Management, 4e*

OutSource, Inc. - Statement of Cash Flows for
The Year Ended December 31, 2007

Cash Flows from Operating Activities

Net Earnings (Loss)	$40,616
Depreciation	21,978
Amortization of software & development	5,111
Decrease (Increase) in trade & other receivables	(24,440)
Decrease (Increase) in inventories	7,921
Decrease (Increase)in other current assets	(11,808)
Increase (Decrease) in deferred income	9,602
Increase (Decrease) in accounts payable	12,800
Increase (Decrease) in income taxes payable	7,836
Increase (Decrease) in employee compensation and benefits	1,205
Increase (Decrease) in other accrued expenses	905
Increase (Decrease) in other current liabilities	(12,577)
Increase (Decrease) in deferred income taxes	1,934
Net cash provided by (used for) operating activities	61,083

Cash Flows from Investing Activities

Expended for capital assets	(36,619)
Goodwill amortized	8,400
Net cash provided by (used for) investing activities	(28,219)

Cash Flows from Financing Activities

Payment of long-term note	(4,138)
Payment of short-term note	(18,411)
Preferred dividends paid	(11,000)
Common stock dividends paid	(24,429)
Net cash provided by (used for) financing activities	(57,978)

Net Cash Flows Provided (Used)	**(25,114)**
Cash at beginning of year	**$169,838**
Cash at end of year	**$144,724**

ADDITIONAL ACCOUNTING INFORMATION

OSI's financial statements for 2007 appear in Table 1. The following list of information is pertinent to calculating a firm's EVA extracted from the footnotes to OSI's annual report for 2007.

A. Inventories are stated principally at cost (last-in, first-out), which is not in excess of market. Replacement cost would be $2,796 greater than the 2006 inventory balance and $3,613 greater than the 2007 inventory balance.

B. On July 1, 2005, the company acquired CompuPay, a payroll processing and reporting service firm. The acquisition was accounted for as a purchase, and the excess cost over the fair value of net assets acquired was $109,200, which is being amortized on a straight-line basis over 13 years. One-half year of goodwill amortization was recorded in 2005.

C. Research and development costs related to software development are expensed as incurred. Software development costs are capitalized from the point in time when the technological feasibility of a piece of software has been determined until it is ready to be put on line to process customer data. The cost of purchased software, which is ready for service, is capitalized on acquisition. Software development costs and purchased software costs are amortized using the straight-line method over periods ranging from three to seven years. A history of the accounting treatment of software development costs and purchased software costs follow:

	Expensed	Capitalized	Amortized
2005	$166,430	$ 9,585	0
2006	211,852	5,362	$ 4,511
2007	89,089	18,813	5,111
	$467,371	$33,760	$ 9,622

ADDITIONAL FINANCIAL INFORMATION

OSI's common stock is currently trading at $2 per share. A preferred dividend of $11 per share was paid in 2007, and the current price of preferred stock is approximately at its par value. Other information pertaining to OSI's debt and stock follows:

Short-term debt	$ 8,889	8.0%
Long-term debt:		
Current portion	$ 18,411	10.0%
Long-term portion	$ 98,744	10.0%
Total long-term debt	$117,155	

Stock market risk-free rate (90-day T-bills)	=	5.0%
Expected return on the market	=	12.5%
Expected growth rate of dividends	=	8.0%
Income tax rate	=	35.0%

REQUIRED:

1. The management of OutSource, Inc. has asked you to prepare a report explaining EVA (Economic Value Added), how it is calculated, and how it compares to traditional measures of a firm's financial performance. As part of your answer, calculate EVA from OSI's financial report.

2. What are the advantages and disadvantages of using EVA to evaluate OSI's performance on an on-going basis, as well as in assessing the performance of individual managers throughout its organization? How might EVA help OSI attain its strategic goals?

3. OSI management wants to know if EVA can be used as part of an incentive program for its employees, and if so, how it should be implemented.

Blocher, Stout, Cokins, Chen: *Cost Management, 4e*

©The McGraw-Hill Companies, Inc 2008

Readings

19.1: USING SHAREHOLDER VALUE TO EVALUATE STRATEGIC CHOICES

By Nick Fera

Creating shareholder wealth or value has become the mantra for most corporate boards, especially in the United States. Yet as recently as the mid-1980s, the idea of "shareholder value" or "shareholder wealth" was not an overwhelmingly accepted principle. But as academics began to teach the principle in business schools around the world, such noted authorities as Professor Alfred Rappaport of Northwestern University's J. L. Kellogg Graduate School of Management, author of *Creating Shareholder Value*,[1] began to apply it to corporate mergers and acquisitions in the 1980s. Shareholder value, or free cash flow analysis, became the measurement standard for the 1980s and into the 1990s. Given today's increased demand for international capital returns, as well as the proliferation of private baby boomer pension funds in the United States, investors have imposed new stringency in their vigil against corporate wealth destruction. Even the brightest stars are not immune to the pressure of pension funds or Wall Street. Witness the pressure that CALPERS (the state of California's teachers' retirement funds) placed on Michael Eisner at Walt Disney Co. despite Eisner's laudable success in Increasing Disney's market value from $5 billion to more than $42 billion during his first 10 years in office. During a 10-year period from January 1986 to December 1996, Disney's stock price grew at a cumulative annual growth rate of more than 21%, while the S&P 500 index has returned approximately 15%. Historical performances are not always enough; investors continue to ask for more.

Measuring performance no longer can be left to the traditional accounting department's calculations of earnings per share (EPS) or return on equity (ROE), as these accrual-based accounting measures aren't always useful indicators of future growth or performance. Thus, it is necessary to understand and adopt measurement techniques that will help make decisions while driving increasing profitability. One of the economic measurement techniques that can be used is free cash flow analysis or Shareholder Value Analysis (SVA).

SHAREHOLDER VALUE ANALYSIS

Because managers began to realize that businesses needed a more realistic means of assessing their value than accrual-based accounting standards offered, such respected academics as Professor Rappaport sought to develop sophisticated economic models for strategic evaluations. As a result, shareholder value analysis was conceived. SVA works by explicitly measuring the economic impact of each strategy on the value of a business. Any strategic decision, regardless of whether it involves internal or external investment, should be evaluated. Examples of such strategic decision-making situations include mergers and acquisitions, joint ventures, divestitures, new product development (R&D), and capital expenditures (major plant and equipment investments).

The actual measurement of shareholder value combines three main factors: 1) cash flow, 2) cash as measured over a given period of time (value growth duration), and 3) risk, otherwise known as the cost of capital. (See Fig. 1.) With a basic understanding of these three components, you are well on your way to valuing a business or entity. Next, let's discuss the difference between corporate value and shareholder value.

---

[1] Alfred Rappaport, *Creating Shareholder Value: The New Standard for Business Performance*, New York: The Free Press, 1986.

CREATING VALUE

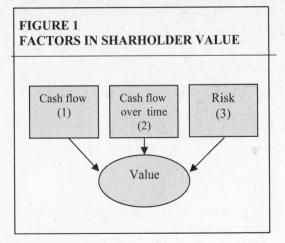

FIGURE 1
FACTORS IN SHARHOLDER VALUE

Cash flow (1) · Cash flow over time (2) · Risk (3) → Value

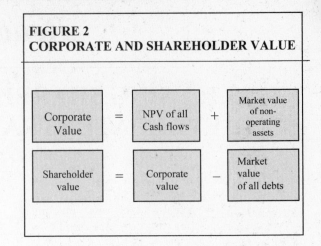

FIGURE 2
CORPORATE AND SHAREHOLDER VALUE

Corporate Value = NPV of all Cash flows + Market value of non-operating assets

Shareholder value = Corporate value − Market value of all debts

Corporate value is equal to the net present value of all future cash flows to all investor types, including both debt and equity holders. Shareholder value is the corporate value minus all future claims to cash flow (debt) before equity holders are paid. Future claims typically include both short-and long-term debt, capital lease obligations, underfunded pensions, and other claims such as contingent liabilities—lawsuits brought against the company. (See Fig. 2.) Another way to define shareholder value is to say that it is equal to the net funds a company generates that shareholders could receive in the form of a cash distribution, such as a dividend.

Be careful not to confuse this figure with the actual dividend a company pays. A company's dividend policy has little or nothing to do with the actual cash the company generates. Look at the high growth of businesses such as computer software or biotechnology. Few pay dividends because they have strategic opportunities to reinvest cash flows and earn the higher returns investors desire.

Generally, it's easy to determine the market value of future obligations or debt. In most cases, it's the accumulation of several debt instruments. To obtain the market value of these financial instruments, use the yield to maturity to calculate the *market value* of each debt instrument. Avoid adding the face value of each debt or bond issue. The question to ask is, "If this obligation were to be paid in full today, how much would the lender need to retire it?"

MEASURING CASH FLOW

After determining corporate and shareholder value, the next step is to measure cash flow. The most tangible measurement of cash flow (also referred to as operating cash flow or free cash flow) can be calculated as shown in Table 1.

Notice that the calculation focuses on the relationship between operating cash income and expenses, specifically by using operating cash taxes rather than the provision for income taxes. It accounts for the investments made on the balance sheet. Many companies measure cash flow by looking at net operating profit after taxes (NOPAT), but it tells only part of the story. Investments to grow the business, either by expansion of the plant and facilities or with working capital policies such as extending the receivable period from net 30 to net 60 days, have a significant impact on the capital employed. Remember: Shareholders are looking for returns on their capital invested in business growth, which requires well-planned capital expenditures. Failure to account for the investment makes for a crucial mistake in the evaluation of strategic alternatives.

CALCULATING CASH FLOWS

The calculation of cash flow illustrates a high level of performance in an organization and produces a result that approximates the net cash of a company. In effect, these funds are a potential dividend to shareholders because they reflect optimal use of shareholder monies for ongoing growth. That is why dividend policy and free cash flow are not synonymous. Few companies base their dividend payout on net cash flow, while others are justified in generating free cash flow, without paying dividends.

To forecast cash flow, most companies require a more detailed formula, as presented in Table 1. In most cases, sales growth tells very little about actual sales activity, so companies use metrics such as price, volume, GNP, and other micro or macroeconomic factors to forecast revenues and costs more realistically. This calculation usually is

Blocher, Stout, Cokins, Chen: *Cost Management, 4e*

TABLE 1
MEASURING CASH FLOW

	Formula	Example	Value Drivers
	Sales	$1,000	Sales growth (Sg)
Less	Operating expenses	–$ 600	Margin (P)
Equals	Pre-tax profit	$ 400	
Less	Cash taxes	–$ 100	Tax rate (T)
Equals	Net operating profit after taxes (NOPAT)	$ 300	
Add	Depreciation expense	$ 75	
Less	Fixed capital investment	–$ 125	Fixed capital investment (F)
Less	Incremental working capital investment	–$ 50	Working capital investment (W)
Equals	Operating cash flow (free cash flow)	$ 250	

conducted at a strategic business unit level and then consolidated for corporate purposes. The key is to plan accurately at the appropriate level of business activity (business unit, value chain, or some other distinction).

Sales or market growth estimations can be achieved many different ways. Predicting price and volume, for instance, provides for a more manageable metric that can be evaluated readily and used later for compensation purposes. In other words, sales growth is a "*value driver.*" But what *drives* the value drivers? Herein typically lies the metric operational professionals can get their hands on. Planning and forecasting can become a real *operating activity rather than a boardroom exercise.*

CASH FLOW OVER TIME

Once cash flow has been defined, the next step is to determine the length of the forecast period. The definition of cash flow over time or value growth duration is the length of time expected for a company to invest in opportunities that will yield internal rates of return (IRR) above their weighted average cost of capital (WACC). This premise is the core of value creation—performing above expectations for a sustainable period of time.

Management usually plans for cycles of three to five years. If this is the case and if the cash flows are discounted over a period of time, the valuation probably will be inaccurate as it does not allow for fluctuations in cash flow throughout the requisite growth period. To determine the appropriate length of the forecast period (or the value growth duration), consider several factors.

One is Michael Porter's work on the competitive structure and five forces of industries (see Fig. 3). Porter says that management's responsibil-

ity is to map the company and its competition according to several factors. Some areas to consider are distribution channels, established brand names, and research and development. Take the pharmaceutical industry, for instance. It has a relatively long value growth duration because of patented products, proven processes, and research and development investment that raise the barriers of entry.

Also, read Alfred Rappaport's discussion of the use of public information to assess the market's expectation for a company's value growth duration.[2] He suggests gathering forecasting information on a particular company as well as identifying competitors. He also advises managers to employ the researched information and forecast the cash flows, as discussed previously. But rather than changing any value driver assumptions, change only the length of the forecast until the present value of the cash flows less debt equals the market value of your company. Surprisingly, most companies in a given industry tend to fall within a certain range; thus, the market is suggesting an implied value growth duration. These "market signals" are helpful for starting an internal analysis and discussion.

RESIDUAL VALUE

Once you have determined the value growth duration, you must address the value of the cash flows beyond the current period. This determination is called the terminal or residual value. Assume that, after the forecast period, new investments (fixed and working capital) will yield returns equal to the

---

[2] Alfred Rappaport, "Stock Market Signals to Managers." *Harvard Business Review,* November-December 1987, pp. 57-62.

cost of capital. In other words, the internal rate of return is equal to the weighted average cost of capital. Therefore, the net present value of cash flows from new or incremental investments beyond the value growth duration will be equal to zero. The only cash flow left to value in the residual period is the preinvestment cash flow, or NOPAT (see Table 1). Note that depreciation is *not* included because it is viewed as a proxy for reinvestment. Given that the cash flows are valued infinitely, the business probably would not continue to generate the same level of cash flow if the plant, equipment, or other physical assets were allowed to deteriorate fully. In fact, some companies recognize a higher level of "maintenance" spending and will adjust the cash flow in the residual period to reflect higher replacement costs.

TERMINAL VALUE

At this point, it is necessary to discuss some assumptions of terminal value. The net present value of the residual cash flows is equal to an infinite stream of cash flow (as measured by NOPAT) discounted back at the WACC. Mathematically, this is NOPAT at the end of the value growth duration divided by the WACC. Once this calculation is complete, it is necessary to discount the value back to the current period. The formula is presented in Table 2 (assuming a five-year value growth duration and 12% WACC).

DEFINING RISK

The last component of determining the value of an entity is deciding on the overall risk. The risk of a company usually is measured with WACC. The approach assumes there is some mixture of debt and equity that is financing the company. The cost of debt is measured as the after-tax cost, that is, the cost accounting for the tax deductibility of interest payments. The marginal cost of debt is not necessarily the average coupon rate on various debt instruments. Instead, it is the rate for which banks will lend the company an incremental dollar.

  The cost of equity is somewhat more complex. If companies use the Capital Asset Pricing Model approach developed by economists Sharpe, Lintner, and Treynor in the mid-1960s, the cost of equity has two basic components: a risk-free return required by investors and a premium for investing in equities that are of higher risk. The risk-free rate is the treasury rate on 30-year U.S. government bonds. This standard generally is used because these bonds typically are seen as delivering the most risk-free, long-term returns investors can earn. The second component is the premium

Measurement Methodologies:
1. Economic Principles
  Shareholder Value Analysis
  (SVA)—also known as Discounted Cash Flow analysis (DCF) or Net Present Value (NPV)

- Evaluates cash inflows to cash outflows on a risk-adjusted basis

- Most widely accepted approach to business evaluation

  Economic Value Analysis (EVA)

- Primarily used as a performance measurement tool to calculate period-by-period performance

- Helps an organization to focus on value creation or increased cash flow

- Measuring the change in EVA also may be an effective financial measurement tool

  Cash Flow Return on Investment (CFROI)

- Derived from market data to determine cash flow growth and the overall discount rate

- Helps an organization to focus on value creation or increased cash flow

- Seen as a complex financial measurement device

2. Accounting Principles
  Return on Capital (ROC)
  Return on Invested Capital (ROIC)
  Return on Equity (ROE)
  Earnings per Share (EPS)

for investing in something that is of higher risk than the U.S. government. This element is called the market risk premium (MRP itself and a multiplier, called beta, for investments that are more or less risky than the market portfolio.

Blocher, Stout, Cokins, Chen: *Cost Management, 4e*

MARKET RISK PREMIUM

The market risk premium is calculated and published by sources such as Ibbotson Associates in its annual SBBI (Stocks, Bonds, Bills, and Inflation). Historically, the premium for holding a portfolio of equities, as opposed to investing in a risk-free instrument, is between 6% and 7%, depending on whether you use the arithmetic or geometric average.   Beta is a measure of the relative riskiness of an individual company or portfolio as compared with the market. Thus a beta of 1.0 correlates exactly with market returns. Beta is measured by comparing the returns of an individual security or portfolio with those of the market. Sources of beta estimates include Merrill Lynch, ValueLine, and Alcar.

There is another way to measure the MRP that is consistent with a forecasting approach. This tack uses estimates of the expected return on the market for the next year. Each month Merrill Lynch publishes a 12-month expected return on the market (S&P 500). Using this forecast, you can determine the expected MRP by subtracting the current risk-free rate, as measured by 30-year treasuries, from the current forecast of market returns. As of October 1, 1997, Merrill Lynch's forecast of market returns was 10.9%, while the risk-free rate is currently 6.38%. As a result, the expected market risk premium is 4.52%. Some companies prefer to use the ex-ante approach because it matches the *forecasting* of cash flows with the *forecasting* of expected returns.

Putting all the components of the cost of equity equation together yields the following formula:

Cost of Equity = Risk-free rate + Beta * (Market Risk Premium) or, $K_e = R_f + \beta * (MRP)$

Once you have calculated the cost of equity and the cost of debt, you may use the WACC approach to combine both costs (debt and equity). In calculating the WACC, use the market values of debts and equity, not the book values, because the market costs of each source of financing are being measured. The equation is as follows:

WACC (K_c) = % of Debt * [Cost of Debt (K_d)] + % of Equity * [Cost of Equity (K_e)]

Let's look at an example involving a manufacturing company using risk estimation:

A U.S. manufacturing company is publicly traded and has a market capitalization of $550 million. Its outstanding debt totals $250 million at a marginal borrowing rate of 8.5% (assume this is the market value of debt and includes all obligations of the company). The current risk-free rate is 7%, the expected return on the market is 12%, the beta of this company has been published as .90, and its marginal tax rate is 28%. What is the weighted average cost of capital (WACC)?

MRP	= 12 − 7	= 5%
K_e	= .07 + .9(.05)	= 11.5%
K_d	= .085 * (1 − 28)	= 6.12% (after tax)
WACC	= (250/800) * .0612 + (550/800) * .115	= 9.8%

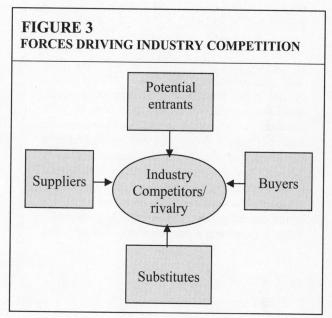

FIGURE 3
FORCES DRIVING INDUSTRY COMPETITION

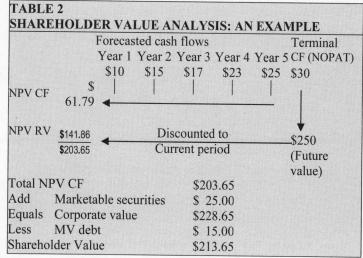

TABLE 2
SHAREHOLDER VALUE ANALYSIS: AN EXAMPLE

	Forecasted cash flows					Terminal
	Year 1	Year 2	Year 3	Year 4	Year 5	CF (NOPAT)
	$10	$15	$17	$23	$25	$30
NPV CF	$61.79					
NPV RV	$141.86	Discounted to				$250
	$203.65	Current period				(Future value)

Total NPV CF		$203.65
Add	Marketable securities	$ 25.00
Equals	Corporate value	$228.65
Less	MV debt	$ 15.00
Shareholder Value		$213.65

FROM THE BOARDROOM
TO THE SHOP FLOOR

Once you have established the methodology, take it out of the boardroom (as a planning exercise), and implement it at all levels, including the shop floor (or any manufacturing or operating activity). The importance of moving the analysis out of the boardroom and into regular practice is that managers and shareholders will have the same economic interests. If managers are compensated on accrual-based accounting measures, they may optimize their own interest when there is a conflict between cash flow and accrual accounting. But if you align the interest and performance measurement of all managers to be the same, both are optimized.

Moving the methodology to the shop floor may pose a challenge. Not only is it more difficult to identify key value drivers on the shop floor (such as production yield, waste, inventory management), but there also is an important educational component. Not all managers have been introduced to the concepts and methodologies of financial metrics. Many still are entrenched with the simpler accrual-based accounting measures. Yet once key drivers are identified and their relative impact on value is measured, managers relate to the results.

ONGOING MAINTENANCE AND
PERFORMANCE MEASUREMENT

Once the methodology is in place, the final challenge is to put it into practice every year. What adds to the complexity of the implementation is the ability to monitor performance in a timely manner due to the multitude of manual and multiple systems currently in place to do the job. Many companies implement and attempt to monitor their performance with the use of disconnected spreadsheet technology. Beyond all the difficulties of performing rigorous economic analysis in a spreadsheet (with factual integrity and documentation leading the pack), the use of spreadsheets can create pockets of information that are disjointed from the rest of the organization. These pockets of information make it difficult to monitor performance, test new scenarios regularly, and make new, informed decisions on a timely basis.

Fortunately, the recent development of new technologies that interface seemlessly with each other is making it easier to gather data quickly and spend the majority of analytical time on planning, testing, and choosing new strategic alternatives. Thus, the planning process is changing from an annual event generally found on the bookshelf to a regularly used strategic exercise that becomes a living document, enabling companies to manage their business by making value-based strategic choices in our ever-evolving environment.

Blocher, Stout, Cokins, Chen: *Cost Management, 4e*

19.2: THE ROLE OF STRATEGY

By Priscilla Q. Clock, CPA, Ph.D, and Kevin Devine, Ph.D.

A primary challenge facing many U.S.-based multinational corporations (MNCs) is the evaluation of foreign strategic business units (SBUs). The way an organization evaluates and measures performance determines the motivation behind the decisions and actions of an SBU's managers. Failure to consider the strategic objectives of an SBU or the cultural identity of its management is an error many MNCs commit when they export the evaluation systems of the parent entity to the foreign SBU. This often results in decisions by the SBU's managers that are incongruent with corporate goals and objectives.

The consideration of cultural differences is particularly important when the management of an international SBU is delegated to host country personnel. All too frequently, multinational corporations mistakenly evaluate their performance using return on investment (ROI) or one of its variants, such as residual income (RI) or economic value added (EVA), regardless of the business unit strategy. This can lead to management control systems that result in suboptimal decision making, conflicting corporate and SBU objectives, and a negative impact on morale. Return-based measures play a role in evaluating performance, but, used improperly, they perpetuate a short-term orientation and may be inconsistent with the cultural preferences that motivate the local manager.

When developing control systems to evaluate the performance of an international SBU—and rewarding its managers—companies should design performance measures that consider the impact of business unit strategies and cultural differences. In this article, we will present competing business unit strategies and suggest variants to the control system to compensate for these differences. We also will discuss cultural dimensions as identified by Geert Hofstede and make a case that the impact of these cultural differences needs to be incorporated into the design and implementation of management control systems for foreign

SBUs.[1] Finally, we suggest performance measures to emphasize and implementation issues to consider when designing accounting control systems that integrate strategic and cultural differences.

STRATEGIC OBJECTIVES

There is no one-size-fits-all answer for the effective design of control systems. When an SBU manager's reward system is matched with the SBU's strategy, performance will match corporate strategy, and objectives will be enhanced. Failure to match strategy and reward will adversely affect the manager's motivation and efforts. The strategy for an SBU is dependent on its mission and the consideration of environmental opportunities, internal strengths, and the resources available to accomplish its goals and objectives.[2] Three approaches to control system design that foster goal congruence are: situation specific, universalistic, and contingency.[3] The situation-specific model views each situation as unique, so application of general rules is not possible. Universalists argue that an optimal control system design will be effective in all settings. The contingency approach, which has become the prominent paradigm, is positioned between these two extremes. It suggests that the appropriateness of the control system depends on the business setting (like the situation-specific approach), but generalization (universalistic approach) can be made across similar settings. If the SBU mission or competitive strategy varies across divisions within the organization, the control system must be modified to capture the relevant performance measures and motivate SBU managers accordingly.[4] Strategic mission or business unit strategies are commonly grouped into the following areas: build, hold, harvest, and divest.[5] Competitive strategies include: low cost, differentiation, focus, defender, or prospector.[6]

STRATEGIC MISSION

The mission of an international SBU is related to lifecycle concepts. A build mission implies the goal of increasing market share and typically applies to any SBU with low market share in a high-growth industry. In order to build a competitive advantage, it may be necessary for the manager to sacrifice short-term earnings and/or cash flow. Also, a build strategy implies an increase in production, which results in additional use of the firm's resources. Performance measures that focus mainly on profit or return would be in conflict with the overall mission of the SBU. The manager, therefore, should be evaluated and rewarded primarily on achieving a targeted increase in sales or market share, with profitability measures (with a great deal of slack) a secondary objective.

The hold strategy applies to an SBU with a high market share in a high-growth industry. Though profit oriented accounting performance measures would be appropriate, nonfinancial measures also should be incorporated, such as customer service, maintaining market share, and quality measures.

The goal of a harvest SBU is to maximize short-term cash flows and earnings at the expense of market share (high market share, low-growth industry). These earnings can then supplement other business units that may be in build strategies. To align management decision making with the harvest strategy, the control system should evaluate performance using one of the conventional return measures, such as ROI, RI, or EVA. Measures of cash flow also may be appropriate. Profit and return measures have a much tighter acceptable range and should be adhered to strictly. In a low-market-share, low-growth industry, the SBU's strategy may be to divest through a process of slow withdrawal or outright sale. The appropriate control system at this stage is unique to the particular situation. Presumably, the objective is to maximize cash flows. This strategy represents the end of the life-cycle stages, however, and is a unique situation with a limited ability to generalize. Therefore, we will skip the discussion of control models for the divest strategy.

COMPETITIVE STRATEGIES

An SBU with a low-cost competitive strategy attempts to achieve lower costs relative to competitors. Typical low-cost actions include taking advantage of economies of scale; learning-curve effects; reducing customer service, research and development, advertising, and/or sales force; and maintaining a stable product line. Strict adherence to cost standards through variance analysis and other measures of operating efficiency, such as cycle time and inventory turnover, would be appropriate measures to evaluate and control performance in this competitive environment. Further, A. A. Thompson and A. J. Strickland, III, suggest that significant cost advantages can emerge from an analysis of an entity's internal and external value chain.[7]

Low-cost participants must be careful, however, because the marketplace will still demand a minimum level of product quality and functionality. A differentiation strategy focuses the SBU manager's attention on brand loyalty, customer service, product design, and technology. The goal is to create a product that customers view as unique and exclusive. Product innovation is critical. To create uniqueness, the SBU is likely to have a more diversified set of products or functionally superior products compared to a low-cost competitor, and it must invest in research and product development, technology, marketing, and customer service. Achieving a target ROI does not measure progress effectively within this strategy. While traditional financial performance measures still play a role, nonfinancial performance measures, such as quality, on-time deliveries, customer satisfaction, and number of new products to market, must be emphasized.

An SBU with a focus strategy targets a narrow competitive market within an industry segment. The specific objectives could be either low cost or differentiation. Design of the control system must be tailored to the selected objective. SBUs with a defender strategy engage in limited product/market research, have limited product lines, and have a stable environment. Defenders compete through cost and quality control. This strategy is consistent with the features of the hold and harvest missions. ROI, RI, and EVA may be effective control measures if they are incorporated with variance analysis, operating efficiency measures, and quality variables.

Prospector SBUs, similar to differentiators, compete by focusing on market development, new product development, and searching (prospecting) for market opportunities. These SBUs are often in a build strategic mission. Profit-oriented performance measures would not capture progress toward goals and objectives. The number of new products to market, customer satisfaction, quality, sales from products developed in the last 24 months, and market share would evaluate and control the manager more appropriately.

As we said, there is no single performance measure or control system applicable across different business unit strategies that provides a basis for aligning management decision making with corporate goals. The specific control system must be modified and aligned with the particular strategy of the SBU. The preferences of the SBU manager in the design of the control system, therefore, must not be ignored. For example, the preferences of international SBU managers for autonomy, level of uncertainty, risk, participation, group versus individual rewards, and short- versus long-term rewards may be influenced by their cultural identity. In turn, consideration of

Blocher, Stout, Cokins, Chen: *Cost Management, 4e*

cultural differences in the design of a control system can increase its effectiveness.

CULTURAL FACTORS

These days, more and more MNCs use local management talent to operate a foreign subsidiary rather than relying on "imported" expatriates.[8] U.S. MNCs frequently export the home country control system to the host country SBU but fail to consider the impact of cultural factors. Effectiveness of the management control system depends on whether the local manager of the SBU perceives the control system as aligned with the shared values maintained in the host country.[9] Hofstede defined culture as "the collective programming of the mind that distinguishes the members of one category of people from those of another."[10] In perhaps the most extensive and most frequently cited research conducted with respect to cultural differences, Hofstede identified five underlying cultural dimensions—power distance, uncertainty avoidance, individualism versus collectivism, masculinity versus femininity, and Confucian dynamism—and assigned scores on them to more than 50 countries.[11] Table 1 shows the relative scores for some of these countries.

Let's look at these dimensions. **Power distance** indicates the extent a society accepts an unequal distribution of power, and this is one of the most important dimensions to consider when designing a control system. A manager of an SBU in a high power distance culture (Malaysia, Guatemala, Mexico, Singapore, Brazil, Hong Kong) is more likely to accept tight budgetary controls, discretionary bonuses, and subjective performance evaluation. Managers and subordinates in a low power-distance country (Austria, New Zealand, Sweden, U.K., Germany, Canada, U.S.) desire more equity in performance evaluation, less budgetary control, participative budgeting, standardized (perhaps formula-based) rewards, easy access to superiors, and open channels of communication. An autocratic manager in these countries is likely to run into resentment and discontent from subordinates.

Uncertainty avoidance refers to the society's preference for risk-free, unambiguous situations. A culture with a high uncertainty-avoidance score (Greece, Guatemala, Japan, Chile, Argentina, Spain) reflects a preference for control systems that adhere to clearly defined performance measures with unambiguous links to performance evaluation and reward. A low uncertainty-avoidance culture (Singapore, Hong Kong, Sweden, U.K., Malaysia), on the other hand, is more open to less structured control systems where rewards are either discretionary or include a bonus scheme rather than fixed compensation. With a preference for uncertainty avoidance, security in one's position is paramount and rigid, and specific rules that reduce uncertainty are generally accepted. Ambiguity in the control system may be perceived as a continuous threat and result in low morale, high turnover, and increased stress and anxiety.

In Hofstede's research, there appears to be an interaction of power distance and uncertainty avoidance. Though the surveyed countries scatter across all four quadrants, there is a significant grouping of countries in the low power distance, low uncertainty avoidance sector (Sweden, U.K., U.S., Canada) and in the high power distance, high uncertainty avoidance quadrant (Spain, Mexico, Argentina, Chile, Brazil).[12] The countries in the former group prefer participation in the budget process, but they also would accept increased risk in the reward structure. Countries in the latter group represent cultures that accept inequality in the power structure and a lack of participative budgets, but they would demand certain fixed rewards.

Individualism versus collectivism represents the degree that members of a society perceive themselves as individuals rather than as members of a group. Countries with a high score on this dimension (U.S., U.K., Canada, New Zealand, Italy, Sweden) reflect a culture with preferences for individual versus group rewards, independence, and recognition of personal achievement. Tight budgetary controls can be perceived as stifling individual performance. In contrast, a control system with slack budgetary controls and individual rewards imposed on a collectivist culture (Guatemala, Singapore, Hong Kong, Malaysia, Mexico, Greece, Brazil, Chile) would be perceived as contrary to societal norms. Such a system highlights individual differences and promotes competition and interpersonal rivalries, contrary to a preference for group harmony and equality.

Masculinity versus femininity indicates the extent that the "masculine" values of assertiveness, ambition, independence, competitiveness, and male dominance are revered over the "feminine" values of nurturing, interdependence, service motivation, quality of life, and equality between sexes. In Hofstede's research, the higher a country scored on masculinity, the greater the gap between the values of its men and women. In a high-masculinity country (Japan, Austria, Mexico, Germany, U.K.), managers are more accepting of stretch budgets and would prefer a focus on individual achievement with performance evaluated relative to peers. In a high-masculinity country such as Japan, the high

Confucianism factor (discussed next) and relatively low individualism score may mitigate the desire for individual recognition. In addition, anecdotal evidence suggests that managers of SBUs in some high-masculinity countries may be open to stretch budgets, but when they fail to deliver they still expect their fixed reward. In low-masculinity countries (Sweden, Chile, Spain, Singapore, Brazil, Canada), a strong emphasis on bottom-line profitability with little concern for members of the organization will be met with resistance and is therefore counterproductive to achieving SBU goals. Quality-of-life values such as a friendly work environment, cooperation, and intrinsic rewards are likely to be motivational factors combined with a preference for group performance evaluation versus individual, incentive-based rewards.

The fifth cultural dimension, **Confucian dynamism,** reflects the relative importance of persistence, perseverance, ordered status, and thrift. These characteristics have been interpreted to refer to differences between Eastern and Western cultures and the extent that a culture pursues long-term orientation and growth. A proactive approach prevails in high-Confucianism countries, resulting in a willingness to sacrifice current success in exchange for future profitability. The SBU manager in a country scoring high on Confucianism (Hong Kong, Japan, Brazil) can be motivated by deferred compensation plans with a focus on growth and less emphasis on current financial performance measures. The manager in a low-scoring culture (New Zealand, Canada, U.K., U.S.) is oriented toward the past and present with a preference for evaluation of the unit's ability to meet short-term financial goals.

The potential exists for conflict in preferences across cultural factors within the same country. In a high uncertainty-avoidance culture, the manager's preference would be for tight budget control with a fixed performance reward. If the country also scores high on individualism, however, a tight budget control would conflict with the manager's preference for independence and performance-based rewards. When factors conflict within a single culture, the control system should target congruence with the dominant cultural dimension as well as align with business strategy.[13]

INTEGRATION OF STRATEGY AND CULTURE

A thorough discussion of each combination of business unit strategies and cultural factors is beyond the scope of this article, but Table 2 does present a summary of both the performance measures to be considered (what) and the manner in which these factors should be determined, budgeted, and rewarded (how) across competing strategies and cultural dimensions.

The performance measures to be considered—the "what"—are factors "a" through "f" in the Table key. The "how" to measure is represented by factors "g" through "z." The columns of Table 2 list business unit/competitive strategies, and the rows list high or low scores on each of the five cultural dimensions. For example, the first two rows present how evaluations and rewards should be determined for managers of SBUs in countries scoring high or low on individualism. If the country scored high, the reward system should permit slack in the process, reward individual effort, and reward the business unit rather than utilizing company based rewards ("h" is slack in budgetary controls; "j" is individual rewards; "l" is business-unit versus companybased rewards). Note that for each row the factors related to how ("g" through "z") are consistent across the respective high or low cultural dimension.

Each cell also integrates the appropriate performance measures (what) to consider across competing business unit strategies or competitive strategies within this cultural dimension. Within each strategy, these factors are also consistent across all cultural dimensions. For example, when the business unit strategy is hold, the suggested performance measures are: maintain market share (b) and quality and/or customer service measures (d). Thus, each cell of Table 2 considers the joint impact of strategy and culture when indicating the most appropriate performance measurements and evaluations.

For an SBU with a harvest strategy in a culture with high scores on individualism, the suggested measurement tools are return metrics, but these measurements should be calculated and evaluated at the business-unit level rather than being incorporated into measures of overall company performance. In addition, the manager would tend to have a strong aversion to tight or strict standards and would more than likely prefer individual versus group rewards. An SBU pursuing a differentiate strategy in a high-masculinity culture should be evaluated using quality and/or customer service measures and number of new products to market. The manager of this SBU will be motivated by extrinsic rewards and individual evaluation relative to peers.

If an SBU in Mexico, which has high scores in power distance and uncertainty avoidance, has a build mission and a differentiate competitive strategy, the performance measures should emphasize market share as well as quality, customer service measures, and the number of new products brought to market. Cultural dimensions suggest that the manager will accept tight budgetary controls with respect to targets but would like some input in setting these targets. In addition, high uncertainty avoidance predicts the manager will prefer frequent fixed rewards with a short-term orientation. High power distance, however, indicates the manager will be open to subjective evaluations and discretionary bonuses. Where cultural dimensions are in conflict like this, the dominant dimension should be given more weight. A control system that provides for evaluation using a strict profit orientation with no input from the manager into the budget process would be frustrating, dysfunctional, in conflict with both strategic and cultural factors, and probably would result in low morale and decision making in conflict with the SBU's strategic objectives.

As these examples suggest, the integration of strategy and culture in the design of control systems can be difficult. The complexity of this task increases when a company considers different approaches to the development and the management of international business units. For example, some MNCs may choose to rely heavily on local managers while others may export management from their home country. When local management is used, there can be significant variation in the degree of experience the local manager has within the parent company. A local manager who has extensive experience with the parent entity and has been indoctrinated in the MNC's home country culture may be less affected by the dominant cultural dimensions in the host country. In each of the examples, the importance of the host country's dominant cultural dimensions may vary. Similarly, the competitive strategies we discussed may not be all-inclusive. Some MNCs may continue to operate SBUs that would otherwise be divested because they provide a source of raw materials or meet the needs of strategically important customers. In such cases, the parent entity should adopt a control system aligned with the purpose of the SBU.

Evaluating the performance of foreign SBUs and their managers is an imposing task for multinational companies. Critical to the design of management control systems is the need to consider both the mission of the SBU and the cultural identities of its management. We have proposed guidelines related to which performance measures are most appropriate for a given business unit or competitive strategy while providing insight into how control system measures should be implemented across different cultures. Consideration of what to measure—as well as how to measure it—will result in the design of control systems that increase goal congruence and reduce conflict between an SBU and its parent entity. Failure to consider the impact of strategy and culture in the design of control systems can result in dissonance, suboptimal decision making, dysfunctional behavior, and managers who lack motivation and suffer from low morale.

Table 1: Relative Scores for Selected Countries on Cultural Dimensions

Country	Individualism	Uncertainty Avoidance	Power Distance	Masculinity	Confucianism
Argentina	46	86	49	58	NA
Austria	55	70	11	79	NA
Brazil	38	76	69	49	65
Canada	80	48	39	52	23
Chile	38	86	63	28	NA
Germany	67	65	35	66	31
Great Britain	89	35	35	66	25
Greece	35	112	60	57	NA
Guatemala	6	101	95	37	NA
Hong Kong	25	29	68	57	96
Italy	76	75	50	70	NA
Japan	46	92	54	95	80
Malaysia	26	36	104	50	NA
Mexico	30	82	81	69	NA
New Zealand	79	49	22	58	0
Singapore	20	8	74	48	48
Spain	51	86	57	42	NA
Sweden	71	29	31	5	33
United States	91	46	40	62	29
Range	6-91	8-112	11-104	5-95	0-96
Median	38	68	60	49	2

Blocher, Stout, Cokins, Chen: *Cost Management, 4e*

©The McGraw-Hill Companies, Inc 2008

Table 2: Performance Evaluation Measures and Control Characteristics
Integrating Strategy and Culture

Cultural Dimension	Business Unit Strategy			Product Line Strategy				
	Build	Hold	Harvest	Low Cost	Differentia-tion	Focus	Defender	Prospec-tor
High indi-vidualism	a,h,j,l	b.d.f.h.j.l	e.f.h.j.l.	e,h,j,l	c,d,h,j,l	a,h,j,l	d,ef,b,j,l	a.c.d.h.j.l
Low indi-vidualism	a,g,i,m	b,d,f,g,i,m	e,f,g,i,m	e,g,i,m	c,d,g,i,m	a,g,i,m	d,e,f,g,i,m	a,c,d,g,i,m
High Power distance	a,g,o	b,d,f,g,o	a,f,g,o	e,g,o	c,d,g,o	a,g,o	d,e,f,g,o	a,c,d,g,o
Low power distance	a,h,n	b,d,f,h,n	e,f,h,n	e,h,n	c,d,h,n	a,h,n	d,e,f,h,n	a,c,d,h,n
High uncer-tainty avoidance	a,g,n,w,z	b,d,f,n,w,z	e,f,n,w,z	e,n,w,z	c,d,n,w,z	a,n,w,z	d,e,f,n,w,z	a.c.d.n.w.z
Low uncer-tainty avoidance	a.h.o.v	b,d,f,h,o,v	e,f,h,o,v	e,h,o,v	c,d,h,o,v	a,h,o,v	d,e,f,h,o,v	a,c,d,h,o,v
High mas-culinity	a,k,r,y	b,d,fk,r,y	e,f,k,r,y	e,k,r,y	c,d,k,r,y	a.k.r.y	d.e.f.k.r.y	a.c.d.k.r.y
Low mascu-linity	a,i,q,s	b,d,f,i,q,s	e,f,i,q,s	e,i,q,s	c,d,i,q,s	a,i,q,s	d,e,f,i,q,s	a,c,d,i,q,s
High Con-fucianism	a,v,x,z	b,d,f,v,x,z	e,f,v,x,z	e,v,x,z	c,d,v,x,z,	a,v,x,z	d,e,f,v,x,z	a,c,d,v,x,z
Low Con-fucianism	a,p,t,u	b,d,f,p,t,u	e,f,p,t,u	e,p,t,u	c,d,p,t,u	a,p,t,u	d,e,f,p,t,u	a,c,d,p,t,u

a) focus on market share and/or sales growth
b) maintain market share
c) new products to market
d) quality and/or customer service measures
e) cost management/efficiency measures
f) return-based measures (e.g., ROI, EVA)
g) tight budgetary controls
h) slack in budgetary controls
i) group-based rewards
j) individual-based rewards
k) preference for evaluation relative to others
l) business units vs. company rewards

m) company-based vs. business unit rewards
n) formula-based evaluation/rewards/bonuses
o) subjective evaluation/rewards/bonuses
p) pay for performance/contingent rewards
q) performance-based rewards less motivating
r) desire for incentive based extrinsic rewards
s) intrinsic rewards likely to be valued
t) focus n short-term financial performance
u) past/present orientation
v) future orientation/long planning horizons
w) preference for immediate rewards
x) motivated by deferred compensation
y) acceptance/desire for stretch budgets
z) preference for interactive budget process

ENDNOTES

[1] Geert Hofstede, "Motivation, Leadership, and Organization: Do American Theories Apply Abroad?" Organizational Dynamics, Summer; 1980, pp. 42-63; Geert Hofstede, Cultures Consequences:International Differences in Work-Related Values, Sage Publications,Newbury Park, Calif., 1984; Geert Hofstede and Michael Harris Bond, "The Confucius Connection: From Cultural Roots to Economic Growth," Organizational Dynamics, vol. 16, no. 4,Spring 1988, pp. 5-21.

[2] J. Fisher and V. Govindarajan, "Incentive Compensation Design, Strategic Business Unit Mission, and Competitive Strategy," Journal of Management Accounting Research, vol. 5, Fall 1993, pp.129-144.

[3] J. Fisher, "Contingency-based Research on Management Control Systems: Categorization by Level of Complexity," Journal of Accounting Literature, vol. 14, 1995, pp. 24-53.

[4] The contingency model proposes that, in addition to mission and competitive strategy, other contingent factors include the external environment, technology, firm diversification and size, and the ability to observe effort and output. Modifications to the control system in this article are limited to discussion of the impact of alternative missions or competitive strategies. In order to generalize a contingency model across similar business situations, however, the cultural dimension (discussed later) must also be similar.

[5] B.D. Henderson, Corporate Strategy, Abt Books, Cambridge, Mass., 1978; R.D. Buzzell and F.D. Wiersema, "Modeling Changes in Market Share: A Cross-sectional Analysis," Strategic Management Journal, vol. 2, no. 1, January-March 1981, pp. 27-42. These mission-driven strategies are more recently discussed in numerous strategy and accounting textbooks, including: R.N. Anthony and V. Govindarajan, Management ontrol Systems, 9th Edition, McGraw-Hill/Irwin, Boston, 1998,p. 53-589

[6] M.E. Porter, Competitive Strategy, Free Press, New York, 1980;.E. Miles and C.C. Snow, Organizational Strategy, Structure and Process, McGraw-Hill, New York, 1978. Miles and Snow also consider analyzer- and reactor-type strategies. These strategies are adaptations of defender and prospector and will not be considered. See pages 68-93 for further discussion.

[7] .A. Thompson and A.J. Strickland, III, Strategic Management: Concepts and Cases, 13th Edition, McGraw-Hill/Irwin, Boston, 2003, pp. 151-163.

[8] R.M. Hodgetts and F. Luthans, "U. S. Multinationals' Expatriate Compensation Strategies," Compensation & Benefits Review, January/February 1993, pp. 57-62. R.M. Hodgetts and F. Luthans, "U. S. Multinationals' Compensation Strategies for Local Management: Cross-Cultural Implications," Compensation & Benefits Review, March/April 1993, pp. 42-48.

[9] G.L. Harrison, "Reliance on Accounting Performance Measures in Superior Evaluative Style—The Influence of National Culture and Personality," Accounting, Organizations and Society, vol. 18, May 1993, pp. 319-339; S.J. Kachelmeier and M. Shehata, "Internal Auditing and Voluntary Cooperation in Firms: A Cross-Cultural Experiment," The Accounting Review, vol. 72, no. 3, July 1997, pp. 407-431.

[10] Hofstede, 1988.

[11] In addition to reporting scores for 50 specific countries, Hofstede(1984) grouped 14 countries into three cultural regions: East Africa, West Africa, and Arabic-speaking countries. Several companies that specialize in global consulting and cross-cultural training rely extensively on the research of Geert Hofstede. For example: ITAP International refers to the work of Geert Hofstede as the "gold standard" of cultural profiles. The company uses the Hofstede cultural dimensions extensively in its programs (see www.itapintl.com/ITAPCWfr.htm). ITIM, one of the leading companies worldwide in the field of management and culture, incorporates the findings of the Hofstede research into its consulting and training practices (see www.itim.org/3.html). Also see Grovewell LLC (www.grovewell.com). Hofstede's (1988) study identified the fifth dimension, "Confucianism," after analyzing data from 22 countries, 20 of which were overlapped from the 1980 report.

[12] Hofstede (1980) presents a map of countries that cluster into four quadrants: 1) high power distance, high uncertainty avoidance, 2) high power distance, low uncertainty avoidance, 3) low power distance, high uncertainty avoidance, and 4) low power distance, low uncertainty avoidance.

[13] The country scores on cultural dimensions in the Hofstede studies are relative scores. Scales were chosen in such a way that the distance between the lowest- and highest-scoring country was approximately 100 points.

Chapter 20
Capital Budgeting

Cases

Readings

20-1: "How Forest Product Companies Analyze Capital Budgets" by Jack Bailes, James Neilsen, and Stephen Lawton, *Management Accounting* (October 1998), pp. 24-30.

This article presents the result of a survey on the uses of capital budgeting techniques by forest product companies. Capital budgeting for this industry has become more challenging and riskier because of increasing competitiveness and government and environmental pressures.

Discussion Questions:
1. The survey result shows that more firms use one or more discounted cash flow methods in evaluating timber-related capital investments. However, more firms use payback period methods to assess plant and equipment purchases. What are reasons for these differences?
2. List changes in the uses of capital budgeting techniques over the years.
3. List some of the methods for adjusting risks in capital investments.
4. What is post-audit? How do forest product companies conduct post-audits?

20-2: "How ABC Was Used in Capital Budgeting" by Steve Coburn, Hugh Grove, and Tom Cook, *Management Accounting* (May 1997), pp. 38-40.

This article presents a case study on the difference that ABC makes on the investment decision of a new project. A business forecast signaled "Go" to an interactive TV project, but the ABC analysis said, "Stop." The article discusses the utilization and limitations of activity-based costing (ABC) in capital budgeting including capacity to predict operating and capital costs, benchmarking model and steps in using ABC in capital investment project.

Discussion Questions:
1. What is the general business case approach to capital budgeting?
2. How does an ABC model approach to capital budgeting differ from the general business case approach?
3. What are the roles of value chain in capital budgeting?
4. List advantages and limitations of ABC approach to capital budgeting.

Cases

20-1 The Case of the Almost Identical Twins

Once upon a time twin boys were born into a typical Ozian family. The boys, named Spender and Saver, were alike in every respect except the one indicated by their names. While they were in high school, both worked at part-time jobs earning the minimum wage of $4.445 per hour for the maximum hours permitted by law, viz., 44 hours per month. There was no income tax in Oz. Spender found many things on which to spend all of his income, while Saver arranged with his parents to add his monthly income to their money market fund which earned 8% per *annum, compounded monthly*.

At the end of four years of high school, each of the boys bought a car costing the amount of Saver's accumulated savings, which he withdrew from his parents' money market account to pay for the car. Spender financed his car on a "no money down," 18% per annum, compounded monthly contract for 48 months. Thus, during four years of university, both boys had cars, both spent the same amounts on other things, but Saver invested each month an amount equal to what Spender was paying on his car, the saving again being at 8% per *annum, compounded monthly*. Both boys financed their expenses while at the university in the same way: partly by working and partly with help from their parents.

When they graduated from the university, the two men continued their identical spending patterns, except that Saver was able to buy a home, using the accumulation of his savings from avoiding car payments in the previous four years as the down payment (20% of the purchase price), financing the remainder on a *10% fixed* rate mortgage, payable monthly over 30 years. Spender rented a similar home, paying (the first year) "net rent" equal to Saver's monthly mortgage payments. Spender's lease also required that he reimburse his landlord for property taxes and insurance on the rental unit-amounts equal to Saver's costs for those items. Thus, Spender continued his pattern of spending all of his income, while Saver paid off his mortgage over 30 years.

Unfortunately for Spender, his "net rent" increased at the rate of 5% per annum, so his housing costs escalated considerably over the 30 years. In the meantime, Saver invested the difference between Spender's escalating "net rent" and his own fixed mortgage payment. Each year he accumulated the monthly saving in his 8% money market fund, then at the end of the year invested in a mortgage bond mutual fund yielding the same rate as he was paying on his own mortgage: 10% per annum, *compounded* monthly. His investments and earnings in that fund continued to compound over the remaining life of his own mortgage.

Upon "burning his mortgage" at the end of 30 years, Saver, now 52 years of age, let his accumulated investment in the mortgage bond mutual fund continue to earn interest for two years but did not add to it. Instead, he departed from his brother's spending pattern by *adding consumption expenditures* equal to what Spender was paying in "net rent." Two years later (age 54) Saver retired to Eve off the income earned on his mortgage bond mutual fund, but kept *the* level of principal unchanged for the rest of his life, leaving it to his heirs. Spender, alas, was in a different position. What does the future hold for him?

REQUIREMENTS:
1) Specific calculations to be made; please describe any shortcuts or approximations you use:
   a) How much did each lad spend on his car upon graduating from high school?
   b) How much did Saver pay down on his home? What was the total purchase price?
   c) What were Saver's monthly mortgage payments?
2) Saver invested the difference between his mortgage payments and his brother's rents. What had this investment accumulated to at the mortgage burning date? At age 54? (Note: The calculations involved here may be quite time-consuming; some planning might pay off.)
3) What annual income did Saver have from age 54 until his death?
4) Describe the differences between Spender's and Saver's consumption expenditures over the several segments of their lives and the positions of their heirs upon their deaths.
5) Which bits of information given, or assumptions made, do you regard as unrealistic on the basis of your own experience? Roughly speaking (or precisely, if you wish), how would the results be affected by substituting your more realistic calculations?

Blocher, Stout, Cokins, Chen: *Cost Management, 4e*

©The McGraw-Hill Companies, Inc 2008

20-2 ACE Company (A)

ACE Company is the technology and market leader in the portable electronic games industry. The company is currently enjoying great success with its Model X, which has been on the market for several years. ACE's management believes that because of increased competition from other types of entertainment, the demand for Model X will dry up after three more years. The company has forecast Model X's net cash inflows in the next three years to be $400 million, $300 million, and $200 million, respectively.

NEW PRODUCT DEVELOPMENT

ACE's senior managers are considering the development and introduction of a replacement for Model X, to be called Model Z. According to the engineers, ACE already possesses the technical expertise to develop Model Z. However, the earliest that this product can be introduced into the-market is one year from now, as it will take this long to develop and test the new product, coordinate with suppliers for parts, set up the production process, and arrange for other related logistic activities. The total cost of these development activities is estimated at $550 million.

All of ACE's top managers agree that Model Z's market potential in terms of net cash inflow would be $200 million in year 2, $400 million in year 3, $300 million in year 4, and $100 million in year 5. They also agree that Model Z would maintain ACE's leadership position in the portable electronic games industry.

Management expects that in addition to developing its own customer base, Model Z also would draw some sales away from Model X. The expected amount of this "cannibalization" is $100 million of net cash inflows per year. The following table summarizes ACE's prediction of net cash flows (in millions) for the next five years for Model X by itself and with the introduction of Model Z at the end of year 1 (or, equivalently stated, the beginning of year 2). For simplicity, cash outflows are assumed to occur at the beginning of the year while cash inflows are assumed to occur at year end. Thus, for example, the $550 million development cost in year 1 is assumed to occur at time zero, while the net cash inflow from introducing Model Z at the beginning of year 2 is assumed to occur at the end of that year. Also note that in the table, net cash inflows of $100 million per year are shifted from Model X to Model Z in years 2 and 3.

Year	Model X Only	Introduce Model Z After One Year				
		Model X	+	Model Z	=	Total
0	$ 0	$ 0	+	$ (550)	=	$ (550)
1	$400	$ 400	+	0	=	$ 400
2	$300	$ 200*	+	300*	=	$ 500
3	$200	$ 100*	+	$ 500*	=	$ 600
4	$ 0	$ 0	+	$ 300	=	$ 300
5	$ 0	$ 0	+	$ 100	=	$ 100

* Reflects $100 cannibalization of Model X by Model Z.

EXTENDING THE DEVELOPMENT PERIOD FOR PRODUCT Z

Several members of top management are concerned about Model Z's erosion of Model X sales. They propose that it would be better to spread the development of Model Z over two years and to introduce it at the beginning of year 3 instead of year 2. They suggest that this plan has two major advantages: (1) it would avoid the $100 million erosion in Model X's net cash inflows in year 2; and (2) the engineers have projected that extending the time for the development process will yield substantial savings due to efficiencies in scheduling. They have estimated that the two-year plan would reduce Model Z's total development cost to $300 million. Half of this total would be spent in each of the two years.

The table below summarizes the estimated net cash flows (in millions) for the two-year plan. Compared to the one-year plan, Model X's year 2 net cash inflow is higher by $100 million. This is due to avoiding cannibalization by Model Z in year 2.

Year	Model X Only	Introduce Model Z After One Year				
		Model X	+	Model Z	=	Total
0	$0	$ 0	+	$ (150)	=	$(150)
1	$400	$ 400	+	$(150)	=	$ 250
2	$300	$ 300	+	0	=	$ 300
3	$200	$ 100*	+	$ 500*	=	$ 600
4	$ 0	$0	+	$ 300	=	$ 300
5	$ 0	$0	+	$ 100	=	$ 100

*Reflects $100 cannibalization of Model X by Model Z.

Proponents of the two-year plan acknowledge that delaying Model Z's introduction by one year would require foregoing its year 2 $300 million net cash inflow. But they emphasize that this sacrifice is more than made up by the additional $100 million cash inflow from Model X in year 2 and the $250 million savings in Model Z development costs.

OTHER CONSIDERATIONS

Supporters of the one-year plan argue that proponents of the two-year plan have overlooked a major factor: that the timing of Model Z's introduction could have an impact on competitors' actions. They maintain that if ACE does not introduce Model Z as quickly as possible, ACE's major competitor would most certainly come in with a comparable product. In response to a query from these managers, ACE's engineers have conducted a study of the competitor's current capabilities. They have reported that due to the competitor's less sophisticated technologies, it will require two years to develop a comparable product for market introduction.

The nature of the industry is such that there is a significant first-mover advantage. Similar products that reach the market at the same time tend to get equal shares of the market. But once a product is introduced, it tends to get so entrenched that comparable products introduced subsequently can gain only inconsequential market shares.

REQUIRED

1) Using net present value (NPV) computations and ignoring income taxes, analyze the one-year and two-year development alternatives. At this time, ignore the potential introduction of a comparable product by ACE's major competitor. Should either alternative be selected? If so, which would you recommend? ACE's cost of capital is 10 percent.

2) How would you modify your analysis in part (1) to address the potential introduction of a competing product by ACE's major competitor?

Blocher, Stout, Cokins, Chen: *Cost Management, 4e*

20-3 ACE Company (B)

Upon receiving the analysis of the data provided in ACE Company (A), the firm's managers wanted to better explore the effect of competition on whether and how to introduce Model Z. Diane Callahan, the Marketing Director, believes that the analysis is incomplete. She argues:

I believe that accelerating the development of Model Z is the right choice if we will not receive any new data. Accelerated development eliminates the possibility of our competitors introducing a product that will significantly erode our market share. Thus, even though accelerated development results in greater cannibalization of our current product (Model X), it is better than spreading the cost out over two years. However, phased development does give us some flexibility that is not available with accelerated development. In particular, if we phase in developmental costs for Model Z over two years, we only commit $150 toward developmental costs in year 1. At the end of that year, we will have a much better idea of total market demand for Model Z. If the demand turns out to be bad, phased development gives us the option of abandoning Model Z without spending too much money. My department has put together some data on expected market conditions (**Table 1**). From that data, I would guess that we may be better off abandoning Model Z unless the market conditions are good. Such an option is not available with accelerated development because it requires us to spend all of the developmental money of $550 in the first year itself. Ignoring the value of the option on further development could have given us an incomplete understanding of the tradeoffs.

Norm Peterson, Director (Product Development), then commented:

What Diane says make sense to me. In fact, if we defer the decision to introduce Model Z by a year and wait for new market information, there is a third development choice. In particular, we can do all of the development during year 2, *after* we have made the decision to launch or abort. This choice would cost $400. I did not bring this choice up earlier because the phased development strategy of developing Model Z over two years seems to dominate this delayed development strategy.[1] But, Diane's comments indicate that we should consider this alternative as well. After all, if there is a possibility we will abort Model Z at the end of year 1, why waste $150 in year one under the two-year development time table?

Sam Mask, the CEO, summarized as follows before adjourning the meeting.

I think we have made substantial progress in understanding the tradeoffs in timing the development of Model Z. I suggest we revisit the issue taking Diane's and Norm's comments into account. For simplicity, let us assume a 40 percent chance that a competitor will emerge and a 50-50 chance that the market will have strong demand for Model Z. Finally, let us retain the simplifying assumptions about the timing of cash flows and do the analysis ignoring tax considerations. Why don't we meet early next week to figure out the best strategy?

---

[1] Case B compares this new strategy (delayed development) with the strategies considered in case A. From case A, notice that phased development (i.e., developing Model Z over two years) costs $300. Also, Model Z would only get introduced at the start of year 3 ($t = 2$) under both the phased and delayed development strategies. Hence, absent information regarding market conditions, delayed development has no incremental benefit but, even with discounting, has a higher cost relative to phased development. Also, notice that delayed development has lower development costs than accelerated development (i.e., develop Model Z in year 1 itself and introduce at the start of year 2) even though both choices develop Model Z in one year. The lower cost is expected because the firm would have learned from its experience with other projects and changes in technology.

REQUIRED

1. For this question only, assume that competition will never emerge and that ACE will obtain no new information regarding market conditions. Notice that expected cash flows, using the CEO's suggested probability estimates, are identical to those given in case A. Compute the expected cash flow for the delayed development strategy. Determine if this alternative is preferred to accelerated or phased development.

2. For this question only, assume that ACE will obtain no new information regarding market conditions. How does the analysis change if there is a 40 percent chance that competition will emerge?

3. Assume that ACE will obtain information regarding realized market conditions at the end of year 1. How does the rank ordering of the development choices change? Why?

COMPUTATIONAL HINTS

1. For all three questions, discount cash flows using a 10 percent rate. Assume that all cash outflows occur at the beginning of the year and all cash inflows occur at the end of the year. It also is helpful to construct a timeline for cash flows. Label the first node (start of year 1) as $t = 0$, the next node (end of year 1 and start of year 2) as $t = 1$, etc.

2. To determine whether or not to proceed with Model Z at time $t = 1$, construct a payoff matrix with 4 cells corresponding to Ace's and the competitor's entry choices. To minimize the potential for errors, look at time $t = 1$ NPV of cash flows at or after time $t = 1$. After you determine optimal choices at $t = 1$, step back to construct a payoff matrix where the rows correspond to Ace's various product development strategies and the columns correspond to the competitor entering and not entering.

Blocher, Stout, Cokins, Chen: *Cost Management, 4e*

©The McGraw-Hill Companies, Inc 2008

TABLE 1
Estimated Cash Flows from Model X and Model Z Under Different Scenarios

Panel A: No Development of Model Z

| | Market Condition: Good | | | | Market Condition: Bad | | | |
| | Competitor Enters | | Competitor Does Not Enter | | Competitor Enters | | Competitor Does Not Enter | |
Time (t)	X	Z	X	Z	X	Z	X	Z
0	0		0		0		0	
1	400		400		400		400	
2	300		300		300		300	
3	25		200		175		200	
4	0		0		0		0	
5	0		0		0		0	

Panel B: Accelerated Development of Model Z

| | Market Condition: Good | | | | Market Condition: Bad | | | |
| | Competitor Enters | | Competitor Does Not Enter | | Competitor Enters | | Competitor Does Not Enter | |
Time (t)	X	Z	X	Z	X	Z	X	Z
0	0	-550	0	-550	0	-550	0	-550
1	400	0	400	0	400	0	400	0
2	150	500	150	500	250	100	25	100
3	25	850	25	850	175	150	175	150
4	0	550	0	550	0	50	0	50
5	0	150	0	150	0	50	0	50

Panel C: Phased Development of Model Z

| | Market Condition: Good | | | | Market Condition: Bad | | | |
| | Competitor Enters | | Competitor Does Not Enter | | Competitor Enters | | Competitor Does Not Enter | |
Time (t)	X	Z	X	Z	X	Z	X	Z
0	0	-150	0	-150	0	-150	0	-150
1	400	-150	400	-150	400	-150	400	-150
2	300	0	300	0	300	0	300	0
3	25	425	25	850	175	75	200	150
4	0	275	0	550	0	25	0	50
5	0	100	0	200	0	0	0	0

Panel D: Defer Development Decision on Model Z

| | Market Condition: Good | | | | Market Condition: Bad | | | |
| | Competitor Enters | | Competitor Does Not Enter | | Competitor Enters | | Competitor Does Not Enter | |
Time (t)	X	Z	X	Z	X	Z	X	Z
0	0	0	0	0	0	0	0	0
1	400	-400	400	-400	400	-400	400	-400
2	300	0	300	0	300	0	300	0
3	25	425	200	850	175	75	200	150
4	0	275	0	550	0	25	0	50
5	0	100	0	200	0	0	0	0

1. All cash-flows are assumed to occur at the beginning of the year. Ignore taxes in your analysis. Time $t = 0$ corresponds to the start of the first calendar year and $t = 1$ corresponds to the end of year 1 and the start of year 2.
2. There is a 50% chance that market conditions will be good.
3. There is a 40% chance that the competitor will develop a product that competes with Model Z. The competitor's decision, however, is independent of realized market conditions. The competitor only has the choice of developing the product over 2 years and, thus, makes the launch/abort decision at time $t = 0$ itself.

20-4 Component Technologies, Inc.: Adding FlexConnex Capacity

In 2002, Component Technologies, Inc. (CTI)[1] manufactured components, such as interconnect components, electronic connectors, fiber-optic connectors, flexible interconnects, coaxial cable, cable assemblies, and interconnect systems, used in computers and other electronic equipment. CTI's global marketing strategy produced significant growth; CTI was now one of three major suppliers in its market segments. Major customers included other global companies, such as IBM, HP, Hitachi, and Siemens. These companies, in turn, manufactured and marketed their products worldwide.

FlexConnex, one of CTI's largest selling products, was very profitable (see **Exhibit 1**). The Santa Clara, California plant that manufactured the FlexConnex component was projected to reach its full capacity of 75 million units in 2003. With sufficient capacity to meet demand, CTI expected its sales of FlexConnex could continue to increase 10 percent per year as applications of computer technology extended into industrial products and consumer products such as automobiles and appliances.

PLANNING MEETING

At a meeting of his staff, Tom Richards, director of manufacturing planning, stated that they needed to plan to bring additional capacity for FlexConnex online in about two years. He suggested that they begin by proposing possible alternatives. The staff quickly identified three promising alternatives:

1. The Santa Clara plant had been designed for future expansion. Additional space was available at the site, and new production capacity could be easily integrated into the existing production processes as long as compatible manufacturing technologies were employed.
2. CTI owned a plant in Waltham, Massachusetts that manufactured a product line that was being phased out. Some existing equipment in the Waltham plant was compatible with the Santa Clara plant's manufacturing technology and could be converted to the production of FlexConnex. Half of the Waltham plant would be available in 2003, and the remainder in 2005.
3. CTI could build a greenfield plant[2] in Ireland, close to its major European customers. To attract such industries, the Irish government would make a site available at low cost. A new technology currently being Beta-tested[3] by an equipment manufacturer could be used to equip this plant.

Tom believed that these three were promising proposals. To ensure CTI could bring additional, profitable, FlexConnex capacity online in two years, Tom felt that they should begin developing plans for these alternatives. Nonetheless, he wanted the staff to keep an open mind to additional alternatives even as they evaluated these three. As the discussion started to wind down, Gracie Stanton, an engineer, said that she had a suggestion.

Gracie: Before we spend our time developing these three alternatives in detail, I'd like to get a rough feel for the potential profitability of each alternative. We shouldn't waste our time developing detailed plans for an alternative if there is no chance it will ever show a positive NPV.

Tom: Good point, Gracie. Let's break up into three groups, and do back-of-the-envelope calculations based on what we currently know about each alternative. Gracie, would you head up the Santa Clara group, since you were part of the engineering team for that plant? Edward Lodge, how about Waltham? Ian Townsley, could you and your folks take a look at Ireland? To start, what are the facts and assumptions about each facility?

---

[1] This case is based on decisions faced by an actual company. Component Technologies, Inc., is a disguised name. Other facts have been changed for instructional purposes.

[2] The term "greenfield plant" is commonly used to refer to a brand new plant built entirely from scratch, as contrasted with the expansion, conversion, refurbishment, or renovation of an existing plant.

[3] A "Beta-test site" refers to equipment being tested using an actual workload at a customer site. Beta-test is often the final testing phase before the equipment is released as commercially available to customers. A customer who consents to be a Beta-test site agrees not only to use equipment that is not fully tested (thus being, in the American vernacular, a "guinea pig"), but also to provide the vendor detailed feedback on operations and problems encountered. In return, the equipment manufacturer often provides incentives such as financial discounts, extra on-site vendor personnel, etc.

Blocher, Stout, Cokins, Chen: *Cost Management, 4e*

Gracie: Well, there's enough space at the Santa Clara site to produce an additional 30 million units annually. I expect it would cost about $23 million to expand this plant, and bring its total capacity to 105 million units. Of the $23 million, we would spend $5 million to expand the building, and $18 million for additional equipment compatible with Santa Clara's existing manufacturing process. All $23 million would probably be spent in 2003, and the plant would be ready for production in 2004.

I assume that the selling price per unit will remain at its current level; further, since the same manufacturing technology will continue to be used, the variable manufacturing cost will remain the same as we show on the 2002 Santa Clara Cost Analysis Sheet [**Exhibit 1**]. Expanding the existing plant would allow some fixed manufacturing costs, like the plant manager's salary, to be shared with the existing facility, so I estimate that the additional fixed manufacturing costs, excluding depreciation, will be $2.1 million annually beginning in 2004. In 2006, these fixed costs will rise to $2.4 million and remain at that level for the foreseeable future.

Edward: Well, the Waltham plant is smaller than the space available in Santa Clara, so I think its capacity will be about 25 million units. It will require renovations to adapt the plant to manufacture FlexConnex, say, about $2 million, and approximately $12 million for equipment. Half of this would be spent in 2003, and half in 2005. Initial production would begin in 2004; half of the 25-million-unit capacity should be available in 2004; two-thirds in 2005; the remainder in 2006.

Since the Waltham plant will use the same technology as Santa Clara, we can assume that the variable manufacturing costs will be the same as Santa Clara's. Selling prices will also be the same. However, since Waltham will be a stand-alone faculty, its fixed manufacturing costs, excluding depreciation, would be somewhat higher: $2.4 million annually beginning in 2004. In 2006, however, fixed costs will increase to $2.6 million annually, where I expect them to remain for the foreseeable future.

Ian: I just visited the Beta-test site for the manufacturing equipment using the new technology that I propose we use for the greenfield plant. There I learned that the economic size for a plant using this technology to manufacture a product such as FlexConnex is about 70 million units, so I propose that we prepare our estimates for Ireland based on a 70-million-unit capacity plant. Of course, this will cost more, since it is much larger than other sites. With the help of the Irish government, an appropriate site can be obtained for about $1 million. A building large enough to produce 70 million units can probably be built for about $10 million, and equipping the facility with the new technology equipment will cost about $50 million. Most of this would be spent in 2003, although as much as 10 percent might be spent before the end of 2002 to acquire and prepare the site. The plant would begin production in 2004; some areas of the plant would not be complete, however, and as much as 20-25 percent of the investment would remain to be spent during 2004.

Although FlexConnex's worldwide selling price will be the same as for the other facilities, the new equipment will lower the variable manufacturing cost to $0.195 per unit. The efficiency of this new plant will help keep fixed manufacturing costs down, as well, but since the facility will be so large, fixed manufacturing costs, excluding depreciation, would be higher than the other two facilities: $2.8 million annually beginning in 2004, rising to $2.9 million annually beginning in 2008.

Tom: These assumptions sound like reasonable first cuts to me. Let's just start with a five-year analysis, 2003 through 2007, using the discount rate of 20 percent, which the corporate finance manual states is the hurdle rate for capital investments. For simplicity, let's assume all cash flows occur at the end of the respective year. Discount everything to today's dollars, that is, as of the end of 2002. And, consistent with corporate policy, we'll do a pretax analysis; we'll ask the corporate finance staff to evaluate the tax implications later.

A few minutes later, the buzzing of the small groups died down, and the tapping on the laptop keyboards had ceased.

Tom: Well, what have you learned from this first glance?

Edward: The Waltham site looks promising.

Ian: Not Ireland.

Gracie: This is odd. The Santa Clara plant is right on the margin, and that surprises me since the existing manufacturing facility is one of CTI's most profitable, and we get further economies of scale by expanding that plant. I wonder if the discount rate we are using is too high. At the "Finance for Manufacturing Engineers" seminar I attended recently, we discussed the problems associated with using a discount rate that was too high. The professor stated that there was a sound theoretical basis for using a discount rate that approximated the company's cost of capital, but many companies "added on" estimates for risk, corporate charges, and other factors that were less well grounded. Based on what I learned in that seminar, I tried to estimate CTI's actual cost of capital; it was about 10 percent. I wonder what would happen if we used 10 percent instead?

Tom: With these laptops and spreadsheet programs, that's easy enough; let's check it out.

A few seconds later . . . .

Gracie: Now, that's better!

Edward: Ours too.

Ian: Well, at least we're moving in the right direction. But it doesn't make sense to me that a facility with lower variable cost per unit, and lower average fixed cost per unit at capacity, shows a negative NPV when the others are positive. We checked our calculations; what's the story? Could it be that Ireland would not even be up to capacity production in five years because the plant is so big?

Gracie: Maybe, but our plants are being penalized, too; after all, even though they reach capacity in the first five years, they will presumably continue to produce FlexConnex. Although there is constant technological change in this industry, there is a reasonable probability that demand for FlexConnex will remain strong for at least 10 years.

Ian: Well, then, let's look at each of the three plants over a ten-year period, using Gracie's 10 percent discount rate.

Later . . . .

Edward: Aha! Waltham continues to improve.

Gracie: However, Santa Clara has you beat now!

Ian: I've got bad news for both of you!

REQUIRED:

1. Prepare the manufacturing staff's calculations for the three alternatives:
   a. In the first set of calculations, the staff used a discount rate of 20 percent, a five-year time horizon, and ignored taxes and terminal value. What is the relative attractiveness of these three alternatives?
   b. In the second set, they used a 10 percent discount rate. What happens to the NPV of each alternative? What happens to their relative attractiveness? Why?
   c. In the third set, they changed the time horizon to ten years, but kept the 10 percent discount rate. Why does Ian say he has "bad news" for the others?

2. In addition to reducing costs, the new technology proposed for the greenfield plant would increase manufacturing flexibility, which would enable CTI to respond more quickly to customers and to provide them more custom features. Should these factors be considered in the analysis? If so, how would you incorporate them?

3. Should other factors be taken into consideration in choosing the location of the FlexConnex plant? If so, what are they?

4. Should Tom Richards continue to develop more detailed plans for these three alternatives? If not, which should be eliminated? Are there other alternatives that his staff should consider? If so, what are they?

Blocher, Stout, Cokins, Chen: *Cost Management, 4e*

EXHIBIT 1 FlexConnex Cost Analysis Sheet
Santa Clara Plant, 2002

Plant Capacity: 75 million units

Selling Price/Unit: $0.85

Variable Cost/Unit: $0.255

Fixed Manufacturing Cost: $9.5 million annually (includes $2.5 million depreciation)

Estimated Plant Profitability at Capacity:

Revenue $63,750,000

Variable Cost   <19,125,000>

Fixed Manufacturing Cost   <u><9,500,000></u>

Plant Profitability [a]   <u>$35,125,000</u>

[a] Excludes interest expenses and corporate selling, general and administrative expenses.

20-5 General Medical Center

The phone rang in the office of Gwen Allbright, a partner in a consulting firm that specializes in health services management. On the line was Dr. George Westford, Chief of Cardiovascular Medicine at General Medical Center (GMC) and Gwen's next-door neighbor. Dr. Westford explained that he needed Gwen's help in understanding an analysis prepared by Brian Alexander, General Medical Center's Chief Financial Officer, of the pending purchase of new imaging equipment for the evaluation of patients with suspected coronary artery disease (CAD). GMC is evaluating two types of imaging equipment—a Thallium scanner and a Positron Emission Technology (PET) scanner. Dr. Westford explained the situation as follows:

> Based on his cost analysis, Brian Alexander has recommended that the hospital purchase the Thallium scanner rather than the PET scanner. The physicians in the cardiovascular medicine department are very upset by this. They want the hospital to purchase the PET scanner because it incorporates the latest imaging technology. In addition, I am not convinced by Brian's analysis that the Thalhum scanner is really the better choice even from a purely financial perspective.

Dr. Westford asked Gwen to evaluate the analysis prepared by Mr. Alexander and to recommend changes to his analysis if she felt that they were warranted. He agreed to bring the analysis to Gwen's house later that evening.

GENERAL MEDICAL CENTER

General Medical Center is a not-for-profit 500-bed community-based hospital. It is located in a metropolitan area with a population of one million people, which has six major hospital systems that provide cardiovascular services. It is the third "busiest" cardiovascular center in the metropolitan area when judged on the number of cardiac catheterizations performed.

GMC recently has become part of an integrated health care delivery system for its metropolitan area. Now that GMC participates in a capitated payment system, its revenue is much more "fixed" than it was under the former fee-for-services arrangement. Capitated payments are per-patient payments to a health care provider (hospital or physician group) for a defined set of benefits for a defined period of time. In a strictly capitated system, a provider receives a predetermined amount for each beneficiary.[1] The actual costs of caring for a beneficiary may be more or less than this predetermined amount. When the actual costs of care are less than the predetermined payment, the provider keeps the "profit." When actual costs exceed the payment, however, the provider is financially responsible and incurs a "loss."

This is in stark contrast to the former fee-for-services system in which the hospital was reimbursed for each imaging procedure performed and for all follow-up procedures (such as cardiac catheterizations) that were triggered by the imaging results. Under the fee-for-services arrangement, the provider's profit increased as a direct function of the number of imaging and follow-up procedures performed, so long as the fee for each exceeded its cost. In effect, the former system rewarded the misdiagnosis of normal individuals as diseased, because of the revenue impact of additional procedures.

Under a capitated system, however, costs that are triggered by misdiagnoses are borne by the hospital. In effect, this payment method merges the insurance function with the provider function in that a portion of the financial risk is borne by the provider. By merging the insurance and provider functions, the capitated payment system encourages the provider to analyze the appropriateness (quality) of care. However, it also provides the short-term financial incentive to reduce costs by under-treating patients. For example, referrals to specialists may be reduced, further testing curtailed, or less costly (but less effective) approaches to treatment prescribed.

---

[1] While this case assumes strict capitation for all payors, such a system is the exception and not the norm—both in the U.S., generally, and in the particular market served by GMC. A more realistic analysis would recognize that (1) patient care may be reimbursed under various combinations of arrangements—including by capitation, by diagnosis and by fee-for-service or discounted fee-for-service schemes; (2) different payors—which include for-profit and not-for-profit private-sector organizations, government and individual patients—are involved; and (3) the relative amount of reimbursement for Thalhurn and PET may differ across the various payors (in fact, some payors may consider a particular technology "experimental" and provide no reimbursement). Thus, the payor mix is an extremely important consideration in a decision such as that faced by GMC. For pedagogical reasons, however, the case abstracts from this complexity on the revenue dimension in order to focus on the role of costs in this decision setting.

Blocher, Stout, Cokins, Chen: *Cost Management, 4e*

Future costs of under-treating patients may not be borne by the hospital due to the high mobility level of the working-age patient base.

Dr. Westford and the other physicians in the cardiovascular division realize that in a capitated system the division will be evaluated more on the appropriateness and cost of its care. Since revenues will not increase with the number of procedures performed, they will need to be concerned about performing unnecessary catheterization procedures. The capitation approach strives to lower the cost of care, subject to quality standards, and match the financial risks with the quality of care. Dr. Westford and the other physicians are convinced that the higher accuracy of the PET scanner vis-à-vis the more conventional Thallium scanner will result in more medically appropriate referrals of patients for cardiac catheterization. Dr. Westford is concerned that Mr. Alexander has failed to consider the cost of *inappropriate* referrals in his analysis of the imaging equipment purchase. This is also of concern to the physicians since they typically are directly penalized in their compensation for inappropriate patient referrals.

HEART DISEASE AND CARDIAC IMAGING

Patients undergo diagnostic imaging to provide physicians with information that will be used to verify a diagnosis, order further testing, or prescribe treatment. A patient with suspected heart disease undergoes a tiered diagnostic process to provide a diagnosis in a cost-effective manner. This process can be represented by a type of decision tree that dictates the sequence of diagnostic testing and/or treatment. A simplified version of such a tree appears in **Exhibit 1**.

As the tree demonstrates, the physician uses a combination of clinical judgment and diagnostic testing results to determine which patients will undergo cardiovascular imaging and perhaps further procedures. Once a patient is referred for cardiovascular imaging, the results of that procedure dictate whether the patient will proceed to diagnostic cardiac catheterization. Patients with normal cardiac imaging results have no further evaluation, whereas almost all patients with abnormal imaging results undergo cardiac catheterization. Currently at GMC, this catheterization costs $2,000 and carries a 0.01 percent mortality rate. The catheterization procedure is used to determine whether the imaging technique has correctly identified the patient as having heart disease. If the imaging technique has correctly identified the patient, the catheterization provides the physician with information that is useful for deciding among medical treatment, coronary angioplasty and coronary artery bypass surgery as the preferred treatment for the disease.

Since the results of the cardiovascular imaging procedure dictate whether the patient will be subjected to cardiac catheterization, it is easy to see why the diagnostic accuracy of the imaging procedure is of paramount importance. An ideal or perfect imaging procedure would correctly differentiate those patients who do and do not have heart disease. A technique that fails to correctly identify patients who actually have heart disease may allow the disease to go undetected for some time, possibly resulting in greater health care risks and costs when the disease later becomes clinically evident. Likewise, a technique that incorrectly diagnoses a healthy patient as having heart disease will result in inappropriate and costly referral for diagnostic cardiac catheterization. The misdiagnosis of a healthy patient as diseased can be a significant factor in the cost analysis of imaging equipment.

GMC is considering two alternative imaging technologies: Thallium and PET. The Thallium scanner has been the standard in cardiovascular medicine for many years. It offers the advantages of lower initial capital outlay, lower annual maintenance costs and a general acceptance by the medical community. The more technologically advanced Positron Emission Technology (PET) scanner was largely restricted to academic medical centers until a few years ago because of its cost. More recently, commercial PET scanners have become available that offer greater clinical accuracy than Thallium scanners. Although the initial costs and maintenance fees of PET have come down in the last few years, they are still substantially higher than those associated with Thallium imaging.

EXHIBIT 1
Decision Tree

Patient has Symptoms

⇓

Examination by Physician

↙ ↘

No Further Evaluation   Cardiac Imaging

↙ ↘

Positive Scan
(Abnormal Result)

Negative Scan
(Normal Result)
(No Further Evaluation)

⇓

Cardiac Catheterization

↙ ↘

No Evident Coronary Problem
(No Further Evaluation)

Evident Coronary Problem

↙   ⇓   ↘

Medical Treatment   **Coronary Angioplasty**   **Bypass Surgery**

THE CFO's ANALYSIS

Brian Alexander, the CFO, analyzed this equipment purchase using an equivalent annual cost (EAC) method. Because the Thallium and PET scanners have different useful lives, EAC appeared to be the best way to determine which type of equipment would be more cost effective for the health care system. Essentially, EAC is the amount of an annuity that has the same life and present value as the investment option being considered. EAC can be viewed as the annual rental payment that would cover both the purchase of the equipment and its operating costs, or the annual amount that GMC would pay if it chose to outsource the scanning procedure. Thus, Mr. Alexander based the cost comparison on the initial outlay costs of both types of imaging equipment and on the annual maintenance, personnel-related and other costs associated with the two equipment types. His

Blocher, Stout, Cokins, Chen: *Cost Management, 4e*

cost estimates are listed and explained in **Exhibit 2**.

Mr. Alexander had to make several assumptions in his analysis. These assumptions, described in **Exhibit 3**, relate to the expected number of cardiac scans in a typical year, the expected useful life of the two scanners, the predicted inflation rate for the various costs associated with scanning and the likely base rate of cardiac disease in the hospital's patient population. Two assumptions are particularly important: the "sensitivity" and "specificity" of the alternative imaging techniques.

Understanding sensitivity and specificity is essential for a comprehensive evaluation of the Thallium and PET scanners. Realizing this, Mr. Alexander included as an addendum to his analysis the definitions of sensitivity and specificity, as well as the definitions of four additional terms on which sensitivity and specificity depend. Mr. Alexander's addendum is summarized in **Exhibit 4**.

Mr. Alexander applied the EAC approach using the relevant data and assumptions from **Exhibits 2, 3** and **4**. The results are presented in **Exhibit 5**. Mr. Alexander determined from this analysis that the EAC for the Thallium scanner is $745,818 and the EAC for the PET scanner is $1,148,004. Based on these calculations, he recommended the purchase of the Thallium scanner because it results in lower cost for the health care system.

SUGGESTED ASSIGNMENT QUESTIONS

1) Evaluate the strengths and weaknesses of the analysis prepared by the CFO.
2) Use the information on sensitivity, specificity and disease prevalence in the population to develop a framework for incorporating the costs of misdiagnoses into the CFO's analysis.
3) Quantify the costs of the expected annual number of cardiac catheterizations that will result from both the Thallium scanner and the PET scanner. After taking these additional costs into account, is the purchase of the Thallium scanner still indicated?
4) How should the costs of the False Negative diagnoses (i.e., classifying diseased patients as normal) be handled?
5) What additional considerations are relevant?

EXHIBIT 2
Cost Information

Cost Classification	Thallium Scanner	PET Scanner
Purchase Price of Equipment	$450,000	$1,600,000
Equipment Maintenance (Per Month)	$3,750	$13,333
Medical Supplies (Per Patient)	$100	$100
Nuclear Isotope (Per Month)	$20,000	$27,000
Lease Space (Per Month)	$2,000	$3,000
Utilities (Per Month)	$500	$1,000
Secretary (Per Month)	$1,667	$1,667
Nuclear Technician (Per Month)	$2,500	$2,500
Nursing Personnel (Per Month)	$2,917	$2,917
Employee Benefits (% of Salary)	28%	28%
Cost of Cardiac Catheterization	$2,000	$2,000

Explanation of Cost Classifications:

Purchase Price: Guaranteed by the manufacturer to be the lowest price offered to any other hospital in the preceding 12-month period.

Equipment Maintenance: First-year maintenance is included in the purchase price. Continuing maintenance is fixed for the life of the equipment at 10 percent of the purchase price.

Supplies: These include patient gowns, EKG electrodes and paper, intravenous kits and pharmacological agents.

Isotope: For the PET technology, a nuclear generator is purchased each month, which supplies the nuclear tracer used in the imaging technique. For the Thallium technology, the nuclear tracer is purchased on a per-dose basis from a nuclear pharmaceutical firm.

Lease Space: The PET equipment requires 50 percent more space than the Thallium equipment.

Utilities: The back-up electrical generators and specialized cooling for the sophisticated computer bank results in twice the utility requirements for the PET scanner as for the Thallium scanner.

Personnel: The two technologies have the same staffing requirements.

EXHIBIT 3
Assumptions

Category	Thallium Scanner	PET Scanner
Sensitivity	85%	95%
Specificity	65%	95%
Useful Life of Equipment	7 years	10 years
Patient Scan Days Per Month	20	20
Patient Scans Per Day	8	8
CAD Rate in Patients	25%	25%
Hospital Cost of Capital	10%	10%
Inflation Factor for Catheterization Procedure	3.2%	3.2%
inflation Factor for Personnel	3.5%	3.5%
Inflation Factor for Other Costs	2.8%	2.8%
Tax Rate for Hospital	0%	0%

Explanation of Assumptions:

Patient Scan Days Per Month: Each manufacturer guarantees equipment "up-time" of approximately 92 percent. The scanners will operate Monday through Friday. Thus, approximately 240 scan days are available each year.

Scans Per Day: This assumes that each scanner will scan the number of patients that currently are referred for imaging. Any potential annual increase in volume is assumed to be offset by the effect of implementing appropriate guidelines for the referral for this type of imaging procedure.

Thallium Specificity: The medical literature provides a range of values. For a community-based patient population, the best studies indicate a specificity of 55 percent to 65 percent. The value of 65 percent was chosen to provide a best-case analysis.

Thallium Sensitivity: The medical literature provides a consensus that this value is 85 percent.

PET Specificity: The medical literature provides a consensus that this value is 95 percent.

PET Sensitivity: The medical literature provides a consensus that this value is 95 percent.

Prevalence of Heart Disease: A review of the hospital's experience, along with reports from the medical literature, reveals that the best estimate of this value is 25 percent.

Useful Life of Imaging Equipment: The manufacturers have provided historical data and engineering projections for these estimates.

Hospital Cost of Capital: The CFO estimates that the hospital's cost of capital in the new integrated health care system will be approximately 10 percent.

Inflation Factors: The CFO has used information from similar integrated health care systems in the region for estimates of inflation rates.

Tax Rate for the Hospital: Since both the hospital and the integrated health care system are not-for-profit, there are no corporate taxes.

Blocher, Stout, Cokins, Chen: *Cost Management, 4e*

©The McGraw-Hill Companies, Inc 2008

EXHIBIT 4
Definitions of Key Terms

True Positive: A test result is positive (abnormal) in a patient with disease. Correct labeling of a diseased patient as having disease.

False Positive: A test result is positive (abnormal) despite the fact that the patient actually does not have disease. Incorrect labeling of a normal patient as having disease.

True Negative: A test result is negative (normal) in a patient who does not have disease. Correct labeling of a normal patient as not having disease.

False Negative: A test result is negative (normal) despite the fact that the patient actually has disease. Incorrect labeling of a diseased patient as not having disease.

Sensitivity: The proportion of diseased patients diagnosed correctly. The ratio of true positives to all patients who have disease (sum of true positives and false negatives above). The ability of a test to correctly identify patients with disease.

Specificity: The proportion of normal patients diagnosed correctly. The ratio of true negatives to all patients without disease (sum of false positives and true negatives above). The ability of a test to correctly identify normal patients.

EXHIBIT 5
The CFO's Analysis

Thallium Scanner Cost Analysis

Year	Initial Cost	Maintenance	Personnel[a]	Other[b]	Total	Present Value
0	$450,000				$450,000	$450,000
1		-0-	$108,810	$462,000	570,810	518,918
2		$45,000	112,619	474,936	632,555	522,772
3		45,000	116,560	488,234	649,794	488,200
4		45,000	120,640	501,905	667,545	455,942
5		45,000	124,862	515,958	685,820	425,840
6		45,000	129,232	530,405	704,637	397,749
7		45,000	133,756	545,256	724,012	371,533
Total						$3,630,954

Equivalent Annual Cost for *Thallium* Scanner: $745,818 [$3,630,954/4.86842 (PV factor for 7-year, 10% annuity)].

PET Scanner Cost Analysis

Year	Initial Cost	Maintenance	Personnel[a]	Other[c]	Total	Present Value
0	$1,600,000				$1,600,000	$1,600,000
1		-0-	$108,810	$564,000	672,810	611,646
2		$160,000	112,619	579,792	852,411	704,472
3		160,000	116,560	596,026	872,586	655,587
4		160,000	120,640	612,715	893,355	610,173
5		160,000	124,862	629,871	914,733	567,977
6		160,000	129,232	647,507	936,739	528,765
7		160,000	133,756	665,638	959,394	492,320
8		160,000	138,437	684,275	982,712	458,443
9		160,000	143,282	703,435	1,006,717	426,946
10		160,000	148,297	723,131	1,031,428	397,660
Total						$7,053,989

Equivalent Annual Cost for *PET* Scanner: $1,148,004 [$7,053,989/6.14457 (PV factor for 10-year, 10% annuity)].

[a]   [($1,667 + $2,500 + $2,917)1.28] x 12 = $108,810 for year 1, increasing by 3.5% each year.

[b]   ($20,000 + $2,000 + $500)12 + $100(1,920) = $462,000 for year 1, increasing by 2.8% each year.

[c]   ($27,000 + $3,000 + $1,000)12 + $100(1,920) = $564,000 for year 1, increasing by 2.8% each year.

20-6: Floating Investments

This case examines capital budgeting issues related to the construction and operation of a marina. The case requires students to identify the relevant cash flows and discount these to establish a net present value (NPV) for the investment. Issues addressed through the case include incorporating inflation into cash flows and the choice of appropriate discount factors; i.e., nominal and real, tax issues relating to the treatment of cash and non-cash items, the determination of terminal values, and the impact of depreciation on after-tax cash flows. The case extends beyond a simple calculation of NPV to the derivation of an appropriate breakeven rental in the first year of operations.

CASE BACKGROUND

Jim was excited as he drove into the car park at Floating Investments Limited. The senior management meeting was scheduled for 9 AM and his proposal was the major item on the agenda. Jim's official title was Projects Manager and he was responsible for initiating and overseeing new projects. This particular project was close to Jim's heart because it involved sailing—an activity that Jim had spent many years pursuing both socially and competitively. Jim believed that his project was well suited to Floating Investments as it was an extension of existing business.

Floating Investments Limited specializes in marine investment projects. Projects previously undertaken by the company include construction of canals and moorings for a major residential development and redevelopment of 'Fisherman's Wharf' in the downtown area. Given the nature of these projects, including the length of time over which the initial investments were recovered, the degree of risk involved was generally higher than more traditional investment projects.

Although Jim had completed a business degree at University, he was determined that his accounting background would not overshadow his career choice as an operational manager. Last night he had told his wife: "This project sells itself. The idea is good. I know the sailing world and we've got the big picture sorted out. Newland Harbor has only one marina to serve over 6000 boats, 80% of which cannot get marina berths and use moorings that sailors must row to. We've already got the site and the contractor lined up to build a new marina. All we need is management's go ahead. The accountants can sort out the dollars and cents later."

The Chief Executive Officer (CEO) opened the meeting and after the preliminaries gave Jim the signal to present his proposal. Jim knew the CEO was an experienced yachtsman and was confident that he would support the project. He started his proposal by describing the current shortage of marina berths and the size of the market, emphasizing that the local Port Authority owned the only existing marina. Because the Authority charged only a minimal rental, anyone who possessed a berth generally kept it and there was an elaborate (and lucrative) black market in trading the license to those on the waiting list.

Jim continued, "The proposed marina is designed for 500 boats and we estimate that it will take two years to build commencing 1 November 2001. Because of the shortage of marina berths it is expected that all berths will be leased from 1 November 2003. The 50-acre site we intend using for the project was purchased several years ago for $268,000 as part of the Fisherman's Wharf development, although it was never used for that project.

Construction of the marina falls into three stages:

1. Construction of sea walls, dredging the seabed, excavations for marina offices and service facilities, and road access.
2. Inserting piles and assembling pontoons.
3. Constructing buildings and facilities such as marina office, chandlery, repair workshops, and waste disposal.

The most favorable tender, from a reputable construction company, indicates a total construction cost of $12,000,000 payable as follows:

10% payable prior to commencement (31 October 2001)
40% payable one year later
40% payable on completion (31 October 2003)
10% retention payable one year after completion.

There will be three categories of berths:

    Category A for boats between 12 and 18 meters in length: 50 berths.
    Category B for boats between 8 and 12 meters in length: 300 berths.
    Category C for boats between 6 and 8 meters in length: 150 berths.

I am sure you will agree that this is an excellent project and an exciting opportunity for the company."

Jim sat down. The CEO spoke: "That site you had in mind. We've just had an offer from a real estate developer of $7000 per acre. How does that affect your project?" Peter Shrivers from marketing also asked: "How much are you going to charge for the berths? I know that the Port Authority charges $4500 for my 10-meter ketch. How does this compare? And what is the bottom line on this?"

Jim was silent. He hadn't thought that management would want the financial details so soon. Help came from an unexpected quarter. Emma Nautically, the Financial Controller spoke: "Figuring out a price is not going to be easy because there has not been a proper market for marina berths in Newland before. A sensible first step would be to calculate the minimum rental for the project to break even. At the same time we can commission a market survey to find out what price boat owners will be prepared to pay for the berths. We also need to consider other issues such as tax effects, inflation, and the opportunity cost of funds. Why don't Jim and I sit down and sort out a formal financial analysis and present it at the next management meeting this time next month?"

To Jim's great relief, the meeting agreed to Emma's suggestion. He was off the hook, at least for the moment. After the meeting had ended, he thanked Emma. She laughed: "It always pays to buy some time particularly when it's a big project. You had the big picture okay but at the end of the day, the financials have got to be sorted out. I know you majored in management accounting at University so you can probably remember how to do this type of analysis. Let me give you some further information." Jim started taking notes.

Emma continued: "The tax rate is 50% and 4% depreciation on a straight-line basis will be allowed for 80% of the construction cost. The company's cost of capital is 16.6% after allowing for tax and inflation. Based on current needs and past experience, 16.6% should cover the required rate of return to shareholders, debt repayment, and include a factor for the risk involved in this type of investment. Let's assume that cash flows take place at the end of each year. What about operating costs and working capital?"

Jim replied: "I estimated that the lease rentals, maintenance and supervisory costs and land values will rise in line with inflation, which is expected to be 6% annually over the life of the marina. Annual maintenance and supervisory costs are estimated to be $60,000 at current prices. Working capital requirements are not expected to be significant."

Emma asked: "What will the time horizon be? We will need to think about terminal values as they can often determine the success or otherwise of a project."

Jim considered her question: "We intend that the lease periods for each berth will be for a twenty-year period; in other words, the period from 1 November 2003 to 31 October 2023. It's probably safest to assume initially that the land will be the only valuable asset at the end of 2023."

Emma gave Jim's reply some thought and then said, "Okay, I think that we have enough information now to do the analysis. There are two things we need to do. First, we have to calculate the amount of annual, pre-tax lease rental that must be generated in order for the project to break even. Calculate this amount for the first year of operations."

"Second, using this first year amount, calculate how much an owner of a 10-metre yacht will pay in the first year. We can then compare this with the amount Peter Shrivers pays. I guess a simple way of doing this is to use the mid-points of the size ranges to calculate the total meters."

Jim returned home that evening. "How did it go?" asked his wife. Jim confessed: "I think I would have been out of a job if it hadn't been for the accountants. Have you seen my old management accounting books? I'm going to need them."

REQUIRED

Identify the information that Jim needs to present to the Board at the next meeting, providing calculations using the data supplied. Set out all the assumptions that need to be made and examine their reasonableness and consequences if violated.

    Include in your information set an analysis of the risks inherent in this type of investment and discuss the ways in which management of these risk factors can be incorporated in the project.

20.1: HOW FOREST PRODUCT COMPANIES ANALYZE CAPITAL BUDGETS

by Jack Bailes, James Nielsen, and Stephen Lawton

Twenty years ago we conducted a survey of forest products companies to investigate the nature of the capital budget project evaluation techniques, methods of risk analysis, and post audit procedures. Because the forest products industry has changed so much, it is appropriate to once again look at the issue of capital budgeting practices within the industry.

A survey was sent to the chief financial officers of 87 U.S. forest products companies, consisting of all of the independent firms (i.e., separate divisions of a single parent company were not included) currently participating in the Oregon State University Forest Products Industry Monograph Program.[1] The survey questionnaire was completed by 29 firms, representing a response rate of 33%—slightly lower than the 47% response rate received in the 1977 survey. Sixteen of these firms operated in the wood products side of the industry. There were only two firms operating exclusively in the pulp, paper, and packaging side of the industry, and the remaining 11 firms sold both wood and paper-related products. This industry breakdown of firms was similar to the breakdown of firms responding in 1977.

Although there are still a number of smaller forest products companies operating in the U.S., the largest percentage of firms (over 33%) had annual sales and total asset levels exceeding $500 million. Such a finding was not surprising given the consolidation that has taken place within the industry in the past 20 years.

The companies also were asked to report the dollar amount of their annual capital budgets for both timber-related investments and plant and equipment. These results are shown in **Table 1**. As was the case in 1977, the annual capital budgets were found to be approximately 10% of total assets.

CAPITAL BUDGETING EVALUATION METHODS

The survey provided description of the four major capital budgeting techniques used most often by financial analysts in order to determine the degree to which sophisticated capital budgeting methodologies were being used. These techniques include accounting rate of return, payback period, internal rate of return, and net present value. The company was asked to identify which of these methods were used in the capital budgeting decision-making process and whether or not they were used as a primary evaluation technique, secondary evaluation technique, or only a project screening technique. This was done separately for timber-related investment decisions and plant and equipment investment decisions. In addition, each company was asked to describe other formal evaluation techniques that they employed as well as other factors they considered relevant to the capital budgeting process.

PRIMARY EVALUATION TECHNIQUES

Several interesting results emerge from the data showing the number and percentage of firms using each of the four methodologies as a primary evaluation technique to judge the acceptability of both timberland and plant and equipment purchases. First, a far greater percentage of firms use one of the discounted cash flow techniques in evaluating timber-related investments (76%) than they do in the case of plant and equipment purchases (55%). These results are conceptually reasonable because the long life of timber-related investments makes the time value of money particularly important. By the same token, fewer companies use pay-back period as a primary evaluation technique when making timber investment (15%) than in the case of plant and equipment purchases (33%). The payback period is most useful as a short-term screening technique; therefore, it should be less useful when looking at timber purchases (**Table 2**).

The most significant finding, however, is the fact that the discounted cash flow techniques of internal rate of return and net present value are much more widely used today as a primary evaluation technique than they were in 1977 when they were used by only 44% of the forest products companies. Furthermore, in 1977, several of the smaller companies reported that they only used subjective judgment in making capital budgeting decisions. Only one of the smaller companies in the current survey relied solely on subjective judgment.

Table 1. SIZE OF CAPITAL BUDGET

Capital Budget (in millions)	Timber Investments	Other Capital Investments	Total Capital Investments
Less than $5	7 Companies	12 Companies	11 (38%) Companies
$5 to $10	5 Companies	1 Company	2 (7%) Companies
$11 to $50	4 Companies	6 Companies	6 (21%) Companies
Over $50	2 Companies	9 Companies	10 (34%) Companies
Total	18 Companies	28 Companies	29 Companies

Table 2. PRIMARY EVALUATION TECHNIQUES

Capital Budgeting Technique	Timber Investments	Other Capital Investments
Accounting rate of return	3 (9%) Companies	6 (13%) Companies
Payback period	5 (15%) Companies	15 (33%) Companies
Internal rate of return	13 (38%) Companies	15 (33%) Companies
Net present value	13 (38%) Companies	10 (22%) Companies
Total	34 Companies	46 Companies

Table 3. SECONDARY EVALUATION TECHNIQUES

Capital Budgeting Technique	Timber Investments	Other Capital Investments
Accounting rate of return	5 (23%) Companies	6 (22%) Companies
Payback period	8 (36%) Companies	13 (48%) Companies
Internal rate of return	5 (23%) Companies	3 (11%) Companies
Net present value	4 (18%) Companies	5 (19%) Companies
Total	22 Companies	27 Companies

Table 4. PROJECT SCREENING TECHNIQUES

Capital Budgeting Technique	Timber Investments	Other Capital Investments
Accounting rate of return	1 (6%) Company	4 (15%) Companies
Payback period	4 (24%) Companies	11 (42%) Companies
Internal rate of return	6 (35%) Companies	8 (31%) Companies
Net present value	6 (35%) Companies	3 (12%) Companies
Total	17 Companies	26 Companies

SECONDARY EVALUATION TECHNIQUES

The number and percentage of firms using each of the four methodologies as their secondary evaluation technique has not changed much from the 1977 results (**Table 3**). The payback period is still the dominant secondary technique although it is more widely used for plant and equipment decisions than for timber investments. In addition, the accounting rate of return is used substantially more as a secondary evaluation technique than as a primary evaluation technique for all types of investment decisions.

While arguments can be made that neither the accounting rate of return nor payback methods consider the time value of money and the economic impact that this has on the market value of the firm, both of these methodologies have some redeeming features. Both are intuitive and easy to understand. Both are easy to calculate. In the case of the payback period, the focus is on liquidity, which is clearly an important issue for a capital-intensive firm. Moreover, accounting information is almost always available for the project under consideration and for the firm as a whole. Thus, the calculation of accounting rate of return is a normal by-product of the companies' financial accounting information systems.

PROJECT SCREENING TECHNIQUES

In the 1977 survey we did not ask about the use of any of these four methodologies as screening techniques in the capital budgeting process. These results for 1997 in **Table 4** show once again the emphasis forest products firms place on the discounted cash flow methodologies in evaluating timber investments. Seventy percent of the firms find these techniques useful even at the project screening stage. On the other hand, payback is the most commonly used screening technique for investments in plant and equipment.

COMPANY SIZE AND EVALUATION TECHNIQUES

In an analysis of the size of the forest products companies in relationship to the type of evaluation techniques, we see that size is still the dominant factor when it comes to using discounted cash flow analysis in analyzing anything other than timber investments. For timber investments, even the smaller companies favor the discounted cash flow techniques. On the other hand, in plant and equipment decisions, the combined accounting rate of return and payback method responses equaled or exceeded the discounted cash flow responses in all companies whose sales were less than $500 million.

It is also interesting to note that none of the largest forest products firms used either accounting rate of return or payback when evaluating timber purchases, and only two out of the 12 largest firms used accounting rate of return when evaluating plant and equipment. The shares of many of these firms are publicly owned, so it is not surprising that investment decisions tend to be market driven. Because book value and net income do not have much to do with cash flow and market value, accounting rate of return measures do not tell the managers of these publicly owned firms what they really need to know.

OTHER FACTORS RELEVANT TO THE CAPITAL BUDGETING DECISION

When we review the comments that were received from respondents regarding capital budgeting decisions, two conclusions emerged. In the case of timber investments, the most important issue centered on strategic wood supply considerations—namely, current availability, expected acquisition cost, location, age, and class of timber, as well as what was likely to happen to any of these factors in the future. To firms selling wood, pulp, paper, or packaging products, this issue of availability is of prime importance. To remain in business, firms need an ongoing supply of timber. As a result, financial analysis techniques that emphasize the accounting concepts of breakeven analysis and shutdown costs are getting increased attention by forest products firms.

On the plant and equipment side, it was not surprising to learn that one of the most important issues has become the need to comply with the regulatory standards concerning health, safety, and the environment. With more and more of these types of pressures likely in the future and with the dollar cost of failing to satisfy these concerns rising, traditional financial analysis may very well become a secondary criterion used to evaluate investment options. Two companies also mentioned the importance of the custodial role they feel forest products companies have with regard to maintaining the timber resource and the overall welfare of their employees.

RISK-ADJUSTMENT METHODOLOGIES

An extended time horizon is implicit in all capital projects. This factor is particularly true in timber acquisition projects and increases the difficulty of accurately forecasting the future costs and returns in these projects. For this reason, risk is an important concern in capital budgeting. Traditionally, there have been three common quantitative methods of adjusting capital projects for risk. The first technique is to raise the cost of capital used as a cutoff rate or used in discounting future cash flows in the net present value methodology. The second technique is to adjust the project life downward. The third approach involves the use of sensitivity analysis where a range of future expectations is considered in the project analysis. In particular, the projected costs can be increased, and/or the projected benefits can be decreased. This approach can determine the extent to which the actual costs and benefits could deviate from the most likely estimate before an acceptable project would become unacceptable.

In 1977 only 44% of the respondent companies reported using one of these three quantitative risk adjustment techniques. Moreover, the majority of the companies used the sensitivity analysis approach. In the 1997 survey, the percentage of companies using formal risk adjustment had risen to 76% (22 of the 29 firms). Only 17% (five firms) reported that they do not adjust for risk at all in evaluating capital budgeting decisions. The remaining 7% (two firms) attempted to consider risk subjectively. These results support the finding noted earlier that forest products companies are becoming more sophisticated in their capital budgeting methodologies.

While sensitivity analysis continues to be the risk adjustment technique of preference for all size categories of firms, and there does not appear to be much difference in the type of risk adjustment technique used in analyzing timber and nontimber investments, some of the larger forest products firms are beginning to use other methods to analyze risk. Some of these techniques include the use of formal probability analysis, in which firms actually attempt to calculate the probability of investments earning a return greater than the cost of capital or earning a positive net present value, and less formal methods such as shortening the payback period and reducing the amount initially invested for projects involving higher risk.

Blocher, Stout, Cokins, Chen: *Cost Management, 4e*

AN INDUSTRY IN TRANSITION

The forest products industry—an industry composed of firms selling wood, pulp, paper, and packaging products—plays a significant role in the global economy, accounting for nearly 3% of the global Gross Domestic Product. A distinguishing feature of this industry is its degree of capital intensity; the assets of firms operating in this industry consist primarily of timber holdings and substantial plant and equipment.

In recent years, the forest products industry has been transformed by external forces that have exerted pressure for new forestry techniques and an overall structural change within the industry. Inflationary pressures alone have caused the cost of timber and timberland to rise to unprecedented levels. Population and economic growth combined with the increased standard of living in many countries has resulted in an increasing demand for forest products. Heightened government regulation and environmental legislation will continue to increase as society places greater emphasis on non-timber benefits that accrue from forests such as bio-diversity, wildlife habitat, water storage, recreation, and aesthetics.

The forest products industry is responding to these forces by implementing capital and technology intensive strategies throughout its operations from the forest to the marketplace. Many forest products firms are shifting their timber supply from natural forests to plantation forests that utilize costly genetics and breeding technologies in their intensive silvi-cultural practices. These plantation forests are vertically integrated with capital intensive, eco-efficient production facilities. Those firms that have not been able to meet the above challenges either have had to close down operations or they have been acquired by competitors. The net result has been a significant decline in the number of firms in the industry.

Furthermore, one company reported using a decision tree approach in evaluating plant and equipment purchases. Under this technique, a firm would attempt to lay out several different scenarios, assign probabilities to each scenario, and then calculate expected profitability measures based on either the firm's cash flow or accounting net income. This technique would appear to be particularly relevant in the case of changing regulatory environments or widely fluctuating timber prices noted earlier.

POST-AUDIT PROCEDURES

It is generally recommended that companies should conduct a post audit to compare the actual results of a capital project with the original forecasts that were used in determining that the project was acceptable. This procedure not only can serve as an evaluation of project implementation but also as an evaluation of the entire capital budget planning process. Companies can use this information to evaluate the accuracy of their forecasts and whether they have been using the appropriate project analysis techniques. In 1977, two thirds of the forest products companies conducted some form of formal post audit of their capital projects. In the 1997 survey, over three quarters of the respondents report that they do post audits of their capital investment projects.

All 12 of the largest companies in the survey do use post audits for their capital projects as do most of the firms in the $50-$100 million and $101-$500 million categories. In fact, post audits seem to be the general practice in all but the smallest companies where only one of the respondent firms has a post audit procedure in place.

Comments about post auditing procedures indicate that post audits typically were conducted between six months to one year after projects were fully operational. Second, in most cases, post audits were mandatory on all large projects (i.e., over $5 million) with the results being reported to the board. Conducting post audits on smaller projects typically was at the discretion of the audit committee, company president, or business unit vice president depending on the size .of the firm involved. Third, most firms conducted post audits on only the first-year results, with one firm reporting that it audited up to five years' results in the case of very large investments.

The most interesting comment received regarding post audits was:

"We pick a finance person and a manufacturing person from a different plant/mill to act as a team to perform the audit. They are given a copy of the project and all backup information and are given three to four months to complete the audit, while continuing with all their normal job requirements. They prepare the audit report and then give a presentation to our audit committee. Normally, only larger projects are post audited. All other financially justified projects are reviewed in a less formal process. These reports are completed by the responsible plant/mill and routed around for review."

The fact that this firm used individuals from both finance and manufacturing in addition to requiring that they be from a different operating unit increases the likelihood that the post audit results for the major investments would be unbiased.

MORE COMPANIES USE IRR AND NPV

On the basis of the survey, the following conclusions can be made regarding capital budgeting practices in the forest products industry in the last 20 years. First, there has been a significant increase in the use of the more sophisticated and theoretically preferred discounted cash flow methodologies of internal rate of return and net present value for all capital investment decisions. While firm size continues to be the dominant factor when it comes to the use of these methods in evaluating plant and equipment purchases, even smaller firms use them in the case of timber investments. Moreover, a greater percentage of firms are now applying discounted cash flow techniques in the preliminary or project

screening stages of their capital budgeting process.

Second, risk analysis has taken on increased importance. A greater percentage of firms are using quantitative techniques, and those that do not at least attempt to consider risk subjectively.

Third, only smaller firms have failed to implement post audit procedures on a consistent basis as a way to both monitor and control their major capital investments. Post audit procedures in medium-sized and large firms not only are becoming more formal in terms of reporting requirements, they are also more extensive in terms of the actual analysis procedures being employed.

Fourth, other procedures such as breakeven analysis, probability analysis, and decision trees are coming into use as relevant capital budgeting methodologies. In addition, noneconomic issues are taking on a greater degree of importance in the decision-making process. The issue most often cited is the changing regulatory climate in the forest products industry especially as it relates to health, safety, and the environment. Each of these areas relates to the company's custodial role concerning both timber resources and employees.

---

[1] In 1977, there were 241 companies participating in the Oregon State University Forest Products Monograph Program.

20.2: HOW ABC WAS USED IN CAPITAL BUDGETING

by Steve Coburn, Hugh Grove, and Tom Cook

How do you estimate cash flows for capital expenditure projects in your company? Many firms use broad strategic approaches for estimating cash flows that are not closely tied to detailed tactical assumptions about future operations. These forecasts may not be very reliable because cash flow projections of new products can have a 30% to 40% margin of error.

A new division of a Fortune 500 company was established to analyze new business opportunities in the electronic (broadband) marketplace of interactive television. The company and data have been disguised here for confidentiality purposes. The initial investment proposal was to develop a "cybermall," similar to the way marketing service organizations bring together sellers and buyers in the traditional television marketplace. At the time, this cybermall proposal was a new idea without any close counterparts in this emerging electronic marketplace.

Senior management of this new division initially had focused upon the marketing strategy of "speed to market" for this cybermall project. Thus, the business case forecast was done at a broad strategic level with few supporting details. A consulting firm provided general forecasts of the electronic market size and market share which it converted into aggregate forecasts of revenue, operating costs, and capital costs. Driven by this "speed-to-market" strategy senior management was willing to commit $50 million to this cybermall project, based upon the business case forecast.

The chief financial officer (CFO) of this new division, however, successfully argued for a tactical translation of the business case's broad strategic view into a detailed analysis of the cybermall's projected business processes and activities. Senior management approved the CFO's proposal because it still had concerns about how the technical development and deployment of the electronic marketplace would impact the cybermall financial forecasts. The CFO's proposal became an activity-based cost (ABC) model (with benchmarking) that created a pro forma process engineering approach for analyzing this business opportunity.

Process analysis typically has been used for reengineering existing—not pro forma—processes.[1] In contrast, this business opportunity

related to an emerging industry with new processes. Also, ABC has been advocated for use in annual, not capital, budgeting.[2] Using ABC for capital budgeting analysis of this cybermall project created an example of activity based management (ABM), which has been defined as providing economic information for management decision making.[3]

The ABC model (with benchmarking) forecasted business processes, activities, revenues, operating costs, and capital costs for this cybermall project. This tactical ABC approach generated forecasts that differed significantly from the forecasts of the strategic business case. For example, the ABC model forecasted that an additional $10 million of capital costs would be needed. Also, revenue forecasts were slowed down and startup cost forecasts were increased. Senior management used these ABC results to reverse its initial decision to go ahead with this cybermall project.

Thus, the CFO provided strategic AEM information and became part of the business decision-making process. Senior management also has decided to use this ABC approach for evaluating future business opportunities. Such a strategic role has been advocated as the most important goal for a CFO's mission statement and the future of management accounting.[4]

The ABC analysis provided an understanding of projected business processes and activities that allowed senior management to have more confidence in the detailed tactical ABC forecasts, rather than the initial, broad strategic forecasts. This pro forma ABC approach also is a logical next step for companies currently using ABC and bench-marking to understand existing business processes and activities.

We describe here an overview of the business case and the ABC model approaches; then a description of the ABC approach for analyzing this cybermall project is provided. Finally, the forecasts from both approaches are compared.

BUSINESS CASE VS. ABC MODEL APPROACHES

Figure 1 provides an overview of the business case approach to capital budgeting for this cybermall project. The strategic business case forecasts started with broad market assumptions concerning electronic market size and share provided by a consulting firm.

These consultants then converted this market data into general projections of revenues with few supporting details. They also used general cost assumptions to project variable and fixed expenses without any detailed cost analyses.

deployment schedule by benchmarking with external parties to obtain detailed data concerning the build-out of the broadband infrastructure for the electronic marketplace. The ten largest cable or multi-system operators (MSOs) were projected to build or deploy broadband infrastructures over five years, starting in 1996, and all other MSOs to

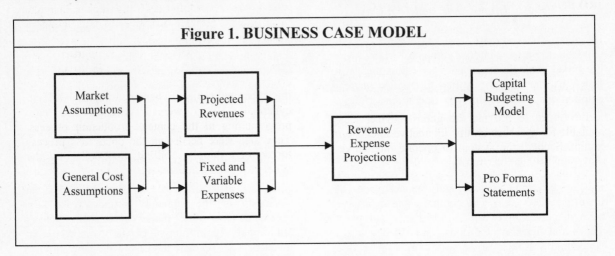

Figure 1. BUSINESS CASE MODEL

For example, the budget line items of technology development, video production, and network

operations were mainly aggregate fixed cost forecasts. The few variable cost forecasts were based upon general revenue projections, such as distribution access as a flat fee per subscriber and order processing as a specified amount per customer. A key capital infrastructure forecast used just one type of client/server technology for all interactive television markets although four different types of client/server technology were being deployed by cable system operators.

The business case provided general revenue and expense projections and pro forma financial statements. Also, the business case provided senior management with capital budgeting information for the decision criteria of net present value (NPV), internal rate of return (IRR), and payback.

Figure 2 provides an overview of the ABC approach to capital budgeting for this cybermall project. The tactical ABC model forecasts were based upon detailed benchmarked data from the cybermall business process analyses provided by the CFO. Using benchmark assumptions, the ABC approach developed a broadband deployment or build-out schedule of the electronic marketplace for potential interactive television subscribers. It also developed a transaction volume schedule for potential cybermall customers. Both schedules were used to help generate the revenue, cost, and capital assumptions and projections of the ABC model.

The ABC model created a broadband network

deploy over seven years, starting in 1997. This deployment was projected to start in the 50 largest cities or suburbs named as areas of dominant influence (ADI).

Using this deployment schedule as a starting point, the ABC model created a detailed transaction volume schedule by benchmarking shopping participation, purchase frequency, and average spending for this cybermall project. Because no interactive television operators existed for this emerging market, the traditional television marketing operators, Home Shopping Network (HSN) and the QVC system, were used as indirect or "out of market" benchmarks. For example, HSN had about five million active shoppers representing 8.3% of the homes reached, and QVC had four million shoppers representing 8.0% of the homes reached. Also, HSN repeat customers had made purchases between five and seven times a year. Average spending per shopping household for repeat customers was about $300 for HSN and about $500 for QVC.

The tactical ABC model used detailed revenue assumptions and forecasts for this cybermall project, as opposed to the general ones of the strategic business case. The ABC model forecasted slower access to cybermall customers, primarily due to delays in developing and provisioning the broadband network. Accordingly, the revenue forecasts for the early years were lower than in the business case. Concerning the ABC pool costs, the ABC model used a pro-forma process engineering approach to construct activity resource

Blocher, Stout, Cokins, Chen: *Cost Management, 4e*

©The McGraw-Hill Companies, Inc 2008

consumption profiles and transaction (cost) drivers that were multiplied together to derive the ABC expense projections. A cybermall value chain of workflow or business processes was specified with key activities and cost drivers. This pro forma process engineering approach is described below.

PRO FORMA PROCESS ENGINEERING

A pro forma process engineering approach was used by the ABC model to forecast operating and capital costs for the cybermall project. A cybermall value chain was created with six sequential workflows or business processes as shown in **Table 1**. First, cybermall seller relationships must be developed to provide the goods and services available for purchase on this interactive television system. Second, the system to operate interactive television applications must be developed. Third, content programs must be purchased or produced. Fourth, the ongoing operations of this interactive television system must be performed, especially the

capital costs in **Table 1** represented four initial broadband deployments. Each deployment used a different type of client/server, and each server type was estimated to require $0.5 million in capital costs. Over the initial 10-year period of this cybermall project, 120 network deployments were estimated for total capital costs of $60 million, which was $10 million or 20% higher than the business case estimate of $50 million, as shown in **Table 2**.

Also, three types of external parties were identified because they were needed to perform critical activities in various business processes for this cybermall project to become operational. First, cybermall sellers were needed to do core programming in the content production process. They also were needed in the operations process for selling, shipping, billing, and collecting the cybermall goods and revenues. Second, software vendors were needed to develop and test network applications, video content programs, and network operations for the cybermall. Third, distributors

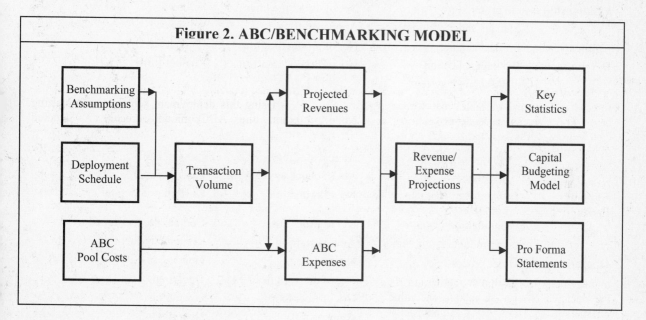

Figure 2. ABC/BENCHMARKING MODEL

processing of cybermall buyers' orders. Fifth, the marketing of the cybermall must be done. Sixth, the network distributors and access fees must be managed.

Major activities were identified for each of these six business processes in the cybermall value chain. Resource consumption profiles and cost drivers were identified for the major activities. Cost pool rates were calculated and multiplied by the number of cost drivers needed at various transaction volumes to project the ABC process expenses as summarized in Table 1.

Detailed capital costs also were forecasted for various levels of activities. The $2 million total

were needed to develop, operate, and deploy the interactive broadband network where the cybermall will be located.

Seller relationship process. The seller relationship business process for the cybermall has three major activities. First, for the activity of acquiring cybermall sellers, account managers are needed to obtain and maintain sellers of goods and services. One full-time equivalent (FTE) manager and one secretary are projected for 1995, increasing to a cap of seven FTEs by 1997. Second, for the promotion activity, the cybermall will be publicized with an annual budget for promotional mailings to potential sellers and distributors. Third, a general manager is needed for managing seller relationships. One half-time position is needed in 1995, increasing to a cap of two FTEs by 1997.

Application development process. Application development business process for the cybermall has four major activities. First, product concept will be defined and evaluated with product research, product specifications, and simulated operations. Capital costs of $350,000 are needed for simulation equipment, a client/server, workstations, and personal computers. Second, two key types of design application activities are needed. An asset management system will be developed with a simulated startup for this

cybermall. Capital costs of $150,000 are needed for video equipment, software, and production workstations. Also, an automated order processing system for cybermall customers will be developed with $100,000 of capital costs.

Third, for the database activity, a database operations center will be developed. Capital costs of $300,000 are needed for the central hardware to coordinate the workstations. Fourth, two key types of technology activities are needed. For the planning activity, three technical employees and $50,000 for test equipment each year are needed to maintain technical core competency and to update technical strategy

Table 1. KEY ACTIVITIES, DRIVERS AND COSTS IN THE CYBERMALL VALUE CHAIN

Business Processes	Major Activities	Cost Drivers	Process Expenses	Capital (000,000)
Seller	Acquire sellers	No. of sellers	Selling	$0
Relationship	Do promotions	No. of direct mailings	Selling	0
	Manage seller relationships	Annual staffing	Selling	0
Application	Product concept	No. of product start-ups	Product R&D	$.4
Development	Design application:	No. of Product Start-ups	Product R&D	
	Asset mgt. system			$.1
	Order process sys.			$.1
	Develop database	No. of product start-ups	Product R&D	
	Technology:			
	Planning	Annual staffing	Product R&D	0
	Deployment	No. of client server types	Product R&D	$.4
Content	Brokerage of Program purchases	No. of programs	Content production	0
Production	Program production	No. of programs	Content production	0
	Post production guidelines	Annual staffing	Content production	0
Operations	Order processing	No. of orders	Operations	$.1
	Customer service	No. of network head-ends	Operations	$.1
	Provision network	No. of fiber loops	Operations	$.5
	Seller interface	Annual staff	Operations	0
Marketing	Buyer acquisition	No. of buyers	Marketing	0
	Advertising	No. of ads	Marketing	0
	Public Relations	Annual staffing	Marketing	0
	Buyer maintenance	Revenue Percent	Marketing	0
Network	Distributor Relationships	Annual staffing	Distribution	0
Distribution	Access Fee	No. of buyers	Distribution	0

Capital Costs in Table 2: 4 types of Deployment * $.5 = $ 2.0

Total Capital Costs in Table 1: 120 Deployments * $.5 = $60.0

continuously. For the deployment activity, this cybermall project will be adapted to four

technology types of client/servers and will cost $100,000 for each type of server. Thus, capital

Blocher, Stout, Cokins, Chen: *Cost Management, 4e*

costs of $400,000 are needed initially to provision four servers (one for each server type).

Content production process. The content production business process for the cybermall has three major activities. First, for the brokerage of program purchases, rights to use existing programming will be purchased when appropriate for this cybermall. Estimated annual costs are $100,000 in 1995, increasing to a $700,000 cap by 2000. Second, for the program production activity, programs for video content describing the cybermall sellers will be produced in-house or outsourced. It is assumed that the company and the sellers will split these costs equally, which are similar to the brokerage program costs. Third, concerning post-production guidelines, costs to monitor and manage programming and production are estimated as one technical employee in 1995, increasing to cap of four FTEs by 1997.

Operations process. The operations process has four major activities. First, for the order processing activity, there will be two cost structures. Manual processing will be used from 1995 through 1997 until higher cybermall shopper volume is obtained. Thereafter, automated processing will be used with capital costs of $100,000. Second, concerning customer service, employee costs are estimated at one third FTE for each network head-end. Capital costs of $100,000 are estimated for workstations and software.

Third, to provision an interactive (broadband) television network, this cybermall project must be deployed on fiber loops, requiring video server equipment. Each server may feed up to four head-end networks and up to 500,000 interactively passed homes. Capital costs of $500,000 are estimated for the video servers, storage units, and personal computer systems to interface with the fiber loops. Fourth, for cybermall seller interfacing, one manager and three technical employees are needed for the post-production functions of program content and network operations.

Marketing process. The marketing process has four major activities. First, for the buyer acquisition activity, sales persons are needed to obtain cybermall shoppers or buyers. Related selling costs also are included. Such buyer acquisition costs are estimated to decrease over time. Second, advertising primarily via television and radio promotions is necessary. Costs for preparation of such advertisements are budgeted for $200,000 in 1996, increasing up to a $500,000 cap by 1999. Third, public relations activities included marketing management. Personnel are estimated at two FTEs in 1995, four FTEs in 1996,

and eight FTEs thereafter. Fourth, concerning buyer maintenance, costs to maintain cybermall shoppers are estimated as a percentage of total revenue.

Network distribution process. The network distribution process has two major activities. First, account managers are needed to manage relationships with the distribution networks used by this cybermall. Personnel are estimated at one half time position in 1995, increasing to a cap of two FTEs by 1998. Second, concerning network access fees from 1995 through 1997, charges are based upon the number of cybermall shoppers making purchases and are paid monthly to the network provider. Thereafter, the charges will be based upon a percentage of total shopping purchases.

In summary, the tactical ABC model engineered pro forma business processes, activities, and cost drivers to calculate detailed revenue and resource consumption patterns, as opposed to the general assumptions of the strategic business case approach. Also, to help senior management make this capital budgeting decision, key operating statistics were compiled by the ABC model. Such statistics were not provided by the business case because it was done without detailed analyses. These statistics were classified by four types of metrics: buyers, sellers, networks, and infrastructure, as shown in **Table 3**.

If comparisons had been available, the ABC model generally would have provided less optimistic forecasts of operating statistics because its related revenue forecasts were lower and startup cost forecasts higher than the business case. For example, the acquisition cost per buyer would have been higher and the revenue per seller, lower. In the network and infrastructure metrics, the access costs and the cost per minute/content both would have been higher.

If the cost drivers were not already represented in the benchmarked transaction file, they were added to these existing transaction volumes. For example, a new cost driver for the number of client/servers was measured by the interactive television deployment sequence under the cybermall revenue assumptions. From the pro forma engineering analysis, an activity resource consumption profile was established to measure the cost of a client/server. Then, the number and cost of the client/servers were multiplied together to project the ABC expenses at various levels of interactive television deployment. Thus, detailed resource consumption patterns and transaction (cost) drivers were used to generate the ABC expense and capital forecasts, as opposed to general assumptions in the business case forecasts.

Table 2. COMPARISONS OF ABC VS. BUSINESS CASE
(In millions and 10-year totals)
Panel A: Key Projections:

	Business Case	ABC Model	Variances Increase (Decrease)	Percent
Total revenues	$1,650	$1,480	($170)	(10%)
Total cash operations expenses	$1,000	$ 950	($ 50)	(5%)
Total net income aftertax	$ 250	$ 175	($ 75)	(30%)
Total capital expenditures	$ 50	$ 60	$ 10	20%
Total net cash flow	$ 400	$ 320	($ 80)	(20%)

Panel B: Key Decision Criteria:

	Business Case	ABC Model	Variances Increase (Decrease)	Percent
1. Without Residual Value:				
Internal rate of return	43%	33%	(10%)	(23%)
Net present values:				
@20%	$ 60	$ 35	($25)	(42%)
@30%	$ 20	$ 4	($16)	(80%)
@40%	$ 3	($ 8)	($11)	N/A
Discounted payback @20% in yrs.	7	9	2	29%
2. With Residual Value:	61%	50%	(11%)	
Internal rate of return				(18%)
Net present values:				
@20%	$225	$190	($35)	(16%)
@30%	$100	$ 80	($20)	(20%)
@40%	$ 40	$ 25	($15)	(38%)

For example, the application development and design costs were forecasted using the number of product startups as the cost driver. (A fixed cost was used throughout the business case.) For another example, manual order processing initially was assumed due to low customer volume in the startup phase. Subsequently, automated order processing was assumed. (A variable cost per customer was used throughout the business case.) The ABC model forecasted specific network operating costs using the cost drivers of network head-ends and fiber loops. (Aggregate amounts of fixed costs were used in the business case.) The ABC model forecasted capital costs that represented four types of broadband deployments, one for each of the actual types of client/servers being deployed by cable television operators. (Only one client/server type was used in the business case.)

The ABC model calculated key operating statistics and differences between the ABC and the business case dollar projections and NPV, IRR, and payback results. The operating statistics are described in **Table 3**. The ABC model also generated pro forma financial statements. All this information was provided to help senior management make its final decision on this cybermall project. The ten different categories of the ABC model in **Figure 2** were linked together as a series of related Excel spreadsheets to facilitate risk analysis. The final ABC model used six megabytes of random access memory.

COMPARISONS OF FORECASTS

For this cybermall project, 10-year financial forecasts are summarized in **Table 2**. Panel A has comparisons of key dollar projections for the business case and the ABC model. Panel B has comparisons of key capital budgeting forecasts for the business case and the ABC model. In **Table 2**, the residual value for this cybermall project represented the net present value of its sales price in year 10. The ABC spreadsheet model calculated both dollar and percent variances between the two approaches as shown in **Table 2**.

Key projections of 10-year financial amounts for both approaches were summarized in Panel A of **Table 2**. For the business case, key dollar projections were (in millions): $1,650 revenues; $1,000 cash operating expenses; $250 net income after taxes; $50 capital expenditures; and $400 net cash flow without residual value. For the ABC model, key dollar projections were (in millions): $1,480 revenues; $950 cash operating expenses; $175 net income after taxes; $60 capital expenditures; and $320 net cash flow without residual value. Concerning the variances, all the business case forecasts were from 5% to 30% higher than the ABC model forecasts, except for capital expenditures, which were 20% ($10 million) lower. Consequently, the ABC dollar projections, especially the 20% reduction in net cash flow, generated lower capital budgeting forecasts than in the business case.

Blocher, Stout, Cokins, Chen: *Cost Management, 4e*

Capital budgeting forecasts for both approaches are summarized in Panel B of **Table 2**. For the business case, the internal rates of return were 43% without any residual value and 61% with the residual value. The net present values were $60 million, $20 million, and $3 million, using cost-of-capital rates of 20%, 30%, and 40%, respectively, without any residual value. With the residual value, the net present values were much larger at $225 million, $100 million, and $40 million, respectively. The discounted cash flow payback was seven years, using a 20% cost of capital rate.

For the ABC model, the internal rates of return were 33% without any residual value and 50% with the residual value. The net present values were $35 million, $4 million, and negative $8 million, using cost of capital rates of 20%, 30%, and 40%, respectively, without any residual value. With the residual value, the net present values were much larger at $190 million, $80 million, and $25 million, respectively. The discounted cash flow payback was nine years, using a 20% cost-of-capital rate.

The variances for the capital budgeting forecasts showed that the ABC model results were significantly lower than the business case results. The internal rates of return decreased by 23% and 18%, without and with the residual values, respectively The net present values were reduced from 16% to 80%, depending upon which cost of capital rate was used. The discounted cash flow payback was increased by two years or 29%. With higher capital forecasts and lower revenue and cash flow forecasts, the ABC capital budgeting forecasts were less favorable for this cybermall project than the business case forecasts.

From the ABC analysis, the electronic marketplace deployment and resulting market share and revenues were too slow while the startup and investment costs were too big and too early to justify the cybermall project at this time. Also, the operating leverage for profit growth did not become favorable until the mid-life point of this cybermall project, as opposed to an earlier prediction in the business case.

Table 3. KEY OPERATING STATISTICS

Buyers:	Networks:	Infrastructure:	Sellers:
No. of shoppers	Homes passed	Programming shelf life	Items per view hour
Purchases per year	Access cost percent of revenue	Cost per minute/content	Number of sellers
Return percent	ADl coverage percent	Connect time	Revenue per seller
Browse time	Network profitability	Percent automatic fulfillment	Transactions per month
Repeat time	Number of platforms supported	Cost per transaction	Percent ship date target
Acquisition cost per buyer	Number of shopping applications	Transaction response time	Seller renewal rate

ABC PROVIDES TACTICAL APPROACH

The ABC model provided a methodology to analyze future business opportunities concerning new types of products and services in emerging markets. The additional level of detail was the key difference from the business case approach for this cybermall project. The pro forma analysis of the business processes and activities with linkages to revenue and cost structures provided critical information for the final decision on this cybermall project.

This approach appears to be applicable to all types of capital budgeting decisions and should provide a unique opportunity for senior management to understand how business processes and activities impact revenue and cost forecasts. As in this cybermall project, the business case approach typically analyzes the symptoms of changes using various levels of market shares, revenues, and costs, but no clear analyses of the causes or drivers of these changes are provided. By contrast, such causal analyses *are* provided by this ABC approach which attempts to understand how changes in business processes and activities impact market share, revenues, and costs.

The ABC information provided a better understanding of the cybermall business processes and activities. This additional knowledge allowed senior management to have more confidence in its strategic decision making for this project. Senior management agreed that the additional costs spent on the ABC and benchmarking analyses were justified by the benefits of more detailed operating and financial information.

For example, the following key uses of this ABC model were identified for this cybermall project in the emerging electronic marketplace:

- Establishing linkages between technology (the electronic market deployment and distribution of interactive services) and financial forecasts,
- Using indirect or "out of market" benchmarks for revenue and cost forecasts,
- Creating a dynamic model that showed how unitized ABC costs behaved and changed over time in providing interactive services, and

Cases and Readings

- Specifying operating leverage more precisely with different step-cost functions at different levels of volume.

These key uses also helped clarify marketing strategies for this emerging industry; i.e., broad market coverage versus narrow or niche market development of interactive services.

As shown by the comparisons in **Table 2**, the tactical ABC model produced less favorable forecasts for the capital budgeting decision criteria than the strategic business case. Thus, senior management decided not to do this project at this time. Because the ABC model also was a working spreadsheet model, sensitivity and "what-if" risk analyses were performed but the final decision was to reject the project. Senior management decided not to be a first or early entrant into this emerging electronic market.

This ABC model provided a detailed tactical methodology to analyze business opportunities in emerging markets, as opposed to the general strategic view of the business case approach. The initial "speed-to-market" strategy in the business case was tempered by the tactical ABC analysis of the cybermall project's feasibility Forecasts of the ABC model created more confidence in making this cybermall decision; therefore, senior management has decided to use this ABC model for analyzing subsequent business opportunities in the electronic marketplace. Thus, by using this ABC and bench-marking methodology to provide strategic information, the CFO became part of the strategic decision-making process in accordance with the key goal for a CFO's mission statement and the future of management accounting.

ENDNOTES:

[1] Refer to M. Hammer and J. Champy, *Reengineer-ing the Corporation,* Harper Business, New York, 1993.

[2] Refer to J. Schmidt, "Is It Time to Replace Tradi-tional Budgeting?" *Journal of Accountancy,* November 1992, pp.103-107.

[3] Refer to R. Kaplan, "In Defense of Activity-Based Cost Management," *Management Accounting*, November 1992, pp. 58-63.

[4] Refer to A. Pipkin, "The 21st Century Controller," *Management Accounting*, February 1989, pp. 21-25; and W. Birkett, "Management Accounting and Knowledge Management," *Management Account-ing*, November 1995, pp. 44-48.